MW00580280

HOW SEXUAL DESIRE WORKS

There are countless books on sex and an endless fascination with the subject. Varieties and vagaries of sexual desire have long been documented, but there has been little engagement with cutting-edge scientific research to uncover the biological and psychological bases of sexual desire. Here, Frederick Toates uses the insights of modern science to show how a wide range of desire-related phenomena – fantasy, novelty-seeking, sexual addiction, sex–drug interactions, fetishes, voyeurism, and sexual violence and killing – start to make sense. For example, the role of the brain's neurochemical dopamine can now be much better understood in terms of wanting, and a distinction between wanting and liking has been established. Also, an understanding of the layered organization of the brain, sometimes described as hierarchical, can be used to explain temptation and conflict. This is a fascinating book with great social relevance to society and its problems with sexuality.

Frederick Toates is Emeritus Professor of Biological Psychology at The Open University and Vice-President of The Open University Psychology Society.

How Sexual Desire Works

THE ENIGMATIC URGE

Frederick Toates
The Open University
United Kingdom

CAMBRIDGE
UNIVERSITY PRESS

University Printing House, Cambridge CB2 8BS, United Kingdom

Cambridge University Press is part of the University of Cambridge.

It furthers the University's mission by disseminating knowledge in the pursuit of education, learning and research at the highest international levels of excellence.

www.cambridge.org
Information on this title: www.cambridge.org/9781107688049

© Frederick Toates 2014

This publication is in copyright. Subject to statutory exception and to the provisions of relevant collective licensing agreements, no reproduction of any part may take place without the written permission of Cambridge University Press.

First published 2014

Printed in the United Kingdom by Clays, St Ives plc

A catalogue record for this publication is available from the British Library

ISBN 978-1-107-05001-3 Hardback
ISBN 978-1-107-68804-9 Paperback

Cambridge University Press has no responsibility for the persistence or accuracy of URLs for external or third-party internet websites referred to in this publication, and does not guarantee that any content on such websites is, or will remain, accurate or appropriate.

Every effort has been made to secure necessary permissions to reproduce copyright material, though in some cases it has proved impossible to trace copyright holders. If any omissions are brought to our notice, we will make every effort to correct this in future reprintings.

I dedicate this book to my wife, Olga.

CONTENTS

FIGURES

PREFACE

Sexual desire could at times appear to bring pleasure and misery in some-what equal proportions. It is my firm conviction that a better understanding of it can help to tilt the weight away from misery, the present book being based upon the belief that knowledge is empowering. For example, rightly or wrongly, people sometimes think that their tastes are socially and morally unacceptable and better knowledge could prove valuable in seeing how the taste might have arisen and coming to terms with it. Similarly, couples frequently find that discord arises from divergent tastes or intensities of desire. Insights into how desire works might yield greater tolerance of differences and thereby harmony. To give a full account of the range of desires, Chapters 20–1 describe the nightmare world of sex-ual violence, for which, of course, there can be no degrees of tolerance. I believe that a greater insight into the causes of sexual violence could help to combat it. However, the reader seeking only insight into harmonious and consensual sex might wish to skip these two chapters.

I have a wide range of different readers in mind, such as neurosci-entists, psychologists, psychiatrists, philosophers, counsellors, teachers, social workers, police and probation officers, as well as the general public. I have tried very hard to write it in a style that is accessible to such a spectrum of different readers and I can only hope that I have succeeded. To respect such a spectrum, some information on, for example, details of brain processes is put in footnotes, which can be ignored without losing the story-line.

My attempt has been to give a balanced account using the most relevant sources that I can find. However, without doubt, a massive amount of highly relevant material has been omitted and I can only apologize to the multitude of authors whose work has not been included.

I would like to express my appreciation of the efforts of Barry Singer, who gave me the initial momentum in this area of research, and of Erick Janssen, whose invitation to speak in Amsterdam was the trigger for a revised model of sexual desire and thereby for the appearance of this book. I am very grateful to Kent Berridge and my wife, Olga Coschug-Toates, for reading and critically commenting upon the whole book. My gratitude is also owed to a number of people who scrutinized one or more chapters: Lesel Dawson, Ellen Laan, Karen Littleton, Jaak Panksepp, Julia Robertson, Mark Spiering, Sandie Taylor, Madeline Watson and Lance Workman, as well as the anonymous referees. For IT help and patience, I wish to thank Stanislav Coschug, Becky Efthimiou, Becky Loake and David Robinson. For their support throughout this project, I am very grateful to Chloé Harries, Hetty Marx, Carrie Parkinson, Sarah Payne and Becky Taylor of Cambridge University Press and to the Open University library staff and Giles Clark. Anna Oxbury made a superb and tireless job of editing the work and has vastly improved it. I wish to express my appreciation of her skill and patience.

If anyone has any comments on the book, I would be pleased to hear from you and will do my best to answer.

ONE

WHAT IS ENIGMATIC ABOUT SEXUAL DESIRE?

> Consider the time, I hope recently, when you saw a woman or man (fill in your preference) who awoke in you, within a matter of seconds, a distinct state of lust . . . The object of origin for that awakening presented itself, in all its glory, probably not whole but in parts. Maybe what first arrested your attention was the shape of an ankle, how it connected with the back of a shoe and how it dissolved into a leg, no longer seen but just imagined, under a skirt . . . .Or maybe it was the shape of a neck sticking up from a shirt. Or maybe it was not a part at all but the carriage, moves, energy, and resolve that propelled a whole body forward.
>
> (Damasio, 2003, p. 93)[1]

It would be informative to discover how Damasio's readers (and indeed mine too) have reacted to this invitation to reflection. If they are like the population sampled by sex researchers, some would find it hard to recall any such lust-filled moments, whereas others would be inundated with recent memories jockeying for occupation of the conscious mind. Some would doubtless find their desire triggered instantly by such parts of the whole as an ankle or leg, whereas a number might find it fuelled by the shoes worn. Others would only be excited slowly by a whole speaking and socially interacting personality.

The enormous variation in the reactivity of human sexual desire is why I use the term 'enigma' and is a feature that must be accommodated by any attempt to explain desire's foundations. What are the implications of this wide spectrum of responses? Is there a healthy norm, while deviations to either side indicate that something is wrong? Accounts by individuals, both famous and not, on their experience of desire are invaluable in understanding how it works and they will be used widely throughout the following pages.

Personal anecdotes and explanations

Insight from biographies

I respectfully held out my hand to her and she took it with an air of utter indifference, but she pressed it firmly as she climbed into the carriage. The reader will be able to imagine the flame which this sent racing through my blood. (Casanova, 1798/1958, p. 192)

Leaning toward the table, she revealed nearly everything I desired. Then, slowly straightening up, she handed me the chemise. I was trembling so violently that I was unable to hold it. (Casanova, 1798/1958, p. 52)

I was a furnace of desire, and it was becoming impossible for me to resist the flame that was consuming me. (Casanova, 1798/1958, p. 81)

. . . but how could I go to sleep? I was still heated from the flame which Lucrezia had ignited in me. (Casanova, 1798/1958, p. 29)

The squeeze on Casanova's hand was interpreted by him, rightly or wrongly, as a signal of reciprocity and encouragement. It would appear to exemplify a fundamental feature that can be associated with desire and serve to accentuate it: the *resolution of uncertainty*. In such terms, the 'flame racing through the blood' following the squeeze would have been triggered by a combination of an initial desire and the sudden assessment that desire might shortly be fulfilled. Investigators can now identify changes in the activity of the brain that form the basis of desire. Casanova used the metaphor of heat and flames and he documented the attention-grabbing aspect of desire associated with persistence of erotic images in his conscious mind. He witnessed the ability of erotic thoughts to interfere with sleep, a feature shared with fear and anxiety.

Remaining at the extreme end of the range of sexual desires, a century or so after Casanova there is a special place for a Victorian English autobiographer, known as 'Walter'. Like Casanova, Walter would have found Damasio's question very easy to answer, and might only have wondered why the suggested reaction time was as long as 'a matter of seconds'.

> I was maddened by desire... at the sight of the fresh, modest, naked girls cleaning themselves so unsuspectingly... (Walter, 1995, p. 328)

> Then a thrill of desire shot through me and staggered me. I trembled as the want overtook me, and drew her closer to me... (Walter, 1995, p. 400)

Casanova and Walter document the power of the visual image to trigger their desire, a tendency to approach the source of desire, accompanied by a powerful emotional bodily reaction. Subsequent chapters will address the role of bodily changes, such as an accelerated heart rate and knotted stomach, in sexual desire. Are they simply the consequence of the desire or a contributory trigger to its intensity? Are they necessary for the experience of desire and can they act as a measure of its intensity? These bodily reactions seem similar to those associated with fear and anxiety. It will be suggested that this similarity is a key to understanding features of sexual desire.

> I sicken with carnal passion, pining for as yet unseen, unknown women... My life is almost unbearable from unsatisfied lust... It is constantly on me, depresses me, and urges me to yield. (Walter cited by Kronhausen and Kronhausen, 1967, p. 184)

Here Walter reveals the role of the imagination in inventing scenarios to trigger sexual desire, their motivating power and the tension that is created when the goal of the associated craving is not attained. Later chapters will explore the link between sexual fantasy and sexual behaviour.

The mysterious author, only ever known to us as 'Walter', endowed the world with a vivid depiction of his series of sexual adventures in Victorian London, a study entitled *My Secret Life*. The quest for sexual novelty was enough to sustain the intrepid author's fascination and vigour during a life that seemed to feature precious little else. Whether the vicarious re-living of this life is sufficient to hold the average reader's attention through Walter's 11 volumes, consisting of no fewer than 4,000 pages of unremitting graphic detail, is perhaps a moot point. By contrast, Casanova is at least a relatively short read, interspersed liberally with commentary on eighteenth-century European social history. Walter's writing gives insight into the role of fantasy and novelty in inflaming desire and preventing the onset of psychological fatigue by escalating the intensity of the content:

> I wish to refresh my memory by repeating the amorous exercises.... it rather seems as if it were strong animal want which is stimulating my desires and exercising my brain to invent even [more] voluptuous combinations. (Walter, cited by Marcus, 1966, p. 180)

Influential books and learned chapters have been written about Walter, where his exploits are scrutinized, surely the ultimate accolade for any writer of autobiography. Experts tend to agree that Walter's is not a work of fiction and that he can be used as evidence for the notions of sexual addiction and 'excessive appetite' (Orford, 2001), important topics when trying to understand so-called normal desires. Walter is an extreme case but a valuable one to study, since he illustrates how sexual desire *can* sometimes work, given ready availability and opportunity. Somewhat lacking subtlety and finesse in his approach, totally unrestrained and undeterred by threats such as sexually-transmitted diseases, it appears that Walter's desire was fired simply and instantly by the physical characteristics of the women to whom he was attracted. The variation in levels of restraint shown between individuals is another feature of desire that is central to its understanding.

Because of its relative simplicity, his life is like a laboratory for the study of exaggerated and undiluted lust. Born into a well-to-do family, social class meant little or nothing to Walter. Indeed, most of his liaisons appeared to have been greased by the woman's prospect of financial gain, which in most cases doubtless provided her with a temporary respite from grinding poverty. Although Casanova and Walter represent an extreme end of the spectrum, they are, of course, by no means unique in their instantaneous excitation and quest for novelty. A twentieth-century life illustrates this:

> When I met a woman, my desire for her was immediate and crippl-ing – a hammer blow to the heart...In the beginning there was just that longing, and the sense of myself as a starved orphan gazing through a window at a room where a happy family is sitting down to dinner. (Trachtenberg, 1989, p. 16)

As a measure of its intensity, the American author Peter Trachtenberg relates desire triggered by an attractive other to the associated bodily reaction:

> Once more I was intolerably drawn to other women – some I knew and some I just glimpsed across a subway platform on my way to work. I say 'intolerably' because what overcame me in their presence left me trembling and labouring for breath and sometimes brought tears to my eyes. God knows what those women thought when they saw a strange man gazing at them with such waif-like yearning. (Trachtenberg, 1989, p. 262)

The author of autobiographical detail expressed at such intensity is most commonly a male but females are also represented, albeit with not quite such an abundance or shade of desperation, as illustrated by the French writer Catherine Millet and the American writer Susan Cheever:

> crossing the huge lobby of an International hotel; the elegant and distinguished assistant who has been travelling across the country with me for two weeks catches hold of my arm when we have just said goodnight to each other, pulls me to him and kisses me on the mouth. 'In the morning, I'll come and see you in your room.' I can feel the spasm rising right up to my stomach. (Millet, 2003, p. 84)

> I would come to a rendezvous already in a state of exacerbated desire. From the very first full-on kisses, from the first moment when his arms crept up under my clothes, the pleasure was violent. (Millet, 2003, p. 207)

> For a while there is no such thing as 'too much' with the object of desire. The world shrinks down to a universe of two.
>   When the dose wears off, however, the sex addict doesn't need more of the same person, he or she needs a new person. (Cheever, 2008, p. 131)

This raises the topic of whether (a) there is such a thing as sexual addiction and (b) whether women as well as men are vulnerable. If the latter is the case, does this undermine any simple distinction in intensity of desires ('sex drive') between men and women? Is the expression 'addiction', which is usually framed in comparison to drug addiction, appropriate when it is applied to sex? It will be argued later that this notion with its drug-related connotations gives some valuable insights.

Moving towards the other end of the spectrum, there is the Scottish author and playwright J. M. Barrie, the creator of *Peter Pan*. One of the two boys who were closest to him observed (Chaney, 2005, p. 214):

> Of all the men I have ever known, Barrie was the wittiest, and the best company. He was also the least interested in sex.
>
> I don't believe that Uncle Jim ever experienced what one might call a stirring in the undergrowth for anyone – man, woman, or child.

If Walter is at one end of the spectrum and a lack of interest in sex in the middle, at the opposite pole from Walter is the experience of an aversion to sex. This might be in a general sense or specifically in the context of a particular relationship. It is exemplified in the account by the New Zealand writer Katherine Mansfield, which is thought to be autobiographical:

> She threw off her clothes, hastily, brushed out her long hair, and then suddenly looked at the wide, empty bed.
>
> A feeling of intolerable disgust came over her.
>
> By Lord Mandeville's pillow she saw a large bottle of eucalyptus and two clean handkerchiefs. From below in the hall she heard the sound of bolts being drawn – then the electric light switched off . . .
>
> She sprang into bed, and suddenly, instinctively with a little childish gesture, she put one arm over her face, as though to hide something hideous and dreadful as her husband's heavy, ponderous footsteps sounded on the stairs. (Mansfield, 2012, p. 543)

Anonymous reports

Some use drug-related metaphors to express how their sexual desire feels:

> I view sex as a fun experience and enjoy the thrill of meeting someone and seducing them. The feeling of having a conquest is exhilarating, like a high. (Predominantly heterosexual woman; Meston and Buss, 2009, p. 87)

Falling in love is always a big letdown. It's like doing cocaine. You get high, but sooner or later you know that you're going to run out and you're going to come down. And it's the same with love: the rush ends after three or four months. (Saul, American fashion executive; Trachtenberg, 1989, p. 46)

Casanovas often view sex as a progression of thrills, each of which must somehow surpass the one before it. When talking with them, one often hears that they are seeking an 'ultimate sexual experience'. (Trachtenberg, 1989, p. 56)

As exemplified by Saul and the insights of Peter Trachtenberg, regular sex can come to yield diminishing returns and then some people make attempts to compensate by increasing the intensity. The drug-related phenomenon of tolerance comes to mind here and later chapters will look at similarities. Walter's fantasy scenarios (just described) illustrate the same point. This quest can take the form of seeking variety and greater risk in order to attain an elusive super-high.

Conversely, some people feel no sexual desire at all but are quite happy with this and do not wish to change it (Brotto et al., 2010, p. 611):

Everyone in the asexual community wants to spread the message that it's [asexuality] not a disorder and it's not something that's a problem and needs to be fixed.

And from one asexual individual (Brotto et al., 2010, p. 611):

I've never had the interest and so, even if today you could say, 'Oh here . . . here's a pill that will fix you' . . . no, that's okay, thanks.

Fictional depictions of desire

Her skirts flew up as she fell to the ground, and she choked with laughter, saying she had not hurt herself; but as he felt her burning, sweating body against his face Jean clasped her firmly. The bitter female smell and the violent perfume of beaten hay in the open air intoxicated him and tensed all his muscles in passionate, angry desire. (Émile Zola, 1887/1975, p. 63)

Various sources of publicly available information, accurate or inaccurate, inform us on the triggers to sexual desire and how it appears to be manifest in behaviour. Great writers have portrayed desire, as in the fictional heroines Lady Chatterley and Emma Bovary. Film-makers have tried to capture the causes of desire and the settings in which it arises. Some individuals probably get much of their information from pornography, in which case they might absorb the erroneous impression that female desire is ever-ready, uninhibited, indiscriminate, and without complications, restraints or any requirement of reciprocity (Lederer, 1980).

A desire for pictorial sex

Casanova and Walter describe undiluted and uninhibited desire. However, we can make things even less complicated by considering desire for visual representations and what they reveal about real desire triggered by another human. Erotica and pornography permit understanding of how sexual desire works, since in some ways 'art' imitates the reality of what the consumer desires. Viewing it says something about sexual desire unrestrained by the problems of gaining access and the risk and prospect of rejection, failure and disease.

Pornography offers the prospect of heightened bodily arousal and of endless novelty and uncertainty:

> Even though we were having sex nearly every day, I still needed my porn fix. Instead of buying magazines, I switched over to going to adult bookstores. They had these little booths with porn films, so I'd pop my quarters in there. No matter how much sex my wife and I had, I still needed the vicarious thrill and stimulation of watching porn to satisfy me. (Rob; Maltz and Maltz, 2010, p. 92)

Some people derive instantaneous soothing from pornography:

> Porn gives me momentary relief from the pains of life. I don't care about the future. What matters is I have escaped for now. (Albert, a middle-aged American father of three; Maltz and Maltz, 2010, p. 62)

> I turned my sexual attention more to the pornography and less to the relationship with my fiancée. I developed a pattern of masturbating to porn whenever I was feeling lonely, frustrated or bored. Our decision to hold off on sex, coupled with how easy it was to access Internet porn at my job, turned my porn use into an addiction. (Corey, an American computer analyst, aged 34; Maltz and Maltz, 2010, p. 56)

As these quotations illustrate, the expression of sexual desire both in reality and in viewing pornography brings short-term positive mood changes and this would be expected to increase the target's future potential to attract the person. As with Corey, the virtual world of pornography can sometimes displace real sexual relationships. It becomes a 'supernormal' stimulus to sexual desire and triggers an escalation of intensity, a feature shared by some people's desires directed to real humans.

> Watching Internet porn began as a natural thing but quickly turned into a compulsion. It became a craving, like a drug. It felt unnatural if I didn't look at porn in the evening.

> When I get really stressed out and feel like a failure in life, it's like a little movie projector in my brain kicks on and starts showing the porn I've already seen to make me feel better. Then I get triggered to go buy and look at more porn. (Marie, an American widow, distracting herself from grief; Maltz and Maltz, 2010, pp. 92 and 200)

> I was looking for the ideal woman, like the ones who exist in porn. Porn hadn't prepared me to be with a real woman. I wanted perfection or nothing.

> I progressed from *Playboy* and soft-core magazines to the very edges of child pornography. And the progression was almost unnoticeable to me. It felt natural. I needed different and deeper stimulation. *Playboy* didn't satisfy me because it's too plain, too common. I wanted magazines that were barely legal. I also began using porn in combination with alcohol and other drugs to heighten the effect. (Hank; Maltz and Maltz, 2010, pp. 125–6)

These accounts reveal the phenomenon of escalation in an attempt to find perfection, a feature shared with sexual desire towards real humans. Note Hank's use of drugs to try to obtain the 'super-high'. The interaction of drugs and sex gives insight into how desire works, discussed later. We need to ask why only certain individuals are attracted to pornography and experience a need to escalate its intensity. Equally important to understand is the existence of many who view pornography but without its use becoming problematic in any way.

Linking the objective and subjective

How does sexual desire work and why does it not work in the same way for everyone? Comparing different people, from where does the enormous variety in desire's form and intensity arise?

Personal reports in surveys that ask questions concerning what desire feels like and the conditions most likely to trigger it start to fill in the puzzle. Consider also posing the closely related questions – what does it feel like to experience sexual frustration? What is an orgasm like? Surely, the only source of evidence is to ask the person having such experiences.

However, valuable as they are, personal reports leave much unexplained, since many factors that contribute to desire lie outside conscious awareness. By simply investigating how sexual desire appears to the individual concerned, there is no way of identifying these additional factors. Consider the following phenomena that call for a very different source of insight:

• Why do some otherwise similar people differ so much in what excites them sexually?
• How do hormones, which are simply chemicals, help to excite a mental state, sexual desire? Why do they not invariably have this effect on everyone?
• Why do some people wish desperately to be fired sexually by a devoted partner but are puzzled that they simply can't get aroused?
• Why does desire for a given individual often fade over time and how do some hormones and psychoactive drugs boost a flagging desire?
• How can a woman show the objective signs of sexual arousal, measured at the genitals, but report no subjective feeling of desire or sexual arousal?
• How do sexual desire and the pleasure of sex sometimes become uncoupled?

The answers are not self-evident to the person feeling the sexual desire or wishing that they could feel it.

How can we understand the desire felt by others? Having no personal experience outside conventional bounds or even with a particular taste that violates these bounds, many people have great difficulty fathoming some of the 'less regular' or 'less acceptable' forms that other people's desire can take. For example:

• A devoted spouse who reports a good sex life cannot see why a partner would view pornography or commit adultery.

- Why would a man climb a drainpipe for a brief glimpse of a woman undressing when he could more safely and reliably witness this at a perfectly legal establishment?
- How could an intelligent and well-informed judge or clergyman be so foolish as to be caught downloading illegal pornography?
- Why does his knowledge of the potential for ruin not deter a seemingly devoted father from seeking sex with one of his own children?
- What kind of brain process would lead someone to risk death through strangulation in a search for the ultimate sexual high?
- Why would a pop star or Hollywood actor having available a devoted following of admirers and financial resources be fired by seemingly sordid illicit sex in a car or public lavatory?
- Why, knowing of the risk of AIDS, would someone deliberately seek unsafe sex with an HIV-infected partner?

The subjective experience of one's own desire and what triggers it, as well as a normal experience of fear and disgust, might prove very inadequate guides to understanding such behaviour.

What is meant by 'sexual desire'?

It might seem obvious what the expression 'sexual desire' means. However, an attempt to state exactly what we mean by it could prove useful. To Stoléru (2006), it involves 'a mental representation' of a goal involving sexual pleasure. One might add that the goal is normally another individual and this *conscious experience* of desire is emotionally charged. When such desire triggers action, it is on the basis of an expectation of sexual pleasure. A person could articulate this in words. Sometimes hedonistic imagery just pops into consciousness as if from nowhere and forms the focus of attention (Kavanagh et al., 2005), erotic imagery exemplifying this. For such imagery to be used as an index of desire, its immediate consequences might be considered. If a conscious effort is made to elaborate on the imagery so as to enrich it, particularly if to plan future engagement with the individual portrayed, this would constitute a feature of sexual desire in the terms used here.

How, you might wonder, could things be otherwise? In principle, we might be drawn like iron to a magnet or a moth to a flame with no conscious expectation of an outcome and indeed some aspects of sexual behaviour appear to be understandable in such terms. However, the fact that desire as consciously experienced has the qualities of conscious *seeking* and *wanting* in its nature is crucial to its fuller understanding.

Much processing of information occurs at an unconscious level and forms the basis on which the conscious experience of desire is built. For example, a perfume or a part of town might have formed an association with desire in the past and is currently triggering conscious desire. We might have only the outcome of such processing available to consciousness; that is, the erotic imagery, not the nature of the means by which it was produced.

One might perform sexual behaviour for reasons other than an expectation of sexual pleasure, for example acting out of fear, sympathy, duty, or for the hope of health, social or financial gain. 'Sexual desire' will be used here to mean only desire having the intention of gaining personal sexual pleasure. The desire for pleasure might merge with other motives that are the necessary condition for permitting sexual behaviour, such as a search for emotional oneness or commitment. In other cases, a person might engage in sexual behaviour for an ulterior motive with no expectation of sexual pleasure.

It might sound perfectly normal for a person to say something like 'I really desire you' or 'my desire is intense' but slightly odd to walk into a café and say 'I desire a cucumber sandwich.' But why, since in each case there is a wanted goal of the desire associated with pleasure and action is taken to reach it? It would seem that 'desire' implies a very high hedonic and emotional value, more than for the prospect of a cucumber sandwich, and the choice of the word is designed to convey this meaning (Schroeder, 2004). To say on an erotically charged evening 'I now desire dark chocolate' might not sound so odd, since desires can intermingle.

Consideration of what the word 'desire' means raises the possibility of fundamental differences in desire between men and women. It is probably no accident that most of the quotes given here, particularly the more explicit, are from males. The following chapters will address this topic.

Bringing science and the personal together

Scientific studies offer insights on how sexual desire arises in the brain. For example, new technology permits the activity of the brain to be scanned while a participant is triggered by sexual stimuli, such as an erotic film. This is called 'brain imaging' or 'functional neuroimaging'. Changes in blood flow in the regions of the brain that occur in response to the film can be measured, sometimes revealing abnormalities in activity corresponding to abnormal desires. Such a scientific study does not provide better evidence than the subjective witness of the individual. It is just *different* and, at least in principle, entirely complementary evidence. The description given by the participants is still vital in scientific studies; correspondences between what they report and the activity of the brain can be mapped. For example, the person's subjective desire triggered by a film clip can be ranked on a scale of one to ten and matched against both activity patterns in the brain and the flow of blood to the genitals.

Activation or its lack in different brain regions can be linked to how the psychological experience of desire arises and how the brain either translates desire into sexual behaviour or inhibits its expression. Equally insightful is when a person reports an absence of sexual desire even in the presence of what would normally be adequate trigger stimuli, such as erotic images, or when a person resists sexual temptation. The brain activity of an individual who reports low or absent desire can be contrasted with controls having normal desire, with the possibility of better therapeutic interventions. Of course, with the body restrained in a neuroimaging apparatus, the scope for sexual action is somewhat limited, except in the imagination! But this restraint in itself can give useful information and the imagination is a powerful aspect of human sexuality.

Such questions as 'how does sexual desire work?' and 'how does desire translate into a flow of blood to the genitals?' have something in common with other 'how does it work?' questions. For example, to answer how the blood circulation works under different circumstances, one would need to consider the parts that make up the circulation: the blood, the heart with its chambers and valves and the control that the brain exerts on the heart and the blood vessels. Examining these bits and seeing how they interrelate gives understanding of how the whole works. From this, we might better understand how the circulation can go wrong in the case of, say, a heart attack or how beta-blockers that restrain the activity of the heart or drugs that lower cholesterol work. To see how things can go wrong is a valuable way of understanding how they work normally.

In a similar way, understanding sexual desire involves consideration of a number of 'components' that contribute to desire: the sight of an attractive other individual or the fantasy about them, sexual arousal by the brain, an accelerated heart rate, the anticipation of pleasure, the action of hormones on the brain and signals running both ways between the brain and genitals. How do these act together in creating sexual desire? The present book aims to give some answers. An understanding in such terms can then be used to address differences in desire between individuals, excesses of desire, aberrant desire and how medicine can increase or lower desire.

Yet, sexual desire is more complex than analogies with the circulation can suggest. It has unique subjective aspects and reflects cultural and historical change, making any understanding extremely challenging. What is an acceptable desire with widespread manifestations in one culture might be a capital offence in another. Although kissing is widely seen as erotic in Europe and America, there are other cultures in which it is absent (Gebhard, 1971). Even in the United States, deep kissing tends to be shunned by the so-called 'lower-level male'; at least it was in 1948 (Kinsey et al., 1948)! So, considering such cross-cultural differences, it appears that the sexually maturing body emerges with certain potentials for attributing desire to particular bodily regions and behaviours and which of these are realized depends in large part upon learning and culture.

Curiously, the reasons *why* people have sex have not been widely researched, except in recent years (Meston and Buss, 2007). Much research on the motivational basis of sex is based upon rats. For humans, there is a mass of information on sexual *behaviour* and bodily arousal both in the popular and academic literature; indeed, it must be one of the most described subjects of all time. However, the *desire* that underlies this behaviour earns not even a single index entry in the classic texts of Kinsey on the sexual behaviour of the human male and female (Kinsey et al., 1948, 1953). Equally curious is the observation that sexual *pleasure* has not played a large role in the history of sexology and does not even earn as much as an index entry in some of the classical texts (discussed by Abramson and Pinkerton, 1995), though one might have thought that it would be fundamental. It earns a single entry in the Kinsey study on the male (Kinsey et al., 1948) but none on the study of the female (Kinsey et al., 1953). This might be a hangover from Victorian prudery and shyness, though such writers as Casanova and Walter would appear to bear witness to pleasure's centrality. The present book will discuss the role of pleasure in how desire works, as well as considering the vagaries of how pleasure is sought.

An endless variety

Yes, sometimes I'll have desire and not necessarily want to consummate it. (Norma, 40-year-old woman; Brotto et al., 2009)[2]

Anyone investigating sexual desire soon confronts a dilemma: can you meaningfully study it in isolation? In one regard you have to, since, even with such simplification, it is hard to understand. However, investigators need to remember the multiple goals that people try to juggle, attain simultaneously, blend or pit against each other. These include a search for improved self-image, short-term excitement or long-term attachment. In some cases, sexual desire doubtless merges with an extraneous goal, whereas at other times one can imagine that sexual behaviour is purely instrumental to another goal and there need be little sexual desire present. Some experience sexual desire but inhibit it in the interests of such goals as safety, celibacy, fidelity, maintaining professional etiquette or keeping an image. Understanding the sources of such restraint can tell us much.

'Low-level' factors such as a magnetic pull of sexual attraction, which probably have much in common across species, co-exist with some high-level goals, such as to seek marital harmony. Some motives seem idiosyncratic and perhaps the only way of getting access to them is to ask the one having the desire. These goals are mediated by more recently evolved brain regions and can be consciously articulated.

According to self-reports based upon people's own conscious insights into their desires, the reasons for having sexual behaviour include to feel wanted and desired, to be accepted into a gang, to gain promotion, simply to please a partner, to appease a partner or to infuriate and punish a partner, to come nearer to God or to move away from God, out of a sense of adventure or to boost flagging self-esteem, to assume status in the eyes of others or to look bad in the eyes of others, to relieve boredom, loneliness, headaches, depression, anxiety or insomnia. The list is indeed already a long one (Cooper et al., 2006; Meston and Buss, 2007; 2009; Tuzin, 1995).

Motives can be roughly categorized into (a) those that involve gain (e.g. feeling more confident as a person) and (b) those that produce escape from aversion (e.g. fear of losing a partner). The expectation of pure *sexual* pleasure might or might not interact with such goals and it might or might not be attained.

Researchers conduct surveys in which they ask those who are willing to reveal how their own sexual desire feels, when it occurs, who and what incites or kills it, and what they tend to do about it, if anything. Of course, many individuals would be more prepared to disclose their innermost secrets to an anonymous Internet-based questionnaire than in the form of a face-to-face account. Using this method, people are good at describing what sexual desire feels like and the circumstances that trigger, inhibit or dampen it.

A landmark study was performed by Meston and Buss (2007), as published in their article 'Why humans have sex' and their book entitled *Why Women Have Sex* (Meston and Buss, 2009). It revealed great complexity of motives and many surprises. My hunch is that a comparable book entitled *Why Men Have Sex* would be considerably shorter.

The research revealed 237 different reasons given for having sex. These ranged from the most obvious, such as to obtain pleasure or babies, to the unbelievably obscure and Machiavellian. This section gives a sample of some of the reasons reported to Meston and Buss and other researchers.

Gaining control

A feature of not only human make-up but that of many non-human species too is the motivation to exert control over the environment, including the social environment. Sexual behaviour offers a potent means of doing so.

> I was suffering with bulimia. I was having serious control issues and it felt good to me at the time to have complete sexual control over someone, especially a man. (Heterosexual woman, aged 23; Meston and Buss, 2009, p. 206)

> I had sex with a couple of guys because I felt sorry for them . . . I felt power over them, like they were weaklings under me and I was in control. It boosted my confidence to be the teacher in the situation and made me feel more desirable. (Heterosexual woman aged 25; Meston and Buss, 2009, p. 206)

Maintaining self-image

Humans appear to have a need to maintain a certain self-image (Baumeister and Vohs, 2001). For some, this is of such intensity that the expression 'narcissistic' is applied. Earning the admiration of sex partners, finding reciprocity in flirting or even achieving some degree of sexual competence in the eyes of peers must surely contribute to sexual desire. People tend also to be motivated to seek a self-identity such that they stand out from the mass of humanity (Berger and Shiv, 2011). This is manifest in such activities as buying clothes that are distinctive and presumably some people seek a sexual identity that equally gives them distinction. As the English comedian Russell Brand is witness (Brand, 2007, p. 112): 'For me, it was more important that people knew I was having sex than having sex.'

The search for perfection

The capacity to imagine worlds beyond one's actual reality means that humans are very good at thinking of sexual scenarios that they are not currently experiencing. The disparity between reality and what can be imagined can set them off on a search for the elusive perfect experience, involving some escalation of their activities (C. Wilson, 1988). Part of the problem is the tendency to satiate on constant levels of stimulation; what was novel yesterday is familiar today, a phenomenon termed 'habituation'. The perfect solution is often one characterized by high arousal, described shortly, and a dimension of the forbidden (C. Wilson, 1988).

Producing children

Some feel sexual desire for the conscious intention of producing children, but this motive appeared not to come very high on the list presented by Meston and Buss. In principle, evolutionary processes might have taken a different direction and created a strong desire for children as the means of transmitting genes. This is not how it has turned out. Rather, evolutionary processes have produced a strong desire for sex, which, unless the situation is artificially manipulated, tends, with some probability, to produce children! The conscious desire for children is presumably a peculiarly human feature, added on to the basic desire process at a late stage of evolution.

Avoiding pain, distress and discomfort or relationship difficulties

Desire can arise since it has relieved physical or psychological distress in the past. A significant percentage of males report increased interest in sex at times of depression or anxiety, reporting that sex, particularly mastur-bation, lowered their level of negative emotion (Janssen and Bancroft, 2007).

> The physical pleasure of sex is one of the best ways for me to relieve menstrual cramping. I've had sex for this reason many times as a comfort-based motivation. (Heterosexual woman of 47 years; Meston and Buss, 2009, p. 239)

> Many times, in most of my long term relationships, I have had sex because I felt that to go for too long without sex would risk having my partner leave or go somewhere else for sex. (Heterosexual woman of 33 years; Meston and Buss, 2009, p. 110)

For some, sexual desire is weak or non-existent but, nonetheless, they force themselves to engage in sexual behaviour, another feature of how human motivation is organized.

> My sex drive is really pathetic so sometimes I push myself to have sex now and then even though I'm almost never in the mood. (Pre-dominantly heterosexual woman of 27 years; Meston and Buss, 2009, p. 120)

> Sometimes, it was easier to just give in and do it when he wanted to rather than put up with listening to him whine and complain. (Heterosexual woman of 29 years; Meston and Buss 2009, p. 118)

Revenge

Occasionally, a truly ulterior motive exists.

> I decided that I wanted to sleep with this man, just to sort of get back at my friend, and to sort of prove that I was the more attractive/better one of us. (Heterosexual woman of 22 years; Meston and Buss, 2009, p. 91)

> I didn't find the woman I had sex with to make her jealous [to be] attractive and would not have had sex with her if I had not felt I had

something to prove. (Gay/lesbian woman of 21 years; Meston and Buss, 2009, p. 101)

So, what is a suitable framework for understanding such complexity?

Culture and biology

Avoiding false dichotomies

For too long, arguments have raged over whether social influences *or* biology can best explain sexuality, including its diversity. Expressed in other terms – is human desire more a social or biological phenomenon? This discussion is unproductive and will be actively avoided. A modern understanding of brain–environment interaction reveals that these influences are intertwined in such a way that it is meaningless to give relative weights to them. Changes in desire and behaviour might result from initial changes in either culture or an individual human's biology but invariably we must take both into account. Any viable attempt to understand sexual desire will need to tackle this complexity head-on.

It is amazing that false dichotomies such as 'biology *versus* social' have endured for so long, fuelled by competition in academia. As Tolman and Diamond (2001) argue (p. 34):

> We maintain that neither a purely biological nor a purely sociocultural approach can encompass the complexity of sexual desire and thus neither is fully satisfying on its own.

They continue (p. 34):

> This seems so commonsensical as to hardly merit discussion – who could argue with studying culture *and* biology instead of culture *or* biology? Yet this is not the impression one would gain from the contemporary empirical literature on gender and sexuality.

The kind of evidence

The enormous range in the forms of human sexual desire and the intensities of its expression across cultures and between individuals might appear to support the notion that social and cultural factors predominantly account for it. This is unlike the behaviour of non-humans. However, it does not undermine the importance of biology in explaining human sexuality. The fact that most people are heterosexual and attracted to mature adults doubtless owes something to cultural norms and expectations. However, the tendency would appear to be rather too universal to be simply due to that. It seems reasonable to speculate that culture mirrors biological tendency in this regard. Although such strong tendencies to conventionality emerge, because the human brain has evolved with a powerful general capacity for flexibility, learning and creativity, many different pathways to gaining sexual pleasure are also available.

The brain mechanisms underlying the flexibility and diversity of human behaviour co-exist and intermesh with some rather fixed brain structures that are somewhat similar comparing different species (Panksepp, 1998). The evidence to be reviewed later will suggest that the biological bases of sexual desire, whether gay, bisexual or straight, whether directed straightforwardly to humans or fetishes, whether legal or illegal, whether social or solitary, show certain similarities in terms of basic mechanisms of desire, arousal and pleasure. Inhibitory processes to varying degrees of intensity and effectiveness also seem to apply throughout. It appears that many, if not all, forms of desire can become addictive, reflecting, I would suggest, the common feature that the mechanisms of desire can move behaviour out of kilter with ideal wishes.

The group membership of an individual has a powerful role in his or her sexual behaviour (Henslin, 1971). Consider some differences that are evident over periods of time, such as why one decade is more permissive than another. While not ignoring the biology, an explanation would most likely need to focus initially upon *changes* in culture over time, rather than to try to find changes in biology as the instigator (Udry, 1995). However, cultures can surely exert little influence on desire and behaviour except by acting via a biological organ, the brain. Brains are at the physical basis of desire and they make some of its forms much more likely than others. Irrespective of the culture, brains are the embodiment of the control of sexual action, excitation, inhibition and pleasure.

People's sexuality tends to tap into cultural stereotypes, social norms and roles. However, some individuals do not invariably follow the conventions, rules and expectations that could be most effortlessly absorbed from their social context. If things were straightforward, we would not expect to find so many sexually abusive parents, terrified and guilt-ridden masturbators, defrocked priests, disowned and even imprisoned homosexuals, banished daughters and executed adulteresses. The tally is a long and depressing one that cuts across cultures and predilections and it surely bears witness to the power of the discovery of sources of desire and pleasure not entirely restrained by social convention.

Within a given culture, there exist subcultures often suggesting different standards from the conventional as their social norm. For example, in violent pornography, the portrayal of women as sex objects and suitable fodder for violent male fantasies has probably much to answer for in terms of sexual harassment and assault. It is insightful to consider the conditions that set desire in a direction that conforms or does not conform to cultural norms, values and stereotypes.

So much for the cultural factor, now consider a given society and point in time and focus upon biological differences. As Bancroft (2000, p. 191) observes:

> We must take the individual biological variability into account when striving to explain the fact that in a given cultural setting, individuals vary considerably in the extent to which they conform to the cultural pattern.

Differences in sexual behaviour between individuals appear to arise in part from genetic differences, which are mediated via differences in their brains (Ellis, 1989; Udry, 1995). For example, differences in novelty-seeking seem to be explicable in part on the basis of genetic differences. Similarly, within a particular individual, certain chemical changes (specifically elevated levels of dopamine[3]) in the brain, as in some treatments for Parkinson's disease, can amplify sexual desire to the point of addiction and can unmask new features of desire (Politis et al., 2013). In trying to understand this, the focus would be upon changes in the individual's brain caused by the drug. However, the changed behaviour necessarily depends upon the possibilities offered by the particular social context, and will surely further change this context.

Even where desire takes an unusual form, as in coercive and violent sexual behaviour, its roots can still be understood better in terms of the intermeshing of biological and social factors, rather than either factor alone. Researchers can identify the properties of particular brain regions and how they appear to deviate from normal in the case of sexual offenders (Raine, 2013). Of course, such brains exist in an environment of the individual's upbringing, which all too often contains identifiable aspects of abuse, and this environment might be assumed to lock into interaction with the brain to affect brain development and to contribute to later deviance.

Emerging sexual desire at adolescence is triggered in part by increasing levels of sex hormones. It tends to be restrained in its expression by social controls, for example parental (Udry, 1990). To ignore either source of influence would lead to erroneous conclusions.

The bigger picture

Accounts of sexual desire do not exist in a social vacuum (Tolman and Diamond, 2001). Rather, societal attitudes, prohibitions and morals to some extent reflect the contemporary understanding of desire and con-tribute to theories on its nature. Suggested advice and therapeutic inter-ventions build upon such understanding. Popular articles, books and magazines explain how to boost desire by the correct choice of diet and life-style, or what to do in terms of dress, gestures, language and body image to trigger irresistible desire in others. Apart from religious texts, few instruct us on how to live with frustrated desire or how to resist temptation. As will be described later, insights into how desire can be increased or reduced illuminate its bases.

Whether men and women are treated as equals surely relates to an understanding of the bases of sexual desire. Traditionally, male sexuality has been described as something ubiquitous, ever-ready and relatively straightforward. By stark contrast, over the centuries women have var-iously been portrayed as, on the one hand, essentially devoid of any intrinsic sexual desire and simply the passive targets of men's desires, but on the other hand, as beings with insatiable drive (Sherfey, 1973), who present devious lures for men's downfall (discussed by Hrdy, 1999; Laqueur, 1990; Tolman and Diamond, 2001). In the latter terms, men are said to have conspired to suppress female drive. The present book will argue that neither extreme position is strictly true, and will attempt to give balance to this debate.

Scientific explanations and lay accounts often appeal to metaphors and analogies and these say much about the interpretation of sexual desire within different cultures. For example, reflecting on his upbringing, the British art historian and journalist Brian Sewell wrote (Sewell, 2011, 169):

> I had too to contend with the increasing pressure of sex and its conflict with piety. I could no longer persuade myself that masturbation was no more an assisted bodily function, a purging as natural and necessary as the emptying of bowel and bladder –'Think no more of it', my parish priest once said, 'just as you think nothing of going to the lavatory'.

Evolutionary psychology

Evolutionary psychology spawns passionate disciples and opponents in roughly equal measure. It follows in the tradition of sociobiology but starts from psychological considerations. Features of desire often fit its predictions on what has proved successful in reproduction during the evolutionary history of humans (Buss, 2003). For example, this perspective makes sense of the observation that men tend to find younger women more attractive than older, since the younger usually have a higher reproductive potential. Similarly, sexual jealousy and mate-guarding make sense since they help to protect against infidelity. Gender differences in sexual behaviour feature at centre-stage in evolutionary psychology, and the underlying assumptions will be examined later.

The brains that emerged in evolution now find themselves in a twenty-first-century society, very different from that in which they evolved. Therefore, in the spirit of evolutionary psychology, it will be argued that consideration of the intermeshing of evolved brains and contemporary culture is again the only way to gain insight.

The framework

Understanding sexual desire and behaviour requires a new organizing framework, one that does justice to the influences of both biology and culture and which can mesh with evolutionary psychology. This will go some way towards showing how desire works, encompassing its constant features as well as its richness and diversity. The framework needs to account for the fact that social and biological factors are not in competition in terms of their relative weight in the control of desire. Rather, it needs to show how biological and social contributions interweave. It must be able to accommodate the fact that different influences arising from cultures can be assimilated by the brain and contribute to differences in sexual desire. Some individuals, because of a combination of biology and life-time experience, either feel no sexual desire or are able to suppress such feelings with little discomfort or harm.

Byrne (1986) argued that sex research has been bedevilled by a tendency to look at the bits rather than the whole. He sees the problem as rather similar to that of one individual describing a trunk, another legs and a third portraying tusks and so on but missing the notion of a whole elephant. This book will try to sketch the whole elephant.

The direction to be taken here

I have spent my academic life researching motivation, including sexual desire. Advances in experimental psychology and neuroscience, particularly since around 1980–1990, now offer some important new insights. However, this information on the brain is not enough. We need all the help that we can get and I will call upon evidence from biology, evolutionary psychology, sociology, feminist studies, psychiatry and clinical psychology, as well as seeing what classical literature and philosophy have to offer. Crucial to understanding desire is the personal witness of the experience and this will also play a key role by being integrated with a scientific perspective.

There are two principal and interacting strands of the research with which I have been closely associated and these will be brought together and set into a broader context of sex research. They are described now.

The difference between wanting and liking

In 1990, working as an academic at The Open University in England, I had a visit from a good friend, Kent Berridge, an experimental psychologist from the University of Michigan at Ann Arbor. I had spent some years studying the psychology of motivation – what moves us? How do desires arise? Based upon ideas advanced by the late Canadian psychologist Dalbir Bindra, I had developed a theoretical model that offered some new insights and could start to accommodate diversity of desire (Bindra, 1978; Toates, 1986). However, this research needed to be grounded better in how real flesh-and-blood brains work and how their chemical messengers underlie desire.

Kent described some surprising results that he and his Michigan colleagues had obtained (Berridge and Valenstein, 1991). These findings appeared to overturn a cherished belief, shared initially by the researchers themselves, on the role of the brain's chemical messenger, dopamine. Previously, it had been thought that dopamine is the brain chemical that confers pleasure on the events of life. That is to say, the pleasures of food, drugs, gambling or sex, or whatever, are a result of the activity of this chemical in the brain. For example, a cold drink to a dehydrated person would taste pleasant because the water on the tongue sends messages to the brain that cause it to release dopamine. To the same person when not dehydrated, the water on the tongue would trigger the release of little or no dopamine and there would not be such an intense hedonic feeling. When viewed in such terms, orgasm would represent an enormous burst of activity by dopamine.

Contrary to established belief, the Michigan researchers' evidence showed that changing dopamine levels did not alter the apparent pleasure that rats derive from tasting food. Therefore, this suggested that dopamine did not mediate the pleasures of life. Rather, dopamine appeared to mediate *wanting* of such things as food, sex, and so on. So, it would follow that some other substance in the brain (introduced later in the book) must serve the role allocated to dopamine as the physical basis of *liking*, also expressed as pleasure and hedonics. To many investigators, this represented a radical shift in thinking. To be precise, the new results showed that dopamine is not involved in the pleasures of eating and drinking with a likely extension to sexual contact and orgasm. However, this substance might still have some role in other pleasures, such as the pleasure of contemplating, pursuing and achieving a goal (Klein, 1987), a theme that will be investigated later.

Many scientists, myself included, do not necessarily welcome radical change, preferring to see confirmation of what we know already with a few new i's dotted and t's crossed. Surely, I protested, common sense dictates that we want what we like and like what we want and the two invariably go up and down in parallel. The thirsty person both wants and likes water. So, why should evolutionary processes have 'invented' two distinct mechanisms, each exploiting a different chemical, to solve this one problem? The researchers were as surprised by the results as I was but they had had more time to assimilate them.

That evening over a drink in the local pub, Kent countered my scepticism by pointing out that one of the intellectual foundations for their new ideas on the role of dopamine in mediating wanting was my own theoretical research (Toates, 1986). Sharing the trait of vanity with most of the world, scientists are particularly susceptible to their own research being cited and I am no exception to this. I started to lower my resistance.

Within two years of his visit, Kent Berridge sent me the first draft of a paper that he and Terry Robinson had written, in which they applied their distinction between wanting and liking to drug addiction. Dopamine was given a role in only the wanting aspect. There is a fracture line: the dopamine-mediated wanting of drugs can go up as addiction progresses, while liking them can even come down over the same time. This paper (Robinson and Berridge, 1993) has gone on to become one of the most (if not *the* most) cited articles of all time in biological psychology. Their perspective has now given a whole new meaning to the relationship between desire and pleasure. The paper dispelled any doubts, convincing me of the distinction and reinforcing my curiosity in tackling the issue. Of course, sex is not exactly like taking drugs but there are some common features and the book applies related ideas to sexual desire.

On reflection, should we have been surprised that dopamine is implicated in wanting? On the one hand, scientific articles, textbooks and the popular media told us that dopamine equals hedonism (see the account by Salamone et al., 2007). At the time of writing, a Google search putting in the words 'dopamine' and 'hedonism' yielded 3,230,000 hits. On the other hand, there were already suggestions that the link is with wanting. Jaak Panksepp, then at Bowling Green State University in Ohio, published a review paper in 1982 in the influential journal *The Behavioral and Brain Sciences*, in which he described an 'expectancy system' that pulls animals, human and other, towards such things as food, drugs and sex

(Panksepp, 1982). He suggested that dopamine is the most likely candidate to serve as a chemical messenger in this system. Ironically, I had worked with Jaak Panksepp some years before this and had published a commentary on his paper. At times we are so inundated with information that we simply don't make the right mental connections.

Levels within the brain

A second theme of the book will be that the brain is organized at different levels, as a kind of hierarchy. This is not a new idea since numerous scholars have suggested it over many years. However, understanding of how this organization is embedded in the brain and the wide implications of it for understanding sexual desire is new (Toates, 2009). Furthermore, the role of dopamine acting at different levels is now better understood.

The human brain contains regions that are old in terms of evolution and have much in common with those in other species ('old brain levels'). These regions co-exist with other regions that have evolved relatively recently, which offer peculiarly human possibilities for flexible and creative behaviour and which can assimilate rich and complex information from culture ('new brain levels'). For example, humans can perform what is probably a unique task of mental time travel, reflecting on early experiences and anticipating future mental states such as sexual pleasure or guilt. The capacity for time travel would seem to be highly relevant to sexual desire, which can be expressed in a wide range of different forms.

Such hybrid brain organization has been compared to a jet engine being added to a horse and cart, something likely to create more than the occasional problem. Only by seeing how this combination of brain regions works can we understand the idiosyncrasies of human desire.

These two sources of understanding, the role of dopamine and the way that the brain is organized in levels, are brought together with other information in the present book. Its central theme is that sexual desire can be much better understood in terms of how several such processes interact. If the logic to be developed here is correct, sexual differences (e.g. in tendencies to addiction or use of fetishes) do not require the postulation of completely new factors; rather, they arise from differences in settings and inputs to what are universal processes.

The next chapter turns to the basic principles underlying the explanation of sexual desire.

In summary

- An explanation of sexual desire must tackle the immense variation between people with regard to its intensity.
- To understand sexual desire two sources of evidence need to be brought together: (a) subjective reports from individuals about their feeling of desire and its expression; and (b) objective scientific findings.
- Sexual desire is that associated with the intention of attaining sexual pleasure.
- Sexual behaviour is not always motivated by sexual desire. Various other (some 'ulterior') motives can exist.
- Culture and biology intertwine as determinants of sexual desire and behaviour.
- Wanting can be distinguished from liking and these two factors sometimes get out of alignment.
- The organization of the bases of desire is by means of levels in the brain.
- At one level, the brain processes underlying sexual desire and arousal show certain similarities when we compare species.
- In spite of similarities across species, there are some peculiar ('highly evolved') features of human brains and behaviour that exist alongside the more basic and general features. Flexibility and creativity are at their most refined in humans.
- By considering how the *general* features and the *peculiarly human* features co-exist and interact in their effects, we can understand the complexities of human sexuality.
- The vagaries and varieties of sexual desire can be better understood by examining how some component processes in the brain interact.

TWO

EXPLAINING DESIRE: MULTIPLE PERSPECTIVES

> The clashing point of two subjects, two disciplines, two cultures – of
> two galaxies, so far as that goes – ought to produce creative chances.
> In the history of mental activity that has been where some of the
> breakthroughs came.
>
> (C. P. Snow, 1965, p. 16)

This chapter looks at several types of explanation that can be applied
to sexual desire and the links between them. It starts by considering
desire in the here-and-now; that is, events in the mind and brain as
individuals experience sexual desire. Some basic psychology and biology
will then be introduced. The book suggests that we can gain insight by
exploring similarities between sex and a number of other activities, for
example feeding, gambling and drug-taking. The chapter then asks how
the processes underlying sexual desire came into being. Two very different
time scales will be considered: the evolutionary history of humans and
the development of the individual.

The 'here-and-now': broad principles

The study of desire in the here-and-now is in terms of brains and minds, as
well as such things as heart rate and blood flow to the genitals. Of course,
desire is often triggered by the perception of an attractive person. This
much would be obvious simply from talking to the one feeling the desire,
quite apart from monitoring events in the body and observing behaviour.
In the physical absence of an attractive other, representations of such an
individual in the form of pictures or simply memories in the mind can

trigger desire. Sensations arising in the genitals also contribute to desire and lock into interaction with the factors just described.

How are objective and subjective linked?

How does sexual desire arise? What might inhibit putting desire into effect? We have two different and what are sometimes seen as competitive types of answer. Some rationalists, believing in free will and the inscrutability of another's mind, might suggest that answers are beyond the realm of science. Only the one doing the desiring can give an answer. By contrast, scientists sometimes argue that subjective conscious insight into the causes of behaviour is fallible, unable to be tested and therefore of no help to understanding. Rather, only the objective techniques of science, such as looking at the activity of a person's brain or their genetics and life-history, can provide testable answers. The present book rejects both of these extreme positions and uses subjective and objective evidence.

The relationship between brains and conscious minds has proven conceptually difficult for scholars over at least two thousand years. Clearly, it is not going to be solved here! However, some words are needed on the approach adopted. It is assumed that, for events in the mind, there are corresponding parallel events in the brain. This is taken to be true of the mind's conscious and unconscious aspects. For example, the conscious feeling of desire corresponds to activity in particular regions of the brain, whereas the pleasure of orgasm might correspond to activity in different regions. So, as a short-hand, the term 'brain/mind' will be used to indicate activity in particular brain regions and the associated mind events.

Taking care with dichotomies

A dichotomy pervades public discourse on minds, brains and behaviour. It is expressed in different but related ways, usually as 'mind *versus* body' or 'psychology *versus* biology' and has echoes of that between biology and social factors (Chapter 1). The dichotomy is exemplified by such claims as – 'the problem is purely psychological' or 'could there be a biological reason for this?' Such logic is fraught with hazards, leading to much confusion.

Suppose that, as a treatment for cancer, a woman's ovaries or adrenal glands are removed. This would cut off the supply of hormone secreted by the gland. Similarly, a man with prostate cancer might take medicine to lower the level of the hormone testosterone. Following these interventions, suppose that sexual desire falls. It would be correct to describe this as a *biological* cause of the loss of desire. However, to the individual concerned, sexual desire and its loss represent *psychological* phenomena. So, even though the initial cause can be described as 'biological', the effect of the hormonal change is experienced as psychological. So, how can a biological change have a psychological effect?

According to the perspective advanced here, any psychological changes correspond to changes in the brain. Sex hormones are released into the blood by glands and travel to the brain, where they sensitize particular regions, making them more responsive to sexual stimuli and thoughts. Therefore, following a loss of hormones (a biological event), the activity of particular parts of the brain changes. This is simultaneously experienced as the psychological state of loss of desire. Restoration of the lost hormones would re-sensitize the brain regions and might well be experienced as a recovery of sexual desire.

Reciprocally, events described as 'psychological' can have effects throughout the body. For example, a change of sexual partner can increase sexual motivation, with effects on the hormones of the body (Woodson, 2002). Anticipating a sexual encounter can increase levels of the hormone testosterone (Zillmann, 1984). Consider erectile dysfunction as a result of blockage of the blood vessels of the penis by fatty deposits, so blood cannot get in sufficient quantities into the penis. This is a biological change. Yet, suppose that it sets up a vicious circle with anxiety, which makes the problem still worse, a psychological change (Bancroft, 2009). Contrast this with a situation where there is an initial psychological cause of sexual dysfunction. Suppose that a man becomes unemployed and falls into depression, a psychological cause for a loss of desire. Yet this change in the man's mind is accompanied by corresponding changes in his brain, biological changes. As a result of the lowered activity in particular brain regions, the secretion of testosterone lowers, which in turn sets up a vicious circle by lowering sexual desire still more.

So, one can describe *initial* psychological or biological changes that trigger a sequence of events. However, events in the brain/mind are simultaneously biological and psychological. This has a powerful implication, described next.

Responsibility and blame

Attempts to explain an individual's desire can trigger soul-searching moral issues. Sexual transgression, like little else, evokes blame and strong social disapproval. Even violence, as depicted in TV and movies, is not censored to the same extent. I have not heard of anyone being dismissed from work or getting a divorce on the grounds of surreptitious viewing of even extreme violence, and yet social and employment rules are often draconian where it concerns pornography.

Belief in human rationality, where people freely and inscrutably decide their own actions and destiny, leads to the notion of personal responsibility and accountability (Bolles, 1975). The torments of hell were said to await the sinner who voluntarily opted for the wrong choices. Unsurprisingly, transgressors usually search for an escape clause. For example, the theologian Paul Tillich[1] had a history of extramarital affairs (C. Wilson, 1988), his widow providing evidence (Tillich, 1973). C. Wilson (1988, p. 215) suggested:

> Is it not, for example, inevitable that a man who cannot keep his hands off his female students will emphasize human helplessness and man's inability to resist sin?

Understanding sexual desires and actions in terms of brains, their evolution and development might afford a mitigating circumstance, particularly since some behaviour that deviates from norms can be associated with particular unusual brain function (Raine, 2013). So, if it can be argued that deviant behaviour has a biological basis, people and indeed courts of law are more inclined to take a sympathetic view. Examples include unexpected desires that occasionally arise from brain damage, as in traumatic accidents or from Parkinson's disease.

Space precludes a discussion of these issues here. Suffice to note that authors on the topic of sexual violence frequently caution that to explain is not to excuse.

Some basic psychology

Principles of organization

Throughout the brain/mind, some fundamental principles of organization can be identified; that is, the same basic 'design' is repeated.[2] Our perception of the world, mental life and behaviour, sexual and non-sexual, are organized and controlled by some similar types of processes. Understanding their properties gives insight into how sexual desire, arousal and behaviour are organized.

Consider the simplest case, a reflex, exemplified by the pupil of the eye widening on going into the dark and constricting in the light. This happens quickly and automatically, involving no intention or conscious awareness. A stimulus, a change in illumination, triggers it; the reflex is 'stimulus-bound'. Similarly, the digestion of food and the beating of the heart are organized automatically; you do not decide consciously when to start or stop them. It is just as well; chaos would ensue if we had much voluntary control over the insides of our bodies.

In evolution, relatively simple processes that are self-regulating have been selected where the solution can be built in and there is a regular trigger to a straightforward action. For example, there would be nothing to gain and much to lose by a facility for conscious intervention in the pupil light reflex. It would waste valuable brain capacity in solving a problem for which the solution can be built in. Similarly, the system that causes the withdrawal of a hand from a hot object is best done by an automatic and non-conscious reflex. In protecting the body, speed is of the essence and the stimulus of heat triggers action very rapidly. Imagine that you had to decide consciously and form an intention to pull the hand away. This would waste valuable time and risk serious injury.

For many other tasks, it is impossible to produce a brain with the requisite solutions preformed and ready to go. So, what factors underlie whether automatic and non-conscious reflexes or full conscious control are responsible for a given bit of behaviour?

Contrast such automatic reactions with those that require full conscious awareness. For example, imagine that you are lost in a strange environment. Full conscious awareness is brought to bear on trying to navigate your way. There is no stimulus to trigger automatic behaviour. Novel problems, such as this or how to negotiate a deal with a stranger, demand novel solutions and they cannot be built into the brain in advance. They involve assimilating information from past experiences, searching memory for relevant information and exploiting this information on the particular and often unique features of the current situation. They involve complex intentions, like what you hope to get out of any social negotiation.

Involuntary unconscious processes exist alongside conscious processes that bring flexibility and creativity. Speech exemplifies this. Our utterances are novel in terms of the intentions underlying them and the meaning that we wish to convey. We often operate in full conscious control as we speak, responding flexibly moment by moment to the changing circumstances triggered by the interaction with our interlocutor. Nonetheless at another level speech depends upon being able to call upon a bank of preformed expressions, some clichés, which run off in a more automatic mode, triggered by appropriate turns of the conversation. The two types of process integrate their control and often a given instance of behaviour is based upon a combination of them.

Some behaviour can be done *either* with full conscious awareness *or* automatically. For example, many people brush their teeth while on 'autopilot', by repeating the same sequence of movements every day. Yet this task can be done with full conscious awareness directed to it, as recommended by dentists and mindfulness meditation gurus alike.

Reflecting these considerations, a fundamental distinction in the way that behaviour is organized by the brain, including sexuality, is between what are termed *automatic* and *controlled* processing.

Automatic and controlled processing

Imagine walking down a sloping pavement, while your conscious mind is fully engaged in conversation. You pay no attention to what your legs are doing, even though walking is a skilled activity involving complex calculations by the brain. The walking part of your behaviour is on 'automatic' control, acting in a *non-conscious* mode. This frees those parts of your brain that are running in the *conscious* or 'controlled' mode to deal with the conversation, to interpret the meaning of the words that you are hearing and articulate your reply.

Now imagine the same situation but this time there is ice under foot and you start to slip. You would instantly stop the conversation and bring full controlled conscious processing to bear on the task of staying upright. Your conscious controls would be engaged with looking for possible supports such as a handrail and selecting parts of the path that appear to be ice-free. In other words, according to circumstances, responsibility for a given task can move between automatic and controlled modes.

Learning

Learning plays a central role in sexual desire and behaviour. There are a few terms associated with learning that require some explanation.

The expression 'habituation' refers to a decline in the intensity of a reaction after repeated exposure to a particular stimulus when there is no important consequence. An example is our tendency to ignore the harmless ticking of a clock after repeated exposure.

The term 'reward' refers to those things with which an animal, human or otherwise, strives to maintain contact and which are assumed to have a pleasant effect. Food, water and sexual contact are described as 'rewards'. The expression 'incentive' has some similarities in meaning but with an emphasis upon the reward's power to attract the animal towards it. For example, a location in the past associated with mating to which an animal is drawn would be described as an 'incentive'.

There are different types of learning, some common across species and some that appear to be particularly human. In the first category, classical and instrumental conditioning are found.

Classical conditioning is exemplified by Pavlov's experiment on salivation in dogs, triggered by food (Figure 2.1a). A tone with no capacity to trigger salivation was sounded immediately prior to giving food. After a few joint presentations of tone and food, the tone acquired the capacity to trigger salivation. The tone became a 'conditional stimulus' to

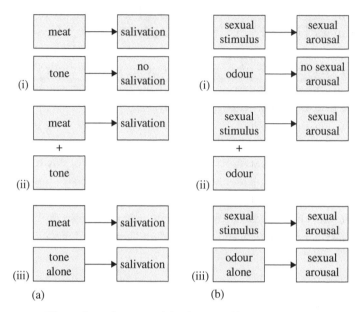

FIGURE 2.1 Classical conditioning: (a) salivation (i) prior to pairing, (ii) pairing and (iii) following pairing; (b) sexual arousal

salivation. The term 'conditional' is used, since the *condition* for the tone to have such a capacity is its pairing with food. This much is common across species, but in humans conscious awareness of the link between the two events can play a role in forming an association between them.

Classical conditioning features extensively in discussions of sexuality (Bancroft, 2009; Pfaus et al., 2013). Across species, cues that have been paired with sexual activity acquire potency ('incentive value') to trigger directed activity and searching ('sexual arousal'). The importance of this in nature is easy to appreciate. Suppose a particular odour has been paired with a sexual stimulus. This odour can label a partner or location as sexually desirable, so that in future the animal is motivated to pursue the odour. In humans, a range of different otherwise neutral events can become associated with sexual arousal, for example by chance pairing (Figure 2.1b). This is particularly evident in the case of men and it probably contributes to the surprisingly wide spectrum of desires that they exhibit.

Instrumental conditioning is where the consequences of behaviour change the future probability of showing that behaviour (Figure 2.2), and is exemplified by the maze. Typically, a hungry rat learns to navigate

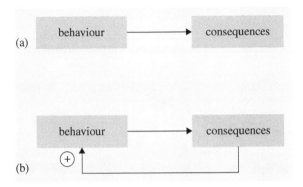

FIGURE 2.2 Instrumental conditioning

a maze since it obtains the reward of food at the end. The chances of taking the correct turns increase as a result of the reward. Another form of instrumental conditioning is termed 'operant conditioning' and is exemplified by the Skinner box. A hungry rat learns to press the lever in the box since the lever-press is followed by, say, the presentation of food.

Food is said to *reinforce* the behaviour of lever-pressing, meaning that the future behavioural tendency to press is strengthened by the food. Food is an example of *positive* reinforcement since the reinforcing event is presented as a result of behaviour. There is also 'negative reinforcement', where the strengthening occurs as a result of the *removal* of something as a result of behaviour. This is exemplified by the termination of a loud sound by an action. Orgasm exemplifies positive reinforcement, while an escape from, say, boredom by means of sexual behaviour exemplifies negative reinforcement.

In addition to such conditioning, people form peculiarly human cognitions about the social world, such as gender identity based upon their observation of gender differences (Bancroft, 2009). Bodily and psychological changes at puberty are assimilated into the growing child's identity, which leads logically to a consideration of biology.

Some details of the relevant biology

The psychological phenomenon of desire, its loss and restraint can be linked to underlying processes in the brain. Parts of the brain that are

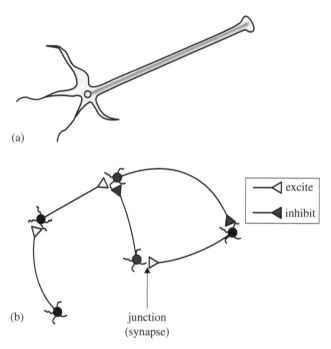

(a)

excite

inhibit

(b)

junction
(synapse)

FIGURE 2.3 Neurons: (a) individual neuron; (b) neurons forming systems

active at times of sexual desire can be identified by neuroimaging and hence some brain correlates of desire found. Changes in desire and its expression or inhibition following damage to identified brain regions can be studied. Evidence derived from non-human species can be cautiously extrapolated to humans. To do this, the means of communication and control of the body need to be examined.

Neurons and hormones

Neurons are a particular class of cell found in the brain and throughout the body (Figure 2.3). The nervous system consists of all the neurons (and some closely associated cells) of the body (Figure 2.4). There are billions of neurons and they transmit and process information. The activity of particular combinations of neurons in the brain is the basis of our thoughts, perceptions and desires. One circuit of interacting neurons would form the basis of, say, sexual desire and a different circuit might

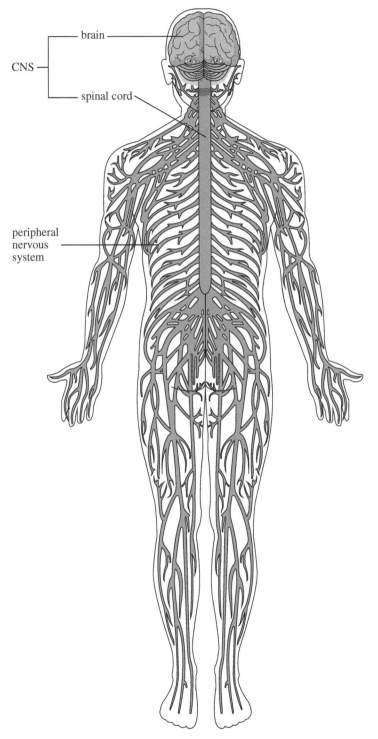

brain

CNS

spinal cord

peripheral
nervous
system

FIGURE 2.4 The nervous system comprises the central nervous system (CNS)
and the peripheral nervous system

underlie orgasm. Investigators try to find the location of such circuits in the brain and define the pathways of neurons that form them.

Neurons also transmit information from one bodily region to another. For example, when a region of the body is stimulated by touch, a message is sent to the brain in the form of electrical activity ('action potentials') in neurons that form a pathway to the brain. In the brain, the message is interpreted in terms of the touch's location, intensity and any emotional significance.

When neurons are electrically active, that is processing information, they require a source of nutrients and oxygen brought by the blood. The more active they are, the greater is the demand for fuels. The technique of functional neuroimaging exploits this fact in order to observe which bits of the brain are most or least active under different conditions, such as viewing erotic pictures as compared to neutral pictures.

Neurons communicate with each other at junctions, known as synapses (Figure 2.5a). Typically, one neuron (A) contains a chemical substance, known as a neurochemical (in many cases, more specifically a 'neurotransmitter'), at its terminal. When the electrical signal arrives at the terminal, it causes the release of this neurochemical into the gap and the occupation of receptors on neuron B. This then affects the activity of B. The neurochemical can excite further electrical activity in B (Figure 2.5b) or it might inhibit activity in B (Figure 2.5c). A number of such neurochemicals are involved in sexual desire and behaviour. The best known are probably dopamine, serotonin and a class known as opioids.

Drugs such as cocaine and heroin powerfully alter the activity of particular classes of synapse in the brain and thereby mimic effects that would under more natural conditions be brought about by, say, sexual events. They target synapses in brain regions normally involved in conventional wanting and liking, and thereby offer powerful interactions with natural activities such as sex.

Another means of communication is by hormones. These are chemicals that are secreted (often from a gland) into a blood vessel and transported by the blood from a site of release to a site of action (Figure 2.6). The hormones of most interest here are:

• The class termed 'androgens', that of prime concern being testosterone. They are secreted from the testes in men, the ovaries in women and the adrenal gland in both sexes.

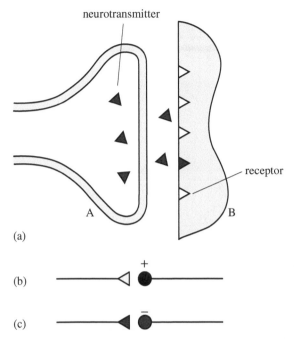

FIGURE 2.5 Synapse between neurons: (a) synapse; (b) one neuron excites another; (c) one neuron inhibits another

- The class termed 'oestrogens', present in both sexes. In women, they are secreted from the ovaries and to a limited extent, the adrenal gland.
- Adrenalin and noradrenalin (known respectively as 'epinephrine' and 'norepinephrine' in the American literature), secreted from the adrenal glands.
- Oxytocin, which is secreted from the pituitary gland.

Starting from about the eighth week following conception, males have a higher concentration of androgens in the body than do females (Hines, 2004). Partly extrapolating from studies on non-human species, the effects of androgens in humans fall into two classes:

- *Organizational effects*: before birth, in males they act on the brain to sculpt those processes (survival of particular neurons and establishment of connections between them) that will later come to play a role in masculine desire. In females, the relatively low concentration of androgens is not sufficient to cause this masculinization and therefore

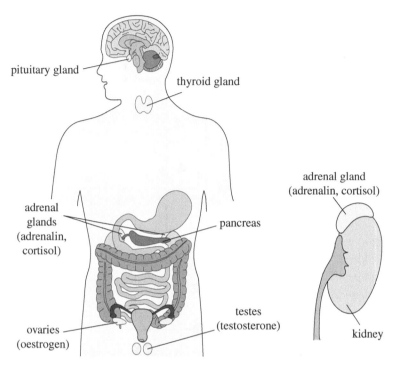

FIGURE 2.6 Some of the glands of the body

the processes of desire assume a feminine form (sometimes termed a 'default position'). These are permanent (or semi-permanent) effects.

- *Activational effects*: following sexual maturity in both sexes, androgens act on these same brain processes that were formed earlier to sensitize them, so that sexual stimuli and thoughts give rise to desire. This is largely a transient effect, present only so long as the hormone is present at the neurons.

It is entirely possible that oestrogens act on the female brain to sculpt desire processes ('active feminization'), but the effects are less clear than for androgens (Hines, 2004; McCarthy, 2008). However, early female development seems to be mainly a consequence of the absence of andro-gens. In adult females, oestrogens appear to operate in concert with testosterone in activating desire.

At times of excitement and challenge, adrenalin and noradrenalin are secreted from the adrenal gland, transported in the blood, and have various effects throughout the body, such as to accelerate the heart rate. Oxytocin is released under various circumstances (e.g. nursing) and has effects of calming and strengthening trust and social bonds.

Basics of the brain

This section can only highlight a few of the regions implicated in sexual desire. In generating desire, these regions and several more interact in complex ways, but this is beyond the scope of the present study.

Psychologists and lay folk alike sometimes discuss which brain region is most evident in human behaviour, the primitive (often expressed as 'animal brain') or the recently evolved (so-called 'civilized brain'). The expression 'he acted like an animal' implies such a distinction. The discussion often takes a naïve form, since it is safe to assume that all levels of brain organization will be involved at all times. However, as already noted, evidence points to a layered organization of brain function. Different layers can exert different weights of control and weight can shift between them according to various factors such as age, pathology and alcohol ingestion.

Within one influential perspective, the human brain is described as the 'triune brain' (MacLean, 1990), meaning three dynamically interacting layers in one brain (Figure 2.7). This reflects the brain's emergence in evolution. In evolutionary terms, the reptilian brain, made up of the brain stem and a number of other structures, is the oldest part, something that we share with reptiles and birds. It is concerned with such things as the organization of relatively simple automatic actions and respiration. The newer paleomammalian brain, shared by all mammals, builds upon this. Complex emotions, such as those underlying the subtleties of social bonding and caring, start to emerge at this level, which corresponds to what is known as the 'limbic system'. Finally, the evolutionarily newest part of the brain, the neomammalian brain, is evident in primates and reaches its most elaborated structure in humans. The neomammalian brain is necessary for what are thought to be peculiarly human attributes such as self-awareness, complex language and the ability to project the imagination backwards and forwards in time. The control of human behaviour requires integration between these brain layers, one especially evolved in humans and the other two largely shared with

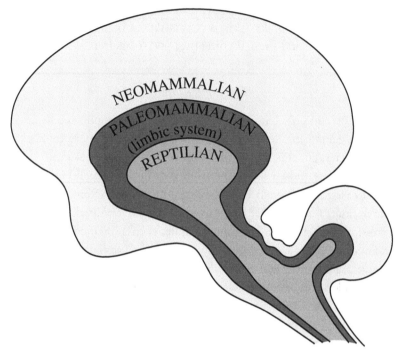

FIGURE 2.7 The triune brain

some other species, something that appears to give rise to more than the occasional problem!

An analogy, albeit highly simplified, is sometimes used with a building.[3] Suppose that the basic construction of a cottage was done in the sixteenth century but plumbing was not installed until the nineteenth century, when a new wing was added. Finally, electricity was added in the twentieth century. It is still the same cottage, with its original foundations and low beams, but the overall functioning of the cottage has changed over the centuries.

Sometimes this layered organization is described as a 'hierarchy' (MacLean, 1990). One might logically assume that the neomammalian brain is at the top of the hierarchy and the reptilian brain at the bottom. Things sometimes do work roughly in this way, as in putting conscious intentions, assumed to arise largely in the neomammalian brain, into effect by the muscles of the body. However, the brain does not always

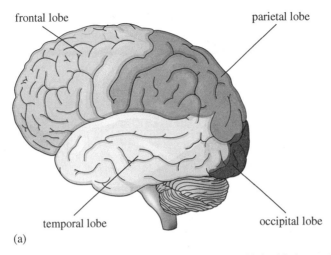

frontal lobe

parietal lobe

temporal lobe

occipital lobe

(a)

FIGURE 2.8 The human brain (a) showing the lobes; (b) highlighting the prefrontal cortex (shaded dark)

work like a well-disciplined army with a commander giving orders that are faithfully followed by lower ranks. At times, the better analogy is with a rebellious army, where the foot soldiers often usurp control. As Price (2002) observes (p. 108):

> When treating patients with depression and anxiety, the clinician finds it obvious that higher centres do not control the lower ones. No patient with his rational brain can command his emotional brain to feel less depressed or anxious.

The same might be said about the stubbornness of unwanted sexual desires when corrective therapy is tried.

On the experience of pleasure, Smith et al. (2010) suggest that 'basic liking' is embodied in mechanisms shared with other mammals. The neomammalian brain contributes a fine-tuning. Of course, one imagines that the appreciation of a Beethoven symphony is a peculiarly human phenomenon requiring neomammalian structures. However, in all probability the pleasure of orgasm and even that of the symphony depend also upon paleomammalian structures.

Figure 2.8 shows the human brain, indicating the lobes, and highlighting a part of the frontal lobe: the prefrontal cortex. The outer layer of the brain, the cortex with its wrinkled structure, is the part most

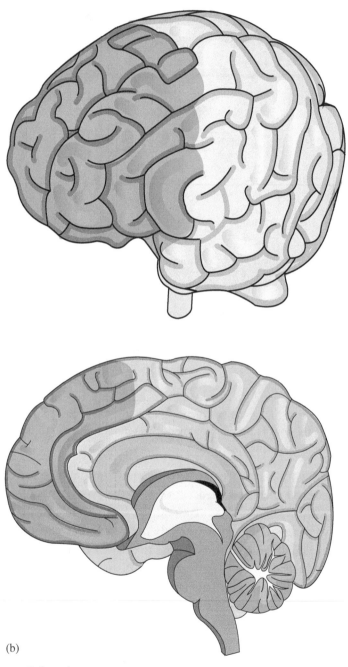

(b)

FIGURE 2.8 *(cont.)*

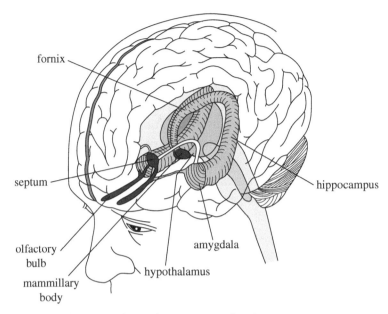

FIGURE 2.9 The human brain showing some of its deep structures

strikingly different in humans as compared to any other species. It largely corresponds to the neomammalian brain. All brain structures not in the cortex are termed 'subcortical'. Figure 2.9 is an X-ray view of the brain highlighting some subcortical ('limbic system') structures.

Sexual desire arises from a combination of sensory stimuli, that is visual, smell, sound and touch, acting in the brain at both a raw level and in the context of memories and meanings with which they are associated. Information on these sensory stimuli is carried by nerves (bundles of neurons) to the brain.

A special type of neuron in the brain, known as a 'mirror neuron', has come into prominence recently and might be involved in sexual desire, particularly where it involves visual erotica (Mouras et al., 2008) (Chapters 8 and 16). They are located in regions of cortex at the frontal and parietal lobes. A mirror neuron is active when either a particular action is being performed or when another individual is observed to be performing the same action.

Consider, for example, triggering of desire by visual stimuli. Light strikes the retina of the eye and information on the image is then transmitted by neurons to various brain regions. There is a fast route to the amygdala (there are two amygdalae, one in each half of the brain, though the singular is usually used), where certain basic features of the image are rapidly processed outside conscious awareness (LeDoux, 1999). Another parallel route that information takes is a slower and more refined one to the visual cortex (located at the back of the occipital lobe) and beyond (through the temporal lobe). Here information is processed and detailed meaning on the nature of the object is extracted for fine-grained image identification. Further detailed processing is carried out in other brain regions, for example the frontal lobe, where the information is put into a context of meanings and personalized memories, associated with conscious awareness (Kringelbach, 2010). A feature of this further processing is to attribute *nuanced value*, for example erotically desirable or not, to the event in the world. This could depend upon such things as the meaning of any potential sexual interaction and the nature of the social relationship with a given individual.

The amygdala (Figure 2.9) attaches crude emotional and motivational significance to events in the world (Mahler and Berridge, 2012). Information in both the slow and fast routes projects to the amygdala. For example, an erotic picture would be labelled as such ('erotic salience attribution'), in part by processing of the information derived from it by the amygdala. The amygdala, in turn, conveys information to other structures, such as the hypothalamus (Georgiadis and Kortekaas, 2010) and the nucleus accumbens (described shortly).

The hypothalamus (Figure 2.9) consists of several sub-regions, each concerned with the organization of one or more particular form of behaviour and control of hormonal events in the body (Hines, 2004). Certain hormones are released from the pituitary gland under the influence of the hypothalamus and they in turn exert a role over the release of oestrogens and androgens from the ovaries and testes.

A region of the hypothalamus, the 'anterior hypothalamus/preoptic area' (AH/POA) has a pivotal role in the control of sexual behaviour. Neurons in the AH/POA are responsive to sexual stimuli and contain receptors that are occupied by testosterone brought via the blood. On engaging with the receptors, testosterone sensitizes these neurons, so that they are particularly responsive to sexual stimuli, underlying presumably part of sexual desire and possibly sexual pleasure (Georgiadis

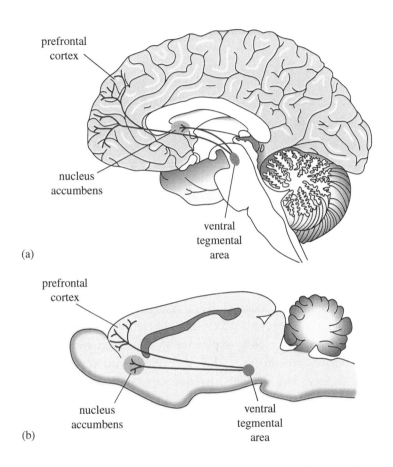

FIGURE 2.10 Pathways of neurons that use dopamine: (a) human; (b) rat

and Kortekaas, 2010). Conversely, loss of testosterone (e.g. following disease) is associated with desensitization of these neurons, with some loss of desire. A sub-region of the AH/POA, termed the INAH-3, is larger in men than women and contains more neurons (described later). In response to erotic stimuli, activation of the hypothalamus is lower in women than in men (Hamann et al., 2004), which might say important things about the roots of desire.

Figure 2.10 shows pathways of neurons that use dopamine as their neurochemical. They project to several regions of interest here. One

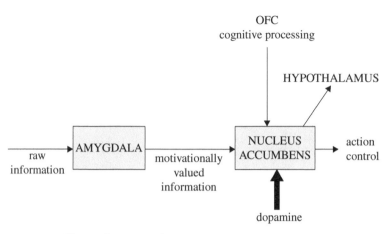

FIGURE 2.11 The nucleus accumbens

place at which they terminate and release dopamine is known as the ventral striatum, which contains the nucleus accumbens. Activity of part of the nucleus accumbens underlies the raw pull that certain events, such as sex and drugs, can exert on behaviour. A different part of the nucleus accumbens has a role as a basis of pleasure (Kringelbach and Berridge, 2010). The nucleus accumbens is a hub that receives information about such things as food and sexually attractive targets and then transmits signals to parts of the brain that organize action based on this (Robbins and Everitt, 1996) (Figure 2.11). The nucleus accumbens is sensitive to conditional stimuli associated with rewards. For example, a conditional stimulus such as a tone sounded just before the appearance of a sexual partner would excite activity there, leading to directed attention and searching. Neurons using dopamine also project to the prefrontal cortex and to the amygdala.

A region of the prefrontal cortex that is associated with attributing value to events is the orbitofrontal cortex (OFC). Neurons that are active here encode the hedonic value of particular stimuli (Rolls, 2012). For example, in the case of taste, early processing (before the OFC) detects, say, a curry taste and its raw hedonic value, whereas later stages of process-ing by the OFC attribute a more refined hedonic value of liking or not to the taste. The liking value arising here depends in part upon the intrinsic taste but also (a) the level of nutrients in the body, (b) how much food of this particular taste has been recently ingested and (c) high-level associations such as any verbal descriptions and cultural meanings related to the taste. So, the OFC, constituting a nexus, is informed of all these factors. Taking them into account, the activity of particular OFC neurons is part of the brain embodiment of the pleasure derived from a taste. Other OFC neurons encode unpleasant events such as unpleasant touch or smell.

Extrapolating to sex, a combination of, say, touch, perceived attractiveness of a partner and meaning would similarly converge onto a different set of neurons in an adjacent OFC region. If one can extrapolate from monkeys, neurons in the OFC are responsive ('selectively active') to particular faces (Rolls, 2012). Regions of human OFC are more strongly activated by what are judged as attractive faces, something of obvious relevance to human sexual desire. The OFC is then an integrator, which extracts signals corresponding to the holistic quality of events put into context. Other neurons encode when an expected event fails to occur. Neurons project from the OFC to the nucleus accumbens (Rolls, 2012), where they appear to inhibit or enhance the strength of signals arising from low-level processing (Figure 2.11).

Other regions of the prefrontal cortex are also relevant here (Figure 2.10). Neurons employing dopamine ('dopaminergic' neurons) make projections from the VTA (ventral tegmental area) to the dorsolateral region of the prefrontal cortex, which is involved with holding memories in awareness and using them in the control of behaviour (Luciana, 2001).[4] Extrapolating from studies on monkeys, this area might be expected to be activated when a sexual incentive not physically present, that is distant in space and time, is being pursued, and during sexual fantasy. Dopamine most likely gives strength ('salience') to the activated memory so that it can occupy consciousness and on occasion take command of the control of behaviour.

Of course, there are also inhibitions on sexual desire and its expression. Inhibition arises from, amongst other things, sexual satiety following orgasm and the assessment of risks attached to sexual advance. Inhibition can be linked to particular brain regions. Damage to the temporal lobes is sometimes associated with heightened sexuality, suggesting that parts of this cortical region normally have an inhibitory effect (Georgiadis and Kortekaas, 2010). One might speculate that the arousal some find in autoerotic asphyxiation, by strangling, could arise from a cut-off of blood supply and hence relative inactivation of the cortex as compared to other brain regions. Parts of the OFC (as distinct from those described earlier) are activated at times of sexual satiety, suggesting a restraining role. The OFC is associated with 'urge suppression'; it plays a role in restraining behaviour motivated by short-term gain in order to avoid long-term costs (Bechara et al, 2000). Damage there can be followed by the manifestation of inappropriate sexual desires.

The parts of the brain do not develop at the same rate. Of interest here, the prefrontal cortex is slow to develop, not reaching full maturity until well into the twenties (Steinberg, 2007). Corresponding to this reorganization, new processing properties become possible, such as the capacity to hold items in memory, to plan and to inhibit behaviour.

The autonomic nervous system

The 'autonomic nervous system' is a division of the nervous system that controls the activity of the inside of the body, such as the stomach, intestine, genitals and heart (Figure 2.12). It controls the flow of blood to the various parts of the body, by means of neurons that contact the muscles located at the local blood vessels.

It is called 'autonomic' because it is to a considerable degree self-governing, for example, we do not consciously decide when to start digestion or accelerate the heart beat. As many soon discover, an exertion of conscious will can prove quite ineffective in diverting blood to the genitals. Signals to the autonomic nervous system and hence to the bodily organs are computed in the hypothalamus and other brain regions. There is a strong link between activity in the hypothalamus and penile erection (Georgiadis and Kortekaas, 2010).

There are two divisions of the autonomic nervous system: the sympathetic and parasympathetic. The sympathetic is active at times of challenge and is responsible for activation, for example increased heart rate and blood pressure. The parasympathetic is dominant at times of relaxation and has effects such as to lower heart rate. Neurons with their tips in the organs such as the heart and genitals transmit signals back to the brain concerning such events as respectively heart rate or touch.

In seeking insight, the book will look at sexual desire in the context of a range of other desires, discussed next.

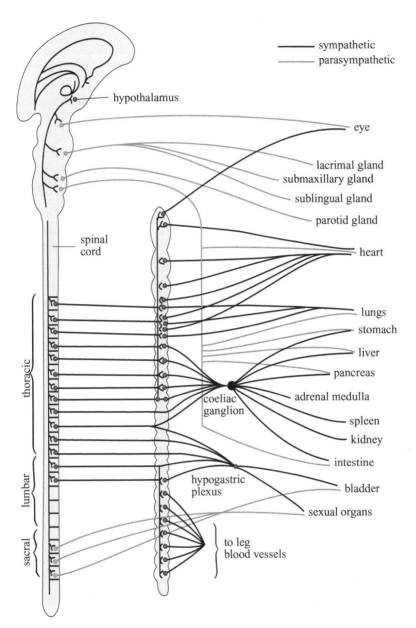

FIGURE 2.12 The autonomic nervous system

Insight through comparison with other desires

> But is it not equally difficult to understand fully anybody who is wholly dedicated to any other single interest, be it money, power, beauty, study, or some special hobby, when one does not feel capable of being so absorbed oneself? To some men there is, for instance, nothing more interesting than, say, sports cars or horse races. (Kronhausen and Kronhausen, 1967, p. 187, on Walter)

One approach to understanding sex is to employ analogies, metaphors or comparisons with other desires. Does sex work in a similar way to anything else, so investigators in different areas can pool insights? In psychology textbooks, sex is often grouped with feeding, drinking and drug-taking, under the general heading of 'motivation'. Some similar, if not identical, brain processes underlie each (Robbins and Everitt, 1996). Everyday expressions compare sexual desire with other desires, as in 'hungry for sex' or 'you are like a drug to me'. These are more than colourful metaphors, but rather they tap into a common feature of all such desires and dopamine systems (Figure 2.10) are central to how desires work. In each case, there can be strong craving to answer the desire and pleasure associated with its satiety (Georgiadis et al., 2012).

One benefit in investigating, say, feeding or gambling is that they are relatively easy to study under semi-natural ('ecologically valid') conditions. The gambler and a casino or the eater and a mini-cafeteria can be brought into the laboratory to study. The person addicted to nicotine or alcohol can be observed as they engage in their behaviour or try to resist it. They can be offered their favourite substance in the laboratory or asked to work to obtain it and the reaction observed. For rather obvious reasons, it is well nigh impossible to follow, say, the lecher on his adventures under anything like ecologically valid conditions or to bring sexual uncertainty and variety into the laboratory and observe their role in triggering desire.

Sex shares the common feature with feeding and drug-taking that the presence of the triggering stimulus causes the future to be devalued ('discounted') (van den Bergh et al., 2008). Hungry people prefer a small immediate food reward rather than a delayed bigger reward. People addicted to heroin or nicotine show a preference for an immediate reward of a small amount of drug, as opposed to a later larger amount of drug. The personal assessed risk of getting a sexually transmitted disease is lowered by showing men sexually attractive images or asking them to do the assessment during masturbation (Ariely and Loewenstein, 2006).

Comparison with feeding and drinking

Feeding and drinking maintain chemical and energy levels within the body. Without force-feeding, death will obviously follow loss of desire for food. On some occasions, people do abstain from feeding, as in hunger strikes or anorexia nervosa. The consequences are, of course, ultimately lethal and surely this is not a life-choice willingly and happily sought. In this regard, sex appears very different. However, the fact that the consequences of being without something are different should not detract from some similarities in how sex, feeding and drinking work.

Like sex, both feeding and drinking are also associated with strong desires, and particularly in the case of feeding with considerable variation between individuals in the intensity with which it is expressed in behaviour. Feeding and drinking are associated with pleasures, sometimes intense, that encourage us to repeat the activities, particularly when in a bodily state of deficiency. Given the opportunity, variety plays a dominant role in the desire for food, as is evident by the marketing strategies of supermarkets or the range of ethnicities of restaurants in any town centre. Who has not found their appetite suddenly revived when a new course is presented? For both feeding and sex, some people are better at restraint in the face of plenty and variety than are others. Stress can trigger 'comfort eating', something similar being found for sex. Certain foods appear to lift mood, as is the case for sex (Meston and Buss, 2009).

As with sex, humans put tastes into a complex context by labelling their meaning, involving the prefrontal cortex (Rolls, 2012). For example, smoked-salmon ice cream has almost no pleasantness rating when it is called 'ice cream'. However, a label of 'savoury mousse' or something quite arbitrary such as 'food 386' gives it a strong positive hedonic value (Yeomans et al., 2008). I will leave it to the reader's imagination to find examples where the way in which something sexual is construed makes all the difference to its hedonic value.

Feeding, like sex, can serve several goals simultaneously. A person might eat with little thought of anything but correcting hunger. On another occasion, nutrient regulation might play less of a role; eating in a restaurant might involve stimulating conversation, passing time and creating the right impression. More food is eaten by people in company than eating alone (Wansink, 2006).

Comparison with drug-taking

Drugs improve mental states, offering temporary relief from anxiety, stress or a depressed mood, as does sex (Meston and Buss, 2009). They are associated with a 'high', which has been compared to orgasm, the culmination of first obtaining and then taking them.

Despite being in an environment where there is peer pressure to take drugs, some people shun them entirely. Some take them in moderation and as part of a healthy life-style without getting addicted. Others get addicted to either drugs or sex or both simultaneously. Following addiction to drugs, people can risk life, limb and liberty to get them. In the absence of their drug, they might feel withdrawal symptoms and crave drugs, a similar experience to some deprived of sex. Craving (intense wanting) seems to be a common feature of desires (Kavanagh et al., 2005). Stress can trigger a desire for drugs as it can for sex (Chapters 15 and 17). A craving for drugs can be situation-dependent; an environment that in the past was associated with taking drugs can trigger craving because of the cues present (Robinson and Berridge, 1993). Similarly, potent cues such as a region of town associated with past sexual encounters or the keyboard on a computer used for viewing pornography can trigger sexual urges.

Some addicted people can quit even hard drugs for life (Heyman, 2013), as do some people manage to quit sex. Drugs can be something of an acquired taste (Alexander, 2008; Robinson and Berridge, 1993), as can sex (Levin, 2006), with initial experiences not being that great and a dependence upon context.

Such drugs were surely not an integral part of our evolution and neither are we naturally equipped with brain processes that lead us to seek them out. Rather, they appear to hijack brain processes that evolved to serve such normal desires as for food and sex (Nesse and Berridge, 1997), most clearly those involving dopamine (Figure 2.10). However, a study of this hijacking can in itself reveal much about the particular brain processes that are hijacked and which normally serve conventional activities such as sex and feeding.

Comparison with shopping

Some purchases are made impulsively, apparently serving psychological needs of comfort, improving self-image and status, rather than being based on rational and purposive choice (Dittmar and Drury, 2000; Rook, 1987). This can get out of control and lead to a full-blown addiction (O'Guinn and Faber, 1989). The perception of the object itself creates a powerful desire for it, a principle that applies to such things as clothes and jewellery rather than to toilet paper or lettuce. Stress tends to increase the desire for impulsive shopping. Behaviour is not simply a response to being by chance in a shopping situation. Rather, the memories are such as to lead people to make an effort to move towards shops. Shopping stampedes can prove lethal.

Many left-at-home partners can surely observe with only thinly disguised envy the ability of advertisers to create inordinate levels of wanting. Uncertainty over what might be the next bargain seems inherent to the attraction. However, the large number of household gadgets gathering dust, unworn clothes, unread books and little-played CDs seem to point to a rather lower intensity of liking.

Comparison with gambling

Gambling, with its associated risk of addiction, has features in common with what some people find attractive about sex: uncertainty of outcome, high arousal and the potential for big rewards. The gambler never knows what is going to happen next and how big the winnings, if any, will be. The gambler's heart rate accelerates while engaging in the activity. Anticipation of winning triggers some of the same brain regions as are excited when a drug-user anticipates getting a shot of drug (Breiter et al., 2001). Some people spend enormous amounts of time and money gambling, occasionally losing their last dime, their family and even their lives in suicide as a result. Some are lured to Las Vegas from thousands of miles away, by the promise of uncertain reward, somewhat comparable to the behaviour of sex tourists.

The casino is rich in stimulation, gaming machines, music and lights, associated with occasional and unpredictable winnings. Internet gambling captures some of this in an even more accessible way. One feature shared between contemporary gambling and the environment in which humans evolved is surely the *uncertainty* of gain. The individual who persisted in the pursuit of goals, for example food, mates, shelter, in the face of such uncertainty might have been at an advantage in terms of genetic perpetuation. Risk-taking within limits could well have been an adaptive trait in our early evolution, allowing colonization of new habitats and finding new mates and so on.

Comparison with other recreational activities

Finally, consider curiosity and exploration of the environment and how this compares with sex. For some, a holiday is a waste of time that would be better spent at work. For others, a regular annual holiday by the seaside with nothing much going on is perfectly adequate to satisfy their limited curiosity about the world. Still others pay large sums and incur enormous inconvenience and danger to visit remote parts of the world. Some travel the world to follow their favourite football team.

Why do some people opt to cross deserts, explore jungles and climb Everest? Why do others play chess, do crossword puzzles or frighten themselves by watching horror movies? Surely, seeking uncertainty, arousal and novelty and then trying to 'resolve' it is a fundamental feature of the human condition. There is satisfaction in, for example, bringing the order of a solution to a crossword puzzle. To Gopnik (1998), the similarities between curiosity and sex are so striking that she entitled an article 'Explanation as orgasm'. We are moved to understand chosen parts of the world and when we find an explanation, as in the missing answer to a crossword, there is a sudden burst of pleasure that motivates us to repeat the experience.

There is suspense in the chess game or football match, resolved by the outcome. The tension of a crime novel or horror movie such as *Psycho* is resolved with the denouement. The exotic island gives up its mystery as it becomes slightly familiar. The uncertainty, suspense and eager anticipation of the football match is relieved by a winning goal and particularly by ending the match with one. A group of England football supporters on their way to an international competition once described to me the similarities with sex, adding that a winning goal was even better than orgasm. This might come as little surprise to some stay-at-home wives. In spite of the similarities, it is probably best not to mention a comparison with watching football, and even more so with horror movies, too soon after the start of a new erotic liaison.

Think of the angler sitting for hours in all weathers waiting for the perfect catch. This behaviour seems motivated by the uncertainty of when the catch will happen and its form. This is resolved once the line is tugged. To catch a visible fish from a small tank, though more certain, would presumably be less appealing. Is this experience of waiting and suspense not similar to that felt by the voyeur sitting for hours in the bushes waiting for the perfect image of a woman undressing, or the exhibitionist investing hours in finding the optimal location for exposure?

Advantages of a broad approach

Quite apart from the relative ease of doing research in areas other than sex, there are good reasons to consider sex in the context of activities such as taking drugs, curiosity, feeding and drinking. First, as just noted, there are similarities between them. Indeed, I will suggest that this arises since they share some common brain processes that involve dopamine and other chemicals. Of course, there are also differences in these activities and investigating these can also enhance our understanding.

Secondly, these activities can interact (Chapter 15). Often drugs are taken to enhance sexual desire, while the urgings of curiosity are sometimes given as a motivation for sexual exploration. A number of women report that they initiated sex out of the simple curiosity that they 'wanted to see what all the fuss was about' (Meston and Buss, 2009). In one sample, curiosity topped the list of reasons for loss of virginity (Shope, 1971). Gambling and sex sometimes go together (Chapter 17).

The brains that we study in the here and now are the product of evolution and individual development, and considering these aspects reveals much about sexual desire, to which the discussion turns next.

Evolutionary perspectives

Basics

It is widely agreed that humans are the product of a process of evolution taking place over millions of years. In sexual reproduction as exemplified by humans, genes from male and female are combined at the time of fertilization. The combination of genes, termed the 'genotype', is then locked into dynamic interaction with, first, the environment of the fertilized cell, the womb and then the external environment, with its physical and social aspects. The animal is placed in a competition for survival and reproduction. Some animals are more successful than others and thereby their genes tend to get transmitted to future generations. Over many generations, evolution occurs such that the animal is said to be *adapted* to its environment.

There is some new terminology to introduce in the context of evolution. A 'functional explanation' is one in terms of how an aspect of behaviour helps an animal to transmit its genes. It asks what is the function of any instance of behaviour and stands in distinction to the 'causal explanation', discussed earlier. Causal and functional can ideally be fitted to give a more comprehensive understanding. For example, consider that an animal can often be sexually re-aroused by a change of partner (Chapter 11). A causal explanation for this would be in terms of events within its brain, specifically activity in pathways using dopamine. A functional explanation would be in terms of spreading the animal's genes more widely. Of course, no one is suggesting that the animal has any conscious intention to spread its genes. It is simply assumed that those animals showing this effect left more descendants than those not showing it and hence the genes having such an effect have been more successful in propagation. Another term employed here is 'fitness'. This is a measure of the success shown in genetic perpetuation. Animal A shows greater fitness than B if A leaves more viable offspring than B. Fitness used in this sense is not to be confused with the narrow sense of physical fitness, though doubtless physical fitness contributes to fitness used in the broader sense.

Considerations of function lead to the notion of 'parental investment' (Trivers, 1972). This term refers to the cost in evolutionary terms of producing offspring. For a woman, the cost is much greater than for a man, since her reproductive system is out of action for more than nine months. She needs to supply nutrients to the growing foetus as well as incur an increase in weight. The cost is measured against what she might be doing if not producing this offspring (Gangestad and Simpson, 2000). By contrast, the investment of the male might be as little as the time spent in mating. From these considerations it is argued that women should be relatively more cautious and discriminating about engaging in sex.

Evolutionary psychology is the study of psychology from the perspective of evolution and adaptation. It asks how the characteristics that are evident today served an adaptive function in our early evolution. Evolutionary psychology has had much to say about human sexuality (Workman and Reader, 2014), an approach that has yielded some profound insights.

Evolutionary psychology and the notion of 'design'

One way of asking 'how does sexual desire work?' is to pose a closely related question – 'how was it "designed"?' I put 'designed' in inverted commas to indicate the sense of metaphor as it is employed by evolutionary psychologists. That is to say, brains that form the basis of sexual desire have presumably been 'designed' by evolutionary processes, since such desire was part of the means for passing on genes. Evolutionary psychologists frequently use 'design' by analogy with design in technology. In trying to understand how, say, a television or computer works, it is useful to know something about what it was designed to do. Evolutionary psychologists suggest that it is *as if* brains were designed and they ask what each feature of brain and behaviour was designed to achieve.

Evolutionary psychologists describe their endeavour as 'reverse engineering'. An engineer designs something either from scratch or by modifying an existing design. By contrast, the end product, the human, has already been 'designed', so the task is to speculate on what functional considerations were involved in this construction.

The design was made way back in our evolutionary history and the environment has changed massively since then. The primary concern here will be how does this pre-stone-age design trigger desire in the twenty-first century? We ask how the brain that emerges is able to produce behaviour, ranging from sexual disgust and celibacy through blissful fidelity and monogamy to agonizing temptation, death-defying sexual risk-taking, extremes of promiscuity and sexual addiction.

It is *as if* desire was 'designed' by evolutionary processes to trigger mating and thereby the production of offspring. However, the issue is more subtle and nuanced, since desire fluctuates. It is turned on and off, expressed or inhibited, according to various internal and external conditions. The design metaphor is useful in understanding how and why these conditions exert their effect. This can be interpreted in terms of the role that fluctuations in desire served in maximizing the chances of successful reproduction in our early environment (Workman and Reader, 2014).

A principal area of interest is differences between the sexes in terms of the desire for sexual variety, casual and indiscriminate sexual behaviour and viewing pornography. In general, women appear less attracted than are men to these aspects of sexuality. Evolutionary psychologists suggest that this difference in sexual strategy reflects a difference in what was optimal for spreading genes. According to this perspective, women have more to lose by an indiscriminate mating strategy, whereas men have relatively little to lose and much to gain.

Evolutionary accounts also ask the question of when in evolution a particular characteristic appeared, for example, the link between sexual behaviour and forming pair-bonds. Not all species show pair-bonding; some of our close ape relatives do not. So, under what circumstances did pair-bonding appear in evolution and what are the implications for sexual desire?

Evolutionary mismatch

The notion of evolutionary mismatch helps us to understand contemporary sexual desire. It refers to the disparity between the current environment and that in which our evolution occurred. For example, humans fear snakes and spiders, whereas these days guns and cars present a vastly increased risk in industrial societies. Fear of guns and cars has not evolved since they have not been around for long enough. That is to say, there is mismatch between what is feared and what presents the most danger to humans living today. Another example is the mismatch between the availability of food in rich countries and the evolutionary design under-lying control of feeding.

As a slight but relevant digression, consider again the similarities between feeding and sex. The term 'addiction' is increasingly applied to excess in either area. Supermarkets offer an abundance of foods of high fat and sugar content. These might be termed 'supernormal stimuli' to our appetites. Through endless permutations of ingredients, cookery programmes and advertising, such stimuli excite our gastronomic desires excessively.

Rather as with sex, the outcome of this food-related stimulation is mixed. The gastronomic experience is hedonically potent, which might sooth a stressed brain in the short term, but the ills of superabundance include diabetes, obesity, heart disease and tooth decay. In the environment of our early evolution there were no refined foods. Whereas foods were obtained only after extensive foraging, hunting and exertion of effort, they now require little more than depressing the pedals of a car and steering to the nearest supermarket, take-away or burger bar. Yet, rather as with perceived excessive sexual behaviour, being obese carries something of a social stigma.

The design of sexual desire similarly arose in an environment very different from that in which most people live today. Even in two or three decades, amounting to not even the blink of an eye in evolutionary time, major changes in the 'sexual environment' have appeared. Yet, it is a brain designed so long ago that finds itself in this current environment. Humans evolved in a social environment in which they relatively rarely met a stranger or non-kin individual (except possibly in conflict), whereas these days we might well pass thousands every day (Feierman and Feierman, 2000). Opportunities for at least attraction, if not contact, are now incalculably more frequent. For many people these days, there is also more time available to pursue sexual desires and more free conscious capacity to be engaged with sexual fantasy (C. Wilson, 1988). The key to understanding so much of the contemporary manifestation of sexual desire is to consider how such a brain works in the current environment, which is so different from that of early evolution.

Once cultures acquired increasingly refined technology to change the body's appearance, people used their ingenuity to find ways of increasing their desire value – in effect, to present supernormal stimuli. For example, on going to a social event, it is said that Venetian women dropped belladonna into their eyes to increase their pupil size. Thereby, a woman exaggerated her apparent level of interest in her male interlocutor and correspondingly increased her attraction value.

In the contemporary sexual landscape, particularly in affluent countries, there is an abundance of supernormal stimuli. The triggers to sexual desire are ubiquitous and are enhanced artificially, such that their exaggerated presence becomes the norm. Many women dress provocatively and use hair dyes, padded shoulders, high-heeled shoes, artificial nails, elaborate hair-styles and make-up applied to lips, eyelashes and fingernails and toenails, as well as carefully crafted perfume, in an attempt to magnify their attraction value. Female dress is often chosen to make women look taller and thinner (Buss, 2003). In the countries where most readers will be living, female dress reveals more of the body than probably at any time in recorded history, something to be witnessed on weekend nights in British town centres even in the depths of winter. For those who prefer to stay indoors and watch television, Saturday night game shows offer comparable amounts of bodily exposure. Males are catching up fast with special fragrance products, amongst many other things.

For those with money, perceived desire value can be increased by plastic surgery, so as to alter cheek bone structure or breast size, to straighten a nose, to increase lip size with the help of collagen, to make a face more symmetrical or a body curvier.

Through billboards, magazines, television and the Internet, advertisers bombard us with triggers to sexual desire. Scantily clad models displaying erotically tailored clothing are shown in even long-established and traditional clothing stores. I just witnessed this even in the window of the charity shop Age UK in Milton Keynes! Specialist shops dedicated to the purchase of supernormal stimuli, in the form of erotically designed dresses, shoes, boots and stockings, are now a regular feature in many town centres. So-called 'top-shelf magazines' cater almost exclusively to the triggering of sexual desire, often with suggestions of how it might be linked to sexual opportunity. Explicit heterosexual, homosexual and bisexual pornography is available in what are often termed 'adult' bookshops as well as via the Internet. The uncertainty and novelty value of both moving and stationary erotic images available through the Internet would seem sufficient to satisfy the curiosity of even the most demanding sexual connoisseur for several life-times. The search for the best-ever image is almost bound to be endless.

The triggers to desire and the means to translate this into novel sexual behaviour are probably more accessible to most people than at any time. I suggest that the knowledge of this availability contributes to triggering desire, and a paradoxical combination of ready availability and inherent transgression in gaining access is probably particularly potent. Locks on doors, rented rooms, employment away from home and fast transport offer the possibility of sexual liaisons undetected by snooping eyes.

The formal and legal rules on what is available have probably seldom, if ever, been so relaxed. In Britain and other countries, so-called massage and escort services are advertised even in the local press. Cheap flights mean that sexual tourism is brought within the reach of many more people. In terms of finding novelty outside the marital bond, there are Internet sites for those seeking adulterous liaisons, whereas other Internet sites and retreats/clubs are available for those who prefer to seek novelty together as couples. Sexual minorities have not been left out of this erotic charging by supernormal stimuli. Specialist magazines, clubs and Internet sites cater for a wide range of legal and other tastes. This change in the landscape needs to be understood before we can make sense of such things as sexual addiction.

The brains of animals are equipped with a process of cost–benefit analysis (Assadi et al., 2009). The decision-making takes both the estimated benefits and costs of any activity into account in choosing a course of action. Researchers are now able to attribute responsibility for this calculation to particular brain regions.[5] It seems logical to suppose that in our present environment the estimated cost–benefit of sexually motivated decision-making is skewed towards the benefit.

It is not just modern, sexually charged environments where evolutionary considerations give insights into behaviour. For example, people in the Ituri region of Zaire show high levels of promiscuity and sexually transmitted disease leading to infertility (Bailey and Aunger, 1995). From evolutionary considerations, why do some groups show behaviour that is likely to be counterproductive to genetic perpetuation? Why has evolution not provided a design that, metaphorically speaking, takes the danger into account and restrains promiscuity? Evolutionary mismatch is a possible answer: today's diseases were not around during most of human evolution and therefore no psychological defence mechanisms have evolved. It would be difficult for evolutionary processes to have provided a psychological defence. Presumably, if the diseases were manifest externally by, say, sores, this would act as a signal and deterrent to sexual activity, but they often remain hidden.

Bailey and Aunger (1995) found that the Ituri people were fully aware of the link between promiscuity and sexually transmitted diseases. It seems then that the cultural transmission of information by word of mouth on the risks of promiscuity can be inadequate in providing inhibition. A sexual encounter poses a theoretical risk, not a certain one that can be assessed there and then. Any negative consequences in the form of disease follow later. Under conditions of high desire, such theoretical risks can often be ineffective as deterrents.

Development

Desire might be non-existent, straight, gay or bisexual, or with an abnormally strong attraction to certain body shapes or hair colours. There might be a fetishist element to desire, where it requires leather or shoes for its triggering. Fetishes reveal much about desire (Chapter 19). Sadly, desire might be directed to a target of a kind where any sexual action would be illegal, as in paedophilia or rape. How does the individual adult brain acquire these particular features that characterize its desire?

We start life as a single fertilized egg cell in the womb. This cell splits into two, and these two cells in turn divide. This process continues until there are the billions of cells that make up the adult. In the womb, there is the physical environment of the mother's body. Following birth, there is an environment having both physical and social dimensions. To understand the emergence of human sexuality, a study of development is essential.

Investigators are increasingly coming to recognize the tight interlocking of genes and environment as determinants of development. Consider that men tend typically to find casual sex more attractive than women do. According to evolutionary psychologists, this is to be understood in terms of evolutionary strategies for maximizing reproductive chances. Thereby, genetic differences between men and women bear the weight of responsibility. However, according to Sarah Blaffer Hrdy, the social controls that men apply to women's sexuality, such as severe punishment for infringement of the moral code, mean that girls assimilate the cultural rule that they are not supposed to feel, let alone express, sexual desire (Hrdy, 1999). Either way, there are problems in trying to understand what is going on. Evolutionary psychologists point out that the gender difference is found across all cultures, which suggests a genetic explanation. A feminist counter-argument is in terms of male domination. A possible resolution will be described later.

The next chapter looks at some of the history of attempts to explain desire, which then leads into a modern view of how sex works.

In summary

- Sexual desire is manifest in conscious experience and in corresponding activity in particular regions of the brain.
- Automatic and controlled processing underlie behaviour.
- Some brain processes operate outside conscious awareness and others are associated with full conscious awareness.
- Classical and instrumental conditioning are involved in sexuality.
- Communication of information involved in sexual desire and behaviour is by means of neurons and hormones.
- The role of particular regions of brain (e.g. the nucleus accumbens) and particular neurochemicals (e.g. dopamine) can be identified.
- Similarities between sexual behaviour and other activities provide insights into how desire works.
- A functional explanation is in terms of how behaviour contributes to genetic perpetuation.
- Evolutionary psychology, the account of how the features of human sexuality were designed in our early evolution, has given powerful insights, as in the notion of evolutionary mismatch.

THREE

SEXUAL DESIRE IN A BROAD CONTEXT

The greatest enterprise of the mind has always been and always will be
the attempted linkage of the sciences and the humanities.

(Wilson, 1998, p. 6)[1]

What is to be explained?

Sexual desire arises within an historical, cultural and religious context, which powerfully influences how it is interpreted (Hawkes, 2004).
Assumptions on how desire works are made and assimilated into cultures.
Discussion of this issue is much more than armchair philosophy; what is
believed about desire tends both to reflect and inform laws, social and
religious attitudes, and policy. This chapter cannot give an even remotely
comprehensive view of this vast subject. All it can do is give some examples of the various assumptions that surround the nature of desire, show
their implications and relate them to a modern interpretation. Throughout history, eminent thinkers have suggested how sexual desire arises and
what the consequences are for well-being of either following its call or
voluntarily resisting it. The effects of thwarted and frustrated desire have
also attracted speculation.

To modern scientifically informed minds, early attempts at explanation
can sound comical, but modesty here would not be out of place. In past
centuries people were, of course, without any knowledge of evolution,
modern anatomical description, neuroimaging and chemical analysis.
However, concerning their own desires and behaviour and the behaviour
of others, they were probably no less astute observers than we are. Early

68

explanations say much about ubiquitous aspects of the experience and expression of sexual desire.

So, which features of sexuality might be equally as evident to pre-scientific as to present-day people and would prompt a search for understanding? Consider the following.

- Desire has much to do with (an) attractive other(s), as well as events within the body, often with a focus on its lower parts.
- Denial of a sexual outlet can be distressing, while engaging in sexual activity can at least temporarily lower desire.
- Some factors act in the opposite direction to desire, either to lower it as such or to leave it unchanged but lower its chances of expression in sexual behaviour.
- Intense desire can cause people to act against their better judgement, leading some to argue for a lack of 'free will'.
- Desire can sometimes be a mixed blessing, when it brings social problems in its wake, and moral advice, if not social/legal sanctions, might be needed to curb its excesses.

Over the centuries, the assumption has commonly been made that sexual behaviour serves as a 'regulator' of particular events within the body; something needs to be maintained within an alignment and healthy limits.[2] People are 'driven' into sexual activity by a misalignment. Successful sexual activity then reduces the strength of this 'push'. Implicitly or explicitly, two related assumptions have frequently been made about this push:

- It is aversive, harmful or at least undesirable in quality, so that its reduction brings some relief.
- It can arise within the body but outside the brain.

Doubtless such arguments arose partly from analogy, e.g. a full bladder triggers the desire for urination, which, when acted upon, lowers the strength of the trigger. Sometimes the role of an attractive individual in triggering or enhancing the push is described and attempts made to link such external and internal triggers.

Closely related to the issue of what gives rise to sexual desire has been that of the consequences of either expressing it in sexual activity, resisting its pull or being denied the chance of an outlet. Opinions have ranged from, on the one hand those describing sexual desire as an imperative, the command of which must be respected in order to attain bodily health, to on the other seeing it as an unfortunate distraction that is best suppressed or ignored in the interests of moral virtue and sanity.

By not engaging in sexual behaviour, a particular bodily disturbance might increase over time, with possibly harmful effects on body and mind. How early writers envisaged such a disturbance and its link to desire gives insight into attitudes towards sexuality prevalent at the time. So, the present chapter will look at prominent ideas that were based upon disturbance to the body: what is the nature of the disturbance, how does it link to desire and what are the consequences of thwarting its expression?

Some have argued that a disturbance from equilibrium could arise with sexual under-activity; that is, sexual behaviour is regulatory. For example, as a possible index of a belief in sex as a regulator, the early church condemned prostitution but nonetheless showed some tolerance towards it 'as a kind of sewer' (Bullough, 1987). In this way, it was seen as providing a relatively harmless outlet for male sexual needs. Similarly, the virtues of masturbation as a safety valve have sometimes been championed. It is perhaps no coincidence that the only form of sexual release outside marriage that has not attracted universal moral censure is that of nocturnal orgasm (Kinsey et al., 1948). Presumably, this has been seen as totally involuntary and serving some kind of regulatory function, provided it is not induced by prior lascivious thoughts.

By contrast, others have taught mainly of the perils of sexual over-activity (Money, 1990). To them, excessive sexual activity or even inappropriate sexual activity was considered to be seriously debilitating and in the extreme even lethal, depleting the body of vital resources and causing madness. This is a non-regulatory view. Various 'experts' described the horrific consequences of misuse of the sexual function, as in masturbation. Therefore, any regulation of a bodily condition would be far from perfect, otherwise behaviour would switch off when the optimum was achieved and serious disturbances accompanying excessive masturbation could not arise.

Historically, in terms of regulation, the male has sometimes featured at centre-stage. Correspondingly, women have been viewed rather ambivalently, some writers claiming that, unlike the male, they lack any intrinsic sexuality. Still others advanced egalitarian unisex theories (see Tolman and Diamond, 2001). In the medieval period, long-term virginity was seen as something of a health hazard associated with a closed body, a condition that could be treated by marriage. Where marriage was not yet appropriate, girls were sometimes given instructions in masturbation by midwifes (Meston and Buss, 2009). Up until the eighteenth century, doctors were worried about the dangers to health of protracted virginity, believing that ailments would find a natural home in the closed body. In earlier times, it was generally assumed that it was necessary for women to have orgasms in order to conceive (Everaerd et al., 2000a), based upon the belief that orgasm triggered the fusion of male and female seed. Midwifery manuals of the sixteenth century described this (Wagstaff et al., 2000). The Victorian period was one during which women's intrinsic sexuality was largely denied (Crepault et al., 1977).

Such issues have been central to shaping laws and moral conventions (Kinsey et al., 1948). The notion that sex should serve reproduction means that it can occur only in the context of marriage and even then only when there is some chance of conception. Non-reproductive outlets such as masturbation and homosexuality clearly stand outside these criteria and it is not surprising that they have been strongly condemned. A counter-view to this, which many have advanced, is that consensual sex is a legitimate source of pleasure even where conception is specifically avoided.

I will start with what could be described as a non-regulatory perspective.

Buddhism: a non-regulatory perspective

As described in the classic text *What the Buddha Taught* by Walpola Rahula, the Buddha (born the son of a ruler in the sixth century BC), lived a life of splendour in a royal palace with a beautiful princess as his wife. However, wandering out one day, he was struck by the misery that he witnessed. The Buddha attributed this unhappiness to several factors, that of most interest here being excesses of desire ('craving'), sometimes described as a 'thirst' for things. Sexual desire is one such; indeed, the strongest, according to the Buddha (Kaza, 2004). The Buddha abandoned his palace and wandered the land, teaching the way to achieve peace of mind, which included trying to quell desire. According to the Buddha's teaching, all suffering in the world, such as envy, poverty and wars, arises from greedy self-centred wants. The road to true happiness is to conquer excessive desires. An emphasis should perhaps be placed on the word 'excessive', since the philosophy does not involve curbing all pleasure (Kalupahana, 1987). However, anyone seeking to become a Buddhist monk or nun is required to dedicate their life to abandoning desires, and respecting celibacy. The state of Nirvana corresponds to the emancipation from attachment to desires.

Kaza (2004, p. 24) interprets Buddhist teaching in the following way: 'Quite quickly, in a single moment, craving can lead to attachment to the feelings (positive or negative) generated by contact . . . A lot of attachment keeps one firmly in the grip of the endless cycle of desire.' As Kaza notes (p. 24), 'For some, attachment can arise from addiction to stimulation and arousal, the need for constant sensation' and 'Another danger is attachment to power within a sexual relationship.'

Buddhism has spawned followers throughout the world and these have occasionally experienced serious problems in controlling lust. However, as Kaza (2004, p. 23) observes, sexuality 'is not easily uprooted even for lofty spiritual ideals'. Somewhat paradoxically, there was a mushrooming of Buddhist centres in the 1960s in the United States at the same time as the flower-power hippie generation was experiencing the liberation of sexual behaviour.

There is an important similarity between Buddhism and Christianity in that both describe a predicament which is an inevitable conflict in life arising from the existence of desire (Numrich, 2009). Both offer insight and solutions for its resolution. However, a fundamental difference is that the Christian church has made frequent attempts to curb desire by sanction based on divine authority of what is right and wrong. By contrast, Buddhism has no divine authority backed with external sanctions and its philosophy is a pragmatic one (Kaza, 2004): desires stand in the way of enlightenment. Buddhism teaches its followers to inspect their own minds for the existence of lusts ('impure thoughts'), to deliberate upon and relinquish attachment to them. The only 'sanction' arises from the suffering of the individual.

Some Christian groups have also advocated celibacy as the answer to conflict arising from desire. Implicit in such arguments is the notion that no harm comes to the body in ignoring its urges. Other thinkers in the Christian tradition have taken a diametrically opposite position, describing disturbances to the body and the psychological harm that arises from a thwarting of sexual desire (described shortly).

Modern psychology relates to Buddhist philosophy in a number of ways. Psychological evidence documents some of the hazards associated with uncontrolled desires, as in addictions to drugs, sex or purchasing, amongst other things (Chapter 17), and the pressure to escalate the intensity of such activity in the quest for increasing 'highs'. The distinction between wanting and liking (Robinson and Berridge, 1993), introduced in Chapter 1, is relevant here. A large investment of time and effort in the search for pleasure is not necessarily rewarded with a commensurately high intensity of pleasure when the goal is reached. Evolution has 'designed' us to keep seeking incentives and the price can sometimes be an uncoupling from pleasure. Clearly, the process of the active *inhibition* of desire (Chapter 12) is at centre-stage in such Buddhist deliberations. Problems associated with the suppression of unwanted ('tempting') thoughts are discussed in Chapter 12. The search for eternal youth and virility might also be seen as somewhat counterproductive when viewed in the light of the Buddhist emphasis upon impermanence of all things.

Although Buddhist philosophy appears to deny any regulatory role to sexual behaviour, it might be seen as regulatory at another level in terms of maintaining mental stability by avoiding excesses. The discussion now turns to perspectives in which regulation by sexual activity of some sort is explicit or at least implicit.

Finding a balance: the classical period of antiquity

In ancient Greece, scholars such as Hippocrates (born 460 BC) articulated the argument that health consists in attaining a balance between different factors within the body. Disease arises when one such gets out of alignment from its healthy state. Furthermore, the body was believed to take corrective action to restore harmony. Males could, it was thought, be debilitated by excessive loss of seminal fluids (Gaca, 2003),[3] a theme destined to surface again centuries later. More specifically, it was types of fluid in the body, known as 'humours', that principally lay at the basis of health and disease (Conrad et al., 1995). This period of antiquity also saw the recognition that the brain rather than the heart is the principal basis of our mental functions.

Black bile was said to be the humour of most relevance to sexual desire and it possessed negative properties in that vomit and excreta facilitated its expulsion from the body in correcting an excess level (Conrad et al., 1995). Some in ancient Greece interpreted erotic passion as a disease, with associated mental disturbance (Dawson, 2008). In terms of humours, erotic passion arose from excess levels of black bile getting to the brain. A boiling of the blood was another interpretation. Such ideas might logically lend themselves to the notion of sex as a necessary evil to be tolerated in the service of regulation and reproduction. Early Arab writers reinforced the disease model and a fusion of such ideas permeated the West.

Plato (born 427 BC) has had a profound impact on Western thought for some two thousand years and set the scene for much subsequent interpretation of desire and its inhibition. From the theorizing of Hippocrates and Plato, an image of human nature as being in three parts emerged: the reasoning and decision-making part was located in the brain; the emotions were found in the heart; while the part responsible for appetites for food, water and sex was housed in the area of the belly and liver (Bendick, 2002; Conrad et al., 1995).

Sexual excess was thought to arise from moisture in the marrow of the bone and a consequence of this theorizing was profound in its implications for desire, free will and moral responsibility. Thus, Plato (1965) wrote of the male who gives in too easily to temptation (*Timaeus*, part 45, p. 115):

> his desires and their satisfaction cause him on each occasion acute agony and intense pleasure; for most part of his life he is maddened by this intensity of pleasure and pain, his soul is deprived of health and judgement by his physical constitution, and he is commonly regarded not as a sick man but as deliberately wicked. But the truth is that sexual incontinence is generally a mental disease caused by a single substance (the marrow) which overflows and floods the body because of the porousness of the bones.

In places, Plato was more specific and described the male seed as having 'caused there a vital appetite for emission, the desire for sexual reproduction', with the consequence that: 'a man's genitals are naturally disobedient and self-willed, like a creature that will not listen to reason, and will do anything in their mad lust for possession'. Plato describes the womb of the woman as being unsettled and causing distress by its wandering around the body, settling only when fertilization occurs.

Of course, medical science has moved on since antiquity! However, certain psychological and moral principles described by Plato have survived the centuries:

- If a physical basis for behaviour can be identified, does this absolve the individual of personal accountability? These days, the physical basis of 'excessive desire' is most likely thought to be an abnormality in structure or activity in parts of the brain.
- Plato suggested that something arising elsewhere in the body influences the brain/mind to trigger desire, an idea popular with some even today. There is satiety and regulation implicit within the account, for the man it is exemplified by ejaculation and for the woman by fertilization.
- It seems that in antiquity the expression of sexual desire outside specified bounds was as much a mixed blessing as it is these days.
- There is a source of restraint, expressed by Plato as (*Timaeus*, Part 48, p. 119): 'We should think of the most authoritative part of our soul as a guardian spirit given by god, living in the summit of the body.' In present times, the restraint is still understood to be 'at the summit', as exemplified by the Freudian superego or the activity of the prefrontal cortex (Chapter 2) in modern neuroscience. In Plato's view, God implicitly seemed to need some help and therefore society should be designed with rigid and authoritarian controls. By offering restraints on the various aspects of human waywardness, civic virtue and social justice would prevail (Gaca, 2003). This appears to extend to sex the kind of controls exerted in modern society by, for example, tax inspectors and traffic wardens, probably earning thereby a similar degree of public affection.

Plato acknowledged the need for expression of sexual desire but took a decidedly negative attitude towards it, viewing its unruly nature with a combination of indifference and distaste. Indeed, his emphasis was upon the restraint of such physical pleasures and their inferiority as compared to more cerebral pursuits, such as philosophy. Plato was one of the first to articulate the notion of conflict for the control of behaviour. His work entitled *The Republic* describes this (Plato, 2003, p. 147):

And isn't the element of prevention, when present, due to our reason, while the urges and impulses are due to our feelings and unhealthy cravings?

The ideas of Plato are timeless, as still reflected in the struggles of sexual temptation and addiction. Any restraint that can be mustered is based upon long-term and rational considerations, in opposition to the pull of desire in the 'heat of the moment'. Calling sexual desire 'tyrannical' in its capacity to defeat reason, Plato also seems to have been aware of what would be termed today 'behavioural sensitization' and the associated 'escalation' of behavioural intensity (Plato, 2003, p. 311):

> When a master passion within has absolute control of a man's mind, I suppose life is a round of extravagant feasts and orgies and sex and so on.

Plato's writing articulates the roots of a conundrum and ethical dilemma, which were to reappear in various guises in the subsequent centuries. Plato understood sex to be an appetite that corresponds to a bodily 'want', like hunger and thirst (Gaca, 2003). Yet the latter are required for bodily survival, so the argument leads logically to the necessity for a minimum level of sexual outlet. Indeed, abstinence was seen as unhealthy since it led to an unhealthy accumulation of seed in men and disturbed the womb in women. So, what is this minimum level of outlet and what forms can answer the body's sexual want? Plato feared that young Athenian men, typically driven relentlessly by excessive levels of seed, would protest the loudest against his arguments for restraint. Nonetheless, he tried to divert their lust into the study of philosophy and suggested obligatory city-organized workouts to draw off ('sublimate') surplus energy. A principal contributor to excessive lust was thought to be excessive food intake, another theme that was destined to reappear over the centuries.

By building upon earlier thinkers, Galen (born AD 129) had an enormous influence on Western medical thought. As with Plato, he appears to have had a negative view of all but conventional sexuality (Hankinson, 2008). There were higher things to be pursued in life; apparently following Plato, he saw an intrinsic conflict between reason and passion. However, Galen managed to combine his dim view of sexuality with a belief in a regulatory principle at its basis and an acknowledgement of pleasure's role in the continuation of the species. According to Galen, even a slight retention of seminal or menstrual fluids could produce grave physiological consequences. Therefore, a regular and corrective sexual outlet is justified physiologically, even if one ought not to enjoy the experience too much! Masturbation was regarded by Galen as a morally superior regulator to the use of 'loose women'. If only some artificial trigger to discharge, such as a herbal remedy, had been available, one imagines that this would have been considered ethically desirable.

Bodily and psychological distress from deprivation and temptation

> For the flesh lusteth against the spirit, and the spirit against the flesh: and these are contrary the one to the other; so that ye cannot do the things that ye would. (The Epistle of St Paul to the Galatians 5:17)

Religious texts

The Old Testament illustrates the belief that thwarted desire can cause a disturbance to the body, exemplifying what subsequently has been interpreted as 'lust sickness':

> And Amnon was so vexed, that he fell sick for his sister Tamar; for she *was* a virgin and Amnon thought it hard for him to do any thing to her. (2 Samuel 13:2)

A question posed to Amnon by his friend Jonadab reveals one aspect of the disorder in the body, reflecting possibly something like anorexia nervosa:

> Why *art* thou, *being* the king's son, lean from day to day? (2 Samuel 13:4)

A theme running through much religious discourse, both Jewish and Christian, is the notion of an inherently sinful body held in check by a virtuous soul (Cohn-Sherbok et al., 2013; Hawkes, 2004). For example, St Paul wrote of his struggles, locating the 'law of sin' in the body. The conflict was seen as between bodily urges and restraint within the spirit, a form of mind–body dichotomy that modern science would reject.

Nonetheless, he correctly identified layered control and the ubiquitous struggle with which it is associated.

Also pointing to an aversive quality of deprivation, St Augustine described, 'scratching the itching sore of lust' (*Confessions*, ix.1). Two influential religious figures from the fifteenth and sixteenth centuries appear to have been powerfully influenced by ideas arising in ancient Greece concerning regulation and restraint on desire. However, these ideas led them to rather different conclusions and social prescriptions, as described next.

Martin Luther

The German monk, Martin Luther, who led the revolt against the Church of Rome, was born into a world where it was taught that sin and temptation are inherent to the human condition and the body is fundamentally unclean morally (Friedenthal, 1970). Not surprisingly, women were regarded as man's principal source of temptation: the 'lust of the flesh'. The official position was one of rigorously imposed celibacy for monks and nuns. A monk could be condemned as a sinner for merely holding his gaze on a woman for longer than a fleeting instant. Any of his colleagues who bore witness to such a moral lapse were obliged to report this to their superiors.

Reality was rather different from the 'ideal'; promiscuity, adultery and prostitution were rife. Not all monks honoured the conventions of the church or their own solemn vows of chastity; doubtless, more than a few surreptitious gazes were made. Indeed, the monks' reputation, as portrayed in popular sayings and humour, was one of lechery. Even certain convents acquired a 'bad name'. Rome, the ultimate source of spiritual authority, was hardly in a position to preach with integrity, for a number of popes had fathered children. People with money could obtain forgiveness for their sins by paying indulgences to the church, the required sum reflecting the gravity of the sin.

Luther was incensed by what he saw as unbridled hypocrisy. His opposition to the prescribed sexual code was a significant factor fuelling the Reformation of the church and the split with Rome. There was perfect compatibility between Luther's references to sexuality and his arguments in favour of marriage for monks and nuns. Thus, he appealed to a God-given 'natural state' of humans and used a regulatory view of sexual desire as a form of liberation (Friedenthal, 1970, p. 431):

> Grow and multiply. This is not a command but something more than a command, it is a work of God that is not for us to prevent or permit; it is as necessary as for me to be a man and more necessary than eating and drinking, sleeping and waking. It is in our nature, implanted in us, just as are the parts of the body essential to it.

He objected to celibacy for monks and nuns on the grounds that a natural urge exists (p. 431):

> if they hamper it, you can be sure that they will not remain pure but will inevitably be defiled by secret sins or whoredom.

Such logic provided the intellectual rationale for Luther's actions in, for example, finding husbands for nuns. He described a regulatory model, which appears to owe much to ancient Greek thinking (p. 431):

> Therefore the physicians do not argue amiss when they say that if we forcibly curb this work of nature it must react on the flesh and the blood and become poison.

Again using a notion of regulation, Luther spoke of 'pollutions', that is masturbation, in terms of the 'needs of the body', a discourse that encouraged hair-splitting discussion of whether, in answering needs, pleasure was permitted (Friedenthal, 1970, p. 33).

Thomas More

Writing in *Utopia*, Sir (later to become Saint) Thomas More also appeared to have been influenced by a similar regulatory notion adopted from antiquity (1516/1975, p. 96):

> Physical pleasures are subdivided into two types. First, there are those which fill the whole organism with a conscious sense of enjoyment. This may be the result of replacing physical substances which have been burnt up by the natural heat of the body, as when we eat and drink. Or else it may be caused by the discharge of some excess, as in excretion, sexual intercourse, or any relief by rubbing or scratching.

However, despite such theorizing and his progressive and egalitarian policies concerning many aspects of life in *Utopia*, More was no sexual progressive and seemed not to be too fond of desire. Indeed, compulsory celibacy for life was the penalty imposed for having sex before marriage, whereas repeated adultery carried a death sentence, perhaps not everyone's idea of utopia. His grouping of sexual intercourse with excretion has some rather obvious failings since it would be odd to devise laws to prohibit excessive excretion or set an age limit on when excretion can begin. In the tradition of Plato, More saw sex and feeding as physical pleasures with all the inherent down-sides, while mental pleasures, such as 'contemplating truth' and music, were superior.

Despite permitting *Utopian* brides and bridegrooms to inspect each others' naked bodies to ascertain that they were satisfied before tying the knot, marital life in *Utopia* took an inevitable strain. Sexual prohibitions seemed rooted in an acknowledgement that novelty plays a role in desire (Chapter 11 of the present book), again pointing to a distinction with excretion (1516/1975, p. 103):

> Then Utopians are particularly strict about that kind of thing, because they think very few people would want to get married – which means spending one's whole life with the same person, and putting up with all the inconveniences that this involves – if they weren't carefully prevented from having any sexual intercourse otherwise.

Accordingly, More arranged things so that the chances of temptation arising were limited (p. 84):

> There are no wine-taverns, no ale-houses, no brothels, no opportunities for seduction, no secret meeting places. Everyone has his eye on you, so you're practically forced to get on with your job, and make some proper use of your spare time.

Martin Luther was described as an open incestuous lecher by More for getting married (p. 145).

Sixteenth- and seventeenth-century green sickness

In sixteenth- to seventeenth-century thought, both sexes were said to produce seed and its agitation underlies desire. In men, the seed is released at ejaculation and a lowering of lust follows. Similarly, the health educator, William Vaughan wrote that for women the build-up of seed is the basis of (Dawson, 2008, p. 25): 'secret flames and unbridled affections which dispose their mindes to waiwardness and extravagant imaginations'. Thus, it would seem that any partner would suffice to release the tension. A failure to discharge the seed means that it turns malignant and harms body and mind alike. The generic notion of 'pent-up seed' provided the basis for a unisex model of desire, while sexual intercourse was the cure for both sexes. Opposite to some later assumptions, if there were any difference, it was female rather than male sexuality that was rooted most firmly within the lower parts of the body.

The so-called 'green sickness', also termed the 'disease of virgins' and the 'white fever', came into prominence as a female disorder in sixteenth- to seventeenth-century Europe (something apparently identical was documented in young men and women in 1027 by the Islamic scholar Ibn Hazm). The disorder was associated with a pale complexion and weakness (Dawson, 2008). For females, it was thought to have a *biological* cause: an accumulation of seed, associated with a disruption of menstruation. The trapped seed could excite sexual desire and, reciprocally, desire could exacerbate the condition. Whether or not sexual desire was triggered, the most reliable cure was thought to be penetrative sex. This would open up the veins and release trapped seed, so marriage was prescribed. However, one can speculate that green sickness was sometimes used as the explicit rationale for 'therapeutic seduction'.

The disorder was not thought to have a psychological trigger in the form of a desired person, which marks a distinction with lovesickness, described shortly. Any possessor of an adequate penis was good enough to bring a cure. So, it might seem that emotional empathy was no more necessary than in acquiring the professional services of, say, a chimneysweep or a plumber.

It was said that, if untreated, green sickness might turn into a still worse disorder, known as 'uterine fury' associated with heat in the womb or vapours released from trapped seed, which culminated in nymphomania. Women in this state were prone to loss of all reason, open expression of matters sexual and to exhibit a voracious sexual appetite. Those in an unconsummated marriage and young widows were thought to be particularly prone to this disorder.

Sixteenth- to seventeenth-century lovesickness

In sixteenth- and seventeenth-century England, building on classical accounts of amongst others the tenth-century Iranian physician Ibn Sina, medical texts described 'lovesickness'. Dawson (2008, p. 2) observes: 'intense unfulfilled erotic desire is classified as a species of melancholy'. And various authors (p. 2) 'held erotic obsession to be a real and virulent illness'. The initial cause of lovesickness was understood to be the mind's obsessive fixation on a *particular desired person* involving the mind's chewing over ('rumination') of the image of this individual. Other thoughts, perceptions and memories were driven out. Lust and sexual desire were seen as an important ingredient of lovesickness. A modern interpretation of lovesickness would be in terms of a combination of sexual desire and unrequited romantic attachment.

In turn, the mental fixation was believed to disturb ('scorch') the humours of the body. Vapours from the external object of desire were thought to lock into interaction with the bodily condition. Love is (Dawson, 2008, p. 15): 'caught through the eyes and triggers an immediate physical reaction: the spirits grow distracted, the liver malfunctions, the blood becomes muddy, and the body deteriorates'. In both sexes, another biological consequence of the mind's fixation was understood to be excess seed in the body. An individual who was simply lustful might have some similar disturbances to the body but was not plunged into melancholy as a result.

Playwrights at this time depicted the lovesick as having a disturbance of fire in the liver, bowels, veins or genitals (Dawson, 2008, p. 21). To us, such descriptions sound bizarre, but in principle they capture one feature of modern understanding: sexual desire and romantic fixation involve an external–internal interaction. The prior state of the body, as an imbalance of humors, was such as to make the individual particularly vulnerable to catching lovesickness. Reflecting its roots in Iranian medicine, this period was characterized by a form of explanation that has a surprisingly modern flavour in that it involved an inseparable link between body and mind.

Lovesickness appeared to be a real illness that involved a serious disturbance to body and mind alike. Personal diaries, accounts by doctors and playwrights converge in portraying genuine suffering, which, in the extreme, was thought to lead even to death from 'wasting away'.

The sickness exemplifies a culturally relative feature of sexual desire and how sending diametrically opposite bodily signals can achieve the same goal. People wishing to succeed in the mating game today, particularly if they have even a superficial acquaintance with evolutionary psychology, might typically try to signal their candidacy by displaying a good complexion, upright posture, polished white teeth, accompanied by smartness of dress and grooming. Thereby, they would advertise their health, affluence and vitality. By stark contrast, during the sixteenth and seventeenth centuries, a pale, dishevelled, unkempt and slouching presentation, probably signalling to modern people little more than clinical depression, could incite the attention and presumably passion of another. However, lovesickness signalled not only fervour and determination but also membership of a noble social elite, since not all classes alike were vulnerable to catching it. Furthermore, it was known to be a transient state corrected by forming the desired erotic bond.

Prior to the Renaissance, lovesickness was generally, though not exclusively, seen as a male disorder. From that time on, women increasingly come into their own as the sufferers from the disorder (Dawson, 2008).

Treatments for lovesickness were both biological and psychological. In the former category was bloodletting, seen as a kind of catharsis, performed in the expectation of correcting the underlying disturbance to the body. In the psychological dimension, the afflicted individual was urged to stay busy, listen to music and, as a means to distract the mind, to travel. Having sex was said to help by restoring the level of seed to a more tolerable state as well as providing psychological therapy. Where union was not possible, and as a striking precursor to modern aversion and cognitive therapy, cures involved devaluing the love object (e.g. in the case of a man, by drinking the blood of the desired one or by exposing him to what purported to be one of her garments 'tainted' with menstrual blood) or trying to construe love itself as an infantile and humiliating affliction.

For some people, lovesickness was a visible sign of a bodily condition, which, if not permitted to run its logical course of uniting the sufferer with the love object, could lead to insanity or even death. The suitor was not acting as a rational being but as an innocent and helpless victim. Thereby, one who was otherwise unacceptable to the parents of the intended might become tolerable. Indeed, lovesickness was occasionally used as evidence in courts of law to permit marriage in the face of parental opposition. In some cases, the disorder was used in seduction as emotional blackmail in portraying victim status, of the form 'look at what you have done to me'.

In modern terms, how might we understand these phenomena? A thwarting of goals can have negative psychological consequences, with possible manifestations also outside the brain, for example in hormonal levels in the blood. These disorders would seem to exemplify something like a grief reaction, which could be viewed as the ultimate thwarter of aspirations. We like to think that we live in a sexually enlightened age, and doubtless in many regards we do. However, consider what sort of reaction you might get if you were to make an appointment with your family doctor to request a treatment for sexual frustration or lovesickness.

A nineteenth-century account

From personal experience, the Russian writer Count Tolstoy described a body/mind distinction and seemed to imply something like sensitization of desire with subsequent battle-fatigue (A. N. Wilson, 1988, p. 431):

> All life is a struggle between the flesh and the spirit . . . Gradually the flesh triumphs over the spirit.

The nineteenth-century literature contains numerous accounts that sexual deprivation is aversive. For example, in adolescence, Tolstoy experienced 'ghastly spells of lust, which tormented him (A. N. Wilson, 1988, p. 34). Things hardly improved with age, the adult Tolstoy reporting 'As for women, there seems to be no hope ... Sensuality is tormenting me' (A. N. Wilson, 1988, p. 114). Here the focus is upon the external trigger to desire, particularly aroused by novelty.

Regulation with a danger of excess

> [Y]ou squander half your force with women. You'll never really do what you should do, with a fine mind such as yours. Too much of it goes the other way. (D. H. Lawrence, 1928/1993, p. 36)

Eleventh century

Early in the eleventh century, the Islamic scholar Abu Ali Sina (Avicenna) in his classic *The Canon of Medicine* reasoned that sleep corrects weakness induced by, amongst other things, emotional disturbances, anger and sexual intercourse. Dryness of the skin was said to be a symptom of excessive indulgence (Avicenna, 1025/1999).

Eighteenth century

The eighteenth century advanced the idea that unruly sexual desire, as manifest in nymphomania, was due to ingesting rich sauces and spiced meat and thereby causing the blood to be 'too abundant', whatever that might mean (Orford, 2001). We normally consider the Victorian era to be that most closely associated with the horrors of masturbation, but the fears were implanted well before then and were promoted in the eighteenth century. They appear to derive from a misunderstanding of the action of Onan (Genesis 38:8–10), where he let his seed fall onto the ground (MacDonald, 1967). A reading of the Biblical text could leave little doubt that Onan's true sin was coitus interruptus, but the idea of wasting seed in masturbation took hold. A number of publications appeared in the early eighteenth century, in which the moral sin of masturbation was associated with almost every imaginable disturbance to the healthy equilibrium of the body. The idea of bodily debilitation by loss of seminal fluids was advanced, one feature being a draining of nervous energy from the brain, hence causing damage to this organ.

Nineteenth century

Throughout the nineteenth century numerous eccentric ideas on the basis of sexuality entered public discourse, one being that excessive sexual desire corresponded to inflammation of a part of the brain, the cerebellum (Orford, 2001). A major influence on nineteenth-century thinking about male sexuality was the English doctor William Acton. Apparently, female sexuality hardly existed and desire posed little problem for the vast majority of women. Acton wrote (Marcus, 1966, p. 31): 'As a general rule, a modest woman seldom desires any sexual gratification for herself. She submits to her husband, but only to please him.' In the rare cases where female desire got out of control, the result was insanity. According to Acton, there was a very narrow window of opportunity for healthy sexual expression; deviate to either side and the consequences were dire. This involved both regulatory and non-regulatory features. As clear non-regulation, he helped to secure broad acceptance of the view that masturbation in males seriously depleted the body of vital forces, even equating an ounce of semen to the loss of forty ounces of blood. Sexual excess in marital intercourse could lead to heart failure, loss of memory and disturbed vision. However, triggering desire without sexual outlet could lead to impotence, a softening of the brain and mental derangement. Thus, in summary Acton wrote (Marcus, 1966, p. 28): 'excitement of the sexual feelings when not followed by the result which it should produce, is ... an unmitigated evil'. Clearly, to the Victorian mind, the only way to attain any semblance of physical and mental health was to exert strong control over lustful feelings.

The Victorians popularized the notion of 'spending resources' in sex, particularly orgasm, though the roots of the idea go back centuries (Cohn-Sherbok et al., 2013). This notion appears in the autobiography *My Secret Life* (Walter, 1995, p. 44):

> Every half-holiday, he made me spend with him in walking, and riding; he insisted on my boating, cricketing, and keeping at athletic games when not at my studies. The old doctor I expect guessed my temperament, and thought, by thoroughly occupying and fatiguing me, to prevent erotic thoughts.

Walter proposed a unisex model of desire and spoke of women 'spending' fluids, in some cases needing to do so, in much the same way as for men (Kronhausen and Kronhausen, 1967, p. 231).

The Victorian British were noted for their sexual eccentricity but this was by no means peculiar to them. For example, regulation was expressed by Tolstoy:

> every day each of us eats perhaps two pounds of meat, game and all kinds of stimulating food and drink. Where does it all go? On sensual excesses. If we really do use it up in that way, the safety valve is opened and everything is all right. (Tolstoy, 1889/2007, p. 34)

In nineteenth-century medical discourse, as a result of the work of a number of researchers, most famously Freud, the experience of love took something of a back seat to sexual desire (Tallis, 2005). Love came to be seen as a variation on the theme of sex, something subordinate to sexual desire. The later decades of the century saw a shift of locus of sexual desire towards the lower regions of the body (Orford, 2001). Tragically, various targets, such as the ovaries, labia and the clitoris, were surgically removed in order to try to cure excessive female sexual desire.

Freud, psychoanalysis and regulation

> According to rabbinic theology, the evil inclination (*yetzer ha-ra*), which in part was understood as the sexual drive, was viewed as the source of energy for properly sublimated activities. (Cohn-Sherbok et al., 2013, p. 4)[4]

Basic notions of desire

Freud suggested that motivation is based upon regulation and a human tendency to try to correct disturbances from equilibrium. All behaviour was thought to be based upon this basic principle, with instigating factors inside the body (Person, 1990). Freud's philosophical foundations derived from, amongst other sources, ancient Greece, pleasure being felt in the "restoration of harmony or return to equilibrium" (Glick and Bone, 1990, p. 2).

Freud theorized by analogy with physical principles, for example, calling the driving force, the id, a 'great *reservoir* of libido' (italics mine; Freud, 1955, p. 51). Libido is a force that is instinctive and which 'presses for gratification' (Person, 1990, p. ix), that is to say, a lowering of tension. When gratification occurs, that is a discharge of libido, this is associated with pleasure, whereas a failure of gratification is associated with increased tension and psychological pain. In 'Beyond the pleasure principle', Freud described what was termed 'psychic energy' (Bowlby, 1982), writing (Freud, 1955, p. 9):

> the mental apparatus endeavours to keep the quantity of excitation present in it as low as possible or at least to keep it constant.

He argued (Freud, 1953, p. 168):

> The source of an instinct is a process of excitation occurring in an organ and the immediate aim of the instinct lies in the removal of the organic stimulus.

So, in the case of sexual desire, where is the source of this psychic energy and motivational tension? Freud was attracted to the idea that pressure in the vessels that hold seminal fluid prior to ejaculation (the seminal vesicles) constitutes the internal factor (Freud, 1953, p. 213). There is obviously some correlation between loss of these fluids at ejaculation and loss of sexual desire. However, as Freud went on to note, the theory can hardly account for continuing sexual desire in castrated males, who have lost the source of seminal fluids. Animals with seminal vesicles removed still show sexual motivation. One could speculate that earlier cycles of tension and release somehow got memorized by the brain and some autonomy was gained. As Freud also acknowledged, and doubtless the reader will have already spotted, the model has even greater difficulty with that half of the population who possess no seminal vesicles.

Despite such an apparently fatal flaw, Freud proceeded to argue (p. 214):

> Nevertheless it may at once be admitted that it is possible to find means by which the theory may be made to cover these cases as well.

He continued (p. 217):

> this sexual excitation is derived not from the so-called sexual parts alone, but from all the bodily organs.

Freud's model arose from analogy with physical energy, as studied in physics and chemistry, and he sought to anchor his ideas within such a scientific framework. Psychic energy was said to seek its own discharge, rather as electrical energy does. Behaviour is triggered by the accumulation of psychic energy reaching a certain level, while the exhaustion of the energy terminates behaviour.

In other words, the nervous system strives to reduce nervous tension, pleasure being associated with a reduction in such tension and so-called 'unpleasure' with an increase. Indeed, neuroses were explained in terms of 'neural poisoning' as a result of the failure to discharge the accumulation.

However, one would be mistaken to link discharge with any orgasm. On the contrary, in keeping with Victorian fears, the abnormal activity of masturbation, amongst others, was accompanied by untold ills such as poisoning of the nervous system. This doubtless owed much to Freud's religious inheritance, in spite of his avowed atheism and wish to build a secular science (Webster, 1995). Thus, only a healthy orgasm was what maintained sexual health. Corresponding to the analogy with physical energy, there is the notion of 'repression', in which the energy is held back from being discharged (Freud, 1953, p. 164). Failing to find an acceptable outlet as in sexual behaviour, it might manifest in, say, hysteria.

Kon (1987, p. 258) notes:

Sexual motivation was considered something entirely biological and instinctive. The culture was regarded as providing the external form, limit, or social control of the libido. It was thought that society may regulate and, to a certain, rather modest extent 'civilize' and 'humanize' the sexual drive but society could not change the libido's primordial, irrational, and aggressive essence.

Sublimation

According to Freudian theory, if libidinous energy is not discharged sexually, it can get transformed and underlie the performance of creative activities ('higher things'). This is termed 'sublimation' and it clearly follows from principles of regulation. The notion is not Freud's original idea but is found in various religious teachings (Kinsey et al., 1948). It has come under criticism, from, amongst others, the Kinsey researchers, whose least sexually active males showed no evidence of sublimation into creative activity. They argue (p. 207): 'Certainly, no one who actually knew the sexual histories of particular artists would have thought of using them as illustrations of sexually sublimated people.' One might apply this logic to the lives of energetic and creative writers (e.g. James Boswell, Tolstoy, Walter) or politicians (e.g. Kennedy, Clinton). One can indeed find people lacking a sexual outlet, who demonstrated high levels of energy and creativity, such as the writer J. M. Barrie, but this is hardly evidence for a diversion of sexual energy. A possible explanation will be advanced in the next chapter.

The Freudian notion of restraint

Civilization and the orderly functioning of society require a powerful source of restraint on the selfish id's cravings. Hence, this sets up an ever-present conflict within the individual. Restraint is provided by what Freud termed the 'superego', the part of the brain/mind that assimilates cultural rules, norms and prohibitions. The superego is the last part of the brain/mind to develop and contains information on the so-called 'ego ideal', the standards of excellence of the individual assimilated from parental authority and cultural norms. It represents the moral part of the brain/mind. The conflicting demands of the superego and the id are mediated by the ego. This idea of Freud's reflects a historical continuity going back to antiquity and has stood the test of time, since it fits well to modern ideas on the layered organization of the brain (Chapter 2).

Some problems with Freud's ideas

Problems with the notion of energy soon became evident to Freud and he struggled with them, as have his followers (Stern, 1990). Most people would accept that something analogous to energy discharge and lowering of tension accompanies sexual orgasm or the hungry baby deriving an adequate amount of milk from the mother. Most would equally subscribe to the hedonism of orgasm, even if being unable to recall the pleasures of breast-feeding! Both pleasures could be based upon opioid substances. However, several complications arise in applying this as a universal basis for desire. Orgasm occurs only *after* a period of sexual searching and interaction, so, although it can reinforce such behaviour, it is hard to see how it can provide the bases of desire. Also, energy discharge in orgasm appears not to be invariably necessary for sexual pleasure. As Apter (2007, p. 8) argues:

> We would expect therefore that Freud would have a great deal to say about the pleasures of excitement. Ironically, the whole tenor of Freudian theory is to see any kind of arousal, including sexual arousal, as something which people try to avoid.

Surely many derive pleasure from flirting and kissing, even in the absence of orgasm. This is presumably associated, if anything, with an immediate *increase* in tension. The pleasure would seem to come from various factors combined with increased arousal, such as stimulation of erogenous surfaces in kissing, cues to possible future sexual progression and confirmation that the flirter is attractive. If the present analysis is correct, any pleasure from tension reduction prior to sexual contact comes from the removal of 'information uncertainty' in establishing a sexually charged social interaction. Similarly, some folk are prepared to pay money to learn Tantric sex techniques, which emphasize the virtues and ultimate pleasures of *restraining* orgasm.

Freud came to acknowledge that both a build-up of tension and a discharge can be associated with pleasure and his followers have sought to understand the interactions between the two, as in a build-up followed by a lowering of tension (Doidge, 1990; Klein, 1987).

Bowlby (1982), a theorist in the psychoanalytic tradition, articulated other objections:

• Behaviour is often repeated immediately after it has ended, where, it would seem, there is insufficient time for energy accumulation to occur. This makes better sense in terms of the consequences of behaviour, for example aggression tends to cease when an intruder flees or submits. Resumption of behaviour occurs if the challenge reappears.
• The theory remains untested, which is a serious failing for something claimed to be scientific.
• The notion of psychic energy does not lead to fruitful interaction with the traditional sciences, where energy of a physical kind is precisely defined and measurable.

Of course, energy might be a useful first metaphor, but it is one that can be improved. Suffice it to note that, making a similar point to that of Bowlby concerning aggression, sexual desire can sometimes be powerfully re-aroused by an external factor, as in a partner change.

A modern view

With biological insight, some contemporary theorists have reinterpreted Freud. Thus, Pfaff (1999, p. 168) writes:

In its simplest psychoanalytic terms, libido is defined as a force originating in physiological signals and acting on the mind.

and

As concepts on the frontier between the somatic and the mental, 'instinct' or 'drive' comprised, for Freud, somatically determined demands made on the mind for psychic work. These demands constituted 'pressures' or 'forces' shaping mental events.

Continuing with

he attempted to provide for the translation of motivational forces from the body into motivational forces in the mind.

This sounds like a dualism between body and mind, which few would accept these days. To repeat, the line argued here is that desire arises in the brain/mind seen as a unified entity and is triggered by attractive individuals, helped by signals from the genitals and sensitized by hormones.

Sex hormones are indeed a factor arising outside the brain/mind and targeting processes in the brain, thereby sensitizing them. It is also true that a loss of hormones can result in a reduction or loss of desire. However, the link between hormones and desire is not a simple one-to-one relationship, as their level can be high and yet little desire be felt. Furthermore, their level is not suddenly reduced following orgasm.

Freud's legacy

No one could doubt the immense impact that psychoanalysis has had on 'opening up the debate' and changing societal attitudes, sexual morals and mores, as well as influencing the intellectual culture of literature, art, theatre and film. This is a quite extraordinary and, outside the spread of religion, perhaps unique achievement, particularly given that the country that was most willing to absorb Freudian ideas was also the one that Freud disliked the most: the United States (Torrey, 1992).

Freud's critics speculate on why the intellectual elite of New York's Greenwich Village, the vanguard of Freud's assimilation within American culture, did not examine more carefully the foundations of psychoanalysis. These would, they argue, have been found to be decidedly shaky, based upon an ad hoc energy regulating contraption, which has been compared to an eccentric mechanical invention of Heath Robinson (Webster, 1995). Maybe this didn't matter too much since large sections of the culture were already prepared to accept these ideas, psychoanalysis being a convenient way of casting off the restrictions of the country's puritan inheritance. One might suggest that a sufficient number of divorces, affairs, 'therapeutic seductions', forgiven transgressions, as well as some enriched and revived marriages, were achieved to guarantee the propagation of Freudian philosophy.

Although various Freudian ideas were assimilated into the culture, the one of most relevance here amounts to the principle of regulation: a healthy sexual life is the necessary condition for psychological health. The notion of sexual repression, presumably corresponding to energy not discharged, was accepted by large sections of the intelligentsia. Abstinence, whether voluntary or involuntary, was something of a health hazard causing energy to be transferred into neuroses. In this regard, Freud's ideas found a natural home with those campaigning for such things as birth control, women's emancipation and a right to divorce. The next chapter will give an alternative perspective on sexual frustration.

Regulation, drive and scientific psychology

Within mainstream psychology, a variant on the theme that sex is regulatory and behaviour is energized by deviations from optimum is captured by the term 'drive'. Despite attempts to expunge it from psychology (Berridge, 2004), the term will probably not go away. Used as a convenient metaphor, for a sexual appetite, it might cause little harm. However, when used to look for some factor in the body that arises intrinsically, it could prove a distraction.

Always searching for an objective foundation for behaviour, the American psychologist, John Watson, the founder of the behaviourist movement, suggested that pressure in the seminal vesicles of males drives them until they achieve release, rather as a full bladder drives urination (Watson, 1930). Of course, as just noted, this leaves unexplained any sexual drive in women. Here Watson recruited the favourite behaviourist stalwart, learning, as an explanation: women learn to be sexually motivated.

In summary

- Spanning the centuries, two design features of sexual desire are commonly described: regulation and mechanisms of restraint.
- Buddhist teaching appears to present arguments that do not involve regulation in the traditional sense. It advises on the wisdom of not allowing desire to turn into craving.
- Concerning the regulatory factor, from Hippocrates and Galen in antiquity, through to Freud and Watson, we see the notion that desire is a reflection of an internal factor getting out of alignment. The nature of this suggested factor has varied over the centuries from black bile, through poison to, more recently, motivational energy and pressure in the seminal vesicles. There are shortcomings to such explanations and later chapters will show where the behaviour and mental states of desire that led to them can be better explained.
- In Plato, we find the notion of an unruly desire held in check by higher rational considerations. St Paul saw the urges of the physical body being restrained by the mind. In Freud, something similar is described in terms of a primitive and immoral id, held in check by the civilizing influence of the superego. These processes can be given a modern interpretation: neuroscience identifies brain regions embodying competition between desire and its inhibition.

FOUR

AN INCENTIVE-BASED MODEL

Some people – probably fewer than are claimed by science and folk-lore – eschew or are denied sexual pleasure for their entire lives, without apparent ill effects. It is all the more remarkable, therefore, that millions of people throughout the ages have eagerly risked life, limb, property, freedom, tranquillity, family, reputation, happiness, have even accepted sure and eternal damnation, all for the attainment, not of offspring, but of sexual pleasure.

(Tuzin, 1995, p. 259)[1]

Is sexual desire part of a regulator?

Sexual desire and behaviour appear superficially to exhibit some features of regulation. However, as Chapter 3 indicated, there is little evidence to support any of the actual regulatory processes that have been postulated over the centuries and considerable evidence against them.

With little controversy, deprivation of sexual opportunity can be felt by some as aversive, while sexual outlet is felt as pleasurable and restorative. This much is in common with feeding and drinking, systems unambiguously concerned with regulation. Or, to take another analogy, there is at least something in common with a full bladder and the urge to urination. However, while acknowledging some level of similarity, one needs to look closer and ask – where lies the source of distress that comes from not being able to express sexual desire? Considering the similarities and differences with feeding and drinking can give useful pointers to the design of sexual desire (Singer and Toates, 1987).

Insight by comparison

Loss of water from the body creates a desire for water and ingested water then switches this off, giving rise to sensations of pleasure. Signals from regions of the body outside the brain are conveyed to the brain informing it of the body's deficit, which excites the desire for water. Similarly, deprivation of food lowers the body's reserves of nutrients and powerfully contributes to the desire for food. Ingesting food tends to switch off the desire, also accompanied by sensations of pleasure.

Now consider similarities and differences with sex. As noted in Chapter 2, the brain processes underlying feeding and drinking have some common features with sex and, as will be described later, some identical bases. In addition to internal factors, feeding is often in response to external events, in common with sexual desire. Except in the extremes of deprivation, our appetite for food is normally mediated by the attraction of foods. This attraction is enhanced by nutrient deficits and lowered by a surplus of nutrients. Pointing to the role of this external factor, the desire for a food can be powerfully enhanced by a change in the available food (Le Magnen, 1967), something often true of sex too (Chapter 11). Social factors, such as being with other people, tend to promote the desire for food. Time of day can influence our feeding and when we are busy we might forget to eat, so clearly there is external–internal interaction underlying the desire to feed. Thwarting of the desire for food, as in finding a restaurant closed or an empty refrigerator, triggers frustration, another feature in common with sexual desire.

Loss of sex hormones can lower desire and boosting their level can increase desire (Bancroft, 2009). So much is in common with factors arousing feeding and drinking. However, corresponding to sexual satiety there is not a fall in hormone levels and so we need to look elsewhere for the signal that switches off desire post-orgasm. Chapter 12 presents evidence that events intrinsic to the brain switch desire on and off. The level of hormones is not regulated by sexual behaviour and there would appear to be little biological value in such an arrangement. Unlike ingested nutrients or water, these hormones serve reproduction not bodily health and integrity.

When taken to extremes of deprivation another difference between feeding/drinking and sex becomes evident. Extremes of hunger or thirst endanger the body tissues and create pathology, which would trigger us to ingest almost anything that is nutritious or fluid respectively, no matter how odious. In such a state and in the absence of anything to eat or drink, most of us would probably opt for the needed substance by the intragastric or intravenous route, to correct the discomfort and pathology. This highlights the biological imperative underlying feeding and drinking behaviour.

Sex doesn't seem to be like this (Ågmo, 2007). Even in the extremes of deprivation, there is not an obvious threatening disturbance outside the brain that increases in magnitude over time. Neither does it appear that desire increases with deprivation in the way that hunger and thirst do. A few men who wish for celibacy or gender reorientation, or have troubling deviant sexuality (Wassersug et al., 2004), opt for surgical castration. However, such troubles all relate to psychological factors and the external world rather than internal events. According to the argument to be developed in the present book, where a failure to find a sexual outlet is troubling, this arises in the context of desires that fail to be translated into sexual behaviour. The trouble starts *in the brain/mind*, not elsewhere.

Any comparison with the bladder and urination makes the same point, though even more strongly. Clearly the tension of a full bladder and the desire for urination serve an intrinsic biological imperative: avoiding involuntary urination or even bursting the bladder. Under medical treatment, a catheter can solve the problem of excessive pressure.

Of course, there is an internal factor underlying sexual desire, which tends to lower its sensitivity for a short period of time following orgasm. It is equally clear that a signal from the genitals can contribute to desire. However, it is the contention of this chapter that for sex no regulatory factor comparable to energy, blood composition or bladder pressure exists. Rather, the internal factor is best described in terms of the activity of particular circuits of neurons within the brain that are responsive to attractive others and are sensitized by sex hormones and signals from the genitals. This brain system is desensitized by orgasm(s), an event intrinsic to the brain.

Sexual activity, health and frustration

In spite of what has just been said, numerous articles and books tell us that sex is good for our mental and bodily health (Shope, 1971). For example, a study of American males concluded that masturbation in young men lent itself to better psychological health than did restraint (Kinsey et al., 1948). Kinsey et al. (1953) noted the neuromuscular tension that arises with sexual arousal and suggested (p. 166): 'Most persons live more happily with themselves and with other persons if their sexual arousal, whenever it is of any magnitude, may be carried through to the point of orgasm.' When sexual arousal stops short of orgasm, some males and females report physical discomfort even pain in the groin area, inability to concentrate and motor incoordination (Kinsey et al., 1953).

The level of pleasure (termed 'affect') rises in the period prior to antic-ipated sexual intercourse and stays elevated for some hours afterwards (Shrier et al., 2010). Negative affect is lowered for a few hours after sex-ual intercourse. One could also argue that sexual health is good for the health of a culture; political and religious cultures that place a high moral premium upon celibacy and virginity are associated with relatively high levels of aggression and authoritarianism (Prescott, 1977).

We do not need to go as far as Freud in asserting that a healthy sex life precludes neurosis (Torrey, 1992) to see that there might be some kind of causal association. Concerning mental well-being, the long-suffering wife of Count Tolstoy reflected upon the author behind *The Kreutzer Sonata* (A. N. Wilson, 1988, p. 395):

> If only the people who read *The Kreutzer Sonata* so reverently had an inkling of the voluptuous life he leads, and realized that it was only this which made him happy and good natured, then they would cast this deity from the pedestal where they have placed him.

Extensive sexual frustration might well have subsequent consequences in the hormones of the body that underlie stress, which could be harmful. Conversely, the achievement of sexual joy and satiety might bring ben-efits in terms of the body's hormonal balance. It is suggested here that adverse effects from sexual frustration arise in only one body organ – the brain/mind, and do so from *psychological* processing that indicates fail-ure and thwarting of sexual goals. Sexual frustration commonly arises in heterosexual partnerships when one party (usually the male) is denied fulfilment of sexual wishes that are judged as offensive or otherwise unac-ceptable by the other party (Zillman, 1984).

As noted in Chapter 3, Freud suggested that energy not discharged sex-ually would be sublimated and find its outlet in, say, neurosis or creative writing. But if there is no such internal regulatory factor, we would question such logic. Any contribution to creativity associated with frustrated sexual desire might be alternatively explained in terms of a sexually deprived person finding other goals in life. The roots of neurosis are to be found in more plausible explanations that might well involve a contribution from sexuality, but do not necessarily feature it, such as a general feeling of frustration, envy and failure.

Concerning a specific feature of bodily biology, there are claims that an accumulation of seminal fluids is not healthy and, therefore, regular sexual outlets could be beneficial. The chances of men getting certain cancers might be lowered by a regular loss of seminal fluids. Pleasurable genital stimulation and orgasm have strong pain-relieving effects (Komisaruk et al., 2010). However, none of this points to an accumulation of seminal fluids as being the trigger to sexual desire.

Masturbation and nocturnal orgasm

If desire were the manifestation of an intrinsic drive we might expect masturbation to occur most frequently in people denied a sexual outlet. However, the evidence suggests that masturbation is not compensation for lack of partnered sex. Highest levels correspond with high levels of partnered sexual activity and the most diverse range of sexual activities (Laumann et al., 1994). Suppose that sexual behaviour is the manifestation of the brain's desire processes involving the imagination, the sensitivity of which is enhanced by sexual activity (except for a period immediately following orgasm). The enormous variation in masturbation frequency and the fact that it often occurs most frequently at times of a new relationship might be expected.

A similar logic would seem also to apply to nocturnal dreams and associated orgasm. Some have argued that nocturnal orgasm represents a safety valve, a natural compensation process for an absence of sexual activity (see Kinsey et al., 1953). However, there is a link between decreasing sexual activity and increasing frequency of nocturnal orgasms in only a minority of women (Kinsey et al., 1953). Even there, the frequency of nocturnal orgasm was very low compared to the frequency of sexual activity prior to the deprivation (deprivation being caused by such things as separation, divorce or incarceration). For a considerable minority of other women, there was a positive association between frequency of nocturnal orgasms and sexual activity. Contrary to compensatory principles, some positive correlation was seen between frequencies of masturbation and nocturnal orgasm.

Differences between cultures, people and situations

Comparing across cultures, or within a given culture, or even within a given individual over phases within a life-time, there are enormous differences in the frequency of sexual outlets, fantasies and desires. For females who engage in masturbation, those with the highest frequency of orgasm achieved something like 240,000 times the rates of those with the lowest (Kinsey et al., 1953). Similarly, males with the highest frequency of sexual outlets had anything up to 45,000 times the frequency of those with the lowest (Kinsey et al., 1948). This figure arose when comparing males who were living in the same area and leading apparently otherwise similar lives. It hardly points to an internal regulation but is entirely compatible with the notion that desire is the outcome of a complex interweaving of external factors and associations, excitations and inhibitions. Indeed, the Kinsey team appealed to conditioning as the process by which much of this range could be explained. In words that have a modern feel (Kinsey et al., 1948, p. 204):

> Whether an individual is located at some lower point or at a higher point on the total curve of outlets depends in part upon the experience which he has previously had and the incentive which that experience provides for a repetition or avoidance of further activity.

Kinsey's conclusion fits with a study of American and Dutch women, comparing those with hypoactive sexual desire disorder and controls (Brauer et al., 2012). Women with hypoactive sexual desire appear to show a weaker positive association with sexual stimuli, possibly built up by a history of negative associations or at least few positive experiences of sexual pleasure.

Kinsey et al. (1948) noted an important social implication of their findings (p. 197):

> The publicly pretended code of morals, our social organization, our marriage customs, our sex laws, and our educational and religious systems

are based upon an assumption that individuals are much alike sexually, and that it is an equally simple matter for all of them to confine their behaviour to the single pattern which the mores dictate.

They continued (p. 199):

> such designations as infantile, frigid, sexually under-developed, under-active, excessively active, over-developed, over-sexed, hypersexual, or sexually over-active . . . refer to nothing more than a position on a curve which is continuous. Normal and abnormal, one sometimes suspects, are terms which a particular author employs with reference to his own position on that curve.

Some people apparently lead a happy life of celibacy. This also suggests that there is not some intrinsic regulatory ('drive') factor at work. Of course, people also differ in how much they eat, but sexual variation, ranging from zero outlet to it being an all-consuming passion, appears excessive, even relative to feeding.

Societies in which there is little tolerance or expression of sexuality have been described, as compared to highly sexually charged and libertarian societies. In the 1950s, the Irish island of Gaeltacht ('Inis Beag') earned the distinction of being the most restricted and sexually naïve that is known to anthropologists. Marital sex, in so far as it existed at all, seemed to be limited to the function of producing children. Sex outside marriage hardly existed, except when local boys met foreign tourists. Female orgasm was reported as being either unknown or regarded as deviant. An anthropologist who studied this population reported (Messenger, 1971, p. 29): 'The seeds of repression are planted early in childhood by parents and kin through instruction supplemented by rewards and punishments, conscious imitation, and unconscious internalization.' The Dani who inhabit west New Guinea also appear to be a somewhat 'sexless' society. Abstinence is practiced for up to five years following childbirth. Whether the inhabitants of such places actually suffer from 'repressed sexuality' in any meaningful sense is unclear, though stress arising from sexual frustration was reported in Inis Beag. The frustration experienced in other societies might owe more to a comparison of one's lot with that of others within society rather than to any intrinsic biological disturbance (Zillman, 1984).

At the opposite pole from Inis Beag, on the Polynesian island of Mangaia there seem to be very few restrictions on sexual expression (Marshall,

1971). Female orgasm is regarded as obligatory in sexual relations and a male is judged as inadequate if he fails to trigger it.

Not something to 'get out of the system'

Linked to the notion of regulation is the idea that extensive sexual experience when young can serve to 'get it out of one's system', sometimes expressed as 'sowing wild oats'. A cross-cultural study found (Suggs and Marshall, 1971, p. 240):

> In none of the permissive societies described in this book, with the possible exception of Mangaia, does premarital sexual freedom seem to have the effect of lowering the rate of extramarital sexual adventures. The popularly held view that a person who can 'get it out of his system' in the premarital state will thereafter be better able to settle down is another reflection of American folklore or cultural bias that seems to be without foundation.

A political dimension

If an intrinsic drive arising in the body tissues exists, no one has been able so far to identify its biological basis. The discussion has a political dimension, since it is sometimes used with reference only to the male. Shere Hite, author of *The Hite Report*, questions the existence of sex drive (Hite, 2003, p. 47):

> It is hard to say if there is such a thing or if it is a product of ideology.

> The common, clichéd view of men's sexuality is that men's bodies contain a powerful mechanism called 'sex drive' connected to 'male hormones', and that sex drive makes men want to 'penetrate' and 'impregnate women with their seed'. Using the phrase 'sex drive' seems to imply that sexual activity leading to reproduction is a biological imperative.

The argument that there is an intrinsic regulatory factor can detract from the crucial motivational role of external factors. Suppose that we focus on such an internal factor with its supposed unremitting push and almost accidental outlet found through sexual activity. We might be in danger of underestimating the importance of context. Thus, a lack of sexual desire does not mean that an internal variable like pressure has been given an abnormal setting. A sexual thermostat has not been set too low as an accident of genes or birth. For much of history, sex for women has been quick and rather brutish, attended by a fear of pregnancy (Abramson and Pinkerton, 1995). It could be misleading to attribute lack of female erotic interest under such conditions to an intrinsically low sex drive.

An alternative: incentive motivation

Background

An alternative to the view that we are pushed by something arising within the tissues of the body and then happen upon a suitable means of discharge is termed the *incentive* view of motivation and is a foundation upon which this book rests. That is to say, people are *pulled* by external stimuli, thoughts about them and their associations. As an alternative to drive theories, various authors have suggested formulations that fit the general umbrella terms of 'incentive' (Ågmo, 2007; Singer and Toates, 1987) and 'desire'. Cameron and Frazer (1987, p. 83) write: 'Whereas desires are intentional and fixed on some object, so that the subject acts to fulfil desire, drives are pushed, so to speak, from behind.' This is much more than a semantic quibble; rather, it is at the essence of understanding desire. In describing conscious desires as 'intentional', they are seen as projecting to the future. Future interaction, usually with another individual, is sought and guides current behaviour. This approach can assimilate the observation that desires can be complex. A person might aim to achieve several things by putting his or her desire into effect, for example sexual pleasure combined with pleasing another and boosting his or her own status and esteem. The *combination* of desires might well very greatly exceed the strength of any component. It is hard to see how such complexity of intentions could be understood in terms of a unitary notion of 'sex drive'. Desire can be very much situation-dependent, reflecting different triggers, something missed by the unitary notion of sex drive.

The first incentive-based interpretation came from Hardy (1964). Central to his thesis was that motives arise from learned expectations that relate particular stimuli to later pleasure. Psychologists usually resist employing a term as simple as 'pleasure' and prefer the more scientifically sounding 'affective' or 'hedonic'. Some of these hedonic expectations might be learned by direct social sexual experience, whereas others might reflect, say, pleasure gleaned from looking at erotic images and masturbating. Further expectations could be built with the help of nothing more than a rich imagination. Any experience of pleasure will strengthen the expectations and thereby increase motivational strength.

Hardy was looking back on an age of innocence, when prolonged courtship was the norm and described the sequence of holding hands, kissing, petting, and the slow build-up of affective associations. He acknowledged that there are problems in how to 'kick-start' such a system initially. A possible solution will be developed later in the chapter.

Such a central principle of incentive motivation is equally applicable to men and women. It does not require hooking motivation to a biological parameter only present in males and then trying to find an auxiliary process that could also extend to women. Rather, typical gender differences in motivation might be explained in terms of subtle differences within the basic process and how it is modulated by context.

Another perspective based upon incentive principles is termed the *sexual behaviour sequence* (Fisher, 1986). This model employs the concepts of *erotophilia*, meaning attraction to erotic stimuli and events, and *erotophobia*, meaning withdrawal from and avoidance of erotic stimuli and events. People differ in their locations on a scale of erotophilia–erotophobia. Someone at either extreme will tend to behave in such a way that their position will be self-reinforcing. The strongly erotophilic individual will seek out sexual stimuli and obtain pleasure from them, which will consolidate their erotophilic tendencies. The erotophobic individual will avoid sexual stimuli, which will leave their tendency intact, or will receive unpleasant experiences, such as coerced sex, which will consolidate their erotophobia. Thus, the same stimulus, for example a picture of an attractive individual, might in one person trigger desire and thoughts of sexual pleasure, whereas for another it might signal predominantly a sexually transmitted disease and mortal sin (Hogben and Byrne, 1998). Location on the scale of erotophobia–erotophilia is not necessarily fixed. For example, a person who starts in the middle of the range but then has a series of pleasant sexual experiences might move in the direction of erotophilia.

Griffitt et al. (1974) exposed participants to a sexual stimulus and observed their immediately subsequent behaviour. Relative to those not sexually aroused, both males and females who found the stimulation to be positively arousing tended subsequently to look more at members of the opposite sex and to sit closer to them. By contrast, those who found it aversive tended not to look more at the opposite sex and even to sit further away from them.

The notion of erotophilia–erotophobia has a certain predictive value (Fisher, 1986), which forms a foundation of what is termed the 'sexual behaviour sequence model'. The essence of this is described in the next two paragraphs. Knowing someone's location on the continuum means that it is possible to predict with better than chance accuracy their reactions to a new sexual stimulus or suggested scenario. For example, in one study, a man's location on the scale predicted better than chance his reaction to buying condoms and even his evaluation of the sales assistant and the drugstore.

People appear to make assessments of the expected outcome prior to engaging in sexual activity (Fisher, 1986). For example, fantasy can be employed in conjunction with images of real people or picture representations. The erotophilic individual will tend to obtain positive feelings from such initial forays and be persuaded to advance, whereas the erotophobic will tend to derive negative assessments that will be associated with withdrawal. Erotophilic individuals tend to talk openly on sexual matters, masturbate frequently, have a wide range of acceptable sexual activities and plan ahead for sexual encounters by taking such actions as acquiring contraceptives.

Clearly, the 'sexual behaviour sequence model' involves a central brain state that modulates the reaction to external events and situations, causing approach or withdrawal. It is entirely compatible with principles of incentive motivation and learning of incentive value and it is hard to see how it would lend support to the notion of sexual drive as some sort of energy that seeks discharge. One would need to propose 'negative drive' to describe those people who react with erotophobia.

Accommodating cultural differences

The model advanced here can accommodate cultural differences in sexuality. In the context of the sexual behaviour sequence model, some cultures are predominantly erotophilic, for example that of Mangaia, whereas others are strongly erotophobic, for example the Irish island of

Inis Beag (Fisher, 1986). Allocation of a culture on this scale allows a prediction of its behaviour at better than chance levels. For example, in Inis Beag a whole range of activities, not only premarital sex but such things as simply revealing too much of the body in swimming, are condemned. A country such as the United States or United Kingdom would be somewhere between the extremes, while Sweden or the Netherlands would be more in the erotophilic direction.

Accommodating gender differences

While noting men's much higher testosterone levels and thereby higher intrinsic contribution to sexual desire, some have speculated that women's sexual desire is more heavily situation-dependent than is men's (Tolman and Diamond, 2001). Women are triggered by a wider range of cues (e.g. emotional empathy) and tend to express a more nuanced desire than men. Some degree of bisexuality is attractive to more women than it is to men. To say that men have a higher sex drive than women could lead to an assumption of some intrinsic property of the body that can be measured outside context. Leiblum (2002, p. 62) suggests: 'women's sexual desire may be more a function of external motivation than internal insistence'. This externally triggered desire might be more easily lowered in women as a result of unpleasant experiences of sexual behaviour, for example clumsy or painful sex or dysfunction in the relationship (Leiblum, 2002; Wood et al., 2006).

Much of the triggering of sexual desire and arousal reflects such intentionality and guidance by future projected events. However, some sexual desire appears to be triggered automatically by powerful stimuli in the environment. It appears that women's sexuality is more determined by expectations of sexual pleasure *set into a context of meaning*, whereas men's is more automatically triggered by physical attributes of the attractive individual. Typically, attachment and emotional empathy are likely to contribute more heavily to women's desire than to men's.

How would the incentive motivation model work?

For sex, the incentive would typically be the pull exerted by another individual. As Hite (2003, p. 48) states: 'Most men in my research feel that their desire is largely inspired by a particular desired individual, or by particular images or fantasy.' The term 'desire' seems to capture the essence of the broader term 'incentive' and of being pulled into action to achieve something presently unavailable to us (Regan and Berscheid, 1999). It reflects a wish for – a 'wanting of' – sexual contact, an engagement of the mind with sexual thoughts, fantasy and imagery.

A similar though simplified principle applies to non-humans. Thus, the pull can also be seen in an animal being attracted to locations associated with a 'mate' such as a location in a maze where sexual behaviour had taken place in the past. It can be measured by how much work an animal is prepared to perform in a Skinner box,[2] to gain access to another animal. Lever-pressing reflects attraction towards a goal of access. For humans, a measure is to ask people about their subjective conscious feeling of desire, a 'psychological state' (Regan and Berscheid, 1999).

Incentives rather than drives

In the view advanced here, rather than internal factors, such as hormone levels, *driving* the animal, human or otherwise, they *modulate* the power of the incentive to exert a pull. Changes in the attraction value of the incentive correspond to changes in sensitivity of regions of the brain, termed motivational processes. These regions are sensitized by sex hormones (Chapter 2). Such a view has now largely replaced drive interpretations inside scientific sexology (Both et al., 2006).

In this view, there are changes in the strength of motivation with changes in the proximity of the incentive. This has health and security implications: good intentions of restraining one's sexuality when at a safe distance from attractive others might get forgotten in a state of heightened arousal triggered by their physical presence. Cognitive distortions can appear that fly in the face of rationality, an important consideration in safe-sex campaigns. A decision to use condoms made when planning an evening doubtless sometimes gets corrupted in the heat of the moment (Chapter 15).

According to an incentive view, the consequences of sexual activity modulate the value of incentives. Successful sexual interaction increases the value of the particular incentive and its context, whereas sexual failure will lower incentive value (Woodson, 2002). People commonly experience a reduction in tension following orgasm (Meston and Buss, 2009). Some bodily condition is clearly rather abruptly reversed. Many women liken the tension release of orgasm to that associated with urination and indeed some of these worry that this might happen (Basson, 2000). However, in incentive terms the tension was not what motivated the initial sexual desire. Rather the tension was introduced into the system by the desire. In incentive terms, the tension release would be expected to modulate future incentive value by making the partner more desirable and thereby the sexual act leading to orgasm more likely to happen in the future. In women, oxytocin levels in the blood rise immediately following orgasm (Blaicher et al., 1999). This could well consolidate the incentive value of the partner and sense of belonging with this person.

So, according to an incentive view, a particular bodily state sometimes termed 'sexual arousal' tends to turn attractive sexual stimuli into wanted stimuli associated with the anticipation that interaction with them would bring pleasure. Evidence to favour this interpretation was provided in a study that first triggered sexual arousal in participants of both sexes by asking them to view an erotic movie. Compared to unaroused participants, those given such prior arousal subsequently rated sexual features of attractive images they viewed as still more attractive (Istvan et al., 1983). However, prior sexual arousal caused participants to rank images that they found sexually unattractive as *even less attractive*. Such polarization argues against a simple drive model of sexual desire and, as the authors argued, arousal enhanced the *salience* of sexual stimuli. There is not some factor inside the body seeking discharge and thereby searching for any means to achieve it. Similarly, bodily arousal induced by physical exertion or humour tends subsequently to make an attractive partner still more attractive but an unattractive partner less attractive (White et al., 1981).

Failure to attain orgasm is something that underlies much of women's lack of satisfaction with sex (Hite, 2000). In incentive terms, this is not a failure to correct a regulatory disturbance. Rather, it is a failure to complete the ascent of a gradient of increasing desire, arousal and pleasure – a failure to attain an ultimate hedonic goal. Prospective manufacturers of 'sexual dysfunction pills' for women are misidentifying the source of the problem (Hite, 2000). The problem does not lie within the biology of the body but in the communicative skills of the couple and stimulation that the woman receives, which is often inadequately targeted to the clitoris in penetrative sex.

To appreciate the essence of an incentive view, consider that gambling can come to exert just as strong a pull on behaviour as can sex (Orford, 2001). Yet, surely, gambling is based upon experience with gambling tasks rather than any intrinsic 'gambling drive'. Once hooked, gamblers can suffer from all manner of bodily disturbances, such as a knotted stomach. However, the bodily disturbance is not the basis of the initial desire to gamble but the outcome of the ups and downs of gambling experience.

To take stock, the essence of the incentive–motivation view is that motivation is triggered by:

- incentive objects (e.g. a partner)
- cues associated with them, through classical conditioning
- use of the imagination to represent absent incentives, that is thoughts of them.

Development: forming incentives

In an incentive view, the interaction between genes and early environment permits a certain range of potential incentives to become real incentives. Which potential incentives (if any) – for example heterosexual, homosexual or bisexual – come to assume that role will depend upon the idiosyncratic dynamics of gene–environment interaction. Adopting an incentive model is not to come down on the culture side of the so-called 'biology versus culture' dispute, since logically there can be no such dispute. Biology is still 'in there' in the form of brain processes that preferentially translate particular stimuli into an incentive motivational pull. Hormones – clearly a 'biological thing' – play a role. Orgasm – surely a biological process – still sits at centre-stage as a reward and reinforcement for action accomplished and a trigger to label and consolidate the incentive as desirable.

The objects of sexual desire do not arise completely unchannelled from the limitless possibilities of early exposure, imagination and masturbation. Societies prescribe certain acceptable targets. Depending upon age and parental influences, adolescent sexual desire encounters both social controls tending to inhibit its expression and peer influences that can either inhibit or excite its expression. These are 'contextual factors' in terms of the present argument.

Celibacy and sexual restraint

For centuries, a number of people in each culture have voluntarily opted for celibacy, often in the cause of religion (Gaca, 2003). As just noted, some cultures experience a highly restricted level of sexual activity (Messenger, 1971). In terms of drive, this would make little sense, since their insides should be disturbed and they should suffer torments. Some doubtless do, but there is no reason to extend this to everyone. In terms of incentives, celibacy makes more sense, since a combination of factors would be seen as responsible. These would include genetics, early development, any sexual experiences and the competition offered by other goals such as to maintain moral virtue. Where a culture emphasizes the necessity for sexual restraint in order to achieve religious salvation, there will be the potential for competition with sexual desire (Messenger, 1971).

Fear and feelings of inadequacy can conspire, it would appear, to produce a kind of involuntary celibacy, a probable example being J. M. Barrie. Chaney (2005) describes the extreme shyness that the creative genius felt towards women (p. 40):

> It was also a natural defence against his sense of failure at making any impression on them at all. But if this young man couldn't attract attention by his appearance, he was to discover there were other ways by which he could hold centre stage.

Being unusually short, Barrie was highly sensitive about this and the failure that he perceived to result from it. Though engaging in 'outrageous flirting' and subject to repeated infatuations, he feared going further than this. Chaney (2005, p. 269) writes:

> Although it is virtually certain that he never consummated any of his numerous flirtations, he doesn't appear to have been essentially different from other trophy-hunting males. He never ceased to need the thrill of collecting a succession of women.

So, where does this incentive-based system and the restraints upon it fit into the notion of levels of control? The next chapter turns to this.

In summary

- Sexual desire is not an aspect of homeostatic regulation of a bodily factor outside the brain.
- Rather than drives triggering the human, sexual incentives are a source of action.
- Hormones sensitize the power of incentives to motivate action.
- Frustration arises from the thwarting of desires.

FIVE

SEX AND LEVELS OF ORGANIZATION

The heart has its reasons of which reason knows nothing.[1]
(Pascal, 1669/1996, *pensée* no. 423)

Charms would not deserve their name if they did not have the power
to silence our reason.
(Casanova, 1798/1958, p. 246)

Having advanced the case for an incentive motivation model of sex,
it is necessary to fit this idea to the notion of levels of organization,
exemplified by automatic and controlled processing (Chapter 2).

Evidence points to behaviour being determined by at least two levels
of control in the brain (Carver et al., 2009; LeDoux, 1999; Toates, 1998,
2006):

- an evolutionarily old low-level system, which is ('automatically') reactive to specific events in the world. It can sometimes operate at an unconscious level;
- an evolutionarily new high-level ('controlled') system that operates at a conscious level and seeks long-term rational goals (e.g. to maintain marital harmony, resist temptation).

The levels of organization can act in the same direction (e.g. both tending
to trigger behaviour) or in opposition (e.g. low level excites behaviour,
while high level tends to restrain).

The low-level system often operates in a way that is not accessible to
conscious awareness, though the endpoint of its processing can engage
consciousness. This system is fast, reacts to the events of the moment, and

poses low demands on processing resources.[2] The high-level system represents the conscious and rational mind.[3] This system takes into account long-term considerations beyond those of the present moment in time and it takes up a large amount of processing capacity.

The low-level system can produce either action or inaction (Carver et al., 2009). Powerful incentives can act through the low-level system to engage appetitive behaviour, whereas aversive events can act to cause withdrawal from a situation or immobility. High-level control, in other words 'executive control', can sometimes override either of these tendencies, to restrain or energize behaviour. When the capacity for executive control is high, people tend to act according to their conscious intentions and long-term goals. When it is compromised, the lower-level control can dominate, sometimes even against the intentions of the higher-level system. The result is 'myopia for the future' and a relative inability to learn from previous mistakes (Schore, 2003). In all of its aspects, human sexuality arises from the complex interdependence between old and new brain parts.

There are various factors that determine the relative weight of control that is exerted at different levels. Each of these is relevant to at least one aspect of sexuality and some of these will be discussed in detail in subsequent chapters. This section gives just a brief overview of these phenomena to show the generality of the principle of levels of control.

Engaging attention and desire – or not

At times, attention is captured automatically ('unconsciously') by particularly salient stimuli in the world or in memory ('low-level control'). This can happen in a way that either runs counter to or matches conscious wishes, goals and intentions. The phenomenon known as 'attentional adhesion' refers to a process whereby the attention of one individual is grabbed by the stimulus of an attractive person and the individual whose attention is grabbed cannot let go (Maner et al., 2007, 2008). At other times attention towards a particular target is under voluntary conscious direction ('high-level control').

Psychologists researching a range of desires and temptations build upon the observation that stimuli can engage processing by the brain at an unconscious level (Hofmann and van Dillen, 2012). When presented with a new stimulus, its qualities of good or bad are extracted first at a rapid unconscious level, and only later, if at all, is the stimulus subject to conscious processing (Elliot, 2008). This rapid analysis gives a predisposition to approach or avoid respectively, though there need be no overt behaviour shown. The quality of the evaluation, good or bad, depends in part upon the individual's current goals (Ferguson and Bargh, 2008).

To some extent, the long-term goal can bias attention towards objects that are compatible with achieving the goal and away from objects that are incompatible (Hofmann and van Dillen, 2012). According to Hofmann and van Dillen, the attention-grabbing strength of the stimulus depends upon three factors: 'stimulus properties', the individual's learned association with the stimulus and 'internal need states'. Since their focus was upon feeding, the third term corresponds to the nutrient needs of the body. On being adapted to sex, it can mean such things as hormone levels and sexual fatigue/recovery, which determine the sensitivity of the brain to sexual stimuli.

The long-term goal (e.g. 'sexual scoring') might be such as to facilitate occupation of the conscious mind with erotic information. Once there, the desire-related goal might be retained in conscious memory,[4] recycled and elaborated upon, triggering strong emotions and associated thoughts and fantasies, exemplified by conscious wanting and craving. The ability to engage conscious processing would depend upon such things as novelty of the stimulus and its hedonic ranking. Occupation within conscious memory can release what is termed 'gravitational pull' or a 'magnet effect', in which further congruent and supportive cognitions (e.g. sub-vocal statements – those words that we silently 'speak' to ourselves – that justify indulgence) are brought into awareness (Hofmann and van Dillen, 2012), which can then trigger consciously mediated action directed at attaining the short-term hedonistic goal.

Under other circumstances, long-term goals (e.g. to maintain diet, keep a vow of chastity) might be at odds with pursuit of a short-term goal; that is, there is temptation (Chapter 12). Under these circumstances, the signal arising from the potential sexual stimulus might be sufficiently inhibited and hence not reach conscious awareness. Inhibition can arise from the presence of long-term goals that bias the early stages of processing, for example to block the processing of sexual stimuli. Even if the desired object is consciously processed, further engagement might still be resisted if the long-term goal is sufficiently strong. However, in any mental struggle the short-term goal, of course, might win. Any counter-statements, associated with long-term goals, might be forced out of conscious awareness.

Consider a person with drug experience, who is not actively seeking drugs at the time and has the general intention of resisting them (Tiffany, 1990). The individual's sensory systems detect a drug-related cue, such as the smell or sight of a drug, and attention is drawn towards it in an automatic fashion. Detection of the cue and the start of approach behaviour might be non-conscious, but then the situation is brought into full conscious awareness with a risk of relapse. Similarly, sex researchers suggest that sexually potent cues, for example the form of an attractive individual in reality or in a picture, can grab attention even before we are consciously aware of their presence. These cues can subsequently be 'demanding' of attention, displacing other items from conscious awareness (Spiering and Everaerd, 2006).

Suppose that, for example, a paedophile has a tendency to move unintentionally near to children's swimming pools and would thereby be drawn towards those habits that he is trying to resist. Forewarned can be forearmed; the person might try to anticipate where trigger cues will appear and avoid such contexts. Failing this, the strategy might be to have a reminder of restraint, such as wearing a bracelet engraved with a warning, which can be consulted when tempted (Chapter 12). Another strategy is to have an incompatible behaviour already primed, so that the individual is diverted from the trigger cues (Tiffany, 1990).

Resisting temptation exemplifies the competition between low-level and high-level controls. The low-level control might effortlessly pull the individual towards the incentive, whereas any resistance will call upon full conscious controlled resources, something which is effortful and can be exhausting (Tiffany, 1990). Again, most research has been done into drug-taking, but the principles would seem to be general.

Of course, erotic targets do not exist only in the outside world but can be generated in the form of imagery (Kavanagh et al., 2005). These can also be automatic (e.g. popping into awareness without effort) or controlled (e.g. a deliberate elaboration of the initial image).

Sexual arousal

How should 'sexual arousal' be measured: as the reaction of the genitals in terms of blood flow (in the male erection) or how aroused the individual *feels*? Arousal of the genitals might correspond to how aroused a person feels but this is not invariably so, especially in the case of women (Laan and Janssen, 2006) (Chapter 9).

For women, a sexual stimulus, such as an erotic picture, triggers a fast automatic reflex-like state of arousal as measured by increased blood flow at the genitals (Laan and Janssen, 2006). However, this does not necessarily correspond to a state of subjective arousal, as measured by how she feels. Subjective arousal results from conscious controlled processing that takes into account not only genital arousal but also various personal assessments, conflicts and intentions. She might feel no subjective arousal, in spite of an objectively aroused state of the genitals. Indeed, the genital reaction still occurs even if the woman later reports that the sexual stimulus was distasteful to her.

Inhibition

Inhibition upon sexual arousal can occur automatically, for example in response to a loud noise or unpleasant odour. However, it can also act at a high level as a conscious intention to inhibit arousal or to inhibit putting desire into action. This is discussed in detail in Chapter 12.

Overcoming resistance

Someone might be depressed, with a tendency to passivity or withdrawal from any sexual contact. However, a higher-level conscious goal might move the individual into sexual activity from a sense of duty or empathy.

In some cases, women engage in unwanted sex to please or appease a partner (Meston and Buss, 2009). Imagine a woman who no longer finds her partner attractive and has no desire for sex. For example, he might have a problem with alcohol and personal hygiene. However, she obliges out of duty and sympathy. This is the opposite situation to one of temptation, described earlier. Her short-term goals might even be based upon an automatic disgust reaction, which, all things being equal, would cause her to distance herself from the situation. However, this influence is overridden by a long-term goal like sympathy or duty. Engaging in sexual behaviour requires the exertion of the woman's conscious effort such as to resist the commands of the short-term goal.

Species differences

The proportion of automatic to controlled processes differs between species. For example, mating in rats is stereotyped, much the same from one animal to another (Beach, 1947). It is largely under the control of structures that specify what to do when in the presence of a sexually motivated partner. A rat *Kama Sutra* would be a rather boring but mercifully very short book. By contrast, evolution has given humans a brain with a great deal of flexibility and, acting at a conscious level, capacity for creativity. This is reflected in the endless variations that people find in terms of the nuances that excite them sexually and the complex agendas that people are able to bring to their sexual interactions (if they choose to!). It is hard to imagine that any other species has anything like the rich fantasy world of humans associated with, say, the sexually exciting notion of the forbidden (C. Wilson, 1988). As the biological basis of this richness, the cortex has taken over more control of sexuality in humans than in other species (Zillmann, 1984).

Gender differences in sexual desire

Men tend to place more weight upon raw stimulus information on the female form in determining their sexual desire and arousal, whereas women tend to place more weight upon meaning (Laan and Janssen, 2006). For example, what a male's behaviour *signifies* to the woman in terms of talent and intelligence plays an important role (Bancroft, 2009).

Learning

As a very general principle, with extensive practice at a given task, the level of control becomes more habitual and sequences of thought and behaviour tend to be run off automatically. As a result of this, automatic control can act counter to conscious intentions. A motorist might repeatedly turn off the motorway to Detroit, such that this move has become automatic or 'habitual'. One day, she is on the same motorway but has the conscious intention to stay on, to go to Ann Arbor. However, she finds herself captured by the familiar road sign and the turn to Detroit, so habit causes her to make the usual manoeuvre. Shortly afterwards, she realizes her mistake and gets back on the motorway.

When a couple first meet, each might have little idea of what to expect from the other, so behaviour is determined in the fully controlled conscious mode. This contributes to high levels of desire. Over extended periods of time, behaviour becomes more habitual with a subsequent lowered desire. Things probably never become fully automated and organized at a non-conscious level, but there can be an increased frequency of lapses, where controlled processing gives way to habits. According to one survey, a move from novelty to habit is a principal factor in the lowering of desire (Sims and Meana, 2010).

C. Wilson (1988) applies this to feeding, but it is equally if not more relevant to sex (p. 89):

> my robot valet takes over and does it automatically; in fact, he does it far more quickly and efficiently than 'I' could. The main trouble with this mechanical valet is that he often takes over functions I would prefer to keep for myself – for example, when I am tired I eat 'automatically', and so do not enjoy my food.

Cognitive load, emotions and stress

A negative emotion can move the weight of control to a lower level, as is witnessed in anger and its 'unthinking' expression in violence. It can presumably also contribute to an engagement in risky 'heat-of-the-moment' sexual behaviour.

The mental challenge posed by stress can decrease the weight of high-level control and increase that exerted at a low level (Tiffany, 1990). Stress appears to be an important contributory factor to sex addiction (Chapter 17) and sexual assault (Chapters 20 and 21). Under stress, a person sometimes reverts back to an earlier apparently long-suppressed form of sexual behaviour, which has been dormant over the years (Money, 1977). For example, exhibitionism might resurface at this time.

There appear to be several reasons for this effect. Stress has been particularly studied in the context of drug addiction, where, amongst other factors, having 'something worrying on your mind' takes up conscious processing capacity and reduces the ability of high-level processes to organize inhibition on lower-level processes, to resist temptation (Baumeister et al., 2011; Tiffany, 1990). The individual is particularly vulnerable to capture by salient cues. For some, a negative mood increases the tendency to take sexual risks, experienced as a feeling 'in this state I don't care about what happens' (Janssen and Bancroft, 2007). As Baumeister et al. (2011, p. 349) express it: 'cognitive load seems to release automatic impulses to dictate actions that conscious reflection would veto'.

Development

The evolutionarily new brain processes that underlie high-level control are the last part of the brain to mature, whereas those acting at a lower level mature at a younger age (Chapters 2 and 13). This means that the levels get out of synchrony and the capacity of adolescents to exert high-level control is weak relative to that of adults. Consequently, adolescents have a relatively high tendency to engage in risky activities, such as drug-taking, dangerous driving and unprotected sex. It can be speculated that young children have even weaker restraint processes but there is relatively little to restrain since the low-level systems have not yet fully matured.

The tendency for stress to shift the weight of control to a low level appears to be greater in those with a traumatic early development, which more usually compromises high-level control (Schore, 2003).

Chemicals

Certain chemicals alter the weight of control between high and low levels. Alcohol decreases the influence of high-level controls and thereby increases that of the low level. It triggers what is known as 'alcohol myopia', a tendency to bias the focus of attention on the *immediate* environment (Steele and Josephs, 1990) and thereby short-term goals. This expression is by analogy with visual myopia, where near things are brought into focus at the expense of more distant things. In other words, alcohol increases the salience of physically present stimuli relative to what is held only in memory (Abbey et al., 2006). It lowers sexual inhibitions that are based upon long-term goals (Chapter 15).

Brain damage

The more recently evolved brain regions that give human behaviour its flexibility tend to be those most vulnerable to damage. In some cases, damage is associated with a lifting of restraint on behaviour, so that the person engages in behaviour that otherwise would have been inhibited (Luria, 1966). Examples of this include the appearance of paedophilia and explicit unwanted sexual advances to family members.

What could stress, alcohol and brain damage have in common such that they tend to shift the weight of control from long-term goals to short-term goals (Hofmann et al., 2009)? Each seems to impair the ability of memories drawn with effort from storage to be held online in such a way as to inhibit the actions of the short-term system. When the high-level system is compromised, as in specific brain damage, excessive alcohol or drug use or stress, the lower-level control can dominate, sometimes even against the intentions of the higher-level system. The result is 'myopia for the future' and a relative inability to learn from previous mistakes.

Fixed and flexible brains: link to evolutionary psychology

What does evolutionary psychology claim?

Evolutionary psychology is concerned primarily with the *function* served by behaviour. Its followers suggest the existence of so-called 'modules': information-processing units, each of which controls one particular mental operation or bit of behaviour (Tooby and Cosmides, 1990). Such modules have, it is argued, been tested in evolution, since they were found to solve one particular problem that facilitated successful transmission of genes. So, for example, there is a jealousy module, which is activated by any threat of sexual infidelity. It is specialized to solve just this one problem. Because an individual has a module primed to react to threats posed by infidelity, compromises to his or her reproductive success have been reduced. Evolutionary psychologists compare their modules to the organs of the body. There is no such thing as a 'general-purpose organ'. Each organ is dedicated to serve a particular function, exemplified by the heart's function of pumping blood around the body.

A broader evolutionary psychology

How are the idiosyncratic dimensions of, for example, human sexual desire to be assimilated into an evolutionary perspective? An understanding of brains can be integrated with the notion of modules to yield a convincing evolutionary psychology of sexual desire. It is necessary to consider the *idiosyncrasy* and *flexibility* of behaviour that is the hallmark of humans, as well as modularity.

Fixed and flexible processes co-exist

Automatic processing appears to map rather well onto evolutionary psychology's 'modules'. The system that automatically triggers genital arousal in response to a sexual stimulus seems like a module (Spiering and Everaerd, 2006). The reaction happens fast, at first at a non-conscious level and the system serves this one specialized and dedicated role in the life of humans. However, such modules co-exist with brain processes offering the possibility of flexibility and creativity.

This evolutionary consideration can be wedded to an understanding of multiple ('layered') controls of behaviour and their embodiment in the human brain. MacDonald (2008) uses the expression 'effortful control' to describe the conscious ('explicit') process that acts to control flexible behaviour, sometimes in opposition to the pull of modules. Such processes make a conscious assessment of the likely benefits and costs of an action, albeit an assessment that is often wrong.

Effortful control is associated with working memory and executive function, embodied in regions of the prefrontal cortex. The exertion of effortful control is a 'resource-limited function', meaning that it shows fatigue with use. Individual differences in effortful control correlate with the personality dimension of conscientiousness. People high on conscientiousness have a high capacity for effortful control and are able to curb short-term pleasure-seeking. MacDonald notes that a number of theorists have suggested that adolescent reward-seeking and risk-taking (described earlier) are due in part to the relative development of approach mechanisms coupled with underdevelopment of prefrontal restraint processes. This imbalance is more marked in boys than in girls.

MacDonald discusses the result that viewing erotic films activates a number of brain regions such as the amygdala. However, viewing them with the instruction to decrease sexual arousal activates regions of the prefrontal cortex but not the amygdala. He notes (2008, p. 1021) 'This study is particularly interesting because the amygdala response to erotic films is an evolutionarily prepared reaction.'

All who subscribe to a Darwinian world agree that brains are 'designed' by evolutionary processes to solve problems that have been confronted in evolution. The solution to some of these can be specified in a modular structure, such as to trigger fear to a large menacing animal quickly and automatically, or disgust in the case of rotting food. These solutions can be hard-wired as modules into the brain. However, there is also 'spare capacity' in the human brain left for flexible solutions to problems and this creates a need to perform juggling between these flexible solutions and the more automatic reactions to events. Sometimes people will override the tendencies of the modules in the interests of serving a conflicting goal. Humans probably more than any other species have to juggle what are often conflicting goals competing for expression in behaviour and have to find creative new solutions to problems.

For example, although most of us are terrified by snakes, reflecting the action of a fixed module, some appear not to be. Some people even show affection towards them as household pets. Were they born lacking the appropriate fear module, or was it, as seems more likely, that an idiosyncratic goal, to overcome fear and gain mastery, has dominated the control of behaviour?

Models have attempted to reconcile the existence of modules with the obvious flexibility of behaviour (MacDonald, 2008; Toates, 2005). Modules are sensitive to the regularities of the environment (e.g. avoid snakes at all times), whereas flexible control is needed in dealing with the irregularities (e.g. approach snakes if you are making a nature film).

The book will follow the logic of Stanovich (2004), who coined the term 'the robots' rebellion'. In such terms, humans are the robots who, metaphorically speaking, staged a rebellion against the hard-wired dictates of genetic destiny. This was possible because of spare capacity that can be exploited in pursuit of goals that are not specified by the brain's collection of modules. Affect is our guide in goal pursuit.

Concerning sexual desire, perhaps the most important shot fired in the robots' revolt was when the first human realized that there is a connection between sexual desire and producing children. This was a necessary step to the invention of contraception in its various forms, which weakened the link between desire and the consequence of having babies. From then on, humans could to varying degrees 'have their affective cake and eat it'.

Sexual jealousy as an example to illustrate the argument

Sexual jealousy can be a particularly powerful emotion, as illustrated by Trachtenberg, (1989, p. 81): 'Suddenly she's an unknown quantity, someone whose failure to call or answer the phone shocks me into spasms of jealousy. I twitch like someone strapped into the electric chair.' The fear of the consequences of jealousy probably represents the strongest single factor inhibiting the expression of sexual desire outside the established bond. Evolutionary psychologists see jealousy as a 'module'. It seems to be universal, triggered automatically and is not open to rational conscious reasoning.

Consider, for example, David and Clara Harris. They appeared to be living the American dream, having achieved prosperity through a chain of orthodontist clinics in Texas.[5] However, after doubting her husband's fidelity, Clara hired a private detective to track his moves. On hearing that David was staying at a hotel with his mistress, Clara drove there with their daughter in the passenger seat and, when the husband and mistress appeared, she drove her car into David three times, killing him at the scene (Buss, 2005).

Jealousy can even be retrospective. A classic account was given by Count Tolstoy's wife, after he had presented his diaries to her as an engagement gift (!), wherein she read of brothels, venereal diseases and so on (A. N. Wilson, 1988, p. 197):

I don't think I ever recovered from the shock of reading the diaries when I was engaged to him. I can still remember the agonizing pangs of jealousy, the horror of that first appalling experience of male depravity.

On meeting one of her husband's former mistresses and the child that he had fathered, she wrote 'I think I shall kill myself with jealousy' (A. N. Wilson, 1988, p. 205).

There is some difference between men and women in the triggers to this emotion. Men tend to find sexual infidelity the most upsetting, whereas women are most disturbed by emotional infidelity. This corresponds to the bedroom versus the candlelit restaurant

Within the social sciences, jealousy has traditionally been interpreted as a product mainly of culture and can correspondingly vary widely across cultures. Indeed, from this perspective, it is often seen as (Meston and Buss, 2009, p. 100) 'an immature emotion, a character defect, and a sign of low self-esteem'. By contrast, evolutionary psychologists suggest that jealousy is a universal adaptive trait that cuts across all cultures and has served a useful role in evolution (Meston and Buss, 2009). Indeed, one might suppose that an ever-responsive jealousy module would form an indispensable part of any viable individual, as omnipresent as an organ for cleaning the blood. For the male, the fitness cost of his partner's infidelity is so high that evolutionary psychologists emphasize the particular premium on men's sexual jealousy (Pinker, 1997, p. 488): 'A woman having sex with another man is always a threat to the man's genetic interests' and 'Men should squirm at the thought of their wives or girlfriends having sex with another man.'

Jealousy is indeed represented very widely across cultures (Marshall and Suggs, 1971). However, the circumstances that trigger it can sometimes be quite subtle, as can those in which it is *not* triggered or at least not expressed. There are some important cross-cultural differences in how marital 'infidelity' is treated or even, one might suppose, how it is felt. The evolutionary psychologist David Buss acknowledges (Buss, 2003, p. 11): 'Jealousy is not a rigid, invariant instinct that drives robotlike, mechanical action. It is highly sensitive to context and environment.' The Toda ethnic group in India are widely tolerant of what would be called 'adultery' in Western cultures (Ford and Beach, 1951). Indeed, bad feelings are generated not so much by 'adultery' but by trying to thwart a married woman's opportunity for it. Jealousy between brothers who share the same wife is apparently very rare. In some societies extramarital sex is permitted on certain specific occasions such as festivities and ceremonies (Ford and Beach, 1951; Gebhard, 1971). Amongst some Aboriginal Australians, group sex involving pair-bonded partners was incorporated as part of fertility rituals (Gregersen, 1986; Roy, 2005). Gebhard (1971, p. 212) speculates: 'in most human societies the regulatory concern is not with the extramarital coital act itself but is rather with its social implications. Does it constitute a defiance of the spouse and society?' A wife on the Polynesian island of Mangaia will occasionally show jealousy at a husband's infidelity, specifically if he had not told her about it (Marshall, 1971). Amongst the Ammassalik Inuit, under certain conditions that were culturally sanctioned (the invitation of 'turning out the lamp'), a man could offer his wife to a visitor for a period of sexual pleasure (Hupka, 1981). Of course, this could be seen as reflecting male power, but nonetheless does not suggest uncontrollable male jealousy. Such 'sex hospitality' was also found in certain Australian aboriginal cultures (Gregersen, 1986). However, outside this accepted framework of mutual agreement, intense jealousy could be triggered even leading to murder. At the start of the twentieth century, the Toda community of southern India practised a form of polyandry, within which sexual relations with the spouse of another individual were acceptable, provided all parties agreed to this (Hupka, 1981).

Some in the Western world might doubt anthropological accounts from remote cultures, so let us look nearer to home. Consider the phenomenon variously known as 'co-marital sex' or 'swinging'. It is hardly the case that the male is invariably suffering under duress or simply seeing this as quid pro quo for access to someone else's wife.

People in the group sex situation report little jealousy and much less than they would feel in the case of non-consensual adultery (Smith and Smith, 1970). When the situation is not evaluated as one of threat, some apparently are even excited sexually by their intimate partner's 'infidelity', as witnessed at swinging clubs. It could be that the aroused state deriving from infidelity detection has been recruited into the service of a goal not of anger and hostility but of sexual arousal and permissive tolerance with a bonus of earning sexual novelty in the bargain.

So, even this basic and primitive emotion can only be understood in terms of any module being embedded within some sophisticated and peculiarly human brain processes. Jealousy is determined in large part by how the situation is interpreted and evaluated (e.g. as threatening to the bond) within the particular couple and broader culture (Hupka, 1981). A possible solution is that we are all equipped with a jealousy module but human ingenuity and discovery are such that the module's potential role can sometimes be overridden ('corrupted') by other brain processes, according to context. Again this points to the plasticity of the human brain with the possibility of subtle nuances of emotional reactivity. Thus, a module is not exactly like an organ. The heart can serve only the one role of moving blood around the body and cannot temporarily be commanded to suspend its activity in the interests of another organ. The modules of evolutionary psychology appear to be more flexible in their operation.

MacDonald (2008) discusses Buss' argument that sexual jealousy is a powerful cue for aggression. Given the threat to genetic perpetuation posed by infidelity, it is easy to appreciate that such a jealousy module might emerge in evolution. However, as MacDonald argues, its effect can often be overridden by mental representations of longer-term gain (maintenance of family, stoical resignation), as well as anticipation of negative consequences of violating the law. Such assessment of costs and benefits is likely to be highly specific to the social context and culture. They could not represent evolutionary regularities and thereby genetically transmitted information.

Given the wide variety of different reactions to infidelity, some have speculated about whether a dedicated jealousy module actually exists. The reaction to infidelity can variously trigger fear, anger, disgust or sadness, or some combination of these, according to cultural norms, individual experience, expectations and intentions (Hupka, 1981). Maybe the reaction is to be understood in terms not of a dedicated jealousy module but as a combination of these more general-purpose systems.[6]

So, now let us turn to sexual attraction and see where these ideas can be applied.

In summary

- Sexual desire, arousal and behaviour are based upon automatic and controlled processes.
- Acting in an automatic mode, the brain would seem to fit rather well the notion of 'modules', as advanced by evolutionary psychologists.
- The brain can multi-task and set idiosyncratic goals. Culture appears to exert a profound role in human sexuality. So, in addition to modules, the brain has a capacity for flexible control.
- Sexual jealousy illustrates rather well how any module is embedded within some rather rich and flexible brain processes.

SIX

SEXUAL ATTRACTION

Beauty may be in the eyes of the beholder, but those eyes and the minds behind the eyes have been shaped by millions of years of human evolution.

(Buss, 2003, p. 53)[1]

Attractiveness is, of course, not the same as sexual desire. For example, a heterosexual man might judge another man to be attractive without feeling any sexual desire towards him. In one experiment, heterosexual women did not show a change in pupil size (an index of desire) on viewing an image of a woman whom they described as attractive (Laeng and Falkenberg, 2007). However, an effect seen across cultures is that normally a necessary, though not sufficient, condition for someone to elicit strong sexual wanting is that they would be judged as 'attractive' (Ford and Beach, 1951). Physical appearance ('attractiveness') is valued highly by both men and women in terms of what triggers desire (Regan and Berscheid, 1999). There is a sex difference in that men tend to find women more attractive than women find men attractive (Istvan et al., 1983).

What is attractive?

Features and qualities

The quality of attractiveness is not simply a product of Hollywood and the advertising industry, though doubtless this has a role in promoting certain stereotypes. In experiments, even human infants as young as 2–3 months of age spend more timing looking at those women's faces which were judged by adults as attractive (Langlois et al., 1990). By 12 months of age, they spend more time interacting with strangers wearing attractive masks as compared to unattractive masks.

Although there are such universals, there are also idiosyncratic culture-dependent aspects of exactly which features are judged as attractive (Ford and Beach, 1951). People occasionally express surprise at whom they find attractive, feeling that one should be able to offer a rational analysis for taste. However, appraisal of stimuli in terms of their value occurs at a largely unconscious level (LeDoux, 1999), and so we should not expect to find all the answers by conscious introspection.

Some place a premium upon eyes whereas others emphasize ears. For women, smell plays a very important role, as do height and symmetry of the face (Meston and Buss, 2009). As the opposite side of the same coin, there are some universals in what is found to be unattractive (Ford and Beach, 1951), for example a face scarred by acne and what are judged as bad breath and body odours.

Levels of analysis are evident in the assessment of attractiveness. The attraction value of a female to a man is more clearly defined largely (though, of course, not wholly) in terms of physical features, whereas male attractiveness to a woman has more to do with features set into context, such as what they indicate about the man's social status (Ford and Beach, 1951; Symons, 1995). That is to say, women tend to place less emphasis upon physical looks, this being a consistently reported sex difference across cultures (Buss, 2003). Exactly corresponding to the heterosexual difference, homosexual males place a high premium on youth and looks, whereas homosexual women attach relatively little importance to these factors.

A preference for female thinness or plumpness as attractive features to a male seems to vary with culture. In cultures where food has been scarce, there is a tendency to favour plumpness over thinness (Buss, 2003). Buss suggests that there is not an evolved predisposition to favour a particular body size, but rather the evolved disposition is to favour status, and what signals such status varies according to culture.

Of course, it is not just physical characteristics that define attractiveness. Rather, psychological and behavioural features can also play an important role. For example, people find creativity, kindness, altruism and a sense of humour attractive (Laham, 2012). Meston and Buss (2009, p. 22) write:

> The tendency to be attracted to those who make us laugh and elicit a positive mood can partly be explained in terms of conditioning. After pairing a particular mood with a particular person on multiple occasions, eventually the person alone will elicit that mood. Indeed, studies have found that when women view photographs of strangers while enjoyable music is playing, they are more attracted to them than when they listen to music they find unappealing.

A woman of 29 years reported (Meston and Buss, 2009, p. 22): 'I had a relationship with someone who was very, very ugly but who made me laugh. He was very self-confident, as funny people tend to be I guess, so that was what attracted me to him.' Similarly, the pop singer Madonna reported (Madonna, 1992, p. 83): 'If I see someone who's not necessarily conventionally beautiful, I can still be attracted based on their intellect or whatever.' A general principle is that 'mere exposure' to something increases its attraction value and this principle applies to people too. Mere repeated exposure to someone has a tendency to increase their attraction value (Meston and Buss, 2009).

The brain and attractiveness

A region at the front of the brain[2] seems to be involved in allocating attraction value; for example, it is activated in men by presenting pictures of women whom they judge to be beautiful (Stoléru and Mouras, 2006).

An evolutionary psychology perspective

Basics

Evolutionary psychology explains why weight is placed upon certain stimulus characteristics: their value in signalling fitness. Hence evolutionary processes have built in such automatic assessments since they have paid over generations in terms of passing on genes. As with explanations in terms of what causes desire in the here and now, when the explanation is in terms of function, incentive motivation can also yield insight. By a selective attraction to certain female characteristics, the male maximizes his chances of successful genetic perpetuation, since they are indicative of good health. In other words, as Symons (1995) expresses it (p. 87): 'male sexual attraction was designed to vary in intensity directly with perceived cues of female mate value'. He argues (p. 80):

> I will use sexual attraction/attractiveness as an index of sexual pleasure. That is, I will assume that if X perceives A as more sexually attractive than B, then X typically would experience more pleasure (and would anticipate experiencing more pleasure) from copulating with A than with B.

In these terms, the fact that A is more attractive than B reflects the higher reproductive viability of A.

He suggests that (p. 81): 'human males evolved psychological mechanisms that selectively detect and respond to certain specific characteristics (such as smooth skin and bilateral symmetry) of women's bodies'. Some qualities that contribute to female attractiveness, for example good skin, teeth and hair, are rather obviously related to physical health (Buss, 2003), whereas others, for example particular facial features, are not. However, sense can be made of the latter from an evolutionary perspective. Symmetry of the face is also a quality of high attractiveness and is an index of healthy development of the body.

According to evolutionary psychologists, there is nothing arbitrary about what is attractive, since female attractiveness is indicative of reproductive potential. If attractiveness were entirely arbitrary, it would be unpredictable. For example, we might tend to find cultures in which acne and wrinkles were highly valued, others in which they were seen as unattractive and still others where they were irrelevant to attraction (Symons, 1995). All things being equal, men tend to be attracted more to younger than to older women, since the younger are more likely to be able to produce children.

What is judged as attractive tends to be the *average* face of the population (Langlois and Roggman, 1990). This was determined experimentally by taking a series of images of faces and by means of a computer forming the average of them. The average tended to be more attractive than any individual face. A possible explanation for this is that such average faces are by definition ones in which there are no deviations from the average, since deviations could indicate a less healthy form (Symons, 1995).

Women tend to find men of high status to be attractive, which makes good evolutionary sense in terms of survival and giving a head start to children (Buss, 2003)

Some qualifications to evolutionary psychology

Having noted the contribution that evolutionary psychology can offer, it is important to add a qualifier. There are some important cultural variations in what is judged as sexually attractive. The female breast, so prized by men in Western society, offers little or no attraction to males on the Polynesian island of Mangaia (Marshall, 1971). Similarly, the Kinsey researchers reported that in regions of tropical Africa, where the breasts are normally exposed in public, they hold little erotic value for the male (Kinsey et al., 1953). This suggests eroticization of the unknown and forbidden.

Evolutionary psychologists acknowledge that changing conditions across cultures and times might mean some variation on what is judged as attractive (Symons, 1995). Clearly, there is a role of culture involved in what is an attractive body size. Beauty as portrayed by Rubens is of a much larger body size than that shown in *Playboy* magazine (Doidge, 2007). As another example, the modern Western emphasis upon slimness might reflect knowledge about the health hazards of obesity in modern societies. There is little reason to suppose that slimness was favoured in an environment of our early evolution, where food was probably scarce.

In keeping with the general theme being developed here, it seems that evolutionary factors select a kind of favoured or default position for attraction but then personal and idiosyncratic experience fills in the rest. In some cases, personal experience might even dominate in determining attractiveness. The obvious, albeit extreme, example of this is sexual fetishes (Chapter 19); a feature that surely does not signal health and reproductive potential, such as a squint or the stump of an amputated limb, might be judged to be particularly appealing.

In summary

- Attractiveness can be assessed without desire being present though strong wanting is associated with attractiveness.

- There are some universals of attractiveness but also some idiosyncratic features.
- In functional terms, evolutionary psychologists suggest that certain features are attractive since they convey good reproductive potential.

SEVEN

SHADES OF DESIRE FROM SIMPLE TO COMPLEX

> The world is an inherently complex place which to a large extent is too complex to be grasped and comprehended by the human intellect. Faced with this complexity we do the best we can – we formulate models which represent our limited grasp of reality.
>
> (Bancroft, 2000, p. 204)[1]

This chapter looks in more detail at both universal and idiosyncratic features of desire. The contribution of arousal is considered mainly in Chapter 9.

Two principal and closely related themes run through this account of desire:

- Different levels of control underlie desire.
- Some aspects of desire can be understood through the subjective insight of the person having the desire. Other aspects are beyond such insight and can only be studied with the tools of objective science.

So, what exactly triggers sexual desire?

The diversity and richness of sexual desire

At the basic level

Imagine a man walking near a red-light district and suddenly being propositioned. His thoughts and intentions might have been far from the erotic but sexual desire and arousal were instantly created by the invitation. The woman's physical properties dominate the 'stimulus-driven' control of the client's behaviour. Just one goal, immediate unconditional pleasure, dominates, with little or no emotional empathy, concern for the pleasure of the woman or thought of the future.

Some people might describe such behaviour as 'animal-like' and they would capture a part of the truth: the brain processes underlying it probably have much in common with those of non-humans (Pfaus, 2009). By analogy with purchasing goods (Hoch and Loewenstein, 1991), the behaviour might be 'purely on impulse', the defining characteristic being that the man would have rejected the option if asked in advance what he would do in such a situation and might regret his behaviour later. However, there could be more than one goal pursued simultaneously, for example to overcome long-term inhibitions and confirm his virility.

Where the transaction seems a simple commercial one, insight might be gained by adapting a theory on customer behaviour (Hoch and Loewenstein, 1991), which fits well to incentive motivation ideas. Researchers distinguish between (a) deliberate, rational purchases, in which the purchase is intended before setting out on the shopping trip and not regretted later; and (b) sudden hot ('impatient') purchases, which were not intended and might be regretted later. A given purchase might result from a combination of these two factors, that is an initial intention that sets the scene for a somewhat impulsive purchase.

Researchers have identified the factors that lead to, and the psychological states that accompany, impulsivity. The trigger and defining feature of impulsive purchasing is the physical proximity of the item to be purchased, with no delay in its acquisition. This would seem to be analogous to using the services of street prostitution. After first engaging in such behaviour, it is likely to be strongly reinforced since the reward of sexual access follows very swiftly after first perception of the attractive stimulus.

Whether impatience is triggered or not, some individuals in this situation do, of course, resist the lure. The term 'willpower' is commonly used here. One obvious way of resisting is to increase physical separation from the temptation. If consumer purchase of goods is any indicator, then, once wanting is triggered strongly, to refrain from making a purchase causes psychological distress (Hoch and Loewenstein, 1991).[2] The ensuing state of frustration might itself trigger giving in to temptation as a means of lowering the aversive state.

Exemplifying 'automatic control', acting very rapidly at an early stage in visual processing, that is before conscious awareness has been triggered, a man's attention is engaged by women whom he finds attractive (Maner et al., 2007). It is easy to appreciate the functional significance: attention is drawn to those stimuli in the environment that are of adaptive importance. The effect is particularly pronounced in so-called 'sexually unrestricted men', those who favour promiscuous strategies. Although women prefer to look at attractive men, the study found no evidence for a process of automatic early-stage capture by such stimuli.

Some women also exhibit relatively uncomplicated desires, though usually of a slightly more reserved kind than that just described.

> Bumping into him again was perfect timing . . . I asked him if he'd like to come over for a couple of hours . . . Sex is for pleasure, he was a sure thing. It was as simple and complex as 'I want you.' (Heterosexual woman of 41 years; Meston and Buss, 2009, p. 30)

> After years of feeling conflicted about the idea of having sex with someone simply because of attraction and the thought that the experience may be fun and satisfying, I have completely owned that desire. I regularly enjoy the thrill of seduction and guiltless, enjoyable sex. (Predominantly heterosexual woman of 33 years; Meston and Buss, 2009, p. 30)

> There have been times when I wasn't emotionally connected to the person I had sex with but I did it because I wanted to feel the physical pleasure of sex and orgasm . . . One instance was a friend of mine for a few years. I hadn't had sex in awhile and needed a release. We had dinner at my house, and later that evening wound up in bed. I felt comfortable with him because he was a friend, and the sex was really enjoyable. (28-year-old predominantly heterosexual woman; Meston and Buss, 2009, p. 41)

At the more subtle level

By contrast, sexual desire can involve complex and subtle dynamics of social interaction. Interviews asking people 'what triggers sexual desire?' show that it is often characterized by multiple levels of organization and complex ways of reaching sexual goals. This is particularly the case in women. The ways in which desire is experienced are likely to be so idiosyncratic that careful coaxing from a sympathetic interviewer is required. It would be impossible to understand these aspects by ticking boxes on a form, and it requires what psychologists call a 'qualitative approach'. In a study by Brotto et al. (2009) of women living on the United States west coast, a number of those sampled found it difficult to articulate exactly what sexual desire meant. Consider the following:

> For me [the trigger of desire] was probably my own memories . . . if a song plays that I associate with positive memories from our past that might click for me and make me think 'yeah, tonight maybe . . . tonight I'm feeling pretty good'. (Joan, aged 49, cited by Brotto et al., 2009, p. 393)

Recall of past experiences of desire and pleasure can contribute to present desire.

> Certainly the way he is touching me and what he's saying to me and where he's putting his hands on my body . . . Definitely the feeling that he is attracted to me, and feeling the strength of his desire which is something that makes me have even more desire for him. (Stephanie, aged 43, cited by Brotto et al., 2009, p. 393)

A factor contributing to Stephanie's desire is an observation of the man's behaviour, accompanied by 'mind reading' that suggested to her the existence of *his* desire.

> It could start with emotional factors, like thinking about my boyfriend in the morning, and then I think coinciding or soon after that the physical stuff starts. (Marge, aged 36, cited by Brotto et al., 2009, p. 392)

The thought of an emotional attachment to one particular individual might be necessary to trigger sexual desire.

> I think that if I could consistently, or even 50% of the time, feel aroused, then that would set up a Pavlov's dog idea like . . . connecting this person to the arousal, and therefore lead me to feel desire. So the next time I see this person I will think 'Oh, I know I'm going to have an orgasm!' (Jill, aged 43, cited by Brotto et al., 2009, p. 393)

A prior condition would be the experience of arousal, which could then be linked to the particular individual.

> My husband is very . . . sort of . . . low ability to hang onto his erections. He needs to do it [sex] and to do it now because he can't really keep it going for a long time . . . and I think it gets in the way [of my desire]. (Elana, aged 53, cited by Brotto et al., 2009, p. 393)

> So I'll have a thought of desire, then I'll think 'Oh, it was so painful last time' and so, it's starting to interfere with the more natural conclusions that would go with desire. (Holly, aged 53, cited by Brotto et al., 2009, p. 393)

The last two cases exemplify that desire involves anticipation of the future. If this is of something painful, or at least less than satisfactory, it can inhibit desire in the here and now. Someone with a depressed mood also tends to lower the partner's desire.

> I see someone and I guess that would be called desire. When you do a little fantasizing in your head . . . even if it's a total fantasy and it would never happen. I guess that would be desire. (Stephanie, aged 43, cited by Brotto et al., 2009, p. 393)

Sexual fantasy (Chapter 16) is a common experience and amounts to a safe way of 'testing the system'.

> I used to feel it really genitally. I used to feel sexually engorged, and now it's more as if I can become sexually engorged as we're starting to have sex, but it's not as much beforehand. (Elana, aged 53, cited by Brotto et al., 2009, p. 391)

The triggers to desire can change as a function of age.

So, can we assimilate such diversity into a general principle that meshes with the scientific study of desire? The common feature of desire in most such cases is that a trigger sets up the *intention* to achieve intimacy and sexually related pleasure in the future and the *expectation* of achievement. In one study, almost all women described an 'intentional object of desire' (Brotto et al., 2009). If the anticipation associated with a sexual inter-action is of disappointment, something at odds with the intention, this can preclude or lower desire. Such a definition excludes sexual behaviour characterized by pure altruism, coerced sex, that to achieve monetary gain or someone seeking a professional advantage or to set a honey-trap, as involving sexual desire. Though they involve a sexually linked intention and behaviour, the individual's goal is not one of sexual pleasure for the self.

Sexual arousal seems to be only one possible contributor to initial desire, albeit often an important one. Someone might have a desire to attain intimacy and emotional oneness without necessarily *feeling* any lust, pure sexual desire or arousal initially. Sexual desire and arousal might gradually switch on as the interaction progresses. A common report was that, once sexual desire started, the woman was moved to continue and to escalate the intensity of the associated sexual pleasure. In some cases, arousal might come first, being triggered by some non-sexual but shared event, such as an exciting fairground ride and this subsequently contributes to sexual desire.

A person might be suffering from depression with low libido but they might *wish to feel libido*. Given such a 'want to want' libido, maybe the chances of sexual desire actually emerging are greater than if there were no 'want to want'.

Not a universal model

A survey of nurses in the United States asked which model of sexual desire best fitted their own personal experience (Sand and Fisher, 2007), contrasting those in which:

1 sexual desire started the sexual behaviour sequence;
2 there was 'sexual neutrality' at the outset and sex was initiated for reasons other than sexual desire, such as intimacy and, out of this, sexual desire emerged.

Women fitted roughly equally in their agreement with these two models. Those who had no problems with their sexuality tended to subscribe to the first. Those who reported problematic and unsatisfying sexuality, with low orgasmic capacity, tended to subscribe to the second. Pre-menopausal women tended to subscribe to model 1, whereas post-menopausal women tended to subscribe to model 2. There was a tendency for women in a relationship of less than five years' duration to endorse model 1. The word 'tendency' needs some emphasis since these trends were no more than that.

Gender differences

An instant turn-on and acceptance of sex with a complete stranger is generally something more desired and accepted by men than women, though of course there are exceptions (Buss, 2003). Women are more likely than men to give extra reasons for agreeing to sex, such as trying to establish a meaningful bond. Women's willingness to engage in sex depends to some extent upon social context, for example the ratio of women to men in a given society, reflecting, it would seem, evolved strategies to maximize the chances of genetic perpetuation.

A study by Clark and Hatfield (1989) is regularly cited to support a strong gender difference in the attraction of casual sex. Male and female students were approached by a stranger of the opposite sex and invited to engage in sex. A large percentage of the males agreed but none of the females. The study suggests that males are simply excited by physical appearance, whereas for females things are more complex. However, even in males, sexual desire is not simple (Janssen et al., 2002). For example, desire is excited more strongly by sexual films that represent a consensual interaction, rather than a coercive interaction.

Women are more likely than men to perceive danger in a casual situation and less likely to anticipate pleasure from the outcome (Conley, 2011). Interestingly, if the proposer were either familiar or a famous handsome individual, women expected themselves to react more positively in the situation.

Levels of control

Evidence presented in Chapter 5 points to behaviour being determined by at least two levels of control (Carver et al., 2009; Meyer et al., 2012; Toates, 1998, 2006). In the case of desire, these are:

1 A low-level control that acts somewhat as a magnet causing the attraction towards a sexual stimulus. This can act at least in part at an unconscious level.
2 A high-level control involving conscious processing and intentions.

To reiterate briefly, circumstances can be such that level 1 acts in the same direction as level 2, that is both causing a move towards the attractive other. For example, a stimulus whether drug, food or sex-related could trigger unconsciously a magnetic-like pull and when this reaches conscious awareness, the intention is put into effect in keeping with the low-level lure. However, factor 2 can also act in the opposite direction to 1 causing restraint on behaviour (Chapter 12). High-level control ('executive control'), can override the low-level system. When the capacity for executive control is high, people tend to act according to their conscious intentions and long-term goals. This is exemplified by low-level 'automatic' desire being restrained by a ('higher') rational level of inhibition that anticipates future problems. Conversely, the low level might be resisting sexual behaviour (e.g. as a result of disgust or a depressed mood), whereas the high level is tending to trigger it (e.g. perceived duty or for financial gain). Inhibition will be described later, while the emphasis of the present chapter is the excitation acting at either level or both simultaneously.

The action of these two levels of control is evident in the wanting phase of sexuality. Incentives can act through the low-level system to engage appetitive behaviour, whereas aversive events can act to cause withdrawal from a situation or immobility. The low-level system would take a considerable weight of the control of sexual behaviour in a case where an individual pursues an instant turn-on, exemplified by the male being turned on by the sex worker.

The high-level system calls up memories, anticipates the future and takes into account long-term considerations and it takes up a large amount of processing capacity. This system might add to the effect of the low-level system, for example a person is happy to be captured by a sexual stimulus and carefully pursues it. I would suggest that the high-level system dominates the control of behaviour in those cases just used to exemplify where desire was not automatically triggered by physical properties. Rather, it took time to emerge, dependent upon memories, emotional connectedness and interpretation of the behaviour of the partner.

A common incentive system

Basics

Obviously we know whether we are feeling lust or hunger! There are distinct systems in the brain underlying particular wants. However, evidence also suggests a *common* process that contributes to any want (Panksepp, 1982); an 'incentive approach system' serves the range of motivations, for example sex, food and drugs, described as a 'common currency' (Berger and Shiv, 2011). Any such incentive can engage the common system, which brings the person into closer contact with the incentive.

A consequence of the common mechanism is that there can be 'spill-over' between different incentives. That is to say, excitement by incentive 1 (e.g. the sight of a drug to someone using drugs) might also be seen in a stronger approach to incentive 2 (e.g. sexual incentive). Incentives 1 and 2 might be simultaneously present and add their effects together or the effect of incentive 1, presented on its own, might be seen in increased wanting towards incentive 2 that is presented immediately afterwards. The common approach ('wanting') system would seem to form the basis of the ubiquitous observation that advertisers exploit sex to create or amplify other wants. There is no better demonstration of this than motor shows, where the latest fashionable model usually has at least one scantily clad female draped over its bonnet.

Future discounting

The phenomenon termed 'future discounting' or 'future myopia' (Wilson and Daly, 2004; van den Bergh et al., 2008) also points to common features of different desires. Numerous studies have shown that people are *impatient* in that they prefer to obtain a reward today rather than tomorrow and prefer a smaller reward (e.g. £10) over a bigger reward (e.g. £15) in one month.

Sexual arousal causes discounting of the value of future monetary gain, as does heroin or nicotine craving. Sexual cues make males impatient to get soda pop and candy bars! Wilson and Daly exposed men to images of women whom they found attractive and this increased the men's tendency to discount the future in terms of monetary reward. This was observed not only for images of women but also by viewing and touching a woman's bra, as compared to a T-shirt. This triggered impatience for a candy bar (van den Bergh et al., 2008). Women exposed to images of attractive men did not show an increased tendency to discount the future[3] and neither did men exposed to images of women that they did not find attractive.

Differences between individuals in their wanting

Some bases of desire remain idiosyncratic. However, certain differences between individuals can be understood in terms of identifiable processes.

Personality

Motivation can arise from either the pursuit of attractive goals (the approach system, exemplified by seeking sexual pleasure) or the avoidance of aversion (a so-called avoidance system, exemplified by having sex to avoid relationship conflict or social rejection). Individuals differ in how much relative weight is placed upon these two systems (Cooper et al., 2008). If someone seeks help for loss of desire, it could be useful to look carefully at the goals set within any relationship. Setting *approach* goals (e.g. to plan to take a holiday together) might spill over into increased sexual desire. This is in contrast to setting avoidance goals (Impett et al., 2008).

Sometimes women feel bad after engaging in consensual but unwanted sex (Meston and Buss, 2009). Whether they feel good or bad depends largely upon whether the sex was engaged in as part of approach or avoidance motivation. If the intended goal was a desired one, such as to please a partner, women tend to feel good afterwards. If it was a goal of avoiding an undesirable effect, such as losing the partner, the consequences are more likely to be negative, involving such feelings as shame. Rather than being analogous to resisting addictive drugs, the situation would be rather like forcing oneself to take a bad-tasting medicine.

Individual differences in the strength of wanting can be linked to differences in the relative sensitivity of the approach system (van den Bergh et al., 2008). Extraverts are characterized by a large weight upon approach motivation, high sensitivity to social rewards and relatively high pleasure levels derived thereby (Larsen and Augustine, 2008). This is a feature of Jeffrey Gray's 'reinforcement sensitivity theory' (see Corr, 2008). Individuals showing a high level of 'reward sensitivity', i.e. 'wanting sensitivity', were found to show a relatively high level of discounting of the future (van den Bergh et al., 2008). A predictor of promiscuous sexual activity is the personality characteristic of extraversion and impulsive sensation-seeking (Schmitt and Shackelford, 2008).

Risky sexual behaviour can also be based upon avoidance motivation (Cooper et al., 2008). Escape from aversion can dominate behavioural control and negative moods can exacerbate the strength of incentive pull, associated with short-term relief from aversion but with long-term risks. Neuroticism is associated with strong avoidance tendencies (Cooper et al., 2008).

The personality characteristics of agreeableness and conscientiousness correlate negatively with the tendency to uncommitted sexuality. The extravert need for variety can perhaps most obviously be satisfied on the basis of a change of partner. Low conscientiousness would surely help to promote short-term mating, especially if infidelity were involved.

Some combination of an intrinsic personality factor and social context predicts a number of aspects of behaviour better than chance. A general personality factor of 'intolerance of deviance' is predictive of resistance to such things as drug-taking in both sexes and early loss of virginity amongst girls (Orford, 2001).

So, where is the incentive process embodied in the brain? The next chapter addresses this.

In summary

- Sexual desires arise from raw stimulus features as well as meanings and goals associated with others.
- The control of desire is organized into layers, evolutionarily old and new co-existing.
- There is a common incentive approach system associated with different desires.

EIGHT

DETAILS OF THE BRAIN AND DESIRE

For suddenly he was aware of the old flame shooting and leaping up in
his loins, that he had hoped was quiescent for ever.

(D. H. Lawrence, 1928/1993, p. 120)

Swelling detected at the genitals appears to add to desire arising from
the stimulus of a potential partner (Georgiadis et al., 2012) and might
even provide the principal stimulus to desire (Laan and Both, 2008). Positive feedback seems to be involved (Mouras et al., 2008); in response to a
visual stimulus, desire would contribute to genital arousal and, by means
of signals from the genitals to the brain, there would be an amplification
of desire.

The bits that make up the whole

Knowledge of the brain bases of desire comes from several sources
(Chapter 2):

1 research on non-humans and cautiously extrapolating to humans;
2 looking at changes in the sexual desire of people following brain damage
   or disease;
3 using neuroimaging to examine activity in the brains of people exposed
   to erotic images.

Neuroimaging reveals a network of interacting brain regions, parts of
which are excited and others of which are inhibited by erotic visual stimuli (Georgiadis et al. 2010; Redouté et al. 2005). Researchers distinguish

regions serving some closely related but nonetheless somewhat conceptually distinct roles:

1 to make an initial assessment of the sexual value of the content of the image;
2 to produce a signal that is sent to the genitals to trigger swelling;[1]
3 to receive feedback from the genitals on their arousal[2] – this signal is thought to contribute to the conscious awareness of the state of the body, particularly the dimension of eroticism;
4 to create a motivational signal, having unconscious and conscious aspects,[3] which tends to direct behaviour towards the sexual stimulus – a feature of this is conscious desire.

Images are categorized and assessed in terms of their sexual content. Attention is focused upon the image and emotional value ('intensity') is attributed to it. If the imagery concerns sexual action, the brain[4] is likely to represent this as a simulation of the viewer performing this same action, so-called 'mirroring'. By extrapolation from evidence on other desires, the insula appears to be a brain region that is sensitive to both external images (in this case, erotic images) and arousal from the body (Craig, 2002). It appears to combine these signals as part of the generation of a desire signal, which then excites the dopamine-rich brain regions, described shortly.

Asymmetry in the cortex

Evidence suggests that the left prefrontal cortex has a predominant role in behavioural approach and the right prefrontal cortex has a role in behavioural restraint and inhibition (Sutton and Davidson, 2000). Presenting such incentives as money, a pleasant-tasting food or the opportunity to view a pleasant film causes activation particularly in the left hemisphere. The prefrontal region appears to embody representations of goals and is involved in movement towards them. Those individuals with a higher left-hemisphere activity will be biased towards acquiring incentives and experience high levels of positive affect in their acquisition.

Similarly, when moving further back in the brain to the temporal lobes, the two hemispheres play somewhat different roles in sexual desire and the exertion of restraint on this. Damage to this lobe in the right hemisphere is often followed by hypersexuality, whereas that to the left is more commonly followed by hyposexuality (Braun et al., 2003).

The discussion now focuses on the approach system.

The approach system

Brain regions underlying approach motivation[5] can be distinguished from those involved in remaining passive or general emotional arousal. The role of dopamine in approach and wanting is manifest at both a conscious level of desire and at the level of the unconscious capture of processing by sexual stimuli (Oei et al., 2012).

Acting 'like a magnet', the dopamine-based system underlies attention, wanting, movement towards and pursuit of incentives (Meyer et al. 2012). This provides the common currency of wanting (Berger and Shiv, 2011). For example, the low-level system involving dopamine is excited by anticipation of financial gains by gamblers and drugs by people addicted to them (Breiter et al. 2001).[6] Dopamine acting at the level of the nucleus accumbens plays a role in the activation of behaviour and in motivating the individual to overcome obstacles in order to reach a goal (Salamone et al., 2007). It appears that there is a system involving various brain regions and performing a cost–benefit (e.g. instant hedonism versus danger) analysis of behavioural options (Assadi et al., 2009). Dopamine can tilt the bias in favour of immediate gratification, downplaying costs.

Dopamine appears to be involved in only the seeking ('goal-directed') aspect of behaviour. If we can extrapolate from rat studies, when the goal is reached dopamine is deactivated (Blackburn et al., 1992).

Different individuals can be compared in this regard. Generalizing from other tasks to sexual desire, high levels of dopamine activation underlie high degrees of persistence in the face of obstacles, delays and uncertainty of getting a reward (Treadway et al. 2012). The extreme persistence of some individuals in sexual pursuit, for example stalking, appears to have a basis in abnormally activated dopamine levels accompanied by relatively low levels of serotonin (Meloy and Fisher, 2005). By contrast, the dopamine-deficient individual is lacking in energy and appears apathetic. Given that many situations of sexual and romantic attraction are those of high arousal, we might expect hormones associated with stress to be active at such times (Fisher, 2004). Stress hormones are known to excite dopamine activity.

In males, even so-called subliminal sexual images (i.e. not triggering conscious awareness) activate various brain regions containing dopamine, including the nucleus accumbens, compared to neutral or unpleasant images (Oei et al., 2012).[7] Boosting dopamine levels artificially was associated with still higher levels of activation in these regions in response to the erotic stimuli. Such unconscious triggering of desire, in a world full of sexual imagery (termed a 'running start' by the authors) is surely relevant to the difficulties some people experience in resisting sexual desire.

By comparison with drug-taking, the notion of *incentive salience* (Robinson and Berridge, 1993) is relevant here. This term refers to the 'magnet-like power' of incentives to engage and attract attention and behaviour. Acting through dopaminergic brain systems, repeated use of certain drugs, such as nicotine or heroin, increases their incentive salience. Their sensory representation in the brain become 'tagged', such that they exert an increasing control of behaviour and increasing occupation of the conscious mind with thoughts of the drugs. Although, say, sex and gambling do not, of course, involve taking a chemical into the body, their effects seem similar to that of drugs (Pitchers et al., 2010). The consequences of such behaviour involve intrinsic chemical changes in the brain that underlie increasing incentive salience. An exaggeration of this process might underlie hypersexuality (Oei et al., 2012), as in sexual addiction (Chapter 17).

Knutson et al. (2008) presented erotic images to heterosexual males, while observing (a) activity in different brain regions by means of neuroimaging and (b) the choice made in a subsequent gambling task, whether opting for high risk or low risk. Seeing erotic images tended to move participants towards the high-risk choice. Other studies also point to future discounting after exposure to erotic images. Compared to viewing neutral images, activity triggered by exposure to erotic images was pronounced in the region of the nucleus accumbens, a good predictor of the move to a risky choice.

Relatively high levels of dopamine activity at both a prefrontal cortical location[8] and a subcortical location[9] correlate with the strength of an individual's willingness to exert effort to obtain monetary reward under uncertain conditions (Treadway et al., 2012). Similarly, dopaminergic activity in these regions might be necessary for a person to be motivated to pursue sexual incentives where effort is needed and there is an uncertain outcome. In early human evolution, considerable effort and uncertainty were probably involved in securing sexual partners. This should be contrasted with the experience of some in today's culture, where no more than a telephone call is needed to obtain 'room service'. The notion of evolutionary mismatch (Chapter 2) seems to be applicable.

The high-level conscious and intention system of wanting seems to be less dependent upon dopamine than the low-level system (Meyer et al., 2012). Nonetheless, there is evidence for dopamine acting there. It is commonly assumed that human action is motivated by the conscious future expectation of pleasure and pain (Gilbert and Wilson, 2007; Sharot et al., 2009). An experiment investigated the effect of artificially boosting dopamine levels. When a stimulus (a holiday location) was simply imagined under a condition of elevated dopamine level, subsequently the person estimated a higher hedonic rating of experiencing that stimulus (being in the location) in the future. This suggests a role of dopamine in so-called 'anticipatory pleasure'.

Hormones

What is the role of hormones in sexual desire? At puberty, do they literally 'drive' the unfortunate teenager to distraction? Some might argue that hormones are what give drive to sexual behaviour. However, should we not expect that their level would fall with satiety? There is no evidence for this. As an alternative, how might hormones fit an incentive interpretation? This section will suggest that certain so-called 'sex hormones' modulate the strength of incentive motivation.

Comparison with non-human species

Insight might be gained from non-human species (Beach, 1947), though there is a risk of uncritical extrapolation to humans. The female rat shows a four-day cycle of changes in sexual activity, from interest through lack of interest, and this depends upon her four-day cycle of hormones. However, unlike primates including humans, she needs a minimum level of hormone *to be able physically* to assume the posture for mating. Humans, of course, do not need to adopt one particular position to facilitate intromission, the imagination being the most obvious parameter to set limits.

Going from rats to non-human primates and finally to humans, a progressive loosening of the link between hormones and behaviour occurs (Ford and Beach, 1951). Some women are able to experience desire even though they appear to be deficient in hormones. Ford and Beach suggest that a relaxing of hormonal controls is accompanied by an increasing role of so-called higher brain regions.[10] These regions mediate learning so that desire reflects knowledge of what is happening, for example concerning contraception and pregnancy.

Monkeys permit controlled studies, which give pointers to the role of hormones in humans (Wallen, 2001). Observations suggest a cycle of female motivation that reflects her underlying hormonal cycle. Such a cycle appears when monkeys are housed in a large enclosure that provides for rich behavioural opportunities. Similarly, where the female is placed in a Skinner box and earns a limited period of access to a male by lever-pressing when she chooses to do so, there is clear evidence of peaks and troughs of motivation, corresponding to her hormonal cycle. Some women might envy the degree of freedom of the subjects in these experiments. When the female is placed in a small cage with a male, the observation that sexual activity occurs throughout the cycle might point to male rather than female choice.

Human sexual desire: general principles

In humans, there appear to be both general and human-specific factors in the link between hormones and sexual desire. This points to a complex interaction between biological and social factors in the determination of behaviour. The fact that humans possess an understanding of the implications of the menstrual cycle for pregnancy doubtless also plays a role.

The so-called 'sex hormones' (oestrogens and androgens in women and androgens in men) act on the brain regions concerned with sexual desire (Regan and Berscheid, 1999; Wallen and Lovejoy, 1993). One of their principal roles is to sensitize incentive pathways, thereby making it more likely that a given incentive will trigger approach. Androgens sensitize the dopaminergic input to the nucleus accumbens (Hermans et al., 2010).

Although hormones play a role in desire, there is not a one-to-one link. Thus, there are examples of very low desire in people with normal hormone levels. In keeping with incentive theory, Wallen and Lovejoy suggest that in humans (1993, p. 92) 'hormones set the basic responsivity of individuals to their sexual environment'. In other words, the link between stimuli and the arousal of desire is modulated by sex hormones, which make sexual interaction more desired and more pleasurable when it happens. Sex hormones increase the frequency of sexual fantasies (Abdallah and Simon, 2007). Is sexual desire idiosyncratic and closed to scientific scrutiny or does it show universal properties rooted in biology? Clearly the answer is 'both'. For example, fantasy takes many different forms but, whatever its content, the frequency is increased by the presence of hormones.

Human males

Testosterone is the hormone of most importance to human male sexuality. Its level in the blood shows a positive relationship to frequency of sexual interest (O'Carroll and Bancroft, 1984; Regan, 1999). The evidence suggests that testosterone acts on attentional processes such that sexual stimuli increase in *salience* (Alexander et al., 1997). For men with a hormone deficiency, supplementary testosterone increases sexual desire and frequency of sexual thoughts and fantasy (Jockenhövel et al., 2009). Development of androgen receptor blockers provides some hope of a treatment for sex offenders. These drugs tend to lower desire, but the ability to engage in sexual behaviour once in an appropriate sexual situation is less disrupted than is desire (Wallen and Lovejoy, 1993). However, even surgical removal of the testes does not invariably lead to a loss of all desire (Kinsey et al., 1953).

One study looked at the activity of the brain in men with a low testosterone level (Redouté et al. 2005). Relative to controls, a number of regions were underactive, including the orbitofrontal cortex,[11] but their activity was restored to nearer normal after administration of testosterone.

For men, the sexual attractiveness of women's body odours reaches a peak at the time of the women's ovulation, which would presumably increase the chances of mating and insemination (Kuukasjärvi et al., 2004). This effect was not found when the odours were from women taking the contraceptive pill. So ovulation, often described as 'concealed' in humans, is not entirely concealed.

Human females

From an evolutionary perspective, one might expect cycles in desire corresponding to the female menstrual cycle. In reality, the results are confusing (Ågmo, 2007). Clearly, women are able to have intercourse at any point in the menstrual cycle. A question is whether, left to their own choice and ignoring complications, they *desire* it at the same intensity throughout.

As might be predicted from functional considerations, desire tends to peak at the time when the chances of fertility are at their maximum: ovulation (Stanislaw and Rice, 1988). Some, but not all, evidence points to women being more responsive to sexual stimuli at this time (Krug et al., 1994). In one experiment, very brief images were flashed on a screen. Images of a naked male were perceived more readily at the time of ovulation. Women made more errors then in 'seeing' sexual images that were not actually being presented.

At ovulation, women are most likely to masturbate or initiate sexual activity (Adams et al., 1978). Masturbation is presumably a good index of the hormonal contribution to desire, uncomplicated by issues of pregnancy. It appears that oestrogens, which peak at mid-cycle, are responsible for the effect. Women taking the contraceptive pill show relatively little such fluctuation over the menstrual cycle, this being further evidence of the normal role of hormones. Loss of oestrogens either through surgery or menopause is associated with some loss of desire. During pregnancy there is generally a decline in sexual desire (Regan and Berscheid, 1999), as would be expected from considerations of function. Of course, hormones might well be only one factor underlying this effect. The woman's knowledge of her pregnancy and feelings of inappropriateness of desire could also contribute.

Gizewski et al. (2006) looked at changes in activation in brain regions concerned with emotional processing over the menstrual cycle.[12] In response to viewing erotic films, greater activation was found at the time of maximum fertility and this correlated with subjective reports of the women's desire.

Subjective reports on fluctuations in sexual desire over the menstrual cycle are not the only source of information and certain techniques allow objective measures. For example, the pupil tends to dilate in response to viewing sexually attractive images. Over the menstrual cycle, researchers investigated its dilation in response to such images consisting of the women's boyfriends and favourite actors (Laeng and Falkenberg, 2007). The reaction was the greatest, indicating highest sexual interest, in the most fertile ('ovulatory') period of the cycle. The authors noted that the pupil reaction is automatic and unconscious. In keeping with a hierarchical understanding, the authors suggested that the pupil reaction gives a 'raw' measure, an automatic and unconscious index of sexual attraction. This is uncontaminated by any complex social interpretation, beliefs or inhibition that the conscious mind might link to desire.

Mass et al. (2009) investigated the facial reaction of women to the stimulus of a nude male over the menstrual cycle, specifically the muscular reaction in forming a smile.[13] This measure was based upon the logic that a smile is an indicator of positive emotion, a necessary prior condition for sexual desire. The reaction of the muscles in forming a smile was stronger at the time of maximum fertility, as was the subjective measure by the women of their desire. Facial muscles might also present a spontaneous and automatic read-out of desire, unaffected by more consciously mediated 'higher' factors.

There is an important social consequence of this cycle of female desire. A significant number of young Americans are now taking pledges of sexual abstinence until marriage. Of course, these pledges sometimes break down and contraception is not being employed. Unfortunately, this is perhaps most likely to happen when the young woman is most fertile.

One study failed to find an effect of phase of cycle on the ranking of attraction of sexual images (Griffith and Walker, 1975). This presumably points to the multiple factors involved in desire and behaviour, such as fear of pregnancy.

Intercourse frequency is probably a compromise between male and female wishes. For some women, desire tends to be high immediately pre- and post-menstruation (Ford and Beach, 1951), presumably reflecting the diminished fear of pregnancy at those times combined with a deprivation effect. This illustrates the peculiarly human role of conscious insight, that is knowledge about the chances of pregnancy, which would interact with any more basic effects of hormones on desire. Cultural factors like having Saturday and Sunday as a holiday also play an important role in determining sexual activity (Wallen, 1995). Lesbian couples allow the influence of desire to be seen, unaffected by a male presence and fear of pregnancy. A mid-cycle increase of desire is seen.

Surgical removal of the ovaries, and thereby loss of oestrogens, is not necessarily associated with reduced desire (Ford and Beach, 1951). It is sometimes followed by increased desire, probably resulting from removal of the fear of pregnancy. Where there is a loss of desire, this probably has as much to do with the psychological interpretation of the surgery rather than a hormonal effect. There can be a possible indirect effect of oestrogens on sexual desire. Since their reduction can be associated with reduced vaginal lubrication, the consequences of sexual desire can be less good. This might lower desire.

Testosterone also plays a role in women's sexual desire and some argue that it is the dominant hormonal influence (Ågmo, 2007). Blood levels of testosterone show a positive link with desire and frequency of sexual thoughts (Regan, 1999). Surgical removal of the adrenal glands and thereby loss of the principal source of testosterone is followed by a reduction in sexual desire. For a group of women having had surgical removal of the ovaries, supplementing oestrogen replacement with testosterone greatly increased reports of desire and arousal (Sherwin and Gelfand, 1987).

Pheromones

Historically, a link between odours and sexual attraction has long been recognized and this link might be assumed to form an important foundation of the perfume industry (Bhutta, 2007). The term 'pheromone' refers to a class of chemical that is released into the air by one member of a species and which influences another of the same species. Pheromones have been most extensively studied in non-humans, particularly mice, where they play an important role in mating. Their influence is to trigger behaviour or to alter biological events (e.g. hormonal release) within the body of the recipient animal.

Jacob and McClintock (2000, p. 59) state: 'We cannot expect humans to behave like moths flying up the concentration gradient toward the desirable source.' Indeed, evidence suggests a role of pheromones in human sexual desire, albeit a more subtle one than for non-humans. For example, odours from lactating women increase sexual desire in other women (Spencer et al., 2004). For women with a partner, this was manifest by increased expressions of sexual desire towards their partner. For those without a partner, there was increased sexual fantasy. In other words, the pheromone exerts an effect that is not stereotyped. Rather, it varies according to circumstances; the pheromone appears to play a modulating ('sensitizing') role in sexual desire. The study suggested that participants had no conscious insight into the relationship between the pheromone and its effect on sexual desire. It is possible to make some functional sense of this phenomenon. The presence of lactating women could signal an environment that is currently favourable for reproduction.

Women prefer the odour of men with symmetrical facial features, pointing to a convergence of attractive qualities stimulating the visual and olfactory senses (Cornwell et al., 2004).

Evidence suggests that, comparing heterosexual men and women, the difference in the target of their desire is associated with differences in the activation pattern of particular brain region (Savic et al., 2001). The triggers are hormone-like substances secreted in the sweat and then vaporized, and so detected through the nose. A part of the hypothalamus is activated by an 'androgen-like' substance in women,[14] whereas in men a different part is activated by an 'oestrogen-like' substance.[15] The substances are secreted in the sweat of mainly men and women respectively and could contribute to the direction of heterosexual orientation of desire.

Approach motivation and differences between individuals

Some fortunate individuals experience actual levels of arousal and desire close to their wishes. Others find that their level of arousal is lower than desired and they seek various means to elevate the level, such as by drug-seeking or engaging in high-risk sexual activities (Alcaro et al., 2007). One suggestion is that dopamine is linked closely to arousal. It appears that low levels of dopaminergic activity are associated with low arousal and a search for ways of boosting arousal. This could be part of the process of escalation seen in some forms of sexual behaviour, whereby increasing intensity of activity, for example greater risks, are seen over time (Chapters 17 and 21).

At a general level, differences between individuals in the reactivity of dopaminergic systems appear to underlie differences in the strength of approach to incentives (King et al., 1986). However, it is also possible to discriminate between individual desires. Demos et al. (2012) examined activation of the nucleus accumbens in response to food, erotic or neutral images. The degree of activation in response to erotic images predicted sexual desire expressed in the subsequent months, whereas reactivity to food cues predicted weight gain. The effect was specific – food reactivity did not predict sexual desire/activity nor vice versa. Evidence obtained from people undergoing therapy for drug or food craving suggests that such interventions reduce the activation at the nucleus accumbens. So, craving appears to arise from a balance between activity in regions such as the nucleus accumbens and restraint arising from executive regions.[16]

Sexual taste

A study looked at two groups of people who had differing subjectively reported tastes in sadomasochistic sex (SM): (a) SM devotees and (b) 'conventional heterosexuals' who found the imagery to be disgusting (Stark et al., 2005). The reactions of the 'conventional heterosexuals' to conventional erotic images and SM folk to SM images were similar in a number of brain regions known to be implicated in approach motivation. By contrast, the reaction of the brain of 'conventional folk' to SM images was very different, being comparable to their reaction to unambiguous disgust-evoking images.[17]

Desire and disorders

Bipolar disorder

People with bipolar disorder alternate between phases of mania (heightened arousal, activity and goal-seeking) and low mood. In the manic phase, they sometimes exhibit hypersexuality. Krafft-Ebing (1978) described (p. 321):

> maniacal exaltation in men, courting, frivolity, and lasciviousness in speech, and frequenting of brothels.

Whether simply a sign of the times, women exhibited more restrained 'excesses':

> inclination for the society of men, personal adornment, perfumes, talk of marriage and scandals.

The manic phase is associated with excitation of a behavioural activation system and heightened dopamine activity. This is manifest as a range of exaggerated desires, excessive seeking of goals, elation and racing thoughts, relative to normal (Cousins et al., 2009). The elevated wanting is commonly associated with increased sexual desire, as indexed by an increased frequency of sexual thoughts, flirting and sexual behaviour, as in promiscuity. Features of this behaviour are described as 'impulsive' and 'risky', meaning triggered by a sexual situation without regard to long-term negative consequences (McCandless and Sladen, 2003). The pleasure of anticipation appears to be heightened in this state (Klein, 1987). Children sometimes show flirtatious behaviour towards medical staff (Geller and Tillman, 2004). Occasionally, hypersexuality is one of the first indicators of the appearance of mania (Tsuang, 1975). Treatments include reducing the dopaminergic activity by employing dopamine-blocking drugs. For some people with mania, there is simply a shift between mania and normality. In other cases, phases of depression alternate with mania and the depressed phase is commonly associated with a loss of interest in sex.

For some, manic phases are also associated with increased drug use (Meade et al., 2008). Cocaine can exacerbate the hypersexuality, leading to unsafe sex practices and thereby to a still higher risk of HIV infection. Since cocaine boosts dopamine activity, this points to a double contribution through this route.

Encephalitis lethargica ('sleeping sickness')

Evidence from encephalitis lethargica ('sleeping sickness') points to the role of dopamine in *wanting* sex. In one study, patients were treated with the dopamine-boosting substance L-Dopa. Typical of the results are those of Mrs B and Miss R (Sacks, 1976, p. 96):

Previously indifferent, inattentive, and unresponsive to her surroundings, Mrs B became, with each week, more alert, more attentive, and more interested in what was taking place around her.

For Miss R, Sacks noted (p. 108)

captivation or enthralment of gaze . . . she had been forced to stare at one of her fellow patients, and had felt her eyes 'drawn' this way and that, following the movements of this patient around the ward.

Concerning Mr P's sexual wanting (p. 152):

Sexual and libidinous arousal was still more marked and the transit of any female personnel across Mr P's field of vision would immediately evoke an indescribably lascivious expression, forced lip-licking and lip-smacking movements . . . and uncontrollable watching; he seemed – visually – to grab and grasp the object of his gaze, and to be unable to relinquish it till it passed from his field of vision.

Following the use of L-Dopa, Mr V became hyperactive, amorous and adjusted his spectacles 200–300 times an hour (p. 197). Mr G experienced increased libido with L-Dopa (p. 217).

The evidence of Mr L points to activation of a general incentive system by the treatment (Sacks, p. 249):

Mr L passed from a gentle amorousness to an enraged and thwarted erotomania.

Fantasies were of a hypersexual form. He masturbated for hours each day. At other times extreme hunger and thirst were triggered.

Parkinson's disease

Parkinson's disease arises from the loss of a particular set of neurons, which employ dopamine.[18] A pathway of neurons involved in the control of movement is severely disrupted, whereas the pathway underlying wanting (Figure 2.10) is left relatively intact. Treatments involve trying to boost the activity of dopamine in the neurons of the disrupted pathway but this is non-selective and has the side effect of increasing activity in the relatively intact wanting pathway.

These treatments sometimes have the unwanted side-effect of triggering addictive-like activities, amongst others gambling, shopping or
hypersexuality (Mendez and Shapira, 2011; Politis et al., 2013). Hypersexuality is mainly, if not exclusively, a male phenomenon, whereas binge
eating is predominantly female. Sometimes treatments boost the desire
for conventional sexual behaviour, as in making excessive demands on
a partner or can even trigger sexual desires of a novel form. Again the
evidence points to activation of a dopaminergic pathway common to a
number of activities. The increased motivation is specific to one or two
heightened activities, such as sex or gambling or both together, rather
than being a general elevation in wanting (Politis et al., 2013). Therefore heightened dopamine activity appears to lock into interaction with
a particular incentive(s) to produce the specific wanting. The incentive
might well have been one of importance to the individual prior to the
onset of the disorder.

Consider the case of a 64-year-old retired steelworker in Sheffield,
who was treated with the dopamine-boosting substance, L-Dopa (Harvey,
1988, p. 834):

> a young female patient, whom he hardly knew, showed the staff a lurid
> letter he had sent her in which he made her the object of his fantasised
> sexual activities . . . This was most unexpected since his mood was still
> sombre and at times tearful . . . he had also started making nocturnal
> visits to a 12-year-old neighbourhood girl.

In a study of patients treated with dopamine-boosting drugs in Rochester,
Minnesota, a 52-year-old man (Klos et al., 2005, p. 383):

> began buying pornography tapes and admitted to recent extramarital
> affairs. He denied having any prior interest in pornography. In addi-
> tion to the pathological hypersexuality, he started gambling, losing
> hundreds of thousands of dollars, intensified his smoking habit from
> one to two packs per day, and reported hyperphagia with weight gain
> of 50lb in 6 months.

A 54-year-old-man (p. 384):

> propositioned his daughter's friend for sex in return for money to relieve
> her financial difficulties. In addition, he requested that his son and
> daughter-in-law 'form a threesome'.

A 59-year-old patient in Los Angeles described (Mendez and Shapira, 2011, p. 1095):

> constantly seeking sexual gratification including going to massage parlours and spending a great deal of money on prostitutes. He began downloading pornography from the Internet, and although not previously known to be sexually interested in children, became especially interested in child pornography.

Behaviour normalized with the discontinuation of this treatment.

Those patients most likely to display addictive-like behaviours tend to be characterized by relatively high levels of impulsivity and novelty-seeking (Politis et al., 2013).

Neuroimaging reveals increased activity in the wanting pathway in medicated patients showing hypersexuality as compared to medicated Parkinson's patients not showing this (Politis et al., 2013). Increased desire does not appear immediately upon taking the medication but is a gradual process over repeated use, suggesting increasing incentive salience. In response to erotic images (about two-second presentations), patients with hypersexuality showed elevated activity in a number of brain regions,[19] including that in which the nucleus accumbens is located, as compared to non-hypersexual Parkinson's patients. The effect was specific to sexual images and not seen for other incentive presentations such as food. The *combination* of sexual stimulation and sensitized dopaminergic brain systems is necessary to see the enhanced effect in brain regions linked to desire. Although *wanting* was increased under these conditions, *liking* of the images did not increase in parallel. The rated level of sexual desire correlated with activity in the nucleus accumbens and in certain cortical regions.[20] From this, the researchers suggested that cortical activity formed the basis of the conscious experience of desire.

Schizophrenia

A distinction that corresponds to that between wanting and liking can be applied to people with schizophrenia and might prove relevant to their sexuality. Although they do not necessarily show a reduction in *liking* things, they typically show a reduction in *wanting* them. Gard et al. (2007) use the expressions coined by Klein (1987) of 'anticipatory pleasure' (the future-orientated pleasure associated with goal-directed activity towards gaining things) and 'consummatory pleasure' (the pleasure of engaging with desired things in the here and now). It is the former rather than the latter that is often disrupted. Anhedonia (loss of pleasure) has long been described as a characteristic of schizophrenia, but closer scrutiny suggests the necessity for such a qualification of the description.

Although there is some inconsistency, most evidence points to a reduction in sexual desire in schizophrenia (Kelly and Conley, 2004). However, there is indirect evidence that sexual pleasure is not decreased to the same degree. Thus, masturbation frequency is often high (Assalian et al., 2000), suggestive of a maintained capacity for pleasure. Occasionally, hypersexuality in the form of a large increase in masturbation frequency or public displays of sexuality is shown (Lukianowicz, 1963; Tracy et al., 1996), along with other behaviours suggestive of a lowering of inhibition. Arieti (1974, 1975) observed a change in the behaviour of patients with schizophrenia over the years. Prior to around 1960, patients rarely showed much expression of sexuality. Some years later, sexual 'acting-out', even exhibitionism in the hospital, had become common at the start of a schizophrenic episode.

It seems that high-level controls underlying anticipation and planning can be compromised (Andreasen, 1987) leaving the lower-level controls intact or even over-sensitive. An increase in a range of behaviours such as sexual behaviour and drinking water is sometimes seen (Luchins et al., 1992), suggesting removal of inhibition on certain activities that are triggered with little effortful cost. Conversely, an abnormally high perceived cost of gaining rewards associated with schizophrenia appears to deter goal-directed action (Gold et al., 2013). Evidence points to abnormalities in the activity of dopamine. There is a loss of sexual desire following treatment of schizophrenia with drugs that block the action of dopamine (Labbate, 2008).

Depression

Anhedonia is described as a defining characteristic of depression. Depression is commonly associated with a loss of sexual desire (Baldwin, 2001). There are various aspects of depression, and the distinction between anticipatory pleasure and consummatory pleasure (just described) applies here too (Sherdell et al., 2012). In healthy controls, consummatory pleasure predicts the amount of work people are prepared to perform to gain a desired object. However, in depressed people there is a fracture line; the amount of work performed to gain a reward, corresponding to anticipatory pleasure, might be low, while consummatory pleasure can be comparable to that of controls.

There is a small amount of evidence to suggest dissociation between anticipatory and consummatory measures of sexuality in depression. Kennedy et al. (1999) suggest that: 'depression is more likely to influence the early stages (desire and arousal) of sexual performance'. Klein (1987) described depressed patients who still enjoyed the pleasure of food and sex but made little effort to obtain it. Lukianowicz (1963) found only a slight reduction in masturbation frequency in depression but a drastic reduction in frequency of coitus.

Link to evolutionary psychology

The notion of 'encapsulated modules', sometimes fails to do justice to insights from a study of the brain. For example, Cosmides and Tooby (1995) argue:

> There is simply no uniform element in sex, eating, drinking, staying warm (but not overheating), and so on, that could be used to build a general architecture[21] that could learn to accomplish these behaviours.

Contrary to this claim, there appears to be a common system based upon dopamine, which underlies all approach behaviours (Panksepp, 1982). A system of restraint might also be common to any behaviour. This might be a more parsimonious design than for each motivation to have dedicated approach and restraint processes. Cosmides and Tooby (1995, p. 58) argue:

> the 'sex drive' is a construct completely inadequate to cope with the structural richness of the factors involved in the differentiated sexual psychologies of males and females.

Drive is not a construct that is favoured in the present study, in agreement with Cosmides and Tooby. However, their conclusion, that there are totally different processes underlying sexual motivation in men and women, is not favoured here. Rather, it is suggested that there are different weights attached to some common neural processes. There appears to be more weight associated with inhibitory and attachment processes in women. Although there is a difference in the averages, there is nonetheless some overlap between genders concerning desired number of lifetime partners and desirability of casual sex (Simpson and Oriña, 2003). The characteristics that men and women regard as desirable in a partner show considerable overlap (Wilson, 1999). Differences between the sexes, rather than simply being the outcome of a genetically determined module, might, at least in part, arise from different developmental trajectories reflecting social norms (Baldwin and Baldwin, 1997).

Wanting is clearly linked to arousal and the consequences of sexual behaviour, the topic of the next two chapters.

In summary

- The approach system underlying the experience of sexual desire employs dopamine as a neurochemical.
- The expression 'incentive salience' refers to the automatic magnet-like pull of incentives.
- In addition, a goal-directed aspect of desire corresponds to conscious intentions.
- Hormones acting on the brain play a role in sensitizing desire.
- A number of disorders appear to exemplify the role of dopamine in desire.

NINE

AROUSAL

As everyone knows, ever since Eve forbidden fruit has always been the
most delectable.

(Casanova, 1798/1958, p. 90)

Evidence suggests that general arousal triggered by a range of non-sexual
events can sometimes spill over into sexual arousal. The chapter will
address the issue of the relationship between sexual arousal and sexual
desire. The chapter will consider first 'general arousal' and then more
specifically 'sexual arousal'.

Anecdotal evidence on general arousal and its spill-over

Basic principles

Some environments are said to be arousing, even some colours are given
this description, while other colours are described as relaxing (Apter,
2007). When humans seek to increase arousal, to find excitement, they
might go to a busy part of town or engage in a challenging and even
dangerous activity. By contrast, to decrease arousal, they might lie on a
tranquil beach. Such observations lead to the notion of an optimal level
of arousal and humans can try to bring their actual level towards this
optimum. People differ in their optimal levels; one person will commonly
seek sources of high arousal, while another will try to avoid them.

Much human behaviour seems to be explicable at least in part as
attempts to elevate a level of arousal (Apter, 2007). Methods range
from activities such as mountaineering and swimming with sharks, to the

socially undesirable, such as making bogus phone calls to the emergency services. Vandalism seems to be motivated by little more than trying to exert action to escape boredom. Other activities appear to have an intrinsic underlying motivation that can get locked into association with arousal. Exemplifying this second type would be a risky business deal or a crime such as bank-robbery. These are motivated in part by a desire to get money but excitement often appears to play an interacting role. A common feature of behaviour that elevates arousal seems to be an element of novelty, unpredictability and often danger, combined with transgression, even illegality.

There can be both pleasant and unpleasant arousal (Apter, 2007). Pleasant arousal is triggered by a range of desirable situations, including sexual behaviour, whereas unpleasant arousal is characterized as fear and anxiety. Apter observes that the bodily states of pleasant and unpleasant arousal overlap considerably, for example in both conditions heart rate accelerates.

The writer Graham Greene described his survival of Russian roulette as a young man (Greene, 1971, p. 128):

> My heart knocked in its cage, and life contained an infinite number of possibilities. It was like a young man's first successful experience of sex – as if among the Ashridge beeches I had passed the test of manhood... At fairly long intervals I found myself craving for the adrenalin drug, and I took the revolver with me when I returned to Oxford.

Unintended spill-over to sexual arousal

Ovid reported that witnessing the blood and gore of a gladiatorial combat enhanced the attraction that young men and women felt for each other. Numerous anecdotes suggest that what is forbidden sexually ('sexual taboos') can assume heightened attraction (Kronhausen and Kronhausen, 1967). For example, the Victorian writer Walter found it appealing to be intimate with someone of a 'lower class'. To Walter's class, it was taboo for a woman to adjust an item of clothing, such as a garter, in public. However, his female companions were prone to do this, which fired Walter sexually. Bertrand Russell, the philosopher, documented that the intensity of sexual passion of one of his affairs was enhanced by the experience of fear in the London blitz (Zillmann, 1984). A law-enforcement officer from Nevada reported (Apter, 2007, p. 120): 'My problem is that I get no thrill when I'm with a legal prostitute, so I find myself drifting over to the big city across the county line where prostitution is against the law. I realize that this is illegal and probably unsafe, but it seems to be the only way I can get any satisfaction.'

It appears that, by a revival of memory, fear can still be arousing years after the event. Hatfield and Rapson (1987, p.2 73) observed:

> J.R. a 50-year-old man, reports that when he was 18 and attending an elite Ivy League school, he dated a Smith[1] girl. He was sexually inexperienced. She was not. In the car, she began to touch him. He panicked. She said, incredulously: 'You've never had any experience have you?' Thirty years later, his dreams were still filled with the delicious sexual excitement of this arousing but terrifying experience.

Transformation of negative emotion into sexual desire can be illustrated by a scenario in which a promising date has been agreed but the individual fails to appear. Forty minutes go by, with rising levels of unpleasant emotion, alternating between anxiety/frustration and anger: 'Was she serious or just leading me on? Has there been an accident?' One hour late, the promising date materializes, harassed and full of apologies 'Terribly sorry. My mobile is not working and I was stuck in traffic.' My hunch is that the intensity of emotion would not drop suddenly to zero but would maintain its value and be redefined in terms of increased attraction.

Selecting an arousing sexual option

Commonly sexual desire appears to interact with general excitement-seeking. The human brain has the ability to fantasize about future prospects and their anticipated arousal value. The other side of the same coin is the ability to remember past situations of high arousal and compare one's current arousal level with what it was like back then. Examples of where the seeking of arousal gives amplification to sexual desire are many and span the range of its forms.

Apter (2007) writes (p. 120): 'The fact that a sexual act is also a sin can undoubtedly make it wickedly attractive to some people.' Much sexual interaction, starting with low-level flirting, has the dimensions of high levels of uncertainty and suspense – who knows the outcome? People in established relationships occasionally choose to have sex in places where there is some risk of detection, as on a beach or in a car. Of course, if all that fails, then seeking novel partners would appear to be an effective means of raising arousal.

Curiosity might be fitted to the notion of aiming to elevate arousal. A number of women in the survey of Meston and Buss (2009, p. 146) reported having sex out of curiosity, 'to see what sex was like with someone other than their current partners, act out a fantasy'. One reported:

> After I broke up with the first person that I had sex with, I wondered if sex with different people was dramatically different, so I had sex with another boy that I knew and . . . yeah, it was definitely different. (predominantly heterosexual woman, age 18; Meston and Buss, 2009)

Seeking a boost to arousal by breaking boundaries of conventionality is dramatically illustrated by such activities as voyeurism, frotteurism (uninvited rubbing of the body against another, a hazard for women on the Japanese subway system) and exhibitionism, to be described later.

That danger can trigger desire in certain women was evidenced by the presence of devoted and sexually aroused groupies at the trial of the serial sex-killer Richard Ramirez (Carlo, 2010). One reported (p. 291):

> It used to turn me on . . . he was so dangerous and so near . . .

Large amounts of fan-mail from eager women overseas were witnessed by prison guards, this not being an isolated case (Berry-Dee, 2003; Buss, 2005; O'Brien, 1985). The biographer of the Austrian serial killer Jack Unterweger speculated that the attraction that women showed towards him was in large part due to the sense of danger that he triggered (Leake, 2007). A report of his trial describes some twenty adoring women in the courtroom.

The forbidden seems to be a crucial element in the sexual turn-on of some people, characterized by Doidge (2007) with the term 'perversion', where such individuals (p. 124):

> often celebrate and idealize humiliation, hostility, defiance, the forbidden, the furtive, the lusciously sinful, and the breaking of taboos; they feel special for not being merely 'normal'. These 'transgressive' or defiant attitudes are essential for the enjoyment of perversion.

For some, physical pain can lower desire and sexual performance, whereas for others it can increase sexual desire. Which of these effects it has depends in part upon earlier experience of pain (Ford and Beach, 1951). Cultural factors play a role here; where a society traditionally sees a certain amount of pain (e.g. from scratching and biting) as being an integral part of the sexual act, then the individual is more likely to exploit pain in the service of sexual arousal. For individuals in other cultures, pain will tend to be a turn-off. This again points to the central role of learning in sexual desire and arousal.

Sexual arousal, experimental evidence and theories

General principles

What do hard physical exertion, genital/sexual arousal and negative emotions such as anger (described later) and fear have in common? They all activate the sympathetic branch of the autonomic nervous system (ANS) (Zillmann, 1986).[2] Thereby, they also share much of the underlying bodily reaction, for example elevated heart rate, adrenalin secretion and blood pressure (Kinsey et al., 1953; Zillmann, 1984, 1986).[3]

An emotion such as fear can sometimes *enhance* sexual arousal, since the arousal of the ANS that it triggers becomes available to sexual arousal (Barlow, 1986). Even simultaneously with experiencing fear, this effect can sometimes be seen. Also, autonomic arousal, such as that induced by vigorous exercise or fear, does not dissipate immediately when such triggers are removed, so it is potentially available to enhance later sexual attraction (Zillmann, 1984). Murstein (1986, p. 108) concluded:

> All in all, it appears that men aroused by a neutral stimulus[4] can be influenced to misattribute the source of arousal if the salience of the neutral arousal is minimized and the salience of cues regarding the attractiveness of the target is maximized.

Reciprocally, consider when the triggers for anger are present. If any arousal arising from an immediately preceding sexual stimulus or from physical exertion is still present, this can contribute to anger (Zillmann, 1986).

People tend to make sense of their bodily reaction by labelling it in terms of its most likely cause. Where there is ambiguity, they might misperceive the cause of their arousal. To what the subjective arousal is attributed depends in part on the time interval between the arousal trigger and the attribution process. If this is short, attribution is made to the correct stimulus, a bit longer and it is sometimes made to some other candidate, but if left too long arousal dissipates and there is no effect of the initial arousal (Zillmann, 1984, 1986).

Arousal induced by physical exertion, humour or exposure to erotic stimulation tends to make an attractive partner still more attractive but an unattractive partner still more unattractive (White et al., 1981). Arousal is interpreted in terms of the available stimulus. Following a bout of strenuous exercise with obvious cues such as heavy breathing still present, arousal is likely to be attributed correctly to the exercise. A bit later, if sexual cues are present the arousal actually arising from exercise can lock into interaction with the sexual cues and contribute to sexual desire.

Fear

An individual who takes a ride on a fear-evoking fairground amusement subsequently tends to see an attractive person as being even more attractive. This is unless the aroused individual has correctly attributed their heightened arousal to the ride (Zillmann, 1984). Laboratory experimentation indicates that under some conditions a prior experience of anxiety can be followed by increased genital arousal (Hoon et al., 1977).

A study in Vancouver, known as the 'rope bridge experiment' (Dutton and Aron, 1974), is a classic of social psychology but must surely rank amongst psychology's more eccentric designs. The researchers wondered whether the bodily arousal associated with a naturally induced fear would increase the attraction felt for another person. So, they located a 450-foot-long suspension bridge, constructed of wooden boards attached to wire cables, that crossed the Capilano River. What were described as its 'arousal-inducing features' included a tendency to sway and wobble, which created the impression that the unwitting participants were about to fall 230 feet to rocks below. It is easy to imagine that this would be fear-inducing: it certainly is even for the present author at a safe distance.

A female confederate of the experimenters approached young males making the crossing and asked for their participation in a study. Subsequently, sexual themes appeared in their interpretation of a picture and they tended to contact the confederate after this. The suggestion is that the fear increased their attraction for her. The control condition was to do the same thing with males crossing a firm and stable bridge just 10 feet above a stream and was associated, it would seem, with lower sexual motivation. Fisher (2004) suggests that the men crossing the rope bridge might have had a surge of dopamine activation.

The experiment has provoked controversy. The result is compatible with the authors' conclusion but so can it be fitted to other interpretations. Any woman sufficiently courageous and risk-seeking to cross such a bridge might have been thought to be adventurous and therefore an interesting contact. It might have been that the sight of the woman served to reduce anxiety (Kenrick and Cialdini, 1977).

What is sexual arousal?

Anyone who has experienced sexual arousal knows something about it, but how is it to be defined and measured exactly? This has proven problematic. At least three different types of definitions have been proposed:

- Sexual arousal is the same as sexual desire, in which case we would hardly need two words to describe the same thing. Sachs (2000) argues persuasively that arousal and desire are distinct processes but with reciprocal excitatory links ('strong positive feedback') between them.
- Sexual arousal is the reaction of the genitals, in terms of the amount of blood flowing there. Genital swelling is known as 'vasocongestion', perhaps not the most erotic of terms. I shall use the possibly more palatable 'genital swelling'.
- The definition which is favoured here: sexual arousal is something situated between desire and the genital reaction, which both influences, and is influenced by, desire and the genital reaction.

Arousal is not the same as desire. There can be serious failures of arousal as indexed by the genital reaction even in people who report normal levels of desire (Nobre and Pinto-Gouveia, 2008). Conversely, asexuals can exhibit sexual arousal and pleasure but feel no sexual desire directed to another individual (Brotto and Yule, 2011). Women with persistent genital arousal disorder experience unwanted arousal in the absence of desire (Leiblum and Nathan, 2001). As described in Chapter 7, desire might trigger sexually-directed behaviour (contact-making, searching one's memories for erotic associations) even in the absence of any felt arousal. Bancroft (2009) speculated that sexual arousal appears first in development and desire is then shaped from this by linking arousal to attractive others. Arousal might be construed as normally providing a modulator between genital touch and the pleasure derived from this, which then links to desire. Arousal is also associated with preparing the body for action. This includes elevating heart rate and putting the muscles involved with the body into a state of readiness (Both et al., 2005).

Objective and subjective arousal

General features

For men, the objective measure of sexual arousal, the swelling of the penis, correlates well with their subjective feeling of sexual arousal. Although the correspondence between objective and subjective is not perfect, it is much closer in men than in women (Chivers and Bailey, 2005; Laan and Janssen, 2006). In women, the objective arousal response of the genitals is generally measured by inserting an apparatus into the vagina to measure the blood flowing there (Bancroft and Graham, 2011). In response to sexual stimuli, there is highly likely to be an increase in this blood flow, a reliable automatic reaction. Objective arousal tends to occur to a wide range of sexual stimuli, for example an erotic film, including even a film of pygmy chimpanzees copulating! Objective arousal is seen whether or not the woman finds the stimuli attractive and even when her subjective reaction is negative. Presumably, rather few women would opt for the sight of copulating chimpanzees as an aphrodisiac. Similarly, women occasionally report vaginal lubrication even when the feeling of subjective arousal is lacking (Laan and Janssen, 2006).

In both sexes, it appears that subjective sexual arousal, the *consciously felt* level, depends upon a combination of two sources of information (Janssen et al., 2000; Spiering and Everaerd, 2006):[5]

1 Automatic ('low-level') arousal, as reflected in the state of the genitals and other bodily reactions such as heart rate. This is, at first, a fast, non-conscious response, which is triggered by sexual stimuli (e.g. an erotic film) and is measured objectively as increased blood flow at the

genitals (Ponseti and Bosinski, 2010). Information on this bodily state is transmitted to the brain. If the bodily arousal persists at sufficient strength, the signal of it contributes to conscious awareness of arousal. Even when a sexual stimulus is presented visually for such a short duration that the person is unaware consciously of it, there is still some arousal response at the genitals (Both et al., 2008a; Ponseti and Bosinski, 2010; Spiering and Everaerd, 2006).

2 A subjective ('high-level') cognitive interpretation of the situation, a form of labelling – is the detected bodily condition specifically one of *sexual* arousal? Subjective arousal depends upon the meaning attached to the bodily state and the apparent sexual stimulus that triggers it. The subjective feeling calls upon attitudes, intentions, memories, beliefs and so on.

To summarize, a sexual stimulus triggers: (a) objective bodily arousal and (b) the search for an explanation for this arousal (Everaerd et al., 2000a). The same stimulus might tend to trigger arousal that is labelled as anger or fear, so the emergence of the sexual label is not inevitable. Learning is involved in linking external sexual stimuli and bodily sensations in order to yield subjective sexual arousal. The combined role of factors 1 and 2 above exemplifies how any attempt to allocate relative weights to which is most important in human sexuality, biology *or* social environment, is misguided. A biological factor is labelled in terms of social meaning.

According to one interpretation, sexual desire does not lead to sexual arousal but arousal can lead to sexual desire, depending upon an interpretation process (Laan and Both, 2008). Maybe it is safest to see a reciprocal relationship between desire and arousal, where each can influence the other, that is desire ↔ arousal.

Gender differences

How is the lack of correspondence between objective and subjective arousal in women to be explained? Is the signal from the genitals to the brain weaker in women, so that they are less well informed on the arousal of their genitals? This appears not to be so. A region of brain, the insula, is excited by bodily reactions including those triggered by erotic stimuli. It shows equal excitation to an erotic film in men and women (Karama et al., 2002). So, what can explain the gender difference in subjective arousal? As a general factor, women are less good than men at monitoring their bodily conditions (Pennebaker and Roberts, 1992).

A number of interacting processes could be implicated (Laan and Janssen, 2006). It might be that, although the signals reaching the brain are little different between men and women, there is a sex difference in the tendency of these signals to enter conscious processing. In addition to internal signals passing from the genitals to the brain, a boy's genital arousal is more evident externally, that is visually and in touching by the hands, than is a girl's. In Western countries, fewer girls than boys masturbate, which could be a learning experience linking genital sensations to erotic labelling (Laan and Janssen, 2006).

Laan and Both (2008) studied objective genital and subjective responses to two erotic films. Each contained depictions of explicit sexuality. One was 'female-friendly' and took the woman's perspective, including time spent showing the development of the relationship between the actors. The other was 'male-typical', with a focus upon the male perspective and the genitals. Males did not differ in their response to the two films. For women, the subjective feeling was greater for the 'woman-friendly' film as compared to the 'man-friendly', although the genital response was the same for both. Such studies suggest that pharmaceutical interventions to treat female sexual arousal disorders, which target the genitals, are likely to be disappointing. Rather, the emotional and social context would be better targeted.

A wide range of sexual stimuli that are presented so briefly that they do not reach conscious awareness nonetheless tend to trigger some genital arousal in women (Ponseti and Bosinski, 2010). For men, the range of stimuli having this effect is more limited than for women.

It appears that, whereas increased activity by the sympathetic branch of the autonomic nervous system increases a woman's sexual arousal as measured by vaginal blood flow, it decreases men's sexual arousal, as measured by erectile capacity (Meston and Buss, 2009) (though see also Chapter 20).

The role of learning and memory

Sexual arousal depends in part upon learning and this can operate at more than one level (Hoffmann, 2007; Spiering and Everaerd, 2006). Some learned associations operate quite automatically and the person might have no conscious awareness of their presence or role. However, conscious awareness that conditioning is being attempted can also enhance its strength.

In males, sexual arousal, as measured by the erectile reaction of the penis, can be conditioned. Plaud and Martini (1999) paired a neutral stimulus, an image of a penny jar, a number of times with an image of a sexually attractive female. After this, just presenting the image of a penny jar on its own triggered an erectile response.

A particular location or odour might in the past have been associated with arousal or conversely with fear and now acts on objective arousal below the level of conscious awareness. Hans Eysenck told a tale of a patient who was somewhat baffled by being sexually dysfunctional in a new partner's bedroom and it was found that the wallpaper was the culprit, because the paper's pattern had earlier been associated with an assault. True to form, Eysenck could not resist adding that the solution required the professional services not of a psychoanalyst but of a paperhanger. I think that the story was apocryphal but, even if so, it serves to make the point rather well!

By contrast, other memories can be tapped in a fully conscious mode and they might increase or decrease subjective sexual arousal. For example, fantasies of past sexual experiences might be exploited to enhance current arousal. Conversely, the conscious recall of such things as a memory of a pledge of fidelity, or of a recent advertisement on sexual health or of having forgotten to take the contraceptive pill might lower arousal.

When objective and subjective match

Objective and subjective factors might act in the same mutually reinforcing direction. Women commonly report the genital swelling with blood in such terms as 'tingling' and 'throbbing' and being sexually motivated to 'resolve the build-up'. This is sometimes described in such terms as an itch that needs scratching (Meston and Buss, 2009, p. 32). To some extent, the contractions of orgasm reverse this state of genital swelling. If orgasm does not occur and the swelling is not resolved, this can lead to an uncomfortable feeling of frustration.

When subjective is at odds with objective

In women, hard physical exercise, a trigger to increased sympathetic activity, increased objective measures of arousal triggered by an erotic film but not subjective arousal (Meston and Gorzalka, 1996).

If the meaning of the situation is negative, for example disapproval, in spite of there being a genital arousal response, subjective arousal can be negative. Under conditions of sexual dysfunction, the meaning-related information, involving say guilt or performance anxiety, could act in the opposite direction to the more automatic genital response. For women with sexual arousal disorder, the objective measure, the genital response to an erotic video, does not differ from that of control women but their subjective feeling is less positive or even negative (Both et al., 2011).

Victims of sexual assault, male and female, sometimes show objective sexual arousal even though subjectively they hate the experience (Levin and van Berlo, 2004). It has been speculated that this automatic genital reaction evolved as a means of protecting women from injury and infection during intercourse (Bancroft and Graham, 2011; Chivers and Bailey, 2005), though this might not explain its existence in males too. The arousal accompanying sexual assault might also be in part a spill-over of arousal from fear. Assailants sometimes wrongly claim that their victim's reaction shows evidence of consent rather than resistance.

A sample of men viewing a film depicting a rape scene showed relatively high levels of arousal but low levels of desire (Janssen et al., 2002).

Biological bases

A brain region, the insula, is responsive to bodily states such as fear, anger, sadness, happiness and disgust, as well as sexual arousal (Stoléru and Mouras, 2006). Pointing to overlap in brain regions embodying arousal, one study found that brain regions activated by recalling an erotic episode were similar to those excited when participants recalled their participation in a competitive event or success in a sporting challenge (Rauch et al., 1999). When sex hormones are deficient, this region fails to respond to erotic stimuli.

Therapeutic implications

Sexual behaviour is often accompanied by thoughts that automatically enter conscious awareness, triggered it would appear by the particular sexual/emotional state (Barlow, 1986; Nobre and Pinto-Gouveia, 2008). Some of these are erotic, of a kind that would be expected to increase arousal. Other thoughts concern personal inadequacies such as loss of physical attraction and performance failure, which might be expected to lower arousal. Not surprisingly, people suffering from sexual dysfunction report many more negative thoughts than do functioning controls. What causes what? Logically we might suppose that the direction of causation can be reciprocal (Barlow, 1986). This would give rise to either a virtuous circle of self-reinforcing sexual cues and arousal, or a vicious circle, for example the sexual context triggers intrusion of negative (failure-related) thoughts, which lower arousal and increase the intensity and frequency of the negative thoughts. A fear of performance failure, particularly on the part of men, can trigger a vicious circle, whereby it causes a focus of attention upon the genitals such as to lead to a self-fulfilling prophecy.

One might suppose that distraction (done experimentally by presenting information irrelevant to the sexual activity, such as listening to a non-erotic reading from a novel while watching an erotic movie) would lower the genital response to sexual stimuli. This is indeed the case for sexually functioning men (Barlow, 1986). They are assumed to have their focus normally on such things as the success of their performance and distraction draws them from this task. However, for men with erectile dysfunction, distraction leaves the genital response to sexual stimuli unaffected.

This makes sense in terms of levels of control. Their cognitive processing is assumed to be occupied normally with thoughts concerning the fear of performance failure. So, it seems that engaging this capacity does not impair things any further. In principle, it might even improve erectile capacity.

The link with desire

Sexual desire and subjective sexual arousal are often perceived in women to be closely connected (Graham, 2010). Disorders of the one correspond to a considerable extent with disorders of the other. So are desire and arousal the same thing? It could be worth distinguishing (a) arousal as the subjective awareness of bodily changes, not exclusively at the genitals, and (b) desire as outward directed goal-seeking that relates to the intention to engage in sexual action (Laan and Both, 2008), though desire does not invariably lead to the wish to have sex (Meana 2010, citing Regan and Berscheid). In such terms, desire would relate to subjective arousal but would not be synonymous with it. There is not invariably a sequence of first desire ('interest') and then arousal, since in some cases arousal is perceived first and desire felt secondly. Desire and genital arousal can lock into a virtuous circle, as two people escalate their sexual activity. Escalation is associated with increasing expectations of success, whereby attention to the genitals reinforces desire and the positive expectation (Wiegel et al., 2006).

Valins (1970) investigated the effect of changes in perceived heart rate on men's assessment of the attractiveness of women. Participants heard what they thought was their heart rate played over ear-phones. As this increased, so did perceived attractiveness. This suggests a cognitive process of making sense of the reaction, that is my heart rate has accelerated so she must be attractive.

The discussion now turns to the consequences derived from sexual behaviour.

In summary

- It is suggested that arousal lies between sexual desire and the reaction of the genitals.
- Subjective arousal should be distinguished from objective arousal as measured at the genitals.
- Particularly in women, there is dissociation between objective arousal, which is triggered automatically, and subjective arousal which involves meaning and goals.

TEN

THE CONSEQUENCES OF SEXUAL BEHAVIOUR
AND ASSOCIATED EXPECTATIONS

Nature has placed mankind under the governance of two sovereign
masters, pain and pleasure. It is for them alone to point out what we
ought to do, as well as to determine what we shall do.

(Jeremy Bentham, 1781/1988, p. 1)

Evidence suggests that they might not be quite the *sovereign* masters
that Bentham supposed, though pleasure and pain feature large in any
explanation of human sexuality.

Basics

Engaging in sexual behaviour has immediate consequences and these
are generally assumed to influence future sexuality in terms of desire
and the chances of sexual behaviour being repeated (Bancroft, 2009).
Consequences of behaviour that encourage us to repeat the behaviour are
known as 'reinforcers' (Chapter 2). Conversely, the consequences can be
such as to reduce the future tendency to repeat the behaviour, in which
case they would be described as 'punishing'.[1] Viewed in evolutionary
terms, reinforcement encourages people to repeat behaviour that has
served reproduction, whereas punishment persuades them to resist, stop,
take stock of the situation and change behaviour. This chapter looks
into the details of these immediate consequences of sexual behaviour and
their link to desire.

Subjectively felt pleasure and displeasure form an obvious feature of
the design of human sexuality. Pleasure normally accompanies behaviour
that is described as 'reinforcing', while displeasure is associated with

'punishment'. Pleasure plays a role in keeping behaviour going – it can create the desire to enhance pleasure by escalating the intensity of the activity and encourages a repeat in the future. The reader not familiar with the esoteric world of psychology might wonder why the terms 'reinforcement' and 'punishment' are used, when pleasure and pain would seem simpler. There are two reasons:

• The language is based upon behaviour and applies equally to humans and non-humans, since we cannot get verbal reports from non-humans on their experience of pleasure or pain.
• A consequence of behaviour might be reinforcing even though it is not pleasurable.[2]

Three features of sexual behaviour can be associated with such consequences:

• Approach behaviour
• Sexual contact
• Orgasm

The next three sections consider these.

Approach behaviour

As a general principle, pleasure is felt when things go according to desires and plans, whereas displeasure is felt when a plan is thwarted or things are significantly below expectations (Carver and Scheier, 1990; Panksepp, 1982). This obviously fits sexual behaviour. Being in a situation of perceived and desired sexual opportunity, detection of a move towards the goal is associated with pleasure, whereas a sign of rejection and movement away from the goal is associated with displeasure. In this stage, pleasure is derived from such things as making a date, receiving a confirmatory telephone call and the date arriving at the agreed location.

Pleasure usually requires not only progress towards a goal but a certain speed of progress being made. Depending upon the overall set of goals, particularly strong pleasure might be felt if progress is faster than expected or an obstacle to progress is suddenly removed. Of course, goals can conflict and this could explain people's experience of rapidly alternating positive and negative affect (Carver and Scheier, 1990). Movement towards one goal, for example a new sexual liaison, might bring pleasure but simultaneously the movement away from a higher goal of an 'ideal self', for example to maintain reserve, could bring displeasure.

In one study, young people gave readings of their levels of affect prior to and following sexual intercourse (Shrier et al., 2010). Positive affect increased in the hours prior to intercourse, presumably in anticipation of the hedonic event and stayed elevated for some hours afterwards. Negative affect was lowered for some hours after the event.

Successful movement towards a sexual goal appears to be a good example of a very general principle: having *control* of a situation is positively reinforcing. Under conditions of stress, exertion of control is associated with a boost in dopaminergic activity in the nucleus accumbens, whereas a failure of control in an aversive situation is associated with a lowering of dopaminergic activity (Cabib and Puglisi-Allegra, 2012). Such dopaminergic activation would be expected to reinforce the action, increasing the tendency to repeat it in the future. It might also be expected to blend with dopaminergic activation arising from sexual desire, enhancing the lure of the sexual incentive.

Engaging in sexual activity

I could never get my pleasure and satisfaction of *her* unless she got hers of me at the same time. (D. H. Lawrence, 1928/1993, p. 214)

Pleasure derives from kissing, and touching the other's body and intercourse, as well as, in the case of empathetic people, signs of pleasure in the partner. As Simon and Gagnon (1987, p. 370) note: 'The sexual actor must not only anticipate and orchestrate the behavior of the other(s), he or she must also anticipate and orchestrate the feelings communicated however uncertainly by that behavior.'

Whether stimulation arising from the erogenous zones of the body is felt as pleasurable depends not only upon the messages sent from these zones to the brain but also upon processing by the brain, indicating the presence of sexual desire. The pleasure of sexual stimulation by tactile contact depends, of course, not only on the signals set up by touch but also the context (Everaerd et al., 2000b). If desire is absent or lost, or arousal not yet sufficiently high, then the signal could be arising in the same way at the genitals but this might contribute to displeasure rather than pleasure. An obvious example is engaging in sexual behaviour under duress or simply out of a sense of duty. Similarly, for a heterosexual male, tactile stimulation by a female might well be very pleasurable, whereas by another male, it would probably be felt as aversive. Pleasure at this stage might be intrinsic to the activity or conditional upon the detection of an escalation of intensity.

Orgasm

This is, of course, something unique to sexual behaviour. It appears that orgasm is a powerful positive reinforcer, encouraging the individual to repeat the behaviour leading to it (Fisher, 1986). An obvious feature of orgasm is a sudden reduction of tension in the body and a return to a more normal state (Kinsey et al., 1948). A powerful orgasm would have the effect of consolidating desire, whereas, if the orgasm is substandard, failing to meet expectations, it might move the individual in the direction of aversion (Fisher, 1986). This emphasizes the role of expectations and interpretations. The more reward obtained from sexual behaviour, the higher the frequency of showing it (Ågmo, 2007). In some cases loss of desire (so-called hypoactive sexual desire) could arise from frustrated expectations, such as failure of orgasm. This can be situation-specific: a person might lose interest in a regular partner but find desire aroused by a different partner. A context such as a particular bedroom might set the scene for a loss of desire, whereas a change of environment revives it. The person with loss of desire can show actual aversion to particular sexual stimuli. Certain therapeutic techniques for loss of desire are based on the principle that any sexual interaction needs to result in reward for both partners. Ågmo sees all this as evidence in favour of an incentive motivation model.

Male orgasm is a powerful reward to encourage the male to persist until this occurs, thereby encouraging ejaculation and permitting fertilization. The function of female orgasm is not so obvious, which has led some to suggest that maybe it has no function and is just an evolutionary by-product. A function has been suggested in terms of (a) moving sperms upwards towards where they can meet the egg cell, (b) reinforcing sexual activity and (c) consolidating the pair bond. Another idea is that female orgasm triggers the male to ejaculate (Meston and Buss, 2009).

Biological bases of sexual pleasure

This subject can best be addressed in a broader context of pleasure, since the relevant experiments mainly involve feeding and drugs. The existence of dedicated brain mechanisms underlying pleasure is indicative of its role in evolution (Berridge and Kringelbach, 2013).

Dopamine is involved in the *wanting* phase of motivation (Chapter 8). This has been established in the context of pleasure reactions to food in the mouth. However, dopamine might also have a role in the pleasure derived from anticipating and achieving a goal (Klein, 1987), such as getting to a place where sexual contact may take place. We simply don't yet know. Some suggest that dopamine has a role in 'enthusiastic positive excitement' and 'euphoric engagement with the world' (Alcaro et al., 2007), which is compatible with the idea that dopamine mediates the pleasures associated with approaching and finally achieving a goal. As introduced in Chapter 8, dopamine levels increase in the phase of goal-directed behaviour leading to a goal and then decline when the goal is reached (Blackburn et al., 1992). This raises the possibility that a rise and then fall in dopamine level is felt as pleasurable.

Rather as with wanting, the brain regions that underlie liking are organized in a layered ('hierarchical') way (Berridge and Kringelbach, 2013). It appears that regions below the level of the cortex form a basis of the 'raw' experience of pleasure and may be common across a number of species (Chapter 2). One of these, the nucleus accumbens,[3] has already been described in the context of wanting. It has sub-regions dedicated to wanting and pleasure. Regions of the prefrontal cortex[4] also play a role in pleasure, probably via projections to the subcortical regions. The prefrontal cortex is expanded in humans relative to other species and thereby appears to contribute to the peculiarly human and meaning-related aspects of pleasure. It is said to 'encode' pleasure and the region's activity probably plays a role in the recall of past hedonic experiences. Much of the brain machinery of pleasure appears to serve various different pleasures (Berridge and Kringelbach, 2013). This would be relevant to the observation that some individuals take drugs such as cocaine to enhance sexual experience (Chapters 2 and 17).

From research on feeding, it appears that substances called 'opioids' are involved in the pleasure derived from, amongst other things, the taste of food. Opioids are the natural equivalents of the opiates, drugs such as heroin. These act in the sub-region of the nucleus accumbens termed a 'hedonic hot-spot', to mediate a range of pleasures (Berridge and Kringelbach, 2013). The fact that some people use masturbation as a means of gaining pain relief (Marchand, 1961) also suggests a basis in opioids.

Levels of the substance oxytocin in the blood increase during sexual activity and particularly at orgasm (Carmichael et al., 1994). Oxytocin could play a role in the pleasure of orgasm, as well as tending to inhibit immediately following sexual activity. Opioids are also simultaneously involved in orgasmic pleasure and post-orgasmic inhibition of further sexual activity (Georgiadis et al., 2012). Feedback to the brain from the muscular contractions that accompany orgasm in men and women might also be implicated in the intense pleasure as well as the satiety effect. The pleasure of sex can sometimes be used as a soothing balm as in post-conflict 'make-up sex' (Dewitte, 2012), which might owe something to oxytocin.

Link between wanting and arousal/liking

Usually pleasure and wanting are closely linked: we like what we want and we want what we like. It would be strange if things were otherwise. Pleasure tends to make the thing triggering the pleasure desired in the future. A possible basis of this is that opioids released during sexual activity sensitize the dopamine-based wanting system. If we can generalize from male rats to humans, when the consequences of sexual activity include ejaculation, durable changes occur in the brain's dopaminergic systems to increase future wanting of sex (Frohmader et al., 2010a). If humans are anything like rats, opioids released within the amygdala act to confer incentive salience on stimuli (Mahler and Berridge, 2012).

However, research strongly suggests that under some conditions, liking does not mirror wanting exactly (Robinson and Berridge, 1993). The research and evidence have mostly involved feeding and drug-taking, but there are a number of indications that a similar principle applies to sex. Even Peter Trachtenberg (1989, p. 81) reported: 'Sex no longer gave me anything more than the physical release of ejaculation.' Although somewhat anecdotal, there are reports that for many people their first experience of intercourse, even of orgasm, was not that great (Levin, 2006). However, this usually does not put them off for life, but rather wanting remains intense. It seems that a process of learning can be involved in forming an association between (a) sexual behaviour and orgasm and (b) pleasure.

A number of women, who are in long-term relationships report little desire but still enjoy sexual behaviour when it happens (Meana, 2010). The pleasure and arousal do not translate into a desire for more frequent sex. In sex therapy, the desire of the male is often much higher than that of the female. In this situation, men frequently cannot reconcile their partner's apparent liking of sex with their lack of desire to repeat the experience.

An example of a woman describing herself as 'asexual' illustrates this point (Brotto et al., 2010, p. 610):

> Even though it is very pleasurable and exciting while I am doing it, I have absolutely no anticipation for it at all. I have no interest or desire that would lead me towards that in the way that I do towards other activities that I enjoy.

It has been noted that while women can be as aroused by sexual stimuli as can men, they usually expend relatively little effort in gaining access to them and a smaller percentage report masturbating than is the case for men (Wallen, 1995). The argument that social prohibitions are responsible for this sex difference is hard to support. Men have traditionally been warned of the dire consequences of masturbation. Biblical prohibitions refer to the male. Since the 1970s, female masturbation has been advised as a part of sex therapy.

Sexual frustration

> All is useless. The desire for change seems invincible... My life is almost unbearable from unsatisfied lust. It is constantly on me, depresses me, and I must yield. (Walter, cited in Marcus, 1966, p. 96)

Sexual frustration in terms of goal failure

Apter (2007) distinguishes between acute frustrations, where the individual perceives that the obstacle can be overcome and where it is thereby arousing, and chronic frustrations, where the situation is perceived as impossible and long-term unhappiness can result. If the analysis of drug-taking by Tiffany (1990) can be extrapolated to sexual desire, cravings and urges will be felt particularly under two different circumstances: (a) when a plan of sexual engagement is thwarted, described as 'frustration'; and (b) when the individual is resisting temptation.

A cross-cultural dimension

> If this chronic state of sexual deprivation on the part of most men (and not a few women as well) has not been more acute in the past, it is largely because the social control of sexual stimuli, i.e. censorship in its various forms, has been so severe as to keep erotic stimulation to a minimum. Likewise, economic conditions have, until now, made the struggle for survival so keen and desperate that only the 'leisured classes' have ever had at their disposal the time, means, and energy for a fuller sex life. This kind of socio-economic picture is however rapidly changing in our times, so that among the industrialised and economically developed countries larger and larger groups of people are beginning to show an interest in such 'luxuries' as a sane and happy sex life. As this sort of change is taking place on a large scale, the sense of sexual frustration will increase painfully for those who had previously plenty of other things to worry about – such as how to obtain the wherewithal for the most basic needs like food, clothing, and shelter, to say nothing of the threat to physical survival itself owing to wars, revolutions, natural catastrophes, etc. (Kronhausen and Kronhausen, 1967, p. 181)

Would we expect sexual frustration to be lowest in a sexually permissive society? Obviously, the more opportunity available, the lower will be the frustration level amongst those engaging in sexual behaviour. But this cannot be the whole picture because, no matter how permissive the society, there will be a proportion of the population who get left out or who perceive themselves to have been left out. There is reason to believe that, amongst this section, frustration will actually be *higher* in

186 • How Sexual Desire Works

a permissive society and possibly rape *more* frequent (Chappell et al., 1971). A comparison of US cities offers some tentative support to this. The authors use the following argument concerning the self-image of a rejected male (p. 176):

> in a non-permissive setting . . . it is the setting itself that is responsible for any sexual setback he suffers. Women are inhibited, church rules are too oppressive, parents too strict, or laws too stringent – any of these conditions may be used to 'explain' an inability to achieve a desired sexual goal. In the permissive setting, the rejected male becomes more hard-pressed to interpret his rejection.

The authors suggest that a man who found himself repeatedly rejected in the gay bathhouses and clubs in pre-AIDS San Francisco would have little explanation except his own lack of attraction. Presumably, the same might be argued for a couple visiting a swinging club. There is probably an additional factor powerfully at work too, as follows. People tend to compare their rewards in life with those of others. For example, a pay rise of £1,000 when others get nothing seems to bring more pleasure than one of £2,000 when others receive £2,500. In a permissive society there will be much more to trigger sexual envy than in a non-permissive society.

Do people in what we might call 'sexually repressed' societies actually suffer in any way? Some have speculated that the answer is 'no', unless they come into contact with societies that have more liberal standards and they are able to put their own situation into context (Zillmann, 1984).

Frustration and the brain

Rage and the expectation of reward appear to be antagonistic emotions (Panksepp, 1982). Panksepp suggested that a thwarted expectation is the trigger to rage. Abler et al. (2005) reasoned that frustration might have features in common with social exclusion. Looking at different regions of the brain and their activity could give insights into frustration and its possible association with other negative emotions. In one study, participants experienced exclusion from a 'virtual game' while having their brains scanned (Eisenberger, 2012). Activation was found in brain regions normally associated with physical pain. Not surprisingly, it is even more difficult, if not impossible, to perform realistic studies on sexual frustration. Therefore, it is necessary to extrapolate based upon studies of the frustration involved in not attaining other desirable goals. Abler et al., looked at participants who were frustrated in not obtaining financial reward in an experiment where such reward was expected. Their brains were scanned to see changes in activity in different regions triggered by the experience of not getting reward. The expectation of a high monetary reward was associated with excitation of the ventral striatum and the right insula. There was a suppression of activity in the ventral striatum when an expected reward failed to materialize.

For some, the quest for enhanced pleasure and the avoidance of frustration leads logically to a search for novelty, the topic of the next chapter.

In summary

- Sexual pleasure arises from a move towards a goal, sexual contact and, most powerfully, orgasm.
- Dopamine might be involved in the pleasure of successful approach towards a sexual goal.
- Opioids and oxytocin are likely candidates as substances forming the basis of the pleasure of sexual action.
- The strength of sexual wanting is not necessarily matched by an equal strength of sexual liking.
- Sexual frustration has something in common with social exclusion.

ELEVEN

SEXUAL FAMILIARITY AND NOVELTY

'I know how to love best. I am your servant, your concubine! You are
my king, my idol! You are good, you are beautiful, you are clever, you
are strong!'

He had heard so often these things said that they did not strike him as
original. Emma was like all his mistresses, and the charm of novelty,
gradually falling away like a garment . . . "[1]
(Gustave Flaubert, 1856/2010, p. 317)

If it is true that variety is essential for the maintenance of a normal,
active sex life – at least for a substantial majority of the male population
and for a certain proportion of females as well – then our social ideals
of life-long enforced monogamy and sexual exclusivism are contrary
to nature and a constantly festering source of cultural and individual
pathology and discontent. Yet, this need for variety is exactly what all
the scientific evidence from both human and animal studies seems to
indicate beyond any reasonable doubt."
(Kronhausen and Kronhausen, 1967, p. 180)

Basic principles

As a general principle applicable across various sexual and non-sexual
situations, a wide range of species, for example rats, monkeys and humans,
show a preference for some novelty (Bardo et al., 1996). That is to say, the
brain is particularly sensitive to *change* in what arrives at the sense organs
relative to an unchanging pattern of stimulation. In experiments, animals
work to achieve change in their physical environment, for example by

pressing a lever to alter the illumination or gaining access to a visual image.

In various species, humans included, novelty can be a powerful stimulus to sexual desire and points to the role of the external incentive. Desire can be re-ignited in a so-called 'sexually satiated' animal, human or non-human, when a new partner appears (Schein and Hale, 1965). Arousal by novelty suggests that motivation arises from an interaction between an internal factor, now re-sensitized, and the incentive.

The search for novelty is an obvious means of sensation-seeking (Chapter 9). Humans, particularly those described as 'sensation-seekers' tend to be attracted to sexual variety, as well as to thrill-seeking in other areas such as dangerous sports and complex music such as jazz (Zucker-man, 1990). A good example of this is the actor Errol Flynn, who led a life largely devoted to risky adventure-seeking, hard drinking and wom-anizing. In terms of different personality types, extraverts are found to be more novelty-seeking than introverts, possibly therefore trying to correct intolerable levels of boredom (Gosselin and Wilson, 1980).

Novelty is not defined in terms of the qualities of the new partner as such – he or she need possess no intrinsically high attraction value. Rather, the property is a function of the new partner set in the context of a nervous system that is 'satiated' by the familiar partner. The features of the novel partner deviate from those of any established partner. In addition to different sensory features, humans know consciously that they are dealing with a different person, who transcends the sum of individual novel features.

A general tendency for humans to seek novelty could have proven advantageous in our evolution, in motivating the exploration of new ter-ritory, finding new foods and new sexual partners. However, it also comes at some cost, namely that of confronting new sources of danger. Some kind of compromise between extreme novelty-seeking and its absence could have proven to be the optimal solution (Bardo et al., 1996).

These days, with life-long monogamous mating being a moral 'norm', an attraction to novelty could seem puzzling. However, the current sit-uation might not reflect what was normal in earlier evolution. Fisher (2004, p. 134) proposes that ancestral humans might have formed a bond with a mate 'only long enough to rear a single child through infancy – about four years'. In group living, it could then have proven genetically advantageous to 'divorce' and find another partner.

Humans compared with other species

Novelty in non-humans

The role of novelty is called the 'Coolidge effect', after US President Calvin Coolidge. The story, which might be apocryphal, has connotations that are anything but Calvinist and will hopefully bear one more repetition.

President and First Lady Coolidge made a visit to a farm. On arrival, they were allocated to separate tours. Mrs Coolidge noticed a cockerel that was particularly sexually active and asked whether he was able to maintain such performance all day. 'Yes, indeed', replied the guide. Mrs Coolidge answered 'So, point that out to the President.' When the President got to this point, the technician directed the President's attention to the sexual prowess of the cockerel. 'Does the cockerel mount the same hen all the time?' asked Coolidge. 'Oh, no, he mounts a different hen every time', replied the technician. To which President Coolidge gave the response that immortalized him in behavioural science: 'You tell that to Mrs Coolidge!'

The adaptive value of the Coolidge effect is clear in terms of the spread of the male's genes. Traditionally, most emphasis has been placed upon the effect in males, but there is one report that female rats are excited by a novel male (Ågmo, 2007). Hrdy (1981) notes the arousal of sexual desire by novelty (i.e. a partner other than the mate) in females of a variety of non-human primate species, such as marmosets. What function could it serve?

Hrdy suggests several possibilities. First, there is sperm competition. If the present mate is substandard, it might not be good to be attached exclusively to him. Second, there is the issue of confusion of paternity. If a female mates with several males, each of them might be the father of any future offspring. Hence, assuming that they can remember their sexual encounter, each might offer some minimal level of support, for example protection and food-sharing or at least not showing aggression. Hrdy speculates that there is not an abrupt transition between non-human and human primates. Rather, there is continuity. Thirdly, non-reproductive mating could offer the female an opportunity to assess the male as a viable partner and potential father, for example to assess his dominance. She could trigger competition between males as part of such assessment.

Novel males can revive sexual motivation even in females who are already pregnant. Hrdy describes (1981, p. 144):

> an aggressive sexuality – by human standards, nymphomaniac – which goes far beyond the necessary minimum for ensuring insemination.

Link to humans

Kinsey et al. (1948, p. 589) concluded:

> that the human male would be promiscuous in his choice of partners throughout the whole of his life if there were no social restrictions.

A number of males in their study remarked that though they desired relationships outside the marriage, they would always resist this on moral and social grounds. By contrast, the researchers marshalled evidence that female desire was much less concerned with variety, including the case of female homosexuality. They continued (p. 589):

> there are a great many human females who find it incomprehensible that so many human males should look for sexual relations with women other than their wives.

Given women's relative sexual modesty, Hrdy reflects on earlier evolution characterized by a more assertive sexuality and asks (1981, p. 176):

> Must we assume that behaviour which was once adaptive is no longer adaptive? How has women's sexuality changed in the intervening five million years or so since we shared an ancestor in common with the chimpanzees?

With concealed ovulation that occurs in human females, for much of the cycle suitors have no way of assessing when fertilization is possible and hence the female can keep them 'hanging on'.

A focus on peculiarly human features

General principles

Consider the enormous variety in what different people desire sexually. One person seeks an endless supply of partners, whereas another is perfectly happy with life-long monogamy and is shocked by any suggestion of extramarital sex. For some, the desire for variety is such that sexual behaviour becomes addictive, 'out of control', whereas most manage to integrate their sexual activities within the remainder of their lives.

As just noted, although novelty plays a role in both sexes, its effects appear to be stronger in men. The gay scene of San Francisco in the 1970s–1980s, prior to awareness of AIDS, can be used to exemplify sex differences in arousal by novelty. It also avoids the complications inherent in heterosexual sex (i.e. different willingness by men and women to engage in casual sex). Whereas a number of gay men achieved astronomically high numbers of partners, lesbians were modest in their number of partners. Gay men commonly cruise in the search for casual sex partners, whereas gay women rarely do so (Buss, 2003).

Novelty plays a differential role even in advance planning of sexual activity. In terms of desired variety of partners, a study by Miller and Fishkin found a large difference between the genders (Buss, 2003). Only female resistance stands as a brake on the expression of male desire for novelty. Novelty also plays a role in pornography, directed primarily to males.

The brain has the property that, for many men and women, desire can be especially aroused by some degree of uncertainty and novelty. It can be that chance and totally unexpected glance or brushing of arms against each other that sets off desire at high intensity. Of course, too much novelty or uncertainty might trigger fear rather than desire, so there is an optimal level. These observations prompt the search for regions of the brain that are particularly sensitive to these factors. Investigators now have some promising leads involving dopamine, which they can link to evolutionary considerations: why has evolution produced a brain with such sensitivity?

When a relationship is fresh, not only is there novelty as such but the novelty triggers each partner to try harder, in terms of gestures, dress and grooming, and so on. So, a virtuous circle arises. Alas, over the years, a virtuous circle can easily turn into a vicious one, with loss of desire triggering a reduction in the effort invested in trying to be attractive to the partner.

Long-term relationships

Loss of sexual desire is an important contribution to dissatisfaction within marriage or other long-term partnerships. In one sample of women, loss of desire corresponded to loss of novelty (Sims and Meana, 2010). Desire was no longer spontaneous but neither was it triggered externally by their husbands.

Another factor could be the generation over time of new associations between the sexual partner and consequences of contact. At first, the partner would be enjoyed in a context of novelty and excitement, for example dating and holidays together. Then with the arrival of a mortgage, children and the added need for washing of clothes and dishes, new associations are formed, those with the mundane, if not distressing, chores of everyday life. An incentive model would suggest where possible the introduction of novelty into any 'satiated relationship', for example by changing locations of sexual activity, routines, dress, appearance or by joint viewing of erotic material. Surprisingly, a study in Germany found that, within a stable relationship, sexual desire declined more strongly in women than in men (Klusmann, 2002). The author could not explain this, since the Coolidge effect was thought to apply more to males than females.

A contribution towards the loss of sexual desire in the elderly who are in long-term relationships is thought to be satiation with the familiar after extensive repetition of the same situation and loss of the anticipation of sexual variety (Kinsey et al., 1948). This is in addition to any bodily changes that accompany the ageing process. Change can often revive a satiated desire.

The intensity of desire felt for a regular partner can decline over time, although the person would ideally wish to maintain a high level of desire.

This change does not simply depend upon increasing age, so what does it depend upon? Consider the following:

> When you've been married for awhile, let's face it – sex just isn't that exciting anymore. It's all so predictable. Even when we try to be 'spontaneous' it's almost comical because I can predict his every move. (Heterosexual woman, age 48 years; Meston and Buss, 2009, p. 133)

Sims and Meana (2010) asked women who had lost desire for their husbands to explain why they thought that this had happened. The predominant reasons given were (p. 364):

> *institutionalization of the relationship, over-familiarity* with one's partner, and the *de-sexualization of roles* in their relationship.

In other words, sex had become predictable and habitual, done largely out of a sense of duty. Fatigue, household chores and the presence of children at home were commonly given as reasons for declining desire. Another factor that emerged was '*lack of transgression in married life*'. The earlier ingredient of risk and uncertainty had been removed, except that associated with children intruding into the bedroom, hardly an aphrodisiac! Consider how this was expressed by women in the study:

> There is no longer that first kiss or that first touch. I think that's why a lot of people cheat. (34-year-old woman)

> Now it's the same guy and there is no novelty anymore. (33-year-old woman)

The authors wrote (p. 376):

> The results of this study question the extent to which women's sexual desire depends on commitment, closeness, and intimacy. These relational qualities may be necessary for some women's desire, but our results indicate that they are hardly sufficient for others. Many of the women in our sample bemoaned the company and security of marriage as *anaphrodisiacs*.

Some women gave loss of romance as a reason for the decline in desire, even though they all reported happy marriages. However, the romance related to a time when they had first met their husbands, presumably when novelty and uncertainty were at their height. The authors suggest that women's sexual desire is something much more heterogeneous than was hitherto thought to be the case. Although all the women studied would be described by some as suffering from 'hypoactive desire disorder', this needs qualification. Many said that a change of partner would rekindle their flagging desire. Hence, a unitary expression such as 'sexual drive' as some purely internal factor divorced from social context would obviously be misleading. The authors suggest the possible value of finding an optimal location on a scale between, at one extreme, no commitment and, at the other, such commitment as leads to total predictability and boredom.

Sims and Meana (2010, p. 378) conclude:

> revisions to a reductionist view of women's sexual desire as a pure drive, divorced from its relational context, were long overdue. It is important, however, to remain mindful to not overcorrect and assume that women's sexual desire is exclusively contingent on intimacy and loving committed relationships.

Ways of achieving novelty

A large family circle

According to family circumstances, there might be little need to venture beyond the home to find sexual novelty. This is exemplified by the Biblical King Solomon, who presumably would have experienced minimal problems with boredom: 'And he had seven hundred wives, princesses, and three hundred concubines' (1 Kings 11:3).

Desire outside the established bond

Flirting by people already in an established pair-bond makes good functional sense even though it can come with some risks (Buss, 2005). By showing interest, a person is in a sense playing safe (cultivating a 'back-up') in that the target of the gesture sees a possible future partner. This could come in handy if the established bond is broken as in bereavement or being abandoned.

Married women tend to seek affairs at times of marital disharmony, whereas men in even happy relationships tend more often than women to seek affairs (Buss, 2003). This fits ideas on the greater interaction of attachment and sexual desire in women as compared to men (Chapter 15).

A survey in Holland showed that, when a person's power increased, as exemplified by the bosses of multinational companies, so did their tendency to commit adultery and their wish to do so (Lammers et al., 2011). This was equally true of men and women. Clearly there could be many factors implicated, such as increased attractiveness and opportunities that come with higher status. It might also be indicative of an interaction between sexual desire and power/dominance (Chapter 15).

Buss (2005) proposes the following logic. Women are often able to secure matings with males who are more attractive than their partners and thereby able to link up with genes that help to encode for attractive offspring.

Co-marital and orgiastic sex

Orgiastic sex can be better understood in terms of the provision of novelty, variety and the forbidden. Some sex workers have always offered their services to males for this (of course, at a price!) and orgies have always formed a very common image in pornography.

Consider also consensual 'extramarital' sex, with which obtaining variety seems to be at centre-stage. Although a minority taste, there is a significant number of married couples who engage in consensual 'extra-pair activities', sometimes termed 'co-marital sex' and 'swinging'. This ranges from the couple parting to different bedrooms, through seeking an extra male, female or couple to join the pair. Participants commonly report deriving pleasure from watching their partner having sex with another person. Later fantasies are often fuelled by such imagery.

One of the principal reasons given for swinging is to obtain sexual novelty and thereby to revitalize an existing relationship (Stephenson, 1973). Another is to feel a buzz by engaging in the forbidden (Jenks, 1998).

The basis in the brain

Zillmann (1986, p. 193) relates the phenomenon of habituation to the loss of arousal of the sympathetic branch of the autonomic nervous system with repeated exposure to the same stimulus and suggests:

> that loss of libido is often nothing less and nothing more than excita-
> tory habituation to sexual stimuli ... The characteristic comment of
> sexually dissatisfied intimates who are breaking up – namely, that 'the
> excitement has gone' out of their relationship – epitomizes the sug-
> gested mechanics. Despite potentially unimpaired genital functioning,
> and frequently because of it, unexcited sexual activities are deemed
> drab and unfulfilling.

Guilt associated with infidelity might, according to Zillmann, be expected
to boost arousal level.

The powerful role of novelty is difficult to reconcile with the notion
that desire is based upon an autonomous intrinsic sexual drive. Rather,
novelty can be better accommodated under the kind of dopamine-based
incentive principles developed here, since evidence points to dopamine
activity being sensitive to novelty.

Novelty appears to be a means of boosting activity in the dopaminergic pathway that projects to the nucleus accumbens (Bardo et al., 1996).
An unexpected reward is particularly strongly excitatory (Panksepp and
Moskal, 2008). Repetition of stimulation and prediction of the response
shifts control away from this pathway and towards brain processes underlying habit (Alcaro et al., 2007). There are differences between animals,
with strong novelty-seekers also being those most ready to self-administer
drugs.

Differences in novelty-seeking and drug-taking in humans, as with
rats, are in part the result of genetic differences between individuals.
Differences between humans in number of sexual partners have been
investigated and linked to genetically based differences in dopaminergic
systems (Guo et al., 2007).[2] One genetic difference[3] was associated with
the number of sex partners in young men but not in young women. The
researchers suggested that social differences could mask the influence
of this particular genetic difference in women. Men with high levels of
testosterone tend to show higher levels of sensation-seeking and have
more extramarital sexual relations than those with lower levels (Booth
and Dabbs, 1993). Testosterone exerts a role via dopaminergic systems.

For sexual behaviour, there are at least two aspects of novelty and both
would be expected to reinforce their effects in terms of the activation

of dopamine and thereby wanting. First, there is the novelty of sensory features; those of the novel potential partner differ from those of any established partner. Secondly, there is the uncertainty of the reaction of the novel partner, the moves being unpredictable.

Let us contrast two extreme cases. First, there is that of meeting someone attractive but totally unavailable, for example someone showing no interest and who is carefully guarded by a jealous partner. The calculated probability of success might be zero. Secondly, there is the case of a long-established partner, with whom sexual behaviour follows a regular and predictable sequence. Here the probability of success might be 100 per cent or close, often with the sequence of moves and reactions highly predictable. Control has shifted to a more automatic mode (Anselme, 2010). If we extrapolate from studies on non-humans, neither a 0 per cent nor a 100 per cent estimate of success in obtaining reward is a powerful trigger to dopamine release (Anselme, 2010). Rather, the strong trigger is somewhere between these extremes, with a maximum at 50 per cent, where uncertainty is at its maximum. A similar logic applies to the addictive lure of gambling, where the pay-off is uncertain.

The quest for novelty and attempts to resist it raise the issue of inhibition, the topic of the next chapter.

In summary

- The term 'Coolidge effect' refers to an increase in sexual desire as a result of the appearance of a novel partner.
- Human ingenuity finds various ways of exploiting the capacity for such elevated arousal.
- The effect appears to involve a heightened level of activity by dopamine systems in the brain.

TWELVE

INHIBITION, CONFLICT AND TEMPTATION

But I see another law in my members, warring against the law of my mind, and bringing me into captivity to the law of sin which is in my members.

(St Paul's Epistle to the Romans 7: 23)

The nature of inhibition

The means by which desire is inhibited ('restrained') represent an important feature of 'how desire works' and will be explored here. St Paul describes one form of conflict: that between the will and desire. Throughout the ages, prohibitions and disapproval of 'inappropriate desire' and its expression seem as evident as desire itself.

Social harmony requires that all societies have curbs on sexual behaviour, whether of an aesthetic, legal, cultural, religious or moral nature. Some potential inhibitors of sexual desire, such as public censure, have eased with more relaxed attitudes. However, jealousy, anger and disgust over what are judged to be unacceptable desires in others are still universal. For some, the existence of desire and its inhibition represent proverbial conflict.

The popular press expose illicit, excessive, dangerous or unconventional desire, where the implicit assumption is that the guilty party should have known better and have exerted inhibition. A favourite target is when behaviour violates fidelity or threatens national security, or both. A person, or society, might wish to increase inhibition, as in restraining personally harmful excesses or socially unacceptable and illegal behaviour. By contrast, others might feel excessively inhibited in their expression of

199

sexual desire, though they rarely make the headlines. They might wish to lower inhibition, as in trying to overcome excessive and unwanted restraints. Erectile disorder caused by excessive worry about performance can be mediated by excessive levels of inhibition (Janssen and Bancroft, 2007).

Inhibition is not the same as absence of excitation (Janssen and Bancroft, 2007). Rather, inhibition is an *active* process, pulling in the opposite direction to excitation. Inhibition either lowers desire or lowers the chances that it will lead to sexual behaviour. This chapter considers the nature of inhibition, how it interacts with desire and what this says about desire.

There appear to be at least three types of inhibition that can be exerted on sexual desire and its expression in behaviour (Bancroft, 2009; Toates, 2009). Inhibition can arise from:

1 orgasm/ejaculation, acting directly to lower arousal and desire;
2 external stimuli, that is physically present unwanted and often aversive stimuli, acting sometimes non-consciously and directly to lower arousal and thereby desire;
3 intentions. Cognitive processing involving a competing goal (e.g. 'I intend to remain faithful') might either lower desire directly or lower the chances that desire will give rise to sexual behaviour. This would arise typically through a conscious cost–benefit analysis of the situation.

The description 'excessive inhibition' might need to include which of the three types of inhibition is excessive (Bancroft and Graham, 2011). One person could have excessive inhibition as an automatic reaction to the situation (factor 2), whereas another might 'put on the brakes' as a conscious choice (factor 3). Women might well be more predisposed to exert greater levels of inhibition (Bancroft, 2009), acting at levels 2 and 3.

Bearing in mind this distinction, the chapter will now describe some triggers to inhibition.[1]

Orgasmic (sexually specific) inhibition

Inhibition triggered by orgasm is specific to sexual desire and is usually more evident in men than women. In men, orgasm normally tends to reduce further desire or makes penetrative sex more difficult due to weakness of erection. It appears not to be the loss of seminal fluids as such that lowers desire, but rather the process of orgasm organized in the brain. Something lowers the degree to which desire can be triggered and it presumably lowers the ability of sexual stimuli to trigger the dopamine system. Accompanying such satiety, other stimuli such as food normally retain their attraction value, so this form of inhibition is specific to sexual desire.

For the male, the functional significance of this inhibitory factor is that, immediately following ejaculation, sexual behaviour would not be successful reproductively. Some minimal time spent away from sexual activity allows the replenishment of the supply of seminal fluids. That women tend to be more multi-orgasmic than men is presumably related to the fact that there is nothing needing regeneration following orgasm and that sex could be pursued with advantage immediately.

Neurochemicals, such as serotonin and opioids, are released at orgasm and implicated in satiety (Georgiadis et al., 2012).[2] Neurons employing serotonin project to numerous brain regions, including the nucleus accumbens. Through this route they could oppose the excitatory influence of dopamine, thereby mediating sexual satiety. Higher than normal levels of serotonin appear to be implicated in low sexual desire. Endogenous cannabinoids[3] are also involved in satiety.

Prolactin appears to be secreted in relatively large amounts at the time of orgasm, acting both on the brain processes underlying desire and genital function (Krüger et al., 2006). However, it is released in both sexes and yet, if implicated, would have much less effect in women (Levin, 2003). The release of oxytocin that accompanies orgasm is another candidate to act in an inhibitory role (Carmichael et al., 1994). The muscular contractions that accompany orgasm in men and women might also be implicated in satiety. For women who attain multiple orgasms, the final and satiating orgasm in the sequence is accompanied by high levels of release of oxytocin and particularly strong muscular contractions.

Differences in feedback from the genitals could play a role in the sex difference. Men pay more attention to genital signals than do women in so far as excitation of sexual arousal is concerned and it could be that such signals play a greater role in loss of arousal.

Whatever the exact process, it is clearly something specific to sexual behaviour and not a general process.

Inhibition from physically present stimuli

There are various physically present events in the here and now that lower sexual desire. Fear and pain, for example pain triggered during sex or a sudden noise indicating that attention might be better directed to defence, can do so. Another example is sexual disgust. Exposure to women's tears shed from emotion has the effect of reducing men's sexual arousal and testosterone levels (Gelstein et al., 2011). This could be a defence mechanism adapted to protect a woman from unwelcome advances. Also in this class of inhibition is the failure of erection, which could trigger the fear of performance failure (Janssen and Bancroft, 2007). In men, this can set up a vicious circle whereby inhibition is exerted on sexual arousal with a subsequent self-fulfilling prophecy of erectile difficulty.

Intentional inhibition

For we know that the Law is spiritual, but I am of flesh, sold into bondage to sin. For what I am doing, I do not understand; for I am not practicing what I *would* like to *do*, but I am doing the very thing I hate. (St Paul, Romans 7:15–17)

Intentional inhibition is conscious, effortful and deliberate (Fujita and Han, 2009). Such inhibition is also characterized as due to 'threat of performance consequences' and arises from cognitive processing in which the prospect of a sexual interaction is put into context (Janssen and Bancroft, 2007). For example, fear of disease is one potential inhibitor, the more positive aspect being a desire for good health. Jealousy and mate guarding, with associated fear of the consequences of transgression, provide other reasons for restraint. People taking high risks sexually tend to be low on this factor.

Sometimes the level of inhibition in the class of 'intentional' proves inadequate in the face of strong excitation. The factors that underlie conscious decision-making on whether desire gets translated into action can be in conflict with each other. Sometimes the actual sexual desire that a person feels corresponds closely to what he or she ideally *wishes to feel*. Such people are the lucky ones, without serious conflict. Alas, in other cases, actual sexual desire does not correspond to how the person ideally wishes ('desires') their desire to be (Irvine, 2007). This was illustrated by the American writer Susan Cheever (Cheever, 2008, p. 127): 'In spite of my love for my daughter, I couldn't stop cheating on my husband, her father. Consciously, I desperately wanted to be faithful.' Of course, this is not unique to sex; for example, many heavy smokers wish that they did not desire their addictive activity to the same intensity.

In such cases, it seems as if two levels of the brain/mind are in conflict and an understanding of brain/mind would suggest that exactly this is the case. Researchers can now identify the brain regions and some of their properties. Conflict is inherent to the human condition, never more so than when it concerns sexual desire arising under the condition described as 'temptation'. A good conscious intention can be inadequate as an inhibitor of desire, as illustrated by the following:

> 'Yes, I will go to her, but like the Saint who laid one hand on the adulteress and thrust his other into the brazier. But there is no brazier here.' He looked round. The lamp! He put his finger over the flame and frowned, preparing himself to suffer. And for a rather long time, as it seemed to him, there was no sensation, but suddenly – he had not yet decided whether it was painful enough – he writhed all over, jerked his hand away, and waved it in the air. 'No, I can't stand that!'
>
> . . .
>
> 'I will come to you directly,' he said, and having opened his door, he went without looking at her through the cell into the porch where he used to chop wood. There he felt for the block and for an axe which leant against the wall.
>
> 'Immediately!' he said, and taking up the axe with his right hand he laid the forefinger of his left hand on the block, swung the axe, and struck with it below the second joint. (*Father Sergius*, in Tolstoy, 1896/2012, p. 326)

Tolstoy must surely have written these words from the heart, understanding that sexual desire, if strong enough, can only be resisted by an even more powerful aversion. Conscious intentions, drawing upon the past, such as early vows of chastity, or upon the future, such as anticipating guilt-ridden years ahead, often prove to be no match for desire in the 'heat of the moment'. Although Tolstoy was never driven to quite the same desperate solution of amputation as his fictional creation, the priest Father Sergius, the author had years of conflict in trying to resist the temptation of sexual desire and being tormented by guilt. By his own testimony, sexual desire almost invariably won (A. N. Wilson, 1988).

Typically, a person might anticipate that there will arise a later feeling of guilt, or fear some kind of religious or cultural sanction if discovered. The prospect of an unwanted pregnancy, eternal damnation or disease would also fit into this category. Inhibition arises, not from a physical event in the here and now, but from anticipation of what *might* happen in future. Richard et al. (1996) asked participants in an experiment to focus on any anticipated negative mood that would follow an unsafe sexual encounter (e.g. regret) and this tended to increase their adoption of safe-sex practices. Intentional and aversive forms of inhibition are perhaps not entirely distinct. For example, revival into memory of a fear of pregnancy or disease might come to act somewhat like a physically present stimulus.

Intentional inhibition can operate at the level of the selection of a target for attention. Thus, a person wishing to maintain fidelity will sometimes voluntarily divert attention from sexually attractive targets other than the partner (Miller, 1997).

Some features of intentional inhibition appear to reflect a general process and not one specifically 'designed' to restrain sexual behaviour. For instance, a weight-conscious person, having to decide between chocolate or celery, would appear to be in a similar dilemma. The hedonic impact of the chocolate is immediate, whereas the aversive consequences of weight gain could only be imagined. The term 'temptation' describes where a long-term goal is in opposition to an immediate desire.

Adolescence is a time of awakening sexual desire as a result of the activation of hormones. The restraint exerted on putting desire into effect tends to arise from social pressures from family, church and so on (Udry, 1990). Sexual culture and habits have changed with technological advance, for example the availability of contraception (MacDonald and Hershberger, 2005). Thus, this contribution to restraint acting at the level of intention has changed over the decades.

The goal in competition with sexual expression might have a positive quality, such as a desired state of celibacy or respecting religious devotion. A given choice of behaviour might be motivated by a combination of positive and negative aspects. Whatever the emotions, they are in competition with current sexual desire triggered by the physical presence of a sexual incentive or moves towards reaching one. Perhaps it is not surprising that the restraint arising from anticipation of the future is often no match for the lure of the present. The strength of temptation would be expected to increase as the tempting incentive is approached (Orford, 2001). However, such potentially restraining things as guilt might not be expected to increase in the same way. Hence, there is the notion of a 'point of no return'. Whether a given level of wanting is translated into action or resisted would depend upon differences in the strength of inhibition exerted on it (Carver and White, 1994), associated with activation of the lateral prefrontal cortex (Chein et al., 2011).

The emotion of disgust, described next, exemplifies a number of features of inhibition, including different levels of processing. It shows where rational choice can prove inadequate in the face of inhibition from physically present stimuli.

Disgust

> [S]he was aware of the spot on her hand that his lips had touched, and she shuddered with repulsion. (Tolstoy, 1877/1977, p. 206)

> And he bent over her gently to kiss her. But at the contact of his lips the memory of the other seized her, and she passed her hand over her face shuddering.[4] (Gustave Flaubert, 1856/2010, p. 411)

Disgust must surely be the most reliable, irredeemable and durable of passion-killers, its effects lingering long after the triggering event. Under some conditions, the other aversive emotions, fear and even anger, can get converted into sexual arousal, but I know of no such conversion of disgust into anything positive.

Disgust can inhibit sexual desire acting at both a raw level based upon simple physical triggers or at a cognitive level after some elaborate processing. This emotion lowers the chances of either engaging in sexual behaviour at all or in those particular forms that trigger disgust. It appears that disgust can be triggered even if the person is unaware consciously of the presence of this emotion (Kelly, 2011).

Cultures that are highly restrictive sexually, such as the Irish island of Inis Beag, tend to see almost any expression of sexuality as being 'dirty' (Messenger, 1971) and by implication disgust helps to set the norms. A survey of Puerto Rican women in the 1950s found that those not enjoying sex with their husbands reported 'disgust and revulsion' (Rainwater, 1971). In the otherwise sexually permissive Mangaia, people caught in incest would suffer filth being thrown at them (Marshall, 1971).

Evolutionary psychologists suggest that disgust has become attached to sexual desire because this served an evolutionary function by restricting mating in situations that were suboptimal in passing on genes (Fessler and Navarrete, 2003). In other words, people could do better by mating with, say, non-relatives or with those lacking unpleasant odours.

In sexual desire, disgust can exert inappropriate inhibition in either of two ways. First, it can be excessive and thwart sexual experience or bring problems to an otherwise harmonious relationship when sexual tastes clash (Borg et al., 2010a, 2010b). For example, the Victorian English writer and social activist John Ruskin never consummated his marriage (Hewison, 2007). He was apparently disgusted by his bride on the first night of their honeymoon, either because of her pubic hair or menstruation. Secondly, by contrast, disgust can be inadequate to serve as a brake on risky or illegal sexual practices (Borg et al., 2008).

The role of raw disgust

Disgust is an 'old emotion' that is assumed to have evolved because it protected the body from poisoning by contact with infectious agents, termed 'pathogens' (Stevenson et al., 2011). Thus, such things as rotting food, blood, faeces, strong body odours and vomit trigger disgust, their sensory properties indicative of the likely presence of pathogens (Danovitch and Bloom, 2009). Disgust is triggered through smell, taste, vision, hearing (e.g. a disgusting sound as in vomiting) or touch (e.g. a feeling of slime). By means of disgust, such sensory events motivate withdrawal from their source and subsequent avoidance.

Raw stimuli trigger disgust rapidly and automatically with little 'higher cognitive' processing (Kelly, 2011; Oaten et al., 2009). Hence, disgust fits the notion of a module, as described by evolutionary psychologists. Bad body odours or bodily sores are usually triggers to disgust and thereby some loss of desire. They are indicative of bad health, signalling that mating might be relatively unproductive. Disgust is associated with nausea and a particular universal facial expression (the 'gape face'), which is recognized as disgust across different cultures (Ekman et al., 1969). It is hard to disguise this facial reaction by the exertion of the conscious will; the expression tends to 'leak out'. Out of politeness, you might say to a dinner host 'it tastes delicious', but non-verbal signals could be telling a different story.

Disgust can override rationality. For example, a sterilized drinking utensil might trigger rejection, if it is known to have been earlier associated with contamination (Rozin et al., 2000). One can speculate that, in the sexual domain, rationality might often be similarly ineffective in the face of a powerful trigger to disgust (Kelly, 2011). A woman might desperately want to overcome the disgust triggered by a bad odour on her partner, but rationality and explicit reasoning that this arises from nothing more infectious than a rotting tooth can be no match for the automatic triggering of disgust.

Disgust is said to be 'on a hair-trigger', primed for rapid action and likely to pick up false positives (Kelly, 2011). Compared to men, women tend to be more sensitive to triggers to disgust and they are better detectors of facial signs of disgust (Tybur et al., 2009). Triggers to disgust are more powerful if they arise from strangers rather than from oneself or kin. One person expressed this as 'other people's dirt is dirtier than my own' (cited in Oaten et al., 2009, p. 310). This makes evolutionary sense in that pathogens are likely to be brought from outside the family.

The function served by disgust is clear (Stevenson et al., 2011). Close intimacy often involves an exchange of fluids as in saliva, semen and vaginal secretions, these being potential sources of pathogens. A running nose, repeated sneezing or scratching are likely to cool a partner's passion.

Cultural and individual variation

By genetic inheritance and early development, humans are given certain strong predispositions for what to find disgusting, for example strong body odours. However, there is not universal agreement and this points to imitation in 'reading this information off' from the culture (Oaten et al., 2009; Rozin et al., 2000). What is one person's 'turn-off', mediated via disgust, might well be another's particular 'turn-on', exemplified by different attitudes towards, say, oral sex. Such attitudes are not invariably set in stone. Even the inveterate lecher Walter started out with an aversion to oral sex, but over the years acquired a liking for it (Kronhausen and Kronhausen, 1967, p. 306).

Thus, so-called deviant sexual acts have the common property of their capacity to trigger disgust in some people, but the exact form of what is judged as deviant varies between individuals and between cultures (Kelly, 2011). Although the disgust system and its effects on behaviour seem to be universal, as is the capacity for extracting inputs to disgust from the environment, there is extensive variation in exactly what these inputs are.

Expressions of disgust on the faces of parents and siblings convey information to the young child. Consider the different reactions to particular foods across cultures. This reading-off gives the facility for fine-tuning of disgust according to the experience within a particular culture. At this level, religious proscriptions, meanings and symbols enter the picture. Disgust tends to be empathetic; seeing an expression of disgust on the face of another normally triggers some disgust in the observer (Kelly, 2011).

The criteria of body cleanliness compatible with sexual desire these days might well have seemed somewhat excessive to most of our ancestors. Clearly, acting at a high level, cultural and social factors relating to individual experience strongly interact with the basic emotion of disgust. So, again the notions of hierarchy and a merging of biological and social influences are evident.

So-called 'social norms' are presumably based in part upon what triggers disgust (Kelly, 2011). For example, the Bible condemns sex with non-human animals:

Whosoever lieth with a beast shall surely be put to death. (Exodus 22:19)

The writer of this edict probably felt a sense of disgust at the prospect of 'lying' with a beast. Most of us probably find sex with non-human animals disgusting, but for some it is a turn-on, with its own scientific name: zoophilia.

Almost all of us would surely feel intense disgust at the thought of intimate 'relations' with a dead body (Kelly, 2011). Yet some men are particularly turned on by intimacy with a corpse, known as necrophilia, and will go to the most extraordinary lengths to achieve it (Chapter 19). Menstruation and its associated cultural taboos might lower a woman's feelings about her own body and thereby her sexual desire (Leiblum,

2002). However, blood, the archetypal trigger to disgust, is a fetish for some people.

An evolutionary trade-off: sexual arousal and sexual disgust

Speaking metaphorically from a design perspective, disgust presents evolutionary processes with a dilemma. Genetic perpetuation invariably involves a trade-off and a compromise (Stevenson et al., 2011). Of course, there are dangers inherent in sexual activity, some of them signalled by disgust. However, there are some obvious disadvantages in *not* engaging in sexual activity! A high risk runs a high probability of disease, whereas taking too little risk could result in missing fruitful mating opportunities. In this context, it seems that evolution has arrived at a brain that performs a cost–benefit analysis.

Consider the thoughts of Count Tolstoy:

> But I do know for certain that copulation is an abomination which can only be thought of without revulsion under the influence of sexual desire. Even in order to have children you wouldn't do this to a woman you love. I'm writing this at a time when I'm possessed myself by sexual desire, against which I can't fight. (A. N. Wilson, 1988, p. 391)

Emma Goldman, American anarchist and devotee of Freud, wrote on her relation to men (cited by Torrey, 1992, p. 2):

> I always felt between two fires, their lure remained strong, but it was always mingled with violent revulsion.

The Victorian sex diaries of Walter reveal that even he occasionally felt disgust after he had finished a sexual encounter and satiation set in (C. Wilson, 1988), exactly the same story being told by 'Casanovas' some hundred years later (Trachtenberg, 1989).

When males are sexually aroused, they tend to lower the disgust value attributed to stimuli associated with sex (Stevenson et al., 2011). There is a conflict involved such that some tolerance of disgust appears to be the optimal strategy. A high arousal value would signal a highly attractive potential partner, with whom there would be much to gain by mating. If not deterred at the outset of the sexual advance, it would make little sense to stop the sexual activity once high arousal kicks in and thereby waste time. By contrast, low arousal value would signal little attraction value and the possible wisdom of exhibiting disgust.

This effect would surely be familiar to many. We might not like to share a feeding utensil with someone else or eat food located in the vicinity of their sneeze, but our disgust is likely to be considerably lower if the other individual is sexually attractive to us. Any disgust at mixing of saliva with another would most usually fall to zero at the time of subsequently exchanging an erotic kiss. However, this appears not to be the case for everyone. There are cultures where such mixing of saliva is considered to be disgusting (Ford and Beach, 1951). This is (or at least used to be) equally true within certain social groups in the United States (Kinsey et al., 1948). Such evidence again suggests a learning and imitation process in what is perceived as erotic and acceptable.

Arousal does not lower the disgust value of non-sex-related disgust stimuli. Whether in a state of high sexual arousal or not, disgust stimuli not related to sex should still be avoided to the same extent. Sexual arousal is irrelevant to the cost attached to interacting with them.

Now the discussion turns to more 'refined disgust': that which involves elaborate cognitive processing.

Cognition, morals, guilt and disgust

The term 'disgust' can refer to both physical events and to morally unacceptable sexual practices. In the latter case there need not be any intrinsic physical triggers to disgust. In common with disgust triggered by physical stimuli, moral disgust also motivates the individual to put a distance, if only symbolic, between him-/herself and the offensive trigger (Kelly, 2011). It appears that evolution exploits ('co-opts') a biologically primitive process and adapts it to serve broader and more cognitively mediated roles. That is to say, built upon the basic brain processes underlying physical disgust, there are more complex and human-specific processes that involve the attachment of meaning, as in morally unacceptable practices.

Incestuous and paedophilic relations exemplify this. Pointing to the role of cognition, disgust at incest does not necessarily involve any undesirable sensory features of the guilty party. Indeed, the trigger might be the disgusted individual's own hitherto much-loved father. Rather, it is the emotion attached to the prospect of sexual interaction, something meaning-related and involving processing beyond the sensory attributes of an individual.

So, does the use of 'disgust' to refer to both moral transgressions and the reaction to certain physical stimuli point to important common features, as implied by the term 'moral dyspepsia hypothesis' (Royzman et al., 2008)? Alternatively, when applied to morality is 'disgust' just a colourful metaphor? The sensations evoked, such as nausea and loss of appetite, are similar in the two cases. There are some common regions activated under both conditions of disgust, one being part of the orbitofrontal cortex (Chapter 2). Another pointer to overlap is that a similar facial reaction is observed in response to both types of trigger (Chapman et al., 2009). So, the expression 'it leaves a bad taste in the mouth' in response to a moral transgression reminds us of genuine overlap in physical and moral disgust.

There is a cultural transmission of information on unacceptable sexual events, which is based upon disgust. Note such expressions as 'moral contamination', 'filthy mind', 'dirty books', 'impure thoughts', 'being sickened by your suggestion' and 'nauseated by paedophilia' to describe unacceptable features of sexuality. Conversely, moral virtue is conveyed by such expressions as 'clean mind' and 'virginal purity'.

Participants were asked to write a story in which they revived an incident from their past associated with guilt. This triggered a desire for physical cleaning (Zhong and Liljenquist, 2006). Related words, such as 'wash', were more easily accessed by the mind. Participants who had guilt triggered were more likely to select a wet-wipe as their reward for participation than were participants who recalled an ethical action. It can surely be no coincidence that the great religions of the world associate physical washing with purification of sins. Consider the biblical book of Jeremiah:

> upon every high hill, and under every green tree, thou wanderest, playing the harlot . . . For though thou wash thee with nitre, and take thee much soap, yet thine iniquity is marked before me, saith the Lord God. (Jeremiah 2:20–2)

Could differences in guilt between people explain, at least in part, differences in sexual desire? There is some suggestion that this is so, described next.

A cross-cultural study

Woo et al. (2011) compared Caucasian Canadians and Canadians of East Asian origin. Women of East Asian origin (China, Japan and Korea) show a more restricted sexuality than do Caucasian Canadian women. Restricted sexuality is indexed by such things as low reported levels of sexual pleasure, desire and arousal, while pain during intercourse is reported more frequently by East Asian women.

The researchers asked – what could mediate this difference in the two groups of women? Could the conservatism of the Asian women, as measured by what is considered appropriate sexual behaviour, reflect a role of increased guilt? Earlier studies showed a correlation between levels of guilt and sexual dysfunction in women. The researchers investigated a possible link between guilt and sexual desire. In their participant pool, Caucasian women experienced greater sexual desire in the four weeks preceding the survey than did the Asian women, while Asian women experienced higher levels of sexual conservatism and guilt. A role of acculturation was evident within the Asian group, with those women reporting greater acculturation to Canadian society reporting less guilt and more desire.

The researchers speculated on the origins of increased sex guilt amongst East Asian women, which led them to consider attitudes found in classic writings of the Confucian philosophy suggesting that sex is just for procreation. They also highlight implicit conservative attitudes towards sexuality by parents in traditional East Asian families, for example condemnation of premarital sex. Where excessive guilt appears to be a serious impediment to sexual functioning, the researchers suggested targeting it specifically by means of cognitive-behavioural interventions.

A hierarchy within morality and disgust

Consider the following (Haidt, 2001, p. 814):

> Julie and Mark are brother and sister. They are travelling together in France on summer vacation from college. One night they are staying alone in a cabin near a beach. They decide that it would be interesting and fun if they tried making love. At very least it would be a new experience for each of them. Julie was already taking birth control

pills, but Mark uses a condom too, just to be safe. They both enjoy making love, but they decide not to do it again. They keep that night as a special secret, which makes them feel even closer to each other. What do you think about that, was it OK for them to make love?

Most people assert that a sexual relationship between siblings is morally wrong. When asked 'why', they search for a reason, arriving at such things as the dangers of inbreeding. On being reminded of the double precaution of contraception, they then find a different justification, such as that the siblings might be psychologically damaged by the experience. Finally, people are likely to say something like 'I don't know why but I just know that it is wrong.' The person acknowledges that their initial rationale was wrong but cannot find a better one, so clings to the initial belief (Kelly, 2011).

The conviction that sex between siblings is wrong appears to be based in large part upon the emotion of disgust. This would normally lower the desire felt by the siblings for each other, though apparently not excessively so with Julie and Mark! When people are presented with this scenario, the gut feeling of disgust is specifically based upon the incestuous nature of the action rather than, say, that arising from its casual and uncommitted nature (Royzman et al., 2008).

Haidt advances a model, in which two layers ('processes') of moral evaluation run in parallel. There is high-level conscious and rational moral reasoning that can generate evidence-based moral decisions and this process has historically dominated academic thinking on morality. The reasoning is open to introspection, something like how a good judge in a court of law weighs up the evidence.

However, according to Haidt, often a different ('lower') level of control takes the weight of responsibility: automatic and unconscious processing is dominant. Acting at this level, moral decisions are based upon the rapid unconscious production of moral emotions, the outcome of which is then presented to conscious awareness. A gut-feeling just pops into consciousness with no effort involved in its production and no insight as to how it was generated. Conscious processes then search for a justification for the moral emotion, for example it is wrong to inflict inbreeding on the world.

Haidt suggests that metaphors serve to link the physical to the moral. That is, the moral feeling of contamination derives from the early understanding of physical contamination in the case of foods that have gone bad or have been poisoned. In some cases, a single exposure to so-called moral impurity is sufficient for a life-time's contamination, as in the case of the shame associated with what is perceived as an inappropriate loss of virginity.

In trying to understand moral emotions, their role in behaviour and why there are such wide differences, it is useful to ask where moral emotions came from in the development of the child. Haidt suggests that morality is not built upon a metaphorical 'blank slate'. Rather, particular brain processes underlie morality and they are formed during early brain development. However, moral reasoning depends also upon an environmental input to the brain and this can vary across cultures. He suggests (2001, p. 826):

> morality, like language, is a major evolutionary adaptation for an intensely social species, built into multiple regions of the brain and body, which is better described as emergent than as learned, yet which requires input and shaping from a particular culture.

Where are the biological bases of these intuitive feelings? Haidt uses the idea of Damasio on somatic markers for insight here, pointing to the role of the ventromedial prefrontal cortex in integrating bodily feelings and cognitions. So, for example, incest might be judged to be wrong since, quite literally, it generates gut-feelings that are integrated with the corresponding cognition at the level of the prefrontal cortex to produce the moral emotion.

Economic exchange and inhibition

In economic transactions, there is the notion of a fair price and a fair exchange. Could this be applied to sex? The notion of economic exchange is not alien to the world of sex and marriage (Huston, 1974). Certain cultures have the notion of a fair exchange in the dowry system. Of course, prostitution is a pure economic exchange. Rich men endow their wives and mistresses with cars and jewels, often it would seem as an exchange for a partner displaying youth and good looks. The kind of complaint 'All he seems to want is sex now. He never brings flowers', is surely not just apocryphal or a feature of bawdy 1950s English film comedies. One hears such comments as '. . . not even if he were the last man on earth. It's disgusting.' The man in question might display no obvious intrinsic triggers to disgust but a sexual liaison would not be perceived as a fair exchange.

A closer look at the nature of conflict and temptation

The notion of temptation suggests the co-existence of a desire and a goal which is incompatible with giving in to the desire. Whether a person succumbs to temptation depends, one supposes, upon the relative strengths of excitation and inhibition. A short-term 'hedonic' goal is pitted against a more 'sensible' long-term goal (Hofmann et al., 2009). The more hedonic option, for example pizza, offers short-term hedonism but alas potential long-term negative consequences, such as a bigger waistline. This is relative to the less hedonic, but more rational, choice, for example to eat lettuce. The reaction to the potent incentive can start in an automatic mode, for instance when attention is grabbed by an odour or a display of pornography, whereas resistance is in the conscious and controlled mode.

Some classical accounts of temptation

The biblical story describing Eve in the Garden of Eden exemplifies temptation. The story is not explicitly sexual. However, the symbolism is obvious and the story has some important messages for the study of sexual temptation. Eve was commanded by God that she could eat from any but the tree of knowledge. She disobeyed God's command and, from then on, all hell was let lose – quite literally so.

In the eighteenth century, Ann Lee, a pioneer of the religious movement 'the Shakers', claimed to have received a message from God that the apple should really be interpreted as sexual intercourse (Wilson, 1999, p. 375). The message was conveyed from England to America and the sect thereafter practised celibacy. Alas, this was not a strategy likely to spawn many offspring and the sect's adherents dwindled in number.

One would surely need to be tough-minded not to have sympathy for Eve, since she appears to have just about everything going against her (if 'sexually attractive other' is substituted for 'fruit' in the below, it makes even more sense):

- The fruit was novel. Whether sexual or food-related, novel stimuli tend to powerfully trigger the incentive system.
- The fruit was present in the here and now, whereas God's command was in the past. To serve as restraint, the memory of this command needed to be brought into active memory. A memory was being pitted against a physically present incentive.
- The fruit was forbidden, which might have increased its attraction value.
- The consequences of any transgression were not immediate but rather delayed. Indeed, we are still said to be paying the price some thousands of years down the line.
- The serpent encouraged Eve to eat the fruit, an example of social facilitation.

Temptation was also described by the Islamic scholar Ibn Hazm. A young man was tempted by the married wife of a friend but then had second thoughts and took pre-emptive action:

> he laid his forefinger against the lamp until it was scorched, and said, 'O my soul, taste thou this: and what is this to compare with the fire of Hell?' (Ibn Hazm, 1027/1953, p. 264)

This enabled him to resist the second advance of the woman. Just as with Tolstoy's story of Father Sergius, temptation might only be resistible by an even stronger aversive force.

Consider St Paul:

> I say therefore to the unmarried and widows, It is good for them if they abide even as I. But if they cannot contain, let them marry: for it is better to marry than to burn. (1 Corinthians 7:8, 9)

Of course, Paul does not address the problem of being married and still burning. Later versions of the Bible make the meaning of the second verse clearer, bringing it into line with modern psychology:

> But if they do not have self-control, let them marry, for it is better to marry than to burn with passion. (New American Standard Bible, 1995)

The modern version is a help to anyone, who like me on first encountering the statement as a worried child, took 'to burn' to be a reference to eternal damnation.

St Paul's advice on resisting fornication exemplifies several things about sexual desire and its possible link to sexual action:

- Desire is a powerful motivator of action. The notion of burning suggests an *aversive* state that arises in the body but which can be corrected by marriage.
- Excitatory and inhibitory determinants of behaviour can be in a struggle for control.
- The restraining control arises from something intrinsic to the individual, later interpreted as 'self-control'.
- Even in the absence of a sexual outlet, a sufficiently high level of self-control is able either to lower the intensity of the burning or at least restrain its effects.

Consider the temptation involved in sexually motivated looking:

> Ye have heard that it was said by them of old time, Thou shalt not commit adultery;

> But I say unto you, That whosoever looketh on a woman to lust after her hath committed adultery with her already in his heart. (Matthew 5:27–8)

The gospel goes on to argue that, if the man's right eye is the weak link leading to such lust, then, interpreted literally, he should gouge it out to avoid damnation. A somewhat more benign solution might be to adopt a conscious high-level strategy to try to divert the gaze, though it could well fail when the high-level control experiences fatigue. Former United States President, Jimmy Carter, famously reported his own, even more benign, interpretation of these Biblical words:

> I've looked on a lot of women with lust. I've committed adultery in my heart many times. This is something that God recognizes I will do – and I have done it – and God forgives me for it.

In what is perhaps history's most famous example of someone hedging bets, St Augustine's prayer must surely trigger the empathy of anyone having experienced such a dilemma:

218 • How Sexual Desire Works

I had prayed to you for chastity and said 'Give me chastity and conti-
nence, but not yet.' For I was afraid that you would answer my prayer
at once and cure me too soon of the disease of lust, which I wanted
satisfied, not quelled. (Augustine, *Confessions*, VIII.7)

Augustine documented the experience of intrusive thoughts, characterized as voices that suggested giving in to temptation. He contemplated a
life free of such temptation:

They plucked at my garment of flesh and whispered, 'Are you going
to dismiss us? From this moment we shall never be with you again, for
ever and ever. (*Confessions*, VIII.11)

The heat of the moment

The notion of the 'heat of the moment' is central to understanding temptation and capitulation to it (Ariely and Loewenstein, 2006; Nordgren
et al 2009). The hot state is triggered by the physical presence of the
tempting incentive. First, consider when a person is in a relatively 'cold'
emotional state, a safe distance from temptation. In this 'cold state', people typically underestimate the strength of temptation that would arise if
they were in a hot state and being pulled by so-called 'visceral impulses'.
This miscalculation is termed the 'cold-to-hot empathy gap'; the inability,
when in a cold state, to empathize with hot feelings. People commonly
exhibit what is termed a 'restraint bias', a tendency to overestimate their
capacity to oppose the lure of visceral impulses and they tend to fall
victim to temptation unexpectedly.

Male undergraduates were asked to self-stimulate short of ejaculation to
achieve the aroused state (Ariely and Loewenstein, 2006). When aroused,
a wider range of sexual stimuli became more acceptable to them, as
compared to when in the cold state.[5] For example, whereas only 7% were
attracted to a 60-year-old-woman when unaroused, 23% were attracted
after prior arousal. When unaroused, only 19% would agree to a threesome
with another man if the woman requested it, whereas, following arousal,
34% would agree. Worryingly, the number who would consider using a
date rape drug increased from 5% to 26% in the aroused state. Arousal
increases risk-taking in that intended condom use tends to go down. It
was not that participants' knowledge went down as a result of arousal;

for example, in response to a question on birth control the answer was equally highly accurate under both conditions. Rather, the change was a motivational one concerning desires, values and intentions.

There are some important implications of the 'heat of the moment' effect. For example, a young person who trusts the message 'just say no', might when aroused find resistance dissolving and being without any protection.

A person might be able to remember being in a hot state in the past, where and when it was, the circumstances that triggered it, and be able to describe its intensity. However, they often cannot simulate its emotional colouring and motivational strength to the degree needed to trigger the necessary pre-emptive action to resist later temptation. For example, a person might harmlessly agree to a date with a former lover on platonic terms, only to find irresistible passion arises on meeting. A person in a cold state might judge another's behaviour as immoral even though that same individual making the judgement might act in just the same way in a hot state (Ariely and Loewenstein, 2006).

Safe sex messages and the practice of unsafe sex tell a similar story. A sample of North American college students performed well in terms of knowledge of HIV/AIDS and yet in the 'heat of the moment' tended to make assessments of risk by using superficial and irrelevant criteria such as how the potential partner appeared (Abbey et al., 2006).

If a person has a low restraint bias or simply knows of the hot-to-cold empathy gap, they might adopt the solution of taking pre-emptive action when in the cold state in anticipation of the hot state. The classical tale of Odysseus is a perfect illustration of such pre-emptive action. Odysseus did not suffer from a restraint bias, so well in advance, he correctly estimated the lure of the song of the sirens pulling him and his boat to the rocks. Therefore, before getting to the tempting location, he had his sailors tie him to the mast of the ship, so he could not alter its course and be drawn to the sirens. His sailors had their ears bunged up with wax so that they would not hear the sound of the sirens.

A puzzle concerning drug addiction might be partly explained by the restraint bias and might apply to sexual desire: why do people commonly relapse long after withdrawal symptoms have faded (Nordgren et al., 2009)? Suppose that craving has abated and with it the capacity to exploit the visceral feeling of craving to guide action. Could it be that, in this 'recovered state', people underestimate the craving that would be triggered by being in a drug-related environment and hence risk putting themselves back in such an environment? This might be particularly so for people with an inflated sense of their own self-efficacy. There could be a lesson here for sexual temptation and addiction.

Similarly, it appears difficult to form an emotionally coloured anticipation of the long-term aversive consequences of sexual behaviour sufficient to kill present desire. After his loss of innocence in a brothel at the age of about 14, Tolstoy wept with guilt. A highly promiscuous life was to follow, peppered with many such instances of morbid guilt and revulsion, which, by obvious implication, did little or nothing to dampen his passions. The pain of infection with venereal disease, which was rife at that time, and the horror of its treatment proved no more effective a deterrent than guilt. As A. N. Wilson (1998) notes (p. 45):

> It is surely a reassuring tribute to the power of nature that the famous lechers of history like Boswell and Tolstoy lost none of their appetite for the chase in spite of the fact that one bit of bad luck could land them once more in the clinic with its primitive syringes and scarcely competent medics.

Self-control and reserve

The terms 'self-control' and 'self-regulation' refer to the capacity to exert inhibition, which, if sufficiently strong, prevents desire giving rise to sexual behaviour (Gailliot and Baumeister, 2007). The expression 'willpower' conveys a similar meaning. Gailliot and Baumeister (2007, p. 184) suggest that:

> self-regulation would be useful primarily when there is conflict between what the individual wants to do sexually and what the individual should or ought to do. Self-control should allow people to behave as they believe they should, even if that is not what they want to do.

The evidence suggests that people who are good at self-control in one area of their lives (e.g. sexual) tend to be good in others (non-sexual), pointing to an all-purpose facility. A capacity for self-control is associated with such things as the practice of safe sex. Conversely, those who have difficulty with self-control in one area (e.g. drug-taking) also have difficulty in others (e.g. sexual).

For a given individual, the capacity for self-control varies over time, somewhat like a muscle of the body, being vulnerable to fatigue with use. Having exerted self-control in one task, the capacity to exert it in an immediately subsequent task is lowered. So, if a person needs to resist putting sexual desires into effect, the theory suggests that it would be good if they are not required to resist, say, fattening foods immediately prior to this. Conversely, the person who feels that their level of self-control in one area is unreasonably high might try depleting it by a prior exercise of resisting temptation!

Gailliot and Baumeister investigated the effect of fatiguing self-control on the tendency to infidelity. You might well have anticipated the problem in bringing this under scientific scrutiny, expressed with some under-statement by the researchers (2007, p. 177):

Ethical and pragmatic obstacles prevented us from measuring actual infidelity in the laboratory.

However, it seems that, if not infidelity, at least the *desire* for it can be brought under scrutiny. Participants were first depleted by being given a linguistic task that required them to override habitual reactions, then placed in an imaginary situation of temptation and asked what they would most likely do. Compared to 'non-depleted' male participants, males 'depleted' by the prior test indicated an increased likelihood of infidelity. The effect was contributed by those males who were assessed as being high in desire for sex outside the established bond and low in self-control. Overall, female participants did not show an effect of depletion.

By definition, depletion is only likely to be a problem where there is a conflict characterized as trying to resist temptation. Someone trying to resist infidelity exemplifies this, as do people with a sexual addiction and those who have proclivities towards illegal sexual activities but try to resist (Gailliot and Baumeister, 2007).

The role of stress

There's no question at times of my life, partially driven by how pas-sionately I felt about this country, that I worked far too hard and things happened in my life that were not appropriate. (Newt Gingrich, former Speaker of the US House of Representatives)[6]

More specifically, the things were acts of adultery. Ridicule and scepticism were poured on this statement, but it might contain a kernel of truth. Evidence suggests that stress tends to favour the short-term hedonic system since the long-term restraint system becomes depleted (Hofmann et al., 2009).

A license to sin

De Witt Huberts et al. (2012) noted an additional factor that can tip the scales in favour of indulging in hedonic activities. Performing an act of virtue (e.g. giving to charity) prior to being in a situation of temptation is felt to give a license to engage in hedonic activity. The researchers looked at the temptations of snacking, but it might be extrapolated to sexual temptation.

Construal interventions

A possible means to reduce the chances of giving in to temptation is to construe the incentive differently, to perform a 'cognitive transformation'. Its appearance might then come to trigger automatic associations that are negative rather than positive. Fujita and Han (2009) investigated construal of food items with some suggestion of possible therapeutic interventions. For example, a candy bar might be construed as a 'sinful diet-buster' rather than as a 'tasty holiday treat'. With the help of exercises in the imagination, a paedophile might try to construe a child as 'jail-bait' rather than as 'desirable'.

The brain and temptation

Some people with damage to the brain show a tendency to go for risky immediate rewards in the face of longer-term negative consequences. Damage particularly to the prefrontal area is sometimes associated with hypersexuality, pointing to its role in inhibition of sexual behaviour (Mendez and Shapira, 2011). Alzheimer's disease is one possible cause.

Krafft-Ebing (1978, p. 38) noted cases of paedophilia triggered after the onset of dementia and recorded:

The libido of those passing into senile dementia is at first expressed in lascivious speech and gesture

and

the intellect may still be sufficiently intact to allow avoidance of publicity and discovery, while the moral sense is too far gone to allow consideration of the moral significance of the act, and resistance to the impulse.

Krafft-Ebing suggested that epilepsy could trigger hypersexuality.

Ideally, people without brain damage would be investigated as bits of their brains are temporarily and harmlessly inactivated. Again, there are problems with trying to identify the brain regions underlying sexual temptation; researchers can hardly present realistic sexual temptations. However, they can study situations which appear to have features in common with sexual temptation.

One technique is that of earning monetary rewards, where there is competition between the temptation of going for an immediate but uncertain large reward (i.e. delivered with only a probability) or a delayed but safe and certain smaller reward (delivered with a 100 per cent probability). Knoch and Fehr (2007) deactivated parts of the brain temporarily by applying a localized magnetic field. When a region of the prefrontal cortex of the right brain (the dorsolateral region) was inactivated, the choice was shifted towards the seductive but risky option. They concluded that this region normally holds in check the tendency to risky behaviour leading to short-term reward.

A hidden consequence of inhibition

Folk wisdom might suggest that even with a gouged right eye or a conscious strategy of avoidance, lust could still arise spontaneously, and modern psychology has given an interesting new slant to this.

Tempting thoughts

The exertion of inhibition is not straightforward, as illustrated by an anecdote concerning Count Tolstoy and white bears (Wegner, 1994). Tolstoy tells of a person who was asked not to think about a white bear for a period of time. The individual was unable to do this, his consciousness being repeatedly subject to intrusion from thoughts of white bears. Thought suppression does not work; try Tolstoy's experiment for yourself. In order to make a conscious effort *not* to think of white bears, one must hold some kind of memory of white bears in an active state and active memories have, by definition, a close link to conscious awareness.

You might guess that lustful thoughts are no easier to suppress than those of white bears and you would be right. Attempts to suppress powerful thoughts such as those of a sexual nature have the effect of making such thoughts pop into consciousness (Wegner et al., 1990).

Tempting actions

The idea that inhibition can be costly has a long tradition. Sigmund Freud (Polivy, 1998) argued that a build-up of tension is the result. He suggested that the conflict remains unconscious, whereas more recent investigators note that it engages the conscious mind, as when a person tries conscious strategies to resist temptation. Polivy (1998) reviews work which concluded that (p. 184):

> restlessness, distress, or increased activity appear to result from blocked action tendencies or inhibition of motivated acts.

According to the evidence (Polivy, 1998, p. 183):

> inhibiting behavior, across a wide spectrum of types of activities, often results in negative affect (discomfort or distress), cognitive disruption (including distractibility and intrusive, obsessive thoughts about the proscribed activity) and maladaptive behavior or excessive display of the suppressed activity (i.e. binges).

Something like drive ('energizing effect') appears within the body, not from any intrinsic source, but from a consequence of thwarting. According to this interpretation, an emotion captured by a term such as 'relief' or 'catharsis' is experienced when this tension is lowered by engaging in the activity.

Polivy assembles evidence from people who have tried to resist their activities, gambling or even television watching, with the consequence of anxiety or depression. Of course, this presents something of a dilemma.

We could hardly encourage the start or continuation of any behaviour on the grounds that trying to refrain or quit might come at a psychological cost. However, it is well to be aware of this factor. It could undermine good intentions in, say, a pledge of chastity or fidelity.

Evidence suggests that when a person must limit the attention she or he gives to a 'forbidden fruit', this makes the fruit all the more salient and desirable (DeWall et al. 2011). The external restraining circumstances might arise from something as obvious as a scowl from a jealous partner.

In one experiment, participants needed to attend to a target image but, to do this, they had to divert their gaze from the image of an attractive person (someone other than the partner). Following this, participants valued their relationship and fidelity towards their partner less favourably. The attractive faces from which attention was diverted stood out particularly well in a subsequent test of memory and the diversion task caused participants' attention to be more strongly captured by attractive faces.

Much seems to depend upon the process underlying the diversion of attention. Doing this voluntarily is associated with greater relationship satisfaction (Miller, 1997), whereas, if the switch is forced by external circumstances, the effect on the existing relationship is a negative one. At least, this is so for psychology undergraduates! The sort of restraint imposed by a jealous partner might well be open to conscious insight, whereas the goal of the experimenters in the task set by De Wall et al. (attention limitation) was not known by the participants. Nonetheless, the task still affected relationship satisfaction. Unrestrained ogling of others might not be recommended as a guarantee of marital harmony, but neither, apparently, could the explicit prohibition of looking. Somewhere a happy mean might exist.

Inhibition and sexual disorders

General principles of conflict

Someone might articulate in words that a particular sexual relationship or activity is morally acceptable. However, at an intuitive level based upon, say, early experience, this person might still feel moral reservation such that the behaviour is inhibited. According to Haidt (2001), the intuitive level is the default option of the system and it provides effortlessly a day-to-day moral compass. The emotions generated at this level might only be questioned when there is competition between levels, for example when the intuitive judgement conflicts with conscious wishes.

Sexual aversion disorder

The term 'sexual aversion disorder' refers to an actual aversion to genital contact with a sexual partner (Everaerd et al., 2000b). People with this disorder experience disgust or anxiety at the prospect of such contact.

Hypoactive desire

A study of women reporting hypoactive sexual desire (Bianchi-Demicheli et al., 2011) measured their brain activity while they view erotic images. Regions of the brain associated with sexual excitation were less strongly activated, as compared to controls who reported normal desire. In addition, a region of brain known from other evidence to exert inhibition on behaviour was *more* active in such women, when compared to controls.[7]

Vaginismus

The disorder termed 'vaginismus' refers to the situation where a woman experiences a chronic difficulty with penetration of the vagina, despite her conscious wish to achieve this (de Jong et al., 2009). It arises from an involuntary contraction of the pelvic muscles that control the tightness of the vagina. Not surprisingly, it is associated with problems of desire (Borg et al., 2010a).

When exposed to erotic stimuli, such women tend to reveal elevated levels of disgust in the pattern of their facial muscles. There appear to be two routes to triggering disgust: (a) a rapid, possibly unconsciously mediated, automatic association with the sexual stimulus; and (b) a slower *conscious* reflective and subjective assessment. The second process seems to be more strongly implicated in the elevated disgust reaction to sexual stimuli shown by women with this condition (Huijding et al., 2011).

Borg et al. (2010b) investigated whether those with conservative values would more readily interpret aspects of sexual behaviour, if not all sexual behaviour, in terms of moral transgression. From an early age, such values might have been assimilated into a set of core beliefs. In the samples studied, women with more conservative core beliefs tended to see sex as sinful and would at most accept only a limited range of sexual activities. So, could such a moral outlook and associated disgust be contributors to vaginismus? Women with vaginismus were found to have low scores on liberal values and high scores on conservative values, while only a relatively narrow range of sexual activities was judged to be acceptable.

These observations do not allow us to conclude what causes what. Although one's intuitive first guess would be that the conservative morality came first and was the cause of the medical condition, things could be the other way around: maybe the condition triggered a new prioritization with sex assuming a low status, subsequently justified by restrictive moral principles. There is the possibility of a vicious circle of inhibitory effects in which biological condition and beliefs reinforce each other.

Sexual pain

In 'dyspareunia', the woman suffers from pain accompanying intercourse (Everaerd et al., 2000a). Some regard it as more parsimonious to see dyspareunia and vaginismus as two conditions lying on a continuum, with disgust also playing some role in dyspareunia (Borg et al., 2010a, 2010b). In addition, by means of classical conditioning, stimuli earlier associated with pain might lower the genital reaction (Both et al., 2008b).

Some divide sexual pain into two types, having either bodily or psychological causes. However, in some cases both factors might be equal contributors. The message from current pain research is that pain can be flexible. It does not bear any simple relation to damage to the body, and cognitive factors, such as beliefs and fears, can play a significant role. There could be a vicious circle set up between bodily and psychological contributions arising from, say, a history of abuse. Some women engage in sexual behaviour in spite of experiencing pain. Investigators speculate that the motives are to please a partner, to avoid conflict and to confirm her image as a 'real woman' (Dewitte et al., 2011). This would constitute a high-level consciously available goal overriding inhibition arising at a lower level.

So far, the discussion has concerned mainly adult sexual desire in the here and now. However, as mentioned in Chapter 2, an entirely complementary way of gaining understanding is to ask how the brain/mind showing sexual desire came into being, the topic of the next chapter.

In summary

- It is important to distinguish between different levels of inhibition: orgasmic, stimulus-triggered and intentional.
- Disgust can inhibit in terms of both raw stimulus features and a more cognitive extraction of disgust, as in incest.
- The word 'temptation' usually describes a situation where there is a powerful incentive lure that is in conflict with a longer-term inhibitory factor.
- The power of an incentive can be particularly evident 'in the heat of the moment'.

THIRTEEN

HOW DID SEXUAL DESIRE GET HERE?

[B]elow the wall, out of sight of their parents but in full view of our porch, their two children, a small boy and girl, were examining each other's private parts. Someone called my mother's attention to this, and she sucked in her breath and said, 'If I caught my boys doing that, I would skin them alive!'

(B. F. Skinner, 1976, p. 60)[1]

Looking back in time, what led to an adult's brain/mind, with its 'regular' as well as idiosyncratic features of sexual desire? Considered in this way, the individual has a history in terms of two related aspects:

- human evolution, starting millions of years ago;
- development of the individual from conception to adulthood.

To understand how desire got here, it can be insightful to look at events happening over these two very different time scales, which is done in this chapter and the next. Such questions arise as:

- What are the roles of nature and nurture in determining human sexual desire?
- What evolutionary factors contributed to contemporary sexual culture and how did they do so?
- How does the early experience of the child lead to the later emergence of sexual desire?
- What is the role of interactions between the child and its parents in leading to a brain/mind that finds other humans attractive?

- What sort of individual becomes the object of desire and how does this occur?
- How can an unusual development lead to unusual sexual behaviour?

The development of sexual behaviour can be best understood in terms of general principles of development, described next.

A broad framework: some general processes underlying development

From conception and starting 'simply' as a single fertilized egg cell, the newly formed individual develops and grows, by means of cells dividing and thereby their number multiplying astronomically. The growing foetus interacts with its physical environment, by absorbing nutrients, making limb movements and bodily adjustments. This is believed to facilitate the wiring of the motor controls of the body, in forming coordination between brain and muscles.

Hormones have effects on sculpting not only bodily sex organs but also the brain mechanisms that will later come to underlie sexual desire (Chapter 2). Comparing boys and girls, there are early differences in testosterone levels, which appear to play a role in producing differences in brain mechanisms. With puberty these mechanisms are activated by the elevated levels of circulating hormones that appear at this stage.

Learning about the environment

The baby interacts with its parents to gain nutrients and warmth and explores its environment by making eye and head movements. The baby assimilates information from the outside world, for example to form representations of important objects, such as the features that define a human face. Nutrients stimulate his/her taste and smell. By eye and head movements, the baby triggers a changing pattern of stimulation of its visual system. Internal bodily conditions, for example temperature and nutrient levels, as well as any serious disturbance to an organ, are monitored and trigger reactions such as crying.

The baby learns that its actions on the environment have consequences. For example, crying brings reassuring comfort, warmth or food, whereas reaching out to manipulate a toy brings feedback on the result of the action. The baby attaches *values* of good and bad to those events in the environment with which he or she interacts. Observations have revealed that a baby spends a disproportionately large amount of time looking at what are judged by humans to be attractive faces (Chapter 6). Herein lies the assimilation of values that are used later in the control of behaviour, including those involved in sexual desire.

Ideally, parents are the source of bringing good things and will be ranked positively in the allocation of value in the child's brain. The parents, as sources of comfort, become attractive stimuli to be pursued. Some children develop attachments to inanimate objects that bring them comfort and which they take to bed with them, such as a teddy-bear or a piece of cloth (Bowlby, 1982, p. 310).

Contrary to what was long believed, infant attachment seems not to be explicable in terms of 'cupboard love', that is a reward or reinforcement system based upon material gain such as food or comfort. Bowlby (1982) writes (p. 260):

> When a mother rebuffs her child for wishing to be near her or to sit on her knee it not infrequently has an effect exactly the opposite of what is intended – he becomes more clinging than ever.

The similarity with some adult relationships is obvious.

A working model

Bowlby proposed that the young child forms a 'mental model' ('working model') of social interactions (see also Collins and Read, 1994). This is an internal representation of (a) the child, (b) others with whom the child interacts and (c) the nature of interactions between the child and others. The working model appears to have profound implications for the nature of later sexual desire, whether it is expressed sympathetically or coercively.

Under optimal conditions, the caregiver offers comfort and is available to meet the security needs of the child. Thereby, the child's working model of the caregiver is as a 'magnet of positive emotion' to which the infant can be drawn and derive security and comfort. This representation will later tend to generalize to the individual's relationship to others beyond the caregivers, who will be treated as trustworthy. The child will tend to develop a feeling of positive 'self-worth'. Most people have a need for 'felt security' (Collins and Read, 1994).

If, however, the caregiver is unavailable for the needs of the infant or is rejecting, the child's representation of others can be one of untrustworthiness. The representation of self might then be one of being unworthy or of having to be self-sufficient.

The theory suggests that a version of this same working model is subsequently used in adulthood to predict the likely behaviour of others in social interactions. Simulations of the world can be performed with the help of the working model and goals set according to anticipated outcomes. Early in life, working models have a relatively high degree of plasticity in that they can alter their predictions in the light of changing social context and caregiver reactions. With maturity, the working model can become less flexible and less able to reflect changing reality.

How does a working model influence later emotions, cognitions and behaviour? In social interactions, the working model is activated automatically and gives direction or at least a bias to cognitive and emotional processing and thereby plays a role in behaviour. It sensitizes particular goals, at a largely unconscious level. Collins and Read (1994, p. 78) write:

> if a partner's behaviour is interpreted as a sign of caring, then a response that communicates positive emotion and is rewarding to the partner may be chosen. On the other hand, if a partner's behaviour evokes anger and is viewed as a lack of responsiveness, a behavioural response that is punishing to the partner is more likely to be selected.

Evidence suggests that the early construction of a working model can depend upon multiple influences, for example mother, father, grandparents, siblings and playmates. The child might develop multiple and interacting working models of these different relationships. Which of these is later activated most strongly can depend upon context. For example, in romantic relationships, the working model of the opposite sex parent appears to play the strongest role. Furthermore, working models involve various bits of information. These include memories of particular incidents from childhood associated with the behaviour of the caregiver, such as acts of affection. Early interactions shape the form of the brain, such that emotions, such as love, joy, empathy, fear and shame, which play a role in good or bad sexual interactions, are formed.

Development of regions of the prefrontal cortex, for example orbitofrontal, occurs post-natally under the influence of social interactions particularly between the mother and child (Schore, 2003). Under the influence of the mother, the infant's dopaminergic, oxytocin and opioid systems develop with the associated processes that underlie seeking her (dopamine) and gaining pleasure from contact with her (opioids and oxytocin).

Healthy development of the prefrontal cortex requires the repeated exchange of positive affect between parent and child in the form of gaze and smiles. Evidence suggests that this region plays a crucial role in the embodiment of the working model of the mother and the emotional ('affective') value attributed to her presence, particularly mediated via facial signals. The orbitofrontal region of the prefrontal cortex comes to embody the highest level of both control over the emotions and evaluation of the emotions of others. In turn, this region is informed of the states of the body such as its emotional reactions. Its damage can disrupt the capacity to exhibit intimacy and the moral emotion of empathy, as well as to inhibit aggression, surely cardinal features of consensual sexual activity.

A focus on the development of sexual desire

> The sexual instincts are noticeable to us for their plasticity, their capacity for altering their aims. (Sigmund Freud, cited by Doidge, 2007, p. 98).

It is useful to trace the development of sexuality back to the beginning of life. Freud recognized that the various forms that adult sexual desire can take do not simply exist preformed ('pre-packaged') in the child to be revealed in time. Rather, early experience plays a decisive role in sculpting the form of adult sexuality.

The genital reaction

In early childhood, 'protosexuality' (early rudimentary features of sexuality) are exhibited (Doidge, 2007). It appears that genital arousal occurs as an automatic reflex even before birth (Langfeldt, 1990; Money, 1990). Having an external organ, the penis, arousal is easier to observe in baby boys than in girls. Technology does not permit any comparable swelling of the vulva to be seen in girl babies. However, it seems reasonable to speculate that something similar happens in both sexes.

Psychologists now recognize the existence of what is called a 'critical period' or 'sensitive period', during which the brain is most sensitive to sculpting. Money describes what he calls 'sexual rehearsal', a kind of simulated run that precedes any actual desire or sexual behaviour. The sexual system might be under construction even during sleep in the young child. This is associated with rapid eye movement sleep (REM sleep), which is later known to accompany dreaming. This dreaming could later take an erotic form. Although penile erection is simply a reflex, there would be feedback from the genitals that could link with brain regions underlying pleasure.

Young infants are responsive to tactile stimulation of the genitals and act in such a way as to trigger it themselves, for example by directed rubbing of the area (Fisher, 1986). As early as the first year of life, children appear to experience sensual signals from their genitals in response to tactile stimuli, and a few years later exhibit rhythmic thrusting of the pelvic area (Money, 1986). This is presumably a candidate for later linking to sensory impressions of playmates. From their facial expressions, it appears that many young children enjoy such sexual self-stimulation (Fisher, 1986), so an intrinsic capacity for pleasure could be a universal capacity given normal development.

In a sample of boys, some 50 per cent reported first memories of erections that were triggered by non-erotic events, most of these occurring in the age range 10–12 (Kinsey et al., 1948; Ramsey, 1943). The situations had the most common general feature of fear and/or excitement and included playing sports, fear of punishment, giving a recital to a class, arson and anger. There was a similar non-erotic content of dreams which were associated with an erection on awakening. This would appear to be evidence of an early precursor of the cross-linkage between different sources of emotional arousal, described earlier. Kinsey et al. (1948) suggested that, building from this diffuse array of triggers to genital arousal, a more specific and discriminatory link is sculpted. That is, with increasing age, sexual stimulation, either tactile or, say, visual or involving the imagination, is needed to obtain an erection, though a range of other sources of arousal might still play some role. Similarly, with development, orgasm becomes closely tied to specific tactile stimulation.

For many, if not most, children, the first experience of pleasure derived from the genitals, as in masturbation, might not be explicitly linked to sexual stimuli in the outside world or erotic images (Spiering and Everaerd, 2006). Only later does this pairing occur and sexual meaning in terms of an attractive other is attached to the genital pleasure. It has been speculated that as much as a year can go by before this association starts to form (Kinsey et al., 1948). This highlights the rich opportunities that exist for the formation of a wide range of different objects of desire according to the idiosyncrasies of individual experience. Even for a significant percentage of adults, particularly women, genital pleasure in masturbation happens without associated sexual imagery in fantasy (Jones and Barlow, 1990).

Masturbation can be an accidental 'self-discovery' or under guidance and instruction from another child or at least with social facilitation (Langfeldt, 1990). Thereby, the child experiences the intensity of the link between arousal of the genitals and the pleasure derived from there. This would encourage a repeat of the experience, something captured in his own inimitable style by the psychologist, B. F. Skinner, describing life in Susquehanna, Pennsylvania. Skinner based his science of psychology on observables and presumably in this case it was his own subsequent behaviour (Skinner, 1976, p. 60):

> another boy and I had gone out of town on our bicycles and walked up a creek, beside which we were later to build a shack. We were sitting in the sun engaged in rather idle sex play when I made several rhythmic strokes which had a highly reinforcing effect. I immediately repeated them with even more reinforcing results. I began a steady movement, making an excited comment to my companion, and then, although I was too young to ejaculate, I had my first orgasm.[2]

Although Skinner's background was somewhat Calvinist and so he had the potential for the development of erotophobia, reading the autobiography shows that peer influences can sometimes rather effectively counter this!

While growing up and later, the two sexes could place different inter-pretations upon bodily signals. The male has an unambiguous interpreta-tion, which provides an input to erotic arousal, whereas in females erotic associations have negative connotations, such as social disapproval and fear. In other words, males tend to put more weight upon raw stimu-lus information arising from the genitals and women more weight upon subtle external cues and the meaning triggered by bodily sensations. For various cultural reasons, girls are more reluctant than boys to label bodily sensations as sexual. They are brought up to be more cautious, if not suspicious, of sensations from the genitals, as evidenced by the notion of the impurity of menstruation (Everaerd et al., 2000a).

Forming the social link

Money (1986) speculated that sexual development has something in common with development of the brain's control of the limbs. The devel-opment of a so-called 'lovemap' begins very early in life (p. xvi):

> a lovemap is not present at birth. Like a native language, it differentiates within a few years thereafter. It is a developmental representation or template in your mind/brain, and is dependent on input through the special senses. It depicts your idealized lover and what, as a pair, you do together in the idealized, romantic, erotic, and sexualized relationship. A lovemap exists in mental imagery first, in dreams and fantasies, and then maybe translated into action with a partner or partners.
>
> . . .
>
> sexuoerotic rehearsal play in infancy and childhood is prerequisite to healthy heterosexual lovemap formation. Deprivation and neglect of such play may induce pathology of lovemap formation, as also may prohibition, prevention, and abusive punishment and discipline. Con-versely, exposure too abruptly to socially tabooed expressions of sexuo-eroticism may traumatize lovemap formation.

From the age of 5 or so, flirtatious rehearsal play sometimes takes the form of boyfriend–girlfriend romance. Hugging, kissing, genital exhibition and even exploration of the genitals of other children is commonly observed at a young age (Ford and Beach, 1951). It appears that rather early in life young children assimilate that there is a mysterious and forbidden aspect to such adventures, presumably a source of arousal. Boys tend to show such sex play, whether heterosexual or homosexual, much more frequently than do girls and often this is with older children (Kinsey et al., 1948). Whether adults approve, ignore or disapprove of such early sexual exploration and play, it is seen widely across cultures (Ford and Beach, 1951).

The degree of flexibility in sexual orientation and desire would be expected to vary between individuals as a function of early hormonal and later social environments. Bancroft (2009) notes that the onset of masturbation occurs (if at all) over a wider range of ages in girls as compared to boys. He speculates that this could reflect a wider range of time course of hormonal sensitizations in girls.

In parallel, with the emerging capacity for pleasure from the genitals occurs something that one might call 'prototype courtship', with boys typically displaying this towards their mothers or other females and girls towards fathers or other males (Money, 1990). Kindergarten romances are seen sometimes with genital play. An absence of so-called sexual rehearsal play might well drive fantasy in unusual (so-called 'paraphiliac') directions (Money, 1977).

Parental reactions could enter into associations with the genital reaction. There is a tendency for erotophilic parents (e.g. who discuss sexual matters openly) to trigger erotophilia in their children, while erotophobic parents (e.g. those refusing to discuss sex) tend to trigger erotophobia. Sexual disapproval can become associated with genital sensations and hence the roots of aversion ('erotophobia') established (Fisher, 1986). At the time when strong emotional attachments to the parents would normally be forged, the child's sexual trajectory is vulnerable to disruption. For example, abuse can get 'wired into our brains' and establish aversive associations, thereby setting desire in a maladaptive direction. The abused child has an increased risk of being an adult abuser or seeking abusive relationships (Doidge, 2007).

Fisher (1986) suggests that early learning can form a foundation for later more sophisticated learning of meanings to be attached to sexuality, for example expectations about sexual action and the emergence of sexual fantasy. A cross-cultural study done in India (Fisher, 1986) compared two groups of Bengali-Hindu students. One group had been brought up in traditional rigid orthodox families and they tended to be erotophobic in outlook, whereas the other group was raised in a more liberal and sexually permissive environment and tended to be erotophilic.

Children pay attention to and react to the behaviour of others. Social learning theory (Akers, 1985; Bandura, 1977) suggests that children learn behaviour by a mixture of reinforcement and imitation of models such as parents, peers and television actors. These days media play a dominant role in providing education on sexual matters, for example in showing what is right and wrong, thereby acquiring the description 'super peer' to teenagers (Samson and Grabe, 2012). The content of other's speech gives indicators as to how to behave. Early in life, the child learns from caregivers ways of social interaction (Schore, 2003). By direct experience, the child's behaviour is rewarded or punished and thereby she or he forms expectations of the kind 'if I do this, I can anticipate this reaction from the other person'. Observation of models being rewarded, as in deriving pleasure from their actions, increases the tendency of the child to try to emulate the actions observed – so-called vicarious reinforcement.

It appears that these processes can contribute to both prosocial and deviant behaviours. For most people controls are such as to maintain conventional standards of conduct but, if lacking or of a deviant kind, they might strengthen deviant behaviour. Sexually aggressive young men usually have sexually aggressive friends (Hogben and Byrne, 1998). If there is little in the way of any such influence, the child is in something of a vacuum and might accidentally discover deviant ways of acting.

Again, the critical eye of Skinner can be relied upon (Skinner, 1976, p. 128):

> I discovered that concealment of sex varied among ethnic groups. I was once crossing a bridge over Drinker Creek just outside of town and saw ten or twelve Italian boys who had been swimming and were now sitting naked on some warm rocks along the bank. They were handling their genitals and the oldest boy was being greatly admired for the size of his erection. The younger were doing their best to emulate him. There was no homosexual contact.[3]

This exemplifies an aspect of social learning (Hogben and Byrne, 1998): the boys were hoping to achieve the result ('reward') being modelled by the oldest boy.

It must be rare that children actually learn by direct observation of sexual behaviour (though internet pornography is now a complicating factor). More generally, they would learn sex roles and who associates with whom on intimate terms.

Of course, parents do not live in a social vacuum but rather their own attitudes and behaviour reflect to some extent the bigger society. The existence of 'social norms' is universal and appears to be old in evolutionary terms, though cultures differ widely in what constitutes their social norms (Sripada and Stich, 2007). Social norms rely upon rewards for conformity, for example social approval, while subtle and not-so-subtle social punishments are given for their violation, such as malicious gossip and ostracism from the group. Most societies have the social norm of condemning incest and most have rules concerning the permitted sexual activity of young people, though what these are varies widely across cultures. To comply with a social norm establishes a powerful source of motivation, though of course not everyone does comply with every social norm. To violate a social norm can trigger anger and outrage. While parents generally have conservative social norms, a peer group might typically be permissive.

Learning specific targets of desire

How does sexual desire come to be directed to particular targets? Laws and Marshall (1990) placed the weight of explanation upon classical and instrumental conditioning (Chapter 2), as follows.

Suppose that, in the child, arousal of the genitals occurs for some reason. Maybe it simply arises spontaneously or physical stimulation of some kind (e.g. auto-stimulation) triggers it. Suppose now that this reaction is accompanied by the sight, sound or touch of a potential erotic stimulus, for example another individual, either in reality or in the imagination. This would commonly be a member of the opposite sex but it might be of the same sex. Because of the coincidence in time, the potential erotic stimulus ('potential incentive') comes to form an association with genital arousal. The potential erotic stimulus becomes an actual erotic incentive.

Based on the ideas of Martin Seligman, the researchers appealed to the notion of 'preparedness' of the motivational system. Certain things, such as particular perceptions, are more likely than others to form an association with genital arousal. From evolutionary considerations, heterosexual stimuli would be the most likely candidates. Conversely, the system would be 'contraprepared' to form associations with inanimate objects. Laws and Marshall note a number of features of such association formation with 'highly prepared' stimuli:

- An association can be formed with only a few pairings of events.
- There is a high degree of specificity and selectivity to a particular stimulus in its capacity to form an association.
- Once formed, it is difficult to break the association (i.e. 'extinction' is difficult).
- Prepared associations are said to be 'non-cognitive (i.e. primitive) and not readily modifiable by information. This explains why deviant sexual behaviour is so resistant to modification' (Laws and Marshall, 1990, p. 211).

Laws and Marshall argue that the consequences that immediately follow sexual arousal triggered by a stimulus can exert a powerful role in changing the future motivational strength of the stimulus. Consider an example of strengthening behaviour, that is positive reinforcement: if a child attains the pleasure of orgasm in the presence of a particular stimulus, the power of that stimulus to produce arousal in the future is increased. Orgasm through masturbation accompanied by particular imagery might consolidate the strength of the imagery as a sexual incentive. Conversely, if something aversive occurs, the future probability of the stimulus triggering arousal might be lowered, that is a procedure described as punishment. Social disapproval is one such example. Alternative unpunished fantasies could arise and possibly lead to unusual sexual preferences. Once the first-order stimulus for arousal has been established, stimuli that are associated with it can also acquire a potential for triggering arousal. The authors suggest that, through masturbation and the use of fantasy, there can be some extension to the range of stimuli that elicit arousal.

Incest and its avoidance

Basic principles

The very young child assimilates into its memory features of the nearest humans, normally the parents. When the child is older, reproductive success requires that similar features, most obviously human facial characteristics, trigger sexual attraction and bonding. Principles of adaptation suggest that the child needs to form an internal representation of an opposite sex individual that has a motivationally attractive value. The first opposite sex individual that the child will encounter is likely to be a parent or sibling.

However, here lies a 'dilemma': it would be maladaptive if the child were to form too close an attraction to the precise features of the opposite sex parent or siblings. This would increase the chances of later incestuous relations developing and decrease the chances of later sexual attraction to those outside the family. One's first reaction is, probably correctly, to think of the risks associated with incest. However, it would seem that there are costs and benefits attached to both incestuous and non-incestuous relationships (Bagley, 1969). As a cost, an incestuous relationship increases the risk of genetically based disorders, but this is only an increased *probability*, not a certainty. Since some degree of incest prohibition appears to be universal, albeit with slightly different precise rules of prohibition across cultures (Ford and Beach, 1951), it would seem that costs have outweighed benefits in evolution.

So, how is the problem solved and incest avoided? A dispute in the history of psychology pitted two perspectives against each other. On one side was the Finnish anthropologist Edward Westermarck, who in 1891 published an influential book called *The Nature of Human Marriage*. How is it, Westermarck asked, that there appear to be universal aversions against sexual relations between close kin? He suggested that there are biological processes that cause a sexual aversion to those with whom one has the most contact in early life, typically, parents and siblings. Since incest brings a heightened risk of the transmission of genetic disorders, it is of adaptive value to develop a sexual attraction only to non-kin. The process might be described as a form of 'negative imprinting'. The term 'imprinting' describes a phenomenon in which young animals (e.g. geese) develop an attraction to the first moving thing that they see after birth/hatching. Negative imprinting refers to the development of an aversion. So, according to this perspective, incest avoidance is mediated through inhibition of sexual desire. A possible candidate to mediate incest avoidance is represented by pheromones; pheromones from one's own family are less attractive than those of others outside the family (Wedekind and Penn, 2000).

A sociological rather than a biological interpretation of incest was proposed by Sigmund Freud. Freud suggested that social taboos act against incestuous relationships in order to avoid the consequences of incest. If there were no incestuous desires to be resisted, there would be no need for such taboos. There is reason to doubt that this captures the whole picture. Are there really strong and burning incestuous desires to be prohibited in the first place? If, on average, incestuous mating is disadvantageous compared to mating outside the family, would evolutionary processes, metaphorically speaking, have left it to cultures and laws to ensure that it does not happen? After all, if adultery and homosexuality are anything to go by, legal and social sanctions do not have a very good track record in suppressing strong sexual desires (Lieberman and Symons, 1998).

It is more likely that the sociocultural and legal prohibitions reflect something observed to occur within the individual, that is some aversion to sex with siblings. In this case, it would fit with the general picture emerging here: a biological level of organization with a cultural overlay. By analogy, there are social and religious prohibitions against sex with animals and corpses but it is hardly the case that most of us have an urge to engage in these activities, only restrained by fear of social censure. More likely the prohibitions are an extension from the individual experience of disgust – others should be protected from an experience that we feel to be disgusting (Fessler and Navarrete, 2004).

The evidence

Among non-human species, such as a number of non-human primates, incestuous mating is almost always avoided. This would suggest a biological basis to the phenomenon. Could this really be lost in the evolution of humans?

Consider both sibling incest and parent–child incest. Concerning the former, a number of studies suggest that close physical proximity in early years triggers sexual aversion (Fessler and Navarrete, 2004). Two cases are frequently cited in support of a biological basis for human incest avoidance, as follows.

In Taiwan, some families fostered their daughters, to be brought up in the homes of boys, who, it was intended, would later become their husbands (Lieberman and Symons, 1998; Wolf, 1995). This would seem to offer a natural experiment to distinguish between biological and socio-cultural accounts of incest avoidance. If the biological account is correct, some sexual aversion would be expected when the children later marry. This would be indexed by such 'proxy measures' as relatively low fertility and high rates of divorce and extramarital affairs. If the sociocultural account is true, no such effect would be expected, since the 'incestuous' relationship was actively encouraged by both sets of parents. It would seem that such marriages were less successful than those between partners not having been brought up together. It appeared that rearing children together lowered later sexual desire.[4]

The other study is that of the Israeli kibbutzim (Shor and Simchai, 2009). It was observed that children growing up in close proximity to each other rarely developed intimate sexual relationships or married one another. Proximity was thought to trigger sexual aversion. However, this has been questioned. A relationship of the marriage kind is not necessarily a perfect measure of attraction and so the researchers conducted in-depth interviews with people who were raised in kibbutzim. Rather than explicit sexual aversion, they found a mixture of indifference or attraction in retrospective consideration of sexual feelings. In contrast, the participants did express aversion to sexual relations with close relatives. Based upon the witness of those brought up in kibbutzim, the reason that they gave for why sexual relationships did not develop was that they would threaten group cohesion and were against society's expectations.

Lieberman et al. (2003, 2007) investigated the relationship between the length of time students had spent in their family with opposite-sex siblings and the disapproval of incest that they expressed. The more contact the student had had, the stronger was the disapproval of incest, supporting the Westermarck hypothesis that contact triggers aversion to incestuous sex. Even when the other children in the family were unrelated (i.e. adopted or from one parent's earlier marriage), an almost equally strong aversion was found. This suggests that the aversion arises from physical exposure rather than genetic relatedness as such. Of course, normally such exposure would be closely correlated with genetic relatedness. Length of exposure predicted aversion to contact with one's own siblings and the degree of disapproval felt to others having incestuous relationships. Thus, incest avoidance cannot arise simply from habituation to a sibling since this would not explain active disapproval of incest by people unknown to the individual. Rather, this points to an active aversion (Fessler and Navarrete, 2004).

As yet another factor, we might expect females to be more sensitive to incest than males, since the cost of suboptimal mating is so much higher in females (Lieberman et al., 2003).

The next chapter builds upon the present one by considering the negotiation of initial and later sexual behaviour.

In summary

- Early experiences mould a child's social reactions and the experience and later expression of sexual desire can be best understood in this broader context.
- There is a developmental process underlying sexual desire and it involves forming links between bodily arousal and stimuli ('incentives') in the environment.
- Incest avoidance appears to arise from a form of 'negative imprinting'.

FOURTEEN

SETTING THE TRAJECTORY: LINK TO ADULT SEXUALITY

We've come a long way culturally in 10,000 years but evolutionary psychologists would argue that if we are to understand the human mind then we would do well to realise that that mind is the same one that scanned the plains of equatorial Africa in days of our Pleistocene ancestors.

(Workman and Reader, 2014, p. 470)

The last chapter looked at how the bases of sexual desire are established in the child. The present chapter revisits this topic in the context of how processes established in the child are revealed in:

- the emergence of adult sexual behaviour;
- changes and stability in adult behaviour.

It first looks at how brain development is manifest in sexual risk-taking (by also drawing on earlier chapters that described levels of the control of behaviour) and it then considers the direction taken by adult sexual desire and expression.

Transitions between adolescence and young adulthood: brain bases

Adolescence and young adulthood represent a stage during which there is a strong tendency to engage in risky activities, including dangerous driving, drug-taking and unsafe sexual behaviour (Steinberg, 2008). For many, it is the time of first sexual intercourse (Hawes et al., 2010).

Educational programmes designed to warn of risky activities by appealing to rational cognition appear to have a very limited effect. Do young people fail to appreciate the risks, as a result of using wrong and irrational calculations? Do they trust in their own invulnerability? It is not a failure of knowledge; the beliefs and calculations of 16-year-olds are much like those of adults.

A study of adolescents found an association between (a) high-risk behaviours such as drug-taking and unprotected sex, and (b) the personality characteristic of impulsive sensation-seeking (Robbins and Bryan, 2004). High-risk behaviours were associated with a low value of 'future orientation'.

In the psychology literature, sensation-seeking and impulsivity are commonly described as synonymous. It is easy to see why: impulsivity could prove an effective means to obtain high stimulation. However, although their effects commonly combine in particular instances of behaviour, they can be distinguished. For example, one could plan to seek high sensations without acting impulsively. Changes in these two features of behaviour occur over development (Harden and Tucker-Drob, 2011). Examining a large sample of the population, the tendency to sensation-seeking was found to increase from age 12 years to 14 years and then steadily decline to age 24. The tendency to impulsivity declines gradually from age 12 to 22.

Concerning the pursuit of rewards, two related questions are:

1 Why is the period between childhood and adolescence one of increasing risk-taking?
2 Why is the period between adolescence and adulthood one of decreasing risk-taking?

The answers appear to lie in the profile of changes over the early years in the relative weights of excitatory (incentive-based) and inhibitory factors. The increase in strength of the dopamine-based incentive factor is such that inhibition does not keep up with it (Luciana and Collins, 2012). The rise of levels of sex hormones at puberty could strongly contribute to the strength of any sexual incentive, making this a likely time for attributing incentive salience to images taken from pornography (Owens et al., 2012). This maturation is thought to contribute to increased sensation-seeking between childhood and adolescence, followed by a levelling-off or decline beyond adolescence (Harden and Tucker-Drob,

2011). The lower-level systems are particularly sensitive to reward and novelty ('sensation-seeking') and their activation appears to give a bias towards relatively risky options with potentially high reward as opposed to more safe options (Casey and Jones, 2010; Steinberg, 2007). There is an increased level of dopamine activity at adolescence (Wahlstrom et al., 2010).

There is slower maturation of the ('high-level') cognitive systems,[1] which mediate more abstract reasoning, long-term planning and underlie restraint (Harden and Tucker-Drob, 2011). This would account for the decrease in impulsivity shown between childhood and adulthood. Of course, differences between individuals of the same age can be considerable and these might be associated with difference in the weight of levels of control.

In evolution, a period of heightened exploration, sensation-seeking and risk-taking coinciding with sexual maturation might well have proven advantageous in, say, colonizing new territories, finding mates or earning status in a social hierarchy. This could have been especially so for boys, who are known to be more prone to risk-taking than are girls (Steinberg, 2008). By definition, novelty involves uncertainty and dopamine systems are particularly responsive to this, motivating engagement with sources of novelty and risk (Wahlstrom et al., 2010).

High adolescent risk-taking is particularly likely to occur when being a member of a group (Steinberg, 2008). For example, whether an individual engages in sexual activity or takes alcohol or illegal drugs is strongly influenced by whether his or her peers do so. This might simply reflect the fact that adolescents spend more time in groups than others do, though this of course raises the issue of why they do this. Evidence suggests that the presence of adolescent peers increases tendencies to risk-taking by sensitizing the incentive-processing brain regions (Chein et al., 2011).

Development, evolution and culture in understanding gender differences

Consider the following interesting observation. Throughout the world, in most societies that have been examined, it is the broadly accepted cultural norm that men alone should be the ones who are permitted to take the initiative in making sexual advances (Ford and Beach, 1951).

However, in reality and in defiance of such norms, for most of the cultures examined by Ford and Beach, girls and women do sometimes take the initiative in looking for sexual liaisons with men.

The reasons that young people give for their first experience of sexual intercourse show a gender difference. Girls tend to express emotional and relationship reasons, whereas boys tend to express reasons of curiosity or lust (Hawes et al., 2010). A significant number attribute their first experience to peer pressure, often under the influence of alcohol. Social context appears to play a somewhat stronger influence in the initiation of girls' sexual activity, whereas boys' initiation can be better explained in terms of rising levels of testosterone (Udry, 1990).

Evolutionary psychology explains gender differences in how sexual desire is expressed as the result of genetically influenced differences between males and females. There is a caution to be sounded here. These behavioural differences might reflect genetically determined sex differences in the processes underlying sexual desire. However, writers taking a feminist perspective argue that they might instead, or in addition, be the outcome of male attitudes to anything but a narrow range of acceptable female behaviour (Hrdy, 1981). It could be that there is some genetically determined tendency acting in the direction of a sex difference, but that this effect is strongly magnified by culture. So, how can this gender difference be explained?

There could well be a biological basis to gender differences but any neat dichotomy needs qualification. Consider by analogy skin colour. Without doubt, this is largely genetically determined. However, imagine growing up in racially segregated society. Based upon this biological factor, a person is in effect allocated to one half of a binary divide: black or white. How that person is then treated depends upon cultural factors such as implicit assumptions, laws, economics, customs and prejudices. It is worth raising the issue that some of the differences in gender roles might similarly reflect social labelling, the label reflecting a biological difference. Furthermore, the individual could assume a self-identity based in part upon such social labelling.

Comparing humans and other species

The history of the application of evolutionary theory to the social sciences has not been a happy one. Social scientists of radical and progressive persuasion have tended to see evolutionary explanations as inevitably supporting the status quo and being male-centric. However, the Harvard anthropologist Sarah Blaffer Hrdy (Hrdy, 1999) is able to reconcile both evolutionary and cultural perspectives.

Hrdy (1999, p. xxvi) asks:

> If our ancient female ancestors were not 'naturally' coy, sexually discreet, monandrous, and modest, then how did women in so many cultures become so sensitive to their social surroundings in that respect? Was the sexual modesty that to varying degrees characterizes women in all societies selected for some time in the Pleistocene[2] because women lived longer if they learned to be sensitive to disapproval? Or did some transformation from a near absence of sexual inhibition (as in chimps and bonobos) evolve earlier or later? Why are women so modest compared with other primates? And within our own species, how much variation exists and why? Is modesty learned, or partly so? This is just one aspect of an ongoing debate over the nature of human nature.

Observers of animal behaviour have tended traditionally to see sexual motivation in terms of males who are aggressive and active choosers, and who select from amongst passive or, at most, receptive females (Hrdy, 1999). However, according to Hrdy, careful observation of non-human primates does not lead to this conclusion.

Hrdy nominates the Barbary macaque as the most 'promiscuous' of non-human primate females. Typically females of this species will mate at least once with every sexually mature male troop member, abandoning a male after each copulation, and, at her peak of fertility, copulating at around once every seventeen minutes. In most cases observed, the female took the initiative in securing these copulations. In some cases, females are particularly solicitous of mating, even at times when fertilization is impossible. Hrdy suggests that this points to a functional value of such mating.

The evolutionary psychologist David Buss acknowledges that casual sexual encounters might have brought some advantages to women in terms of assessing the value of available males and her own value as well as negotiating access to a male's resources, such as meat from a recent animal kill (Buss, 2003). Also, the male in question might serve as a kind of understudy in case the regular partner is deposed, killed or injured. Furthermore, the so-called 'good genes hypothesis' suggests that a female might secure genes from a particularly attractive male by means of a casual encounter, thereby involving a cuckolded partner. It appears that women tend to select men who are facially symmetrical for their affairs and hence likely to produce sexually attractive offspring. Anthropological evidence points to much greater degrees of female activity and promiscuity in societies where women have more power (Goethals, 1971).

Gender differences in child rearing

Some theorists attach weight to social learning (Chapter 13) in determining gender differences. Various processes underlie sex differences in learning and these include reward, punishment and observational learning ('imitation'). Which behaviours are modelled depends upon a number of factors such as the power shown by the model and the consequences of the model's actions. For example, aggression is more likely to be modelled if it has been observed to achieve favourable consequences.

Evidence suggests that children learn socially approved sex-typed behaviours by means of both direct reinforcement of the sex-appropriate behaviour (e.g. by parental approval) and observing the behaviour of models that is followed by favourable consequences. Certain behaviour acquires negative connotations by verbal descriptions, such as sissy (for boys) or tough (for girls). An admission of anxiety is not considered manly and so is less likely to be shown by boys than it is by girls. Aggression fits the notion of sex-typing, with boys showing more physical aggression than do girls. Observations of parental behaviour reveal that boys are not discouraged from expressing aggression to the extent that girls are. Girls both show more dependency upon others than boys and are reinforced more by others for showing it. These could represent developmental precursors of later interactions with sexual desire and modes of expressing that desire.

Sanctions against female sexuality

Almost as a universal, there have been severe sanctions against female adultery, promiscuity or even sex before marriage, enforced by officers of the law and religion, male relatives and partners. In some cultures, this prohibition extends even to showing the face or an ankle in public. In the most extreme cases, women are subject to disfigurement of the genitals in order to deter sexual desire and girls judged not to be virgins at marriage are killed (Hrdy, 1981; Smuts, 1996). Sanctions against unacceptable male sexuality tend to be much milder, if they even exist.

Surgical removal of the clitoris ('clitoridectomy') as a cure for masturbation appeared in England around 1858 but mercifully never became established. In the United States, this and other forms of genital mutilation, as well as removal of the ovaries, were not uncommonly prescribed as a cure for masturbation and survived to at least 1937 (Barker-Benfield, 1976; Moscucci, 1996).

Why, as happens in parts of North Africa, should a man insist that any potential future wife would earlier have received genital mutilation? In some of the forms practised, it is easy to appreciate that this operation was perceived to guarantee her virginity and increase the chances of chastity and later fidelity, thereby increasing his certainty of paternity of any children. Indeed, her marital prospects required this. The belief prevailed that women would otherwise be over-sexed and promiscuous. The Chinese custom of binding the feet of girls appears to have emerged and survived for some thousand years for the same reason: immobility as a guarantee of virginity, chastity and fidelity and a passport to a good economic future (Mackie, 1996). As a bonus, bound feet were something of a fetish for Chinese men and were thought to lead to better sex.[3]

All this, it is argued, has led the developing young woman to associate sex with danger and tends 'to foster a kind of female sexuality that responds to male needs and desires rather than one that has needs and desires of its own' (Smuts, 1996, p. 255). Consider the argument that, because of the dangers to women, a restrained sexual motivation has been favoured by evolution. There are several arguments against this (Hrdy, 1981; Smuts, 1996), including:

- If sexual desire is intrinsically weaker in females, why are such extreme measures taken to restrain it?
- There can be an important reproductive advantage gained by women having multiple partners.
- Non-human primates and women in societies with fewer 'coercive constraints' reveal excitation of female desire by variety.

Barbara Smuts considers Symons' argument that the relatively low numbers of partners of lesbians as compared to either gay or heterosexual males is evidence of the intrinsically weaker level of desire for novelty in women. She suggests that such women are not immune from an earlier, if not current, influence of male-dominated culture.

Smuts (1996) suggests that (p. 254):

> human females are less promiscuous and appear to be less sexually motivated in part because of the effects of male aggression on female sexuality.

This is such that (p. 255):

> in most societies, it is impossible to identify the 'intrinsic' nature of female sexuality based on female behaviour.

Smuts (1992) adds that in some cultures female sexual adventure is more tolerated than in others (p. 30):

> I do not call attention to these considerations in order to argue that in the absence of constraints, female sexuality would be just like male sexuality. Rather, my goal is to emphasize the need to investigate how the experience and expression of female sexuality varies, at both the psychological and behavioural levels, depending on the extent and nature of the constraining influence of male strategies. Until these investigations provide new evidence, the nature of female sexuality must remain an open question.

Orgasm

The function of female orgasm is a topic of much discussion (Chapter 10). It could help the woman to assess the viability of the male with whom she is copulating (Meston and Buss, 2009). The man who hangs around long enough to trigger orgasm might be a considerate and investing type!

Sexual orientation

Closely related to the subject of gender differences in sexuality is that of sexual orientation, similar arguments being raised by these topics. The question usually takes the form – is sexual orientation, whether heterosexual, homosexual, bisexual or asexual, determined *either* biologically *or* socially? This suggests an unrealistically neat dichotomy, as will be shown in this section. Differences between heterosexual and homosexual behaviour, of course, derive primarily from differences in the object (the 'goal') of sexual desire. This is both in terms of the individual's desired partners and the content of his/her sexual fantasy (Bogaert, 2006; Storms, 1981).

Biological perspectives

The biological argument sometimes takes the form: does a gene (a 'gay gene') determine sexual orientation? A genetic contribution does not require that a single gene determines orientation. More likely, a *combination* of genes could yield a *tendency* to a particular orientation. Evidence derives from twin studies, comparing identical and fraternal twins (Hines, 2004). Research tentatively suggests that the 'concordance' (correlation) in orientation is closer in identical twins, who are genetically identical, than in fraternal twins. Attempts have been made to rule out the possible explanation that identical twins are treated in a more similar way than are fraternal twins.

Genes might act on the brain mechanisms underlying sexual desire, which would not preclude a contributory role for environmental influences. However, genes might act on something else, such as personality, physical appearance or style of childhood play (Hines, 2004), which, in turn, via different environmental experiences, contributes to sexual orientation. Examples of a possibility along these lines are given shortly. Adult hormonal profiles do not predict sexual orientation. The idea, once advanced, that gay males are deficient in testosterone and gay females have unusually high levels finds no support.

A comparison of various species of animals leads to the following conclusion, which might tentatively be extrapolated to humans (Woodson, 2002). Hormonal influences acting on the very young brain normally tend to create a bias towards heterosexual attraction. However, early learning experiences also play an important role, such as either to reinforce or to reverse this tendency.

One suggestion that could explain part of the effect is known as the 'nice-guy theory' (Buss, 2003). In these terms, male homosexuality is a spin-off from the selection of characteristics of the 'nice guy'. Such traits as sensitivity and empathy tend to be attractive to women and so their possessors have achieved high levels of mating and thereby these genes have prospered in evolution. The fact that some possessors have an increased tendency to homosexuality is not sufficient to undermine the genes' advantage in a heterosexual context.

Although controversial, researchers have reported differences in the structure of the brains of homosexual men compared to heterosexuals (LeVay, 1991), specifically a nucleus of the hypothalamus (Chapter 2): the INAH-3 nucleus. In the sample studied, this was larger in heterosexual males as compared to homosexual and bisexual males, corresponding to its larger size in heterosexual males as compared to heterosexual women. As LeVay notes, even if substantiated, such a difference does not in itself prove this to be the basis of sexual orientation. Rather, in principle, it could be a *consequence* of differences in life experiences of people with different orientations. However, there are sex differences in a comparable nucleus of the rat brain and these arise from different exposures to testosterone in early development.

Later studies suggested that a broader range of brain regions are different in structure according to sexual orientation (Savic and Lindström, 2008). Also a different pattern of activation of nuclei in the hypothalamus[4] has been observed in response to what are suggested to be human pheromones. In response to stimuli emanating from under the arm of males, homosexual males showed a similar reaction to that of heterosexual females and different from that of heterosexual males (Savic et al., 2005), though the interpretation of this result has been disputed (Burke et al., 2010). Lesbians showed a response pattern similar to that of heterosexual men (Berglund et al., 2006).

Trying to establish a precise timing

A young homosexual man, 18 years old, in Chicago described when he first felt his future sexual orientation. He recalled that (McClintock and Herdt, 1996, p. 178):

he was sitting in the family room with his parents watching the original 'Star Trek' television series. He reports that he was 10 years old and had not yet developed any of the obvious signs of puberty. When 'Captain Kirk' suddenly peeled off his shirt, the boy was titillated. At 10 years of age, this was his first experience of sexual attraction, and he knew intuitively that, according to the norms of his parents and society, he should not be feeling this same-gender attraction.

By the time the boy reached puberty, his sense of 'self' involved a homo-sexual orientation.

Studies give 10 years as the average age when sexual attraction, whether heterosexual or homosexual, is first experienced (McClintock and Herdt, 1996). This runs counter to the common assumption that the emergence of sexual attraction corresponds to the time of maturation of the testes and ovaries (12–14 years). A survey of a group of homosexual boys and girls in Chicago, revealed that the first same-sex attraction appeared at around 10 years of age, the first same-sex fantasy arising a little later at around 11–12 years, followed still later (13–15 years) by same-sex activity.

So, is there a biological event happening at around the age of 10 years, which could help to transform a neutral image into one endowed with sexual attraction? A candidate is maturation of the adrenal glands (Chapter 2), a source of sex hormones[5] in males and females (McClintock and Herdt, 1996). With maturation, the glands appear to secrete relatively large amounts of sex hormone into the blood. The hormone travels around the body and some enters the brain, where it has effects on the organization of brain processes that underlie sexual attraction. It is known that, in adults, sex hormones sensitize erotic thoughts, making them more likely to appear. So it could be that hormonal elevation is responsible for the first appearance of sexual attraction.

Of course, the fact that two events occur together in time does not prove that the hormone caused an effect on the brain processes that underlie sexual attraction. So, McClintock and Herdt were led to con-sider a possible social cause. Could there be some event in the lives of young people that happens at around age 10 and which assumes great significance? The researchers could find no such significant social event normally happening then.

They considered a possible explanation that combined biological, cog-nitive and social factors. The hormonal change might trigger changes in the brain that underlie interpreting the social world, so that the child assimilates notions of sexual attraction observed in adults. They suggest that this could explain the development of heterosexual attraction but not homosexual attraction. Heterosexual development would consist of 'reading-off' the cultural norms of their environment, whereas homosexual development would be counter to cultural norms and might well involve considerable prejudice.

So, a hormonal change at around age 10 years might explain when the process of forming an orientation occurs. It could be seen as switching on a process of assimilating sexual information from the environment. However, it seems not to be able to explain the form of orientation. What is happening at around 10 years of age in the environment to determine sexual orientation? The next sections describe some suggestions.

The role of conditioning

What is considered a normal sexual orientation is surely to some degree set by conventions of society in the form of role models and reinforcement or punishment for signs of attraction to particular types of individual (Akers, 1985). Any reinforcement derived from actual sexual behaviour will tend to be strengthened if there is social approval of the kind of relationship involved. Conversely, disapproval might undermine the potential for positive reinforcement to be derived from an unconventional attraction. Kinsey et al. (1953) found that disapproval of heterosexual activity prior to marriage was a significant trigger to homosexual contact. Presumably in some social contexts, homosexual and heterosexual desires might be equally acceptable and this might contribute to bisexuality.

Children tend to exhibit curiosity about the bodies of other children and many engage in low-level sexual interaction (Van Wyk and Geist, 1984). From peer contact and particularly with those slightly older, children learn the ways of the sexual world and things about the opposite sex (Storms, 1981). Between the ages of 12 and 15 years, ideas that encourage heterosexual behaviour are usually transmitted to the child within groups of same-sex friends.

Other people use the existence of biological sex differences as indicators of how to treat the developing child, that is what is boy-appropriate or girl-appropriate behaviour, and thereby what kinds of behaviour to reinforce. These influences are such that most people become heterosexual, while it is anticipated that signs of homosexual attraction are likely to be punished, either explicitly or implicitly. However, Akers argues, upbringing might, explicitly or implicitly, reinforce homosexual attraction. The criteria and standards set for heterosexual attraction might be perceived as impossible to meet by the developing child, with a correspondingly increased tendency for a homosexual attraction. Excessive moralizing might devalue heterosexual attraction.

Adolescent sex play between boys or between girls might 'accidentally' reinforce homosexual attraction, which could then be further reinforced by fantasy based on the early experience (Van Wyk and Geist, 1984). Sensitized, it would seem, by testosterone, boys tend to be more adventurous than girls and might well find more willing male than female sex partners. This might partly explain the higher frequency of homosexuality amongst males than females. Boys also masturbate more than girls, which could strengthen the role of fantasy. Those boys who learned to masturbate by having this done to them by another male tend to prefer male partners when adult. In addition, some children who grow up to become homosexual claim to have experienced early urges towards homosexual contact prior to any experience, such that first experiences are likely to be rewarding (Akers, 1985). Many adult homosexuals have had earlier heterosexual experiences of some sort but found them less rewarding than their homosexual contacts. Some might have found initial heterosexual advances intimidating (Van Wyk and Geist, 1984). Once a trajectory is started it then tends to be self-reinforcing. Girls who had coerced sexual experience with older males have some tendency to prefer women sexual partners. A whole array of different experiences could blend into a feeling of being gender-atypical.

The first experience of sexual arousal might have a particularly strong effect in setting future orientation, for example first masturbation while viewing an image or holding an image in mind. A study of a group of individuals in San Francisco found that sexual orientation, whether primarily heterosexual or homosexual, followed the orientation of their first sexual experience (Weinberg et al., 1994). However, this did not preclude some later feelings that were discordant with the initial orientation.

Amongst the Sambia people of Papua New Guinea, and some other ethnic groups (Ford and Beach, 1951), boys are initiated into homosexual activity at around 7–10 years of age and this lasts for several years.

Yet Sambia boys do not grow up with an exclusively homosexual attraction. Indeed, they mainly assume a heterosexual identity. This could be interpreted as the cultural norms prescribing acceptable adult behaviour powerfully influencing sexual orientation. It might equally be interpreted as a biologically determined predisposition coming to dominate in spite of early experience.

A social learning model

Storms (1981) proposed a theory of sexual orientation, based upon (a) conditioning and (b) early social experiences, comparing children who went on to become either homosexual or heterosexual. As the basic process of conditioning, he suggests that sexual arousal that is followed by its reduction with orgasm, for example the sequence of masturbation, will consolidate the link to the object of desire that is current at the time, either in reality or in fantasy. This much could be common to either orientation of desire or indeed to bisexual fantasy.

Storms cites Kinsey's evidence that the sexual experiences of boys prior to age 13 are mainly homosexual, whereas beyond this age they are mainly heterosexual. For girls, the pattern of change is similar but less marked. Another observation fits Storms' theory: exclusive homosexuality is more frequent amongst men than amongst women. He accounts for this by noting that, amongst other factors, sexual arousal commonly appears earlier in boys (when still in homosocial groups) than in girls (when they are already in heterosocial groups).

Another theory is discussed next and, beyond its opening assumptions, appears to be at odds with that just described.

Exotic-becomes-erotic?

Bem (1996) advanced the 'exotic-becomes-erotic' theory of desire orientation. It questioned the assumption that heterosexual desire is the unproblematic default position of the brain/mind and only deviations from this require explanation. Rather, following in the tradition of Freud, Bem suggests that the acquisition of either a heterosexual or homosexual orientation requires explanation, something which is accounted for symmetrically in his theory. Both male and female desire are similarly accommodated with the same proposal. One might suppose that bisexuality arises from finding both sexes exotic.

The logic of Bem's 'exotic-becomes-erotic' theory is as follows. For a given individual, whichever gender is perceived to be the most different ('exotic') becomes attractive. Exotic gets transformed into erotic by *labelling* of arousal. The exotic tends to be arousing because it triggers an emotion such as fear, but this arousal tends to get labelled as sexual attraction. If Bem is right, heterosexuality is no more 'wired into' the brain through the genes than is homosexuality. Rather, it is experience-dependent and the experience is within a culture that normally dichotomizes the genders, as exemplified by the term the 'opposite sex'.

The role of later experience

The theories just described refer to different early childhood experiences comparing heterosexuals and homosexuals, whereas Gallup (1986) emphasizes the role of later experience. The foundations of his argument lie in evolutionary principles and the difference in optimal mating strategies ('sexual agendas') of men and women. Gallup suggests that heterosexual mating usually involves a compromise: the male has fewer sexual partners and less immediate gratification than he would desire, while the female must compromise with a less than ideal emotional commitment from the man.

Gallup suggests that females become disillusioned with being lied to, betrayed and coerced, whereas males become disillusioned with limited access to females. In such terms, female homosexuality is a response to the negative experiences they have had in their sexual relations with men, whereas male homosexuality is a response to the frustration of thwarted expectations and limited access.[6] Gallup observes that some 85 per cent of female homosexuals had experience of heterosexual intercourse prior to assuming a gay identity, whereas only 20 per cent of male homosexuals had prior heterosexual experience. Gallup notes that hostility and distrust towards men is relatively common in homosexual women, whereas such feelings directed towards women are uncommon in homosexual men. Following this line of logic, if evolution had been such that mating opportunities for men and women were equal there would be no homosexuality (Gallup, 1986).

In these terms, orientation might not be dichotomous but rather on a sliding scale that can accommodate bisexuality.

Asexuality

Puberty, well uh, you know I had the hormones, uh stuff starting working there but I really didn't have anything, nothing to focus it on. I did you know test the equipment so to say and everything works fine, pleasurable and all it's just not actually attracted to anything. (Participant interviewed by Brotto et al., 2010, p. 612)[7]

Asexual people can be defined by their agreement with the expression 'I have never felt sexually attracted to anyone at all' (Brotto et al., 2010). Defining asexuality in terms of lack of desire is entirely compatible with the definitions of heterosexuality and homosexuality in terms of preferred object of desire *as directed towards another* (Bogaert, 2006). Asexuals are not averse to sex as in feeling fear or disgust, but rather are indifferent towards it (Prause and Graham, 2007). For a number of such 'asexuals', this constitutes an orientation which they are happy with and, they believe, is rooted in biology (Brotto et al., 2010). Asexuals sometimes feel a romantic attraction to others, so asexuality is characterized specifically by a lack of the *sexual* incentive. Asexuals need to be distinguished from those who experience (often temporarily) the distress of hypoactive sexual desire disorder and might well seek treatment for this (Bogaert, 2006). As with the dimension of heterosexuality–homosexuality, one might locate desire somewhere on a continuum from hypersexuality to asexuality (Chasin, 2011). How could the asexual orientation arise?

People self-identifying as 'asexual' commonly report pleasure derived from genital stimulation by masturbation but no link to any attractive other (Brotto et al., 2010). The chapter has earlier described the developmental formation of links between the three components of (a) genital arousal, (b) pleasure from the genitals and (c) attraction to another. So, for asexuals a link can form between the genitals and pleasure but not between this process and an attractive other. How is this lack of a link to be explained? People destined to become asexuals might not *interpret* their arousal as arising from an attractive other and therefore they never form an association between other individuals and their arousal.

When desire can overcome any incestuous aversion

Palmyre stood straight up, and in her panic and misery she flew into a rage.

'And even if it is true what's it got to do with you? The poor boy doesn't have much fun. I'm his sister. I might easily be his wife because none of you girls will look at him'...She earned his keep for him, and at night she could surely give him what everyone else refused him, a real treat that cost them nothing...in the depths of their dark minds lay instinctive desire and unpremeditated consent. (Émile Zola, 1887/1975, p. 62)

Incestuous aversion is not absolute but can under some conditions be overcome: there are a number of exceptions to the universality of the taboo (Bagley, 1969). Incest rules across cultures do not invariably match the criterion of biological closeness. Anthropological reports describe children brought up together but who nonetheless marry each other. For example, some cultures permit brother–sister marriage. Incest was reported as 'not infrequently practiced' on the Polynesian island of Mangaia, including between brother and sister (Marshall, 1971). In the nineteenth century, amongst the isolated Mormon communities of Utah, a man's marriage to his daughter or sister was not uncommon, a similar phenomenon being reported from rural Japan (Bagley, 1969). In the period between the world wars in rural Sweden, father–daughter incest was reported as 'not uncommon'. It occurred in isolated farms, where there was no other sexual outlet for the father and the daughter assumed the role of wife. The actual wife, if she was still around, offered tacit approval to the relationship. Of course, as is commonly concluded from the Taiwanese study (Chapter 13), a marriage or other form of sexual relationship should not be taken as a reliable index of the presence of reciprocal sexual desire.

According to Bagley (1969), the scene is often set for incest in the following way. The dominant participant in incest is detached from mainstream society, either physically, as in geographical isolation or psychologically, as in alienation from the mainstream – for example, in chronic unemployment. Those who can match societies' goals and expectations are less likely to breach society's conventional ethics.

Incest does not only occur in situations of social disadvantage, since quite the opposite conditions can also be associated with it. For example, in the case of the Azande of Africa, a top chief is required to have sexual relations with his own daughter (Ford and Beach, 1951). This violates the otherwise most universal of all incest taboos, that between parent and offspring.

There is, of course, a fundamental difference between sibling incest and parent–child incest, as well as an asymmetry between parent and child. First, there is a rather obvious power differential. In the case of father–daughter incest (probably the most usual form), we might speculate that the fathers felt strong desire whereas the daughters found the experience of incest distasteful. Secondly, the father and mother will have imprinted negatively on characteristics of their own parents and siblings and the process will not thereby be open for imprinting negatively on their own children (though of course common genes need consideration).

Erotic plasticity

Are eroticism and its expression a fixed property of an individual? How constant is sexual desire? Does it fluctuate much over a life-time? How does it vary between cultures? The term 'plasticity' refers to the degree to which the brain/mind can adapt to changing circumstances, that is a point on a dimension opposite to rigidity.

The phenomena to be explained

According to Baumeister (2000), the pattern of male eroticism in terms of target and desired activity, as well as intensity, tends to be 'set in stone' rather early in life. Males show relative constancy in the face of varying life events. For example, following their first orgasm, males tend immediately to adopt a regular pattern of achieving sexual outlets by one means or another (Kinsey et al., 1948). Finding himself in a situation of being between relationships, a highly active male is more likely than a woman to resort to masturbation.

By contrast, female desire shows more plasticity, flexibility and variation as a function of environmental context. This is true both comparing between women and within a given woman over time. During a life-time, a woman tends to show more change in behaviour as a result of changing circumstances. Following their initiation, women can sometimes go for years before resuming any form of sexual expression. Societies can be compared across time and geography. As cultural 'norms' and expectations change, so women's behaviour changes more than that of men. For example, religious institutions and prescriptions have greater influence on women. Women priests taking vows of chastity have greater success maintaining them than do males. Bisexuality is more common amongst women than men. Gay women are more likely to have experienced heterosexual activity than have gay males. Whereas educational level correlates with a broadening range of sexual activities for women, there is little effect on men. Women tend to feel that they have more choice in their sexuality than men. Indeed, women sometimes assume a gay role as a part of an expression of choice within a radical political process. Women who have a particularly high sexual attraction towards men also tend to show an attraction to women (Lippa, 2006), suggesting a more diffuse desire not so closely tied to gendered physical characteristics. By contrast, men with a particularly high attraction to women do not show a simultaneous attraction to men.

Baumeister's argument was triggered by analyses of the so-called sexual revolution of the 1960s–1970s in the USA, finding that this was more a revolution of women's attitude and behaviour than those of men. A greater willingness of women to indulge in multiple-partner sex gave more opportunity to males to express their desires, but it didn't change men's fundamental motivation pattern. It simply lowered male frustration levels as compared to less liberated times.

Adult plasticity and sexual orientation

Tolman and Diamond (2001) note that changes in women's personal circumstances and social context can lead to changes in sexual orientation. In a survey of young women's same-sex experiences, they found (p. 61):

> Many of these young women indicated that as time went by, they became increasingly aware of the way in which sexual identity categories failed to represent the vast diversity of sexual and romantic feelings they were capable of experiencing for female and male partners

under different circumstances. As one woman said, 'I'm really attracted to the person and not the gender, and there's no category for that, not even "bisexual".' Such data demonstrate how much we lose by trying to fit women's (and men's) complex, highly contextualized experiences of same-sex and other-sex sexuality into cookie-cutter molds of 'gay', 'straight', and (only recently) 'bisexual'.

Kitzinger and Wilkinson (1995) investigated the first steps towards experiencing lesbian sex in a sample of adult women who had previously identified as heterosexual. Various factors, such as re-establishing an old friendship, developing non-sexual intimacy or simply curiosity, seemed to be the precursors. Though not stated, presumably satiation within an established relationship would also have contributed. In some cases, a full-blown lesbian identity with rejection of previous heterosexual identity was assumed after consolidating the new relationship. In other cases, the women remained tentative and were wary of assuming a lesbian identity. The authors argue that their results emphasize the fluidity and flexibility of women's sexual desire and they reject the notion of the innate formation of sexual orientation.

Evidence from swinging

A good arena for examining differences in sexual desire is the swinging scene of group sex, described earlier. Bisexual behaviour amongst women is extremely high at swinger gatherings, even defining the norm, whereas amongst men it is very rare (Dixon, 1984; Stephenson, 1973; Symonds, 1971), even being banned at some swinger clubs (Weinberg et al., 1994).

It is more often men who initiate group sex but women discover their bisexuality as a result. Sometimes this discovery comes as a surprise to them, since they have felt no same-sex attraction prior to this (Diamond, 2007). However, it is not always at the swingers' club itself that women first discover their bisexuality. A glance at a British, French or German swingers' contact magazine or web-site reveals the common description 'she bi-curious' but rarely the corresponding description for the male. This difference is also reflected in nominally heterosexual group-sex pornography, in which depictions of woman–woman sex are very common but male–male sex non-existent. Although this is directed mainly at a male audience, it may also say something relevant about female sexual desire.

Woman–woman contact in this context reminds us that a particular incentive can be attractive as a result of more than one underlying motivation. It has been suggested that the links between affectional bonding and sexual desire (Chapter 15) are stronger in women than in men (Diamond, 2003) and this might explain why women are inclined to manifest bisexual attraction.

Dixon (1984) studied the emergence of bisexuality in a population of married American women. All had considered themselves heterosexual prior to the discovery of their bisexuality in the context of swinging. As a group, they appeared to show a relatively high sensitivity to sexual stimulation (high 'erotophilia'). A large percentage started masturbating before the age of 12 and continued masturbation ever since. The sample started heterosexual activity at a relatively young age and continued at a relatively high frequency with their current husbands.

The bases of plasticity

Baumeister (2000) accepts that sexual desire invariably develops from a complex interaction between biology and social context. Also, once matured and expressed, desire is maintained as a result of such interdependence. Of course, he also accepts that behaviour can be a less than ideal correlate of desire. Someone might lack an outlet for their desires or they might comply with sexual wishes in the face of little desire (this usually being a woman). However, even allowing for such factors, he suggested that there are differences between men and women in the way that biology and culture influence desire.

From a functional perspective, how might it have been to women's advantage in evolution to show such flexibility? Firstly, Baumeister considers power, arguing that, in general, men exert more power and are more aggressive than women. In the face of bonding with a partner who is in a stronger position, flexibility could be a distinct advantage to survival and reproduction. Secondly, he notes that, in most societies, women have traditionally been in a situation of saying 'no' to many sexual advances. Sexual behaviour usually proceeds when 'no' transforms to 'yes', a clear requirement for flexibility according to changing circumstances. The capacity to fine-tune desire and behaviour so as to match an estimate of a male's reproductive viability could be a means of maximizing chances of genetic perpetuation. Women have more to lose than men do by getting it wrong. It could be that plasticity is a means of allowing female desire to track assessments of reproductive viability. These would be partly economic and might vary from period to period and culture to culture.

What might we say about causal explanations? Baumeister suggests that women might have a weaker sex drive than men. This raises the problems noted earlier in the use of the term 'sex drive'. Reflecting the confusion endemic in this area, in the same paragraph Baumeister uses 'drive', 'motivation' and 'desire' apparently as synonyms.

Baumeister notes that women have lower levels of testosterone than men. He also suggests that differences in sexual desire might reflect a more general difference between men and women in terms of the sources of emotional information. He calls on research by Pennebaker and Roberts (1992), pointing to men being more sensitive to their physiological responses than females when in an impoverished social environment. This superiority vanishes when there is a context providing cues.

In keeping with Baumeister's interpretation, boys might show rather rapid imprinting on the first sexually appropriate images they experience. There is a 'window of opportunity' in the formation of the target of desire. Once imprinting is done, it is difficult, if not impossible, to substantially rewrite the script. For girls, the motivation system remains relatively open for various scripts to be written, according to experience within a broader culture. Finally, Baumeister suggested that a strong early imprinting process could explain homosexual or heterosexual orientation. Males might strongly imprint on certain characteristics of their same sex. This could also explain the greater incidence of paraphilias amongst men.

Baumeister suggests (2000, p. 369):

> The importance of social, situational, and cultural influences on women suggests that sex depends very prominently on the meanings and interpretations that a given sex act may have. The relative inflexibility of

males with regard to sociocultural factors suggests that meanings matter less than simpler, physical aspects of sex.

Chapter 5 suggested that women are more 'meaning driven' and men are more 'stimulus driven'. One might expect meaning to fluctuate rather widely with fluctuations in social context, for example acquisition of a new faith, marital breakdown and divorce. By contrast, basic sexual stimulus cues are more likely to be ever-present in reality and imagination.

However, Baumeister's argument is not without its problems. Evidence suggests a considerable degree of male plasticity in *certain cultural contexts* (Abramson and Pinkerton, 1995). For example, in the Sambia of New Guinea, boys go through a homosexual phase early in life, which is followed by heterosexual attraction. In ancient Greece, a homosexual role for boys in relation to older men was not uncommon.

Diamond (2007) argues that the idiosyncratic changes often seen in women's same-sex sexuality require a new explanatory framework and suggests that 'dynamic systems theory' could provide the answer. This theory points to how complex systems can reorganize themselves over time, with novel properties *suddenly* emerging. This is manifest as new behaviours and desires. Seemingly small changes in input, for example encountering new sexual opportunities, can cause dramatic changes in the properties of the system. By analogy, certain professional career trajectories can show sudden switches, rather than linear changes. As adults, some women report the sudden and surprising appearance of same-sex desire, experienced not as an orientation that was intentionally sought. The context might typically be, for example, engagement in feminist politics and finding lesbian/bisexual friends. It commonly builds upon an affectional relationship to *one particular female*. This model stands in contrast to the idea that the 'coming-out' of same-sex sexuality represents a gradual and predictable emergence starting with fantasy and culminating in same-sex behaviour and identity. Some women switch equally suddenly from same-sex to opposite-sex orientation, occasionally being, as they express it, 'straightened-out' against their wishes. Others find themselves to be of bisexual orientation.

So far, the discussion has mainly looked at sexual desire in relative isolation. It is now time to see it in interaction.

In summary

- Differences in the experience and expression of sexual desire between males and females arise from a complex interweaving of genetic and environmental factors.
- Theories on the development of sexual orientation attribute roles to early development of brain mechanisms and to later experience with same- and opposite-sex children.
- Women appear to show more erotic plasticity than males.

FIFTEEN

SEXUAL DESIRE IN INTERACTION

Then the lusts of the flesh, the longing for money, and the melancholy of passion all blended themselves into one suffering, and instead of turning her thoughts from it, she clave to it the more, urging herself to pain, and seeking everywhere occasion for it. She was irritated by an ill-served dish or by a half-open door.[1]

(Gustave Flaubert, 1856/2010, p. 187)

Sexual desire probably does not usually exist in isolation, though for some people it might best be understood in these simplified terms. As a more general principle, sexual desire locks into interaction with other processes and only by looking at its interactions can it be understood. This chapter describes three such interactions.

Attachment, care-giving, love and romance

Sexual desire interacts with a motivation that is variously described as seeking 'companionship', 'love', 'attachment' or 'romance'. Attachment is essential for some to express sexual desire, in which case sexual desire needs to be understood in terms of its links with this primary motivation. This is illustrated by a number of personal accounts, such as the following: The pop singer Madonna wrote (Madonna, 1992, p. 3): 'Sex is not love. Love is not sex. But the best of both worlds is created when they come together.' Meston and Buss (2009, p. 30) give the witness of a 25-year-old woman: 'We were both sixteen-year-old virgins and had been dating for three months. I pushed for us to have sex because I wanted to show him that I loved him. I wanted to give him something that no one else could have. . . . I probably lost my virginity out of a need to be loved', and 'Sex to express love is about being able to put feelings into actions. With different kinds of love there are different ways to express that love through action. When I physically and/or mentally desire someone I may choose to show that desire through sexual actions.'

A particular emotional attachment to another person, romantic love, is found across all cultures (Buss, 2005) and something having features in common with this occurs in a number of non-human species (Fisher, 2004). Fisher (p. 22) argues that, even in the face of rational considerations, romantic love is very frequently: 'unplanned, involuntary, and seemingly uncontrollable'. It appears to be the most obvious, universal and potent of the possible interactions with sexual desire and takes the features of a motivational system in its own right (Fisher, 2004). Indeed, the motivation to obtain a feeling of love and commitment commonly combines with sexual desire, particularly in women (Stephenson et al., 2011). When it is triggered by this combined desire, sexual behaviour yields relatively high levels of satisfaction. The relationship is a reciprocal one: sexual contact can promote bonding, while bonding is a trigger to sexual desire (Dewitte, 2012).

For men, one might have thought that making visits to sex workers would exemplify pure lust in the absence of complications. Unsurprisingly, satisfying lust is invariably high on their list of motives. Again pointing to the role of arousal, uncertainty and novelty, the factors of thrill, excitement and the illicit nature of this activity were also found to be attractive to some. However, for a number of clients, lust seems to lock into interaction with a rather different motive. Qualities that can also be valued and sought include companionship, the woman's conversational abilities and her skill at making the man feel special, and 'personal warmth and friendliness', 'emotional intimacy' or to obtain a 'girl-friend feeling' (Pruitt and Krull, 2011).

From functional considerations, such a link makes sense. Given that ovulation in women is hidden, it would pay a man to stay around over extended periods of time to secure fertilization (Buss, 2005). Following fertilization, a pair who have formed a close bond are presumably at some advantage in terms of surviving the period of pregnancy and the subsequent raising of children. Somewhat surprisingly, sex and attachment have largely been studied in isolation from each other, though this is now changing (Dewitte, 2012; Mikulincer and Goodman, 2006).

Individuals differ in the bases of their sexual desire: to achieve intimacy or more individual-based goals (Cooper et al., 2008). Comparing different individuals, there are various attachment styles with their characteristically different features of interaction with sexual desire (Dewitte, 2012). Space precludes an extensive discussion of these and the section considers mainly just a broad principle that applies to what is termed 'secure attachment'.

Characteristics of romantic love

We could do no better than to go back almost a thousand years, to 1027 and the Islamic scholar Ibn Hazm, who described the characteristics of romantic love, as distinct from relatively 'uncomplicated' sexual desire:

> that mental preoccupation, that derangement of the reason, that melancholia, that transformation of settled temperaments, and alteration of natural dispositions, that moodiness, that sighing, and all the other symptoms of profound agitation which accompany passionate love. (Ibn Hazm, 1027/1953, p. 25)

This hardly reads as a prescription for bliss. Indeed, six of the seven defining characteristics would seem to be decidedly negative, while the first mentioned, 'mental preoccupation', is at best somewhat neutral. If this were part of a job description, it would surely entice rather few applicants. The rumination and craving over the theme of the loved one probably owes much to elevated dopamine levels in the brain combined with lower than normal serotonin levels (Meloy and Fisher, 2005). A surge of energy commonly arises when in the presence of the loved one (Fisher, 2004), possibly reflecting dopamine activity. Persistence is a hallmark of courtship in various species, including humans. The phenomenon of love at first sight is reported by a significant number of people (Fisher, 2004) and might well owe something to dopaminergic activation.

Art mirrors reality in this regard; great operas, ballets and novels often have a tragic course and ending, exemplified by *Romeo and Juliet*. Some of the most enduring pop classics of all time include The Righteous Brothers' *You've lost that loving feeling*, Elvis Presley's *Heartbreak Hotel*, Dionne

Warwick's *Walk on by*, Marvin Gaye's *I heard it through the grapevine*, The Supremes' *Where did our love go?* and Little Anthony and the Imperials' *Going out of my head*. Why so many of us actively seek such tales of unremitting misery presents a dilemma for motivation theorists, particularly if they believe that motivation derives from and serves in any simple way the maximization of happiness.

Over 900 years after Ibn Hazm, the researchers Berscheid and Walster (1974) similarly cast doubt upon any simple equivalence between love and happiness (p. 359):

> some practical people manage to fall passionately in love with beautiful, wise, entertaining, and wealthy people who bring them unending affection and material rewards. Other people, however, with unfailing accuracy, seem to fall passionately in love with people who are almost guaranteed to bring them suffering and material deprivation.

According to the 'two-component theory' advanced by Berscheid and Walster, romantic love occurs when there is (a) intense bodily arousal and (b) the situation is such as to label the experience as 'love'. As noted (Chapter 9), intense arousal can arise in aversive situations, characterized as fear of loss and jealousy, just as much as in positive states such as eroticism and elation. Sexual arousal shares some of the same bodily changes of arousal as experienced in negative emotions. The authors suggest that, so long as the context is such as to label the arousal experience as passionate love, this condition will persist. A strong attraction, exemplified by beauty, will presumably trigger both arousal and a tendency to label this as love. The common feature of arousal might explain how the height of joyous passion can all too easily switch into despair at, say, a forced parting of the loved one, a rollercoaster effect. This has been compared to the alternating elation and fear felt by the novice skier (Hatfield and Rapson, 1987). Similarly, high arousal might explain the otherwise puzzling effect that on occasion intense love can rapidly shift to an equally intense animosity or flip-flop between these emotions.

The researchers noted that various arousing negative emotions, such as fear, can increase the attraction felt towards someone, which lends support to their theory. This might arise for example in the fear of being parted from the object of the passion. Similarly, sexual frustration or the distress at rejection might contribute to passion. The story of *Romeo and*

Juliet appears to exemplify how animosity, in this case from the feuding families, can heighten passion (Fisher, 2004). Hatfield and Rapson suggested that the double standard was traditionally such that, whereas men were encouraged to label sexual arousal as just that, cultural norms and prohibitions might have encouraged women to label it as 'romantic love'.

A list of some characteristics of romantic love, expressed in contemporary terms, includes (Reynaud et al., 2010; Tallis, 2005):

- Focused attention – the salience of the object of love is extremely high. Things associated with the loved one are sought out, for example locations known to be associated with his/her presence. Other considerations are often neglected.
- Planning – the person in love makes inordinate effort in planning to secure contact, and even just to be in locations where the loved one might possibly appear.
- Memories – memory retrieval is biased towards things associated with this single individual.
- Invasive thoughts – the conscious mind tends to be repeatedly ('obsessively') occupied by thoughts of the loved one.
- Withdrawal effect – this occurs on breaking contact even temporarily and is similar to that arising from the absence of a drug in the regular user and consists of such emotional qualities as craving, anxiety, depression and anger.
- Loss of reason – the person in love can ignore the risk of adverse consequences of engaging with the love object, a risk that might be evident to everyone else.

These qualities would seem to make romantic love a candidate as an activity that can easily tip into addiction and merge with sexual addiction, a topic discussed later. Tallis (2005) notes the close similarities between romantic love and bipolar illness (Chapter 8), suggesting a common basis for the two phenomena. In the manic phase, the similarities include a lowered need for sleep, racing thoughts, naïve optimism, euphoria, recklessness and over-confidence. The depressed phase of bipolar disorder has similarities to when lovers are separated or the relationship terminates.

Charles Darwin rationally constructed a balance sheet of the pros and cons of marriage (Tallis, 2005, p. 79):

He was able to sit down and calculate the enormous personal cost of marriage: the wasted time, the financial difficulties, the restricted freedom, the obligation to squander hours talking trivia with uninteresting and boring relatives. Yet, in the final reckoning, all Darwin's logic was overthrown because – and only because – he fell madly in love.

Of course, Darwin contributed massively to understanding the function served by this loss of reason: the opportunity for reproduction. His experience exemplifies levels of control of behaviour; long-term rational considerations were no match for the immediacy of the present situation. In Darwin's balance sheet, the negatives were all future ones, whereas the love object was in the here and now.

To understand romantic attachment, insights can be gained from considering its precursor: the attachment formed between an infant and its caregiver. Romantic attachment is thought to build upon this system where we can sometimes see a similar 'irrationality'. Given its very early appearance in the life of the child, attachment is assumed to have a primary role in shaping the nature of the later expression of sexual desire (Schachner and Shaver, 2004).

Although adult attachment to romantic partners has features in common with infant attachment, there are also some differences (Hazan and Zeifman, 1994). Caregivers normally are motivated to give security to infants but do not expect to receive it back. By contrast, in adult attachment, there is usually reciprocity of giving and receiving. It would be expected that such reciprocity would confirm the attraction value of each partner (Mikulincer, 2006), which would be reflected in sexual desire.

Hatfield and Rapson (1987) note (p. 263):

> Often, passionate love seems to be fuelled by a sprinkling of hope and a large dollop of loneliness, mourning, jealousy and terror. In fact, in a few cases, it seems that these men and women love others not *in spite of* the pain they experience but *because* of it.

So, is passionate love simply characterized by unending misery? That might be going too far! Usually people like those with whom they fall in love and so there is initially a minimal level of reciprocal good feelings (Berscheid and Regan, 2005). When the intense phase kicks in, I would suggest that the joy comes in times of approach to the loved one and in confirmation of reciprocated love, as in receiving a comforting gesture, letter or telephone call. Presumably, this serves to reinforce the bond. In some cases, the misery might well represent a much greater percentage of time but it is more delayed and diffuse (e.g. times of separation, doubt or tension or the termination of the relationship). Often the heights of romantic love seem to exemplify the fracture line between wanting (intense and unremitting) and liking/pleasure (mixed). This distinction runs through the present book.

Feeling the mental states of another

Clearly for most people, understanding, feeling and sharing emotional states ('empathy') are an essential ingredient of reciprocity in romantic and sexual behaviour. Where such empathetic emotions are lacking, there is the danger of coercive sex, as in emotional blackmail and rape. Such reciprocated emotions have an identifiable basis in the brain. Concerning empathy for the pain of another, there is activation in particular regions of the brain, which have overlap with regions activated at times when people feel their own physical pain (Lamm and Singer, 2010).[2] For example, witnessing a loved one in pain activates these regions, having some overlap with physical pain. Evolution has built upon basic mechanisms of pain and exploited them for sophisticated empathy reactions. The system of empathy for another in pain or distress makes its appearance early in life, in fact as early as 2 or 3 years of age (Schachner and Shaver, 2004). The primacy of this emotion suggests a fundamental role in shaping interactions with later-emerging sexual desire. Sadly, both sexual desire and the system that would normally underlie empathy can get distorted in suboptimal rearing.

According to so-called 'simulation theory' (Lamm and Singer, 2010, p. 580):

> we understand other people's minds by using our own mental states to simulate how we might feel or what we might think in a given situation, and to infer from this what the other person may actually feel or think.

The interaction with sexual desire

Ibn Hazm articulated that erotic attraction is an ingredient of passionate love:

> when carnal desire moreover becomes so overflowing that it surpasses these bounds, and when such an overflow coincides with a spiritual union, in which the natural instincts share equally with the soul; the resulting phenomenon is called passionate love. (Ibn Hazm, 1027/1953, p. 58)

This fits a modern notion of two interacting systems and little in the way of basic understanding has changed in almost one thousand years. Researchers these days emphasize the importance of sexual desire as an ingredient of romantic love (Regan, 2000). Sometimes lust starts first and then the interaction with romantic attachment is formed, while in other cases there is the reverse sequence (Fisher, 2004).

In the survey conducted by Meston and Buss (2009), the reason a number of women gave for wanting to have sex had much to do with love for their partner. It was either a means of expressing love or a means by which they hoped that love would be triggered. A number needed to feel emotional intimacy with their partners for sexual desire to be triggered (p. 61):

> When I had sex with him, I was elated, almost triumphant, because to my naïve mind, sex was the equivalent of love, and having sex with him was 'proof' that he loved me. (Heterosexual woman, age 25)
>
> I thought that he would fall in love with me if I did the things he asked... He didn't, and I still have feelings for him to this day. (Heterosexual woman, age 46)

Men more frequently fall in love 'at first sight' than do women (Meston and Buss, 2009; Tallis, 2005). This possibly reflects men's instant sexual turn-on by physical appearance, whereas women take more time to form an assessment of potential, yet another example of women's greater use of cognition. Women tend to form stronger links between attachment and sexual behaviour, in some cases demanding at least some commitment before any sexual contact is permitted (Regan, 2000). Traditionally, social norms and ethical codes have permitted a love–sex dissociation for men but not for women.

A study of bisexual men and women living in San Francisco found (Weinberg et al., 1994, p. 7):

For men it was easier to have sex with other men than to fall in love with them. For women it was easier to fall in love with other women than to have sex with them.

Basson (2000 and 2002) proposed a model of female sexual desire, in which emotional interactions described as 'intimacy' are central. She suggested that frequently women initiate sexual activity even in the absence of sexual desire as such. Rather, they are motivated to attain emotional closeness. Sexual desire and arousal emerge as the woman gains a feeling of emotional closeness.

The link between romantic attachment and sexual desire can, of course, have its hazards and people sometimes take pre-emptive action to avoid these. Thus, some who practise sexual relationships outside the established bond take steps to avoid attachment developing (Hazan and Zeifman, 1994). For example, couples who practise swinging occasionally avoid repeated contact with the same partners (Stephenson, 1973). Some gay males avoid kissing except with the established partner.

What is the physical basis of romantic love and its link with sexual desire? Oxytocin has a role in linking sexual arousal to bonding. In addition, oxytocin that is released during sexual intercourse could amplify sexual desire by acting on dopaminergic systems (Reynaud et al., 2010). As Tallis (2005, p. 2 26) expresses it: 'If Cupid's arrows are dipped in anything, they are dipped in oxytocin.'

Companionate love

Intense sexual desire and arousal are more usually associated with the early passionate phase of romantic love. A lower desire usually accompanies the so-called companionate love that was there all along (Berscheid and Regan, 2005) but was somewhat masked in the beginning and is more durable and characterized by feelings of intimacy including the sexual (Regan, 2000). However, this phase can, of course, be strengthened by regular sexual interaction (Dewitte, 2012). A 35-year-old homosexual male reported (Regan, 2000, p. 268):

It's not that I don't love him anymore, it's simply that I don't desire him *as much*. In a way, our relationship is stronger now, built more solidly on other, less sexual feelings . . . It used to be that I would glimpse him making a certain gesture, or hear his voice on the phone, or catch the scent of his cologne, and I would literally be infused with this feeling of desire, of need, of sheer *want*. . . . But we've been together for a long time, and somehow, somewhere that feeling just faded.

Problems within a romantic relationship can have a negative effect on sexual desire, particularly for women (Dewitte, 2012). Loss of sexual desire sometimes reflects simply the passage of time, but it can also be caused by emotional difficulties of a kind that threaten intimacy and attachment (Regan, 2000). Couples seeking therapy for loss of desire might sometimes usefully address this factor. Of course time-related loss of desire and relationship difficulties are not mutually exclusive.

Forms of attachment

For folk who are lucky, so-called secure attachment is experienced as a child and reflected in adult romantic relationships. In the adult, secure attachment is characterized by reciprocal and empathetic sexual relations, associated with affection for the partner and a desire to please them. The securely attached individual appears to be happy with his/her sexuality and experiences relatively low levels of erotophobia and guilt and shows low levels of promiscuity (Cooper et al., 2006). Sexuality tends to thrive in a context of reciprocity, security and reliability, reflecting early childhood attachment (Davis, 2006). The pleasure that the securely attached derive from sexual behaviour is relatively high (Gillath and Schachner, 2006).

Alas, there can be a failure to achieve a harmonious bond with significant others, as an infant and thereby also as an adult. When this happens, there can be one of two basic reactions both described as 'insecure' (Mikulincer, 2006) and both being associated with a lack of reciprocity and an increased risk of coercion (Davis, 2006). The individual can show so-called hyper-activation, in which he or she protests and employs coercion in order to try to obtain an acceptable degree of comfort. The other reaction is known as deactivation, in which he or she turns off the attachment system, shows detachment and does not try to gain an intimate and trusting association.

The two patterns of insecure attachment also have characteristic associations to sexual desire and behaviour (Cooper et al., 2006; Davis, 2006;

Gillath and Schachner, 2006; Mikulincer, 2006). In an established relationship, hyper-activation can be associated with sexual demands and coercive attempts to control the partner, as well as hyper-vigilance for any sign of loss of interest by the partner. This pattern, sometimes described as 'obsessive' and 'dependent', is linked to chronic worries about one's sexual attraction value and ability. It can be associated with the motive for sex being primarily that of trying to confirm one's value, to obtain reassurance and care-giving and to avoid abandonment. There is a tendency for those aspects of sexuality that overlap with affection, like hugging, to be particularly attractive.

By contrast to this, deactivation is associated with very different interactions with sexual desire. Sexual desire can be inhibited but, if not, it can take an egocentric and impersonal quality that de-emphasizes or actively avoids intimacy and reciprocity (Gillath and Schachner, 2006). The sexual preference is for those aspects of behaviour not associated with intimacy, for example intercourse rather than kissing. Somewhat paradoxically deactivation can lead to sexual promiscuity, even though this does not necessarily bring correspondingly high levels of pleasure. Again this suggests a fracture line between wanting and liking, as well as pointing to the misleading use of the notion of 'high sex drive' to account for the number of sexual partners (Schachner and Shaver, 2004). There is a tendency for the motive underlying sex to be one of proving oneself, including to others (e.g. 'gaining status'), rather than sexual desire as such. This strategy is particularly associated with those who exert coercion, which appears to arise through a failure of social skills and thereby an inability to negotiate the social world of consensual sexuality (Davis, 2006).

Selective attention

Earlier we discussed the role of novelty (Chapter 11). However, too much triggering of desire by novelty might be counterproductive and there appears to be functional value in preserving an established pair bond from too much outside interference. Thus, relative to uncommitted individuals, people who are in a committed romantic relationship tend to pay less attention to sexually-attractive others, suggesting a kind of 'perceptual defense'. By an objective measure of arousal, committed people pay less attention to images of attractive others and are less strongly aroused by them (Miller, 1997). They also attribute less attractiveness to others. Miller writes (p. 765): 'Even if the grass is greener elsewhere, happy gardeners may not notice.' Conversely, a high level of distraction by others was predictive of later breakdown in the relationship.

So, although, as a largely conscious choice, people in committed relationships spend less time than uncommitted ones in looking at attractive others, they might still be susceptible to *automatic* capture of attention by attractive others (Maner et al., 2008). Might there be circumstances that can lower such an automatic tendency? Male and female participants were set a task that triggered romantic thoughts and feelings about their partners. After performing this task, they showed less strong automatic distraction by attractive others than they did after performing the control task of simply reviving happy memories. The effect was specific to sexually attractive others, rather than being a general effect on attention.

In another study, participants were first exposed to an image of someone they found to be attractive, other than the established partner (Gonzaga et al., 2008). Subsequently, triggering romantic thoughts of the established partner reduced the frequency of intrusions into consciousness of the attractive other.

From evolutionary considerations, there is a delicate balance between the strategies of fidelity and infidelity. A time of romantic attachment would be one when, to preserve the bond intact, the scales could be tipped against infidelity and this could be served by diverting attention from other attractive individuals. It was speculated that the neurohormone oxytocin is released by romantic thoughts and feelings and it plays a role in drawing attention away from the other target and back to that of the committed bond (Maner et al., 2008).

When sex and attachment fragment

Sexual desire and attachment are distinct systems, which might or might not coalesce in their actions. People differ in the strength of these interactions; for some, sex and attachment operate independently. For example, in the so-called Madonna–whore complex, a man might affectionately regard his wife as saintly but express little sexual desire towards her, while his lust is satisfied with sex workers, whom he regards as whores (Money, 1990). Occasionally, this can take the form of sexual violence towards women outside the Madonna relationship, the 'Madonna' being blissfully unaware of the husband's other role.

In another form of dissociation, an individual feels sexual desire towards one gender but feels attachment towards a person of the other gender (Diamond, 2006). For example, a person might have a heterosexual *sexual* desire but a homosexual *romantic* attachment or vice versa. Diamond suggests that such diffusion of desires across two systems might help to explain the claim (more usual in women than men) that 'I am attracted to the person more than to a particular gender.' This is exemplified by one woman's account (Diamond, 2006, p. 288):

> I guess my attraction to women isn't really all that sexual . . . My imme-diate gut-level physical response is to men, but I want to marry a woman because I find women more beautiful, and I have more enduring emo-tional bonds with a woman. I guess I find women magnetic. I'm not sure that's the same as a sexual attraction.

Asexuals sometimes feel a desire for romantic attachment towards another individual but with a total absence of sexual desire towards anyone (Brotto et al., 2010).

Aggression, power and dominance

Sadly, sexual desire can interact with aggression and domination. Over-whelmingly this refers to male coercion on others, whether male or female, though female coercion also occurs occasionally (Struckman-Johnson and Struckman-Johnson, 1994). Male violence is manifest in violent pornography, which is targeted to a male audience. Quite what constitutes aggression needs some unpacking. Inflicting mild damage and pain is sometimes done by both men and women on their partners during consensual sexual interactions and probably serves to enhance the expe-rience by increasing arousal (Zillmann, 1984). This would not be classed as aggression.

Sexual frustration following strong sexual arousal can trigger aggres-sion, particularly if the woman is perceived to have insulted the man by a refusal to engage in sexual activity (Zillmann, 1984). For males with power and a desire to harass women, when words linked to power are primed the attractiveness of those women over whom they have power is increased (Bargh et al., 1995).

Biology or social or both?

Debate has raged over whether there is a biological component to the link between male coercion and sexual desire. Feminists have argued that the link is an exclusively human one and arises from peculiarly human aspects of society in which males dominate (see discussion in Pavelka, 1995). Doubtless there are features of the link that are exclusively human, such as media portrayals of women as objects, the existence of violent pornography and the cultural transmission of rape myths such as that women secretly want to be raped. However, this should not preclude consideration of two aspects that could be called 'biological':

- Male aggression related to sexual behaviour is evident in other species apart from humans, where such a culture is, of course, not present. Non-human primate species exemplify such mating-related coercion.
- In non-human species quite close to us, for example squirrel monkeys, there is a proximity of brain regions controlling sexual and aggressive behaviours (Zillmann, 1984). This could suggest an automatic spill-over of excitation from one system to the other.

However, Zillmann (1984) argues (p. 75):

> the vast majority of people – both in Western and non-Western societies – fails to behave violently in their sexual endeavors despite the same anatomical and functional constitution of their brains.

This could point to an important role of learning based upon experience, learning which is facilitated by the plasticity of the brain and, in the case of violence, the proximity of some regions underlying sex and aggression.

The roots of human aggression

Much research on sex and aggression has studied incarcerated rapists. However, some of the underlying motivational processes appear also in a study of non-incarcerated college males (Lisak and Roth, 1988). Men who use manipulative, coercive and aggressive tactics in their sexual relations with women frequently feel themselves to have been humiliated, hurt and ridiculed by women. They tend to be impulsive and feel a need to be assertive, with control frequently being lost under the influence of alcohol. Sexually aggressive males show a motivation of dominance.

Agnew (1992) writes (p. 59):

> Anger results when individuals blame their adversity on others, and anger is the key emotion because it increases the individual's level of felt injury, creates a desire for retaliation/revenge, energizes the individual for action, and lowers inhibitions.

Adversity creates arousal which can act to facilitate a range of behaviours.

Anger as motivation

Anger often arises from the advance towards a desired goal being blocked (Carver and Harmon-Jones, 2009; Lewis and Bucher, 1992). It is particularly aroused when one individual perceives another as being responsible for thwarting these aspirations. Anger triggers forms of behaviour that seem to be appropriate for correcting the situation. Viewed in these terms, unreciprocated sexual desire or unwillingness to sexually cooperate would seem to be just such a situation with the potential in some people to trigger anger and thereby threats or other forms of coercion.

What sort of an emotion is anger and how might it link to sexual arousal? At first glance, anger, surely a negative emotion, and sexual desire, surely positive, might seem to be opposite states of brain/mind. However, although this is doubtless true, there is reason to suppose that an excitatory interaction can arise between them (Carver and Harmon-Jones, 2009). Central to this is the distinction between approach and avoidance (Chapter 8). Desires for sex or food are clearly approach motivations, whereas fear and disgust are avoidance motivations, but what is anger? Anger appears to be an emotion underlying approach towards goals, acting to secure the goals of the angered one, often involving the inflicting of discomfort on someone else. From studies on children, the amount of frustration felt when a goal is blocked appears to bear a positive relationship with the strength of approach motivation.

Carver and Harmon-Jones investigated the activity of the brain during anger. Approach motivations are associated with a relative increase in front left brain activity and angered individuals tend to show such an increase, particularly when it is perceived that action is possible to correct the anger-triggering situation. Testosterone has the effect of promoting aggression and anger as well as libido. Elevated levels in humans are associated with dominance-seeking, being assertive and violent, as well as relatively low levels of fear.

Investigators distinguish between two different types of aggression: predatory ('stalking') aggression and rage-induced aggression (Schore, 2003). Tragically, much evidence suggests that both types can interact with ('facilitate the expression of') aberrant sexual desire.

Consequences of anger expression

It is sometimes suggested that an explicit display of anger has a cathartic effect – 'to let off steam'. This is misleading. Although a display of anger might make the individual feel better in the short term, alas its effect appears also to be one of positive reinforcement, that is it increases the future probability of such a display of anger when in a state of frustration (Lewis and Bucher, 1992). This is of obvious importance in the case of sexual violence, which could well be reinforced by both sexual and aggressive consequences of the action in combination (Chapters 20 and 21).

Sexual arousal as a trigger to aggression

Anger can excite sexual desire but is there a reciprocal link, from sexual arousal to aggression? Under some conditions, an angered man shown a highly arousing sexually explicit film appears to exhibit increased anger as a result of the 'spill-over' from sexual arousal (Donnerstein and Hallam, 1978). What appears to have a particularly toxic effect on violence towards women is a combination of anger and viewing a sexually explicit film that involves aggression towards a woman (Donnerstein, 1980). Quite apart from increased arousal, it could be that the depiction of a female victim cues later aggression towards other women.

In various species, including humans, drugs that boost dopamine activity in the brain amplify both sexual activity and aggression, whereas drugs that boost serotonin reduce both of these (Everett, 1975). This suggests at least some common bases in the brain.

A case study in the fusion of aggression and sexual desire

Doidge (2007) treated a patient (called 'A'), a 'single, handsome young man', suffering from depression. A had a history of troubled relationships with emotionally disturbed women and yet it was precisely women who treated him badly that he found attractive, while caring and considerate women bored him. A's mother, an alcoholic prone to violent rages, had been abusive towards A and his sister. A's father was absent most of the time. The relationship between A and his mother had been a 'highly sexualized' one. A was described as having 'excited but furtive' memories of his interactions with his mother. Although during his childhood A felt rage towards his parents, he acquired an erotic taste for violence. A wished to break free from his attachment to the type of woman who was destined to harm him, and to be able to form viable relationships. Doidge described A (p. 122):

> One of his most tormenting symptoms was the almost perfect fusion in his mind of sex with aggression . . . Thoughts of sexual intercourse immediately led to thoughts of violence, and thoughts of violence to sex. When he was effective sexually, he felt he was dangerous. It was as though he lacked separate brain maps for sexual and violent feelings.

Thus, either stimulus triggered the 'desire' processes underlying both sex and aggression. Doidge explains this in terms of the plasticity of the brain; repeated early pairings of aggression and sexuality led to their fusion. As the saying goes 'neurons that fire together, wire together'. Therapy consisted of trying to sever the link between the two desires, a process of unlearning, and constructing two non-overlapping brain maps.

Drugs

Drugs exemplify that insight into so-called 'normal sexual desire' can be gained by observing interactive desire.

Alcohol

Alcohol has various effects upon sexual desire and its link to action, which tend to combine to increase desire and the chances of it leading to sexual behaviour. Alcohol both increases excitation and tends to decrease inhibition, so it might best be avoided when trying to resist temptation.

People commonly report significant aphrodisiac effects of alcohol, and in one study this was particularly the case for women (Rawson et al., 2002). Somewhat paradoxically, alcohol can reduce the level of arousal as measured at the genitals but increase the feeling of subjective arousal (Rosen and Beck, 1986). This was known to William Shakespeare:

> Lechery, sir, it provokes, and unprovokes; it provokes the desire, but it
> takes away the performance. Therefore much drink may be said to be
> an equivocator with lechery; it makes him, and it mars him. (*Macbeth*,
> Act 2, Scene 3)

Alcohol tends to make people look more attractive, summarized in the expression 'beer goggles'. Just the belief that one has been drinking alcohol (without actually doing so) can increase subjective sexual arousal, make people look more attractive and lead a person to think that he or she is more attractive to others relative to the assessment made when sober (Bègue et al., 2013), again evidence of a peculiarly human feature of sexuality. This effect led Bègue et al. to entitle their paper 'Beauty is in the eye of the beer holder.' Alcohol lowers people's ability to detect asymmetry in the faces of others. Since symmetry is attractive, alcohol thereby increases a person's attraction value (Halsey et al., 2012).

Alcohol triggers what is known as 'alcohol myopia', a tendency to focus attention on the immediate environment. Intoxicated people are likely to put weight upon the excitatory cue of a partner's physical attractiveness and their own arousal rather than on the more abstract, probabilistic and remote inhibitory factors of disease potential, pregnancy risk or offending morality (Abbey et al., 2006). Intoxication is associated with decreased likelihood of using a condom (MacDonald et al., 2000). Placed in a simulated situation of sexual opportunity but without access to a condom, more intoxicated males indicated willingness to engage in unprotected sex than did sober participants. The situation of arousal was salient whereas the risks were not. However, the groups were equal in their description of this behaviour as irresponsible.

The popular image of alcohol, that it lifts inhibitions, is often accurate, but there are limits on its validity. More precisely, intoxicated people experience difficulties with response inhibition *where there is a 'compelling predominant response'* (Abbey et al., 2006). If inhibitory cues are made salient, then alcohol does not necessarily lift inhibitions. For example, in one study, patrons entering a bar had a message 'AIDS KILLS' stamped on their arms. Making inhibition more salient in this way reduced the disruptive effect of alcohol on safe decision-making (MacDonald et al., 2000). The advice would be to have condoms available before getting into an intoxicated state. Suppose that the cues promoting condom use are made salient. Alcohol use might then paradoxically be associated with an *increased* use of condoms.

Canadian psychology students watched a film concerning safe sex and were presented with a bracelet to wear as a reminder (Dal Cin et al., 2006). They were asked to think of the film over the subsequent weeks when they looked at the bracelet and to report on how frequently they wore condoms during subsequent casual sex activities. Wearing the bracelet increased condom use, whether or not sex was associated with taking alcohol. Interestingly, the combination of alcohol and wearing the bracelet appeared to be particularly effective in *promoting* condom use. The authors suggested that alcohol makes information retrieval more difficult and a person is more likely to attend only to salient cues present in the environment. In such terms, the bracelet becomes such a salient cue to safe sex.

Do sexual arousal and alcohol interact in influencing the decision concerning condom use (Ebel-Lam et al. 2009)? Suppose that a person is highly aroused sexually. This would constitute a salient cue. What effect would alcohol have here? The researchers suggested that the combination of sexual arousal and intoxication would lead to an increased tendency to have the intention to engage in unprotected sex. This was indeed the case. When tested sober, even sexual arousal did not favour the thought of having unprotected sex. Neither did alcohol when the participants were not sexually aroused. However, participants tested when *both* sexually aroused *and* intoxicated tended to report the 'impelling thought' to engage in unprotected sex.

One experiment simulated a sexual encounter. It found a relationship between, on the one hand, so-called 'cognitive reserve' and 'executive cognitive functioning' and, on the other, the ability to resist unprotected sex while intoxicated (Abbey et al., 2006). These cognitive terms refer to the ability, for example, to plan ahead, devise new strategies in response to a challenge and to switch strategy in the light of changing circumstances.

In a test of the intention to employ condoms in a simulated situation, people high on these cognitive measures prior to intoxication were more likely to resist the temptation of unprotected sex when intoxicated. The term 'reserve capacity' points again to the notion of strength or resource within a competition for the control of behaviour. By implication, such capacity might be used up by stress or competing demands. When intoxicated, people of relatively low cognitive reserve seem to find the processing demands of weighing up conflicting goals to be over-taxing and opt for the path of least resistance.

Knowledge of the effects of drugs on sexual behaviour played a role in a biblical example of incest that was spared moral condemnation. Lot's daughters were keen to preserve the bloodline, but the only available male was their own father. So, aided by alcohol, the seduction was portrayed in terms similar to that associated with a contemporary date-rape drug:

> Come let us make our father drink wine, and we will lie with him, that we may preserve seed of our father.

> And they made their father drink wine that night: and the first-born went in, and lay with her father; and he perceived not when she lay down, nor when she arose. (Genesis 20:32–3)

I find it hard to believe that a seemingly comatose Lot would have been able to perform the task of insemination. An alternative interpretation is that the alcohol lifted Lot's inhibitions.

Marijuana

From at least as far back as ancient Rome, through *Arabian Nights*, and up to the present, marijuana has been used to increase sexual desire and pleasure (Abel, 1981) and to lift inhibitions (Symonds, 1971). However, intentions associated with its use also play a role in its effects. People who use marijuana tend to have a relatively high number of sex partners. This could indicate an underlying effect of sensation-seeking (Abel, 1981, p. 3): 'Those who are most willing to experiment with drugs also seem the most willing to experiment with sex.' In the balmy pre-AIDS days of the 1960s–1970s, the San Francisco region of Haight-Ashbury became a Mecca for free-thinking young hippies. Drugs and sex mixed freely. It also formed something of a natural laboratory for researchers. An investigation into the effect that different drugs had on sexual desire found that marijuana came out top in increasing it (Gay et al., 1975).

It is reported that some ascetics have used marijuana to *lower* sexual desire (Hollister, 1975). Doubtless context and intentions lock into its action. Also, a number of drugs might well have opposite immediate (to excite desire) and long-term (to lower desire) effects, the latter reflecting suppression of the secretion of sex hormones.

Stimulants

For centuries, the coca leaf has been used in Aztec culture as an energizer and aphrodisiac (Cohen, 2010). Stimulants boost dopaminergic activity. An American cocaine user, let us call him Charlie, reported (Washton and Zweben, 2009, p. 56):

> For me, cocaine and sex are one and the same. Every time I feel sexually aroused, my brain immediately thinks cocaine. Last time I tried to give up cocaine, I thought I could do it without giving up the escorts and the wild sex scenes. But I was dead wrong. Every time I got turned on sexually, all I could think of was cocaine. The cravings got so bad that I had to stop everything and call my drug dealer. Sex without cocaine just seemed unexciting to me, even downright boring. I guess I'll have to learn all over again how to enjoy sex without the hookers and the drugs. It wont [sic] be easy, but unless I can break the connection between cocaine use and sex once and for all, I don't see how I can remain drug-free for very long. I don't want to remain stuck in this vicious cycle of cocaine and sex any longer. I feel like a dog chasing its tail.

Typically, a person tries to meet several goals that co-exist, sometimes in coalescence, as with Charlie's drug and sexual highs. The type of drugs that sensitize sexual desire, most obviously cocaine and methamphetamine, act on dopamine. Interactions between drugs and sex are now better understood in terms of such processes (Pitchers et al. 2010). Charlie is seeking to elevate his level of arousal with the help of sex and drugs and he exemplifies escalation, whereby a person chases sexual 'highs' as much as drug 'highs'. The perfectionist search for a 'super-high' can make coming down undesirable. It can be distressing to ponder the prospect of drug-free, and thereby suboptimal, future sexual 'highs'.

Cocaine was ranked high in the Haight-Ashbury study in terms of desire and energizing of sexual behaviour. But for its limited availability and high price in those days, it might have been the drug of choice as an aphrodisiac (Gay et al., 1975).

Up to 70 per cent of people who enter treatment for cocaine addiction are simultaneously addicted to sex (Washton, 1989) (Chapter 17). Cocaine can have a strong effect on sexual motivation as indexed by thoughts and fantasies. It also lowers sexual inhibitions, providing a trigger to combined sexual and cocaine binging (Washton, 1989).

Amongst some of his patients, Freud observed 'violent sexual excitement' that was associated with taking coca (Byck, 1974). In spite of being seen almost universally as a guru of sexual liberation, one hardly gets the impression that sexual desire featured high on Freud's personal list of behavioural priorities. However, cocaine seemed to have enhanced his desire, as suggested by a letter to his fiancée in 1884 (cited by Torrey, 1992, p. 11):

> Woe to you, my Princess, when I come. I will kiss you quite red and feed you until you are plump. If you are froward[3] you shall see who is the stronger, a gentle little girl who doesn't eat enough or a big wild man who has cocaine in his body.

Amongst a sample of patients with bipolar disorder and associated drug use, those using particularly cocaine, rather than alcohol or marijuana, showed a drug-related amplification of sexual risk-taking (Meade et al., 2008).

In a survey of users of alcohol, opiates, cocaine or methamphetamine, methamphetamine came out clearly as the most sexually charged drug

(Rawson et al., 2002). More than any other substance, male and female users reported that it interacted with their sexuality in terms of enhanced pleasure, experiencing 'sexual obsession' and engaging in 'sexual experimentation'.

Taking cocaine or methamphetamine increases libido and decreases inhibition, leading to unsafe sex practices (Washton and Zweben, 2009). A primary site of action of methamphetamine is on dopaminergic systems (Holder et al., 2010). Indeed, evidence suggests that methamphetamine and sexual incentives act on the same population of dopaminergic neurons.[4]

In a sexual context, methamphetamine triggers three closely related effects (Schilder et al., 2005), corresponding to three effects of high dopaminergic activity. Users experience increases in:

- sexual desire
- arousal, activation and 'stamina'
- risk-taking, that is a focus on the immediate situation, with some disregard to the future.

As a gay male reported (Schilder et al., 2005, p. 342):

> I had sex with about eight men in three days. Crystal[5] fuelled marathon sessions. Completely unprotected and not even thinking about it.

Dopamine is involved in forming a cost–benefit analysis of a given situation, that is acting on those brain processes that weigh up the potential benefits as set against any disadvantages (Assadi et al., 2009). Methamphetamine biases decision-making in terms of persistence with the immediate hedonic activity, while disregarding potential future costs.

Methamphetamine use illustrates several further features of sexuality. Users sometimes report such an elevation in the intensity of the experience that it is later hard to come down to pre-drug levels. As one described drug-free sex (Green and Halkitis, 2006, p. 317): 'This isn't very interesting; it's not very developed.' Furthermore, some users seek ever more daring and novel experiences in a form of spiral upwards in intensity of the experience. It would seem that the intensity of a sexual experience can be such as to create such instability. Methamphetamine does not invariably create enhanced lust on first experience (Green and Halkitis, 2006).

Rather, it seems to require a learning effect involving the combination of drug and sexual opportunity. Methamphetamine tends to increase the attraction value of potential partners (Green and Halkitis, 2006).

If the findings on rats can be generalized to humans, taking d-amphetamine causes durable changes in the brain ('incentive sensitization') such that subsequently sexual motivation is also increased (Pitchers et al., 2010). Reciprocally, sexual experience sensitizes the brain to drug use. This again points to a common incentive process.

Heroin

Heroin and morphine usually lower sexual desire (Ford and Beach, 1951). For its aphrodisiac properties, heroin was given a positive ranking by some in the Haight-Ashbury study but not as high as cocaine or marijuana (Gay et al., 1975). Although not ranked highly in terms of sexual desire (some reported a lowering), it did better when it concerned the effects of touching and being touched. The general opinion amongst people addicted to heroin is that it has little effect on sexual desire or even lowers it (De Leon and Wexler, 1973; Hollister, 1975; Rawson et al., 2002). Another study, also done in Haight-Ashbury, and of people using shared needles to inject predominantly heroin, found that the act of social-injecting took on sexual connotations for some (Howard and Borges, 1970). For example, they would try to find a sexually attractive other to inject them. The comment was received that injecting was a 'sexual substitute'.

Mathias (1970) studied sexual desire in heroin addicts, finding it to be of minimal intensity. Whereas a group of non-addicted young men thrown into each other's company would frequently engage in 'sex talk', this was not the case for incarcerated heroin-addicted young men. Mathias reported that the drug knocks out their sexual desire and that (p. 98) 'Heroin replaces sex as the prime interest in their lives.' One prisoner described the substitute nature of heroin-taking: the searching for the drug, the gain of drug, the act of inserting the needle, the immediate orgasmic high and then a post-high phase of relaxation and serenity.

Comparing drugs

Drugs with a primary dopaminergic effect, most obviously cocaine and methamphetamine, amplify sexual desire and energize behaviour. By contrast, heroin primarily targets liking and either lowers sexual desire or gives a sexual connotation to the act of injection. Heroin mimics natural opioids and taps one of the *consequences* of engaging in hedonic activity. The effects of these drugs on sexual desire mirror their effects taken outside a sexual context. Klein (1987) reports that stimulants create the repeated desire for more drug until the drug runs out, comparable to the desire ('positive feedback') phase of sexuality. By contrast, opiates trigger satiation and sedation ('negative feedback'), comparable to orgasm and post-orgasmic satiety.

Part of the biological basis of orgasm and the subsequent satiety effect appears to be a sudden rush of endorphins, natural substances similar to opiates (Pfaus, 2009). Heroin floods the brain with endorphin-like substances that appear to substitute for sexual reward or to trigger something like sexual satiety. Thereby, it appears to act as a substitute for conventional sexual behaviour (De Leon and Wexler, 1973; Kellett, 2000).

Ecstasy primarily targets serotonin rather than dopamine. Like methamphetamine, it is also popular in the club circuit and also lowers inhibitions (Schilder et al., 2005). However, its effect is one of promoting emotional intimacy rather than sexual desire.

In summary

- Sexual desire commonly locks into interaction with romantic love.
- Dominance, anger and aggression can form an interaction with sexual desire.
- Various drugs, such as alcohol, can amplify sexual desire. Drugs that target dopamine such as cocaine and amphetamine are particularly effective in this regard.

SIXTEEN

REPRESENTATIONS OF SEX

I found everything that the most voluptuous pens have written about
pleasure: seductive books whose incendiary style forces the reader to
seek in reality what they depict in imagination.

(Casanova, 1798/1958, p. 94)

Basics

The use of representations of aspects of life is part of what it is to be human
(Byrne and Osland, 2000). Representations exist outside the brain on
film and paper and in its inner workings of fantasy. Our early ancestors
left us cave paintings depicting hunting scenes and wild animals. In the
period up to 600 BC, Etruscan art was already explicit in its depiction of
heterosexual and homosexual activity (Byrne and Osland, 2000). These
days we have films, the Internet, television, photographs, novels and
paintings to convey other worlds to our imaginations, including those of
sexuality and its possibilities.

Representations of sexuality can trigger arousal in the present as well
as plans for the future and reflections upon the past. In the absence of
a partner, as in masturbation, or even in their presence during sexual
activity, people commonly employ 'virtual' means of boosting sexual
excitation: erotic visual images, stories and the use of pure fantasy in the
imagination (Byrne and Osland, 2000).

It appears that representations of emotionally loaded events trigger a
similar set of brain regions as are triggered by the corresponding real
events, though with less intensity (Lang and Bradley, 2008). Knowing that they are not real, erotic images might create a preparation

('disposition') to action in the absence of overt action, which could be inhibited by the context. The startle reflex is inhibited by attractive erotic images and some internal physiological changes (heart rate, sweating) occur.

Erotic and pornographic images

General principles

There is commonly overlap between the terms 'erotic' and 'pornographic', the distinction sometimes appearing to be in the eye of the beholder. However, some use 'erotic' to denote the depiction of consensual and egalitarian sexual activities, whereas 'pornographic' is reserved for degrading and non-consensual activities, such as sexual violence and where exploitation is suspected (Byrne and Osland, 2000; Steinem, 1980).

Both men and women show a strong genital arousal to viewing explicit erotic depictions, as in films (Laan and Both, 2008). Whether women feel subjective arousal depends upon an interpretation of the images (Chapter 9). Much research on the brain's reaction to sexual stimuli comes from presenting erotic images, still or moving, to participants and observing changes in the activity of the brain (Stark et al., 2005). During the viewing of images that are judged to be sexually attractive, particular brain regions are excited.[1] From this and other evidence, for example on the reaction to food or drugs, these regions are thought to be associated with incentive motivation. In one study, erotic stimulation was triggered by asking participants to relate a highly arousing sexual experience (Rauch et al., 1999). The story was then recorded and later played back to them. Some brain regions implicated in motivation were activated in this way.[2]

Areas of the brain associated with the planning of actions[3] are also triggered into activity by watching erotic scenes, suggesting that the viewer is in some sense simulating the action (Stoléru and Mouras, 2006). Mirror neurons (Chapter 2) might well be implicated here (Mouras et al., 2008), their activity providing a measure of the desire to perform it. Of course, sitting with the head in a scanning device somewhat limits the potential for sexual action, and activity is also observed in brain regions that inhibit the translation of planning into action.[4]

One might suppose that watching such material in the absence of a partner would lead only to frustration, so a paradox associated with pornography as with strip-tease and live sex shows is as follows (Zillmann, 1984, p. 170): 'The enormous popularity of erotic fare has, of course, always been at variance with such a frustration argument. Are people seeking exposure time and time again in order to frustrate themselves?' Evidence suggests that such experience brings pleasure, but exactly why this is remains something of a puzzle.

The biggest gender difference in viewing erotica appears not to be in *liking* it, since women are able to be as aroused as men by its more subtle forms, but in *wanting* it (Leitenberg and Henning, 1995). Traditionally women have done little to obtain erotica/pornography, men being the prime consumers. By contrast, women are the prime consumers of romantic fiction and derive as much erotic stimulation from reading it as do men (Kinsey et al., 1953). Of course, overwhelmingly most pornography is geared to male sexual tastes. The advent of the Internet, with its perceived anonymity and the ready availability of pornography, has increased the number of women consumers (Chapter 17).

Does exposure to erotic representations change behaviour in encouraging people to try to repeat the actions? One only has to note the use of sex in advertising to suggest that representations do trigger desires as well as actions (Byrne and Osland, 2000). The multi-million dollar advertising industry, often using sexual images to sell anything from cars to soap, surely cannot be based wholly upon psychological misunderstandings (Rush, 1980). Several experimental findings across various cultures point to a boosting of sexual desire to engage in sexual activity as a result of viewing sexual imagery (Byrne and Osland, 2000). Of course, there is no simple one-to-one link. Furthermore, sexual representations often tap into powerful pre-existing desires.

X-rated movies typically show sex that is devoid of any restraints, precautions or negative consequences such as disease or unwanted pregnancy. This type of film might encourage a lack of responsibility in sexual behaviour and even promote promiscuity by over-estimating its extent current in society (Samson and Grabe, 2012). It appears to tilt the balance of excitation/inhibition in favour of excitation and serve the role of 'super-peer'.

Being sexually aroused by witnessing others' sexual activity is not confined to cultures that possess the technology for representation. In the Polynesian island of Mangaia, people are sexually excited by the sounds of others copulating. In some cultures, displays of copulation are performed to stimulate observers into action (Suggs and Marshall, 1971).

Habituation and escalation

In one regard, pornography mirrors reality: the multi-million dollar industry seems to bear witness to the tendency for habituation to set in with lengthy exposure. Surely, imagery of copulating bodies cannot go out of fashion that quickly, nor, even with extensive use, do any physical materials such as books and DVDs disintegrate. Indeed, controlled studies show that people become less aroused after repeated viewing of the same film, arousal being revived by a change of either actors or acts performed (Kelley and Musialowski, 1986). Extensive exposure turns some off pornography entirely or at least temporarily (Reifler et al., 1971), whereas others are motivated to seek more extreme forms, a familiar process of escalation. Over the years pornography has become more extreme, including increasing sadomasochistic themes (Doidge, 2007), suggesting an escalation in terms of satiety with earlier ('tame') forms setting in.

Watching pornography can create dissatisfaction in established relationships when the partner fails to live up to the standards of those in the film (Owens et al., 2012). The criterion of excellence has been elevated ('escalation'), so that what was previously exciting is no longer and such excitement that is obtained requires the person to fantasize about the scenes in the porn film. As a porn user known as Len observed (Maltz and Maltz, 2010, p. 89):

> Out of curiosity and for a change of pace I'd read most anything – stories of bondage, incest, gang rape, torture, and all of those sorts of bizarre things that you don't normally find . . . It's a matter of becoming accustomed. I'll find anything new and interesting at first. Then it becomes familiar and isn't as exciting.

Wanting and liking

It appears that for some people, as the intensity of wanting pornography goes up, so the liking of it does not increase in parallel, as with sexual addiction. It can now be better understood in terms of emerging knowledge about how the brain controls desire. As the psychiatrist Norman Doidge observed (Doidge, 2007, p. 107): 'Paradoxically, the male patients I worked with often craved pornography but didn't like it.'

Violent and coercive forms

Police reports indicate that violent sexual offenders commonly view pornographic materials prior to offending (Rush, 1980). Of course, we should not form any simple equation that viewing violent pornography produces sexual violence (Buss, 2005). Sexual violence predates historically the availability of pornographic representations and is found in cultures having little or no exposure. However, pornography could be one amongst many factors.

John Court reported (cited by Lederer, 1980, p. 17):

> a chain reaction with people constantly seeking stronger stuff...
> increased availability of material dealing with sadomasochism, bond-
> age, abuse of young children ... and ritual murder and torture for sexual
> pleasure.

Many people viewing violence have no wish to replicate the acts seen, but sadly some do. There is inconsistency concerning whether specifically aggressive pornography encourages sexual aggression, but the evidence suggests that it does (Owens et al., 2012; Lederer, 1980). Given the early plasticity of the brain (Chapter 2), we might expect adolescents to be particularly vulnerable to powerful visual images.

Of importance in understanding the role of pornography is which model ('theory') of behaviour we accept. These come in basically two kinds: the cathartic model and the imitation model (Bart and Jozsa, 1980). According to the cathartic model, a person watching pornography achieves release ('sublimation') of sexual and/or aggressive tendencies. This acts as a safety valve and reduces his or her subsequent tendency to commit the type of act in question. Of course, this raises the question of how long any cathartic effect lasts. A short-term effect could be followed by a longer-term tendency to copy the behaviour. If the catharsis model were true, one might expect that, as the availability of violent pornography has increased, so the frequency of rape would decline, whereas the opposite is the case (Bart and Jozsa, 1980). The imitation model suggests that the actors serve as role models and this increases the subsequent tendency for the viewer to enact the scenes.

At least one report suggests that watching what the researchers term 'erotic' rather than 'pornographic' material actually reduced males' sexually coercive attitudes (Russell, 1980).

Fantasy

[T]he image of Françoise perpetually returned, he was obsessed by the idea that she was coming to him, that he was taking her, consuming her in his embrace . . . But as soon as he got up and put his head in a bucket of cold water the idea shocked him, for he was too old for her; yet the next night the torment would begin again. (Émile Zola, 1887/1975, p. 94)

Basic principles

Presumably, the evolutionary function of 'hot imagery' is that people imagine what is (or might be) in the world even in the absence of the corresponding sensory stimulation (Kavanagh et al., 2005). It can energize behaviour and bridge the gap until contact is made or help avoidance strategies. By means of fantasy, people can simulate possible scenarios, 'testing the water' safely (Fisher, 1986). 'All my life I have gone back over, tinkered with and developed these few imagined situations with the application of someone composing a fugue, and those that serve me today are more or less altered versions of these originals' (Millet, 2003, p. 40). Mental images in the form of sexually arousing fantasy play an important role in the sexual experience of many, if not most, people, both when alone or during sexual interaction with others. This imagery appears to play a role in people's future sexual motivation, desire and planning, but much of it probably constitutes no more than unrealizable acting (Zillmann, 1984).

Fantasy can be triggered by externally produced stimuli, such as the sight of another person or viewing pornography, or might have little apparent relation to any external triggering. Having formed images of sexually desired others and interactions with them, those having the fantasy can then enjoy this as they manipulate it in their conscious minds. With luck on their side, in this fantasy world, people have control over their interactions with their partner and setting, limited only, quite literally, by their own imagination. Fantasy might also serve to fuel bizarre behaviours or trigger frustration as imagined events fail to occur in reality (Zillmann, 1984). As Kavanagh et al. (2005, p. 462) note in the context of drugs, but presumably of broader application: 'The relish seduces us into successive elaborations of the desire, but the piquancy of this relish also amplifies a sense of deprivation and torture when the target cannot immediately be obtained.'

Fantasy need not be contaminated by the embarrassments, fears and dangers nor the legal and social sanctions and practical difficulties that are involved in real sexual action. There are no government health warnings to restrain us, no nosey neighbours, no one to police and censor the experience, though it is not entirely free of guilt for everyone (Ellis and Symons, 1990). Given that it is not subject to such practical restraints and considerations, accurate accounts of fantasy could prove a valuable source of insight into 'unconstrained' desire (Hicks and Leitenberg, 2001). Evidence on fantasy is, rather obviously, derived primarily from the self-report of the person experiencing it. However, for the psychologist, fantasy can be used as a revealing probe of sexual interest and desire.

The activity has not always been so free of harmful consequences: under pressure in the Inquisition, confessing to the fantasy of committing adultery with the devil could lead to being burnt at the stake (Money, 1977). These days, for many people, fantasy is a world in which they need not fear shame, humiliation or rejection, unless, of course, that is necessary to excite them! Exceptions to this blissful state include when the fantasy is unacceptable either to the individual concerned (when it assumes the form of an obsessive disorder and thereby forms a different category of experience) or to society.

Spontaneous and responsive desires

A distinction is commonly made between spontaneous and responsive desires (Meana, 2010; Nobre and Pinto-Gouveia, 2008). Sexual fantasy can also be induced by a deliberate effort. A spontaneous desire is triggered in the imagination, whereas a responsive desire is triggered externally. It is frequently claimed that men show more spontaneous desire than women do. It would be hard to claim that every spontaneous desire simply pops from nowhere into the conscious mind. They presumably arise from an unconscious memory store, often primed by subtle environmental cues or conscious thoughts. There might be some external triggering by cues associated with desire, even unconsciously. So, spontaneous desire and responsive desire could lie on a continuum of being more or less externally triggered.

If the conscious mind is engaged in some incompatible activity, such as public speaking, any erotic imagery might be no more than fleeting. Otherwise, it might be elaborated (Kavanagh et al., 2005).

Frequency

Surprisingly, a poll carried out by the *New York Times* in 2000 found that 48 per cent of people did not approve of fantasy about someone other than the individual's current partner (Hicks and Leitenberg, 2001). Former US President Jimmy Carter famously admitted to having committed adultery 'in my heart' (Chapter 12), which he distinguished from physical adultery, the former being forgivable. Fantasy might not always be free of danger; Carter's poll ratings slipped after this confession. However, a survey at the University of Vermont, Burlington found that a large majority of men and women had sexual fantasies in the preceding two months (Hicks and Leitenberg, 2001). For those who feel guilt about their fantasies, this knowledge could offer some comfort.

Content

The precise content of fantasy surely takes many forms, but popular themes involve having sex with someone other than one's partner, having sex with a random stranger and group sex. In the University of Vermont study, 98 per cent of men and 80 per cent of women entertained fantasies about someone other than their partner (Hicks and Leitenberg, 2001).

Fantasy sometimes involves a complex story-line of sequential moves but at other times just a single brief passing scene of sexual encounter. Reliving a sexual encounter from the past is a popular theme (Crepault et al., 1977). Another theme is straightforward intercourse with a past or current partner (Doskoch, 1995). Common themes amongst women are ones that involve passivity and loss of responsibility, as in a masochistic interaction (Crepault et al., 1977). Of course, in such a fantasy women still remain in control, which makes the experience very different from reality (Russell, 1980).

Fantasy not only mirrors reality in terms of intensity and frequency but also in content (Byrne and Osland, 2000). Those having a fantasy involving coercion are also more likely to try coercive techniques in reality. A sample of women engaging in swinging and having their first homosexual experience in this context was examined (Dixon, 1984). Of those reporting masturbation, only 4.5 per cent of them fantasized about homosexual contact prior to the experience, whereas 61 per cent did so afterwards, exemplifying how fantasy can be fed by reality.

Context

Sexual fantasy can occur at any time, including during masturbation and non-sexual activities as well as sexual interactions (Jones and Barlow, 1990). During a sexual interaction, it can concern the present situation (e.g. a self-directed silent message of the kind 'of all the men I know, I must be the luckiest') or some hypothetical situation and partner. Erotic imagery can sometimes take on an obligatory component for a person to attain sexual arousal, with a particular detailed theme being repeated on each occasion (Crepault et al., 1977). Some men prove impotent without having their favourite fantasy as a prop (Money, 1977). In a sample of women, fantasy was particularly evident in the phase prior to orgasm and seemed to be a necessary trigger to attain this (Crepault et al., 1977). There is the occasional report such as the following of a woman for whom (Greenson, 1977; p. 226):

> In order to reach orgasm it was necessary for her husband to tell her stories of some sexual perversion which he had committed or imagined in the past.

Fantasy is especially evident in long-term relationships, where presumably it helps to compensate for reduction in desire (Crepault et al., 1977).

In surveys, of the people who report masturbating, the majority also report having fantasies while they do so, with males showing a higher percentage of fantasy than females (Leitenberg and Henning, 1995; Kinsey et al., 1953). In masturbation, males normally find it difficult, if not impossible, to reach orgasm in the absence of fantasy, whereas females more commonly achieve this (Kinsey et al., 1953). A high percentage of people report occasional fantasies during intercourse, with males and females roughly equally represented (Leitenberg and Henning, 1995).

Gender differences

Both men and women tend to enjoy and feel excited by their sexual fantasies and experience a rich and varied content. Men report more frequent sexual fantasy than do women (Ellis and Symons, 1990; Jones and Barlow, 1990), but we have only the sampled individuals' word for this difference.

There is some gender difference in the contents of fantasy, though this represents only a trend rather than an absolute distinction. As such, 'art' again imitates reality. Men tend to fantasize in terms of rich, explicit and rather basic visual 'anatomical' detail. For women, the tendency is to attach meaning, that is a context of relationship, romance and emotional empathy (Ellis and Symons, 1990; Leitenberg and Henning, 1995; Meana, 2010). Compared to the fantasy of females, that of males is more likely to be with a stranger, to be anonymous, to involve a much larger number of imagined partners, to accelerate rapidly in intensity and to switch partner mid-fantasy (Ellis and Symons, 1990).

It appears that men and women are about equal in terms of the amount of internally generated fantasy that they experience whereas males experience twice as much externally triggered fantasy, for example that in response to an attractive person in the street (Jones and Barlow, 1990). So, fantasy mirrors reality and again points to the layered nature of motivation, with women attributing meaning. Women's fantasies tend to situate them more frequently in the role of passive recipient, while men's concern the active initiator (Leitenberg and Henning, 1995).

The greater the number of sex partners a person has had, the greater is the tendency to fantasize about someone other than the current partner, a correlation that is particularly strong in women. Hicks and Leitenberg (2001) suggest three possible reasons for this:

- People with a relatively large number of past partners might have led the kind of life that subsequently triggers fantasy.
- A rich fantasy life might trigger people to try out novel partners.

- There could be a common factor of sensitivity to novelty underlying both number of partners and tendency to fantasize outside the current relationship.

Emergence of the fantasy's theme

Fantasy is believed to be involved in the development of sexual desire, whether conventional or deviant (Storms, 1981). Any association with masturbation is thought to strengthen the content of the fantasy. One particular fantasy acquired early can come to dominate fantasy life. This is exemplified by Catherine Millet: 'the very first narrative that accompanied my masturbating – and one that I used again and again for very many years – put me in a situation where I was dragged into one of these shelters by a boy. I saw him kissing me on the mouth and touching me all over as his friends came to join us' (Millet, 2003, p. 38).

Money (1977) suggested that, from puberty, men and women tend to have an ideal 'turn-on' fantasy that is persistent and stable for life. However, certain variations on such a theme can occur, corresponding to the phenomenon of escalation that is seen in sexual behaviour. Crepault et al. (1977 p. 269) write:

> eroticism does not require full perfection but a lack of such which ensures its eternal striving to attain such perfection, and fantasy is part and parcel of this striving toward a goal which is always one step removed from reality.

Suppose that a first or at least early experience of sexual arousal was triggered by a particular event, such as passionate kissing or watching a pornographic movie (Leitenberg and Henning, 1995). A high level of arousal could increase the strength of consolidation of memory. Therefore, this memory is likely to pop back into conscious awareness subsequently. It might occur spontaneously, by triggering from external cues similar to the arousing event or as a directed search of memory done with the goal of finding a fantasy and thereby triggering sexual arousal. Subsequently the fantasy can be 'cut and pasted' and enriched to incorporate new features or delete features that are no longer so arousing (e.g. a change of fantasy figure with a change of relationship). Masturbation can be used to consolidate the latest edit, with orgasm acting as a powerful reinforcer of the fantasy, thereby increasing the probability of its reoccurrence. This kind of process can be exemplified as follows.

The Victorian writer Walter described his first experience of an orgy (Walter, 1995, p. 354):

> I thought of nothing else for a long time. Nothing has ever yet fixed itself in my mind so vividly, so enduringly, except my doings with my first woman, Charlotte.

Serving in the Second World War, a Scottish man had his first experience of sex in brothels in Asia (McGuire et al., 1965). He was from a strictly religious background and believed that respectable women simply didn't consent to sex. After getting married, he fantasized that his wife was a prostitute and his potency depended upon such fantasy.

Sometimes the initial experience that sets the scene for fantasy does not need to be sexually arousing or even perceived to be sexually associated. However, on later reflection in fantasy the event might take a sexual character, which then can be amplified by masturbation (McGuire et al., 1965). An example concerned a Scottish boy who had been seduced when age 15 by a man on a train. He reported being frightened by the incident and shortly afterwards was punished for a sexual advance towards a girl. Later the incident on the train was used as a prop for masturbatory fantasy and subsequently the man developed a homosexual identity. Note that the early incident was not erotic or even pleasant, but it was emotionally potent, which might have facilitated its consolidation in memory and its later conversion to an erotic stimulus.

Freud and fantasy

Freud and his followers took a negative view of fantasy (Leitenberg and Henning, 1995), arguing for a so-called 'compensation model', sometimes termed a 'deficiency theory'. According to this, activity in the imaginary world is a correction for sexual deficiency in the real world and thereby reflects unsatisfied wishes. Given the Freudian notion of an internal equilibrium of pressure or energy levels that the individual strives to maintain within limits, it is easy to appreciate how one might arrive at such a view. What is not 'coming out' in reality does so in fantasy.

Contemporary theorists take a very different view from that of Freud, suggesting that not to have sexual fantasy is a sign of something being wrong, indicative of 'inhibited sexual desire' (Leitenberg and Henning, 1995). The *Diagnostic and Statistical Manual of the American Psychiatric Association* (DSM-IV) defines hypoactive sexual desire in terms of the criterion that 'desire for and fantasy about sexual activity are chronically or recurrently deficient or absent' (Pfaus, 2009).

People scoring high on sexual guilt and negative attitudes to sex score low on sexual fantasy frequency. Sex therapists encourage non-orgasmic women to employ fantasy during masturbation and intercourse (Leitenberg and Henning, 1995).

A contemporary incentive perspective

In incentive terms, human and non-human animals are pulled to sexual incentives and, in addition, we humans uniquely (?) can be 'pulled' in our world of fantasy. Evidence suggests that the brain processes underlying desire for a physically present individual have overlap with those underlying fantasy about the individual. Thus, sensitization of these common processes by, for example, hormones is reflected in enhanced desire for sexual activity and increased fantasy. Conversely, lack of interest tends to be reflected in low or absent fantasy. So, fantasy reflects reality, actual and desired.

As noted in Chapter 14, a sample of children first recognized the appearance of a sexual attraction, whether heterosexual or homosexual, at around the age of 10 years (McClintock and Herdt, 1996). Fantasy corresponding to their sexual orientation appeared about a year and a half later and actual orientation-specific sexual contact at around 13–15 years of age.

There is no evidence of a deprivation effect on fantasy; absence of sexual outlet does not increase the frequency of sexual thoughts (Leitenberg and Henning, 1995). If anything, fantasy frequency *increases* in parallel with sexual activity. The lack of a deprivation effect is unlike hunger, where there is an increased frequency of food-related thoughts with food deprivation. The lack of a deprivation effect is not surprising on the basis of incentive principles. A short-term deprivation might initially lead to increased sensitization of fantasy, as it does with desire and male ability.

However, beyond this short time sexual activity, real, in the immediate past or in prospect, contributes to sensitization of fantasy and thereby increased frequency.

In one sample of women, the earlier the age they started masturbation, the more frequent were their sexual fantasies as adults (Crepault et al., 1977). A life-time absence of masturbation was associated with a low frequency of fantasies. People who show the highest sexual activity, most frequent orgasms and the fewest problems experience the most sexual fantasies (Gosselin and Wilson, 1980; Jones and Barlow, 1990; Leitenberg and Henning, 1995; Shope, 1971). Those with the greatest variety of sexual experiences similarly have the greatest variety of sexual fantasies. In other words, a high desire and high arousability of desire circuitry is also reflected in an active fantasy life (Gosselin and Wilson, 1980). Women from the late twenties up to the time of menopause tend to exhibit a heightened sexual sensitivity, relative to both younger and older women (Easton et al., 2010). This is indexed by their frequency of sexual fantasies and such things as willingness to engage in sex after knowing a man for a short period of time.

The direction of what causes what could go either way: actual sexual activity could sensitize fantasy or fantasy could lead to increased activity, discussed next. Most likely both of these things occur in parallel.

Have fantasies a role in behaviour?

Intuitively, one might suppose that what a person entertains repeatedly in fantasy, often accompanied by masturbation, corresponds to what, given the chance, they would tend to put into practice in reality. Of course, out of fear, shame or guilt, some might be inhibited in putting their fantasies into effect and would see them as pure fantasy. Others might wish to put their fantasies into effect but lack a willing partner.

Suppose that it was known that, for an individual performing a particular sexual action, this had been preceded by extensive corresponding sexual fantasy over weeks or years. This would not prove that the fantasy played a role in *causing* the behaviour. As every psychology student soon learns, correlation does not prove causation. So, are fantasies mere incidental by-products of brain activity ('epiphenomena'), having no impact on actual behaviour? In principle, this is possible. Alternatively, does the fantasy make a contribution to later behaviour? This contribution might act in either direction. Does a history of fantasy about something increase or decrease the chances of putting the fantasy into effect if the opportunity arises?

There is little direct evidence on sexual behaviour, so we are forced to speculate, based upon other behaviour, where the evidence suggests that fantasy can alter subsequent behaviour. Practising a skill in the conscious mind can improve its subsequent performance in reality (Baumeister et al., 2011). This is particularly likely to be so at the start of acquiring a new skill, before it has become automatic. Fantasy can take the form of rehearsing plans of the kind, 'if I encounter situation X, do Y'. Subsequently, encountering situation X, behaviour Y is more likely to occur as a result of the mental practice.

One report suggests that triggering an increase in sexual fantasy can have an excitatory effect on subsequent sexual behaviour (Eisenman, 1982). Students had their sexual fantasy primed by being read an erotic passage and then they were asked to generate their own extensive fantasies and to write them down. In the immediately following period of days, an increased frequency of sexual activity was reported, though with no new sexual variations appearing in the repertoire.

Another report suggested that certain types of fantasy, which concern future negative emotion, can have an inhibitory effect on subsequent sexually linked behaviour (Richard et al., 1996, cited by Baumeister et al., 2011). Participants were asked to consider how they might feel after practising unsafe sex and this was associated with a lower risk of performing unsafe sex.

The possible role of fantasy assumes a particular importance when it concerns illegal sexual activity (Chapters 20 and 21). Many people who commit sex crimes report a prior phase of fantasy (Leitenberg and Henning, 1995), and the assumption is commonly made that repeated fantasy contributes to the corresponding action. However, as just noted, correlation does not prove that the fantasy had any effect on behaviour. In principle at least, it might have had no effect at all or it might have served for at least some of the time as a safety-valve. It might even have two effects acting in the opposite direction in the same person: a very short-term satiety effect as a result of its association with masturbation but a long-term sensitization effect.

Not all sex offenders report a prior history of fantasy. A caution needs reiterating here: we only have the word of the offenders and, of course, they are likely to be more motivated to create the right impression rather than to contribute to psychological research. A contrite account that attributes their behaviour to, say, an unexpected and chance moment of madness while stressed and intoxicated could well go down better with a parole board than would the confession of an extensive prior history of deviant fantasy. So, the figures might underestimate the frequency of prior fantasy in offenders.

Some insights into the possible role of fantasy in behaviour might be gained by studying the activity of the brain, discussed next.

Biological roots

Evidence on the role of hormones suggests a common incentive process that underlies desire, arousal and fantasy. Thus, hormones have a similar effect on fantasy as they do on sexual behaviour and, in men erectile capacity. The level of testosterone in the blood is a principal determinant of the level of desire and the frequency of sexual fantasies in males and females; as the level rises, so does the frequency of fantasies (Regan and Berscheid, 1999; Leitenberg and Henning, 1995). In men, a drastic lowering of testosterone levels as a consequence of treatment for prostate cancer is followed by a sharp reduction in the intensity of sexual fantasy (Bokhour et al., 2001). Some women are able to achieve orgasm by means of fantasy alone, suggesting brain processes that are common with arousal triggered by sexual contact (Whipple et al., 1992).

What parts of the brain are involved in sexual fantasy? It is believed that the relatively large cerebral cortex in humans provides the biological basis for the capacity to exploit fantasy in rich and creative ways (Abramson and Pinkerton, 1995). However, other brain regions are doubtless also involved in giving fantasy its emotional and motivational colouring.

Neuroimaging provides insight into fantasy and its possible link to actual sexual behaviour. Results of experiments on feeding and drug-taking can be cautiously extrapolated to sex. Some of the brain regions most closely associated with the desire to pursue physically present incentives can be identified (Chapter 8). These same regions are also involved in fantasy about them. Craving for drugs such as cocaine is associated with activation of the same brain regions[5] as are excited by the sight of drugs (Kilts et al., 2004).

Reading pleasant stories, as distinct from unpleasant or neutral stories, activates the incentive-related brain regions: the nucleus accumbens and medial prefrontal cortex (Costa et al., 2010). This suggests the possibility of overspill from fantasy to reality, in that excitation of these brain regions triggered during fantasy would make an approach towards actual sexual incentives more likely. This observation also raises the distinct possibility that repeated excitation of these particular brain regions by fantasy could sensitize them so that they have increased responsiveness to actual sexual stimuli. This could make subsequent approach to these incentives more likely.

Some research into the dynamics of the mind is relevant to the role of fantasy, though it was carried out in the context of politics rather than sex (Westen et al., 2006). It was grounded in what is termed 'motivated reasoning'. This term refers to the observation that human reasoning is guided not just by rational principles but by the outcomes of the reasoning. The human is motivated to reason in such a way that outcomes maximize pleasure ('positive affect') and minimize displeasure ('negative affect'). This was articulated by Sigmund Freud as the phenomenon of 'defence', by means of which people act on their cognitions to seek to avoid psychological distress.

So, in making a judgement on, say, a statement by a political candidate, a person's judgement would be guided by both a rational analysis of the content but also by how comfortable the individual is with the outcome of the analysis. Hearing a statement that is at odds with one's convictions might be expected to activate parts of the brain concerned with emotional processing and this could prompt a search for a so-called exculpatory ('get-out clause') cognition that would lower the intensity of the negative emotion.

Neuroimaging was employed to observe the activity of the brain when politically partisan people were given a sequence: (a) a statement made by their favoured candidate, (b) an apparently incompatible statement and (c) an exculpatory statement (i.e. one that could lower the disparity felt on exposure to statements (a) and (b)).[6] Resolution of the conflict by presentation of the exculpatory statement was associated with activation of the ventral striatum, a region containing the nucleus accumbens.

The researchers argued that since this brain region is activated by the presentation of conventional rewards such as food, the resolution seen in the study also constitutes a form of reward. There was a parallel lowering of activity in brain regions associated with negative emotion,[7] giving thereby, as the researchers express it, a source of double reinforcement. One can speculate that this reinforcement will increase the power of such exculpatory statements to trigger this reward process in the future.

It is reasonable to extrapolate this to the mental life surrounding sexual desire. The experiment suggests that the outcome of emotionally coloured cognitive reasoning can activate the same brain pathways as conventional rewards. This raises the issue that 'successful' resolution of the story-line involved in sexual fantasy could strengthen reward pathways and make it more likely for the fantasy to be enacted in reality. This assumption runs implicitly through the literature on forensic psychology and here lies a possible biological basis. While we are with the subject of exculpatory statements, it is relevant to note that these form the stock-in-trade of sex offenders, both in their intrinsic mental functioning and exchanged with other offenders (described again later). These include 'you are really doing the child a favour' and 'women say no when they mean yes'.

Sexual dreams

> One dream haunted her almost every night. She dreamed that both were her husbands at once, that both were lavishing caresses on her.... And she was marvelling that it had once seemed impossible to her, was explaining to them, laughing, that this was ever so much simpler, and that now both of them were happy and contented. (Tolstoy, 1877/1977, p. 151)

Dreams are a form of fantasy in that the brain runs simulations of possible scenes in their physical absence. They could reflect a problem-solving exercise – testing out possibilities, however improbable they might be. Explicit sexual dreams appear to be more frequent in males than in females (Ellis and Symons, 1990). The erotic content of dreams tends to correspond with the waking desires and activities of the dreamer, for example heterosexuals tend to have heterosexual encounters in their dreams (Kinsey et al., 1948).

Freud went to great lengths to describe the coding of the hidden sexual themes of dreams in terms of a non-sexual content. However, Webster (1995) notes the extraordinary fact that Freud does not try to account for dreams that have an explicit sexual theme and often reflect the same fantasies as those entertained in daily life. Kinsey et al., (1953) argue that dreams might represent sexual desires unrestrained by social conventions and inhibitions. Furthermore, they rapidly lead to orgasm in many cases.

It would seem that over two thousand years before Freud made his counter-intuitive claims, Plato was already much nearer the truth. Plato suggested that dreams expose raw desire lifted from its usual restraints such that all sorts of forbidden partners can be recruited. Consider the following (Plato, *Republic*, 571c, p. 308):

'But what are the desires you mean?'

'The sort that wake while we sleep, when the reasonable and humane part of us is asleep and control is relaxed, and our fierce bestial nature, full of food and drink, rouses itself and has its fling and tries to secure its own kind of satisfaction . . . It doesn't shrink from attempting intercourse (as it supposes) with a mother or anyone else, man beast or god.'

Indeed, this has a modern feel to it; there is evidence that the prefrontal regions of the brain are tuned down in sleep (Madsen et al., 1991). Freud might have been spared such nocturnal temptations, but others concur with Plato on what is surely for many a very familiar experience. For example, St Augustine recorded God's ability to 'quench the fire of sensuality which provokes me in my sleep' (*Confessions*, x.30).

William Acton, an English Victorian 'sexologist', wrote extensively on the dangers of masturbation. Although few would give credence to such views today, Acton was probably right about erotic dreams (quoted by Marcus, 1966, p. 24):

if a man has allowed his thoughts during the day to rest upon libidinous subjects, he finds his mind at night full of lascivious dreams . . . A will which in our waking hours we have not exercised in repressing sexual desires, will not, when we fall asleep, preserve us from carrying the sleeping echo of our waking thoughts farther than we dared do in the daytime.

Since they are involuntary, an interesting moral issue can arise in the context of nocturnal orgasms. Catholic doctrine traditionally regarded them as without sin even if enjoyed, provided that they were neither deliberately induced (e.g. by prior tactile stimulation) nor *consciously* welcomed (Kinsey et al., 1953).

In summary

- Viewing pornography can be associated with habituation and escalation in an attempt to maintain its value.
- Pornography could increase the chances of trying to enact the scenes depicted.
- Most people experience sexual fantasy.
- Sexual fantasy is not a response to sexual deprivation but often occurs most frequently at times of highest sexual activity.
- Fantasy appears to utilize some of the same brain processes as are used in sexual wanting and behaviour.

SEVENTEEN

SEXUAL ADDICTION

O Lord, my helper and my Redeemer, I shall now tell and confess to the glory of your name how you released me from the fetters of lust which held me so tightly shackled and from my slavery to the things of this world.

(Augustine, *Confessions*, VIII.6)

The phenomena to be explained

If psychotherapists and gossip columnists had been plying their trades at the time of St Augustine, some would surely have diagnosed 'sexual addiction'. These days, when news breaks on a sex scandal involving a public figure, pundits are sought in an attempt to answer the question: 'Why on earth take the risk, since surely he must have known of the potentially disastrous consequences?' The cases of Bill Clinton and Tiger Woods come to mind. Television journalists, psychiatrists and psychologists argue for and against the validity of the term 'sexual addiction'.

Alas, such discussions are likely to descend into semantic hair-splitting. Those interviewed often cannot even agree that sexual addiction exists as a useful diagnostic category, let alone whether a particular individual qualifies for the label. (For a criticism of the notion of 'sexual addiction', see Ley, 2012.)

At what point, does a so-called 'womanizer', 'philanderer' or 'ladies' man' become an addict?[1]

So, what is in a term? In this case, a great deal, it would seem. People use 'addiction' to serve distinct ends, pointing to an element of social construction in its meaning. Consider, for example, a woman in the

314

divorce courts who wishes to damn her cheating husband, win a handsome settlement and gain custody of the children. To her, 'addiction' might mean feckless, immoral and freely choosing a selfish life-style, which makes the husband worthy of the kind of social disapproval more commonly directed to street junkies. By contrast, to a woman trying to find reconciliation, sympathy and forgiveness for an errant husband, or to a defence counsel in a criminal trial seeking mitigation, the same term might imply an unintended and involuntary course of action. Addiction is sometimes construed as a loss of control as a result of a process going seriously wrong in the workings of the brain. In the spirit of the more sympathetic perspective, to give uncontrolled sexuality the designation 'addiction' brings it nearer to a medical interpretation. Similarly, in using such terms as 'shackles' and 'slavery', St Augustine points to a perceived loss of control. Also, in keeping with this perspective, for people said to be addicted to sex, there are in-patient clinics, self-help books and web-sites, sufferers' groups modelled on Alcoholics Anonymous, as well as at least one treatment-related learned journal. As far as I can discover, there exists nothing equivalent targeted to 'philanderers'.

Use of the combination of words 'addict' and 'treatment' implies distress; something has gone seriously wrong, either for the addicted person or his family or both. Words convey subtle meanings and intentions. To a growing number in the caring professions, 'addiction' seems to imply something out of kilter in the body, such that the power to make free and informed choices has been compromised, if not lost. Thereby, the scales are tipped, even if only slightly, towards sympathy and help rather than moral blame and censure. The term 'compulsion' points the same way but perhaps even more strongly.

An observation of only the behaviour itself in terms of its type and frequency of expression might not yield a diagnosis of addiction (Orford, 2001). Rather, it is the *conflict* underlying the behaviour and its consequences that leads to this term or to the alternative 'excessive appetite'. One could imagine secular contemporaries of St Augustine acting in much the same way but experiencing little or no guilt or conflict, and one might feel it inappropriate to employ the term 'addiction' to describe them. Conflict necessarily implies forces acting in opposite directions, that is excitatory and inhibitory. Where behaviour is excessive, excitatory factors obviously outweigh inhibitory. Inhibition might normally derive from personal guilt or social controls, such as the weight exerted by family pressure or religious institutions. This is the definition to be adopted here, but I cannot claim any absolute authority and doubtless controversy will remain.

Arguments on free choice and being 'out of control' often seem to come down to issues of philosophy and ethics, areas that might derive some illumination from psychology but rarely any resolution. However, we should not allow quibbles over terminology to halt progress since there exist many terms, such as 'moral virtue' and 'free will', which are equally hard to define but are nonetheless pragmatically useful. The term 'addiction' captures a real feature of behaviour, describing important aspects of how sexual desire can seriously malfunction. Furthermore, under this label, much distress and need for help can be subsumed.

Given that sex is one of the most intense of hedonic experiences, if not the most intense, it would be very surprising if something like an addiction were not an associated risk (Orford, 2001). Estimates of the prevalence of sexual addiction lie between 0.7 and 6 per cent of the US population (Gold and Heffner, 1998; Ley, 2012). Since sexual addiction can be associated with disease, financial and professional ruin and family breakdown, as well as, in a few extreme cases, serious crime, it is difficult to exaggerate the importance of gaining understanding of it.

Some of sexual addiction's essential features are excitement, destructiveness and lack of one-to-one reciprocity with an 'object' of desire (Carnes, 2001). The rest of the addict's life can become subordinate to the addiction, while the toll on family, social and professional spheres can be insufferable. Addicted people are usually in a situation that they would rather not be in and they dislike themselves for being in it. However, some only recognize their addiction in retrospect when they review their life histories and then feel regrets.

In each form of sexual addiction, the individual's mind can be taken over, engrossed trance-like with the search for a specific sexual achievement. Rerunning past encounters in the imagination can yield a 'high' and serve as a distraction to divert the mind from current concerns, for example professional or family. The quest can take on ritualistic properties of needing to repeat a particular regular sequence of activities. As

Carnes expresses it (p. 20): 'It is the pursuit, the hunt, the search, the suspense heightened by the unusual, the stolen, the forbidden, the illicit that are intoxicating to the sexual addict.' Often the addictive activity is non-threatening in one sense: there is little chance of rejection. The expectation of ultimate 'success' must be high, especially in the cases of watching pornography or compulsive masturbation! It must be relatively rare that sex workers reject a client, whereas pornography shops and sex theatres probably do so even less frequently. In the case of some other targets, the addicted person's victim has little or no say concerning rejection. Paradoxically, in spite of their powerlessness in the face of the addiction, the individual has at last found a source of 'high' over which he has a degree of prediction and control. In some cases, he can hone and perfect his skills.

There are several related issues to be developed in the present chapter:

- The discussion of whether sex can be addictive is useful in highlighting important features shared by several behaviours, some drug-related, such as heroin use, and others non-drug-related, such as sex and gambling. A few differences between drug and non-drug addictions also emerge.
- A comparison of sex addiction with more uncontroversial addictions, such as those to certain drugs, reveals common underlying processes in the brain, while the subjective experiences of addicted individuals are similar (Orford, 2001).
- It is difficult to perform realistic laboratory experiments on any addiction, perhaps most of all to sex, and so psychologists can gain insight by cautiously extrapolating from research on the more tractable drug and gambling addictions.
- Sex addiction shows where the processes that underlie non-addictive ('conventional') sexual behaviour, introduced in earlier chapters, can 'become excessive'. Thereby, excess illuminates so-called normality. In the terms of the present book, the processes involved are those of incentive motivation and levels of control, so the model suggested in earlier chapters will be applied to sexual addiction.
- Addiction to sex often does not exist in isolation but can co-exist and mutually reinforce other addictions, such as to drugs or romance.

What constitutes addiction and does sex qualify?

Back to the original meaning

In the United States, the website of the National Council on Sexual Addiction and Compulsivity defines the phenomenon as:

> a persistent and escalating pattern or patterns of sexual behaviours acted out despite increasingly negative consequences to self or others.

The original meaning of the word 'addiction' is simply that of excessive devotion to something, and is equally applicable to, say, sex, religious worship or work, as to heroin or alcohol (Alexander, 2008; Orford, 2001). However, in the first decades of the twentieth century the term came to be used mainly, if not exclusively, to refer to an addiction to drugs and this still has a pervasive influence. Later in the twentieth century, some investigators argued for a reversion to the original meaning. Thereby, excesses of feeding, sex, shopping, gambling and exercise could be included under the heading. The term 'sexual addiction' only emerged in the early 1980s, though such behaviour has surely been around for a very long time (Turner, 2008). So, one aspect of sexual addiction is the behaviour's excessiveness relative to some standard of normality (Orford, 2001). Of course, what constitutes 'normal activity' is open to discussion, and cultural relativity is enormous.

To merit the term 'addiction', it appears that the activity needs in some way to be disruptive or harmful to the addicted person or others (Orford, 2001). Heroin addiction can lead to death through infection, overdose or criminal activity. Nicotine addiction can cause various diseases. Some argue that 'addiction' should be applied only where intake of a chemical is involved, since the other behaviours are not lethal. Is this true? Excessive sex does not, of course, usually compromise the integrity of the body, except in the cases of, say, infectious disease or violence. However, in the rare instance, a jealous partner can kill or be killed. Loss of job and family and even suicide can follow disclosure.

One way of viewing addiction is that the individual devotes an excessive ('sub-optimal') allocation of time and effort to a restricted range of activities or even a single activity (Brown, 1997). Normally, various behaviours compete for expression. Time is allocated to them such that each makes a balanced contribution by which our hedonic tone is more or less maintained at a reasonable level. Addictions can distort such time management by capturing decision-making. A very high incentive salience is attributed to the addictive activity. Undue time, effort and money are often allocated to gaining its short-term effects and it displaces more reliable means of raising hedonic tone over the longer term, albeit less dramatically so. Addictive activities have immediate positive effects, while the negative consequences are delayed and hence do little to undermine its potency.

Depending upon the particular individual and their addiction, different states accompany the rise in hedonic tone. In some cases, a move from a low level of arousal ('boredom') to a desired state of a higher arousal is achieved. Sex would be expected to fit this pattern. High arousal while engaged in the activity might normally be followed by calming. So, a desired alteration of the 'state of consciousness' is a common feature of addictions (Brown, 1997).

Does an addiction need to be chemical?

The logic that only chemicals could truly be 'addictive' was rooted in the observation of unpleasant bodily withdrawal symptoms when drug use was discontinued. Then came the realization that there could be addictions to drugs, for example to cocaine, with few if any physically evident signs of withdrawal. Rather, there was the psychological distress of a depressed mood associated with craving and the search for more drug. Conversely, a non-chemical addiction, gambling, can be associated with insomnia and such bodily disturbances as colitis, constipation, a knotted stomach and excessive perspiration (Orford, 2001). Such evidence has contributed to a reinterpretation of the criteria of addiction. A new model emerged, in which any addiction reflected an attempt to self-medicate mental distress and sex was an equally viable candidate to take the label 'addictive' (Alexander, 2008; Washton and Zweben, 2009).

Suppose someone argues that a necessary feature of addiction is the use of a chemical substance. In such terms, one could be addicted to chocolate or French fries but not to sex. This hardly seems a useful distinction. Furthermore, according to a contemporary understanding of brains and minds, each type of behaviour is, at the same time, both chemical and psychological. That is to say, behaviour depends upon chemical events in the brain. In turn, behaviour, whether that of taking a chemical into the body or not, alters these same chemical events. Based upon the insights of modern neuroscience (Berridge and Kringelbach, 2013), it seems reasonable to speculate that the hedonic consequence of any addiction is rooted in opioid processes in the brain (Chapter 10). Excitement is also associated with a surge of adrenalin, amongst other bodily chemicals, which could contribute to sex's addictive potency (Carnes, 2001).

At once, psychological and physical

While acknowledging that addictions come in a wide variety, some authors distinguish between *physical* addictions (e.g. to heroin) and *psychological* addictions (e.g. gambling, sex). As a description of the target of addiction and the nature of the immediate interaction, that is either a chemical substance or non-substance, this has validity. However, as a description of the addiction itself, it is problematic. It suggests that a range of behaviours are in some sense 'non-physical', even though we know that they are organized in the brain and can identify the brain regions and neurochemicals involved. Conversely, it suggests that addictions to chemicals are 'non-psychological', yet surely craving for anything has to be psychological. Similarly, we know that psychological factors such as despair and alienation are crucially important in triggering urges to take drugs (Alexander, 2008). Social and other environmental factors play a crucial role in drug urges and relapse. So, although some addictions involve taking in chemicals and others do not, all addictions are simultaneously physical and psychological.

What constitutes 'natural' in the twenty-first century?

Yet another argument used against the notion of 'sex addiction' is that, unlike taking drugs, sex is a perfectly natural activity, an essential part of our evolution. The same logic suggests that there could not be an 'eating addiction'. This seems an illogical criterion.

By analogy, the capacity to experience, say, sadness at a social loss or fear when confronted by threats is surely 'natural' and a part of our evolutionary history, serving to preserve social bonds and to protect us from danger. However, when these emotional reactions take the form of clinical depression or anxiety, they can become a serious medical problem.

Just because feeding and sex are evolutionary adaptations does not mean that they are immune from pathology best described as addiction. Remember 'evolutionary mismatch' (see Chapter 2); we did not evolve in a world of fast food and refined sugars and surely neither did we evolve surrounded by drop-in bath-houses, sex shops and Internet porn. Both food and sex as presented in the twenty-first century constitute 'supernormal stimuli' to our motivational processes, making them liable to switch into an addictive mode.

Is it an illness?

Is an addiction an illness? This of course depends upon how you define an illness and I cannot arbitrate here. Former US President Gerald Ford, speaking of Bill Clinton, argued (cited in DeFrank, 2007, p. 132): 'Betty and I have talked about this a lot. He's sick – he's got an addiction.' Unlike unambiguous illnesses, such as cancer or influenza, for sex addiction there is no obvious and measurable disturbance in the body. However, the same could be said of anxiety and phobias. If distress is the criterion then the term might be applicable, provided that genuine suffering is involved.

Sex in comparison with other addictions

> I needed to distract myself, so I went off to gamble; gambling is some-times an excellent sedative for love. (Casanova, 1798/1958, p. 77)

Different addictions show similarities in terms of observable events in the body, behaviour and subjective experience (Orford, 2001). People addicted to sex, alcohol, gambling or eating all reveal several or all of the following:

- A feeling of being 'out-of-control' and driven. The behaviour is excessive by conventional standards.
- Mental preoccupation with the addictive activity.
- An experience of conflict and guilt.
- Failed attempts at restraint.

The addictive behaviour might sometimes take certain features of a habit, a kind of automatic reaction to a particular stimulus. It is well established that drug addiction shows this property (Tiffany, 1990). For sex, St Augustine described this: 'Habit was too strong for me when it asked "Do you think you can live without these things?"' (*Confessions*, VIII.11). An escape from boredom and the achievement of euphoria are common features underlying chemically based and non-chemically based addictions (Chaney and Chang, 2005; Orford, 2001). Various addictions, including sex and gambling, are also associated with the attainment of so-called 'dissociated states' of mind. Thereby, the normal flow of conscious mental life is disrupted and distraction occurs so that the focus moves from anxious thoughts, such as rumination about personal inadequacies (Kuley and Jacobs, 1988; Orford, 2001).

Unlike some other addictions, the sexually addicted person is almost inescapably bombarded day and night with visual trigger cues to their addiction. The streets throng with sexual cues and, even at home, TV and Internet advertisements tell of the association between sex and success as measured by such things as the value of one's car. Going to a self-help group might unavoidably put the addicted person in close proximity to precisely the trigger to their addiction, rather as if meetings of Alcoholics Anonymous were to be held in a bar.

In comparison with gambling

In gambling addiction, the person can gain relief from painful thoughts and act out fantasies of boosted esteem. The majority of heavy gamblers gave positive answers to each of the following questions concerning their gambling experiences:

- Did you feel as if you were in a trance?
- Did you feel outside yourself watching yourself from another vantage point?
- Did you feel as if you had acquired another identity?
- Have you ever had a memory blackout whilst gambling?

People addicted to gambling also tend to be sensation-seekers, putting a value on variety and novelty. They offer accounts of the experience in such terms as 'relief of boredom', 'oblivious to surroundings', 'adrenalin rush' and being on a 'high'; occasionally the experience is compared to sexual excitement (Orford, 2001). Similarly, people prone to impulsive buying occasionally report being 'overwhelmed', 'out of control' and 'hypnotized' as they interact with prospective purchases (Rook, 1987). Subsequently, goods bought impulsively can lead to long-term distress.

Sexually addicted people report a similar altered state of consciousness to gambling addicts (Chaney and Chang, 2005; Schwartz and Southern, 2000). Engaging in the addictive activity triggers a boost of self-esteem, combined with dissociation, loss of the sensations of time, boredom and self-identity. From addicted patients, Bancroft and Vukadinovic (2004) recorded 'nothing else under consideration', 'kills time and pain' and 'feel detached from what is happening'. This suggests a shift to a lower level of control of consciousness and behaviour, in which present external stimulation is 'in the driving seat'.

The altered state of consciousness that can be gained by engaging in sexually addictive behaviour was illustrated by Ryan (1996, p. 3):

> It's as if an electronic magnet in my solar plexus were switched on. At its most intense, I'd go into a kind of trance, dissociated, beamed in from Mars, my mouth dry and my heart pounding, my usual waking consciousness hovering somewhere outside my body while I was taken by the pull.

A primary factor in gambling addiction appears to be the generation of excitement, with large heart rate increases as a gambler starts to get near to the gambling location and throughout the gambling activity (Brown, 1997). It seems that increases in arousal are an ingredient in increasing hedonic tone and in turning the gambling situation into a trigger to addiction. This factor could equally apply to sexual addiction. Gambling also suggests another factor that might generalize to sexual addiction: the disparity between current hedonic tone and a memory of the highest hedonic tone ever experienced. Presumably, a big and unexpected win is comparable to an early mind-blowing sexual encounter or porn image. Over weeks and months, the individual is motivated to try to close this gap.

A profoundly important feature of both gambling and sexual addictions is the uncertainty of reward. To those of a behaviourist orientation, reinforcement is said to be 'partial' rather than 'continuous'. The gambler does not know when luck will change and high winnings will arise. Similarly, neither does the sex addict know who might appear in the nightclub next time or when reward in the form of the perfect image will follow the click of a mouse. When high reward follows the click, it does so without delay, another contribution to the strength of reinforcement. As discovered by B. F. Skinner, such a so-called 'schedule of reinforcement' is one that is particularly effective in strengthening behaviour and causing its persistence in people, rather as with rats and pigeons pressing a lever for food.

In comparison with drugs

In the case of drugs, the prime trigger for the move to addiction is a sub-stance taken into the body that has effects ('incentive sensitization') on the brain. Subsequently, as a result of classical conditioning (see Chapter 2), particular features of the environment (e.g. places where the drug is taken) then get locked into a new mode of interaction with the chemically changed brain. That is to say, these features of the environment acquire conditional incentive properties such that they can trigger changes in the brain that underlie drug-wanting.

As noted earlier, if we generalize from studies on rats (Pitchers et al., 2010), sexual experience sensitizes dopaminergic systems underlying wanting. One could speculate that such sensitization is excessive in the case of sexual addiction. In sex and drugs, a similar set of chemical effects within the brain seems to be triggered (Pitchers et al., 2010), but in the case of sex, both initially and subsequently, the trigger is from *outside* the body (e.g. by repeated contact with pornography). By conditioning, this then sets up links with other features of the environment (e.g. the red light signalling brothels comes to trigger wanting/desire). Thus, expressed in physical terms, in each case a crucial link in the addictive sequence is the effect on the brain (Gold and Heffner, 1998).

Of the people interviewed by Giugliano (2008), some did not stop their sexually addictive activity for long enough to experience withdrawal symptoms. Others did report withdrawal effects and they consisted of such features as:

- depression
- anger and irritability
- insomnia

- anxiety
- fatigue
- guilt and shame
- inability to focus
- physical ailments

That symptoms of withdrawal from sexual addiction have features in common with those of withdrawal from drugs points to the broad validity of the term addiction (Maltz and Maltz, 2010).

Ambivalence and conflict

For each addiction, the addicted person can be in conflict, often torn between carrying on and trying to quit (Orford, 2001). Maltz and Maltz (2010) suggest that sexually addicted people are (p. 2): 'unable to stop using pornography even when they are aware of the negative consequences it is having on their lives'. Ambivalence is best conveyed in the words of people who have experienced out-of-control sexual behaviour. Consider this example (Giugliano, 2008, p. 148):

> I remember throwing away porn and my heart went (hand gesture – indicating breaking) and then I went back to the trash and took it all out again.

There is also the insight of the English comedian Russell Brand (2007, p. 10): 'It felt strange to be chatting up the airhostesses on the American Airlines flight, knowing that I was on my way to a residential treatment centre for sexual addiction.' Occasionally, ambivalence is felt already in the immediate after-effects of engaging in the activity. This is illustrated by the American writer Michael Ryan, who was 'basically heterosexual' but engaged also in homosexual activity (Ryan, 1996, p. 330):

> [T]o have sex with men, was my deepest degradation. It enacted my calcified childhood shame. Of all my shame-based sexual behaviours, this was the most shameful to me.

In some cases, the conflict arises more from the pressure of others, for example courts and the probation service, than from regrets or a wish to acknowledge the problem and try to quit. Salter (1988, p. 87) writes: 'For many clients child molestation is an addiction. They are more frightened by being without the addiction than of continuing it.'

The danger of relapse is common to addictions as are some of the conditions likely to trigger it, for example being in a mood associated earlier with addiction, reviving a memory of the addictive experience or being in an environment earlier associated with the activity. Chapter 12 described the so-called 'cold-to-hot empathy gap': that is, a person in a cold emotional state has difficulty empathizing with how they would feel and their ability to resist temptation when in a hot state. This can be a problem in sexual addiction, where a person in a cold state is tempted to do a test of their reaction and, say, take just a quick look at porn (Maltz and Maltz, 2010).

Tolerance and escalation

Another criterion leading to the description 'addiction' is that the behaviour shows tolerance over time, for example increasingly larger doses of drug are required to obtain the same high. Something analogous to this is found in sexual addiction (Chaney and Chang, 2005). Tolerance in this case is closely linked to the phenomenon of habituation or satiation to a constant incentive and the revival of desire that is triggered by novelty. Consider the case of Tom (Maltz and Maltz, 2010, p. 135):

> I never found the perfect picture, but I would find one that suited me in the moment, that helped me reach climax. I never returned to the same one. Every night was a different picture. Each one I looked at quickly got old and lost its power. I became really desensitized.

Note that the *consequence* of engaging with porn shows habituation, while wanting porn is as strong as ever or even stronger, exemplifying the wanting–liking distinction. One could speculate that the feedback consequence of engaging in sexual behaviour is something like a rush of endorphins. Presumably, over repeated experience the size of the rush diminishes, yet the memory of the earlier rushes is still present.

A 30-year-old American male reported how his criteria of acceptance have changed:

In the last couple of years, the more porn I've viewed, the less sensitive I am to certain porn that I used to find offensive. (Schneider, 2000, p. 257)

The following cases lead to a similar conclusion (Giugliano, 2008, p. 147):

Yes in the initial experience of going to a bathhouse if I ended up with two people that was like, 'Wow my God, I'm a slut.' But over the years two is like nothing. I know it may sound very crude but to be with 3 or 4 people at different times doesn't seem to be a big deal anymore.

One of the things I did not engage in before, which became common-place, is engaging in sex with more than one person at a time. I've had sex with four people in my room. You need to experience more and more intensity or it becomes boring after a while.

I took bigger risks. Over time I would go towards prostitutes that would not require condoms. It started monthly then weekly.

It increased in time and frequency. It started out weekly and ended up daily. And I would spend more time having phone sex.

In other words, the only way is up. Rather as the heroin addict might well scoff at cannabis, so the sex addict will not find satisfaction in what earlier was attractive. Previously satisfying sexual activities, for example marital sex, can seem boringly tame by comparison.

The notion of tolerance in the face of danger (Apter, 2007) could well apply to some situations of sexual addiction. As a given 'dose' of danger is repeatedly experienced, a perception of safety increases. Hence, the danger level needs to be increased to obtain the same thrill, rather as a mountaineer who acquires skill will require ever more challenging climbs.

This might provide insight into a strange phenomenon, so-called 'bug-chasing' (Moskowitz and Roloff, 2007). This consists of gay men who are not HIV-positive seeking out HIV-positive sex partners for unpro-tected sex. The researchers suggest that, through stages of escalating risk, bug-chasers are led to seek the ultimate risk: that of death. As the authors express it (p. 26): 'They have an increased tolerance for their sexual behaviours, and as a corollary, need to escalate the risk and significance of the sexual act to get "high".'

Is out-of-control sexual activity an addiction, a form of compulsion or an impulse control problem?

Would the phenomenon termed 'sexual addiction' be better described under the heading of 'sexual obsession and compulsion', an example of an obsessive-compulsive disorder (OCD)? Is it like compulsive checking or hand-washing? Alternatively, is it an 'impulse control disorder'?

Similarity to OCD

There are some common features with OCD, expressed as a shift of weight of control to a lower level. A low serotonin level appears to be implicated in OCD, hypersexuality (Kafka, 1997) and love addiction, possibly associated with elevated dopamine activity (Fisher, 2004). Also, the same medication, boosting serotonin levels, is employed to treat both OCD and sexual addiction. In each case, the person can feel out of control and driven, sometimes engaging in futile self-destructive behaviour and wishing they could quit. Conflict is the hallmark of each condition, where things can get more severe over time. Stress, anxiety and depression can exacerbate both conditions and experiencing unstructured time can be dangerous. In each case, temporary relief is sought in an activity that only serves to make matters worse in the longer term. However, the criteria just described apply equally to drug addiction as to sex addiction.

Difference from OCD

There is a fundamental difference between OCD and addiction. At their roots, addictions appear to tap into a basic biological incentive ('go') system that normally moves the individual *towards* contact with something positive. This process might well have got corrupted, has become counterproductive in any biological sense and no longer serves the interests of the individual. It might no longer bring as much pleasure as in the beginning, but the activity normally has the capacity to give intense pleasure, in the case of addictive activity particularly in the early stages (Giugliano, 2008).

In the sample of fourteen men studied by Giugliano, only one reported that he engaged in the activity 'to neutralize anxiety rather than for sexual pleasure'. So, an addictive activity is multi-purpose according to context – to give pleasure and avoid pain. Sexually addicted people spend enormous amounts of time thinking about sex, but do not generally describe their erotic thoughts as 'intrusive', unlike people with OCD (Giugliano, 2008). An exception is certain paraphiliacs, such as paedophiles trying to quit, who often experience their sexual imagery as intrusive and demanding (Schwartz and Masters, 1983).

In OCD, by contrast the individual is invariably trying to escape from something aversive, such as apparently contaminated hands, the insecurity of an unlocked door or the pain of an unacceptable mental image (Toates and Coschug-Toates, 2002). The obsessive imagery is usually intrinsically aversive, unlike that of most sexual addictions. Pleasure is never the expected goal in OCD; rather the goal is invariably the alleviation of suffering (Giugliano, 2008). At its basis, the engagement of an 'avoid' or 'escape' system places it in distinction to addiction. Certain forms of therapy also point to the logic of a distinction between OCD and addiction. In OCD, the individual is gradually coaxed *into* contact with the feared object whereas in addiction he or she is coaxed *away from* contact with it. However, as a similarity with OCD, some forms of therapy try to induce satiation with the content of the addiction, rather like trying to associate relaxation with the obsession.

In comparison with impulse control disorders

When sexual behaviour is out of control, it can also exhibit features in common with impulse control disorders, which are defined as a failure to resist a harmful impulse, drive or temptation. On these disorders, Giugliano (2008) notes that: 'The individual feels an increasing sense of tension or arousal before committing the act and then *experiences pleasure, gratification, or relief at the time of committing the act*' (p. 144). In such terms, one sexually addicted person gave the following account (Giugliano, p. 146):

> It's like the pleasure one gets from scratching an itch . . . it's the pleasure of letting a sneeze go.

When in the presence of the target incentive, addictive sexual behaviour appears to show features of an impulse control disorder. People describing themselves as sex addicts do occasionally experience spontaneous 'acting-out' when finding themselves in this context (Giugliano, 2008). However, this can only be part of the picture. More generally, the sexually addicted person takes such purposive actions as to *move towards* situations in which subsequently he or she cannot resist. Hours of meticulous planning might be involved in moving to engagement with an incentive and to maximize the size of the hit, as in advance booking of a hotel room and arriving there equipped with a stock of pornographic movies and cocaine.

The forms that sexual addiction can take

Some of the targets of the addictions are either illegal or at least strongly disapproved of by society (Carnes, 2001). Activities include incest, child molestation, voyeurism, exhibitionism, child pornography and rape. Others, though reluctantly tolerated by society, are still outside the bounds of conventional morality, such as use of prostitutes and pornography. Impersonal casual sex and masturbation are included as addictions if they reach levels of excess and disruption and are associated with despair.

Interaction with real humans

Paraphilias are possible candidates for addictive sex, but there is not a one-to-one equivalence between paraphilia and addiction. Some people manage to live with their paraphiliac desire unexpressed, express it only rarely or integrate it into a balanced life-style. Conversely, someone can show addiction to 'conventional' and perfectly legal heterosexual or homosexual sex. So, to repeat, addiction is not defined in terms of the activity itself but rather in the nature of the relationship of the activity to the rest of the person's life (Goodman, 1998).

The investment in addiction can be enormous. As Carnes (1989, p. 62) expresses it:

> This kind of preoccupation is time-consuming. In fact, most of the sex addict's time spent in the addictive cycle is spent in preoccupation. The office, the shopping mall, the bus on the way home – all the everyday situations are transformed with sexual energy.

The world is scanned rigorously for any cue that is sex-related.

Family and work might get neglected. Vast sums of money are sometimes spent on sex workers, at the expense of necessities for the family. There is often a risk of disease and violence. Hours might be invested hiding in a neighbour's bushes, while staring at a window to get a brief glimpse of a naked woman. There can even be a cost in petrol, as the exhibitionist spends a whole day driving around to find the perfect moment for exposure. The risk of being caught and the potential shame in the eyes of family, friends and employer present a terrifying image to addict and non-addict alike.

Cyber activities and addiction to viewing portrayals of sexual activity

The phenomenon of altered consciousness is exemplified by a 35-year-old divorced American lawyer, who was addicted to chat rooms, posing as a 13–15 year old boy:

> I would spend up to 8 hours online, trying to escape from my problems and trying to get a porn and sexual fix. I would not eat or drink during this time. Emotionally, I was as detached as though I was in a coma. Nothing else mattered. I didn't think about the illegality of what I was saying or doing on the computer. (Schneider, 2000, p. 251)

Similarly, consider Albert, an American, a divorced father of three children (Maltz and Maltz (2010, p. 62):

> Porn gives me momentary relief from the pains of life. I don't care about the future. What matters is I have escaped for now.

Michael Ryan wrote (Ryan, 1996, p. 339):

> I had watched hundreds of porno-movies, some of them in hellish-smelling booths in adult book-stores pumping in quarters every ninety seconds.

In some cases, early exposure to pornography can trigger a kind of imprinting process in which the imagery takes on a particular unforgettable significance in the sexual life of the individual and can fuel later addiction (Maltz and Maltz, 2010). In one sample of women exhibiting cybersex addiction, the majority reported relying on abusive fantasy to get aroused (Corley and Hook, 2012). For some people, their first sexual encounter is with porn; the chances of this happening are greatly increased with the advent of the Internet. The Internet has massively increased the chances for addiction to occur, some individuals spending up to seventy hours a week online searching for sexual targets (Schneider, 2000). Consider the following:

> When Jack got married for the second time, he told doubting buddies, 'I mean it, this time no extramarital secret life.' One wedding present, a home computer, gave Jack entry to a whole new world – the Internet. Unknown to his friends and new spouse, within six months of being married, Jack was involved nightly in three different online, or virtual affairs, had downloaded more than 1,200 pornographic images, and was spending fifteen to twenty hours a week in sexual chat rooms and 'membership clubs', trading and downloading new pictures – all of it a secret from his wife and accessed from his study at home.

> Before their marriage, Jack and his second wife, Jody, had enjoyed an active and exciting sexual relationship, but gradually, as Jack's hidden Internet life became more arousing to him than sex with his wife, he grew more detached and withdrawn. (Schneider and Weiss, 2001, p. 1)

The Internet and cybersex have introduced new risks, while occasionally reducing others. In order now to achieve a variety of 'forbidden highs', addicted individuals might need to venture no further than their own sitting room. Through cybersex, the addict can occupy hours on end in an altered state of mind and heart rhythm, searching for the perfect porno image or virtual partner. The addicted person might spend all night sending come-on messages to a sex chat room. Some people only realize that they were addicted to sex years later, after their cybersex addiction causes them to do a life review (Schneider, 2000).

Apparently, feeling anonymous and safe, an increasing number of women are becoming addicted to cybersex. Turner (2008) writes of such a person: 'The intensity and excitement draw her away from her reality and responsibilities.' In keeping with the argument developed earlier, women tend to be more addicted to chat rooms where there is at least some modicum of reciprocity, rather than viewing erotic images, the staple diet of males with such problematic sexual behaviour (Schneider, 2000).

However, some women report addictive sexuality very much like men. Consider the case of a single 37-year-old female executive:

> I'd get in a chat room looking for a man with whom I could have sex. I'd meet him at a hotel or at my house and have sex. When I travelled, I'd set up meetings in towns where I knew I would be staying. None of these meetings were ever romantic interests. I was clear from the beginning that it was about sex and nothing else. I also had pornographic sites which I frequented when on line but not in the chat room. Those sites mainly functioned to add to the file footage which was continually running in my brain. (Schneider, 2000, p. 251)

Similarly, a 35-year-old married American woman wrote:

> My husband could no longer satisfy me. I wanted what I saw in the videos and pictures, and was too embarrassed to ask him for it. (Schneider, 2000, p. 262)

The individual, even one who is unsuccessful in attracting partners, can fantasize that people with perfect bodies reciprocate his desire. As Tim, a librarian in his forties, responded:

> All these women perform for me – dancing, gyrating, and showing their bodies. They're under my control, performing for me. (Maltz and Maltz, 2010, p. 20)

A drive that is too high?

Consider those people who led an uneventful sex life until finding cyber-sex and then got hooked (Schneider, 2000). Surely it adds little, if anything, insightful to say that their drive was suddenly boosted. In some cases, addicts shun conventional and potentially available safer sexual outlets, for example with a stable partner (though in other cases the unsuspecting partner even reports a good home sex life (Schneider and Weiss, 2001)). An American male of 38 years, who sought help for sexual addiction, wrote:

> I would rather look at porn than be with my girlfriend. Sometimes I resent her presence as it keeps me away from the Net. (Schneider, 2000, p. 260)

Most people with a particularly high sexual interest and activity usually do not display features of addiction. In therapy for addiction, the high drive argument would sound like a prescription for despair – how do you lower such a setting? This line of explanation might even serve to fuel the addiction – 'I need sex all the time and there is nothing I can do about a design flaw in my basic biology.'

Contrary to the old drive models (discussed earlier), sexual addiction seems not to be driven by some bodily event that is independent of stimuli, has got massively out of equilibrium and needs the correction of very frequent orgasm. Rather, incentive theory can offer insights. Thus, addiction should be distinguished from the state of simply having a high sexual appetite ('hypersexuality') that is realized in the context of mutually rewarding relationships and is not associated with powerful negative feelings.

An incentive perspective

An historical shift

Over the period 1985–2000, there was an important shift of thinking amongst researchers into addiction (Orford, 2001). Prior to this, excessive behaviour was thought to represent an attempt to correct a bodily deficit or aversion.[2] Such correction can indeed *sometimes* be a contributory factor, as in trying to escape from boredom, depression or painful withdrawal symptoms. Evidence suggests that any intense hedonic experience, whether drug-based or not, *can* be followed by a negative rebound, described as 'withdrawal symptoms'. However, this is not now thought to be the defining and universal feature of excessive appetites. For example, withdrawal symptoms from drugs do not predict when users will crave drugs or return to drug-seeking (Robinson and Berridge, 1993). Rather, the common feature of addiction, especially at the start, is one of approach, that is pleasure-seeking.[3] This fits incentive motivation.

In incentive terms, sexual addiction represents a massively focused capture of behaviour by a restricted range of sexual stimuli, very often, if not always, involving novelty employed as a means of finding the perfect 'high'. One or just a few classes of incentive come to assume a disproportionate weight and displace other candidates for control of behaviour.

Sometimes the setting of the addictive activity can be highly specific. For example, one patient compulsively masturbated while viewing Internet pornography (Bancroft, 2007). Yet, when brought into the laboratory, the erotic materials on display held no interest for him.

Central to the incentive interpretation is the motivational pull of things associated with the sexual goal. Thus, the lure of the neighbour's bushes signalling the chance to glimpse a naked body, the red lights of a region of town or even the sound of switching on the computer can come to acquire enormous incentive salience, presumably as a result of conditioning (Orford, 2001). Some addicts binge, with periods free between binges. This suggests that the addictive activity fuels further activity rather than satiating it.

Schneider and Weiss (2001, p. 31) note:

> For the cybersex addict and sex addicts in general, the goal of all the looking, cruising, contacting, and downloading is not necessarily the orgasm. In fact, orgasm is not always a welcome or desired part of the process. Most porn and cybersex addicts look at images or remain in sexual chat rooms for hours on end, maintaining the desired level of self-stimulation – but once orgasm occurs, the game is over and reality sets in.

Proximity to temptation

There is an important feature of an incentive interpretation of addictions (Orford, 2001), mentioned under the heading of 'temptation' (Chapter 12). The addicted person is in some conflict and might wish to quit but simply can't. This is like the person encountering temptation, but in the case of addiction it is a state of *chronic and unremitting* temptation.

The excitatory factors can arise particularly strongly from the physical presence of particular incentives, for example the sight of the computer on which pornography is watched or the presence of a sex worker. As a physical goal (e.g. a brothel, porno cinema or the keyboard of a computer) is approached, so the strength of approach motivation increases with decreases in distance to the goal.

However, addictive activity does not just suddenly appear when the addicted person happens to find himself in the presence of the incentive. Rather, as with conventional sexual desire, representations are formed in memory and these can be used to guide pursuit of the appropriate incentives.

So, what offers restraint, albeit ineffectively so? Certain restraining factors such as fear might also increase as distance decreases. If the activity is illegal, the presence of a police officer could exemplify this. However, a number of potential restraining factors, such as catching a disease are *hypothetical possibilities*, not necessarily physically present and certainly not apparent at the time of temptation. Other factors, such as guilt or fear of a partner's reaction, are abstract, cognitive and probably only emerge with a delay relative to the time of indulgence. They would not normally be associated with the location and would therefore not be expected to increase in a similar way to the incentive stimulus. So often it appears that they are no match for the lure.

Proximity would be expected to be an important factor in triggering relapse. It could be that beyond the tipping point, the feeling of being out of control arises. This can trigger panic with a subsequent loss of control, panic that might well be reduced by engaging in the addictive activity and thereby providing yet another factor that strengthens the addiction (Orford, 2001). In this way a vicious circle is reinforced. For feeding, gambling and drug addictions, replace sexual goal with supermarket/restaurant, casino or bar/pusher, respectively.

Wanting and liking

As noted earlier, the incentive system has a potentially strong association with pleasure. However, that does not mean that it invariably triggers intense pleasure. Some addicted people report that they 'repeatedly participate in sexual behaviours *despite* finding them *aversive* or *unsatisfying*' (Gold and Heffner, 1998). As with drugs (Washton and Zweben, 2009, p. 50), the pleasure of sex can decline over time. Similarly, Doidge, (2007, p. 107) reported:

> Pornographers promise healthy pleasure and relief from sexual tension, but what they often deliver is an addiction, tolerance, and an eventual decrease in pleasure. Paradoxically, the male patients I worked with often craved pornography but didn't like it.

Giugliano (2008, p. 146) obtained the reports from two sexually addicted males:

> There was no bad sex when I was 18 to 21 years old. All sex was great sex. The feeling of disgust came in later.

> When I was a teenager, it felt great. I put everything out of my mind. I noticed a change in my 20s. The sex no longer felt great. The way it felt was more empty than anything else.

Again, such observation underlines the fundamental strength of the incentive-seeking system, even if it sometimes gets uncoupled from pleasure.

Therapeutic implications

Incentive ideas give hope for therapy, in terms of teaching addicts about alternative sources of pleasure and fulfilment, often in trusting social networks of the kind that they have feared and shunned. In some cases, faulty reasoning of the kind 'I am wholly a bad person', 'women really want to be groped' or 'men can never be trusted with love' can be challenged. A new cognition 'others can answer my needs if I am honest with them' can be learned. As with alcoholics, to some people God can play a role in therapy. In this case, when one admits powerlessness and seeks help, there emerges a new relationship: one with the Almighty. Meditation can be employed to occupy otherwise empty time. In therapy, steps can be encouraged whereby any particularly potent incentive trigger cues to the addicted person (e.g. the sight of a computer in a secluded part of the office or house) are eliminated or actively avoided.

The link with negative emotion

General principles

In incentive terms, a sexual object can become particularly attractive at a time when a negative mood is experienced (e.g. anxiety, frustration, loneliness, depression, boredom or stress) (Maltz and Maltz, 2010). After initial contact, the incentive can consolidate its strength through its association with a reduction of negative emotion that closely follows sexual engagement. Contextual factors, such as alienation, difficulty in establishing trusting relationships, a history of sexual abuse when young and low self-esteem, can set the scene for capture by one particular activity. Consider a man described by Trachtenberg (1989, p. 81): 'When Anthony leaves his home for the cruising circuit, he sloughs off his ennui and comes alive for the first time. His pulse speeds up. He feels vital and witty and desirable.'

Sexually addicted people commonly suffer simultaneously from disorders such as anxiety and depression (Kafka, 2000). For some, these conditions trigger increased sexual interest (Bancroft and Vukadinovic, 2004). Negative emotions are commonly experienced prior to acquisition of the addiction or in parallel or both. In these terms, consider the description 'compulsive sexual behaviour as mediated by anxiety reduction, rather than by sexual desire *per se*' (Leiblum and Rosen, 2000, p. 471). This appears to be a false dichotomy: in incentive terms, the strength of sexual desire is maintained in part by any associated anxiety reduction.

Attributes found in a group of sexually addicted people undergoing treatment included (Reid and Carpenter, 2009, p. 300): 'depression, anxiety, difficulty with social norms, and difficulty managing thoughts, lowered inhibitions, behavioural control, and social alienation'. A significant percentage were plagued with doubts over self-worth. Ryan (1996, p. 330) described his craving as being most strong when:

I just couldn't stand being in my own skin.

and explained this in terms of (p. 353):

a lifetime of desperate attempts to feel worthwhile – driving myself mercilessly, clamouring for approval and impossible sexual validation.

However, over a third of the sample studied by Reid and Carpenter exhibited no psychological problems, apart from the addiction itself. They appeared to be moved simply by the intrinsic sexual reward.

Finally, can an incentive view have anything to do with the observation that a rather high percentage of sexually addicted people were themselves victims of childhood sexual abuse? This raises the prospect that repeated traumatic flashbacks might somehow get converted into sexual incentives. Turner (2008) suggests how addiction could emerge out of childhood neglect or abuse. Children discover coping strategies such as masturbation or over-eating. She writes: 'Whatever "escape" gives the greatest "rush" away from psychic pain and promotes survival will be used again and again until it takes a life of its own.'

Later sexual promiscuity provides a way of earning a feeling of power and worth.

Often states of high anxiety, depression, shame and guilt form part of a withdrawal syndrome that follows each sexual outlet (Schneider, 2000). The only way to gain even temporary relief is to engage in the addictive activity. For others, the state to be escaped is best described as 'boredom' and they get locked into an endless cycle in which behaviour is reinforced by removal of boredom (Chaney and Chang, 2005).

Stress

At one stage, Walter (see Chapter 1) was seriously troubled by financial worries and felt himself to be in complete mental breakdown. He observed the role of sex workers in alleviating distress and also the substitutability of different activities (Kronhausen and Kronhausen, 1967, p. 176):

> They came to my rescue and gave me forgetfulness, a relief far better than gambling or drinking, the only other alternatives I could have recourse to.

A man reported the following experience, which illustrates both the role of stress and escalation:

> My live-in girlfriend and I were going through a rough time in our relationship. She left town for a few days and I decided to look at porn on the Internet to satisfy me. Up 'til then I'd never been interested in porn. I began on a Friday afternoon looking at the free peeks. By Saturday I was into the sex chats, and by Sunday I had joined a swinger site. (Maltz and Maltz, 2010, p. 11)

Stress often instigates or exacerbates addictions or causes relapse. Several processes would be expected to be implicated in this effect.

- Stress is a negative emotion and engaging in an addictive activity can lower the level of such emotion. Therefore, a learning process is involved in which the addicted person forms an association between their activity and a lowering of negative emotion.

- Extrapolating from drug addiction, stress engages conscious cognitive processing resources (Tiffany, 1990). These resources are needed in resisting temptation and their occupation by the content of the stress means that behavioural control shifts in favour of more automatic routines.
- Stress triggers the release of so-called stress hormones, which sensitize the dopaminergic incentive system (Pitchers et al., 2010).

Often sexual addiction arises at times of particular stress (Schneider and Weiss, 2001) – stress is known to exacerbate chemical addictions too. Time allocation and the opportunity for capture of behaviour are crucial elements. As Carnes (2001, p. 24) observes:

> Graduate school, for example, is often when addicts first encounter compulsiveness. The stress of proving one's self in an arena where every inadequacy is evaluated is a potent flash-point for the ignition of sexual addiction. So are new jobs, promotions, and solo business ventures. Unstructured time, a heavy responsibility for self-direction, and high demands for excellence seem to be the common elements in these situations that are easy triggers for addictive behaviours.

When placed in a situation of stress, people take corrective action so as to try to reduce the stress. Sometimes they stumble upon their particular effective action by accident. One way is through taking a chemical cure in the form of drugs such as alcohol. Others discover that sexual stimulation, as in Internet pornography, is a way of lowering stress levels or soothing negative emotions of some form (Turner, 2008).

Soldiers returning from war, as in Iraq and Vietnam, often experience high levels of stress, including flashbacks to horrific experiences. Occasionally they arrive at pornography as a form of self-medication (Howard, 2007). Alas, such behaviour can then take over the person's life in the sense that other activities are squeezed out; priorities change and a large part of the waking hours are occupied with thoughts of the activity. Addiction to consensual sexual activity among Vietnam War veterans has been frequently observed (Trachtenberg, 1989). Howard (2007) describes a veteran of the Iraq war (p. 84):

> It didn't take Jim long to make the mental association that while viewing pornography online, he didn't think about war or combat. In fact, it was as if the war never existed.

Jim spent increasing amounts of time online, six to eight hours per day, and his family relationships deteriorated in parallel. Pornography served as a soothing balm to cope with the family disruption as well as the traumatic memories. Therapeutic intervention that only addressed the addiction might well prove inadequate. The underlying triggers needed to be addressed.

Link with drugs

Recreational drugs

The literature contains a number of accounts of the link between recreational drugs and sexual desire, as in:

> I stepped up my usage of drugs and alcohol to keep myself from cheating on my wife and found instead that I could cheat when I was too high to speak coherently. (Trachtenberg, 1989, p. 266)

> The persistence of symptoms is also evidenced by the number of Casanovas who are multiply addicted, who not only womanize but gamble, drink or take drugs and who sometimes attain momentary relief from one disorder only to plunge headlong into another. (Trachtenberg, 1989, p. 267)

> Once I started to feel a bit more confident, and realised there was now a great gaping hole in my life that wasn't filled by drugs and booze any more, my tendency to pursue women – which had always been quite rapacious – somehow became enhanced further. (Brand, 2007, p. 379)

Often addictions co-exist (Orford, 2001; Washton, 1989). For example, the sexually addicted individual not uncommonly has simultaneously an addiction to alcohol or illicit drugs. This suggests that there is a 'common incentive process' that gets captured and exploited by more than one addiction, with cross-sensitization between them. Given the known effects of addictive drugs in sensitizing dopamine systems (Robinson and Berridge, 1993), it is not surprising that drug-taking can sensitize sexual addiction. As noted earlier, if we can extrapolate from rats, sexual activity can sensitize drug-seeking (Pitchers et al., 2010). It appears that the chances of relapse in sexual addiction are increased by taking certain drugs, including alcohol (Maltz and Maltz, 2010). As an additional factor, drugs, for example alcohol, can impair inhibitory processes. Sex and cocaine are sometimes exploited only in combination and specifically use of prostitution and gambling are not uncommonly found together.

Many people taking cocaine or methamphetamine discover that it increases their sexual desire, fantasies and stamina, while lifting inhibitions (Washton and Zweben, 2009). Such hypersexuality is found particularly in male drug-users. The combination of drug and sex yields a 'super-high' brought by interlocking rewards and having an addictive potential that is stronger than sex or the drug alone. Not surprisingly given the longer-lasting effect of methamphetamine as compared to cocaine, the sexual effects last longer for methamphetamine and are sometimes associated with 'marathon sexual binges' of up to seventy-two hours. Sexual experimentation is occasionally initiated in association with these drugs, as in group sex, high-risk unprotected sex, using sex workers, or homosexual behaviour by otherwise exclusively heterosexual individuals.

For some people addicted to cocaine or methamphetamine, sexual stimuli are a particularly potent trigger to drug-craving (Washton and Zweben, 2009). Even sexual fantasies can trigger intense drug-craving. If such a person wants to quit drugs, not only do trigger cues to drugs need to be avoided but so do sexual triggers. This is of course easier said than done, particularly when the triggers can arise in the imagination. However, triggers that might be successfully avoided could include erotic Internet sites, pornographic books, and advertisements for escort services.

Concerning relapse to drug-use, a cocaine-addicted patient of Washton and Zweben, (2009 p. 137), who was trying to quit, recorded:

> At first I didn't throw out every bit of my paraphernalia. I kept a little memento – a collector's item – just to remind me of my foolishness, so I thought. When I finally admitted this to my therapist, she said I was playing with fire – trying to keep my relationship with cocaine alive and keep the door open for an easy return to the drugs and sex scene. I guess she was right. I went back and threw out the little rubber fixture from my freebase pipe, a porno DVD that would set off my sexual compulsion, and the phone numbers of escorts and drug dealers. I felt greatly relieved after getting rid of one more set of temptations.

A problem amongst some people with a combined sex–drug addiction is that the prospect of drug-free sex ('ordinary sex'), for example with a regular partner, seems boring by comparison with drug-fuelled sex (Washton and Zweben, 2009), again pointing to the role of expectations and desired levels of hedonism.

Not all users of cocaine or methamphetamine find their drug use gets locked into interaction with sexual desire. For some, the desire is for the drug alone and hence sexual desire might get downgraded. Presumably, the chances of the drug setting up a combined desire with sex would depend upon, amongst other things, the level of sexual desire and engagement prior to drug-taking as well as the frequency of holding erotic thoughts in the conscious mind while under the influence of the drug. Indeed, a prior history of sexual addiction increases the likelihood of a combined addiction (Washton and Zweben, 2009).

Drugs taken to treat Parkinson's disease

As noted in Chapter 8, some Parkinson's disease patients, who are being treated with dopamine replacement therapy, develop addictions (Lawrence et al., 2003). Sometimes the object of the addiction and the associated craving is for the medicine itself. In other patients, the object is gambling or shopping, compulsive eating or particular sexual incentives. Heightened aggression is another possible outcome. In accordance with incentive theory, it appears that elevated dopamine activity locks into interaction with one of several possible behaviours – shopping, gambling or sex – depending presumably upon prior predilections and chance associations between brain activity and the presence of the target activity in the outside world or the imagination.

In one sample of patients with Parkinson's disease and sexual addiction, the majority also developed other addictive activities, gambling, smoking, alcohol abuse, in response to dopamine-boosting medication (Klos et al., 2005). (Three developed OCD.) Again, this points to a dopaminergic process that is common to a number of addictive activities.

Such instances suggest sensitization of particular sexual incentives and thoughts by the increased levels of dopamine activity.

Link with love

Fisher (2004, p. 53) raises an interesting issue: 'Is romantic love an addiction? Yes; I think it is – a blissful dependency when one's love is returned, a painful, sorrowful, and often destructive craving when one's love is spurned.' There are clearly some similarities between sexual and love addictions and they can sometimes merge into one, as suggested by the name of the charity 'Sex and Love Addicts Anonymous'. However, love addiction is usually more closely associated with an addiction to one special individual, at least at any given time. By contrast, sexual addiction is more impersonal and might relate to any number of people or to no particular person, as in an insatiable desire for novelty in searching for pornographic images.

Throughout history, poets, song-writers and novelists have portrayed the swing between the ecstasy when being with a loved one and the despair at being separated. That is, heightened energy as in a hypomanic phase can alternate with anhedonia and irritability. This cycling pattern has features of addiction (Reynaud et al., 2010). However, the kind of love under consideration would need to lead to overall and long-term harmful consequences to qualify as an addiction. Falling in love repeatedly but without any reciprocity would exemplify an aspect of this. Love addiction seems to be more common in women, whereas sexual addiction is more common in men (Reynaud et al., 2010).

Reynaud et al. (p. 263) consider when love becomes addictive:

> The shift from normal passion to addiction may be barely perceivable because dependence and need for the other are present in love passion. Addiction would be defined as the stage where desire becomes a compulsive need, when suffering replaces pleasure, when one persists in the relationship despite knowledge of adverse consequences (including humiliation and shame).

Pointing to the interaction between sex and love addiction, it appears that the chances of love switching into addiction are stronger the greater the intensity of the initial phase, for example a sexually intense period of first encounter (Reynaud et al., 2010).

In summary

- In an exaggerated form, sexual addiction illustrates a number of features of sexual desire and its translation into action.

- Long-term negative consequences of addictive activity prove no match for immediate sexual reward.
- Behaviour is captured by a particular highly arousing type of incentive or a range of incentives, whether real, in books or in cyberspace.
- An altered state of consciousness can be attained.
- Habituation can set in with an associated escalation of the intensity of the sought experience.
- The addicted individual's sexual experience is sometimes compared against a perfectionist standard and attempts made to close the gap.
- An increase in some general sexual drive is not a useful way of viewing addiction.
- The reward deriving from behaviour can be in terms of not just sexual reward but also the lifting of negative emotion, such as that characterized by stress, anxiety or depression.
- Stress can trigger the addictive behaviour.
- Sexual addiction can sometimes be best understood in terms of its interactions with other addictive activities, such as those of emotional regulation, drug-taking and romantic attachment.

EIGHTEEN

VARIATIONS IN DESIRE: GENERAL PRINCIPLES

When I took off my shoes, Paulus became ecstatic about my feet. In later years, I often said that if I hadn't walked barefoot with him that day, we would never have married. That was after I had learned that his preoccupation with feet had always been extraordinary. One of his most erotic sensations – a memory from childhood – was of the mother of a friend of his who behaved unconventionally, not to say audaciously, by walking barefoot in the sand at the ocean.

(Hannah Tillich, wife of theologian Paul ('Paulus') Tillich, in Tillich, 1973, p. 87)

The phenomena

This chapter examines variations in the *form* of behaviour, where it is idiosyncratic. Some of these forms are perfectly harmless exaggerations of 'normal' desire, as in the above, or where some individuals are sexually excited by particular items of clothing, most usually shoes. However, at the other extreme, some are 'all-engaging' and extremely dangerous. One person's desires are fuelled by coercion and violence, whereas most of us are horrified by this. To most, a reciprocating and empathetic human is essential to sexual desire, but a few seek sex with terrified victims or even corpses. Another's fantasies are mainly masochistic. Others are drawn to peeping through their neighbours' windows to glimpse a naked body, whereas some want their own exposed genitals to be displayed. Some of the best known such 'paraphilias' these days, such as voyeurism, fetishism and exhibitionism, are apparently little if at all evident in traditional societies (Gebhard (1971). They might arise in societies where people are able to remain anonymous.

How can we understand these outliers of desire? Chapters 18–21 look at various forms of desire 'at the fringes' and the kind of underlying processes that appear to give rise to them. I cannot provide definitive answers to why someone exhibits a particular 'fringe desire', but there are now some strong pointers. The incentive-based model developed in Chapter 4 can serve as a framework for understanding.

The term 'paraphilia' derives from the Greek *para* (beyond) and *philia* (love). It is a blanket term for conditions in which a person can only be aroused by stimuli that are outside normal bounds. It describes some widely different forms, with doubtless rather different underlying processes and thereby explanations. Some are inherently violent, whereas others are not. For example, someone might feel sexual desire only for children, or be fired disproportionately or even exclusively by a particular dress worn by his partner. An activity might only be classed as a paraphilia if the particular object is *necessary* for arousal to occur. Thus, an individual might engage in sex with, say, children not out of a preference for them but for lack of any other outlet.

In theorizing about atypical sexuality, a working hypothesis is termed the 'sexual preference hypothesis' (Barbaree, 1990, p. 116): 'If a man is maximally aroused by a deviant stimulus or act, his eventual satisfaction or reward will be greater than that resulting from less strong responses to normalized or socially acceptable stimuli or acts.' In the laboratory and clinic, arousal to a deviant image is measured by the reaction of the genitals. If the person is speaking the truth, he or she will admit to being aroused by the deviant stimulus or act. The logic underlying treatment would normally be to attempt to shift the deviant desire and arousal to a more acceptable target or act.

In some cases, fear is necessary to achieve sexual arousal. For many voyeurs and exhibitionists, such fear is that associated with potential capture (Barlow, 1986). Similarly, consider a transvestite, John, who assumed the role of Jenny (Gosselin and Wilson, 1980, p. 62):

we asked him if he would feel happier if people were allowed to dress as they wished, without let or hindrance. From John's rather reserved attitude suddenly sprang something of Jenny's greater mischievousness. 'Heavens, no,' he smiled. 'Merely to be allowed to wear women's clothes in public is nothing. It is the challenge of being so like a woman that no one knows I'm a man that turns me on. The combination of doing something that you want to, that everyone says is impossible and is forbidden anyway produces in me an arousal which, because it is in a sexual context, becomes sexual arousal.'

Unusual sexual preference might arise from the same set of component processes that is responsible for acquiring normal sexual preferences (Laws and Marshall, 1990). The underlying processes might start out being much the same but the social environment in which they develop can be very different, for example abusive as opposed to supportive. That is to say, the external inputs to these processes can be very different. So, to understand some differences in desire, we might not need to propose any factor beyond those involved in normal sexual desire. This chapter will show how general processes of desire, learning, arousal and so on can help our understanding. As a bonus in this investigation, by studying how things can take an atypical trajectory, we might better understand how normal sexuality arises.

For an analogy, albeit an imperfect one, consider learning a language. Children exposed to Japanese learn this language, while American children normally learn English, Spanish or both. In each case, the brain is assumed to start out much the same but then it gets channelled in a particular direction such that later learning of another language without an accent can be difficult, if not impossible. The linguistic environment writes the script onto the developing brain. This can be contrasted with a situation of genetic abnormality or traumatic brain damage such as to disrupt language acquisition. Here an unusual form of speech might arise as a result of disruption to brain processes. By analogy, different social environments write the sexual script on the developing brain. Genetic differences or traumatic brain damage could modify or even seriously disrupt sexual development.

So, the discussion now turns to consider how a difference in the underlying processes and inputs to them could contribute to differences in sexual desire and behaviour. Some processes are within the system of sexuality itself whereas others are in those systems with which it interacts: executive control, attachment, anger/aggression and fear. The notion of levels of control will be shown to be fundamental to understanding different types of fringe sexuality.

Attachment

Specifically humans

Atypical sexuality appears to arise sometimes from sub-optimal attachment formation (Ressler et al., 1992; Smallbone and Dadds, 1998), most obviously where the trajectory leads to socially damaging activities. The assumption is commonly made that the early attachment failures cause adult effects. However, this notion has not gone unchallenged (Hare, 1993). In the case of serious adult psychopathic behaviour, Hare speculates that an early failure to bond might be a *symptom* not a *cause* of the underlying abnormality.

Of course, not everyone with a bad attachment history develops an antisocial sexual desire, otherwise the jails would be overflowing. So, poor attachment appears to be only one possible factor (Rich, 2006). Reciprocally, there might be those with an antisocial aberration who did not have a disturbed early history. However, FBI profilers of serial sex-related killers (Douglas and Olshaker, 2006) and experts on juvenile sexual offenders (Rich, 2006, p. 106) suggest the universality of a disturbed childhood. A healthy attachment history is necessary for full and healthy brain development, while abuse of a young child can impair optimal brain development (Schore, 2003).

Smallbone and Dadds theorize that for sexually mature adults with a secure attachment history (1998, p. 557): 'sexual behaviour may tend to be activated within a context that includes perceptions of security, reliability, and mutuality'. This would reflect early experience of such things as recognition and synchronicity of emotion ('mirroring') between mother and infant, for example, in exchanging smiles (Rich, 2006). By contrast, for sexually mature adults with an early developmental history of being insecurely attached (Smallbone and Dadds, 1998, p. 557): 'sexual behaviour may be activated with less regard to commitment or mutuality and may indeed be activated in response to negative cognitive and affective states similar to those experienced during problematic early attachment experiences'.

Non-human studies

Disturbances to the early mother–baby interaction have been studied in monkeys and rats (Harlow and Harlow, 1962; Lomanowska et al. 2011). These experiments reveal deviations from normal development that have some striking similarities to the effects of disturbed upbringing in humans. For example, animals that have suffered maternal deprivation have difficulty in inhibiting responses and in abandoning unproductive courses of action. They are more attracted to the self-administration of cocaine when they are adult. Such animals show signs of abnormally strong attraction to cues predictive of reward and they develop attachments to seemingly irrelevant inanimate objects. Evidence from non-human species points to sensitization of dopaminergic systems as a result of social isolation during development (Kehoe et al., 1996; Lewis et al., 1990). These deviations from typical development might help us to understand certain features of atypical sexual development in humans, particularly as manifest in violent sexuality. Such experimentation suggests a *causal* role of disturbed attachment in the production of behavioural abnormality.

Learning

Basics

Early learning is thought to be involved in forming sexual desires, that is changing a neutral representation of another person or related object into a sexually attractive ('motivationally charged') incentive. Evidence suggests that the particular content of paraphilias can arise as the result of learning (McGuire et al., 1965) but, of course, researchers cannot do controlled experiments. Sometimes a chance combination of stimulus → arousal seems to be crucial in setting desire off in a particular direction. In some cases, it appears that something unconventional, such as a fetish object is around at the time when there is (a) arousal and (b) a 'window of opportunity' (or 'critical period') available for conditioning of desire (Bancroft, 2009).

In conventional desire, another human and the representation of this human in the imagination are the source of the sexual desire and arousal, while any favourable consequences of sexual 'interaction', in reality or fantasy, consolidate the desire value.

In the examples considered shortly, there is bodily excitement trig-gered by, for example trauma, in the presence of a potential incentive for sexual desire. As a result of this combination, what was a potential incen-tive becomes a real source of desire, which might then be put into sexual action. The consequences of behaviour are assumed to be crucial, exem-plified by a relaxed state following orgasm and its effect in strengthening the value of the particular stimulus.

Evidence suggests that the formation of sexual desires is based upon *early* contact with the class of individual or physical object that later comes to form the object of attraction (McGuire et al., 1965). Three-quarters of the patients in one study reported that the theme of their para-philia reflected their *first* sexual experience. Following the initial phase of experience, the world of fantasy, often associated with masturbation, could come to play a crucial role in consolidating the value attached to the particular event. Very many people are exposed to potential triggers to paraphilia but few develop them. The difference could depend upon whether (a) this was an individual's first experience of sexual excitement, (b) they subsequently fantasize about the experience accompanied by masturbation and (c) alternative and more conventional sources of stim-ulation are unavailable. Boys masturbate much more than girls which could explain in part why paraphilias are mainly a male phenomenon.

The person might find that experimentation with masturbation has the consequence, at least in the short term, of not only the pleasure of orgasm but a lowering of boredom, anxiety or depression. This could add still more motivational strength to the particular incentive. Even though guilt commonly accompanies paraphilias, it arises slowly relative to the immediate impact of orgasm and therefore exerts limited inhibition (McGuire et al., 1965).

Rather than simply looking at why someone is attracted to a paraphil-iac stimulus, we also need to consider the opposite side of the same coin: why they do not acquire a conventional sexual desire. Often paraphiliacs perceive themselves to be very inadequate for a conventional hetero-sexual role (McGuire et al., 1965). There is the possibility of a learned aversion to consensual sex with same-age peers (Heide et al., 2009). Typ-ically, the paraphiliac's early life was devoid of normal sensual contact and healthy associations with the opposite sex (Schwartz and Masters, 1983). That is to say, early social contacts had negative consequences. A deficit in mastery of social skills is evident in such individuals. Repeated rejection might set up aversive links (e.g. anxiety) leaving any potential link between paraphiliac incentives, for example a young child, and sexual arousal intact. Schwartz et al (1981, p. 250) observe:

> Repeatedly, paraphiliacs give a history which suggests that society's definition of normal sexual functioning is associated with excessive taboo, punishment, fear or guilt during their childhood which can greatly distort substitute rehearsal cognition at puberty.

Viewing the acquisition of paraphilias in terms of 'preparedness' might give insight into which associations are likely to be formed (Laws and Marshall, 1990). In evolutionary terms, we might expect humans to be strongly prepared to form associations between adult human partners of the opposite sex and sexual arousal. Inanimate objects having no obvious human link would lie at the opposite end of the preparedness spectrum – to be 'contraprepared'. An attraction to deviant human stimuli and behaviour, such as sex with children or rape, would be somewhere between these extremes.

Paedophilia might usefully be viewed as representing something near to one extreme of a so-called 'normal distribution' of objects of desire, a disorder of 'stimulus acquisition' (Abel and Osborn, 1995). Nubile females represent the peak, with older and younger females corresponding to the extremes to either side. Of course, what can constitute paedophilia in our culture would be considered a perfectly normal sexual attraction in some others, where a girl might be married by the age of 12.

In many cases, a crucial aspect of the development of paraphilias could be the acquisition of control (Chapter 1). The individual who acquires a paraphilia might often be under stress at this stage. The paraphilia would serve as a coping strategy. Experiments with stressed animals have shown that the experience of acquiring control is associated with enhanced dopaminergic activity in the nucleus accumbens (Cabib and Puglisi-Allegra, 2012). This would be expected to increase the future attraction of the activity, possibly with an enhanced strength at a time of acute stress.

The gender difference

The most striking difference in who acquires such things as fetishes is that of gender – overwhelmingly, these are male activities. Gosselin and

Wilson's (1980) explanation should sound familiar. My interpretation of it is as follows:

1 At intervals, arousal of the genitals occurs spontaneously or with various external triggers. This could reflect spill-over from some other source of arousal such as fear.
2 The feedback from aroused genitals is more obvious in boys than in girls.
3 The brain is programmed to set up associations between external events and bodily reactions.
4 A chance pairing of, say, the sight of women's shoes and detectable arousal is more likely to happen in boys than in girls.
5 The chance pairing will endow the shoes with an erotic potential.

Courtship disorder

One approach to understanding paraphilias is summarized by the term 'courtship disorder' (Freund, 1990). Certain paraphiliacs seem to be stuck at an early stage of a conventional courting ritual. Often voyeurism, exhibitionism, spoken eroticism, rubbing and touching form part of conventional sexual 'approach behaviour' that leads to reciprocal sexual behaviour. As such, they are not particularly remarkable. Some paraphiliacs are unable to progress beyond one or more such stages. Possibly anxiety and fear of failure at the prospect of progression means that paraphiliacs cannot proceed beyond the 'chosen point' at which they remain comfortable. Patients being treated for paraphilias often report that a normal sexual experience was not possible for them as a result of perceived inadequacies or a rigid parental influence (Gosselin and Wilson, 1980). Paraphiliacs often vary between such activities, either over a given period of time or sequentially. For example, voyeurs are often also exhibitionists (Feierman and Feierman, 2000). Within the imagination, there is a consolidation of the strength of one or more acts, often accompanied by masturbation.

Gosselin and Wilson (1980, p. 153) report that paraphilia:

is not the deliberate choice of a jaded sexual appetite, whose owner is merely looking for some form of kick. It, is rather, the logical though unfortunate outcome of what appears to a generally shy, introverted and emotionally over-sensitive child to a restrictive sexual upbringing.

354 • How Sexual Desire Works

It is, however, important to note that some people who progress to conventional sexual behaviour, rape and sexual homicide still sometimes engage in fetishism, exhibitionism and voyeurism (Chapter 21).

Fringe fantasy

Fantasy can be a healthy feature of sexuality. However, it can acquire a maladaptive content and actual behaviour can thereby be steered into alignment with its content. Without the consistent presence of appropriate adult role models and the associated restraints ('re-tuning') by positive social interactions, the child's mind can be filled by uncontrolled and deviant fantasy (Ressler et al., 1992).

For many, if not all, those with paraphiliac desires, fantasy is a way of moving affect in a positive direction (Gee et al., 2003, p. 52). The level of affect can start from a negative baseline associated with, say, financial or relationship problems. A negative mood might even be triggered by a paraphiliac's reflecting on his own sexual orientation – a vicious circle.

In fantasy, an individual can gain mastery and control over others that they could not achieve in the real world (Gee et al., 2003). The world of fantasy can start out as one that relies upon pure imagination but, following any first offence, reality can be incorporated into the story-line (Meloy, 2000). Particularly if accompanied by masturbation, the mastery in the fantasy world brings psychological relief ('catharsis') and could reinforce the 'behaviour' within the fantasy, increasing the probability of its future translation into action. Negative mood states characterized as rejection, anger, loneliness and humiliation appear to increase the chances that deviant sexual fantasy will occupy the conscious mind. In turn, whether fantasy translates into action will depend upon the balance of excitation and inhibition. Repeated fantasy scenarios, particularly if accompanied by masturbation, might alter the brain so as to make particular incentives and associated behaviour seem more attractive and viable as future sexual possibilities. This could then lead to, say, grooming of a child (Wolf, 1988).

It appears that repeated use of fantasy in the conscious mind can set up scripts ('prescriptions') for behaviour which are stored at a non-conscious level. Under circumstances beyond the individual's control, such as sudden stress or humiliation, these scripts might be activated and brought to conscious awareness in the service of controlling (deviant) behaviour (Bartels and Gannon, 2011).

Maintaining atypical behaviour

The tendency to paraphiliac behaviour can be increased by a negative emotional state. Paraphiliac behaviour would thereby be reinforced not just by pleasure but by the escape from aversion (McGregor and Howells, 1997). In more cognitive terms, the expectation of the 'high' of sexual contact is described by some sex offenders as giving 'uncontrollable urges'. Potential long-term negative consequences of atypical behaviour are devalued if not ignored. The similarity with addiction is obvious. Any long intervals imposed between behavioural episodes can be filled by fantasy accompanied by masturbation. This might be expected to maintain the strength of paraphiliac tendencies.

If the course of action takes a deviant direction, 'neutralizing definitions' can be assimilated (Akers, 1985). Subsequently, if the individual fits into a subculture of other similar deviants, a new form of social bonding and mutual reinforcement can be provided by exchanging these definitions. For example, in an offending subculture a rapist might acquire and promote the neutralizing definition that 'all women secretly want to be raped', or a paedophile might hear that 'you are doing the child a favour'. Neutralizing definitions serve to undermine the negative quality of the deviation and the criticisms made from outside the subculture.

A tendency to repeat earlier trauma

The 'tendency to repeat trauma' represents an unexpected and counter-intuitive role of arousal and learning in the sexual behaviour of some individuals.

What is it?

A significant percentage of those who display unusual sexual behaviour were subject to intense stress as children, for example in the form of abuse. Such exposure can later create a tendency for people to put themselves back into situations similar to that which caused the initial trauma (Apter,

2007; Chaney and Chang, 2005; van der Kolk, 1989). The phenomenon of trauma-seeking is widespread, not confined to childhood exposure.

Two examples that are not necessarily related to sexual behaviour might point to a common underlying process. Consider the phenomenon of 'combat addiction'. Sufferers appear to crave danger to 'get the adrenalin flowing' and create a psychological state similar to that of the original trauma. Some use the terms 'sexual trip', 'orgasmic' and 'orgiastic' to describe the battlefield (Apter, 2007). Therefore, re-enactments of the original setting of the trauma are sought, with the consequence of a brief improvement in the sense of well-being. For example, one Vietnam War veteran would visit the oriental part of an American town and occasionally find men looking like Vietnamese with whom he could pick a fight. This made him feel alive again and following the fights a sense of calmness prevailed. It would just temporarily lift his loneliness, anger and anxiety.

The bizarre case of Dr Shipman

The British doctor and serial killer Harold Shipman appears to exemplify the 'tendency to repeat trauma'. Shipman represents a slight digression in the story-line but one that might have an important relevance. While still a young man, Harold watched as his chronically ill mother derived pain relief from regular injections of morphine given by a doctor (Whittle and Ritchie, 2004). At age 17 years, Harold was present at her death, which devastated him. His reaction was to go out on a strenuous run, the consequences of which might have had a soothing effect similar to that found in the aftermath of his killings.

Some years later, after qualifying as a doctor, he developed an addiction to pethidine, a drug similar to morphine. Shipman then proceeded to kill his elderly, particularly women, patients by lethal injections of morphine, under circumstances similar to the death of his own mother. He has been described as 'addicted to the adrenalin rush' and searching for the ultimate but elusive 'super-high', revealed in a rapidly escalating frequency of murders towards the end. Whether there was a sexual motivation to his killing is a topic of speculation (Whittle and Ritchie, 2004), the answer to which went to Shipman's grave with him.

According to the interpretation of Hickey (2010, p. 171), Shipman was not a lust killer and felt that his victims: 'would not leave him again without his permission'. Furthermore (p. 171): 'By killing his female patients he controlled the when and how, two issues that he had no control over when his mother died.' Police, lawyers and psychiatrists have failed to find a rational motive behind Shipman's killings; what was it, if not money, revenge or sexual arousal? Perhaps rational analysis led investigators to pose the wrong questions. Shipman might have been simply drawn to experience a motivationally irresistible event of very high arousal value associated with temporary closure and tension relief. Whatever, it would seem that Shipman illustrates an addictive feature of how behaviour can be determined and one that could also play a role in some unambiguously sexually motivated behaviour.

Link to sexual behaviour

There are various forms that re-exposure to trauma can take. A number of children who were sexually abused go on to become sexual abusers[1] or rapists, while many engage in self-harm. In one sample of women who described themselves as sex or love addicts, some 50 per cent had experienced either child sexual abuse or exposure to pornography (Corley and Hook, 2012). Children who have been physically abused sometimes appear to try to provoke attack or emulate their abuser by attacking other children, thereby gaining a modicum of control (Green, 1985). Boys tend to grow up to identify with the abuser and exhibit violence, whereas girls tend to become the passive victims of male violence (van der Kolk, 1989). Boy victims often go on to become abusive husbands. Some men seek re-enactment of their trauma through visiting porno web-sites exhibiting similar events (Chaney and Chang, 2005). Boys who practise autoerotic asphyxiation ('self-strangling') appear to have a history of trauma, sometimes specifically of being strangled (Friedrich and Gerber, 1994).

Girls who were abused have a relatively high later probability of engaging in sadomasochistic sex, prostitution or in other risky sexual activities (Green, 1985; Southern, 2002). For example, Rosemary West who, it was speculated, had been abused as a child, showed extreme sexual precocity, perverse sexuality and engaged in prostitution as well as becoming a sexually linked serial killer (Sounes, 1995). The occasional hostage comes to desire sex with her hostage-taker. Rape victims sometimes bond with their rapist (Ellis, 1989). To the dismay and frustration of police and social workers alike, battered wives often find their path back to their tormentors.

The Victorian English writer 'Walter' reports that his first sexual experience happened between the ages of 5 and 8, when his nursemaid would hold his penis, a painful and traumatic experience, followed by her soothing him (Walter, 1995). Walter developed an insatiable appetite for sex.

Consider also an American businesswoman, Laura, who started to use pornography at age 11 following sexual abuse (Maltz and Maltz, 2010, pp. 41 and 207):

> My two older brothers got into my dad's pornography. They showed me the pictures and read me the stories, and then did to me what they had seen and heard. I became their learning tool. It may sound strange but later on I would sneak into their rooms and look through the magazines by myself. I developed a fascination with stories of women who felt threatened in sex. I had a nightly routine of masturbating to the porn. It gave me an escape from the reality of what my brothers were doing to me and enabled me to get to sleep. I used pornography this way even after they stopped abusing me.

> I've mostly been drawn to written porn about risky sex in which a woman is weak and physically threatened. It's pretty clear that my attraction to this scenario has something to do with how powerless I felt when my brothers molested me when I was a young girl.

Laura's situation was possibly transformed from aversive to attractive because of the control that she gained subsequently with the pornography. The common element of high arousal was carried over between situations.

How do we explain it in terms of the brain?

This phenomenon seems to be a specific example of a general principle described by Sigmund Freud in *Beyond the Pleasure Principle* under the name of the 'compulsion to repeat'. He suggested that it represents an attempt to gain mastery of the situation, which overrides the tendency of the body to seek pleasure (Freud, 1955). One suspects that the term might occasionally have been used as a convenient get-out clause for therapeutic failure (Webster, 1995, p. 152), but that would not undermine its potential explanatory value.

Investigators have subsequently identified the kind of brain processes that trigger such behaviour. A feature of trauma is a high level of brain arousal. Immediately following exposure to trauma, there are consequences that can assume positive motivational qualities. That is to say, high arousal is followed by behavioural calming (Apter, 2007). This sequence sounds remarkably like one aspect of a conventional reinforcing sexual interaction.

Natural opioids are released under conditions of stress and going back into a similar situation appears again to trigger opioid release, in some cases followed by withdrawal symptoms when the effect wears off. Drugs, such as heroin and morphine, that mimic natural opioids, cause motivation to be directed towards repeating the drug experience. It appears that stress-induced opioid release can have a somewhat similar effect in triggering a repeat of the stressful experience (van der Kolk, 1989). Evidence supportive of such an effect is that Vietnam War veterans reported feeling less physical pain when they were allowed to view a movie about the war. This had a similar pain-relieving effect to a shot of 8 mg of morphine. Shipman might have recreated an opioid-based mood change by his murders.

The phenomenon of the abused becoming the abuser says something about reinforcement, classical and instrumental conditioning. To a considerable extent, experiences that were hedonically positive become reinforcers and form associations with neutral stimuli. However, Skinner and his followers pointed out that positive reinforcement does not equate to hedonism in any simple way, and the phenomenon under discussion here illustrates this. Although the experiences of abuse would surely have been felt as aversive (Hogben and Byrne, 1998), nonetheless the individual is moved to repeat something similar.

Excitation and inhibition

As a general principle, sexual interaction, whether atypical or not, contains opposing elements (Chapter 12 and Bancroft, 2009). A behavioural activation system underlies appetitive behaviour, while a behavioural inhibition system tends to restrain behaviour. Inhibition arises from such things as fear of humiliation or possible harm to oneself. It is triggered by the detection of threats, such as cues predictive of aversive consequences.

Some forms of paraphiliac behaviour meet with social disapproval, from mild mocking to severe punishment. Social exclusion, life in prison or even death can form the penalty for the most extreme. This would surely be enough to recruit sufficient inhibition to keep most of us on the straight and narrow, even if we felt any inclination to deviate. Where behaviour is atypical, especially of a socially unacceptable form, excitation might not necessarily be abnormally high but inhibition could be relatively under-active.

Some individuals exhibit a range of different paraphilias (Abel and Rouleau, 1990; Meloy, 2000), so there might be a general deficit of inhibition rather than a multitude of different conflicts each specific to a given paraphilia. Engaging in one paraphilia might lower the inhibition on others. For a subgroup of paraphilias, Wolf (1988) remarked (p. 142):

> once a person is disinhibited to and aroused to one particular focus of sexually aggressive behaviour, it is significantly easier for them to acquire a second or third or fourth focus. This is much in the same manner that it would be easier for a skydiver to take up hang-gliding.

Levels of control in the brain and brain chemicals

Paraphilias are often troubling to those who suffer from them, even if only through the risk of capture, and these individuals often acknowledge the problem and at least consider, if not seek, medical help. This reveals a conflict for the control of behaviour, with a high level of restraint proving inadequate in the face of the pull of the lower-level controls triggered by incentives and their mental representation.

The relative influence exerted by the low-level and high-level systems appears to be dependent upon the amount of the neurotransmitter serotonin in the brain (Carver et al., 2009). If this is decreased, control shifts in favour of the lower level, with a tendency for a person to behave more impulsively, to show a higher reaction to anger and a relatively high degree of sensation-seeking. They are more likely to be captured by the 'cues of the moment'. Conversely, increasing the amount of serotonin is associated with greater conscientiousness and agreeableness. These qualities appear to require taking a more distant perspective in assessing priorities, rather than giving in to impulsiveness, suggesting a tilting in favour of higher-levels of control. There is evidence that drugs that boost the availability of serotonin in the brain are sometimes effective in treating a range of paraphilias (Masand, 1993), suggesting a strengthening of high-level controls. In addition, serotonin could act at the level of the nucleus accumbens to inhibit desire (Pfaus, 2009).

Certain brain structures, for example the prefrontal cortex, that are particularly compromised by early abuse are newly evolved and late to develop fully (Gerhardt, 2004; Rich, 2006; Schore, 2003). These normally exert high-level inhibition on behaviour. Correspondingly, the low-level system takes a disproportionately large weight in the balance of control. Those exhibiting deviant sexuality reveal a rather high probability of having suffered early abuse or at least inadequate mother–child interaction.

The closely-related notions of (a) excitation and inhibition and (b) levels of control appear to be central to understanding psychopathy, to which the discussion now turns.

Psychopathy

Some features of the psychopath

The characteristic of 'psychopathy' does not necessarily link with deviant sexual desire but it sometimes does so in an alarming manner. Some general principles of psychopathy illuminate features of coercive sexual behaviour (Muñoz et al., 2011). As a defining feature, psychopaths are not insane and they exhibit rational decision-making. It is just a rather different rationality, which is based upon an alternative set of values and parameters, as compared to that of non-psychopaths (Hare, 1993). Psychopaths are not lacking in social understanding of the mind-set and intentions of other individuals; indeed, they can be very competent in exploiting flattery, charm, manipulation and lies to get their way (Muñoz et al., 2011), as exemplified by the serial killer Ted Bundy. They have a relatively shallow experience of fear and a weak bodily reaction to what would trigger a pounding heart and sweaty palms in most of us (Hare, 1993). Psychopaths are also often characterized by hypersexuality, in the form of early onset of sexual behaviour, promiscuity and high sexual risk-taking (Kastner and Sellbom, 2012). In an analysis congruent with that presented here, Bailey (2002) suggests that psychopaths have shifted the weight of control to a lower level.[2]

The notions of narcissist and psychopath are linked and appear to be relevant to sexual coercion. Although not all narcissists are psychopaths, probably all psychopaths are narcissists. Narcissists are characterized by a particularly high arrogance, sense of self-importance and self-entitlement, accompanied by a willingness to exploit others to achieve their own ends while showing low empathy with their concerns (Bushman et al., 2003). Narcissists are likely to exhibit relatively high levels of aggression in response to 'threatened egotism', as in for example perceived insults.

Some psychopaths tend to be more strongly weighted towards impulsive control than are non-psychopaths, showing little sensitivity to the future (Hare, 1993) and great difficulty in delaying gratification. However, for other psychopaths aggression tends to be measured and appropriate to the circumstances, which indicates retention of control (Raine, 2013). Psychopaths are very good at allocating undivided attention to a given task and thereby missing signals of danger.

Hare (1993, p. 61) writes: 'Psychopaths have an on-going and excessive need for excitement – they long to live in the fast lane or "on the edge", where the action is.' Breaking the rules can bring them up to a more desirable level of arousal, to a 'high'. One psychopath described the experience of breaking out from prison as 'better than sex' (p. 62).

Personality characteristics of psychopaths include a willingness to exploit manipulation and use aggression, irresponsibility and callousness, accompanied by a lack of guilt and remorse and other similar restraining emotions (Blair, 2006; Gao and Raine, 2010). Some psychopaths make primary use of so-called 'instrumental aggression' ('cool', planned aggression) to gain desired things, such as money, goods or sex. However, for other psychopaths, behaviour is biased towards so-called 'reactive aggression', which is impulsive, anger-related and can be triggered by frustration (Blair et al., 2006). Hence there is likely to be a heightened anger/aggression when such people are thwarted in attaining sexual goals, a tendency that could well be sensitized in cases where there has been a history of abuse when a child.

The married psychopath can sometimes have a good life, particularly if his wife fits the traditional role (Hare, 1993). He can maintain an endless sequence of sexual adventures untroubled by remorse and yet have the security of the wife.

A range of psychopathy

The word 'psychopath' most likely creates an image of a serial killer lurking in the bushes to pounce on an unsuspecting victim. This represents just one extreme. At the milder end of the scale, traits of psychopathy are associated with such things as aggressive sexual coercion of a date partner and use of alcohol as a tool in sexual manipulation (Kosson et al., 1997). In some cases, women who fall on the psychopathy scale also exhibit some sexually coercive tactics (Muñoz et al., 2011). Not surprisingly, these are usually of milder degree than the male equivalents but include the common feature of getting a potential sex partner intoxicated.

Excitation and inhibition as applied to psychopathic behaviour

The notions of excitation, inhibition and disinhibition play a central role in understanding psychopathy and the associated reckless and coercive behaviour (Sewell, 1985; Wallace and Newman, 2008). In terms of behavioural activation, it appears that psychopaths have a relatively high sensitivity, this being triggered particularly by novelty (Kastner and Sellbom, 2012).

For non-psychopaths, at the prospect of engaging in coercive sexual behaviour, there would be inhibitory factors of two rather different qualities:

- At an egocentric level, there would be fear of humiliation or capture or possible harm to oneself.
- At an altruistic level, there would be empathy from signs of negative emotion in the other individual, such as fear or disgust on the face of a child or a woman's embarrassment, resistance or pain or, at the least, lack of interest.

Psychopaths often appear to have a relatively under-reactive inhibition system relative to their activation system, based in part on weaknesses in the control of behaviour by the prediction of aversive consequences of actions (Blair, 2006; Hare, 1993). This deviation from normal could be based in part upon genetic differences from controls, pointing to the need for a biopsychosocial perspective (Kastner and Sellbom, 2012; Muñoz et al., 2011). This is either a permanent feature of their behaviour, or a temporary lifting of inhibition occurs. Such lifting can be triggered by alcohol or anger, often facilitated by maladaptive cognitions ('neutralizing definitions') (Segal and Stermac, 1990).

Many rapists have earlier convictions for property offences (Smallbone and Dadds, 1998). In one sample, 82 per cent had a history of criminal convictions but only 23 per cent had a history of previous sexual offences (Scully and Marolla, 1984). Such evidence points to a weakness in an all-purpose restraint system (MacDonald, 2008).

Psychopathic and narcissistic sexual aberration appears to exemplify behaviour that Gorenstein and Newman (1980) describe as 'disinhibited'. Behaviour is often said to be 'impulsive', acting to gain immediate rewards, although this can incur very serious long-term costs. Such people can articulate verbally that their behaviour is maladaptive in the long term, but this insight is not translated into the necessary restraint. Laboratory studies, for example with monetary rewards, find that disinhibited individuals tend to act so as to get immediate reward in a situation where delay can bring an enhanced reward. That is to say, they get captured by the potency of immediate reward. Disinhibited individuals also tend to be thrill-seekers, finding ordinary experience insufficient.

Some who commit sexual violence do so impulsively and opportunistically in an unplanned and uninhibited way, taking advantage of the situation as it presents itself (Raine, 2013). However, others devote considerable creativity to planning their actions, fine-tuning the strategy moment by moment according to prevailing circumstances, aborting sorties that suddenly appear to have acquired a high risk and performing a cost–benefit analysis. They are not necessarily overwhelmed by sudden temptation; that is, they can exert inhibition. However, the logic would still be that the prospect of reward in the relatively near future motivates such planning, while the prospect of still longer-term punishment exerts inadequate levels of inhibition. Doubtless some exhibit a combination of both these underlying deviations.

The psychopathic brain

Neuroimaging suggests that psychopaths have a relative under-activity in brain regions (cortical) that are characterized as underlying 'high-level' control, involving restraint on lower brain levels (Yang et al., 2008).[3] Conversely, there is heightened sensitivity of the dopaminergic system projecting to the nucleus accumbens, possibly arising from underactive inhibition on the dopaminergic neurons (Buckholtz et al., 2010).

Psychopaths are deficient at processing visual facial and auditory cues to fear and sadness. According to Blair (2006), disruption of the function of the amygdala underlies diminished sensitivity to distress cues exhibited by other individuals. The biological basis of empathy is formed from a number of brain regions, both evolutionarily old and new (Decety and Ickes, 2011). In the latter case, these include the orbitofrontal cortex. In psychopaths, the little empathy that they possess could well be decreased still further as sexual arousal and anger arousal move the weight of control to lower brain regions.

Psychopaths know right from wrong but they simply don't care, since wrong is not emotionally and morally weighted appropriately in the control of behaviour (Haidt, 2001). When tested on laboratory tasks, patients with damage to regions of the prefrontal cortex but no criminal history or tendencies also show evidence of deficits in the inhibition of behaviour (Luria, 1973). As with psychopaths, they show a sensitivity to physically present stimuli and relative disregard of long-term consequences of their behaviour, and can also verbally articulate what is required of them in terms of inhibiting responses but find it difficult to exert inhibition. Of course, brain damage does not usually transform such people into serial killers or violent rapists. Presumably, what stops most of us from engaging in such activities is not that we are actively inhibited from doing so but rather that we have no desire to do so. Hence, there is nothing to inhibit and we can speculate that this is equally true of most brain-damaged patients.

The subtlety of empathy

There are identifiable brain regions involved in forming empathy with others (Decety and Ickes, 2011; Fonagy, 2003), and they would normally exert a restraining influence on aggression and deception.[4] Hence, their disruption might be expected to lead to problems with inhibition of behaviour and a tendency to make decisions that fail to take normal account of long-term punishing consequences of actions or the consequences to others.

Some of the deviations described here necessarily have a victim and one whose suffering would inhibit most people. Empathy for the suffering of another individual is accompanied by activation of a similar set of brain regions as those that are triggered by a noxious stimulus to oneself such as a thorn (Eisenberger, 2012). In this sense, psychological pain is real and has a measurable basis in the brain. Similarly, the perception of disgust in the face of another is normally associated with some activation of disgust in the brain of the perceiver (Kelly, 2011). One could speculate that sexual psychopaths are either insensitive to such signals or, if they detect the signals, are unmoved (or even excited) by them and there is evidence that sexually aggressive males show low levels of disgust in response to simulated sexual aggression (Calhoun and Wilson, 2000).

However, empathy is not some all-or-nothing feature. Rather, it appears to be based in part upon cognitions involving the potential recipient of the empathetic feeling (Decety and Ickes, 2011). For example, even normal individuals qualify their empathy as a result of the perceived deservedness of the recipient. A person with AIDS receives more empathy if she or he caught the virus through transfused blood rather than by drug injection. Empathy increases as the perceived closeness to the sufferer in terms of family or ethnic group increases. There is greater activation of the brain regions underlying empathy when the empathizer is contemplating what is considered to be a psychologically closer or subjectively more deserving individual.

In some cases, individuals showing violent sexual desire entertain highly negative cognitions concerning their intended victims, such as that all women set out to hurt them by their rejections. Similarly, if a man has the goal that the streets should be swept clean of sex workers, or thinks that the wives and daughters of enemy soldiers are equally 'the enemy' and thereby fair game, then he is unlikely to exhibit much empathy.

How does psychopathy arise?

So, what makes a psychopath? This is often expressed as a simple dichotomy: born or made? Perhaps the most likely explanation is a subtle interplay between early biological endowment and experience (Hare, 1993). The psychopathic brain might emerge early with a deficient capacity to form empathetic associations, which means that the experience of empathy is not developed ('downloaded') from early social interactions. Poor parenting, appears often to be a contributory factor in the emergence of psychopathology.

A fundamental assumption of 'social learning theory' is that the roots of deviant behaviour lie in deviant social interactions, for example between parents and child and/or between peers (Akers, 1985; Chan et al., 2010). The child's learning processes could be intact but the content (what is learned) might set development in an abnormal direction. Evidence suggests that sexual aberration can relate to the early learning of deviations in general ways of acting in the world and to underlying brain processes, as well as more specifically to sexual behaviour.

Some of the most serious kinds of sexual deviation involve the use of violence and evidence points to the early learning of aggressive strategies for dealing with social problems. Aggressive behaviour can be reinforced by its consequences, for instance the child getting his own way by bullying, or can be learned by observation of the successful exploitation of aggression in role models (Akers, 1985). The parents of aggressive children tend to exhibit aggression. Those who 'blow their top' and impulsively show violence have often had a history of being reinforced for violence, albeit of a more restrained form. Aggressive young men tend to gravitate towards peers with similar attitudes and thereby derive some reinforcement for their attitudes (Calhoun and Wilson, 2000). In some cases, such activities form part of the trajectory to later more serious offences such as rape and sexual homicide (Britton, 1998; Rule, 1983). Such behaviour could arise from a lack of appropriate restraints on antisocial behaviour combined with failures of expected or actual sexual reciprocity.

Most psychopaths exhibit serious deviant behaviour, such as lying, vandalism and stealing, from an early age (Hare, 1993). Precocious sexual behaviour is another common behaviour. Although many children show at least some of these characteristics, future psychopaths tend to exhibit more of them and at greater intensity.

A common assumption is that psychopaths invariably come from violent, disturbed and abusive family backgrounds and some indeed do. However, in Hare's experience, for every one fitting this image there is another from a loving family, with siblings who show no signs of being psychopaths. For some reason, psychopaths have failed to assimilate the emotional processing that helps to keep the rest of us in line. For example, there are deficiencies in the assessment of the chances of being caught or, if the assessment is correct, it exerts relatively little weight in restraining behaviour. The prospect of future punishment often does little to deter. They lack that 'nagging conscience' or 'inner policeman' that watches over us. There is an 'inner voice' that speaks up against risky and immoral action, even at the planning stage when it is no more than thoughts, and in the case of psychopaths this voice, if it exists at all, lacks emotional impact.

Evolutionary considerations

From an evolutionary perspective, the term 'psychopathy' might be something of a misnomer. Particularly as it applies to sexual behaviour, it represents, not pathology, but rather a particular strategy that has been favoured since it serves adaptive ends (Hare, 1993; Raine, 2013). That is to say, it represents one end of a spectrum: a way of maximizing investment in the future by producing a maximum number of offspring. By chance, some of these will survive and in turn reproduce. The psychopath wastes little time or energy in either the partner or the offspring's welfare, a reminder of the cliché 'survival of the fittest'. The strategy is to mate with a maximum number of partners and to quickly move on to another. The psychopath's skill at deception, lying and cheating lends itself well to this strategy. At the other end of the spectrum the alternative strategy is to have few children but to invest heavily in them.

Having listed some of the component processes and how their variation could underlie variation in desire, the next three chapters exemplify the variety of sexual desire and behaviour at 'the fringes'.

In summary

- Behaviour that is at the fringes of desire appears to arise by means of some similar processes to those underlying conventional desire and behaviour. It is suggested simply that some weightings and parameters within these processes are different.

- In some cases of aberrant sexual behaviour, particularly where violence is involved, there appear to be deficiencies of attachment.
- Learning and fantasy appear to contribute to sending desire in an abnormal direction.
- A chance pairing of a particular stimulus situation with arousal seems to be implicated.
- Some cases involve re-running an earlier trauma.
- In cases of desire at the fringes, inhibition can be deficient.
- Psychopathic sexual desire appears to arise from a combination of a lack of empathy for others, a tendency to instant gratification, and weak inhibition arising from anticipated negative consequences of behaviour.

NINETEEN

SOME FORMS OF DESIRE AT THE FRINGES

Attempts to divide anything into two ought to be regarded with much suspicion.

(C. P. Snow, 1965, p. 9)

The central argument of the present study is that biology and environment are inextricably mixed in the determination of all forms of desire, whether normal or at the fringe. The following examples are based upon this.

Voyeurism

Starting from childhood, the Victorian writer Walter was an insatiable and creative voyeur, an activity which he accompanied by masturbation, but this did not prevent him from developing an active 'conventional' sex life in parallel. Having found a hiding place in a basement and looking up to the street above through a hole, Walter would sometimes wait for hours before catching a glimpse of the legs of an unsuspecting woman. On visits to the Continent, Walter spent hours peering through keyholes watching women or couples. Kronhausen and Kronhausen (1967) observe (p. 318):

> This may sound strange for a man as sexually active as Walter was, but is entirely in keeping with what we have come to know about other individuals like him. In fact it is a fallacy to assume that a sexually active person may not also be interested in voyeurism.

How might it begin?

Consider a Scottish male, who illustrates how chance circumstances can set off this type of desire (McGuire et al., 1965, p. 189):

> This 28-year-old patient, married at the age of 24, had had normal sexual interests. However, his wife proved to be totally frigid so that the marriage was never consummated. In the early months of his marriage, while sexually frustrated, he observed that a young lady in the opposite flat was in the habit of stripping in a lighted room with the curtains open (the patient's wife confirmed this story). The patient found this very stimulating sexually. The marriage had not been consummated when the couple moved house. In his new environment the patient sought opportunities of seeing women undressing and developed the habit of masturbating on these occasions. It is interesting to note that the patient retained all the circumstances of the early stimulus and had no interest in nudist films or strip-tease shows. He came to our notice after his fourth conviction for a 'Peeping Tom' offence.

This case illustrates a narrow focus of attraction, most likely associated with a very high arousal value deriving from its illicit nature. Also there is the search to recapture a trigger to desire which arose initially by chance. The unavailability of the wife for a conventional sexual relationship would have contributed to a vacuum, ready to be filled.

Voyeurism appears to be almost exclusively a male pursuit (Kinsey et al., 1953).

Link to other behaviour

Voyeurism does not, of course, necessarily lead to more serious behaviour such as rape. However, it appears that in some cases, voyeurism serves as a gateway. One example of this is the Canadian rapist and killer Paul Bernardo, who became a peeping Tom when still a young boy (Pron, 1995). Bernardo also illustrates that voyeurism need not be a substitute for sexual activity involving physical contact. While married with his sexually very active partner, and right up to his arrest for rape and murder, he was still prowling as a peeping Tom.

Voyeurism, particularly if accompanied by masturbation, captures the ingredients of what is, to some people, highly motivating sexuality:

novelty, uncertainty, the excitement of the forbidden and the chance to search for perfection. The essential features of the forbidden and risk are evidenced by the fact that these days it is not necessary to run the risk of climbing drainpipes or hiding in bushes to see naked female bodies (Apter, 2007). However, by their legality and relative predictability of outcome, strip-clubs are presumably less arousing.

Voyeurism and the Internet

On the Internet, there are sites catering for the posting of subscribers' favourite pictures, often those of a willing or unwitting wife or girlfriend, a kind of reciprocal altruism between exhibitionists and voyeurs. The control is total and available at the click of a mouse. Nigel, a businessman described his use of Internet pornography, and illustrates the purposive nature of the activity and its inherent uncertainty (Maltz and Maltz, 2010):

> I know exactly what I am looking for in terms of a specific look and a specific type of sex. I know it's there somewhere. I love the hunt, looking and searching for the best and most exciting, my ideal. And there's always the chance I will be able to find something better than I had before.

With Internet porn, it is reported (Maltz and Maltz, 2010, p. 20):

> As with capturing prey, you can look for it, circle around it, target it, and then go in for the 'kill' by purchasing or downloading the porn. Some porn users tell us that the hunt and conquest feeling that blends with sexual arousal is even more satisfying than having an orgasm.

Fetishes, partialism and transvestism

What are they?

In its psychiatric use, 'fetish' refers to something that is *indispensible* for sexual arousal to occur, either when this is linked to a person or even when acting as a substitute for a person. The fetish might actually be physically present or would at least need to be present in the individual's fantasy world (Binet, 1887). However, the term 'fetish' can also be used in a lay sense as something that has a particular sexual attraction and facilitates arousal (Scorolli et al., 2007). Thus, many towns have window displays of items of female attire, such as stockings and high-heeled shoes, designed to excite male sexuality by their association with the presentation of apparent female sexual availability. However, they are not usually an absolute prerequisite to such desire and would thereby not constitute fetishes in the psychiatric sense (Money, 1986). One can speculate that the fetish serves as a token for the whole female, helping the man to fill in the full picture (C. Wilson, 1988). The fetish is a kind of tag, which gives the unlimited and unthreatening fantasy world its emotional colouring and richness.

Male displays designed to arouse female desire are much less evident. If we could explain this, we might understand why fetishes are overwhelmingly a male phenomenon (Kinsey et al., 1953). In giving lectures on this topic, I sometimes ask the students to imagine a female who steals male shoes or underwear to form a collection. This invariably triggers giggles, particularly from women, suggesting its implausibility.

Women do sometimes form associations with inanimate objects. It was reported that they would kiss the paper on which the eighteenth-century writer Jean-Jacques Rousseau (more on him in a moment!) had placed his name and offer a high price for a glass from which he had drunk (C. Wilson, 1988). One might suspect that over the centuries, such stories have been embellished but I witnessed something similar. At a concert in Cambridge by the 1960s pop group The Walker Brothers, I observed girls to tear the sleeve off a member of the group and then shred it, the spoils being shared out (university academics rarely have such an effect on their audience). The important point is that the objects collected by such females owe their strength not to an association simply with a male or even with a strikingly attractive male but with a *particular famous* male, who shows some exceptional behaviour or ability. Again this demonstrates the female attribution of meaning and personal individualistic association to their emotions.

There are several variations of fetish. The expression 'partialism' refers to a type in which a particular part of the body forms an attraction somewhat in isolation from the rest of the body. The transvestite, sometimes termed transvestophile (Money, 1986), derives sexual excitement from dressing in women's clothes. Transvestism might be an extension

374 • How Sexual Desire Works

of fetishism, that is a fetishist attraction to clothes as worn by a woman (Kinsey et al., 1953).

Using 'fetish' in the psychiatric sense, Krafft-Ebing (1978) claimed (p. 35):

> As a rule, when the individual fetish is absent coitus becomes impossible or can only be managed under the influence of the respective imaginary presentation, and even then grants no gratification. Its pathological condition is strongly accentuated by the circumstance that the fetichist does not find gratification in coitus itself, but rather in the manipulation of that portion of the body or that object which forms the interesting and effective fetish.

We should not view fetishes in an entirely negative light. As one man observed (Gosselin and Wilson, 1980, p. 118):

> People should envy us rather than back off from us: we've got a stone cold, guaranteed aphrodisiac that can turn us on at any time, however old we are.

How might fetishes arise?

It is commonly assumed that fetishes acquire their power from association formation (Binet, 1887). What seems to occur is the pairing, even once, of a human-related object or human feature with a powerful emotion, whether positive or negative, such that the object/feature acquires a strong sexual value. In some cases, the initial emotion is one specifically of *sexual* arousal, whereas in other cases the emotion seems not to be initially sexual but comes to acquire this label. Fetishes appear not to arise from conditioning to any object that happens to be around at the time of arousal. As Leitenberg and Henning (1995, p. 485) note: 'Few people are turned on by doorknobs, bedroom dressers, or bathroom fixtures, even though these cues are in the environment when sexual arousal and orgasm take place.' This points to the brain's preparedness to link with particular classes of stimuli.

As the pioneer of sex research, Krafft-Ebing (1978) wrote (p. 145):

> *in the life of every fetichist there may be assumed to have been some event which determined the association of lustful feeling with the single impression.*

This event must be sought for in the time of early youth, and, as a rule, occurs in connection with the first awakening of the sexual life.

In some cases, the person can identify what he believes to be the incident that formed the association and set the whole thing going, whereas in other cases this information has been lost in the mists of time (Binet, 1887). Abel et al. (2008) describe the case of a boy who, at age 6, attended a church party where there were balloons. Some of these popped loudly, which terrified the boy and he ran from the church. Subsequently, he avoided balloons and loud noises. However, when a young teenager, he acquired the habit of masturbating while blowing up balloons. At age 18, he was arrested in a store after a repeated history of asking sales assistants to blow up balloons. He would retreat a distance and masturbate to the sight of the balloon. Abel et al., argue, doubtless correctly, that the arousal triggered initially by fear became labelled sexual with the emergence of sexual maturity. Note that the cue here is a dynamic one: the *change* in shape of the balloon. Stimuli with a defined onset and offset are probably particularly likely to form associations, as opposed to door handles or wardrobes.

In one study in England, people with rubber fetishes gave ages between 4 and 10 years as the most likely for when the attraction first appeared (Gosselin and Wilson, 1980). The authors extrapolated that this would have been at around the start of the Second World War, when anxiety and hence arousal were triggered to a large degree. It was when gas-masks, with their associated rubber, were much in evidence.

Another possible angle on understanding fetishes is to consider the relative value of the object and the person. Could it be that in the life of the fetishist, something has happened to form an aversive association with real people but has left something about them, such as their clothing, unaffected? An experiment suggests this possibility (LaTorre, 1980). Men were duped into believing that women had rejected them and consequently women were devalued. However, their underwear, feet and legs were not devalued. It appears that at times of prominence of sexually transmitted diseases, foot fetishes assume a greater frequency (Lowenstein, 2002). This suggests a fear of the whole person.

Concerning 'fetish' in the mild sense of the word, the ubiquitous use of stockings and suspenders in pornography calls for an explanation.

I can only suggest that it arises from a combination of factors based upon conditioning in the following way. These items are tagged with desire potential ('incentive salience') because of their proximity to the female genitals and their exposure during undressing. In pornography, their appearance has a certain dynamic in terms of erotic progression. In addition, the culture means that they acquire a connotation of the forbidden.

Transvestism

Transvestism ('fetishistic cross-dressing') describes the phenomenon where a male is sexually excited by wearing an item of women's clothes, often leading to masturbation (Stoller, 1971). Sometimes the single item remains constant for life. In other cases, this behaviour starts with wearing a single item of women's clothing and then broadens to include additional items, sometimes culminating in full dressing as a woman. The man normally retains a heterosexual identity and is attracted to women, thereby the phenomenon needs to be distinguished from transsexualism. In the latter case, the male is not happy being a man and is not sexually excited by clothes. Of course, women commonly wear clothing more typically male but they are not sexually excited by doing so.

For transvestophiles, Money (1986, p. 38) observes how a negative emotion can get transformed into a positive one:

> The tranvestophile's tragedy, in some cases on record in his early history, was his mortification at having been paraded in public in girl's clothes, in many instances as a punishment. The triumph is that the mortification is transposed into erotic and genital arousal.

Early dressing in girl's clothes is evident very commonly, if not invariably, in the developmental history of boys who go on to become transvestophiles (Stoller, 1971).

Stoller (1971) describes one of his transvestophile clients in Los Angeles. The man, a machinist in his thirties was married and had three children. He was first cross-dressed at age 4 by an aunt. At age 7, forced cross-dressing as a punishment by another aunt triggered strong sexual arousal. From the time of puberty, sexual excitement required wearing women's shoes, which escalated to full dressing in women's clothes. He had no interest in male bodies. When being with a woman, to attain arousal required either wearing items of women's clothing or having fantasies that he was doing so.

Bodily features and actions as fetishes

Particular human features can acquire fetishist properties. This was articulated almost one thousand years ago by the Islamic scholar Ibn Hazm, in describing men for whom idiosyncratic qualities of their partners:

> had become an obsession with them, the sole object of their passion, and the very last word (as they thought) in elegance.

He added that when the relationship triggering the fetishist element ended, nonetheless the fetishist taste continued:

> those men never lost their admiration for the curious qualities which provoked their approval of them, neither did they ever afterwards cease to prefer these above other attributes that are in reality superior to them. (Ibn Hazm, 1027/1953, p. 60)

Ibn Hazm observed various fetishist elements essential for attraction based upon an initial encounter, including a particularly short neck, shortness of height and a wide mouth, or in his own case, blonde hair.

Another example is the sixteenth- to seventeenth-century French philosopher, René Descartes, who had a particularly strong attraction to cross-eyed women, arising from a childhood crush on a cross-eyed girl (Binet, 1887; Shaffer, 2011). The nineteenth-century French psychologist Alfred Binet described a male patient M.R., who had a fetish about women's hands. M.R. recalled that even prior to puberty he had a peculiar fascination with girls' hands but this was not then sexual in character. Only later did hands assume a sexual quality. Sometimes hands would suddenly appear to M.R. in his fantasy while he was engaged with his work and he would need to try to drive them away in order for work not to be disrupted.

Krafft-Ebing describes a 30-year-old male civil servant who had a particular sexual fixation (1978, p. 155):

Since his seventh year he had for a playmate a lame girl of the same age . . . it lies beyond doubt that the first sexual emotions towards the other sex were coincident with the sight of the lame girl.

For ever after only limping women excited him sexually.

Some attractions to particular bodily features appear to be acquired by what is termed 'one-shot conditioning'. In the following case, this occurs with an arousing and, one might assume, aversive event. Krafft-Ebing (p. 73) describes a 26-year-old man, who had shown no interest in women until a chance event:

when one of his mother's maids cut her hand severely on a pane of glass, which she had broken while washing windows. While helping to stop the bleeding he could not keep from sucking up the blood that flowed from the wound, and in this act he experienced extreme erotic excitement, with complete orgasm and ejaculation.

He then sought out this trigger by requesting of girls that he be allowed to prick their finger and lick the blood.

Some men feel a sexual desire to observe women urinating. This is documented in graphic detail in the autobiography of the Victorian writer 'Walter' (Walter, 1995). While still a boy and prior to sexual development, Walter felt intense fascination with female urination. This was later to translate into a sexual desire and voyeurism directed to witnessing this event, to which he devoted inordinate effort and ingenuity.

The Victorian English sexologist Havelock Ellis also derived a particular sexual arousal from observing women while they urinated (Brome, 1979). This apparently derived from when he was a boy, with his mother walking in the gardens of London's Regent's Park and his mother was 'taken short', needing to go into the bushes. The mother later said 'I did not mean you to see that', which might well have triggered embarrassment in an impressionable young man. C. Wilson (1988, p. 181) reports: 'What seems most extraordinary was not that Ellis persuaded so many respectable young ladies to urinate in front of him, but that he himself was convinced that this was an exquisite aesthetic experience.' How could this attraction be explained? I suggest that it builds upon a childhood fascination with the mystery surrounding the genital region and from where urine comes. This has the character of the secret and forbidden, associated with arousal. The act of urination provides a signal and marker of the existence and exposed function of this part of the female anatomy.

More recently one-shot conditioning was described by Gebhard et al. (1965, p. 489), concerning:

> an individual, now in his thirties, who, when nearing puberty, had not as yet recognized sexual arousal. He became involved in a childhood tussle with a girl somewhat larger and more powerful than he. While struggling and wriggling beneath her he experienced not only his first conscious sexual arousal but in a strong degree. This one experience has dominated his life ever since. He has always been attracted to large, muscular, dominant females; and in his heterosexual contacts he tries to arrange the same wrestling. He has, not surprisingly, developed some additional masochistic attributes.

Gebhard describes another case telling a similar story (p. 489):

> that of a boy who was already in what one might call the flush of sexual excitability which accompanies puberty in most males. During some childhood game he fractured his arm and was taken to a neighbourhood physician. The physician's attractive nurse felt very sorry for the boy. During the reduction of the fracture and for some time afterwards she held and caressed him with his head pressed against her breasts. The boy experienced a powerful and curious combination of pain and sexual arousal. Considerably later in life this man began to notice that he was unusually attracted to brunettes with a certain type of hair style – attracted to an extent meriting the label of fetish. Some sadomasochistic tendencies also existed. After much introspection the man recalled that the hairstyle which was his fetish was the style in which the nurse had worn her hair. This insight did not destroy the fetish.

In this case, as with that described by Krafft-Ebing, a negative emotion seemed to trigger, merge with or become labelled as sexual arousal, a phenomenon that appears frequently in the study of sexual desire. The process of one-shot conditioning might describe the initial phase of exposure but then the person could revive memories of the experience and thereby strengthen its value as a sexual stimulus.

In some cases, the animate stimulus is not human. Krafft-Ebing (p. 83) describes a 42-year-old man who in childhood:

took particular pleasure in witnessing the slaughtering of domestic animals, especially swine. He thus experienced lustful pleasure and ejaculation. Later he visited slaughterhouses in order to delight in the sight of flowing blood and the death throes of the animals.

Fetishes linked to inanimate objects

Binet (1887) described a judge living in nineteenth-century Paris, who had a fetish about the clothes worn by Italian women. The sight of them in the street caused an immediate genital reaction. The man attributed his fetish to an incident when he was a boy of 16 and a group of three Italian women happened to stand near him in the street. He was 'bowled over'[1] by this sight and subsequently trembled at the thought of them such that he was moved to follow any such women he saw in the street. Unlike some other cases, the clothes needed to be actually on the woman to have the effect, those in a window on a mannequin failed to arouse him. One might find this a rather sad and frustrating tale, except that he reported to Binet that the excitement gave him great pleasure. Another Parisian studied by Binet would steal women's handkerchiefs to smell their odours, forming a collection of 300.

Binet suggested that certain inanimate sexual fetishes derive from association with particular body parts. He illustrated this with patient M.R., just described, who had a primary fetish about women's hands but also a secondary fetish about jewellery worn on the hand.

Krafft-Ebing observed the high frequency of foot and shoe fetishes, in some cases not associated with attraction to the whole woman. He reported that glove fetishism was relatively rare as compared to hand fetishism, whereas shoe fetishism is common relative to foot fetishism. He suggested that the reason is that the hand is normally naked whereas the foot is normally covered by a shoe. Occasionally, a boot fetish appears to arise as one-off conditioning, since on an early sexual encounter the woman was wearing boots. Krafft-Ebing describes a man who was introduced to sex at the age of 14 years. Subsequently a woman dressed any way other than the woman of this first encounter failed to interest him sexually.

Freud (1953) noted the high frequency of foot fetishes and suggested that the shoe is symbolic of the female genitalia. He clearly had a rich imagination and also suggested that fur fetishes are due to an association with pubic hair.

A survey of Google fetish interest groups reported in 2007 found that feet and shoes are still the most popular incentives for fetishist attraction and behaviour (Scorolli et al., 2007).

An apparently harmless case

A 15-year-old boy in New Orleans had a shoe fetish, requesting access to the shoes of women in his neighbourhood (Epstein, 1975). He reported that he wished to wet the shoes so as to make them shiny, that shoes occupied his mind for much of the time and entered his dreams. He also derived pleasure from putting a wet shoe on his own foot. The boy reported that the fetish first became apparent after (p. 306): 'being at a swimming pool and feeling he would like to pay one of the girls to step in the water with canvas shoes on.' Presumably, the *transition* from dull to relatively shiny on getting the shoes wet formed part of the fetish.

When fetish turns to tragedy

A tragic case of fetishism was that of Jerry Brudos, who in Oregon went on to become a serial killer (Rule, 1983). He was also a cross-dresser, a feature often associated with fetishism (Epstein, 1975). His fetish appears to have arisen from a chance pairing of a female-related object and a powerful (negative) emotion. When 5 years old, Jerry found a pair of women's shiny high-heeled shoes on a dump and took them home. He used the shoes as his initiation into cross-dressing, whereupon he was severely scolded and punished by his mother, whom he detested. At this time, a neighbour, a girl of 5 with whom Jerry had developed a strong attachment, died. To make matters worse, a neighbouring lady who had befriended him was taken ill and was no longer accessible for friendly contact. It appears that memories of the shoes, the girl and the lady became linked in his mind. Shortly after this, Jerry stole the shoes of a female teacher and, corresponding to his emerging sexuality, shoes become an erotic fixation for him. Pointing to the arousal value of the forbidden, Rule (1983) suggests (p. 180): 'his very need for subterfuge and secrecy made his obsession all the more thrilling'.

Females were either detested, as in the case of Jerry's mother, or had been lost from his life, but the eroticism of their shoes remained intact. The fetish targets now expanded to include women's silky underwear, which he stole from neighbours' houses and clothes lines. The act of intrusion doubtless created excitement and strengthened the future tendency to repeat this behaviour. Each item was added to a growing collection and, in the privacy of his room, Jerry would take out and fondle them while masturbating and would sleep with them. His fantasy evolved into dwelling on the prospect of creating a prison in which he would house chosen women who were to be at his command.

Jerry then escalated his activities to stalking women and seizing their shoes, which he took home and to bed with him. After he married, Jerry insisted that his wife wear high-heeled shoes, even for doing housework. When he felt depressed, he would resume night-time foraging to steal clothes and thereby ease his mood. Putting them on and feeling the sensation against his skin, he would enjoy a kind of token of its original owner. After killing one woman, he even cut off her foot and kept it with the shoe on. After receiving a life sentence for murder, the tedium was relieved by receiving an endless stream of catalogues of women's shoes through the post.

Another example of the tragic consequences of an escalating activity starting with fetishes is the Canadian, Colonel Russell Williams, the highly respected commander of the largest military base in Canada (Gibb, 2011). As far as is known, Williams' path towards fatal addiction and escalation started with entering the homes of unsuspecting women to steal their underwear, even trying it on while still in their homes. His biographer suggests that the adrenalin rush of the illegal entry served to add to the attraction of the activity. When this escalated to rape he would take such items as a souvenir of the event.

There has been speculation (and one can put it no stronger than that) concerning what triggered Williams' intense fetishist attraction, one suggestion being that he caught glimpses of his highly attractive mother wearing just underwear in the home (Gibb, 2011). Sexual advance towards the mother would have been inhibited with a possible accentuated focus upon her underwear. There is also speculation that he felt a parallel animosity towards the mother, for her role in their dysfunctional family.

Why the particular content of fetishes?

McConaghy (1987) recalls the phenomenon of 'preparedness' (p. 295): 'Sexual arousal in male fetishists occurs mainly to objects that are shiny, smooth, silky, and pink or black. Is this a "prepared" association to stimuli similar to the vulva?' Binet (1887) documented fetishes for women's hair and also for their body odours, the latter sometimes overriding all other stimuli.

Pointing to the combination of basic processes of association and more complex uniquely human meaning-related processes, Epstein notes that fetishes (1975, p. 307):

> frequently bear a relationship to body parts or to the person as a whole (shoes, boots, gloves, underclothes, aprons, handkerchiefs) and have the capacity to be applied easily to the body of the self (putting on a shoe). Such an object becomes the equivalent of a body part or person and is endowed with meaning beyond its mere intrinsic qualities.

By wearing the item of clothing, something that has acquired qualities of desire, the fetishist in some symbolic sense achieves a kind of union with the woman.

One can speculate on why, ahead of hands and gloves, it is feet and shoes that top the list of fetishes. Let us suppose that the attraction develops by a process of association between things in the real world and also between their representations in memory. Feet are attached to legs and legs are sexually charged by association with genitalia, more so than arms and, by association, hands. At least in industrial societies, feet are normally covered and the process of uncovering them triggers a change in the stimulation reaching the senses. Ramachandran and Blakeslee (1999) suggests that foot fetishes arise because of the proximity in the brain of sensory regions devoted to processing information from the feet and the genitals.[2] As a general principle, the process that forms associations tends to be insensitive to constant features of the environment, such as the regularly exposed hands, but would register the sudden appearance of naked feet or feet covered by a stocking. This is presumably one reason why door handles and light fittings rarely if ever feature as fetishes. There is a report that in cultures where breasts are normally exposed men do not tend to eroticize them (Symons, 1995), which could point in a similar direction.

An animal model of fetishes?

Investigators have observed fetish-like behaviour in some non-human species and this gives pointers to the kind of process that could underlie a part of the human equivalents. Evidence suggests the attribution of incentive salience by means of classical conditioning. Breland and Breland (1961), two students of B. F. Skinner, carried out an experiment, which involved presenting tokens to various species such as pigs and racoons by means of which they could earn food rewards. The behaviour started off well but then degenerated, in that the token seemed to acquire an inordinate degree of attraction. It was hard for the animal to let go of the token. In a bird species, the Japanese quail, an inanimate object paired with copulation can acquire such a value that the bird tries to mate with the inanimate object (Köksal et al., 2004).

Lomanowska et al., (2011) presented hungry rats with food pellets at unpredictable intervals. Just prior to the food pellet arriving, a lever would slide into the cage. The rat did not have to contact the lever in any way to get the food. So, the optimal thing to do would be to approach the food cup without delay and take each pellet of food, while ignoring the lever. That is to say, the goal of the food cup would dominate the control of behaviour. Nonetheless, a significant proportion of the rats made energetic contact with the lever, pointing to its strong attraction to them. It appeared that in such rats the low-level dopamine-based control underlying approach behaviour was strongly activated in this situation. Those rats which had experienced maternal deprivation were particularly prone to contact the lever (Lomanowska et al., 2011), suggesting that maternal deprivation sensitized the low-level incentive-based system. The life-histories of sex-related serial killers reveal a tendency to have experienced maternal deprivation and fetishes sometimes assume a great importance (Chapter 21).

Could arson be a form of fetish?

At first glance it might seem that there is little link between arson and sexual fetishes. Yet a number of sex offenders have a history of arson and sometimes the act of setting fire is said to take a sexual dimension. For example, the most notorious arsonist in US history, Thomas Sweatt, fits this description.[3] He set hundreds of houses and cars alight in the Washington DC area between 1985 and 2005. Driving away from the fires and later, Sweatt masturbated over the imagery. Sweatt, always an oddball, was socially inadequate and regarded himself as a failure. He had a fetish over uniforms, feet and shoes and would also use shoes as an object of masturbation.

Masochism and being dominated

What is it?

A classical account of masochism was given by the eighteenth-century Swiss philosopher and writer Jean-Jacques Rousseau in *The Confessions*, as he recalled his experiences at age 8 years at the hands of his governess Mlle Lambercier (Rousseau, 1781/1953, pp. 25–6):[4]

> But when in the end I was beaten I found the experience less dreadful in fact than in anticipation; and the very strange thing was that this punishment increased my affection for the inflictor. It required all the strength of my devotion and all my natural gentleness to prevent my deliberate earning another beating; I had discovered in the shame and pain of the punishment an admixture of sensuality which left me rather eager than otherwise for a repetition by the same hand. No doubt, there being some degree of precocious sexuality in all this, the same punishment at the hands of her brother would not have seemed pleasant at all . . .
>
> Who could have supposed that this childish punishment, received at the age of eight at the hands of a woman of thirty, would determine my tastes and desires, my passions, my very self for the rest of my life, and that in a sense diametrically opposed to the one in which they should normally have developed? . . . Tormented for a long while by I knew not what, I feasted feverish eyes on lovely women, recalling them ceaselessly to my imagination, but only to make use of them in my own fashion as so many Mlle Lamberciers.

And describing events somewhat later, he continued (pp .27–8)

> Not only, therefore, did I, though ardent, lascivious, and precocious by nature, pass the age of puberty without desiring or knowing any other sensual pleasures than those which Mlle Lambercier had, in all

innocence, acquainted me with; but when finally, in the course of years, I became a man I was preserved by that very perversity which might have been my undoing. My old childish tastes did not vanish, but became so intimately associated with those of maturity that I could never, when sensually aroused, keep the two apart. . . . I never dared to reveal my strange taste, but at least I got some pleasure from situations which pandered to the thought of it.

To fall on my knees before a masterful mistress, to obey her commands, to have to beg her for forgiveness, have been to me the most delicate of pleasures; and the more my vivid imagination heated my blood the more like a spellbound lover I looked.

Rousseau reported that he desired to repeat the earlier experience of punishment but dared not ask any woman to perform it, and so had to be content with the imagination.

There is a high sympathetic nervous system arousal associated with pain, which, provided it is not excessive, might get attached to sexual desire (Zillmann, 1986). Krafft-Ebing (1978) observed (p. 22): 'It sometimes happens that in boys the first excitation of the sexual instinct is caused by spanking, and they are thus incited to masturbation.' He noted that, in the thirteenth and fourteenth centuries, passive flagellation was at first welcomed by the church as a form of moral purification. However, it was later opposed after it was observed that sensuality was excited by the process. Amongst some of his patients, masochism was (p. 138) 'directed exclusively to purely symbolic acts expressing subjection without any actual infliction of pain'.

In keeping with this interpretation, Baumeister (1988) develops an interesting, albeit speculative, argument on masochism. According to this, masochism is a means for an individual to escape from the self; that is, to get away from meaningful thoughts and painful self-consciousness. In this regard, it is an activity that has the feature of 'mental narrowing' in common with extreme exercise, certain spiritual and meditative techniques, alcoholism and binge eating. Masochism moves the focus of attention to the body itself and thereby increases sexual pleasure. Baumeister suggests that painful self-awareness gets in the way of sexual pleasure and masochism is often accompanied by, or is a prelude to, more conventional sexual activity. The masochist switches off from personal and professional roles in life, and the goals and opinions of others. In masochistic sex, people are not acting as observers of their own performance. Performance failure can hardly feature large in masochistic activities; surely most could be confident of their powers of total submission!

The stereotype of extreme pain is probably a considerable exaggeration if applied universally. Light pain or token pain can suffice for some, as can merely the threat of pain. Madonna (1992, p. 28) observed: 'I talked to a dominatrix once and she said that the definition of S and M was that you let someone hurt you who you knew would never hurt you.' A study of masochists revealed the tendency for pain to be within acceptable limits (Gosselin and Wilson, 1980, p. 50): 'a masochist has little wish to put his head on the block, figuratively or literally, and will only play that role with someone who understands the "rules of the game"'. However, in some cases, 'the rules of the game' appeared to be such that injuries were incurred, as in cigarette burns. Such activities might well hold high arousal value, which can be labelled as sexual arousal (Zillmann, 1984). There are various forms that the loss of control can take, most obviously and usually those of bondage and blindfolding.

In Gosselin and Wilson (1980, p. 56), a neurologist in England gives the following self-report:

> When a person such as myself visits a sympathetic lady so that he might obtain pleasure by her inflicting what most people regard as pain on him, a curious thing happens. With me at any rate, the stimulus must be applied at a very modest intensity at first. As my ritual is carried out, the intensity may be increased without my finding it distressing. By the time climax occurs, the woman is beating me with an intensity that, were it done outside the situation we have arranged, would probably give me a heart attack, whilst my cries would be heard far away. It is by no means easy to explain how such high levels of pain can be not only tolerated but enjoyed.

This escalation in tolerated intensity suggests that, over the time that this occurs, particular changes are gradually happening in the brain. Doidge (2007) suggests that, under these circumstances the brain rewires itself, so that neurons that were previously triggering its pain regions now come to trigger its pleasure regions. It would be expected that any such wiring manifests its influence only in the specific context of the masochistic experience. There would not be a general loss of the sensation of pain.

Who are masochists?

Both males and females are represented amongst masochists, with a slight excess of males. According to Baumeister and contrary to the stereotype of extreme deviation, masochists are generally healthy individuals, 'normal' in every other feature of their lives (Gosselin and Wilson, 1980). Masochists tend to be successful individuals of high socioeconomic status, which Baumeister interprets as reflecting the need to escape from the self. Thus, sex workers who cater for this taste tend to derive most of their clients from the rich and powerful. In Washington DC, judges and politicians are the typical clients. A feature in some cases of masochism is full identity change by taking on female characteristics, specifically dressing in women's clothes.

Baumeister (1991) argues that the greatly increased frequency of masochism seen in recent centuries reflects the move to greater individualism (p. 121):

> Just when our culture started to increase the stressful burden of the self by insisting that each person cultivate a unique, autonomous, individually responsible and authentic identity, the appetite for sexual masochism emerged historically as a response to the spread of individuality – exactly what one would expect if masochism is an escape from the self.

A study of those who engage in hardcore sadomasochism, that is where real physical damage is inflicted, revealed that a large percentage had suffered painful surgical interventions in childhood (Stoller, cited by Doidge, 2007). In some way, their development had been such as to eroticize their suffering.

The nature of pain

Baumeister suggests that pain causes a fundamental shift in the state of awareness with what is termed a 'deconstruction of the self' and a low capacity for abstract thought. The focus shifts to the 'here and now' and away from issues of meaning and of long-term concern. Taking a biological perspective, he suggests that in the masochistic experience just sufficient pain can be triggered to act as a narcotic.

The consequences

Apparently, masochists experience intense orgasms as a culmination of their activity, which according to Baumeister powerfully reinforce the activity, increasing the future tendency to repeat. As he notes, if masochism has a disinhibiting effect, then new aspects of sexuality might appear – those which were previously desired but suppressed. This would follow logically if control moves to a lower level. Some people reported that they engaged in new experiences for the first time in the course of masochistic sex. It was as if responsibility for performing a previously forbidden act was lifted from the participant and put into the hands of the dominant partner.

> It's simply enjoyable to submit, when one has to be in control of one's life all the time. When I have to spend all day every day fulfilling responsibilities and obligations and taking care of business, it's nice to just let go and give someone else complete and utter control. (Bisexual woman, aged 18; Meston and Buss, 2009, p. 207)

> Sometimes being submissive turns me on. Not always...Being submissive sometimes includes having my wrists tied down with rope or having my partner hold my arms down. (Heterosexual woman, aged 33; Meston and Buss, 2009, p. 208)

Exhibitionism

A classical account

Apart from masochism, Rousseau also described exhibitionism. The following events happened when he was about 16 years of age, the result, he suggests, of his chronic shyness, insecurity and inability to establish conventional relationships with the opposite sex. This would seem to be a textbook example of courtship disorder, possibly combined with youthful naïve optimism (p. 90):

> My disturbance of mind became so strong that, being unable to satisfy my desires, I excited them by the most extravagant behaviour. I haunted dark alleys and lonely spots where I could expose myself to women from afar off in the condition in which I should have liked to be in their company...The absurd pleasure I got from displaying myself before

their eyes is quite indescribable. There was only one step for me still to make to achieve the experience I desired, and I have no doubt that some bold girl would have afforded me the amusement, as she passed, if I had possessed the courage to wait.

Later insights

In the clinical experience of Money (1986), exhibitionism can develop very early (p. 20): 'a young boy may over-respond to the excitement and the possible punishment generated by his display of his erect penis to girl playmates so that he becomes addicted to repeating the procedure'. This appears to represent another example of the familiar link between a stimulus situation and arousal generated in that situation.

The experience that appears to be the trigger to exhibitionism need not be sexually related at the time but it assumes this aspect later as a result of, it would seem, fantasy and conditioning. Two men who met this description were treated in Glasgow (McGuire et al., 1965). Each had been urinating at a location described as semi-public when they were disturbed by a woman passing. They had felt embarrassed and had quickly moved on but subsequently masturbated to the image in memory. From this, they were led to exposure in public. Note that, although the initial encounter was not erotically charged, nonetheless it was emotionally potent. This emotional charge could have had the effect of increasing the chances of subsequent aberrant behaviour appearing by means of (a) consolidating the memory of the incident and (b) emotion being transferred from fear/embarrassment to sexual arousal.

Kinsey et al., (1953) suggested that what motivates exhibitionism is the surprise or embarrassment of the accosted female combined with the high of a forbidden pursuit. Another dimension is also possible: a link with aggressive feelings. Based upon the strong male reaction to visual sexual stimuli, Britton (1998) suggests (p. 86):

Some flashers mistakenly assume that if a woman sees an erect naked penis it has a similar effect on her and she'll become so filled with lust, she'll have sex with them . . . There is also sometimes an aggressive or revenge element – something has happened in their own earlier life, they've been rejected or ridiculed by a woman and they want to shock and frighten and dominate.

Consider the case of a 32-year-old patient (J), a factory worker (Rosen and Fracher, 1983). As a child, J and the other children in the family were beaten by the father, said to be 'an abusive drunken tyrant' (p. 151). In adolescence, J would retire for long periods into the shower where he would obtain relief from tension and anxiety by masturbation. This was accompanied by a rich world of fantasy in which he was strongly attractive to the opposite sex. At age 17, J experienced a very bad encounter with his father, which left him feeling anger. So, J exposed himself to a group of girls, supposing that they would find the sight irresistible. J obtained some relief from this and repeated the behaviour frequently in the future. J was a loner during his twenties, finding solace and escape from negative emotions only in masturbation accompanied by deviant fantasy or exhibitionism. The latter gave him a feeling of improved self-esteem. J also developed the habit of voyeurism, using this to fuel his fantasy that the women he spied upon found him desirable.

A similar case concerned L.R., who was a chaplain in the US Air Force, aged 37. Stressed by marital and professional conflicts, L.R. found himself entertaining exhibitionist fantasies at an increasing frequency and intensity. To resist them was becoming more difficult and he cruised through the streets on the look-out for potential female targets. He derived some transient relief from anxiety by exhibitionism.

The exhibitionist can now achieve an outlet in cyberspace by sending anonymous images of himself to unsuspecting recipients, albeit a behaviour somewhat lacking in desired feedback.

Exhibitionism appears to be almost exclusively a male pursuit (Kinsey et al., 1953).

Paedophilia and child molestation

Basics

The paedophile has an attraction ('sexual preference') directed towards children, associated with fantasy (Barbaree, 1990), which triggers a relatively high level of sexual arousal. The use of fantasy is exemplified by an offender's account (Gee et al., 2003, p. 52):

> whenever you are depressed, you would use images of naked kids to pull you out of it.
>
> . . .
>
> inside you had nothing to think about, the boredom, that probably had something to do with it.

At other times a positive mood could be enhanced by fantasy, as in:

> fantasy makes things even more exciting.

Paedophiles exhibit not only an attraction to children but often also a conflict over sex with adults, taking the form of either indifference or disgust (Williams and Finkelhor, 1990). There is a tendency for paedophiles to find children less threatening and more accepting than adults and it is easier to control them (Groth, 1983), suggesting a developmental trajectory directed by interactions with social fear. Some paedophiles are not able to bring themselves to start a conversation with an adult (Pithers et al., 1983). Bancroft (2009) speculates that most boys' first sexual attraction is to girls of a similar age and then the attraction is adjusted with years. Paedophiles appear to be lacking this developmental adjustment. Usually paedophiles do not marry (Hickey, 2010).

There is a distinction between paedophiles and what are termed 'non-paedophiliac child molesters' (Mendez and Shapira, 2011). The latter might well be married and have conventional adult relationships but opportunistically have relationships with under-age children, or they might be adolescents who have difficulty with establishing relationships with peers.

Sometimes a person can inhibit paedophilic tendencies until influenced by stress, alcohol or drugs (Abel and Osborn, 1995), suggesting the lifting of top-down inhibition. Paedophiles commonly hold 'neutralizing definitions', for example 'children need sex for healthy growth and desire sex with adults'. The world can be selectively interpreted in such terms (Ward and Beech, 2006), for example a gesture of friendship might be construed as a sexual advance. If the paedophile was also the victim of sexual abuse, this lends itself to the kind of cognition 'He did it and got away with it, so I can do the same' (Wolf, 1988). It suggests a desire to replicate a paedophilic encounter.

Internet sites provide a forum where deviant fantasies can be socially reinforced by approval from others and increase the chances that fantasy will turn into reality. Female paedophiles exist, which might surprise some people (Ramsland and McGrain, 2010) and certain Internet sites serve them (Lambert and O'Halloran, 2008). One message on a female site pointed to satiety and escalation (p. 290):

> I left the child porn behind. I was bored with it and preferred the erotic stories, they took up less space on my floppy discs. But I eventually got bored with that as well. I wanted real experience with a child.

Psychopaths and sex with children

Some of those having sex with children meet the criteria of being termed psychopaths (Hare, 1993). They are lacking moral restraints and thereby unmoved by the harm that they do. One psychopath guilty of abusing his girlfriend's 8-year-old daughter reported (Hare, 1993, p. 110) 'I just take what's available.'

Brain processes

In some cases, men with a conventional sexual history develop a sexual attraction to children following brain damage, from disease or injury (Mendez and Shapira, 2011). This can be part of a general loss of discrimination shown by an increase in a range of different aspects of desire, such as demanding frequent sex from a partner and inappropriate advances to women in public. Damage to the prefrontal region is commonly implicated. Often such patients can articulate the inappropriateness of their actions but cannot inhibit them, a feature shared with others exhibiting a similar imbalance of controls, whether or not sexual desire is changed.

Therapy

There is at least one report of successful treatment with the dopamine-blocking drug haloperidol, pointing to a reduction in the strength of the incentive-based approach system. Some interventions for paedophiles try to exploit deviant fantasy to a therapeutic end (Salter, 1988). Offenders can be asked to masturbate to satiation and beyond while holding the fantasy in mind, in the hope that it will lose its potency ('habituation'). Therapists can then propose acceptable substitute fantasies (adult and consenting content) as material for accompanying masturbation. Another technique is to try to block a fantasy sequence at an early stage by imposing in the sequence a memory of a real aversive event from the individual's life, such as a drowning incident or an attack of asthma.

Attempts can be made to block paedophilic approach sequences at an early stage (Pithers et al., 1983). The technique taps into the sequence of incentive approach when the person is still relatively 'cool' and less likely to give in to temptation (Chapter 12). For example, a paedophile might carry a 'stop card' and have instructions to read it at the first feeling of attraction to a child. The card might say something indicating that just a friendly chat will lead to making a sexual advance (the attraction might first have been triggered at an unconscious and automatic level). It appears that this technique brings inhibition into the 'here and now' and away from the abstract and remote. By the same logic, the paedophile might need to plan routes ahead and make a conscious effort to avoid locations that are likely to trigger an ascending phase of desire, such as a school playground (Pithers et al., 1983). The individual might be advised to avoid alcohol prior to approaching any high-risk situations.

Multiple factors underlying motivation

That motivation can be very complex is exemplified by Perry, a 16-year-old boy (Rich, 2006). At age 14, Perry started to sexually abuse his stepsister Marcy, who was aged 4. He had tried unsuccessfully to stop, describing the behaviour as 'addictive and obsessive'. He suggested that the behaviour was a means of getting back at his father and step-mother, as well as at Marcy, for his perceived failings. Rich argues (p. 154):

> Perry's sexually abusive relationship with his young step-sister possibly met a complex combination of personal needs. It may be seen as a troubled effort to become connected to someone, combined with being seen, commanding respect, and being in charge (if only in the form of

fear and domination – much like his father), while also meeting Perry's needs to feel that he was experiencing what he imagined other young men of his age were experiencing – sex!

Rich suggests also that sources of reward derived from such behaviour include satisfying curiosity and relief of stress. Taking such a multidimensional approach to understanding Perry's motivation could help to rule out other explanations and suggest more hopeful therapeutic interventions. On Perry's behaviour, he writes (p. 159):

> rather than being the product of deviant sexual arousal – wanting to hurt another individual, wildly out-of-control sexual drive . . . is more directly related to attachment difficulties and his view of himself, others, relationships and their availability to him, and his capacity to have a satisfactory impact on the world.

Thus attachment issues rather than atypical sexual choice could form the most productive target of therapy.

Sadism

Sexual sadism would seem to reflect a development of the sadistic individual in which sexual desire and aggression have fused (Doidge, 2007). There are a number of ingredients of the motivation and behaviour of sadism and it is important to distinguish between what might be called 'benign sadists' and 'toxic sadists'. Concerning the former category, a survey carried out in Great Britain led Gosselin and Wilson (1980) to comment (p. 50): 'it is our impression, based on our interviews and the research of others, that most sexual sadists have no wish to hurt their partner in their sex games any more than is enjoyed or at least accepted by the partner'. An important aspect of the motivation of the more toxic type of sadists is gaining total mastery and control over the destiny of the victim (Gibb, 2011; Schlesinger, 2001). Use of bondage is one vehicle to achieve this. Another factor in the motivational mix is observing the consequences of the actions ('feedback') in the form of fear and pain of the victim.

Indicating the interactive nature of desire in such cases, Krafft-Ebing (1978, p. 54) wrote:

That lust and cruelty often occur together is a fact that has long been recognized and is frequently observed... When the association of lust and cruelty is present, not only does the lustful emotion awaken the impulse to cruelty, but vice versa; cruel ideas and acts of cruelty cause sexual excitement.

Krafft-Ebing reported very few cases of sadism in women. One such, which involved a fetishist component, was as follows (p. 85):

A married man presented himself with numerous scars of cuts on his arms. He told of their origin as follows: When he wished to approach his wife, who was younger and somewhat 'nervous', he first had to make a cut in his arm. Then she would suck the wound and during the act become violently excited sexually.

C. Wilson (1988, p. 113) attributes habituation and escalation to the Marquis de Sade:

when the fairy gold dissolved in his fingers, he decided that the problem was that his goal was not 'forbidden' enough, and looked around for something slightly more wicked.

Wilson continued (p. 246):

he had to conjure up more and more nauseating forms of violation.

A woman fortunate enough to survive the sadistic sexual assaults inflicted by the Gloucester couple, Fred and Rosemary West suggests that they derived pleasure from the signs of fear and pain on the faces of their victims (Sounes, 1995). Of course, fear did not exist in a vacuum. It was the result of violent acts, which were means of exerting control over the social environment.

Necrophilia

The usual interpretation of 'necrophilia' is in terms of desiring sexual 'relations' with dead bodies. However, it literally means a morbid attraction to death, in which case Harold Shipman might be described in such terms (Whittle and Ritchie, 2004).

Apparently, there exist brothels in Seattle (Rule, 2004) and Paris (Krafft-Ebing, 1978, p. 66; Masters, 1993) and doubtless elsewhere catering for this taste, where the sex worker puts on make-up and dresses as in death, while lying in a coffin and with solemn music playing for the benefit of her client. The wives of some married men are said to perform a similar role, though this has never formed a popular topic of conversation in my social circle.

One can speculate that this behaviour might sometimes, if not always, be associated with a fear of contact with real living and reciprocating humans (Schlesinger, 2007). This could include a fear of criticism over inadequacies of performance. Such fear might skew the trajectory of sexual development towards forming a desire for a passive incentive. Thus, Krafft-Ebing (p. 66) speculated:

> it is probable that the lifeless condition itself forms the stimulus for the perverse individual. It is possible that the corpse – a human form absolutely without will – satisfies an abnormal desire, in that the object of desire is seen to be capable of absolute subjugation, without possibility of resistance.

Some cases of sexual homicide (described in Chapter 21) are associated with the killer having sex with the victim only after death (Hickey, 2010). Hickey writes (p. 156): 'In the perception of the offender, a corpse permits him to be intimate without fear of rejection.'

In summary

- The various forms of desire described here illustrate how explanations can be offered in terms of some of the same processes as those that underlie conventional desires, such as the central role of arousal and the use of fantasy.
- The formation of associations between arousal and a sexual stimulus is evident throughout as are the strengthening ('reinforcing') effects of consequences, for example orgasm through masturbation.
- Denial of access to conventional targets of desire could also play an important role in the development of desires at the fringes.

TWENTY

THE TOXIC FUSION: VIOLENCE AND SEXUAL DESIRE

But she hath lost a dearer thing than life,
And he had won what he would lose again;
This forced league doth force a further strife;
This momentary joy breeds months of pain;
This hot desire converts to cold disdain.

(Shakespeare, *The Rape of Lucrece*, lines 687–91)

Rapists come in different varieties with different underlying motivational dynamics (Hickey, 2010).[1] Therefore, it is possible to present here a description in only very broad brushstrokes, highlighting certain features that might usually be present. Some rapes are planned well in advance and target a stranger, whereas others can be the sudden impulsive reaction to thwarting of the male's goals towards a familiar woman, as in date rape. Some appear to be second best to consensual sex, where force is only instrumental to achieve the goal. For others, the element of coercion is an integral part of the desire. So, it appears that rape can serve goals in addition to sexual fulfilment (Marshall and Barbaree, 1990) and interactions of sexual desire with other motivations are evident. A desire for power and dominance can contribute to the motivation (Calhoun and Wilson, 2000). Some rapists use violence only to gain access to a woman, whereas for others the violence continues beyond this point suggesting fusion of sexual and aggressive motivations (Zillmann, 1984). Sadly, rape is evident across cultures, including even the sexually permissive land of Polynesian Mangaia (Marshall, 1971). Novelty, excitement and transgression doubtless often play a role. As the ex-wife of the British rapist known as the 'monster of the M5' expressed it (quoted by Apter, 2007,

p. 152): 'We always had a perfectly healthy sex life – but he always seemed to need that little bit of extra excitement, like a racing driver.'

What goes on in the brain of a rapist?

Hare (1993) estimates that one half of all repeat/serial rapists meet the criteria for being psychopaths. The non-psychopathic rapists would feel some guilt and remorse.

Ramsland and McGrain (2010) suggest that there are a number of personality characteristics of rapists as a group:

- Misogynist beliefs: women are subservient to the interests of men.
- An aggressive style: a willingness to employ force to gain ends.
- Personality style: little personal responsibility.
- Sexual style: dissatisfaction with their sexual lot in life and a failure to achieve sexual satisfaction.

What follows applies mainly to those who plan rapes and are turned on by transgression. Rapists often feel inferior and rape boosts their image of manliness. Where anger is a precipitating trigger, the rape appears to have the consequence of lowering this, an additional source of reinforcement (Rosen and Fracher, 1983). Also, sensation-seeking is very frequently offered by rapists themselves as an explanation (Apter, 2007; Gove, 1994), sometimes described as 'being on a high'. Transgression and risk, probably associated with fear, would add to arousal level and would surely add to the attraction of rape for some (Zillmann, 1984, 1986).

Zillmann (1986) argues (p. 195): 'Sexual access has become a matter of convenience in contemporary western societies, and sexual coercion offers itself as a high-excitement, mania promising solution to the tedium of habitual recreational sex.' Rapists typically experience fantasies and urges for rape prior to committing the offense (Pithers et al., 1983). They commonly try to resist but are overwhelmed by the strength of the urges. Following the rape, fantasy can only go so far in perpetuating the high and, when it subsides, thoughts presumably turn to the next victim. Typically, in the fantasy world of the rapist, the act itself is easier to entertain, for example, based upon memories of previous rapes, than are its longer-term negative consequences. Guilt sometimes follows the rape but the urges then build up in strength again (Abel and Rouleau, 1990). Those fearing that they will submit to the urges might try speaking silently to themselves a preformed statement of the kind 'a moment's pleasure is not worth years in jail'. They could carry an instruction card at all times showing such an expression in words.

Finding deficiencies of attachment amongst rapists, Smallbone and Dadds (1998) write:

> If they indeed seek out adult intimate relationships, they may adopt an uncaring, unsympathetic approach to their partners. Their sexual behaviour may become disconnected from normal (i.e. secure) attachment-related perceptions, such as commitment and mutuality, and may be readily activated or at least may fail to be inhibited in the context of abuse and violence.

Rapists are likely to be high on a scale of narcissism, since several characteristics of this personality type are conducive to coercive sex (Bushman et al., 2003):

1 low empathy when this conflicts with the individual's goals, as in feeling bad about the victim's suffering;
2 high tendency to show reactive aggression when thwarted;
3 elevated sense of entitlement;
4 high need for admiration by others, which would be associated with a strong threat to the ego on rejection but also with the opportunity to brag about the rape to any peers of similar inclination.

Characteristic (2) would be expected to be applicable in situations of date rape as well as stranger rape. In fact, it might be particularly a factor where there has been some consensual erotic contact already and the woman decides to 'put the brakes on' (Bushman et al., 2003). The physiological reaction in sexual arousal has considerable overlap with that of anger (Chapter 15), and hence thwarting of sexual advances could easily transform itself into full-blown anger (Kinsey et al., 1953). Factors (2) and (3) are linked, with narcissists coming out relatively highly in both. A high sense of entitlement is likely to lead to a strong negative emotion on being thwarted.

Rapists commonly acquire various 'rape myths' ('neutralizing definitions') concerning women. Men high on narcissism find such myths more attractive than do non-narcissists (Bushman et al., 2003). Scully and

Marolla (1984) note that rapists learn attitudes of the kind 'women mean "yes" when they say "no"'. Their schemas would often seem to be anger-associated and thereby possibly contributing to rape, such as that women are deceitful and cannot be trusted (Ward and Beech, 2006). Such neutralizing definitions would act counter to any remnants of empathy. Where blame can be placed upon someone else for any perceived unfair situation in which an individual finds himself and corrective action seems possible, anger is a likely emotion (Harmon-Jones et al., 2008). Pornographic representations that show women finally coming to enjoy the rape could be particularly toxic in undermining the little empathy that the potential rapist might feel (Zillmann, 1984). Males' negative attitudes towards rape are lowered by this depiction (Fisher, 1986). Hence, a woman's behaviour of, say, avoidance is likely to trigger such ideas and be interpreted in terms that facilitate assault.

In the case of date rape, there is often a failure to pick up cues given out by a woman. Friendliness is interpreted as a come-on sign and negative signals, such as resistance, are seen as being positive invitations (Calhoun and Wilson, 2000). Alcohol and the man's own sexual arousal often have a role in such misinterpretation.

An aspect of rape that might give insight into it is the observation that this act is sometimes reported as being associated with a 'trance-like state of consciousness' (Rosen and Fracher, 1983, p. 147).

A case study: the tragic role that chance can play

A case illustrates how deviant sexual desire can arise from an apparently chance event (Laws and Marshall, 1990). A boy had a conventional upbringing until he reached age 13 years, when he viewed a film that depicted rape. The adult female victim was highly attractive and the boy attained a full erection while watching the film. It was unclear to a naïve viewer whether the woman was truly resisting or, as is often falsely portrayed (Bart and Jozsa, 1980), enjoying the experience. Subsequently, the boy fantasized about the scene and portrayed himself in the role of the all-powerful rapist, something which produced a high level of sexual arousal. Masturbation to the imagery reinforced this.

When the boy started dating girls, he expected to obtain sexual access as readily as that portrayed in the film but was repeatedly rejected. He was left with his fantasies about the rape scene and adult women intact, which led him to rape an adult woman. Watching violent pornography provided role models for rape. As a result, together with his failure to obtain conventional sexual contact, his own self-image came to be that of 'rapist'.

His subsequent behaviour illustrates the narrow and deviant preference acquired as a boy and also some escalation of intensity of stimulation necessary to arouse him: contact with sex workers needed to be accompanied by ever more violent fantasy. In a similar case, a boy had his first exposure to violent pornography at around 6 years of age (Donnerstein and Malamuth, 1997). He later became an addict to such pornography with an escalation in his viewing times. He subsequently became a rapist and murderer.

Lifting of inhibition

Some rapists appear to be characterized not so much by the attraction of violent sex as such as by a failure of inhibition (Calhoun and Wilson, 2000). In many (but not all) cases, drugs or alcohol have been taken prior to rape. One rapist reported that this (Scully and Marolla, 1984, p. 538):

> brought out what was already there but in such intensity it was uncontrollable. Feelings of being dominant, powerful, using someone for my own gratification, all rose to the surface.

It seems that it is not just the chemical content of the drink but the knowledge that it is alcohol and the expectation of its effect that plays a role in disinhibiting sexually aggressive behaviour (Russell, 1980). This observation points to a peculiarly human factor.

Anger and stress

Immediately preceding anger is implicated in a number of rapes (Lisak and Roth, 1988). Rapists commonly report a traumatic precipitating event, such as anger at a wife or girlfriend (Rosen and Fracher, 1983; Scully and Marolla, 1984). Wolf (1988) remarked (p. 135): 'sexual offenders seem to use sexuality in a self-medicating manner, much in the style of an alcoholic abuser's use of that drug'.

A number of theorists speculate that hostility in such cases is triggered by 'blocked goals' (Malamuth, 1996) and takes the character of
frustration.

The notion of sexual drive, brought under suspicion in earlier chapters,
could lead to a wrong conclusion concerning rapists, namely that they
have inordinately high drives, associated with extreme sexual deprivation (ideas disputed by Quinsey and Marshall, 1983; Malamuth, 1996).
Rather, rapists claim to have a lower frequency of desired sexual outlets
than a control group, though this is disputable (Ellis, 1989). Either way,
there is little reason to think that their behaviour arises from some general 'drive' factor getting out of alignment. Rather, explanation is best
provided in terms of external stimuli and fantasies about them, deficient
attachment and empathy, as well as interactions between sexual desire
and anger/aggression.

Conscience, social controls and social norms

When it is present, inhibition normally arises from conscience, social
controls, fear of injury or capture, and social norms, society's disapproval
(Russell, 1980). In some subcultures, social norms will be such as to
approve of rape, for example in certain Hell's Angels groups. One can
reasonably speculate that the high level of arousal associated with being in
a war can spill over into sexual desire and contribute to a tendency to rape
(Apter, 2007; Zillmann, 1984). This would presumably be reinforced by
the social facilitation of the presence of comrades, a consideration of the
'enemy' as being undeserving of empathy and a low chance of subsequent
capture and punishment. By portraying women as coming to enjoy rape
and the rapist finding successful long-term satisfaction with no capture,
violent pornography could undermine any potential inhibitors (Russell,
1980).

Theories of rape

The best-known theories of why men rape should not all be seen as
necessarily mutually exclusive, since they address different aspects of the
phenomenon. After presenting and commenting on these theories, an
integrative framework will be advanced that can organize our understanding.

The feminist theory

The feminist theory of rape views it as the inevitable outcome of male domination of society and acquisition of resources, whereby women are economically powerless and subservient to men, often regarded as their property (Brownmiller, 1975). Feminist theorists see rape as more motivated by a desire for domination rather than for sexual contact. In the interactive model proposed here it is impossible to allocate such relative weights. In so far as reports by certain rapists are to be believed, their desire is more for a combination of sexual contact and arousal rather than domination (Ellis, 1989). Date rape often only follows a failure of other devious but not explicitly violent attempts to obtain sexual access, such as getting the woman intoxicated.

Social learning theory

Social learning theory suggests that rape arises from exposure to 'role models' where sexual access is gained by coercion, either in reality or in pornography. These tend to excite the desire for this behaviour and cause habituation to any restraints on it (Ellis, 1989). Rape myths of the kind that women secretly want rape can be subsumed under this category. Pornography tends to set a standard of female readiness and unrestrained availability which might, when reality is later found not to match the standard, tend to trigger the desire for rape.

Consider, as a possible developmental influence, the child's observation of aggression within the family, as well as the direct experience of physical and or sexual abuse. This can lead to increased acceptance of violence and its adoption as a coping strategy, either in reality or in the imagination, or both. Marshall and Barbaree suggest (1990, p. 261): 'Poor socialization, particularly a violent parenting style, will both facilitate the use of aggression as well as cut the youth off from access to more appropriate sociosexual interactions.'

Evolutionary theory

One evolutionary theory of rape suggests that the benefits that the human male gained by pursuing a coercive mating strategy outweighed the costs

(Ellis, 1989; Thornhill and Palmer, 2000). Hence, evolution favoured males who followed such a strategy, because they have been more successful reproductively. Proponents of this theory note that female rape victims are most commonly in the ages of maximum fertility, that is between 13 and 35 (reviewed by Ellis, 1989). Furthermore, some kind of male subjugation and violence in the service of obtaining sexual access, for example biting, is very common across a wide range of non-human species, including those most closely related to humans (Zillmann, 1984). Of course, any extrapolation from non-human species is fraught with hazards.

In principle, there could be genes underlying rape that have been selected in evolution because of their contribution to reproductive success. Alternatively, and more likely, there could be a genetic contribution to differences in (a) aggression, (b) strength of sexual motivation and (c) inhibitory processes. Genetically based differences in any of these three could alter the probability of rape.

Of course, there is a large sex difference in rape. As Buss (2003, p. 220) states:

> The fact that there has never in history been a single case of women forming a war party to raid neighbouring villages and capture husbands tells us something important about the nature of sex differences – that men's mating strategies are often more brutal and aggressive than women's.

Comparison

Clearly, there is considerable overlap between the feminist and social learning theories (Ellis, 1989). Both suggest that features of society and culture promote this behaviour. The feminist theory has little to say about why many, if not most, males don't rape or wish to do so, whereas the social learning theory sees this in terms of different degrees of exposure to toxic role models. The feminist and evolutionary theories are usually seen as incompatible. Presumably, according to feminist theory, if a society were to be reformed root and branch to eliminate power differentials, rape would naturally be extinguished. As a point of compromise, it is possible to imagine that rape might have been advantageous in evolutionary history *and* that it is maintained by power differentials and contemporary culture.

Towards some resolution: formation of the brain of a rapist

False dichotomies of (a) *either* biology *or* culture and (b) *either* aggression/dominance *or* sexual desire have only confused this subject. The aggression/dominance part of the second dichotomy usually maps onto the culture part of the first. Once we escape from such false logic, we might be able to make some sense of what is going on. Chapter 15 described the evidence that, if power motivation is triggered even unconsciously, a woman can actually seem more attractive to a man who values dominance.

Evidence reviewed earlier points to sharing between different systems associated with arousal. By a chance association of sexual desire/arousal and experiencing aggressive feelings, a blending of aggression and sexuality could be formed (Maniglio, 2010; Marshall and Barbaree, 1990). Concerning abnormal development that takes a violent form, Marshall and Barbaree (p. 257) suggest: 'the task for human males is to acquire inhibitory controls over a biologically endowed propensity for self-interest associated with a tendency to fuse sex and aggression'. Therefore, attention is drawn to the role of those inhibitory processes that appear underactive.

In sexually linked offenders, disturbances in the dynamics of social interactions with their parents not uncommonly include harsh and inconsistent punishment and being witness to domestic violence (Rich, 2006). Central to theorizing about such sexual deviation, is the notion of *insecure attachment*, arising from a caregiver who was either not available for mutually rewarding interactions (e.g. smiling, comfort-giving) or who actively rejected the child's advances towards the caregiver. Such early dynamics are then reflected in sexual behaviour when the child becomes an adult, if not earlier. A child with such a history is thought to lack social confidence in later dealings with others and to be unable to form social expectations of a positive kind but rather to rely upon coercion to gain social rewards. In a statement concerning general features of development but which obviously relates to later sexual behaviour, Malamuth writes (1996, p. 281): 'Abusive home environments may also interfere with the mastery of critical developmental skills such as managing frustration, delaying gratification, negotiating disagreements, and forming a prosocial identity.' Appropriate parenting teaches empathy with others (Fonagy, 2003) even where such empathy might conflict with one's own goals and facilitates the development of attachment bonds. By contrast, inappropriate parenting can teach that violence is a viable means to achieve goals, which can lead to alienation as an adult, thereby further triggering hostility and aggression.

Evidence (Chapter 15) points to anger being a trigger to the approach system and hence it could add its effect to that of sexual desire. As an approach motivation, anger is associated with increased relative neural activity of the front part of the brain's left hemisphere (Carver and Harmon-Jones, 2009). Such increased activity is particularly evident when there is the *combination* of anger and the perception that action is possible to change the situation. It seems quite possible that the rape victim often serves the dual role of sexual pleasure and anger resolution. Power motivation underlies a number of rapists, who show 'striving to exert control over what threatens them' (Lisak and Roth, 1988, p. 795). It would appear that sometimes apparently consensual low-level sexual behaviour turns even to murder as the man finds his progression resisted and anger at frustration escalates (Britton, 1998)[2].

Clearly, power conflict as advanced by feminist theory and social learning can contribute to a tendency to rape. A brain that has strongly fused aggression and sex could prove receptive to toxic messages. The suggestion of a contribution from reactive aggression that is triggered by thwarting is entirely compatible with such ideas. Genetic contributions to high aggression could all act in the same direction.

Rape is found even in societies that are sexually permissive and there is abundant consensual sexual contact, which might suggest that it is not an act necessarily performed out of deprivation (Zillmann, 1984, 1986). However, even in a permissive society some will feel left out.

One possible scenario for the development of the brain of a rapist is the *accidental* pairing of aggressive feelings with sexual arousal (Zillmann, 1984). Thus, a man might be sexually aroused but rejected by a woman, which leads him to fantasize about forceful sex, maybe accompanied by masturbation. The combination of aggression and sexual arousal then leads to the *deliberate* strategy of seeking sex through violence.

The next chapter illustrates these same points but in an even more extreme form.

In summary

- Coercive sex needs to be understood, not only in terms of what is present, but what is deficient or absent: a role of empathy derived from early social interactions.
- The hierarchical nature of the control of desire is evident, with such factors as stress and alcohol switching weight away from those higher layers of control that are involved in inhibition in the interests of long-term consequences.
- Sexual desire can sometimes only be understood in terms of its interactions with the systems controlling anger and aggression.
- The ubiquitous role of stress as a contributing factor and stress reduction as a source of reinforcement emerge as central to understanding.

TWENTY ONE

SEXUALLY ASSOCIATED (SERIAL) MURDER

But many people are abnormal in their sexual life who in every other respect approximate to the average, and have, along with the rest, passed through the process of human cultural development, in which sexuality remains the weak spot.

(Freud, 1953, p. 149)

What exactly is it?

Sexual homicide consists of (Burgess et al., 1986, p. 252): 'one person killing another in the context of power, control, sexuality, and aggressive brutality'. A defining feature is: 'the infliction of physical or psychological suffering on another person in order to achieve sexual excitement'.

The motivational basis

Not all serial killings arise from sexual motivation, though many do (Hickey, 2010). As a broad generalization, Buss (2005, p. 219): 'serial killers murder because they seek vengeance for status denied'. Non-sexually linked serial killings are motivated by the desire for such things as attention, financial gain, political action (e.g. 'mission killings' to rid the world of undesirables) or 'pure anger' associated with retribution (Holmes and DeBurger, 1998).

So-called lust killers merge the motivations underlying sexual desire and aggression (Ressler et al., 1992) and find sexual arousal, pleasure and temporary satisfaction in their activity (Hickey, 2010). The desire for vengeance merges with sexual desire. Where sexual assault is involved, it is very difficult, if not impossible, to disentangle and attach relative weights to sexual and power/aggression/control motivations. They are interactive in promotion of the behaviour, while the reinforcing feedback obtained from behaviour would presumably sensitize desire. Such murderers report that 'total domination becomes erotic' (Holmes et al., 1998a, p. 115).

Some so-called 'killings without motivation' (Burgess et al., 1986) might involve a sexual element. Although serial killers are psychopaths, it is estimated that for every one serial killer there are 20,000 or 30,000 psychopaths who are not (Hare, 1993). They are probably engaged in domination and power struggles in industry or within their families.

Sometimes sexual homicide is the outcome of motivational escalation from near normal behaviour, similar to addiction. The individual finds conventional and consensual sexual relations inadequate in attaining arousal (Heide et al., 2009; Sounes, 1995). In other cases, rape is preliminary to homicide but this also proves inadequate as a source of arousal (Ramsland and McGrain, 2010). There is sometimes no preliminary phase of consensual sexual activity (Ressler et al., 1992). Some killers find that reality is not as good as fantasy and they kill in order to reach the 'ultimate high', a form of escalation and addiction (Carlisle, 1998; Ramsland and McGrain, 2010).

That there is a change of levels of control at the time of sexually associated aggression derives support from those committing the act. They tend to report opposing forces battling for supremacy and periodically feeling what they term being 'outside my own body' (Ramsland and McGrain, 2010) or even a condition of 'possession' (Masters, 1985). In some cases, an act of sexual homicide reflects careful long-term planning, whereas in others it is somewhat opportunistic (Ressler et al., 1992). There can also be a combination of these: the individual has a desire congruent with killing and then happens upon a suitable situation.

Associated activities

Amongst the principal interests of men who commit sex-related violence are masturbation, pornography, fetishes and voyeurism, activities that do not require any reciprocal personal involvement (Arrigo and Purcell, 2001; Ressler et al., 1992), and have a relatively low immediate risk, if any. Fetishes (e.g. female underwear and high-heeled shoes) were evident in the childhood of the sample studied by Burgess et al. Such items were incorporated into ritualized aspects of the murders that they were later to commit. In some cases, the sequence of escalation passes through fetishes, voyeurism, then rape, and finally to serial murder (Rule, 1983). Each stage brings increasing excitement, but this appears to prove insufficient after a time.

Sometimes fetishes, such as an item of clothing or a body part, play a central role in the killing, being the target of particular attention and occasionally being kept as a souvenir or 'trophy' (Holmes, 1998). Their attraction appears to owe something to classical conditioning. A number of killers take photographs of the victim, such that the crime can later be re-enacted in the imagination (Hickey, 2010; Rule, 1983). A number have even videotaped their rapes prior to killing (Gibb, 2011). Some return to the body to masturbate over it (Ramsland and McGrain, 2010).

Prior to the start of his killing, Dennis Rader of BTK (bind, torture, kill) notoriety had a history of voyeurism, stalking women and breaking into their homes to steal underwear (Wenzl et al., 2008). Subsequently, accompanying the murders, underwear was stolen to play with later and cuttings were made of pictures of women's clothes taken from newspapers. Extensive stalking took place between murders.

What does it feel like?

Prior to the first killing, the Boston Strangler described the motivation as 'building up', while it was perceived as getting out of control (Carlisle, 1998). The Californian serial killer Edmund Kemper used the expression 'an awful, raging, eating feeling that was threatening to consume me from within' (Holmes, 1998, p. 110). This appears to have at least something in common with the kind of deprivation effect described by some in connection with conventional sexual behaviour.

Sexually linked serial killers commonly use strangulation as the method of killing, as opposed to, for example, shooting. This appears to be a way of prolonging arousal and maximizing the degree of control (Gibb, 2011).

Power, anger and control

Some argue that in serial killing any sexual element is secondary to the motivation for power and control. A similar argument is made concerning rape. However, one is left to speculate why the sexual element needs to be included at all since power and domination can be achieved through many different, and it might seem, much less risky, means. Also, offenders frequently reach orgasm in the context of their assault (Myers et al., 2006). Sexual offenders almost always target victims of a gender corresponding to their own sexual attraction. Female victims tend to be of reproductive age. The self-reports of serial sexual murderers, ranging from the fifteenth-century French nobleman Gilles de Rais, indicate typically that they attained a state of heightened sexual arousal and pleasure in their activity.

Stress

In many cases, attacks occur at a time of stress, for example rejection by a girl-friend or dismissal from work (Chan and Heide, 2009; Douglas and Olshaker, 2006; Schlesinger, 2001). Stress can strengthen the dopaminergic systems underlying appetitive activities (Pitchers et al., 2010) and also appears to lower restraint on behaviour. Fantasy seems inadequate as a coping strategy and the scales are tipped in favour of acting out (Heide et al., 2009). Acting out appears to serve as a coping strategy, whereby the individual is driven (Maniglio, 2010, p. 300) 'to gain relief through action' and a sense of equilibrium ('satiety') is achieved, albeit often only temporarily (Hickey, 2010).

Development of a serial murderer

Early traumatic experience

There appear to be multiple trajectories that lead to sexually linked killing. However, it is possible to identify a few common factors. In many, if not all, cases, there was an early traumatic experience that can be captured by such terms as 'pain', 'shame' or 'humiliation', involving loss of self-worth and a feeling of being dealt a bad hand (Hale, 1998; Hickey, 2010; Leake, 2007; Sullivan and Maiken, 1983). There can be a combination of negative feelings, with the term *humiliation* capturing a universal feature. One can speculate that, rather than diminishing over time, this painful emotion becomes 'self-reinforced'. Tragically, this early trauma occurs at an age when the neurons of the brain are rapidly forming new connections. Subsequently, the negative emotion appears to form associations with a range of other triggers beyond the initial ones but which have similarities to the original trigger. Later frustrations excite the sensitized pathways. Years later, the individual feels compelled to offer a violent response to the long-lasting effects of this challenge to self-worth.

Various early initial triggers can instigate these emotions, which some famous cases exemplify. Meloy (2000) suggests that many sexual homicides are generalizations from rage directed at the offender's mother (O'Brien, 1985). In the case of Russell Williams, the striking facial similarity between one of his victims and his mother has been noted (Gibb, 2011). Jerry Brudos detested his mother because of her rejection of him (Hale, 1998). The Austrian serial killer Jack Unterweger gave an account of his early life in his autobiographical novel entitled *Purgatory*. Leake (2007) writes (p. 38):

> A recurring theme in the novel is Jack's quest for his mother. He yearns for her to come and take him away from his unhappy world, but she never does. His grandfather tells him that she is a 'tramp with no time for you'.

In a confession on why he killed his first victim, Unterweger stated (Leake, 2007, p. 48):

> Well, you know from *Purgatory* that my mother abandoned me with her alcoholic father when I was a baby. For so long I was full of rage against her, and I think it affected all my thinking and feeling . . . Something about the way she looked and talked reminded me of my mother.

A trigger is sometimes actual or perceived sexual promiscuity by the mother, exemplified by Angelo Buono, one of the so-called Hillside Stranglers (Schlesinger, 2001). Sexual killers sometimes acquire a straight-laced and double-standard morality.

In a few cases, it seems that early discovery of a family secret having a sexual connotation establishes a pathological trajectory culminating in anger towards women. An example is Ted Bundy's discovery of his illegitimacy, combined with an all-too-familiar pattern of an early absence of the mother, a dysfunctional family, absence of a male role model and possible early exposure to pornography (Rule, 2006). Paul Bernardo learned at the age of 10 that his father was a child molester (Pron, 1995). He was later to discover that the man he took to be his father was not his real father and Paul was called by his mother the 'bastard child from hell'.

Not infrequently, future killers were ridiculed in school for such things as social ineptitude, a stammer, ethnic difference or a bad complexion and made to feel inferior (Douglas and Olshaker, 2006; Pron, 1995; Rule, 2006; Sounes, 1995; Gibb, 2011). Some are described as 'misfits'. Many were raised in households characterized as abusive and either were themselves victims of physical, emotional or sexual abuse or all of these, or at least were witness to it (Hickey, 2010; Meloy, 2000; Ramsland and McGrain, 2010; Sullivan and Maiken, 1983). Harsh and inconsistent physical punishment was an early experience of most serial killers (Anderson, 1994). All such experiences were likely to be highly arousing. In such cases, subsequent sexual assaults appear to act as proxies for ('re-runs of') the murderer's own earlier suffering of abuse. Where such abuse did occur, it is associated with the development of so-called insecure attachment between parent and child (Chan et al., 2010; Ressler et al., 1992). However, of course, only a small percentage of victims of abuse become killers, so clearly this factor must lock into interaction with others to produce the lethal combination (Maniglio, 2010).

Rejection by parents is common amongst these men (Hickey, 2010). In the family backgrounds of many sexual murderers there are family breakdowns, criminal, psychiatric, drug or sexual problems such that parents were 'absorbed in their own problems' (Burgess et al., 1986, p. 254; Pron, 1995; Ressler et al., 1992; Sounes, 1995; Sullivan and Maiken, 1983). The children suffered from such things as shame, isolation and lack of positive social interactions (Berry-Dee, 2007). Development of interpersonal skills was therefore difficult. Moves of the family home and time away from the home, for example in foster homes, tended to be frequent while the killer-to-be was growing up. While still in their youth, most serial killers experienced a break with their parents and had few if any close links with peers.

However, in some cases, though there was a bad marital situation and a painful divorce (Gibb, 2011), the family circumstances could hardly be described as wholly exceptional or massively abusive. One can speculate

that despite only objectively mild triggers, anger subsequently got amplified by a process of mental rumination, accompanied by such sensitizers as
school bullying. Laboratory studies on normal controls show that repeated
rumination involving a transgression can subsequently lead to displaced
aggression in response to only minor transgressions (Bushman et al., 2003;
Fabiansson et al., 2012).

For some, abandonment by a girlfriend has a particularly devastating
effect that seems to add to earlier triggers to negative emotion, exemplified
by Ted Bundy and Russell Williams (Gibb, 2011).

Acquisition of aggression and control

But why specifically is *aggression* triggered? If, in early development, an
aversive state like shame was paired with sexual arousal, why, when
adult, do people not simply become shamed when sexually aroused? This
might happen in some cases, but presumably they fail to make the news
headlines. There is evidence that in various species aversive events can
trigger a variety of actions, such as attack, eating or even sexual behaviour.
What is triggered will doubtless depend upon various factors such as the
availability of a helpless victim to attack. Fear or shame might trigger
anger and aggression in the world of fantasy and subsequently in reality.

Both anger/aggression and sexual motivation are *appetitive* motivations involving forward engagement with the world (Carver et al., 2009).
Turning negative emotion into attack is much more likely in males than
females and indeed, with exceedingly rare exceptions, sexual murderers
are male (though see the section on women's involvement below). Attack
is a coping strategy. There is some consensus that extreme aggression as
shown by serial killers arises from early experience and is perceived to
bring some relief from pervasive lack of self-worth and negative emotions
of conflict that arise from early traumatic experience (Hickey, 2010). The
action brings a sense of ultimate control over an innocent victim.

An animal model of control (Cabib and Puglisi-Allegra, 2012) appears
to be relevant. When in an aversive situation, the acquisition of control
that eliminates or reduces the aversion (a 'coping strategy') is associated
with increased dopamine release in the nucleus accumbens. This has an
energizing effect on behaviour and gives a steer away from passivity. As
noted earlier (Chapter 8), such dopaminergic activation might strengthen

the strategy adopted, in this case the active one based upon a fusion of sexual desire and violence.

The toxic link to sexual desire

The path leading to sexual homicide involves (Maniglio, 2010, p. 299): '[the] combination between early traumatic experiences, deviant fantasy, and social and/or sexual dysfunction.' The frequent, if not universal, feature underlying the early motivational development of sexual serial killers appears to be the *pairing* of (a) negative and/or violent emotions, typically embarrassment, anger or aggression, and (b) emerging sexual arousal (Meloy, personal communication). Sometimes the role of emerging sexual development is only implicit in the association with negative emotion, whereas in other cases, there is an explicit external trigger to sexual arousal that occurs near in time to something traumatic.

Dennis Rader reported that he was aroused by the sight of chickens being slaughtered. He was beaten by his mother when she discovered that he had masturbated, but he derived sexual arousal from this 'punishment' (Wenzl et al., 2008, p. 243). The Chicago serial killer John Wayne Gacy collected items of his mother's underwear. When this was discovered, he was made to wear such an item and was then beaten by his father. As a child of 10, he was beaten for sexual advances to a girl. Gacy appeared to merge anger at his perceived failure in life with an emerging homosexuality (Sullivan and Maiken, 1983). Another toxic combination is witnessing violence towards a woman, either in reality or in pornography, accompanied by sexual arousal. The age of 6–14 years appears to be one of particular vulnerability to such association formation. Some examples include (Meloy, 2000):

- A boy of 14 years, who committed sexual murder and who, at the age of 5, with his father, had started watching sadomasochistic pornography.
- A boy who was subject to physical abuse from his father, followed by sexual soothing from his mother. He committed sexual homicide at age 21.
- A 7-year-old boy, whose mother teased him in public and in front of her female friends by stroking his penis.

A career progression

A number of future sexual murderers were earlier involved in stealing and assault, sometimes marital assault and sexual assault of children in the family, indicative of a failure to acquire normal levels of inhibitory control (O'Brien, 1985). These individuals start with relatively minor sexual deviations and then escalate over time (Britton, 1998). Cruelty to animals and fire-setting, both common features, could serve to reinforce antisocial and aggressive behaviour (Ressler et al., 1992; Schlesinger, 2001; Wenzl et al., 2008). According to FBI investigators, arsonists commonly masturbate as they watch the flames (Douglas and Olshaker, 2006), another example of a powerful and arousing ('traumatic') event apparently forming a link with sexual arousal.

In healthy development, sexual desire and social empathy blend (Britton, 1998). Correspondingly, fantasies involve consensual sex and mutual pleasure. This stands in contrast to deviant sexual development, which misses the link with empathetic development. It could be that many people lack self-esteem and self-confidence sufficient to entertain seriously such consensual fantasies. In some cases, early courting experiences were perceived as failures, leading to resentment. In a small number of such cases, anger emerges and forms a toxic link with sexuality. These individuals' sexual fantasies involve anger, domination and revenge.

The role of fantasy

Fantasy and the link to action

When still young, violent sexual fantasy is sometimes reported by those who go on to commit sexually linked serial killing (Wenzl et al., 2008). Burgess et al. (1986) assume that (p. 257): 'these men are motivated to murder by their way of thinking. Over time, their thinking patterns emerged from or were influenced by early life experiences'. Interviewing them revealed (p. 258): 'long-standing aggressive thoughts and fantasies directed toward sexualized death'. Evidence suggests that rehearsal in fantasy can increase the chances of the content of the fantasy being later enacted (Baumeister et al., 2011) (Chapter 16). If this effect can be observed in a brief laboratory experiment, years of fantasy over a particular sexual theme could be much more potent. To make matters worse, a serial killer will typically feel anger about events in his early life and endless rumination on these will probably serve to strengthen the anger. The fantasy world of serial killers has something of the quality of a hypnotic trance (Carlisle, 1998).

These individuals' backgrounds set the scene for the emergence of deviant fantasy, as they are often lacking any trusting reciprocal sexually attractive contact (MacCulloch et al., 1983; Maniglio, 2010; Ressler et al., 1992). Fantasy is a source of stimulation, sometimes being the only retreat from emotional pain, social isolation, feelings of inferiority and inadequacy. Fantasy is a source of control in a life otherwise often bereft of this, exemplified by the use of the most effective, if not the only viable, kind: aggressive fantasy permitting domination of another. In some cases, fantasy seems to represent a re-run of earlier abuse but with a change of roles, from victim to aggressor (Ressler et al., 1992). For some, while still children, fantasy was translated into 'mini-scenarios' of 'acting-out' that take the form of sexual assaults on other children. As MacCulloch et al. (1983, p. 27) express it, the man 'controls his inner world and in that way becomes the success he would like to be in the real world'.

Successful resolution of the story-line of the fantasy could act as a source of relief, a kind of negative reinforcement, an escape from a world of failure, and thereby a coping strategy. In other words, the fantasy is an operant[1] which increases in frequency as a result of reinforcement. Fear on the face of the victim in the fantasy and later in reality is a form of control, which could constitute positive reinforcement (MacCulloch et al., 2000). If fantasy mirrors reality, acquisition of control in fantasy would be expected to trigger dopamine release, further strengthening the fantasy and thereby increasing the chances of its enactment in reality. In addition, masturbation in a comfortable and safe environment could serve to weaken the power of any inhibitory factors that are also entertained as part of the fantasy, for instance the prospect of getting caught.

In a sample of sixteen men convicted of sexual offences, thirteen exhibited a close connection between the content of their repetitive fantasy and what was actually performed in their offence (MacCulloch et al., 1983). Prior to the final offence, part of the sequence was performed as a 'try-out', for example stalking a target woman. A number of men reported that they varied the content of their fantasy, increasing the intensity so as to maintain arousal. Try-outs were motivated to maintain the fantasy's value. Earlier real 'try-outs' were incorporated into the story-line of the fantasy and accompanied by masturbation. Fantasy subsequent to the try-out might act to hone the skill and lead to 'better performance' next time, since there is always an ultimate 'high' to be attained if only they try hard enough. The arousal value might be increased by planning and then taking greater risks (Anderson, 1994). Pornographic materials depicting violence can offer role models of scenes to be incorporated into the line of the fantasy (Anonymous, 1998). Hence, by operant and classical conditioning, orgasm strengthens the salience of the fantasy (Maniglio, 2010). Hickey (2010) argues that: 'the world of fantasy becomes as addictive as an escape into drugs'.

Like all addictions, there can be escalation to more and more extreme scenarios (Britton, 1998; Douglas and Olshaker, 2006; Gibb, 2011). Also, when the fantasies lose their arousal value they can subsequently be 'acted out' in stalking, cruising, spying and then in actual assaults, presumably with an escalating rush of adrenalin (Britton, 1998; Chan et al., 2010). Interweaving of fantasy and sexually aggressive behaviour is often a graded process starting with relatively harmless activities, such as collecting sexually related items of female clothing and such antisocial but non-sexual acts as assault, arson and burglary, which then escalate. FBI investigators describe Jerry Brudos (Chapter 19), who started with a shoe fetish and systematically refined his fantasies and activities to increase the stimulation level, as a textbook example of escalation (Douglas and Olshaker, 2006).

Sadistic fantasy in a control population

Alarmingly, a significant percentage of a control population also show a tendency to entertain sadistic fantasy (Gray et al., 2003). MacCulloch et al. (1983) ask – given that a number of so-called normal men have such fantasies, why do so few of them escalate into actual violence? Clearly, additional factors are involved with serial killers, such as repeated reinforcement by masturbation and a weakness in the inhibition on expressing such fantasy. It could be that a developmental exposure to extreme negative emotion is a necessary condition to show actual violence.

Conversely, a healthy sex life or at least reciprocal heterosexual contact might exert a protective effect against escalation of deviant fantasy.

The consequences

An immediate consequence of killing appears to be relief of tension, a sense of achievement and temporary closure (Ressler et al., 1992), which might be expected to reinforce the action. Masturbation onto the body or an item of the victim's underwear, as in Dennis Rader (Wenzl et al., 2008), would presumably contribute to the reinforcement. The consequence of engaging in sex-linked killing might be a rush of endorphins in the brain (Anderson, 1994), as occurs with other addictions and harmless ways of boosting emotional state. As one serial killer wrote (Anonymous, 1998, p. 130):

> The acting out of his cherished fantasies, he knows, will elevate him from his intolerable and infuriating psychological low; they will make things 'all right' and cause him to feel good about himself. They will 'prove' without any shadow of doubt, that he is really somebody.

So-called 'signature behaviour' is sometimes carried out at the time of the kill, such as damage to the body (often sexually linked regions), rather as in leaving a calling-card to label the kill as his handiwork (Schlesinger, 2001) and presumably to help intensify memories later. A number return to the crime scene, indicative that it retains motivational potential. Some use the visit to revive the fantasy and a number engage in sexual activity with the corpse. In one case, a map was labelled with the kill sites and pinned to the killer's wall (Douglas and Olshaker, 2006). Things of a fetishist nature are commonly taken from the victim, such as an item of underwear or even a body part (Ressler et al., 1992; Sounes, 1995). These are later used as props during masturbation (Gibb, 2011). In some cases, like that of Dennis Rader, when safely back home the killer took photographs of himself dressed in the victim's clothes (Wenzl et al., 2008).

Following discovery of a sexually linked killing, Britton (1998) briefed the police (p. 402): 'You have to remember, this is the most unique, pleasurable and exciting experience of this man's life and when the urge is strong enough, he's going to want to do it again.' The killer will retain vivid memories of his crime and will typically 'play' these repeatedly in his conscious mind (Britton, 1998). However, sometimes the killing will not live up to expectations and the 'ultimate high' proves elusive (Carlisle, 1998). If the intensity of the replays diminishes, the man will turn to plans for another killing, possibly introducing a novel perverse twist to it in order to increase the intensity and overcome the habituation. The frequency of killings sometimes intensifies over time, apparently also to overcome habituation.

Serial sexual killers are not necessarily totally lacking in all post-killing remorse, shame or guilt, since some are troubled by these emotions and promise themselves 'I will never do it again' (Carlisle, 1998; Holmes, 1998), rather like addicts. However, such emotions involve extrapolation beyond the present and running an emotionally 'hot' simulation of the mind of the victim and his or her loved ones. It would seem that any such simulation is no match for the appetitive lure of sexual action. It is perhaps surprising not that serial killers show so little guilt, but rather that they show any. Guilt is thought to build upon disgust (Chapter 12) and these individuals seem to have an abnormal response to the triggers for the most basic disgust at the sight of wounds and blood. Occasionally, as with the Connecticut killer, Michael Ross, they report a feeling of disgust after the killing (Ramsland and McGrain, 2010).

The bases in the brain

Head injuries are frequently found in those who go on to commit sexual homicide (Hickey, 2010; Sounes, 1995). A high prevalence of convulsions is also evident, which corresponds to neurological malfunction (MacCulloch et al., 1983). On epilepsy, Krafft-Ebing (1978) noted (p. 313): 'numerous cases in literature in which epileptics, who, during intervals, present no signs of active sexual impulse, but manifest it in connection with epileptic attacks, or during the time of equivalent or post-epileptic exceptional mental states'. John Wayne Gacy suffered from epileptic seizures (Sullivan and Maiken, 1983). There is the possibility of oxygen starvation to the brain at the time of birth in the case of Paul Bernardo (Pron, 1995).

The process underlying the formation of toxic associations appears to be one of 'sensory preconditioning' (MacCulloch et al., 2000).

Sensory preconditioning arises when two events occur simultaneously or at roughly the same time. Following this pairing, presenting one of the events revives a memory of the other and the individual acts on the basis of their joint occurrence. Sensory preconditioning is associated with activation of dopamine at the nucleus accumbens (Young et al., 1998), which would be expected to contribute salience to the association. In this case, sexual arousal would be paired with an aversive emotional state, say, shame, humiliation, physical violence or witnessing representations of violence as in pornography. Hence, subsequently, negative emotion as in fear will evoke sexual arousal. Reciprocally, sexual arousal would trigger an aversive emotional state, leading to a vicious circle.

In some cases, there is the possibility of a sensitization of an underlying aberrant sexuality by addictive drugs. One example is Russell Williams, who took large amounts of medically prescribed drugs, including prednisone (Gibb, 2011). There are reports of a link to mania, excessive energy and a feeling of invincibility, even hypersexuality, in a few cases, but I would not want to overplay the evidence.

Who commits serial sexual homicide?

Personality

The characteristics that seem most usually to be found among serial killers are narcissistic personality disorder, associated with an excessive need to be admired and a sense of grandiosity and entitlement (Ramsland and McGrain, 2010). Self-centredness and a lack of empathy are also characteristics. The extreme narcissist is likely to experience intense frustration at rejection by a woman. This was probably a contributory factor in the phase of Ted Bundy's serial killing (Ramsland and McGrain, 2010).

Heide et al. (2009) suggest that (p. 71):

> the personality development of men who commit these crimes must be arrested. We suspect that they are operating on a more primitive level, one seen in the normal course of development, but typically transcended in the course of late childhood or early adolescence.

Offenders have failed to acquire normal levels of control by inhibitory factors, such as empathetic mental simulations of the consequences of their actions.

Not a deficiency correction

Sexual killers are not necessarily deprived of conventional and consensual sexual outlet by, for example, inadequacies in obtaining normal partners, which argues against non-discharged 'excess drive'. Indeed, some, such as the Los Angeles 'Hillside Stranglers' Kenneth Bianchi and Angelo Buono (O'Brien, 1985), led very rich 'conventional' sex lives. The Austrian writer, journalist and serial sex killer, Jack Unterweger, was something of a toast of the town amongst Vienna's cultural elite, surrounded by adoring and sexually available women (Leake, 2007). The Gloucester couple Fred and Rosemary West (Sounes, 1995) enjoyed an endless supply of consensual sexual variety and the rich sex life of the Canadian couple Paul Bernardo and Karla Homolka was doubtless facilitated by their striking good looks. Rather, we need to seek explanations in terms of the specific lure of escalation beyond the consensual.

They appear so normal

[P]eople whose behaviour is in other respects normal can, under the domination of the most unruly of all the instincts, put themselves in the category of sick persons in the single sphere of sexual life. (Freud, 1953, p. 161)

After the conviction of someone committing sexual violence, neighbours often remark 'He seemed so normal and pleasant' (Gibb, 2011). Probably in every aspect of his life that was publically visible, he was indeed normal and pleasant. The fictional story of Dr Jekyll and Mr Hyde contains an essential element of truth. Thus, some speak of 'dissociation and compartmentalization' (Carlisle, 1998, p. 87), wherein at times a function of the brain switches into a different and pathological mode of control. It is even possible that attempts to suppress this 'dark side' increase its strength.

The Wisconsin killer Ed Gein, who formed the role model for a genre of horror movies, was a trusted and respected babysitter, described in terms no more sinister than 'a bit eccentric'. In Wichita, Kansas, it would appear that few, if any, suspected the devoted family man and church president Dennis Rader of being the so-called Bind Torture and Kill (BTK) terrorizer of their city. A part-time university student of criminology, his full-time job involved admission to people's homes to install security systems, equipment doubtless acquired in many cases simply from fear of the BTK killer. On her visit to Canada, Queen Elizabeth would surely have found it hard to believe that Russell Williams, the trusted and highly decorated military hero assigned to be her pilot, was later to be found guilty of rape and sexual homicide (Pron, 1995).

Handsome, articulate and charismatic, Ted Bundy was a university student of law and psychology in Seattle, who worked as a volunteer on a university Crisis helpline and was a political campaign organizer (Rule, 2006). He was entirely reasonable and pleasant until he came under the grip of his murderous urges (Masters, 1993). Similarly, between renovating the house's torture chamber and digging holes in the back yard to bury his victims, the workaholic Gloucester builder, sexual pervert and serial killer Fred West was delighted to take time out to offer the charity of rescuing neighbours who had got into trouble with their DIY (Sounes, 1995).

Of course, the appreciative fellow parishioners and neighbours could hardly discern the preoccupation of the conscious minds of these trusted individuals, which even in church might well have involved the depths of sexual depravity. In a number of cases, apparently neither did their wives detect anything amiss.

Are they insane?

That the behaviour can be so well disguised seems in a macabre way to bear witness to rationality in mental function. Trial lawyers often spend hours discussing whether such killers are insane, the outcome of which could make the difference between the gas chamber and a mental hospital (Sullivan and Maiken, 1983). Usually the guilty are not judged to be psychotic (Schlesinger, 2001). Rather, the winning case tends to be that they exhibited meticulous purposive planning ('goal-direction'), while carefully weighing up costs and benefits, in execution of the crimes and evasion of capture, one index of a rational mind (Sewell, 1985). It would appear that the dopamine-based system of assessing costs and benefits of actions is working normally. Furthermore, they can show high functioning in other aspects of their lives, such as at work (Carlisle, 1998). At some level, they know right from wrong but don't act appropriately on the basis of this.

In most cases, it could not be argued that such killers suddenly and unexpectedly came under the control of an irresistible impulse that was triggered by the presence of a victim. A psychiatrist at the trial of John Wayne Gacy noted that the killer would excavate graves for future victims, remarking that (Sullivan and Maiken, 1983, p. 346): 'I don't think that a person who *plans* to have an irresistible impulse in the future could be considered *having* irresistible impulses.' Having said this, the presence of a suitable victim might greatly and unstoppably increase the desire for attack. Whether this is truly irresistible is an issue perhaps best left to philosophers.

Their perverse goal might well co-exist and compete for time with a range of other quite unspectacular and socially desirable goals, such as entertaining children while dressed as a clown, as exemplified by John Wayne Gacy, or accompanying a son during a stay at a scout camp, as with Dennis Rader. The change of consciousness from benign to deadly was described by Dennis Rader as quickly switching 'from one gear to the next' (Wenzl et al., 2008, p. 342). So, the task is to try to understand how such atypical goals arise and are able to dominate the control of behaviour.

Why so few women?

In the annals of sex-linked killing, there is an overwhelming preponderance of males (Cameron and Frazer, 1987). There have been very few females; experts give the names of only two: Jeanne Weber in France and Jane Toppan in the United States (Ramsland and McGrain, 2010). There is a possible candidate in the USA for an unattached sexually motivated female serial killer: Aileen Wournos, who stripped her male victims naked (Silvio et al., 2006). However, it seems more likely that her underlying motives were simply those of robbery and revenge for the monstrous injustices that had earlier been done to her, rather than sexual excitement. Somewhat more frequently, though still very uncommon, women have been closely involved in sexually linked serial homicide in combination with male partners. Famous cases include that of Myra Hindley (Lee, 2012) and Rosemary West (Sounes, 1995) in England and Charlene Gallego and Carol Bundy (no relative of Ted Bundy) in the USA (Silvio et al., 2006), as well as Karla Homolka in Canada (Pron, 1995) and Monique Olivier in France (Hamon, 2008).

We cannot be certain whether the female partners derived sexual satisfaction from these actions or the satisfaction came just in their supportive role, though some appear to have derived sexual pleasure (Holmes et al., 1998b; Sounes, 1995). Rosemary West had a highly dysfunctional upbringing, was probably abused by her father and seemed to find some salvation in the powerful but perverse bond with her husband. The Wests exemplify the combination of two people each with a disturbed background coming together, which seems to create a particularly lethal cocktail. Karla Homolka's defence was in terms of the battered wife syndrome, something comparable to the Stockholm syndrome, and there is much evidence that she was abused.

Why the lack of women? Girls experience early attachment problems just as boys do. Some girls suffer both physical and sexual abuse, probably more than boys do, and some go on to abuse their children. Girls are often subject to situations that trigger shame and humiliation. Women, albeit many fewer than men, have proven themselves perfectly capable of serial killing, done to gain money, revenge or notoriety. Women are to be found at the outer fringes of sex, albeit in smaller numbers than men. Some single women enter swinging circles (O'Neill and O'Neill, 1972), while others join Satanic cults and many have outlandish fantasies. A few reveal the depths of bizarre sexual taste, in such things as becoming sexually explicit groupies for serial killers (Carlo, 2010), while in one case a groupie even tried to help a notorious serial killer earn an alibi by herself committing a murder and planting bogus evidence (O'Brien, 1985). So, there is something very special and, it would seem, uniquely male about the link between murder and sexual desire. If only we could establish what it is, this could be of inestimable social good.

A stressed animal has a decision to make on how to react: actively, as in escape or attack, or passively (Cabib and Puglisi-Allegra, 2012). It is possible that the female is biased towards coping passively.

Writing from a feminist perspective, Cameron and Frazer (1987) suggest that lust killing arises from men's assimilation of the dominant role from culturally transmitted masculine stereotypes. Males have traditionally played the dominant and violent role in life and it would seem logical that such role models are culturally transmitted through generations. Correspondingly, violent pornography caters for a male rather than a female market. However, this begs the question of how this gender difference arises in the first place. For a number of non-human species, males are more aggressive than females, which surely requires a biological explanation. If we adopt an integrative model of understanding human behaviour (Chapter 1), we would allocate key roles to both biology and social context. The biological difference arose prior to there being human cultures and is still with us, involving such things as the higher levels of testosterone in men as compared to women. This factor would tend to give an orientation to the way cultures institutionalize male dominance. Sex differences in early development in the womb might set the scene for the emergence of such a sex difference in behaviour (see Schore, 2003, p. 254).

The victim

Sexually linked serial killers tend to favour their own idiosyncratic type of victim, such as female, young, blonde and student-looking (Holmes, 1998). These are also the material of their fantasies and they will sometimes go to great lengths to find such a victim (Anonymous, 1998). However, if the ideal is not available, and depending upon the strength of their desire, these men will typically compromise by attacking a victim not fitting the ideal. Some victims are selected on the basis of what they do, such as sex workers or drug addicts, this occasionally being justified as a so-called mission killing. This motivation might well be compatible with a sexual motivation and can be supported by neutralizing definitions of the kind that 'prostitutes are immoral so they are fair game'.

Sexually related homicide can be illustrated by looking at some famous cases.

Some famous cases of homicidal sexual desire

Richard Ramirez

In the 1980s, Richard Ramirez, also known as 'The night stalker', terrorized Los Angeles (Carlo, 2010). His story represents an example of the fusion of sex and violence, later sensitized by industrial quantities of cocaine and other drugs.

Born in 1960 in El Paso, Texas, Richard had, as a boy, read the story of Jack the Ripper, which fired him with the prospect of murder in the pursuit of sexual desire (Carlo, 2010). A violent temper and the administration of severe corporal punishment had been transmitted through generations of Ramirez males. In addition to Richard himself being the recipient, he was witness to merciless beatings of his brothers. As a child, Richard suffered two serious accidental blows to his head, which might have contributed to later troubles, possibly mediated in part through the temporal lobe epilepsy that he manifested.

At the age of 10 or 11, Richard acquired a 'role model', his cousin Mike, who had returned from Vietnam. Mike brought back photos of himself sexually assaulting Vietnamese women, which he shared with Richard. The younger man used these images as a prop for masturbation. Richard repeated the exact form of these assaults during his later spree of terror. The symbiotic bond between these two individuals was consolidated by smoking marijuana, while Mike would brag of his exploits and instruct Richard in the techniques of killing. In the presence of Richard, Mike murdered his own wife. Mike was not the only role model. From his brother-in-law, Richard was taught the skills of voyeurism and found himself turned on by nightly forays around carefully selected lighted windows.

Subsequently Richard dropped out of school, watched horror movies, smoked large quantities of marijuana and committed 'petty' crime. House-breaking was starting to put him on a 'high', as was hunting animals and then dissecting the prey. Estranged from his parents and with El Paso being too parochial, Richard took refuge with a cousin in Los Angeles, where he was dazzled by the pornography shops, the sight of sex workers and the glamour of women bathing on the beach at Santa Monica. From the cousin he refined the art of house-breaking.

Richard Ramirez found a job at a hotel, where he was able to hone his skills of prowling, voyeurism and theft, culminating in one attempted rape. At the relatively benign end of the sexual spectrum, he acquired a strong fetish for women's feet. However, facilitated by viewing pornographic bondage imagery and reading Satanic literature, Ramirez fantasized about domination and violent sex, which he accompanied with masturbation (Carlo, 2010). Attempted rape was followed by 'successful' rape and then the full horrors of the sequence of repeated rape and murder unfolded. Carefully and stealthily planning and then ascending the approach gradient that links fantasies to real action 'sexually charged' him.

Ramirez showed a 'career path' from dropping out of school, delinquency, petty crime and relatively minor sexual offending, through sexual assault and finally to killing. From the role models who were around during the emergence of his sexuality, he was exposed either to pure violence or the explicit combination of sexual stimulation and violent imagery.

Excessive drug-taking could have had two effects to make things much worse. First, there might have been cross-sensitization between the systems underlying (a) drug-seeking and (b) aggression and sexual desire. Secondly, restraint processes are associated with higher brain regions, the activity of which would normally counter putting atypical desire into effect. These would most likely have been severely compromised by the trauma and drugs.

Gary Leon Ridgway

In Seattle during the 1980s, Gary Ridgway murdered sex workers (Hickey, 2010; Rule, 2004). Known as the 'Green River Killer', he was responsible for at least forty-nine killings, thereby, as far as is known, being the most prolific murderer in America's history. His full confession exemplifies the fusion of sexual desire and anger.

With a long-term stable job, he was described as an ideal husband by his last wife and exhibited an interest in spreading Christianity. By all accounts, his final marriage was a very happy one and between marriages there was no shortage of consensual sexual partners. Unlike the stereotype of a serial killer, Ridgeway did not come from a broken home where he had been the victim of violent abuse.

However, his early childhood was seriously troubled. The family moved at frequent intervals such that Gary did not form any close friends. The boy felt himself to be an outsider from his family and school, a non-entity, who came to believe that he was so unlike his brothers that some mix-up of babies had happened in the maternity unit. His home was dominated by his mother, who was over-controlling and subjected the father to mild emotional and physical abuse. Gary wetted his bed, a common feature of those going on to such killing. This annoyed his mother. Indeed, everything in his life seemed to go wrong for him, including being picked on by school bullies. In desperation and in chronic anger, he fantasized about violence and this led to vandalism, animal cruelty and fire-setting. Killing an animal gave him a feeling of strength and control, while he became fascinated by murder.

At puberty, Gary felt simultaneous anger and sexual arousal when, following bed-wetting, his mother would spend some fifteen minutes cleaning urine from his genital regions (Rule, 2004). This triggered humiliation but also gave him an erection and sexual thoughts, which were compounded by her occasionally appearing semi-naked. However, he was brought up to view masturbation as a sin. Gary started to watch neighbouring girls secretly as they swam in the garden. When invited to their house he exposed himself to them. He also became a frotteur, brushing against girls on passing them.

Ridgeway's first two wives made him angry after he discovered that they had cheated on him; boyhood anger developed into adult rage (Rule, 2004). Violent thoughts assailed him for most of his life. Ridgeway exhibited ambivalence in his sexual desire. He was attracted to sex workers but hated them after contracting venereal disease and sought revenge by strangling them during sex. Strangling, he reported, had a more 'personal and rewarding' effect than other methods of killing and was a way to gain control and ultimately, in the deceased body, a possession that was his alone (Rule, 2004, p. 577).

Ridgeway also once subjected his second wife to temporary choking (a phenomenon also reported in some other cases of serial sexual homicide (Pron, 1995)). He reported feeling intense bouts of anger, and the pressure could only be relieved by another murder. Conversely, after a particularly good day at work, the pressure to kill would sometimes temporarily abate.

The image of Ridgeway pursuing drug-addicted sex workers standing alongside the highway is a tragic one. Many of these young women, themselves victims of abuse and desperate to obtain money for their next fix, would ask the naïve and innocent question of each punter: 'Are you sure that you are not the Green River Killer?' In Ridgeway's case, each party was seeking a form of quick and short 'high', traumatized predator and traumatized prey having at least this much in common.

The sites where the bodies were left became attractive to him, a common feature amongst such killers (Douglas and Olshaker, 2006), and he would sometimes later return to the body of a victim and have sex with her. Rule (2004, p. 152) writes about Ridgeway and similar sexual killers: 'For them, murder is addictive, and it takes more and more of the "substance" to satisfy them, or to make them feel, as two infamous serial murderers have said, "normal".' Ridgeway enjoyed having sex with his wife outdoors, chillingly the locations chosen included precisely where the murders had taken place, probably reflecting conditioning of arousal. It seems likely that, by means of fantasy he was aroused by reliving those last moments with his victims.

Ridgeway would seem to exemplify rather well a fusion of negative emotion and sexual desire, both developmentally as a child and as an adult. The early experience of being washed by his mother might well have blended sexual arousal with embarrassment, shame and anger. As an adult, anger helped to trigger thoughts of erotically linked death. Sexual themes associated with prostitution, venereal disease and infidelity seemed to form a strong bond with anger, pointing to a link with mission-killing. Bouts of anger triggered by unfortunate life events served to lift inhibitions and exacerbate the lure of the pathological form of sexual high.

Anger with their victims might not be a necessary ingredient in all sexually related homicides, as the following two cases suggest.

Jeffrey Dahmer

Jeffrey Dahmer murdered seventeen young men in association with sexual activity performed on them before and after their deaths. There was apparently no cruelty or abuse in the family and little suggestion that he felt any contempt or hatred towards his victims. Dahmer confessed to all the crimes in graphic detail, which gave investigators vivid insights.

Dahmer was born in 1960 in Milwaukee and grew up in rural Ohio. He might well have been emotionally traumatized by his mother's depression shortly after the birth, her unavailability for early social interaction and the acrimonious relationship and divorce between his parents. Maternal depression and an absence of early social interaction are disruptive to a child's emotional development (Schore, 2003). When 4 years old, he had a double hernia operation, associated with intense pain in the groin area (Masters, 1993). One can speculate as to how this intrusive trauma might be interpreted by a young child or what permanent changes in connections between neurons in the emotional processing regions of the brain it might have triggered.[2] Whatever such effects, it would appear to have marked a turning point, following which Jeffrey became even more withdrawn from the world (Nichols, 2006).

At school, another boy invited Jeffrey to choke him ('pretend strangulation'), promising not to tell the teacher. The boy betrayed the trust and Jeffrey received corporal punishment, the first in a long series of disappointments and perceived betrayals. By age 8, Jeffrey found himself alone in the world due to parental problems amongst other things, and it was claimed by his father and probation officer that he had been sexually molested by another boy (Davis, 1991).

He would spend time exploring woods and, as with other future serial killers, feeling that he just did not 'belong anywhere', being worthless (Davis, 1991; Masters, 1993). Signs of overwhelming loneliness were evident by the time that he attended junior high school, and the only solution was to withdraw still further from the outside world into one of private fantasy. There was, however, some early sexual experience, when Jeffrey was 13 years of age and with a boy of age 10 years (Masters, 1993). The other boy had taken the initiative and persuaded Jeffrey to undress, whereupon they kissed and caressed. However, fear of being caught caused them to cease this activity.

Jeffrey discovered some fascinating but lonely pastimes in the forests: chopping down tree branches and dissection of the bodies of animals that he found dead (Masters, 1993). It was noted at his trial that an awakening sexuality appeared on the scene at the same time as his engagement with dissection. This raised the question of whether there could have been an early fusion between the brain processes underlying these two aspects. There was also the potent memory of his earlier operation in the groin area, which might have triggered an attribution of 'salience' to this bodily region and its surgical investigation.[3]

Classmates recall Jeffrey being mocked and bullied in school and his reluctance to hit back. He went through a phase of craving recognition, something that was earned by performing clowning antics in public. Towards the end of his junior high school days, Jeffrey discovered alcohol as a soothing balm for his troubled mind, regularly getting drunk, excessive intake being something he was destined never to quit.

By age 17, Jeffrey was performing masturbation on occasions more than three times a day (Masters, 1993). This was accompanied by looking at magazines showing naked men, with a focus of attention upon their chests. The masturbation presumably reinforced a developmental course wherein he became particularly attracted to the single physical feature of the chest area. Jeffrey also developed a fascination with the thought of peering inside the bodies of men and he recalled his own hernia operation, presumably revisiting his trauma.

Jeffrey observed a jogger going past his house each day. The jogger's body was of the kind Jeffrey wished to touch but how could he make the necessary contact? To ask would be to invite rejection and violate the need for total control. In his imagination, Jeffrey fantasized about knocking the man unconscious, dragging him into the woods and there lying with him, kissing but with the man blissfully unaware. One day, he waited for his prey by the side of the road armed with a baseball bat. For the first and almost only time in this tragic saga, fate was on the side of the intended victim; the jogger failed to materialize and Jeffrey called off the plan.

With his parents' separation and divorce, Jeffrey was left alone in the house for days on end with no outside contact and only his bizarre fantasies for company. He masturbated over thoughts of the jogger, which gave him some very short-term satiation. However, over the longer term it would appear that the masturbation strengthened the power of salient erotic thoughts, those of a still and totally submissive, even dead, body.

These thoughts became more pressing and involved picking up a hitch-hiker. Turning fantasy into reality and borrowing his father's car, Jeffrey, now aged 18, went out looking for a victim and soon found one: a young man with chest exposed, just like the scenes within his fantasy. Though not homosexual, the boy agreed to go back to Jeffrey's home to spend some time together. After a few drinks, the boy said that he would now need to leave, a lethal decision, it being the trigger for the reaction that Masters (1993) describes as follows (p. 52):

> The swell of frustration within Jeffrey Dahmer rose until it filled his nostrils and pressed at his temples. He was not going to leave. He couldn't leave. He wouldn't let him leave.

Jeffrey proceeded to knock out and then strangle the young man, where-upon he kissed the body and masturbated over it. Later he disposed of most of the young man's remains, keeping the head as a token and as an object of masturbation (a fetish), a possession that was his alone. Presum-ably, it served as a trophy, a token that at least there was one area in life in which he excelled. Photographs, which Jeffrey then and subsequently took of the bodies, would, it appears, have served a similar role. At age 22, Dahmer was arrested for exhibitionism, behaviour that was to be repeated subsequently (Masters, 1993).

Dahmer found a job in Milwaukee, where he was sexually proposi-tioned by a man and invited to the public toilets, though, presumably through fear of capture or performance failure, he did not pursue this (Masters, 1993). However, after priming by this encounter, his sexual urges increased in intensity and the frequency of masturbation increased correspondingly up to twelve times a day, though even this was inade-quate. He sought out bookshops that specialized in homosexual pornog-raphy and had anonymous sexual contact in darkened booths showing gay films. Dahmer stole a male mannequin from a shop, took it home and used it as a prop for fantasy and masturbation.

In 1985, at age 25, Dahmer discovered Milwaukee's bathhouses, where he was initiated into conventional and some unconventional homosexual activities (Masters, 1993). However, his desire for an entirely passive partner exceeded the boundaries of even this permissive environment. So, he devised a brutally effective solution, quite literally so: a concoction of alcohol and crushed sleeping pills, which he smuggled in and gave to unsuspecting partners. Thereby, for up to eight hours locked in a cubicle, he had a passive partner with whom he could realize the contents of his fantasies, accompanied by masturbation. He would lie with his head on the man's body listening to the heart beat and sound of the stomach, a form of fetish, an erotic focus on just a part of the body.

Alas, escalation set in, so that even the 'pseudo corpse' of a drugged partner was inadequate to match 'perfectionist' desires, and he wanted sex with a real corpse. Fantasy became reality: Dahmer's behaviour escalated to murder followed by sex with the body and eating body parts. Consuming body parts was a form of sexual excitement that brought a bizarre affiliation between killer and victim. With a dead body as a partner, banished were the fears of ridicule, performance failure, humiliation or abandonment, since here was the attainment of the ultimate goal of perfect control (Davis, 1991).

Unusually for a serial killer, nine years elapsed between his first and second killings, which suggests the exertion of considerable inhibition even in the face of strong temptation. After these nine years, he reported feeling hopeless in the face of the temptation (Masters, 1993, p. 87): 'I couldn't quit.' Masters (1993, p. 93) writes: 'The hunt for the perfect prop, the fantastical become real, would henceforth pervade his every thought and grip him with such intensity as to banish all interfering concepts of morality or safety.' The hunt might not have entirely banished such inhibitions – he reported experiencing fear after a killing (Davis, 1991). However, in the competition for the control of cognition and behaviour, once the desire kicked in strongly such restraining factors were clearly inadequate. If Dahmer were like a number of other serial killers, he might well have entertained compassionate thoughts at times and have acted upon them, until in the grip of his particular brand of sexual desire (Masters, 1993).

Dahmer described the sexual thoughts as coming into his head from nowhere (a 'compulsion'; Masters, 1993), which would give them features in common with obsessive compulsive disorder. However, a distinction emerges when we consider his use of the expression 'a craving, a hunger' to describe the immediate consequence of the thought's arrival, which is unlike the aversive quality of OCD.

Towards the end, Dahmer exhibited the familiar phenomenon of escalation: the killings became more frequent (Davis, 1991; Hickey, 2010). This was also the case with Ted Bundy (Sewell, 1985), suggesting the effect of one or more underlying processes: a gradually waning level of satiety ('catharsis' value), a failure to meet expectation or increasingly strong reinforcement.

Jeffrey Dahmer seems to exemplify perfectly the following developmental trajectory. The parents were not available to offer adequate reinforcement for any emerging conventional social behaviour (Nichols, 2006). His actual early social experiences were such as to lead to a failure to establish a generalized internal working model that involved an expectation of positive attainment in dealing with others. His model of the other individual's perception of him was that of worthlessness. Hence, his emerging sexuality could not attach itself to any expectation of success in establishing a relationship. Rather, he resorted to a world of fantasy, in which he was in control by having sex with unconscious or dead men.

It is sometimes said that sexually linked serial killers are not really motivated by lust but rather by the need for control and domination. However, this divides the world in an illogical way. Of course Dahmer wanted control but, according to his own testimony, he experienced 'ungovernable lust' (Nichols, 2006). I would see a coalescence of the need for control, lust and a desire for attachment in Dahmer's motivation.

Dennis Nilsen

A few years before Dahmer's killings, a strikingly similar case emerged in London: Dennis Nilsen (Masters, 1985). Nilsen killed fifteen young men. Like Dahmer, Nilsen was intelligent and highly articulate. He confessed fully and graphically to his crimes.

As a child, he was, in his own words, 'a wanderer at odds with his fellows' (Masters, 1985, p. 41) and living in a world of the imagination. The young boy formed a unique bond with his grandfather, a sailor. It would be hard to overstate the importance of this for the psychological development of Dennis. The grandfather's departures to sea were heartbreaking for the child, since they heralded days to be spent within a meaningless social vacuum, but the grandfather's returns, when he would invariably go first to find Dennis, were uniquely joyous.

One day, when Dennis was not yet 6, he waited in vain for his grandfather; tragically the grandfather had died in his boat. Dennis was later invited to peer into his grandfather's coffin, being told that his grandfather was sleeping. In retrospect, Dennis reported being massively traumatized, as he could not resolve the issue of life and death. It only slowly dawned on him that his soul mate would probably never be coming back. Dennis retreated even further into his self-imposed isolation. He felt alienated from the family, jealous towards his mother's new husband and did not develop trusting bonds. Receiving corporal punishment in school for his poor performance hardly helped.

While still a boy, he was part of a search party for a missing man and was present when the body was found. Dennis reported (Masters, 1985, p. 59):

He reminded me of my grandfather, and the images were fixed in my mind . . . I could never comprehend the reality of death.

Masters (1985) suggests that, at this stage, images of death and love were beginning to converge in his mind. Dennis developed a crush on a boy in his school but the boy was perceived to be of a higher social class and Dennis feared to approach him. The next crush was on a boy used as an illustration in a book. Dennis explored sexually the sleeping body of his brother. By the time that he left school, sexual arousal had been triggered under three conditions which had the feature in common that (Masters, 1985, p. 60): 'safety from rejection was ensured; with a distant idol, with an inanimate drawing, and with a sleeping body'.

After leaving school he had a traffic accident in which he sustained a blow to the head. One can speculate whether this was of any consequence to his later killings. He had some homosexual experience and developed a particular technique of sexual arousal: lying still and viewing his own naked body in a mirror but without seeing his head. In this way, he could imagine it to be another individual but one who was dead.

When 27 years old, his eyes fell upon an 18-year-old man and Nilsen reported (Masters, 1985, p. 76):

As he walked in the door he had the effect upon me of an electric shock.

Subsequently, they were to share a number of activities, including film-making. Nilsen reported it to be 'a source of extreme pain' (Masters, 1985, p. 77) when they were parted for any reason. In their film-making, it was particularly the scenes where the young man was lying still and seemingly playing dead that Nilsen found most attractive. When finally circumstances caused them to part, Nilsen was profoundly depressed.

Finding himself in London, Nilsen frequented gay bars and was involved in endless casual sexual encounters, which he found unsatisfying; indeed, they were even soul-destroying in the frustration of repeatedly being abandoned. However, solace and, as he put it, 'sexual feasts' were found by viewing his own body in a mirror. From an unconscious body, his fantasy evolved into a dead body with memories of the image of his dead grandfather. The dead body was fantasized to play a role in various scenarios in which actors in the fantasy found it arousing and their trigger to masturbation. In 1978, at age 33, he committed his first murder by strangling a young man lying in his bed. In a state of sexual arousal, Nilsen explored the body and masturbated onto it. He then proceeded to dispose of the body. Subsequently, there was a series of further murders associated with necrophiliac sex.

Nilsen said that he felt intense guilt following his capture. He reported that when he ventured out it was not with the intention of killing but rather to find a relationship. He reported that in death the victims looked like his last viewing of his dead grandfather, which (Masters, 1985, p. 189): 'brought me a bitter sweetness and a temporary peace and fulfilment'. On being asked by the police to recall the incidents, Nilsen reported (Masters, 1985, p. 144):

"I seem to have not participated in them, merely stood by and watched them happen – enacted by two other players – like a central cinema".

This suggests an altered state of consciousness, described by the term 'dissociation'.

Masters (1985, p. 295) poses the question:' Why does the word 'love' persistently strike a chord which releases the word 'death' in Nilsen's sentences?' In summary, Nilsen's biography is chillingly like Dahmer's. In each case, excessive alcohol might have caused brain damage in regions that would normally offer restraint, as well as temporarily lifting inhibitions. Each individual craved intimate company that was denied them. A difference would seem to be that Nilsen had an early experience of a real image of death on which he imprinted and with which his emerging sexuality fused. Dahmer generated his own imagery.

General points

A study of some infamous cases points to the necessity to take a broad perspective. The role of biology is implicated in consideration of epilepsy and possible brain damage by traumatic accident (Sounes, 1995) and/or the toxic effect of drugs such as alcohol upon those brain processes that would normally restrain behaviour.

Consider the kind of societal variables that permit this behaviour to arise and why, in the form exemplified here, it is a modern phenomenon (Haggerty, 2009). The killings typically take place in large urban centres such as London, Los Angeles, Milwaukee and Seattle. Even in those pre-Internet days, pornography to cater for every taste was readily available. In such places, people often don't even know who their next-door neighbour is, quite apart from what might constitute his night-time sexual proclivities. The victims were strangers to the killers, while the killers were often strangers to their environment themselves. The notion of a stranger is particularly evident in today's society. In medieval Europe, a person might go for a life-time without ever meeting a stranger. With the exception of the case of Ramirez, the victims tended to be the easiest targets, the disadvantaged and dispossessed: drug-addicted sex workers, the homeless, those living in the poor parts of town and ethnic minorities. Ramirez and Ridgeway would have found life very difficult without a car and highways.

In some cases, the kind of discourse assimilated from society served to provide background props. This is exemplified by the ultimate feminist nightmare, the Hillside Stranglers, who were violent pimps, contemptuous of women, even while seeking them out for sex. In such paired killers there can doubtless be a bond of solidarity established by their shared attitudes, bravado and planning of operations, as well as each holding a secret about the other (Sounes, 1995).

Looking at the sources of reinforcement for serial killers, these would appear to be multiple. Reinforcement deriving from the satiation of sexuality and (in most cases) anger would be the most obvious, combined with that which derives from 'successful' completion of an action. Another source of reinforcement for those such as Ramirez, Ridgeway and the Hillside Stranglers, where bodies were discovered periodically, would seem to be the media attention that was brought into their homes

(Haggerty, 2009; O'Brien, 1985). Kenneth Bianchi, one of the Hillside Stranglers, even requested that the police take him on a conducted tour of the murder sites. Serial killers often collect news cuttings of features describing their activities (Rule, 1983, 2006). This again points to a factor that makes such serial killing a predominantly modern phenomenon. Some serial killers became almost overnight celebrities with fame before and after capture. A number basked in the dubious glory of being able to mislead and taunt the police (Rule, 2006; Wenzl et al., 2008). Given that in most cases they regarded themselves previously as non-entities, it is not altogether surprising that they revelled in fame afterwards. One can only imagine what a mention in the evening news would do for dopamine transmission and incentive salience, thereby helping to keep motivation alive and bridge the gap until the next killing. Press cuttings would serve a similar role. Dennis Rader, wrote (Wenzl et al., 2008, p. 65):

> How many do I have to Kill (sic) before I get a name in the paper or some national attention. (sic) Do the cop (sic) think that all those deaths are not related?

Are such people lacking in empathy? They certainly were deficient in terms of the victims and their families, but did they exhibit a total lack? Ted Bundy was said to resist stealing from poor people (Rule, 2006). One is reminded of the contrast between the vicious cruelty of Fred and Rosemary West as contrasted with the tender romantic love letters that they frequently exchanged (Sounes, 1995). Could it be that empathy was suppressed when their bizarre desires kicked in? It might be relevant here to note the argument of Rich (2006, p. 214) in the context of juvenile sex offenders:

> sex offenders appear to possess the same sort of global, or dispositional, empathy as non-sexual criminal offenders and even non-offenders, and it is only in victim-specific empathy that they differ.

In summary

- There is no single trajectory leading to sexually linked killing but there are some strong pointers commonly evident in comparing examples.
- There appears to be a relatively high frequency of brain damage.

- The early upbringing of sex-linked killers is such that they fail to have healthy available role models and do not make healthy attachments. They often feel a grudge against society.
- Sexual stimulation makes an early fusion with negative emotions, such as anger and resentment.
- Toxic fantasy appears to be a prelude to killing.

TWENTY TWO

CONCLUDING REMARKS

The statements in the lecture were as simple as I could make them.
Any statements which have any reference to action must be simple.
(C. P. Snow, 1965, p. 60)

It is time to return to the enigma described in Chapter 1: the enormous range of different sexual desires, varying from the all-consuming, through indifference, to aversion and from cases where romantic bonding is a necessary condition for desire to the extremes of callous violence. It is hoped that the book has enabled this diversity to be better understood in terms of the role of *differences* in various contributory factors, such as:

- Genetic differences between people, which can be manifest in terms of different contributions to the structure of brain processes underlying desire, arousal and inhibition, as well as differences in hormone levels.
- Different interactions between sexual desire and attachment, drugs and anger/aggression.
- Chance events of an arousal-inducing nature experienced early in development.
- The occurrence of fear-evoking or disgust-evoking situations at any stage of life.
- Different histories of classical conditioning, such that a range of different events can get paired with sexual arousal.
- A variety of events that can reinforce or punish expressions of sexual desire and thereby alter that desire.
- Differences in sociocultural context.

Given this variety of contributory effects, it is not surprising that there is such a range of different desires both in terms of intensity and their target of attraction. Chapter 2 described a number of common features between sex, feeding and drinking. However, Chapter 4 noted a fundamental difference from feeding and drinking, in that these are both necessary for life and they relate to a regulated state of the body inside and outside the brain. Even given the restraint on variation that is imposed by this regulation, the enormous variety of different appetites for food with associated differences in body weight should be noted. It is suggested that a range of environmental and bodily factors play a role here, some probably similar to those involved in the variations in sexual desire.

Consider again two quotes from Chapter 1:

I respectfully held out my hand to her and she took it with an air of utter indifference, but she pressed it firmly as she climbed into the carriage. The reader will be able to imagine the flame which this sent racing through my blood. (Casanova, 1798/1958, p. 192)

the elegant and distinguished assistant who has been travelling across the country with me for two weeks catches hold of my arm when we have just said goodnight to each other, pulls me to him and kisses me on the mouth. 'In the morning, I'll come and see you in your room.' I can feel the spasm rising right up to my stomach. (Millet, 2003, p. 84)

Consider the essential ingredients of the escalation of desire evident in these two quotes:

- There is an intrinsically attractive other individual present and thereby a background level of desire.
- Sexual novelty is present.
- There is a sudden transition from a state of maybe neutral prediction of outcome to one of the encouragement of incentive advance. Things appear to be moving towards a desired goal. If experiments on non-human species are any indication, an unexpected reward is a particularly potent stimulus for the release of dopamine.

There are a number of conclusions from the earlier chapters, many of which are consolidated by comparisons across chapters, as follows:

1 Sexual desire can be best understood by taking both objective and subjective perspectives (Chapters 1 and 7). Some features of desire are open to scientific investigation, whereas others are best understood by qualitative first-person insights.

2 How sexual desire is understood has profound implications for how sexual behaviour is treated in ethical, medical, social, legal and religious contexts (Chapter 3), as exemplified by edicts on the desirability of chastity (Chapter 3) and the meaning attached to 'addiction' (Chapter 17).

3 Sexual desire arises from triggering by sexual incentives in the outside world, acting together with internal representations of these in memory (Chapters 4 and 16). The strength of desire increases with the physical and temporal proximity of the incentive, exemplified by temptation (Chapter 12) and addiction (Chapter 17).

4 Sexual desire towards a particular incentive is strengthened by its consequences such as orgasm (Chapter 10) and the lifting of negative emotional states, seen in addiction (Chapter 17) and sexual violence (Chapters 20 and 21).

5 Desire is sensitized by sex hormones (Chapter 8) and this is reflected in fantasy (Chapter 16).

6 The system underlying sexual desire is constructed in such a way as to assimilate information from the social environment, in the form of imitation and reinforcement, which further undermines naïve dichotomies of the 'nature versus nurture' kind (Chapters 1 and 2).

7 Sexual desire, arousal, pleasure and inhibition (Chapter 12) arise at different levels within the brain, in some cases acting in automatic and controlled modes (Chapters 1, 5, 7, 9, 10 and 12). The differences in weight attached to different levels can vary as a function of species, gender, development, experience, stress, drug-intake and brain damage.

8 Sexual desire can be associated with discounting the future (Chapters 7 and 8).

9 The modules suggested by evolutionary psychology co-exist with some flexible motivational processes (Chapters 2, 5 and 6).

10 The intensity of contemporary sexual desire can be illuminated by the notion of 'supernormal stimuli' and 'evolutionary mismatch' (Chapter 2).

11 Sexual desire has many features in common with hunger, gambling and drug-seeking, such that insight can be gained by taking a broad perspective (Chapters 2 and 4), including towards addiction (Chapter 17). The notion of 'incentive salience' is applicable across several motivations. However, unlike hunger/feeding, there is no obvious harm to the body tissues caused by sexual deprivation. This is exemplified by asexuality (Chapters 9 and 14). Any distress associated with deprivation, it is argued, arises in the brain from frustrated desire (Chapter 3, 4 and 10).

12 Evidence suggests that dopamine lies at the basis of desire (part of a behavioural activation system) and opioids at the basis of the pleasure of sexual activity (Chapters 1, 8 and 10).

13 Anticipatory and consummatory pleasures can be distinguished (Chapters 1 and 10). This distinction is useful in the study of bipolar disorder, depression, schizophrenia and drugs. Dopamine might have a role in anticipatory pleasure (Chapters 1 and 10).

14 The model suggested bears some similarity to that advanced by Freud (Chapter 3). Rather as with the Freudian id, the dopamine-based incentive system can energize and act at an unconscious level. However, its activation is not from an intrinsic energy source but from external incentives and internal representations of them. The cost–benefit calculation of action has features in common with the role of the ego. The process underlying intentional inhibition (Chapter 12) assimilates information from the culture, incorporates the 'inner policeman' (Chapter 18), and has similarities with the Freudian superego.

15 Up to a point, the strength of incentives as triggers to desire is increased by the novelty value of the incentive (Chapter 11) and the uncertainty of gaining it. Experimentation on non-humans suggests a dopamine basis to this. Addiction is commonly directed to particular specific targets (Chapter 17). Hence there is little to support the notion of a diffuse and undirected sexual drive (Chapter 3 and 4).

16 There can be a fracture line between wanting and liking, such that wanting can escalate without a corresponding increase in liking, as in addiction (Chapter 17), or wanting can decrease without a corresponding decrease in pleasure, as in some long-established

relationships (Chapter 10). It seems reasonable to suppose that altered dopamine activity lies at the basis of this.

17 Some individuals show an escalation in the expression of their sexual desire, revealed in such things as taste indexed by pornography (Chapter 16), addiction (Chapter 17) and violent sex (Chapters 20 and 21). This implies a comparison between some actual state and a modelled state, with a desire to bring the former into alignment with the latter.

18 Typically, women's sexual desire is more heavily dependent upon a partner's individual personality and such contextual factors as meaning and relationship dynamics than is men's desire (Chapter 7) and is less strongly expressed in overt wanting and searching. There is no reason to suggest a difference in liking between the sexes. Sexuality taken out of a personal one-to-one context is more of a male than female phenomenon, as revealed in such things as fetishes and anonymous voyeurism and exhibitionism (Chapter 19).

19 Sexual desire can exhibit strong interactions with attachment, anger/aggression and drug-seeking, as well as the reward derived from control (Chapters 1 and 15). When attachment fails and there is early conflict, sexual behaviour can be projected in a seriously aberrant direction (Chapters 20 and 21).

20 The drugs that form the strongest link to sexual desire, namely cocaine and methamphetamine, target primarily dopamine (Chapter 15) and can be associated with combined sex and drug addictions (Chapter 17).

21 In certain disorders, increasing dopamine activity, either naturally as in bipolar disorder or by medication as in sleeping sickness and Parkinson's disease, increases sexual desire (Chapter 8).

22 Stress can increase the tendency to put desire into action, exemplified by addiction (Chapter 17) and violent sex (Chapters 20 and 21), probably by sensitizing incentive salience and lowering inhibitions (Chapters 12).

23 Diffuse arousal can spill over into a specifically sexual arousal and desire (Chapter 9).

24 The direction that sexual desire takes sometimes appears to owe much to chance events early in development or even later (Chapter 18), exemplified by the acquisition of paraphilias, such as fetishes

(Chapter 19). A situation of high arousal, not necessarily sexual and even aversive, can later form a target of sexual desire.

25 Inhibition takes several forms (Chapter 12). Temptation arises from a struggle between desire and intentional inhibition. Inhibition appears to be deficient in cases of coercive sexuality (Chapter 20 and 21).

26 In development (Chapters 13 and 14), the first or at least a very early sexual experience sometimes has a profound effect on setting the direction that sexual behaviour will subsequently take. Behaviour is such as to try to repeat that first experience or masturbatory fantasy.

27 It appears that sexual fantasy mirrors reality and can interweave with it. They exploit some similar brain processes. Reality is incorporated into fantasy and it appears that fantasy can strengthen the tendency to enact the fantasy in behaviour (Chapters 16 and 21). The scenarios envisaged in fantasy can show evidence of escalation. Dopaminergic activity appears to be implicated here.

28 Viewing pornography can exhibit features in common with sexual behaviour in association with real humans, for example habituation, novelty-seeking, temporary relief from distress, escalation and addiction (Chapters 1 and 16).

29 The layered nature of the organization of the brain was revealed in two ways in the previous chapters: desire arising at a basic stimulus-driven level as well as a 'higher' cognitive level (Chapter 5); and inhibition arising from stimulus properties as well as cognitive calculations.

A number of similarities between coercive sexual offending and non-violent addiction are evident (Pithers et al., 1983), suggesting some common underlying features. For both, the individual experiences a transient boost in emotional state on engaging in the activity, often followed by extensive and delayed negative consequences. In both phenomena, the experience of negative emotion is a common precursor to relapse. The violent offender, as with the addicted person and the paedophile, might only escape from relapse by carefully planning ahead to avoid the danger of unexpected high-risk situations.

Consider the following common features between violent offending, exemplified by sexual homicide, and sexual addiction:

- The lure of immediate pleasure is followed by long-term costs.
- There is an ideal incentive that is pursued often with an extensive phase of searching.
- Negative emotional states such as stress can exacerbate each condition.
- Over repeated experiences, habituation can set in such that novelty is sought in order to maintain or increase intensity.
- Escalation occurs over time.
- Deprivation from a suitable outlet is felt as stressful and tension-evoking.
- Use can be made of props such as items of erotic underwear.
- Fantasy, pornography and masturbation provide virtual simulations of the interactions with real incentives.
- A changed state of conscious awareness can be obtained, sometimes termed 'dissociation'.
- Engaging in the target behaviour causes an elevation in mood.
- Following engagement in the behaviour, vows are sometimes made to quit but these usually are broken.
- Behaviour can lock into excitatory interaction with use of alcohol and illegal drugs.

In addition, there are two features which usually apply to sexual addiction and almost invariably apply to sexual homicide:

- It is a male behaviour.
- There is not a one-to-one reciprocal attachment.

There are a number of questions raised by the present study, amongst which are:

- Do genetic differences and early experience both have a role in determining sexual orientation, and, if so, how? Chapter 13 presented two somewhat conflicting accounts of the environmental factor. Is reconciliation possible?
- Do genetic differences and cultural influences intertwine in determining women's greater sexual modesty compared with that of men and, if so, how?
- Rather as with drug-taking, why does sexual activity for some people tip into escalation and addiction, whereas for others it remains under control? Can the notion of increasing incentive salience illuminate this?

NOTES

1. WHAT IS ENIGMATIC ABOUT SEXUAL DESIRE?

1. From *Looking for Spinoza* by Antonio Damasio (2003). Published by Hutchinson. Reprinted by permission of The Random House Group.
2. From 'Narratives of Desire in Mid-Age Women With and Without Arousal Difficulties' by Lori A. Brotto, Julia R. Heiman & Deborah L. Tolman in *Journal of Sex Research* 46:5 (2009). Published by Taylor & Francis Ltd, www.tandfonline.com. Reprinted by permission of the publisher.
3. One of the brain's chemical messengers, described shortly.

2. EXPLAINING DESIRE: MULTIPLE PERSPECTIVES

1. One of the founders of Christian existentialism.
2. The reader fully versed with biological psychology might wish to jump straight to the section 'Sex in comparison with other desires'.
3. I am grateful to Saroj Datta for this.
4. This describes 'working memory'.
5. The basal ganglia.

3. SEXUAL DESIRE IN A BROADER CONTEXT

1. From *Consilience: The Unity of Knowledge* by Edward O. Wilson (1998). Reprinted by permission of the author.
2. The contemporary language is of homeostasis and negative feedback.
3. In the Taoist tradition of China, men were urged not to waste their yang essence by ejaculation (Hatfield and Rapson, 2002).
4. From *Love, Sex and Marriage: Insights from Judaism, Christianity and Islam* by Dan Cohn-Sherbok, George D. Chryssides and Dawoud El-Alami (2013). Published by SCM Press. Reprinted by permission of the publisher.

4. AN INCENTIVE-BASED MODEL

1. From 'Discourse, Intercourse, and the Excluded Middle: Anthropology and the Problem of Sexual Experience' by Donald Tuzin in *Sexual Nature Sexual Culture* edited by Paul R. Abramson and Steven D. Pinkerton (1995). Published by University of Chicago Press. Reprinted by permission of the publisher.
2. See Chapter 2.

5. SEX AND LEVELS OF ORGANIZATION

1. Le cœur a ses raisons que la raison ne connaît point.
2. The brain region termed the amygdala is implicated here (LeDoux, 1999; Spiering and Everaerd, 2006).
3. The prefrontal cortex plays a primary role here.
4. Working memory.
5. http://en.wikipedia.org/wiki/Murder_of_David_Lynn_Harris
6. Panksepp (1982) suggests that jealousy might be a mixture of panic, rage and expectancy.

6. SEXUAL ATTRACTION

1. From *The Evolution Of Desire* by David M. Buss (2003). Published by Basic Books. Reprinted by permission of the Perseus Books Group.
2. The orbitofrontal cortex.

7. SHADES OF DESIRE FROM SIMPLE TO COMPLEX

1. From 'Individual Differences in Sexual Risk Taking' by John Bancroft in *The Role of Theory in Sex Research* edited by John Bancroft (2000). Published by and reprinted courtesy of Indiana University Press.
2. This is comparable to 'frustrative non-reward', though in this case the non-reward is, of course, self-imposed.
3. There was a slight but insignificant effect in this direction.

8. DETAILS OF THE BRAIN AND DESIRE

1. The cingulate cortex, insula (Craig, 2002) and lateral hypothalamus play a role here.
2. The insula and somatosensory cortex are involved in processing and interpreting information deriving from the interior of the body. A reasonable assumption is that this includes signals on the swelling of the genitals.

3. Regions implicated here include the cingulate cortex, claustrum and the nucleus accumbens.

4. Brain areas concerned with planning motor action are implicated here.

5. This refers to a pathway running from the ventral tegmental area of the brain to the nucleus accumbens and to the orbitofrontal region. See Chapter 2.

6. For example, at the nucleus accumbens.

7. Also activated is the dorsal anterior cingulate cortex, a region linked to the nucleus accumbens and involved in emotional processing and decision-making.

8. The ventromedial prefrontal cortex.

9. Described simply as 'the striatum', a region that, depending upon the particular investigator's terminology, either includes or is near to the nucleus accumbens

10. Specifically, the cortex.

11. Also the insula and claustrum.

12. Anterior cingulate, left insula and left orbitofrontal cortex.

13. Using the technique of electromyography.

14. Preoptic and ventromedial nuclei.

15. Paraventricular and dorsomedial nuclei.

16. Particularly the lateral prefrontal cortex (Chein et al., 2011).

17. The ventral striatum, a brain region including the nucleus accumbens, was particularly activated by conventional erotic images in participants with conventional desires but not by SM imagery. This same region was activated by SM imagery in participants with SM tastes. Other regions, e.g. amygdala, were activated under all conditions, pointing to general emotional arousal, irrespective of quality. In the latter case, there might have been differentiation but the resolution was insufficient to reveal it.

18. A pathway projecting from the substantia nigra to the striatum, not shown in Figure 2.10.

19. Orbitofrontal cortex, cingulate cortex, amygdala and hypothalamus.

20. Anterior cingulate and orbitofrontal cortex.

21. This term refers to the structure of the regions of the brain.

9. AROUSAL

1. A reference to Smith College, Massachusetts.

2. See Chapter 2.

3. These involve release of what are termed 'catecholamines', specifically adrenalin and noradrenalin.

4. This term means a stimulus other than an erotic one, for example, physical exercise.

5. The insula region of the cortex appears to form a biological basis where objective signals, e.g. from the genitals, are integrated with cognitive information on meaning and yield subjective levels of arousal (Spiering and Everaerd, 2006).

10. THE CONSEQUENCES OF SEXUAL BEHAVIOUR AND
ASSOCIATED EXPECTATIONS

1. Students often confuse negative reinforcement and punishment but they are quite distinct processes having opposite effects (Chapter 2).
2. Confronted with two levers, drug addicts can come to favour pressing that which delivers a shot of drug to them even though they cannot consciously register the arrival of drug, let alone appreciate any pleasure (see Robinson and Berridge, 1993).
3. A particular region of this nucleus, acting together with another structure, the ventral palladium.
4. The orbitofrontal cortex.

11. SEXUAL FAMILIARITY AND NOVELTY

1. 'Je sais mieux aimer! Je suis ta servant et ta concubine! Tu es mon roi, mon idole! Tu es bon! Tu es beau! Tu es intelligent! Tu es fort!' Il s'était tant de fois entendu dire ces choses, qu'elles n'avait pour lui rein d'original! Emma ressemblait à toutes les maîtresses; et le charme de la nouveauté, peu à peu tombant comme un vêtement...
2. In the basal ganglia.
3. Specifically in variants ('alleles') of a gene mediating differences in the mechanism ('transporter') underlying re-uptake of dopamine from the synaptic gap. This would be seen as differences in the clearance of dopamine following its release.

12. INHIBITION, CONFLICT AND TEMPTATION

1. Concerning the neurochemical basis of inhibition, acetylcholine is a neurochemical having general inhibitory properties on motivation antagonistic to those of dopamine (Hoebel et al., 2008).
2. With orgasm in human males, activity in the lateral hypothalamus falls and that in the anteroventral hypothalamus increases (Georgiadis et al., 2010).
3. Natural substances similar to cannabis.
4. Et il s'inclina doucement pour l'embrasser. Mais, au contact de ses lèvres, le souvenir de l'autre la saisit, et elle se passa la main sur son visage en frissonnant.
5. This result stands in contrast to that obtained by Istvan et al. (1983), described in Chapter 4.
6. CBN interview with David Brody, 9 March 2011.
7. The inferior frontal gyrus.

13. HOW DID SEXUAL DESIRE GET HERE?

1. From *Particulars of my Life* by B. F. Skinner (1976). Published by Jonathan Cape. Reprinted by permission of The Random House Group.
2. From *Particulars of my Life* by B. F. Skinner (1976). Published by Jonathan Cape. Reprinted by permission of The Random House Group.
3. From *Particulars of my Life* by B. F. Skinner (1976). Published by Jonathan Cape. Reprinted by permission of The Random House Group.
4. Alas, the conclusion is not without controversy. It does not necessarily involve comparing like with like (Shaver, 2006). The girls adopted into the family of the bridegroom-to-be were more likely to be ill-treated as compared to those staying with their biological parents, which might have disrupted their subsequent lives.

14. SETTING THE TRAJECTORY – LINK TO ADULT SEXUALITY

1. Including the lateral prefrontal cortex (Chein et al., 2011).
2. This term refers to the period in evolution during which humans evolved into their present form.
3. A fascinating article by McGeoch (2007) suggested why this might be.
4. Anterior hypothalamus/preoptic area (AH/POA) (Chapter 2).
5. Specifically termed 'androgens' in both sexes.
6. Kinsey et al. (1953, p. 14) suggest that, for both males and females, restrictions on 'premarital heterosexual contacts appear to be primary factors in the development of homosexual activities...'
7. From 'Narratives of Desire in Mid-Age Women With and Without Arousal Difficulties' by Lori A. Brotto, Julia R. Heiman & Deborah L. Tolman in *Journal of Sex Research* 46:5 (2009). Published by Taylor & Francis Ltd, www.tandfonline.com. Reprinted by permission of the publisher.

15. SEXUAL DESIRE IN INTERACTION

1. Alors, les appétits de la chair, les convoitises d'argent et les mélancholies de la passion, tout se confondit dans une même souffrance; et, au lieu d'en détourner sa pensée; elle l'y attachait davantage, s'excitant à la douleur et en cherchant partout les occasions. Elle s'irritait d'un plat mal servi ou d'une porte entrebâillée.
2. The anterior insular and anterior cingulate cortex.
3. My computer tried to change this to 'forward' but I insisted otherwise. It means to act in a way that is contrary to what is expected.
4. At least, this is the case in rats (Frohmader et al., 2010b) and it is most likely so in humans too.
5. Another name for methamphetamine.

16. REPRESENTATIONS OF SEX

1. For example, the ventral striatum, a region containing the nucleus accumbens.
2. Specifically, amongst other regions, the ventral globus pallidus, a region that receives an input from the nucleus accumbens.
3. Parts of the parietal lobes.
4. Regions of the basal ganglia.
5. For example, the nucleus accumbens.
6. Typically, the first statement might be that the 'President expressed his total faith in Mr X', the second and contradictory statement might be 'Now that Mr X has been shown to be a crook, the President keeps quiet about him' and the exculpatory statement could be 'The President is silent because he feels shocked and betrayed.'
7. Insula and lateral orbital cortex.

17. SEXUAL ADDICTION

1. The discussion of 'sexual addiction' usually relates to heterosexual men, though, as discussed in this chapter, women and gay men can also meet this description.
2. This is termed 'negative reinforcement'.
3. In other words, positive reinforcement.

18. VARIATIONS IN DESIRE: GENERAL PRINCIPLES

1. Though the claim that paedophilia can be explained in terms of an *invariable* link between early abuse and later becoming an abuser has little support (Feierman and Feierman, 2000).
2. A phenomenon that he terms 'phylogenetic regression'.
3. The orbitofrontal region of the prefrontal cortex is one such, acting in close interaction with the amygdala (Blair, 2006).
4. The prefrontal cortex and amygdala are involved in ethical decision-making, in calculating anticipated consequences of actions and using this information in planning and decision-making (Blair, 2006).

19. SOME FORMS OF DESIRE AT THE FRINGES

1. 'bouleversa complètement'.
2. The so-called 'sensory homunculus'.
3. The Washington journalist Dave Jamieson made a thorough investigation and had extensive exchanges of letters with Sweatt (www.alternet.org/story/53378/?page=entire).
4. In his autobiography, Graham Greene records a somewhat similar experience (Greene, 1971, p. 32). The English poet Algernon Swinburne is another example (C. Wilson, 1988).

20. THE TOXIC FUSION: VIOLENCE AND SEXUAL DESIRE

1. The term 'rape' used here refers to enforced sexual interaction usually involving penetrative sex of a woman victim by a man. However, there can be other forms such as homosexual rape and a woman demanding oral sex of a man at knife-point. The focus of this study is on the more common situation of the rape of a woman by a man.
2. Occasionally, it is argued that sexual arousal cannot be associated with rape since anger triggers the sympathetic branch of the ANS, whereas erection is mediated via the opposite, parasympathetic, branch. However, evidence suggests that both branches contribute to erection acting in combination (Zillmann, 1984, 1986). See also Bancroft (2009). Furthermore, erection is sometimes triggered under such conditions as anger and aggression, even outside an explicit sexual context (Chapter 13).

21. SEXUALLY ASSOCIATED (SERIAL) MURDER

1. The term 'operant' usually refers to behaviour. However, it can also be applied to mental events.
2. A large percentage of those involved with hardcore sadomasochism, where actual physical damage is inflicted, have suffered childhood surgical interventions. Their suffering has subsequently been eroticized (Doidge, 2007). It could be that some similar process was involved in Dahmer's development.
3. Ressler et al. (1992) noted a similar case of early trauma causing salience attribution to parts of the offender's own body.

REFERENCES

Abbey, A., Saenz, C., Buck, P. O., Parkhill, M. R., & Haymn, L. W. (2006). The effects of acute alcohol consumption, cognitive reserve, partner risk, and gender on sexual decision making. *Journal of Studies on Alcohol*, 67(1), 113–121.

Abdallah, R. T., & Simon, J. A. (2007). Testosterone therapy in women: its role in the management of hypoactive sexual desire disorder. *International Journal of Impotence Research*, 19, 458–463.

Abel, E. L. (1981). Marihuana and sex: a critical survey. *Drug and Alcohol Dependence*, 8, 1–22.

Abel, G. G., Coffey, L., & Osborn, C. A. (2008). Sexual arousal patterns: normal and deviant. *Psychiatric Clinics of North America*, 31(4), 643–655.

Abel, G. G., & Osborn, C. A. (1995). Pedophilia. In L. Diamant & R. McAnulty (Eds), *The Psychology of Sexual Orientation, Behavior, and Identity: A Handbook* (pp. 270–281). Westport, CT: Greenwood Publishing Group, Inc.

Abel, G. G., & Rouleau, J. L. (1990). The nature and extent of sexual assault. In W. L. Marshall, D. R. Laws, & H. L. Barbaree (Eds), *Handbook of Sexual Assault: Issues, Theories, and Treatment of the Offender* (pp. 9–20). New York: Plenum Press.

Abler, B., Walter, H., & Erk, S. (2005). Neural correlates of frustration. *NeuroReport*, 16(7), 669–672.

Abramson, P. R., & Pinkerton, S. D. (1995). *Sexual Nature – Sexual Culture*. Chicago: The University of Chicago Press.

Adams, D. B., Ross Gold, A., & Burt, A. D. (1978). Rise in female-initiated sexual activity at ovulation and its suppression by oral contraceptives. *The New England Journal of Medicine*, 299(21), 1145–1150.

Ågmo, A. (2007). *Functional and Dysfunctional Sexual Behavior*. Academic Press: London.

Agnew, R. (1992). Foundation for a general strain theory of crime and delinquency. *Criminology*, 30(1), 47–87.

Akers, R. L. (1985). *Deviant Behavior: A Social Learning Approach* (3rd edn). Belmont, CA: Wadsworth Publishing Company.

Alcaro, A., Huber, R., & Panksepp, J. (2007). Behavioral functions of the mesolimbic dopaminergic system: an affective neuroethological perspective. *Brain Research Reviews*, 56(2), 283–321.

Alexander, B. K. (2008). *The Globalization of Addiction: A Study in the Poverty of the Spirit*. Oxford: Oxford University Press.

Alexander, G. M., Swerdloff, R. S., Wang, C., et al. (1997). Androgen–behavior correlations in hypogonadal men and eugonadal men, 1: mood and response to auditory sexual stimuli. *Hormones and Behavior*, 31(2), 110–119.

456

Anderson, J. (1994). Genesis of a serial killer. Retrieved from www.angelar.com/~jeremy/genesis.html

Andreasen, N. (1987). Affective flattening: evaluation and diagnostic significance. In D. C. Clark & J. Fawcett (Eds), *Anhedonia and Affect Deficit States* (pp. 15–31). New York: PMA Publishing Corp.

Anonymous. (1998). A serial killer's perspective. In R. M. Holmes & S. T. Holmes (Eds), *Contemporary Perspectives on Serial Murder* (pp. 123–131). Thousand Oaks: Sage Publications.

Anselme, P. (2010). The uncertainty processing theory of motivation. *Behavioural Brain Research*, 208(2), 291–310.

Apter, M. (2007). *Danger: Our Quest for Excitement*. Oxford: One World.

Ariely, D., & Loewenstein, G. (2006). The heat of the moment: the effect of sexual arousal on sexual decision making. *Journal of Behavioral Decision Making*, 19, 87–98.

Arieti, S. (1974). *Interpretation of Schizophrenia*. New York: Basic Books.

Arieti, S. (1975). Sexual problems of the schizophrenic and preschizophrenics. In M. Sandler & G. L. Gessa (Eds), *Sexual Behaviour: Pharmacology and Biochemistry* (pp. 277–282). New York: Raven Press.

Arrigo, B. A., & Purcell, C. E. (2001). Explaining paraphilias and lust murder: toward an integrated model. *International Journal of Offender Therapy and Comparative Criminology*, 45(1), 6–31.

Assadi, S. M., Yucel, M., & Pantelis, C. (2009). Dopamine modulates neural networks involved in effort-based decision-making. *Neuroscience and Biobehavioral Reviews*, 33(3), 383–393.

Assalian, P., Fraser, R., Tempier, R., & Cohen, D. (2000). Sexuality and quality of life of patients with schizophrenia. *International Journal of Psychiatry in Clinical Practice*, 4(1), 29–33.

Avicenna. (1025/1999). *The Canon of Medicine*, ed. L. Bakhtiar. Chicago: Kazi Publications.

Bagley, C. (1969). Incest behavior and incest taboo. *Social Problems*, 16(4), 505–519.

Bailey, C. (2002). Upshifting and downshifting the triune brain: roles in individual and social pathology. In G. A. Cory & R. Gardner (Eds), *The Evolutionary Neuroethology of Paul MacLean* (pp. 317–343). Westport, CT: Praeger.

Bailey, R. C., & Aunger, R. V. (1995). Sexuality, infertility and sexually transmitted disease among farmers and foragers in Central Africa. In P. R. Abramson & S. D. Pinkerton (Eds), *Sexual Nature – Sexual Culture* (pp. 195–222). Chicago: The University of Chicago Press.

Baldwin, D. S. (2001). Depression and sexual dysfunction. *British Medical Bulletin*, 57, 81–99.

Baldwin, J. D., & Baldwin, J. I. (1997). Gender differences in sexual interest. *Archives of Sexual Behavior*, 26(2), 181–210.

Bancroft, J. (2000). Individual differences in sexual risk taking: a biopsychosocial theoretical approach. In J. Bancroft (Ed.), *The Role of Theory in Sex Research*. Bloomington: Indiana University Press (pp. 177–212).

Bancroft, J. (2007). Discussion. In E. Janssen (Ed.), *The Psychophysiology of Sex* (p. 431). Bloomington: Indiana University Press.

Bancroft, J. (2009). *Human Sexuality and its Problems*. Edinburgh: Churchill Livingstone.

Bancroft, J., & Graham, C. A. (2011). The varied nature of women's sexuality: unresolved issues and a theoretical approach. *Hormones and Behavior*, 59(5), 717–729.

Bancroft, J., & Vukadinovic, Z. (2004). Sexual addiction, sexual compulsivity, sexual impulsivity, or what? Toward a theoretical model. *Journal of Sex Research*, 41(3), 225–234.

Bandura, A. (1977). *Social Learning Theory*. Engelwood Cliffs: Prentice-Hall.

Barbaree, H. E. (1990). Stimulus control of sexual arousal: its role in sexual assault. In W. L. Marshall, D. R. Laws, & H. E. Barbaree (Eds), *Handbook of Sexual Assault: Issues, Theories, and Treatment of the Offender* (pp. 115–142). New York: Plenum Press.

Bardo, M. T., Donohew, R. L., & Harrington, N. G. (1996). Psychobiology of novelty seeking and drug seeking behavior. *Behavioural Brain Research*, 77(1–2), 23–43.

Bargh, J. A., Raymond, P., Pryor, J. B., & Strack, F. (1995). Attractiveness of the underling: an automatic power → sex association and its consequences for sexual harassment and aggression. *Journal of Personality and Social Psychology*, 68, 768–781.

Barker-Benfield, G. J. (1976). *The Horrors of the Half-Known Life: Male Attitudes Towards Women and Sexuality in Nineteenth-Century America*. New York: Harper Colophon Books.

Barlow, D. H. (1986). Causes of sexual dysfunction: the role of anxiety and cognitive interference. *Journal of Consulting and Clinical Psychology*, 54(2), 140–148.

Bart, P. B., & Jozsa, M. (1980). Dirty books, dirty films, and dirty data. In L. Lederer (Ed.), *Take Back the Night: Women on Pornography* (pp. 204–217). New York: William Morrow and Company.

Bartels, R. M., & Gannon, T. A. (2011). Understanding the sexual fantasies of sex offenders and their correlates. *Aggression and Violent Behavior*, 16(6), 551–561.

Basson, R. (2000). The female sexual response: a different model. *Journal of Sex & Marital Therapy*, 26(1), 51–65.

Basson, R. (2002). Women's sexual desire – disordered or misunderstood? *Journal of Sex & Marital Therapy*, 28, 17–28.

Baumeister, R. F. (1988). Masochism as escape from self. *Journal of Sex Research*, 25(1), 28–59.

Baumeister, R. F. (1991). *Escaping the Self: Alcoholism, Spirituality, Masochism, and Other Flights from the Burden of Selfhood*. New York: BasicBooks.

Baumeister, R. F. (2000). Gender differences in erotic plasticity: the female sex drive as socially flexible and responsive. *Psychological Bulletin*, 126, 347–374.

Baumeister, R. F., Masicampo, E. J., & Vohs, K. D. (2011). Do conscious thoughts cause behavior? In S. T. Fiske, D. L. Schacter, & S. E. Taylor (Eds), *Annual Review of Psychology* (Vol. 62, pp. 331–361).

Baumeister, R. F. and Vohs, K. D. (2001). Narcissism as addiction to esteem. *Psychological Inquiry*, 12, 206–210.

Beach, F. A. (1947). A review of physiological and psychological studies of sexual behavior in mammals. *Physiological Reviews*, 27, 240–307.

Bechara, A., Damasio, H., & Damasio, A. R. (2000). Emotion, decision making and the orbitofrontal cortex. *Cerebral Cortex*, 10(3), 295–307. doi: 10.1093/cercor/10.3.295

Bégue, L., Bushman, B. J., Zerhouni, O., Subra, B., & Ourabah, M. (2013). 'Beauty is in the eye of the beer holder': people who think they are attractive also think they are attractive. *British Journal of Psychology*, 104(2), 225–234. doi: 10.1111/j.2044-8295.2012.02114.x

Bem, D. J. (1996). Exotic becomes erotic: a developmental theory of sexual orientation. *Psychological Review*, 103(2), 320–335. doi: 10.1037//0033-295x.103.2.320

Bendick, J. (2002). *Galen and the Gateway to Medicine*. Bathgate: Bethlehem Books.

Bentham, J. (1781/1988). *The Principles of Morals and Legislation*. New York: Prometheus Books.

Berger, J., & Shiv, B. (2011). Food, sex and the hunger for distinction. *Journal of Consumer Psychology*, 21(4), 464–472. doi: 10.1016/j.jcps.2011.01.003

Berglund, H., Lindström, P., & Savic, I. (2006). Brain response to putative pheromones in lesbian women. *Proceedings of the National Academy of Sciences of the United States of America*, 103(21), 8269–8274. doi: 10.1073/pnas.0600331103

Berridge, K. C. (2004). Motivation concepts in behavioral neuroscience. *Physiology & Behavior*, 81(2), 179–209. doi: 10.1016/j.physbeh.2004.02.004

Berridge, K. C., & Kringelbach, M. L. (2013). Neuroscience of affect: brain mechanisms of pleasure and displeasure. *Current Opinion in Neurobiology*, 23(3), 294–303. doi: http://dx.doi.org/10.1016/j.conb.2013.01.017

Berridge, K. C., & Valenstein, E. S. (1991). What psychological process mediates feeding evoked by electrical-stimulation of the lateral hypothalamus. *Behavioral Neuroscience*, 105(1), 3–14. doi: 10.1037/0735-7044.105.1.3

Berry-Dee, C. (2003). *Talking with Serial Killers*. London: John Blake.

Berry-Dee, C. (2007). *Face to Face with Serial Killers*. London: John Blake.

Berscheid, E., & Regan, P. C. (2005). *The Psychology of Interpersonal Relationships*. New York: Prentice-Hall.

Berscheid, E., & Walster, E. (1974). A little bit about love. In T. Huston (Ed.), *Foundations of Interpersonal Attraction* (pp. 355–381). New York: Academic Press.

Bhutta, M. F. (2007). Sex and the nose: human pheromonal responses. *Journal of the Royal Society of Medicine, 100*(6), 268–274. doi: 10.1258/jrsm.100.6.268

Bianchi-Demicheli, F., Cojan, Y., Waber, L., et al. (2011). Neural bases of hypoactive sexual desire disorder in women: an event-related fMRI study. *Journal of Sexual Medicine, 8*, 2546–2559.

Bindra, D. (1978). How adaptive-behavior is produced: perceptual-motivational alternative to response-reinforcement. *Behavioral and Brain Sciences, 1*(1), 41–52.

Binet, A. (1887). Le fétichisme dans l'amour. *Revue Philosophique de la France et de l'Étranger, 24*, 143–167.

Blackburn, J. R., Pfaus, J. G., & Phillips, A. G. (1992). Dopamine functions in appetitive and defensive behaviors. *Progress in Neurobiology, 39*(3), 247–279. doi: 10.1016/0301-0082(92)90018-a

Blaicher, W., Gruber, D., Bieglmayer, C., et al. (1999). The role of oxytocin in relation to female sexual arousal. *Gynecologic and Obstetric Investigation, 47*(2), 125–126. doi: 10.1159/000010075

Blair, R. J. R. (2006). The emergence of psychopathy: implications for the neuropsychological approach to developmental disorders. *Cognition, 101*(2), 414–442.

Blair, R. J. R., Peschardt, K. S., Budhani, S., Mitchell, D. G. V., & Pine, D. S. (2006). The development of psychopathy. *Journal of Child Psychology and Psychiatry, 47*(3–4), 262–276. doi: 10.1111/j.1469-7610.2006.01596.x

Bogaert, A. F. (2006). Toward a conceptual understanding of asexuality. *Review of General Psychology, 10*(3), 241–250. doi: 10.1037/1089-2680.10.3.241

Bokhour, B. G., Clark, J. A., Inui, T. S., Silliman, R. A., & Talcott, J. A. (2001). Sexuality after treatment for early prostate cancer: exploring the meanings of 'erectile dysfunction'. *Journal of General Internal Medicine, 16*(10), 649–655. doi: 10.1111/j.1525-1497.2001.00832.x

Bolles, R. (1975). *Theory of Motivation*. New York: Harper and Row.

Booth, A., & Dabbs, J. M. (1993). Testosterone and men's marriages. *Social Forces, 72*(2), 463–477. doi: 10.2307/2579857

Borg, C., de Jong, P. J., & Schultz, W. W. (2010a). Vaginismus and dyspareunia: automatic vs. deliberate disgust responsivity. *Journal of Sexual Medicine, 7*, 2149–2157.

Borg, C., de Jong, P. J., & Schultz, W. W. (2010b). Vaginismus and dyspareunia: relationship with general and sex-related moral standards. *Journal of Sexual Medicine, 8*, 223–231.

Borg, J. S., Lieberman, D., & Kiehl, K. A. (2008). Infection, incest, and iniquity: investigating the neural correlates of disgust and morality. *Journal of Cognitive Neuroscience, 20*(9), 1529–1546.

Both, S., Everaerd, W., & Laan, E. (2006). Desire emerges from excitement: a psychophysiological perspective on sexual motivation. In E. Janssen (Ed.), *The Psychophysiology of Sex* (pp. 327–339). Bloomington: Indiana University Press.

Both, S., Laan, E., & Everaerd, W. (2011). Focusing 'hot' or focusing 'cool': attentional mechanisms in sexual arousal in men and women. *Journal of Sexual Medicine, 8*(1), 167–179. doi: 10.1111/j.1743-6109.2010.02051.x

Both, S., Laan, E., Spiering, M., et al. (2008a). Appetitive and aversive classical conditioning of female sexual response. *Journal of Sexual Medicine, 5*(6), 1386–1401. doi: 10.1111/j.1743-6109.2008.00815.x

Both, S., Spiering, M., Laan, E., et al. (2008b). Unconscious classical conditioning of sexual arousal: evidence for the conditioning of female genital arousal to subliminally presented sexual stimuli. *Journal of Sexual Medicine*, 5(1), 100–109. doi: 10.1111/j.1743–6109.2007.00643.x

Both, S., van Boxtel, G., Stekelenburg, J., Everaerd, W., and Laan, E. (2005). Modulation of spinal reflexes by sexual films of increasing intensity. *Psychophysiology*, 42, 726–731.

Bowlby, J. (1982). *Attachment and Loss: Vol. 1. Attachment*. New York: Basic Books.

Brand, R. (2007). *My Booky Wook*. London: Hodder and Stoughton.

Brauer, M., van Leeuwen, M., Janssen, E., et al. (2012). Attentional and affective processing of sexual stimuli in women with hypoactive sexual desire disorder. *Archives of Sexual Behavior*, 41(4), 891–905. doi: 10.1007/s10508–011–9820–7

Braun, C. M. J., Dumont, M., Duval, J., Hamel-Hebert, I., & Godbout, L. (2003). Brain modules of hallucination: an analysis of multiple patients with brain lesions. *Journal of Psychiatry & Neuroscience*, 28(6), 432–449.

Breiter, H. C., Aharon, I., Kahneman, D., Dale, A., & Shizgal, P. (2001). Functional imaging of neural responses to expectancy and experience of monetary gains and losses. *Neuron*, 30(2), 619–639.

Breland, K., & Breland, M. (1961). The misbehavior of organisms. *American Psychologist*, 16(11), 681–684. doi: 10.1037/h0040090

Britton, P. (1998). *The Jigsaw Man*. London: Corgi Books.

Brome, V. (1979). *Havelock Ellis, Philosopher of Sex: A Biography*. London: Routledge and Kegan Paul.

Brotto, L. A., Heiman, J. R., & Tolman, D. L. (2009). Narratives of desire in mid-age women with and without arousal difficulties. *Journal of Sex Research*, 46, 387–398.

Brotto, L. A., Knudson, G., Inskip, J., Rhodes, K., & Erskine, Y. (2010). Asexuality: a mixed-methods approach. *Archives of Sexual Behavior*, 39(3), 599–618. doi: 10.1007/s10508–008–9434–x

Brotto, L. A., & Yule, M. A. (2011). Physiological and subjective sexual arousal in self-identified asexual women. *Archives of Sexual Behavior*, 40(4), 699–712. doi: 10.1007/s10508–010–9671–7

Brown, I. (1997). A theoretical model of the behavioural addictions – applied to offending. In J. E. Hodge, M. McMurran & C. R. Hollin (Eds), *Addicted to Crime?* (pp. 13–65). Chichester: Wiley.

Brownmiller, S. (1975). *Against our Will: Men, Women and Rape*. New York: Simon and Schuster.

Buckholtz, J. W., Treadway, M. T., Cowan, R. L., et al. (2010). Mesolimbic dopamine reward system hypersensitivity in individuals with psychopathic traits. *Nature Neuroscience*, 13(4), 419–421. doi: 10.1038/nn.2510

Bullough, V. L. (1987). A historical approach. In J. H. Geer & W. T. O'Donohue (Eds), *Theories of Human Sexuality* (pp. 49–63). New York: Plenum Press.

Burgess, A., Hartman, C., Ressler, R., Douglas, J. E., & McCormack, A. (1986). Sexual homicide: a motivational model. *Journal of Interpersonal Violence*, 1, 251–272.

Burke, A. R., Renner, K. J., Forster, G. L., & Watt, M. J. (2010). Adolescent social defeat alters neural, endocrine and behavioral responses to amphetamine in adult male rats. *Brain Research*, 1352(0), 147–156. doi: http://dx.doi.org/10.1016/j.brainres.2010.06.062

Bushman, B. J., Bonacci, A. M., van Dijk, M., & Baumeister, R. F. (2003). Narcissism, sexual refusal, and aggression: testing a narcissistic reactance model of sexual coercion. *Journal of Personality and Social Psychology*, 84(5), 1027–1040. doi: 10.1037/0022–3514.84.5.1027

Buss, D. M. (2003). *The Evolution of Desire*. New York: Basic Books.

Buss, D. M. (2005). *The Murderer Next Door: Why the Mind is Designed to Kill*. New York: The Penguin Press.

Byck, R. (1974). *Cocaine Papers by Sigmund Freud*. New York: Stonehill Publishing.

Byrne, D. (1986). Introduction: the study of sexual behavior as a multidisciplinary venture. In D. Byrne & K. Kelley (Eds), *Alternative Approaches to the Study of Sexual Behavior* (pp. 1–12). Hillsdale: Lawrence Erlbaum.

Byrne, D., & Osland, J. A. (2000). Sexual fantasy and erotica/pornography: internal and external imagery. In L. T. Szuchman & F. Muscarella (Eds), *Psychological Perspectives on Human Sexuality* (pp. 283–305). New York: John Wiley.

Cabib, S., & Puglisi-Allegra, S. (2012). The mesoaccumbens dopamine in coping with stress. *Neuroscience and Biobehavioral Reviews*, 36(1), 79–89. doi: 10.1016/j.neubiorev.2011.04.012

Calhoun, K. S., & Wilson, A. E. (2000). Rape and sexual aggression. In L. T. Szuchman & F. Muscarella (Eds), *Psychological Perspectives on Human Sexuality* (pp. 573–602). New York John Wiley.

Cameron, D., & Frazer, E. (1987). *The Lust to Kill: A Feminist Investigation of Sexual Murder.* Cambridge: Polity Press.

Carlisle, A. C. (1998). The divided self: toward an understanding of the dark side of the serial killer. In R. M. Holmes & S. T. Holmes (Eds), *Contemporary Perspectives on Serial Murder* (pp. 85–100). Thousand Oaks: Sage Publications.

Carlo, P. (2010). *The Night Stalker.* Edinburgh: Mainstream Publishing.

Carmichael, M. S., Warburton, V. L., Dixen, J., & Davidson, J. M. (1994). Relationships among cardiovascular, muscular, and oxytocin responses during human sexual activity. *Archives of Sexual Behavior*, 23(1), 59–79.

Carnes, P. (1989). *Contrary to Love: Helping the Sexual Addict.* Center City, MN: Hazelden.

Carnes, P. (2001). *Out of the Shadows: Understanding Sexual Addiction.* Hazeldon: Hazeldon Information and Educational Series.

Carver, C. S., & Harmon-Jones, E. (2009). Anger is an approach-related affect: evidence and implications. *Psychological Bulletin*: 135, 183–204.

Carver, C. S., Johnson, S. L., & Joormann, J. (2009). Two-mode models of self-regulation as a tool for conceptualizing effects of the serotonin system in normal behavior and diverse disorders. *Current Directions in Psychological Science*, 18, 195–199.

Carver, C. S., & Scheier, M. F. (1990). Origins and functions of positive and negative affect: a control-process view. *Psychological Review*, 97(1), 19–35.

Carver, C. S., & White, T. L. (1994). Behavioral inhibition, behavioral activation, and affective responses to impending reward and punishment – the BIS BAS scales. *Journal of Personality and Social Psychology*, 67(2), 319–333. doi: 10.1037/0022-3514.67.2.319

Casanova, G. (1798/1958). *The Memoirs of Casanova.* London: Transworld Publishers.

Casey, B. J., & Jones, R. M. (2010). Neurobiology of the adolescent brain and behavior: implications for substance use disorders. *Journal of the American Academy of Child and Adolescent Psychiatry*, 49(12), 1189–1201.

Chan, H. C., & Heide, K. M. (2009). Sexual homicide. *Trauma, Violence, & Abuse*, 10(1), 31–54. doi: 10.1177/1524838008326478

Chan, H. C., Myers, W. C., & Heide, K. M. (2010). An empirical analysis of 30 years of US juvenile and adult sexual homicide offender data: race and age differences in the victim–offender relationship. *Journal of Forensic Sciences*, 55, 1282–1290.

Chaney, L. (2005). *Hide-and-Seek with Angels: A Life of J. M. Barrie.* London: Hutchinson.

Chaney, M. P., & Chang, C. Y. (2005). A trio of turmoil for internet sexually addicted men who have sex with men: boredom proneness, social connectedness, and dissociation. *Sexual Addiction & Compulsivity*, 12, 3–18.

Chapman, H. A., Kim, D. A., Susskind, J. M., & Anderson, A. K. (2009). In bad taste: evidence for the oral origins of moral disgust. *Science*, 323(5918), 1222–1226. doi: 10.1126/science.1165565

Chappell, D., Geis, G., Schafer, S., & Siegel, L. (1971). Forcible rape: a comparative study of offenses known to the police in Boston and Los Angeles. In J. M. Henslin (Ed.), *Studies in the Sociology of Sex* (pp. 169–190). New York: Appleton-Century-Crofts.

Chasin, C. D. (2011). Theoretical issues in the study of asexuality. *Archives of Sexual Behavior*, 4(4), 713–723.

Cheever, S. (2008). *Desire: Where Sex Meets Addiction*. New York: Simon and Schuster.

Chein, J., Albert, D., O'Brien, L., Uckert, K., & Steinberg, L. (2011). Peers increase adolescent risk taking by enhancing activity in the brain's reward circuitry. *Developmental Science*, 14(2), F1-F10. doi: 10.1111/j.1467-7687.2010.01035.x

Chivers, M. L., & Bailey, J. M. (2005). A sex difference in features that elicit genital response. *Biological Psychology*, 70(2), 115–120.

Clark, R. D., & Hatfield, E. (1989). Gender differences in receptivity to sexual offers. *Journal of Psychology and Human Sexuality*, 2, 39–55.

Cohen, D. (2010). *Freud on Coke*. London: Cutting Edge Press.

Cohn-Sherbok, D., Chryssides, G. D., and El Alami, D. (2013). *Love, Sex and Marriage: Insights from Judaism, Christianity and Islam*. London: SCM Press.

Collins, N. L., & Read, S. J. (1994). Cognitive representations of attachment: the structure and function of working models. In K. Bartholomew & D. Perlman (Eds), *Attachment Processes in Adulthood. Advances in Personal Relationships* (Vol. 5, pp. 53–90). London: Jessica Kingsley.

Conley, T. D. (2011). Perceived proposer personality characteristics and gender differences in acceptance of casual sex offers. *Journal of Personality and Social Psychology*, 100(2), 309–329. doi: 10.1037/a0022152

Conrad, L. I., Neve, M., Nutton, V., Porter, R., & Wear, A. (1995). *The Western Medical Tradition 800 BC to AD 1800*. Cambridge: Cambridge University Press.

Cooper, M. L., Pioli, M., Levitt, A., et al. (2006). Attachment styles, sex motives, and sexual behavior: evidence for gender-specific expressions of attachment dynamics. In M. Mikulincer & G. S. Goodman (Eds), *Dynamics of Romantic Love: Attachment, Caregiving and Sex* (pp. 243–274). New York: The Guilford Press.

Cooper, M. L., Talley, A. E., Sheldon, M. S., Levitt, A., & Barber, L. L. (2008). A dyadic perspective on approach and avoidance motives for sexual behavior. In A. J. Elliot (Ed.), *Handbook of Approach and Avoidance Motivation* (pp. 615–631). New York: Psychology Press.

Corley, M. D. and Hook, J. N. (2012). Women, female sex and love addicts, and use of the Internet. *Sexual Addiction and Compulsivity*, 19, 53–76.

Cornwell, R. E., Boothroyd, L., Burt, D. M., et al. (2004). Concordant preferences for opposite-sex signals? Human pheromones and facial characteristics. *Proceedings of the Royal Society B: Biological Sciences*, 271(1539), 635–640. doi: 10.1098/rspb.2003.2649

Corr, P. J. (2008). *The Reinforcement Sensitivity Theory of Personality*. Cambridge: Cambridge University Press.

Cory, G. A. (2000). *Toward Consilience: The Bioneurological Basis of Behavior, Thought, Experience, and Language*. New York: Kluwer Academic.

Cosmides, L., & Tooby, J. (1995). From evolution to adaptations to behavior: toward an integrated evolutionary psychology. In R. Wong (Ed.), *Biological Perspectives on Motivated Activities* (pp. 11–74). Norwood: Ablex Publishing.

Costa, V. D., Lang, P. J., Sabatinelli, D., Versace, F. and Bradley, M. M. (2010). Emotional imagery: assessing pleasure and arousal in the brain's reward circuitry. *Human Brain Mapping*, 31, 1446-1457.

Cousins, D. A., Butts, K., & Young, A. H. (2009). The role of dopamine in bipolar disorder. *Bipolar Disorders*, 11, 787–806.

Craig, A. D. (2002). How do you feel? Interoception: the sense of the physiological condition of the body. *Nature Reviews Neuroscience*, 3(8), 655–666. doi: 10.1038/nrn894

Crepault, C., Abraham, G., Porto, R., & Couture, M. (1977). Erotic imagery in women. In R. Gemme & C. C. Wheeler (Eds), *Progress in Sexology* (pp. 267–283). New York: Plenum Press.

Dal Cin, S., MacDonald, T. K., Fong, G. T., Zanna, M. P., & Elton-Marshall, T. E. (2006). Remembering the message: the use of a reminder cue to increase condom use following a safer sex intervention. *Health Psychology*, 25(3), 438–443. doi: 10.1037/0278–6133.25.3.438

Damasio, A. (2003). *Looking for Spinoza: Joy, Sorrow, and the Feeling Brain*. London: William Heinemann.

Danovitch, J., & Bloom, P. (2009). Children's extension of disgust to physical and moral events. *Emotion*, 9(1), 107–112.

Davis, D. (1991). *The Jeffrey Dahmer Story: An American Nightmare*. New York: St Martin's Press.

Davis, D. (2006). Attachment-related pathways to sexual coercion. In M. Mikulincer & G. S. Goodman (Eds), *Dynamics of Romantic Love: Attachment, Caregiving and Sex* (pp. 293–336). New York: The Guilford Press.

Dawson, L. (2008). *Lovesickness and Gender in Early Modern English Literature*. Oxford: Oxford University Press.

de Jong, P., van Overveld, M., Weijmar Schultz, W., Peters, M., & Buwalda, F. (2009). Disgust and contamination sensitivity in vaginismus and dyspareunia. *Archives of Sexual Behavior*, 38(2), 244–252. doi: 10.1007/s10508–007–9240-x

De Leon, G., & Wexler, H. K. (1973). Heroin addiction: its relation to sexual behavior and sexual experience. *Journal of Abnormal Psychology*, 81(1), 36–38.

De Witt Huberts, J. C., Evers, C., & De Ridder, D. T. D. (2012). License to sin: self-licensing as a mechanism underlying hedonic consumption. *European Journal of Social Psychology*, 42(4), 490–496. doi: 10.1002/ejsp.861

Decety, J., & Ickes, W. (2011). *The Social Neuroscience of Empathy*. Cambridge, MA: The MIT Press.

DeFrank, T. M. (2007). *Write it when I'm Gone: Remarkable off-the-Record Conversations with Gerald R. Ford*. New York: G. P. Putnam's Sons.

Demos, K. E., Heatherton, T. F., & Kelley, W. M. (2012). Individual differences in nucleus accumbens activity to food and sexual images predict weight gain and sexual behavior. *The Journal of Neuroscience*, 32(16), 5549–5552. doi: 10.1523/jneurosci.5958–11.2012

DeWall, C. N., Maner, J. K., Deckman, T., & Rouby, D. A. (2011). Forbidden fruit: inattention to attractive alternatives provokes implicit relationship reactance. *Journal of Personality and Social Psychology*, 100(4), 621–629.

Dewitte, M. (2012). Different perspectives on the sex-attachment link: towards an emotion-motivational account. *Journal of Sex Research*, 49, 105–124.

Dewitte, M., Van Lankveld, J., & Crombez, G. (2011). Understanding sexual pain: a cognitive-motivational account. *Pain*, 152(2), 251–253.

Diamond, L. M. (2003). What does sexual orientation orient? A biobehavioral model distinguishing romantic love and sexual desire. *Psychological Review*, 110(1), 173–192. doi: 10.1037/0033–295x.110.1.173

Diamond, L. M. (2006). How do I love thee? Implications of attachment theory for understanding same-sex love and desire. In M. Mikulincer & G. S. Goodman (Eds), *Dynamics of Romantic Love: Attachment, Caregiving and Sex* (pp. 275–292). New York: The Guilford Press.

Diamond, L. M. (2007). A dynamical systems approach to the development and expression of female same-sex sexuality. *Perspectives on Psychological Science*, 2(2), 142–161. doi: 10.1111/j.1745–6916.2007.00034.x

Dittmar, H., & Drury, J. (2000). Self-image – is it in the bag? A qualitative comparison between 'ordinary' and 'excessive' consumers. *Journal of Economic Psychology*, 21(2), 109–142. doi: 10.1016/s0167–4870(99)00039–2

Dixon, J. K. (1984). The commencement of bisexual activity in swinging married women over age thirty. *Journal of Sex Research*, 20, 71–90.

Doidge, N. (1990). Appetitive pleasure states: a biopsychoanalytic model of the pleasure threshold, mental representation, and defense. In S. Bone and R. Glick (Eds),

Pleasure Beyond the Pleasure Principle (pp. 138–173). New Haven: Yale University Press.

Doidge, N. (2007). *The Brain that Changes Itself*: London: Penguin Books.

Donnerstein, E. (1980). Aggressive erotica and violence against women. *Journal of Personality and Social Psychology, 39*(2), 269–277.

Donnerstein, E., & Hallam, J. (1978). Facilitating effects of erotica on aggression against women. *Journal of Personality and Social Psychology, 36*(11), 1270–1277.

Donnerstein, E., & Malamuth, N. (1997). Pornography: its consequences on the observer. In L. B. Schlesinger & E. Revitch (Eds), *Sexual Dynamics of Anti-Social Behavior* (2nd ed., pp. 30–49). Springfield: Charles C. Thomas.

Doskoch, P. (1995). The safest sex. *Psychology Today, 28*, 46–49.

Douglas, J., & Olshaker, M. (2006). *Mindhunter*. London: Arrow Books.

Dutton, D. G., & Aron, A. P. (1974). Some evidence for heightened sexual attraction under conditions of high anxiety. *Journal of Personality and Social Psychology, 30*(4), 510–517. doi: 10.1037/h0037031

Easton, J. A., Confer, J. C., Goetz, C. D., & Buss, D. M. (2010). Reproduction expediting: sexual motivations, fantasies, and the ticking biological clock. *Personality and Individual Differences, 49*(5), 516–520.

Ebel-Lam, A. P., MacDonald, T. K., Zanna, M. P., & Fong, G. T. (2009). An experimental investigation of the interactive effects of alcohol and sexual arousal on intentions to have unprotected sex. *Basic and Applied Social Psychology, 31*(3), 226–233. doi: 10.1080/01973530903058383

Eisenberger, N. I. (2012). Broken hearts and broken bones: a neural perspective on the similarities between social and physical pain. *Current Directions in Psychological Science, 21*(1), 42–47. doi: 10.1177/0963721411429455

Eisenman, R. (1982). Sexual behavior as related to sex fantasies and experimental manipulation of authoritarianism and creativity. *Journal of Personality and Social Psychology, 43*(4), 853–860.

Ekman, P., Sorenson, E. R., & Friesen, W.V. (1969). Pan-cultural elements of emotion: new findings, new questions. *Psychological Science, 3*, 34–38.

Elliot, A. J. (2008). Approach and avoidance motivation. In A. J. Elliot (Ed.), *Handbook of Approach and Avoidance Motivation* (pp. 3–14). New York: Psychology Press.

Ellis, B. J., & Symons, D. (1990). Sex differences in sexual fantasy: an evolutionary psychological approach. *Journal of Sex Research, 27*(4), 527–555.

Ellis, L. (1989). *Theories of Rape: Inquiries into the Causes of Sexual Aggression*. New York: Hemisphere Publishing Corporation.

Epstein, A. W. (1975). The fetish object: phylogenetic considerations. *Archives of Sexual Behavior, 4*(3), 303–308.

Everaerd, W., Laan, E. T. M., Both, S., & van der Velde, J. (2000a). Female sexuality. In L. T. Szuchman & F. Muscarella (Eds), *Psychological Perspectives on Human Sexuality* (pp. 101–146). New York: John Wiley.

Everaerd, W., Laan, E. T. M., & Spiering, M. (2000b). Male sexuality. In L. T. Szuchman & F. Muscarella (Eds), *Psychological Perspectives on Human Sexuality* (pp. 60–100). New York: John Wiley.

Everett, G. M. (1975). Role of biogenic amines in the modulation of aggressive and sexual behavior in animals and man. In M. Sandler & G. L. Gessa (Eds), *Sexual Behaviour: Pharmacology and Biochemistry* (pp. 81–84). New York: Raven Press.

Fabiansson, E. C., Denson, T. F., Moulds, M. L., Grisham, J. R., & Schira, M. M. (2012). Don't look back in anger: neural correlates of reappraisal, analytical rumination, and angry rumination during recall of an anger-inducing autobiographical memory. *Neuroimage, 59*(3), 2974–2981. doi: 10.1016/j.neuroimage.2011.09.078

Feierman, J. R., & Feierman, L. A. (2000). Paraphilias. In L. T. Szuchman & F. Muscarella (Eds), *Psychological Perspectives on Human Sexuality* (pp. 480–518). New York: John Wiley.

Ferguson, M. J., & Bargh, J. A. (2008). Evaluative readiness: the motivational nature of automatic evaluation. In A. J. Elliot (Ed.), *Handbook of Approach and Avoidance Motivation* (pp. 289–306). New York: Psychology Press.

Fessler, D. M. T., & Navarrete, C. D. (2003). Domain-specific variation in disgust sensitivity across the menstrual cycle. *Evolution and Human Behavior, 24*(6), 406–417. doi: 10.1016/s1090–5138(03)00054–0

Fessler, D. M. T., & Navarrete, C. D. (2004). Third-party attitudes toward sibling incest: evidence for Westermarck's hypotheses. *Evolution and Human Behavior, 25*(5), 277–294.

Fisher, H. (2004). *Why we Love: The Nature and Chemistry of Romantic Love.* New York: Henry Holt.

Fisher, W. A. (1986). A psychological approach to human sexuality: the sexual behavior sequence. In D. Byrne & K. Kelley (Eds), *Alternative Approaches to the Study of Sexual Behavior* (pp. 131–171). Hillsdale: Lawrence Erlbaum.

Flaubert, G. (1856/2010). *Madame Bovary.* UK: Alexander Vassiliev.

Fonagy, P. (2003). Towards a developmental understanding of violence. *British Journal of Psychiatry, 183,* 190–192. doi: 10.1192/bjp.183.3.190

Ford, C. S., & Beach, F. A. (1951). *Patterns of Sexual Behavior.* New York: Harper and Row.

Freud, S. (1953). Three essays on the theory of sexuality. In J. S. Strachey (Ed.), *The Standard Edition of the Complete Works of Sigmund Freud* (Vol. 7, pp. 123–248). London: The Hogarth Press.

Freud, S. (1955). Beyond the pleasure principle. In J. S. Strachey (Ed.), *The Standard Edition of the Complete Works of Sigmund Freud* (Vol. 17, pp. 7–64). London: The Hogarth Press.

Freund, K. (1990). Courtship disorder. In W. L. Marshall, D. R. Laws, & H. E. Barbaree (Eds), *Handbook of Sexual Assault: Issues, Theories, and Treatment of the Offender* (pp. 195–207). New York: Plenum Press.

Friedenthal, R. (1970). *Luther: His Life and Times.* New York: Harcourt Brace Jovanovich.

Friedrich, W. N., & Gerber, P. N. (1994). Autoerotic asphyxia: the development of a paraphilia. *Journal of the American Academy of Child and Adolescent Psychiatry, 33,* 970–974.

Frohmader, K. S., Pitchers, K. K., Balfour, M. E., & Coolen, L. M. (2010a). Mixing pleasures: review of the effects of drugs on sex behavior in humans and animal models. *Hormones and Behavior, 58*(1), 149–162. doi: 10.1016/j.yhbeh.2009.11.009

Frohmader, K. S., Wiskerke, J., Wise, R. A., Lehman, M. N., & Coolen, L. M. (2010b). Methamphetamine acts on subpopulations of neurons regulating sexual behavior in male rats. *Neuroscience, 166*(3), 771–784. doi: http://dx.doi.org/10.1016/j.neuroscience.2009.12.070

Fujita, K., & Han, H. A. (2009). Moving beyond deliberative control of impulses: the effect of construal levels on evaluative associations in self-control conflicts. *Psychological Science, 20*(7), 799–804.

Gaca, K. L. (2003). *The Making of Fornication.* Berkeley: University of California Press.

Gailliot, M. T., & Baumeister, R. F. (2007). Self-regulation and sexual restraint: dispositionally and temporally poor self-regulatory abilities contribute to failures at restraining sexual behavior. *Personality and Social Psychology Bulletin, 33*(2), 173–186. doi: 10.1177/0146167206293472

Gallup, G. G. (1986). Unique features of human sexuality in the context of evolution. In D. Byrne & K. Kelley (Eds), *Alternative Approaches to the Study of Sexual Behavior* (pp. 13–42). Hillsdale: Lawrence Erlbaum.

Gangestad, S. W., and Simpson, J. A. (2000). The evolution of human mating: trade-offs and strategic pluralism. *Behavioral and Brain Sciences, 23,* 573–644.

Gao, Y., & Raine, A. (2010). Successful and unsuccessful psychopaths: a neurobiological model. *Behavioral Sciences & the Law*, 28(2), 194–210. doi: 10.1002/bsl.924

Gard, D. E., Kring, A. M., Gard, M. G., Horan, W. P., & Green, M. F. (2007). Anhedonia in schizophrenia: distinctions between anticipatory and consummatory pleasure. *Schizophrenia Research*, 93(1–3), 253–260. doi: 10.1016/j.schres.2007.03.008

Gay, G. R., Newmeyer, J. A., Elion, R. A., & Wieder, S. (1975). Drug/sex practice in the Haight-Ashbury or 'The sensuous hippie'. In M. Sandler & G. L. Gessa (Eds), *Sexual Behaviour: Pharmacology and Biochemistry* (pp. 63–79). New York: Raven Press.

Gebhard, P. H. (1971). Human sexual behavior: A summary statement. In D. S. Marshall & R. C. Suggs (Eds), *Human Sexual Behavior: Variations in the Ethnographic Spectrum* (pp. 206–217). New York: Basic Books.

Gebhard, P., Gagnon, J., Pomeroy, W., & Christenson, C. (1965). *Sex Offenders: An Analysis of Types*. New York: Harper and Row.

Gee, D., Ward, T., & Eccleston, L. (2003). The function of sexual fantasies for sexual offenders: a preliminary model. *Behaviour Change*, 20(1), 44–60. doi: 10.1375/bech.20.1.44.24846

Geller, B., & Tillman, R. (2004). Hypersexuality in children with mania: differential diagnosis and clinical presentation. *Psychiatric Times*, 11, 19–21.

Gelstein, S., Yeshurun, Y., Rozenkrantz, L., et al. (2011). Human tears contain a chemosignal. *Science*, 331(6014), 226–230. doi: 10.1126/science.1198331

Georgiadis, J. R., Farrell, M. J., Boessen, R., et al. (2010). Dynamic subcortical blood flow during male sexual activity with ecological validity: a perfusion fMRI study. *Neuroimage*, 50(1), 208–216. doi: http://dx.doi.org/10.1016/j.neuroimage.2009.12.034

Georgiadis, J. R., & Kortekaas, R. (2010). The sweetest taboo: functional neurobiology of human sexuality in relation to pleasure. In M. L. Kringelbach & K. C. Berridge (Eds), *Pleasures of the Brain* (pp. 178–201). Oxford: Oxford University Press.

Georgiadis, J. R., Kringelbach, M. L., & Pfaus, J. G. (2012). Sex for fun: a synthesis of human and animal neurobiology. *Nature Reviews Urology*, 9(9), 486–498. doi: 10.1038/nrurol.2012.151

Gerhardt, S. (2004). *Why Love Matters: How Affection Shapes a Baby's Brain*. Hove: Brunner-Routledge.

Gibb, D. A. (2011). *Camouflaged Killer: The Shocking Double Life of Canadian Air Force Colonel Russell Williams*. New York: Berkeley Books.

Gilbert, D. T., & Wilson, T. D. (2007). Prospection: experiencing the future. *Science*, 317(5843), 1351–1354. doi: 10.2307/20037750

Gillath, O., & Schachner, D. A. (2006). How do sexuality and attachment interrelate? Goals, motives and strategies. In M. Mikulincer & G. S. Goodman (Eds), *Dynamics of Romantic Love: Attachment, Caregiving and Sex* (pp. 337–355). New York: The Guilford Press.

Giugliano, J. R. (2008). Sexual impulsivity, compulsivity or dependence: an investigative inquiry. *Sexual Addiction & Compulsivity*, 15, 139–157.

Gizewski, E., Krause, E., Karama, S., et al. (2006). There are differences in cerebral activation between females in distinct menstrual phases during viewing of erotic stimuli: a fMRI study. *Experimental Brain Research*, 174(1), 101–108. doi: 10.1007/s00221–006–0429–3

Glick, R. A., & Bone, S. (1990). Introduction. In R. A. Glick & S. Bone (Eds), *Pleasure Beyond the Pleasure Principle* (pp. 1–10). New Haven: Yale University Press.

Goethals, G. W. (1971). Factors affecting permissive and non-permissive rules regarding pre-marital sex. In J. M. Henslin (Ed.), *Studies in the Sociology of Sex* (pp. 9–26). New York: Appleton-Century-Crofts.

Gold, J. M., Strauss, G. P., Waltz, J. A., et al. (2013). Negative symptoms of schizophrenia are associated with abnormal effort-cost computations. *Biological Psychiatry*, 74(2), 130–136. doi: 10.1016/j.biopsych.2012.12.022

Gold, S. N., & Heffner, C. L. (1998). Sexual addiction: many conceptions, minimal data. *Clinical Psychology Review, 18*, 367–381.

Gonzaga, G. C., Haselton, M. G., Smurda, J., Davies, M. S., & Poore, J. C. (2008). Love, desire, and the suppression of thoughts of romantic alternatives. *Evolution and Human Behavior, 29*(2), 119–126. doi: 10.1016/j.evolhumbehav.2007.11.003

Goodman, A. (1998). *Sexual Addiction: An Integrated Approach.* New York: International Universities Press.

Gopnik, A. (1998). Explanation as orgasm. *Minds and Machines, 8*(1), 101–118. doi: 10.1023/a:1008290415597

Gorenstein, E. E., & Newman, J. P. (1980). Disinhibitory psychopathology: a new perspective and a model for research. *Psychological Review, 87*(3), 301–315.

Gosselin, C., & Wilson, G. (1980). *Sexual Variations: Fetishism, Sado-Masochism and Transvestism.* London: Faber and Faber.

Gove, W. R. (1994). Why we do what we do: a biopsychosocial theory of human motivation. *Social Forces, 73*(2), 363–394. doi: 10.2307/2579814

Graham, C. (2010). The DSM diagnostic criteria for female sexual arousal disorder. *Archives of Sexual Behavior, 39*(2), 240–255. doi: 10.1007/s10508-009-9535-1

Gray, N. S., Watt, A., Hassan, S., & MacCulloch, M. J. (2003). Behavioral indicators of sadistic sexual murder predict the presence of sadistic sexual fantasy in a normative sample. *Journal of Interpersonal Violence, 18*(9), 1018–1034. doi: 10.1177/0886260503254462

Green, A. H. (1985). Children traumatized by physical abuse. In S. Eth & R. Pynoos (Eds), *Post-Traumatic Stress Disorder in Children* (pp. 135–154). Washington, DC: American Psychiatric Press, Inc.

Green, A. I., & Halkitis, P. N. (2006). Crystal methamphetamine and sexual sociality in an urban gay subculture: an elective affinity. *Culture, Health & Sexuality, 8*(4), 317–333. doi: 10.1080/13691050600783320

Greene, G. (1971). *A Sort of Life.* London: The Bodley Head.

Greenson, R. R. (1977). On boredom. In C. W. Socarides (Ed.), *The World of Emotions: Clinical Studies of Affects and their Expression* (pp. 219–237). New York: International Universities Press, Inc.

Gregersen, E. (1986). Human sexuality in cross-cultural perspective. In D. Byrne & K. Kelley (Eds), *Alternative Approaches to the Study of Sexual Behavior* (pp. 87–102). Hillsdale: Lawrence Erlbaum.

Griffith, M., & Walker, C. E. (1975). Menstrual-cycle phases and personality-variables as related to response to erotic stimuli. *Archives of Sexual Behavior, 4*(6), 599–603.

Griffitt, W., May, J., & Veitch, R. (1974). Sexual stimulation and interpersonal behavior: heterosexual evaluative responses, visual behavior, and physical proximity. *Journal of Personality and Social Psychology, 30*(3), 367–377.

Groth, A. N. (1983). Treatment of the sexual offender in a correctional institution. In J. G. Greer & I. R Stuart (Eds), *The Sexual Aggressor: Current Perspectives on Treatment* (pp. 160–176). New York: Van Nostrand Reinhold.

Guo, G., Tong, Y. Y., Xie, C. W., & Lange, L. A. (2007). Dopamine transporter, gender, and number of sexual partners among young adults. *European Journal of Human Genetics, 15*(3), 279–287. doi: 10.1038/sj.ejhg.5201763

Haggerty, K. D. (2009). Modern serial killers. *Crime Media Culture, 5*(2), 168–187. doi: 10.1177/1741659009335714

Haidt, J. (2001). The emotional dog and its rational tail: a social intuitionist approach to moral judgment. *Psychological Review, 108*(4), 814–834.

Hale, R. (1998). The application of learning theory to serial murder, or 'You too can learn to be a serial killer'. In R. M. Holmes & S. T. Holmes (Eds), *Contemporary Perspectives on Serial Murder* (pp. 75–84). Thousand Oaks: Sage Publications.

Halsey, L. G., Huber, J. W., & Hardwick, J. C. (2012). Does alcohol consumption really affect asymmetry perception? A three-armed placebo-controlled experimental study. *Addiction*, 107, 1273–1279. doi: 10.1111/j.1360-0443.2012.03807.x

Hamann, S., Herman, R. A., Nolan, C. L., & Wallen, K. (2004). Men and women differ in amygdala response to visual sexual stimuli. *Nature Neuroscience*, 7(4), 411–416. doi: 10.1038/nn1208

Hamon, A. (2008). *Michel Fourniret – Monique Olivier: Les Diaboliques face à leurs Juges*. Monaco: Éditions du Rocher.

Hankinson, R. J. (2008). *The Cambridge Companion to Galen*. Cambridge: Cambridge University Press.

Harden, K. P., & Tucker-Drob, E. M. (2011). Individual differences in the development of sensation seeking and impulsivity during adolescence: Further evidence for a dual systems model. *Developmental Psychology*, 47(3), 739–746. doi: 10.1037/a0023279

Hardy, K. R. (1964). An appetitional theory of sexual motivation. *Psychological Review*, 71(1), 1–18. doi: 10.1037/h0047158

Hare, R. D. (1993). *Without Conscience: The Disturbing World of the Psychopaths Among us*. New York: The Guilford Press.

Harlow, H. F., & Harlow, M. K. (1962). Social deprivation in monkeys. *Scientific American*, 207, 136–146.

Harmon-Jones, E., Peterson, C., Gable, P. A., & Harmon-Jones, C. (2008). Anger and approach-avoidance motivation. In A. J. Elliot (Ed.), *Handbook of Approach and Avoidance Motivation* (pp. 399–413). New York: Psychology Press.

Harvey, N. S. (1988). Serial cognitive profiles in levodopa-induced hypersexuality. *The British Journal of Psychiatry*, 153(6), 833–836. doi: 10.1192/bjp.153.6.833

Hatfield, E., & Rapson, R. L. (1987). Passionate love/sexual desire: can the same paradigm explain both? *Archives of Sexual Behavior*, 16(3), 259–278. doi: 10.1007/bf01541613

Hatfield, E., & Rapson, R. L. (2002). Passionate love, sexual desire, and mate selection: cross-cultural and historical perspectives. In A. Vangelisti, H. T. Reis, & M. A. Fitzpatrick (Eds), *Stability and Change in Relationships* (pp. 306–324). Cambridge: Cambridge University Press.

Hawes, Z. C., Wellings, K., & Stephenson, J. (2010). First heterosexual intercourse in the United Kingdom: a review of the literature. *Journal of Sex Research*, 47(2–3), 137–152. doi: 10.1080/00224490903509399

Hawkes, G. (2004). *Sex and Pleasure in Western Culture*. Cambridge: Polity Press.

Hazan, C., & Zeifman, D. (1994). Sex and the psychological tether. In K. Bartholomew & D. Perlman (Eds), *Attachment Processes in Adulthood: Advances in Personal Relationships*, (Vol. 5, pp. 151–178). London: Jessica Kingsley.

Heide, K. M., Beauregard, E., & Myers, W. C. (2009). Sexually motivated child abduction murders: synthesis of the literature and case illustration. *Victims & Offenders*, 4(1), 58–75. doi: 10.1080/15564880802561770

Henslin, J. M. (1971). The sociological point of view. In J. M. Henslin (Ed.), *Studies in the Sociology of Sex* (pp. 1–6). New York: Appleton-Century-Crofts.

Hermans, E. J., Bos, P. A., Ossewaarde, L., et al. (2010). Effects of exogenous testosterone on the ventral striatal BOLD response during reward anticipation in healthy women. *Neuroimage*, 52(1), 277–283. doi: http://dx.doi.org/10.1016/j.neuroimage.2010.04.019

Hewison, R. (2007). *John Ruskin*. New York: Oxford University Press.

Heyman, G. M. (2013). Addiction: an emergent consequence of elementary choice principles. *Inquiry – an Interdisciplinary Journal of Philosophy*, 56(5), 428–445. doi: 10.1080/0020174x.2013.806126

Hickey, E. W. (2010). *Serial Murderers and their Victims*. Belmont: Wadsworth Cengage Learning.

Hicks, T. V., & Leitenberg, H. (2001). Sexual fantasies about one's partner versus someone else: gender differences in incidence and frequency. *Journal of Sex Research*: 38, 43–50.

Hines, M. (2004). *Brain Gender.* Oxford: Oxford University Press.

Hite, S. (2000). *The New Hite Report.* London: Hamlyn.

Hite, S. (2003). Sex, brains, robots and Buddhism: looking for free will. *New Scientist, 178,* 47–48.

Hoch, S. J., & Loewenstein, G. F. (1991). Time-inconsistent preferences and consumer self-control. *Journal of Consumer Research, 17*(4), 492–507. doi: 10.1086/208573

Hoebel, B. G., Avena, N. M., & Rada, P. (2008). An accumbens dopamine-acetylcholine system for approach and avoidance. In A. J. Elliot (Ed.), *Handbook of Approach and Avoidance Motivation* (pp. 89–107). New York: Psychology Press.

Hoffmann, H. (2007). The role of classical conditioning in sexual arousal. In E. Janssen (Ed.), *The Psychophysiology of Sex* (pp. 261–273). Bloomington: Indiana University Press.

Hofmann, W., Friese, M., & Strack, F. (2009). Impulse and self-control from a dual-systems perspective. *Perspectives on Psychological Science, 4,* 162–176.

Hofmann, W., & Van Dillen, L. F. (2012). Desire: the new hotspot in self-control research. *Current Directions in Psychological Science, 21,* 317–322.

Hogben, M., & Byrne, D. (1998). Using social learning theory to explain individual differences in human sexuality. *Journal of Sex Research, 35,* 58–71.

Holder, M. K., Hadjimarkou, M. M., Zup, S. L., et al. (2010). Methamphetamine facilitates female sexual behavior and enhances neuronal activation in the medial amygdala and ventromedial nucleus of the hypothalamus. *Psychoneuroendocrinology, 35*(2), 197–208. doi: http://dx.doi.org/10.1016/j.psyneuen.2009.06.005

Hollister, L. E. (1975). The mystique of social drugs and sex. In M. Sandler & G. L. Gessa (Eds), *Sexual Behaviour: Pharmacology and Biochemistry* (pp. 85–92). New York: Raven Press.

Holmes, R. M. (1998). Sequential predation: elements of serial fatal victimization. In R. M. Holmes & S. T. Holmes (Eds), *Contemporary Perspectives on Serial Murder* (pp. 101–112). Thousand Oaks: Sage Publications.

Holmes, R. M., & DeBurger, J. E. (1998). Profiles in terror: the serial murderer. In R. M. Holmes & S. T. Holmes (Eds), *Contemporary Perspectives on Serial Murder* (pp. 5–16). Thousand Oaks: Sage Publications.

Holmes, R. M., DeBurger, J., & Holmes, S. T. (1998a). Inside the mind of the serial murderer. In R. M. Holmes & S. T. Holmes (Eds), *Contemporary Perspectives on Serial Murder* (pp. 113–122). Thousand Oaks: Sage Publications.

Holmes, S. T., Hickey, E., & Holmes, R. M. (1998b). Female serial murderesses: the unnoticed terror. In R. M. Holmes & S. T. Holmes (Eds), *Contemporary Perspectives on Serial Murder* (pp. 59–70). Thousand Oaks: Sage Publications.

Hoon, P. W., Wincze, J. P., & Hoon, E. F. (1977). A test of reciprocal inhibition: are anxiety and sexual arousal in women mutually inhibitory? *Journal of Abnormal Psychology, 86*(1), 65–74.

Howard, J., & Borges, P. (1970). Needle sharing in the Haight: some social and psychological functions. *Journal of Health and Social Behavior, 11*(3), 220–230.

Howard, M. D. (2007). Escaping the pain: examining the use of sexually compulsive behavior to avoid the traumatic memories of combat. *Sexual Addiction and Compulsivity, 14,* 77–94.

Hrdy, S. B. (1981). *The Woman that Never Evolved* (1st edn.). Cambridge, MA: Harvard University Press

Hrdy, S. B. (1999). *The Woman That Never Evolved* (2nd edn.). Cambridge, MA: Harvard University Press.

Huijding, J., Borg, C., Weijmar-Schultz, W., & de Jong, P. J. (2011). Automatic affective appraisal of sexual penetration stimuli in women with vaginismus or dyspareunia. *Journal of Sexual Medicine, 8,* 806–813.

Hupka, R. B. (1981). Cultural determinants of jealousy. *Journal of Family and Economic Issues*, 4(3), 310–356. doi: 10.1007/bf01257943

Huston, T. L. (1974). A perspective on interpersonal attraction. In T. Huston (Ed.), *Foundations of Interpersonal Attraction* (pp. 3–28). New York: Academic Press.

Ibn Hazm. (1027/1953). *The Ring of the Dove* (trans. A. J. Arberry). London: Luzac.

Impett, E. A., Strachman, A., Finkel, E. J., & Gable, S. L. (2008). Maintaining sexual desire in intimate relationships: the importance of approach goals. *Journal of Personality and Social Psychology*, 94(5), 808–823.

Irvine, W. B. (2007). *On Desire: Why we Want What we Want*. New York: Oxford University Press.

Istvan, J., Griffitt, W., & Weidner, G. (1983). Sexual arousal and the polarization of perceived sexual attractiveness. *Basic and Applied Social Psychology*, 4(4), 307–318. doi: 10.1207/s15324834basp0404_2

Jacob, S., & McClintock, M. K. (2000). Psychological state and mood effects of steroidal chemosignals in women and men. *Hormones and Behavior*, 37(1), 57–78. doi: 10.1006/hbeh.1999.1559

Janssen, E., & Bancroft, J. (2007). The dual control model: the role of sexual inhibition and excitation in sexual arousal and behavior. In E. Janssen (Ed.), *The Psychophysiology of Sex* (pp. 197–222): Bloomington: Indiana University Press.

Janssen, E., Everaerd, W., Spiering, M., & Janssen, J. (2000). Automatic processes and the appraisal of sexual stimuli: toward an information processing model of sexual arousal, *Journal of Sex Research*: 37, 8–23.

Janssen, E., Vorst, H., Finn, P., & Bancroft, J. (2002). The sexual inhibition (SIS) and sexual excitation (SES) scales: II. predicting psychophysiological response patterns. *Journal of Sex Research*, 39(2), 127–132.

Jenks, R. J. (1998). Swinging: a review of the literature. *Archives of Sexual Behavior*, 27(5), 507–521. doi: 10.1023/a:1018708730945

Jockenhövel, F., Minnemann, T., Schubert, M., et al. (2009). Comparison of long-acting testosterone undecanoate formulation versus testosterone enanthate on sexual function and mood in hypogonadal men. *European Journal of Endocrinology*, 160(5), 815–819. doi: 10.1530/eje-08-0830

Jones, J. C., & Barlow, D. H. (1990). Self-reported frequency of sexual urges, fantasies, and masturbatory fantasies in heterosexual males and females. *Archives of Sexual Behavior*, 19(3), 269–279.

Kafka, M. P. (1997). A monoamine hypothesis for the pathophysiology of paraphilic disorders. *Archives of Sexual Behavior*, 26, 343–358.

Kafka, M. P. (2000). The paraphilia-related disorders: nonparaphilic hypersexuality and sexual compulsivity/addiction. In S. R. Leiblum & R. C. Rosen (Eds), *Principles and Practice of Sex Therapy* (pp. 471–503). New York: The Guilford Press.

Kalupahana, D. J. (1987). *The Principles of Buddhist Psychology*. Albany: State University of New York Press.

Karama, S., Lecours, A. R., Leroux, J., et al. (2002). Areas of brain activation in males and females during viewing of erotic film excerpts. *Human Brain Mapping*, 16(1), 1–13. doi: 10.1002/hbm.10014

Kastner, R. M., & Sellbom, M. (2012). Hypersexuality in college students: the role of psychopathy. *Personality and Individual Differences*, 53(5), 644–649. doi: 10.1016/j.paid.2012.05.005

Kavanagh, D. J., Andrade, J., & May, J. (2005). Imaginary relish and exquisite torture: the elaborated intrusion theory of desire. *Psychological Review*, 112(2), 446–467. doi: 10.1037/0033-295X.112.2.446

Kaza, S. (2004). Finding safe harbor: Buddhist sexual ethics in America. *Buddhist Christian Studies*, 24, 23–35.

Kehoe, P., Triano, L., Hoffman, J., Shoemaker, W. J., & Arons, C. (1996). Repeated isolation in the neonatal rat produces alterations in behavior and ventral striatal dopamine release in the juvenile after amphetamine challenge, *Behavioral Neuroscience*, *110*, 1435–1444.

Kellett, J. M. (2000). Older adult sexuality. In L. T. Szuchman & F. Muscarella (Eds), *Psychological Perspectives on Human Sexuality* (pp. 355–379). New York: John Wiley.

Kelley, K., & Musialowski, D. (1986). Repeated exposure to sexually explicit stimuli: novelty, sex, and sexual attitudes. *Archives of Sexual Behavior*, *15*(6), 487–498.

Kelly, D. (2011). *Yuck!: The Nature and Moral Significance of Disgust*. Cambridge: The MIT Press.

Kelly, D. L., & Conley, R. R. (2004). Sexuality and schizophrenia: A review. *Schizophrenia Bulletin*, *30*(4), 767–779.

Kennedy, S. H., Dickens, S. E., Eisfeld, B. S., & Bagby, R. M. (1999). Sexual dysfunction before antidepressant therapy in major depression. *Journal of Affective Disorders*, *56*(2–3), 201–208. doi: 10.1016/s0165-0327(99)00050-6

Kenrick, D. T., & Cialdini, R. B. (1977). Romantic attraction: misattribution versus reinforcement explanations. *Journal of Personality and Social Psychology*, *35*(6), 381–391. doi: 10.1037//0022-3514.35.6.381

Kilts, C. D., Gross, R. E., Ely, T. D., & Drexler, K. P. G. (2004). The neural correlates of cue-induced craving in cocaine-dependent women. *American Journal of Psychiatry*, *161*(2), 233–241. doi: 10.1176/appi.ajp.161.2.233

King, R. J., Mefford, I. N., Wang, C., et al. (1986). CSF dopamine levels correlate with extroversion in depressed patients. *Psychiatry Research*, *19*(4), 305–310. doi: 10.1016/0165-1781(86)90123-x

Kinsey, A. C., Pomeroy, W. B., & Martin, C. E. (1948). *Sexual Behavior in the Human Male*. Philadelphia: W. B. Saunders.

Kinsey, A. C., Pomeroy, W. B., Martin, C. E., & Gebhard, P. H. (1953). *Sexual Behavior in the Human Female*. Philadelphia: W. B. Saunders.

Kitzinger, C., & Wilkinson, S. (1995). Transitions from heterosexuality to lesbianism: the discursive production of lesbian identities. *Developmental Psychology*, *31*(1), 95–104.

Klein, D. F. (1987). Depression and anhedonia. In D. C. Clark & J. Fawcett (Eds), *Anhedonia and Affect Deficit States* (pp. 1–14). New York: PMA Publishing Corp.

Klos, K. J., Bower, J. H., Josephs, K. A., Matsumoto, J. Y., & Ahlskog, J. E. (2005). Pathological hypersexuality predominantly linked to adjuvant dopamine agonist therapy in Parkinson's disease and multiple system atrophy. *Parkinsonism & Related Disorders*, *11*(6), 381–386. doi: 10.1016/j.parkreldis.2005.06.005

Klusmann, D. (2002). Sexual motivation and the duration of partnership. *Archives of Sexual Behavior*, *31*(3), 275–287. doi: 10.1023/a:1015205020769

Knoch, D., & Fehr, E. (2007). Resisting the power of temptations. *Annals of the New York Academy of Sciences*, *1104*(1), 123–134. doi: 10.1196/annals.1390.004

Knutson, B., Wimmer, G. E., Kuhnen, C. M., & Winkielman, P. (2008). Nucleus accumbens activation mediates the influence of reward cues on financial risk taking. *Neuroreport*, *19*(5), 509–513.

Köksal, F., Domjan, M., Kurt, A., et al. (2004). An animal model of fetishism. *Behaviour Research and Therapy*, *42*(12), 1421–1434. doi: 10.1016/j.brat.2003.10.001

Komisaruk, B. R., Whipple, B., & Beyer, C. (2010). Sexual pleasure. In M. L. Kringelbach & K. C. Berridge (Eds), *Pleasures of the Brain* (pp. 169–177). Oxford: Oxford University Press.

Kon, I. S. (1987). A sociocultural approach. In J. H. Geer & W. T. O'Donohue (Eds), *Theories of Human Sexuality* (pp. 257–286). New York: Plenum Press.

Kosson, D. S., Kelly, J. C., & White, J. W. (1997). Psychopathy-related traits predict self-reported sexual aggression among college men. *Journal of Interpersonal Violence*, *12*(2), 241–254. doi: 10.1177/088626097012002006

Krafft-Ebing, R. von (1978). *Psychopathia Sexualis*. New York: Stein and Day.

Kringelbach, M. L. (2010). The hedonic brain: a functional neuroanatomy of human pleasure. In M. L. Kringelbach & K. C. Berridge (Eds), *Pleasures of the Brain* (pp. 202–221). Oxford: Oxford University Press.

Kringelbach, M. L., & Berridge, K. (2010). *Pleasures of the Brain*. Oxford: Oxford University Press.

Kronhausen, E., & Kronhausen, P. (1967). *Walter: The English Casanova*. London: Polybooks.

Krug, R., Pietrowsky, R., Fehm, H. L., & Born, J. (1994). Selective influence of menstrual cycle on perception of stimuli with reproductive significance. *Psychosomatic Medicine*, 56(5), 410–417.

Krüger, T. H. C., Schedlowski, M., & Exton, M. S. (2006). Neuroendocrine processes during sexual arousal and orgasm. In E. Janssen (Ed.), *The Psychophysiology of Sex* (pp. 83–102). Bloomington: Indiana University Press.

Kuley, N. B., & Jacobs, D. F. (1988). The relationship between dissociative like experiences and sensation seeking among social and problem gamblers. *Journal of Gambling Behavior*, 43, 197–207.

Kuukasjärvi, S., Eriksson, C. J. P., Koskela, E., et al. (2004). Attractiveness of women's body odors over the menstrual cycle: the role of oral contraceptives and receiver sex. *Behavioral Ecology*, 15(4), 579–584. doi: 10.1093/beheco/arh050

Laan, E., & Both, S. (2008). What makes women experience desire? *Feminism & Psychology*, 18(4), 505–514. doi: 10.1177/0959353508095533

Laan, E., & Janssen, E. (2006). How do men and women feel? Determinants of subjective experience of sexual arousal. In E. Janssen (Ed.), *The Psychophysiology of Sex* (pp. 278–290). Bloomington: Indiana University Press.

Labbate, L. A. (2008). Psychotropics and sexual dysfunction: the evidence and treatments. *Advances in Psychosomatic Medicine*, 29, 107–130.

Laeng, B., & Falkenberg, L. (2007). Women's pupillary responses to sexually significant others during the hormonal cycle. *Hormones and Behavior*, 52(4), 520–530.

Laham, S. M. (2012). *The Science of Sin*. New York: Three Rivers Press.

Lambert, S., & O'Halloran, E. (2008). Deductive thematic analysis of a female paedophilia website. *Psychiatry, Psychology and Law*, 15, 284–300.

Lamm, C., & Singer, T. (2010). The role of anterior insular cortex in social emotions. *Brain Structure and Function*, 214(5), 579–591. doi: 10.1007/s00429-010-0251-3

Lammers, J., Stoker, J. I., Jordan, J., Pollmann, M., & Stapel, D. A. (2011). Power increases infidelity among men and women. *Psychological Science*, 22(9), 1191–1197. doi: 10.1177/0956797611416252

Lang, P. J., & Bradley, M. M. (2008). Appetitive and defensive motivation is the substrate of emotion. In A. J. Elliot (Ed.), *Handbook of Approach and Avoidance Motivation* (pp. 51–65). New York: Psychology Press.

Langfeldt, T. (1990). Early childhood and juvenile sexuality, development and problems. In M. E. Perry (Ed.), *Handbook of Sexology: Vol. 4. Childhood and Adolescent Sexology* (pp. 179–200). Amsterdam: Elsevier.

Langlois, J. H., & Roggman, L. A. (1990). Attractive faces are only average. *Psychological Science*, 1(2), 115–121. doi: 10.1111/j.1467-9280.1990.tb00079.x

Langlois, J. H., Roggman, L. A., & Rieser-Danner, L. A. (1990). Infants' differential social responses to attractive and unattractive faces. *Developmental Psychology*, 26(1), 153–159. doi: 10.1037/0012-1649.26.1.153

Laqueur, T. (1990). *Making Sex: Body and Gender from the Greeks to Freud*. Cambridge, MA: Harvard University Press.

Larsen, R., & Augustine, A. A. (2008). Basic personality dispositions related to approach and avoidance: extraversion/neuroticism, BAS/BIS, and positive/negative affectivity. In A. J.

Elliot (Ed.), *Handbook of Approach and Avoidance Motivation* (pp. 151–164). New York: Psychology Press.

LaTorre, R. A. (1980). Devaluation of the human love object: heterosexual rejection as a possible antecedent to fetishism. *Journal of Abnormal Psychology, 89*(2), 295–298. doi: 10.1037//0021–843x.89.2.295

Laumann, E. O., Gagnon, J. H., Michael, R. T., & Michaels, S. (1994). *The Social Organization of Sexuality: Sexual Practices in the United States.* Chicago: University of Chicago Press.

Lawrence, A. D., Evans, A. H., & Lees, A. J. (2003). Compulsive use of dopamine replacement therapy in Parkinson's disease: reward systems gone awry? *Lancet Neurology, 2*(10), 595–604. doi: 10.1016/s1474–4422(03)00529–5

Lawrence, D. H. (1928/1993). *Lady Chatterley's Lover.* Harmondsworth: Penguin Books.

Laws, D. R., & Marshall, W. L. (1990). A conditioning theory of the etiology and maintenance of deviant sexual preference and behaviour. In W. L. Marshall, D. R. Laws, & H. E. Barbaree (Eds), *Handbook of Sexual Assault: Issues, Theories, and Treatment of the Offender* (pp. 209–229). New York: Plenum Press.

Le Magnen, J. (1967). Habits and food intake. In C. F. Code (Ed.), *Handbook of Physiology* (Vol. 1, pp. 11–30). Washington, DC: American Physiological Society.

Leake, J. (2007). *The Vienna Woods Killer: A Writer's Double Life.* London: Granta Books.

Lederer, L. (1980). *Take Back the Night: Women on Pornography.* New York: William Morrow and Company.

LeDoux, J. (1999). *The Emotional Brain.* London: Phoenix.

Lee, C. A. (2012). *One of Your Own: The Life and Death of Myra Hindley.* Edinburgh: Mainstream Publishing.

Leiblum, S. R. (2002). Reconsidering gender differences in sexual desire: an update. *Sexual and Relationship Therapy, 17*, 57–68.

Leiblum, S. R., & Nathan, S. G. (2001). Persistent sexual arousal syndrome: a newly discovered pattern of female sexuality. *Journal of Sex & Marital Therapy, 27*(4), 365–380. doi: 10.1080/009262301317081115

Leiblum, S. R., & Rosen, R. C. (2000). *Principles and Practice of Sex Therapy.* New York: The Guilford Press.

Leitenberg, H., & Henning, K. (1995). Sexual fantasy. *Psychological Bulletin, 117*(3), 469–496.

LeVay, S. (1991). A difference in hypothalamic structure between heterosexual and homosexual men. *Science, 253*(5023), 1034–1037. doi: 10.1126/science.1887219

Levin, R. J. (2003). Is prolactin the biological 'off switch' for human sexual arousal? *Sexual and Relationship Therapy, 18*(2), 237.

Levin, R. J. (2006). Discussion. In E. Janssen (Ed.), *The Psychophysiology of Sex* (pp. 313). Bloomington: Indiana University Press.

Levin, R. J., & van Berlo, W. (2004). Sexual arousal and orgasm in subjects who experience forced or non-consensual sexual stimulation: a review. *Journal of Clinical and Forensic Medicine, 11*, 82–86.

Lewis, M. H., Gluck, J. P., Beauchamp, A. J., Keresztury, M. F., & Mailman, R. B. (1990). Long-term effects of early social isolation in *Macaca mulatta*: changes in dopamine receptor function following apomorphine challenge. *Brain Research, 513*(1), 67–73. doi: 10.1016/0006–8993(90)91089-y

Lewis, W. A., & Bucher, A. M. (1992). Anger, catharsis, the reformulated frustration-aggression hypothesis, and health consequences. *Psychotherapy: Theory, Research, Practice, Training, 29*(3), 385–392.

Ley, D. (2012). *The Myth of Sex Addiction.* Lanham: Rowman and Littlefield.

Lieberman, D., & Symons, D. (1998). Sibling incest avoidance: from Westermarck to Wolf. *The Quarterly Review of Biology, 73*(4), 463–466.

Lieberman, D., Tooby, J., & Cosmides, L. (2003). Does morality have a biological basis? An empirical test of the factors governing moral sentiments relating to incest. *Proceedings of the Royal Society of London. Series B: Biological Sciences*, 270(1517), 819–826. doi: 10.1098/rspb.2002.2290

Lieberman, D., Tooby, J., & Cosmides, L. (2007). The architecture of human kin detection. *Nature, 446*, 727–731.

Lippa, R. A. (2006). Is high sex drive associated with increased sexual attraction to both sexes? It depends on whether you are male or female. *Psychological Science, 17*(1), 46–52. doi: 10.1111/j.1467-9280.2005.01663.x

Lisak, D., & Roth, S. (1988). Motivational factors in nonincarcerated sexually aggressive men. *Journal of Personality and Social Psychology, 55*(5), 795–802.

Lomanowska, A. M., Lovic, V., Rankine, M. J., et al. (2011). Inadequate early social experience increases the incentive salience of reward-related cues in adulthood. *Behavioural Brain Research, 220*(1), 91–99. doi: 10.1016/j.bbr.2011.01.033

Lowenstein, L. F. (2002). Fetishes and their associated behavior. *Sexuality and Disability, 20*(2), 135–147. doi: 10.1023/a:1019882428372

Luchins, D. J., Goldman, M. B., Lieb, M., & Hanrahan, P. (1992). Repetitive behaviors in chronically institutionalized schizophrenic patients. *Schizophrenia Research, 8*(2), 119–123. doi: 10.1016/0920-9964(92)90027-3

Luciana, M. (2001). Dopamine-opiate modulations of reward-seeking behavior: implications for the functional assessment of prefrontal development. In C. A. Nelson & M. Luciana (Eds), *Handbook of Developmental Cognitive Neuroscience* (pp. 647–662). Cambridge, MA: The MIT Press.

Luciana, M., & Collins, P. F. (2012). Incentive motivation, cognitive control, and the adolescent brain: is it time for a paradigm shift? *Child Development Perspectives, 6*(4), 392–399. doi: 10.1111/j.1750-8606.2012.00252.x

Lukianowicz, N. (1963). Sexual drive and its gratification in schizophrenia. *International Journal of Social Psychiatry, 9*(4), 250–258.

Luria, A. R. (1966). *Higher Cortical Function in Man*. London: Tavistock Press.

Luria, A. R. (1973). *The Working Brain: An Introduction to Neuropsychology*. Harmondsworth: Penguin Books.

MacCulloch, M., Gray, N., & Watt, A. (2000). Brittain's Sadistic Murderer Syndrome reconsidered: an associative account of the aetiology of sadistic sexual fantasy. *Journal of Forensic Psychiatry, 11*(2), 401.

MacCulloch, M. J., Snowden, P. R., Wood, P. J., & Mills, H. E. (1983). Sadistic fantasy, sadistic behaviour and offending. *The British Journal of Psychiatry, 143*, 20–29.

MacDonald, K. B. (2008). Effortful control, explicit processing, and the regulation of human evolved predispositions. *Psychological Review, 115*(4), 1012–1031. doi: 10.1037/a0013327

MacDonald, K. B., & Hershberger, S. L. (2005). Theoretical issues in the study of evolution and development. In R. L. Burgess & K. MacDonald (Eds), *Evolutionary Perspectives on Human Development* (2nd edn, pp. 21–69): Thousand Oaks: Sage Publications.

MacDonald, R. H. (1967). The frightful consequences of onanism: notes on the history of a delusion. *Journal of the History of Ideas, 28*(3), 423–431.

MacDonald, T. K., Fong, G. T., Zanna, M. P., & Martineau, A. M. (2000). Alcohol myopia and condom use: can alcohol intoxication be associated with more prudent behavior? *Journal of Personality and Social Psychology, 78*(4), 605–619. doi: 10.1037//0022-3514.78.4.605

Mackie, G. (1996). Ending footbinding and infibulations: a convention account. *American Sociological Review, 61*, 999–1017.

MacLean, P. D. (1990). *The Triune Brain in Evolution*. New York: Plenum Press.

Madonna. (1992). *Sex*. New York: Warner Books.

Madsen, P. L., Holm, S., Vorstrup, S., et al. (1991). Human regional cerebral blood flow during rapid-eye-movement sleep. *Journal of Cerebral Blood Flow and Metabolism, 11*, 502–507.

Mahler, S. V., & Berridge, K. C. (2012). What and when to 'want'? Amygdala-based focusing of incentive salience upon sugar and sex. *Psychopharmacology, 221*(3), 407–426. doi: 10.1007/s00213-011-2588-6

Malamuth, N. M. (1996). The confluence model of sexual aggression: feminist and evolutionary perspectives. In D. M. Buss & N. M. Malamuth (Eds), *Sex, Power, and Conflict: Evolutionary and Feminist Perspectives* (pp. 269–295). New York: Oxford University Press.

Maltz, W., & Maltz, L. (2010). *The Porn Trap*. New York: HarperCollins.

Maner, J. K., Gailliot, M. T., & DeWall, C. N. (2007). Adaptive attentional attunement: evidence for mating-related perceptual bias. *Evolution and Human Behavior, 28*(1), 28–36.

Maner, J. K., Rouby, D. A., & Gonzaga, G. C. (2008). Automatic inattention to attractive alternatives: the evolved psychology of relationship maintenance. *Evolution and Human Behavior, 29*(5), 343–349.

Maniglio, R. (2010). The role of deviant sexual fantasy in the etiopathogenesis of sexual homicide: a systematic review. *Aggression and Violent Behavior, 15*(4), 294–302.

Mansfield, K. (2012). 'A Little Episode'. In *The Collected Works of Katherine Mansfield*, ed. G. Kimber & V. O'Sullivan (Vol. X, pp. 543–544). Edinburgh: Edinburgh University Press.

Marchand, W. E. (1961). Analgesic effect of masturbation – masturbation as a clinical sign of painful somatic disorders in psychotic-patients: report of two cases. *Archives of General Psychiatry, 4*(2), 137–138.

Marcus, S. (1966). *The Other Victorians*. London: Weidenfeld and Nicolson.

Marshall, D. S. (1971). Sexual behavior on Mangaia. In D. S. Marshall & R. C. Suggs (Eds), *Human Sexual Behavior: Variations in the Ethnographic Spectrum* (pp. 103–162). New York: Basic Books.

Marshall, D. S., & Suggs, R. C. (1971). *Human Sexual Behavior: Variations in the Ethnographic Spectrum*. New York: Basic Books.

Marshall, W. L., & Barbaree, H. E. (1990). An integrated theory of the etiology of sexual offending. In W. L. Marshall, D. R. Laws, & H. E. Barbaree (Eds), *Handbook of Sexual Assault: Issues, Theory and Treatment of Offenders* (pp. 257–275). New York: Plenum Press.

Masand, P. S. (1993). Successful treatment of sexual masochism and transvestic fetishism associated with depression with fluoxetine hydrochloride. *Depression, 1*, 50–52.

Mass, R., Hölldorfer, M., Moll, B., Bauer, R., & Wolf, K. (2009). Why we haven't died out yet: changes in women's mimic reactions to visual erotic stimuli during their menstrual cycles. *Hormones and Behavior, 55*(2), 267–271.

Masters, B. (1985). *Killing for Company*. London: Jonathan Cape.

Masters, B. (1993). *The Shrine of Jeffrey Dahmer*. London: Hodder and Stoughton.

Mathias, J. L. (1970). Sexual aspects of heroin addiction. *Medical Aspects of Human Sexuality, 4*(9), 98–109.

McCandless, F., & Sladen, C. (2003). Sexual health and women with bipolar disorder. *Journal of Advanced Nursing, 44*(1), 42–48. doi: 10.1046/j.1365-2648.2003.02766.x

McCarthy, M. M. (2008). Estradiol and the developing brain. *Physiological Reviews, 88*(1), 91–124. doi: 10.1152/physrev.00010.2007

McClintock, M. K., & Herdt, G. (1996). Rethinking puberty: the development of sexual attraction. *Current Directions in Psychological Science, 5*(6), 178–183.

McConaghy, N. (1987). A learning approach. In J. Geer & W. O'Donohue (Eds), *Theories of Human Sexuality* (pp. 287–334). New York: Plenum.

McGeoch, P. D. (2007). Does cortical reorganisation explain the enduring popularity of foot-binding in medieval China? *Medical Hypotheses, 69*, 938–941.

McGregor, G., & Howells, K. (1997). Addiction models of sexual offending. In J. E. Hodge, M. McMurran & C. R. Hollin (Eds), *Addicted to Crime?* (pp. 107–137). Chichester: Wiley.

McGuire, R. J., Carlisle, J. M., & Young, B. G. (1965). Sexual deviations as conditioned behaviour: a hypothesis. *Behaviour Research and Therapy, 2,* 185–190.

Meade, C. S., Graff, F. S., Griffin, M. L., & Weiss, R. D. (2008). HIV risk behavior among patients with co-occurring bipolar and substance use disorders: associations with mania and drug abuse. *Drug and Alcohol Dependence, 92*(1–3), 296–300.

Meana, M. (2010). Elucidating women's (hetero)sexual desire: definitional challenges and content expansion. *Journal of Sex Research, 47,* 104–122.

Meloy, J. R. (2000). The nature and dynamics of sexual homicide: an integrative review. *Aggression and Violent Behavior, 5*(1), 1–22.

Meloy, J. R., & Fisher, H. (2005). Some thoughts on the neurobiology of stalking. *Journal of Forensic Sciences, 50*(6), 1472–1480.

Mendez, M., & Shapira, J. S. (2011). Pedophilic behavior from brain disease. *Journal of Sexual Medicine, 8,* 1092–1100.

Messenger, J. C. (1971). Sex and repression in an Irish folk community. In D. S. Marshall & R. C. Suggs (Eds), *Human Sexual Behavior: Variations in the Ethnographic Spectrum* (pp. 3–37). New York: Basic Books.

Meston, C. M., & Buss, D. M. (2007). Why humans have sex. *Archives of Sexual Behavior, 36*(4), 477–507. doi: 10.1007/s10508-007-9175-2

Meston, C. M., & Buss, D. M. (2009). *Why Women Have Sex.* New York: Times Books.

Meston, C. M., & Gorzalka, B. B. (1996). Differential effects of sympathetic activation on sexual arousal in sexually dysfunctional and functional women. *Journal of Abnormal Psychology, 105*(4), 582–591.

Meyer, P. J., Lovic, V., Saunders, B. T., et al. (2012). Quantifying individual variation in the propensity to attribute incentive salience to reward cues. *PLOS One, 7*(6). doi: 10.1371/journal.pone.0038987

Mikulincer, M. (2006). Attachment, caregiving, and sex within romantic relationships: a behavioural systems perspective. In M. Mikulincer & G. S. Goodman (Eds), *Dynamics of Romantic Love: Attachment, Caregiving, and Sex* (pp. 23–44). New York: The Guilford Press.

Mikulincer, M., & Goodman, G. S. (2006). *Dynamics of Romantic Love: Attachment, Caregiving, and Sex.* New York: The Guilford Press.

Miller, R. S. (1997). Inattentive and contented: relationship commitment and attention to alternatives. *Journal of Personality and Social Psychology, 73*(4), 758–766.

Millet, C. (2003). *The Sexual Life of Catherine* M. London: Transworld Publishers.

Money, J. (1977). Role of fantasy in pair-bonding and erotic performance. In R. Gemme & C. C. Wheeler (Eds), *Progress in Sexology* (pp. 259–266). New York: Plenum Press.

Money, J. (1986). *Lovemaps.* New York: Irvington Publishers.

Money, J. (1990). Historical and current concepts of pediatric and ephebiatric sexology. In M. E. Perry (Ed.), *Handbook of Sexology: Vol. 7. Childhood and Adolescent Sexology* (pp. 3–21). Amsterdam: Elsevier.

More, T. (1516/1975). *Utopia.* Harmondsworth: Penguin Books.

Moscucci, O. (1996). Clitoridectomy, circumcision, and the politics of sexual pleasure in mid-Victorian Britain. In A. H. Miller & J. E. Adams (Eds), *Sexualities in Victorian Britain* (pp. 60–78). Bloomington: Indiana University Press.

Moskowitz, D. A., & Roloff, M. E. (2007). The ultimate high: sexual addiction and the bug chasing phenomenon. *Sexual Addiction & Compulsivity, 14,* 21–40.

Mouras, H., Stoléru, S., Moulier, V., et al. (2008). Activation of mirror-neuron system by erotic video clips predicts degree of induced erection: an fMRI study. *NeuroImage, 42,* 1142–1150.

Muñoz, L. C., Khan, R., & Cordwell, L. (2011). Sexually coercive tactics used by university students: a clear role for primary psychopathy. *Journal of Personality Disorders, 25*(1), 28–40.

Murstein, B. I. (1986). *Paths to Marriage.* Beverly Hills, Sage Publications.

Myers, W. C., Husted, D. S., Safarik, M. E., & O'Toole, M. E. (2006). The motivation behind serial sexual homicide: is it sex, power, and control, or anger? *Journal of Forensic Sciences*, 51(4), 900–907. doi: 10.1111/j.1556-4029.2006.00168.x

Nesse, R. M., & Berridge, K. C. (1997). Psychoactive drug use in evolutionary perspective. *Science*, 278(5335), 63–66. doi: 10.1126/science.278.5335.63

Nichols, D. S. (2006). Tell me a story: MMPI responses and personal biography in the case of a serial killer. *Journal of Personality Assessment*, 86(3), 242–262. doi: 10.1207/s15327752jpa8603_02

Nobre, P. J., & Pinto-Gouveia, J. (2008). Differences in automatic thoughts presented during sexual activity between sexually functional and dysfunctional men and women. *Journal of Cognitive Therapy and Research*, 32, 37–49.

Nordgren, L. F., Harreveld, F., & Pligt, J. (2009). The restraint bias: how the illusion of self-restraint promotes impulsive behavior. *Psychological Science*, 20(12), 1523–1528. doi: 10.1111/j.1467-9280.2009.02468.x

Numrich, P. D. (2009). The problem with sex according to Buddhism. *Dialog: A Journal of Theology*, 48, 62–73.

Oaten, M., Stevenson, R. J., & Case, T. I. (2009). Disgust as a disease-avoidance mechanism. *Psychological Bulletin*, 135(2), 303–321. doi: 10.1037/a0014823

O'Brien, D. (1985). *The Hillside Stranglers*. Philadelphia: Running Press.

O'Carroll, R. O., & Bancroft, J. (1984). Testosterone therapy for low sexual interest and erectile dysfunction in men: a controlled study. *British Journal of Psychiatry*, 145, 146–151.

Oei, N. Y. L., Rombouts, S., Soeter, R. P., van Gerven, J. M., & Both, S. (2012). Dopamine modulates reward system activity during subconscious processing of sexual stimuli. *Neuropsychopharmacology*, 37(7), 1729–1737. doi: 10.1038/npp.2012.19

O'Guinn, T. C., & Faber, R. J. (1989). Compulsive buying: a phenomenological exploration. *Journal of Consumer Research*, 16(2), 147–157. doi: 10.1086/209204

O'Neill, N., & O'Neill, G. (1972). *Open Marriage: A New Lifestyle for Couples*. New York: M. Evans and Co.

Orford, J. (2001). *Excessive Appetites: A Psychological View of Addictions* (2nd edn). Chichester: Wiley.

Owens, E. W., Behun, R. J., Manning, J. C., & Reid, R. C. (2012). The impact of internet pornography on adolescents: a review of the research. *Sexual Addiction and Compulsivity*, 19(1–2), 99–122. doi: 10.1080/10720162.2012.660431

Panksepp, J. (1982). Toward a general psychobiological theory of emotions. *The Behavioral and Brain Sciences*, 5, 407–467.

Panksepp, J. (1998). *Affective Neuroscience*. New York: Oxford University Press.

Panksepp, J., & Moskal, J. (2008). Dopamine and SEEKING: subcortical 'reward' systems and appetitive urges. In A. J. Elliot (Ed.), *Handbook of Approach and Avoidance Motivation* (pp. 67–87). New York: Psychology Press.

Pascal, B. (1669/1966). *Pensees*, trans A. J. Krailsheimer. London: Penguin Books.

Pavelka, M. S. M. (1995). Sexual nature: what can we learn from a cross-species perspective? In P. R. Abramson & S. D. Pinkerton (Eds), *Sexual Nature – Sexual Culture* (pp. 17–36). Chicago: The University of Chicago Press.

Pennebaker, J. W., & Roberts, T. A. (1992). Toward a his and hers theory of emotion: gender differences in visceral perception. *Journal of Social and Clinical Psychology*, 11(3), 199–212. doi: 10.1521/jscp.1992.11.3.199

Person, E. (1990). Foreword. In R. A. Glick & S. Bone (Eds), *Pleasure beyond the Pleasure Principle* (pp. ix–xiii). New Haven: Yale University Press.

Pfaff, D. W. (1999). *Drive: Neurobiological and Molecular Mechanisms of Sexual Motivation*. Cambridge, MA: Bradford Books.

Pfaus, J. G. (2009). Pathways of sexual desire. *Journal of Sexual Medicine*, 6, 1506–1533.

Pfaus, J. G., Erickson, K. A., and Talianakis, S. (2013). Somatosensory conditioning of sexual arousal and copulatory behavior in the male rat: a model of fetish development. *Physiology and Behavior, 122*, 1–7.

Pinker, S. (1997). *How the Mind Works*. London: Allen Lane.

Pitchers, K. K., Balfour, M. E., Lehman, M. N., Richtand, N. M., Yu, L., & Coolen, L. M. (2010). Neuroplasticity in the mesolimbic system induced by natural reward and subsequent reward abstinence. *Biological Psychiatry, 67*(9), 872–879. doi: 10.1016/j.biopsych.2009.09.036

Pithers, W. D., Marques, J. K., Gibat, C. C., & Marlatt, G. A. (1983). Relapse prevention with sexual aggressives: a self-control model of treatment and maintenance of change. In J. G. Greer & I. R. Stuart (Eds), *The Sexual Aggressor: Current Perspectives on Treatment* (pp. 214–239). New York: Van Nostrand Reinhold.

Plato. (1965). *Timaeus*. Harmondsworth: Penguin Books.

Plato. (2003). *The Republic* (2nd edn., trans D. Lee). London: Penguin Books.

Plaud, J. J., & Martini, J. R. (1999). The respondent conditioning of male sexual arousal. *Behavior Modification, 23*(2), 254–268. doi: 10.1177/0145445599232004

Politis, M., Loane, C., Wu, K., et al. (2013). Neural response to visual sexual cues in dopamine treatment-linked hypersexuality in Parkinson's disease. *Brain, 136*, 400–411. doi: 10.1093/brain/aws326

Polivy, J. (1998). The effects of behavioral inhibition: integrating internal cues, cognition, behavior, and affect. *Psychological Inquiry, 9*(3), 181.

Ponseti, J., & Bosinski, H. A. G. (2010). Subliminal sexual stimuli facilitate genital response in women. *Archives of Sexual Behavior, 39*, 1073–1079.

Prause, N., & Graham, C.A. (2007). Asexuality: classification and characterization. *Archives of Sexual Behavior, 36*, 341–356.

Prescott, J. W. (1977). Phylogenetic and ontogenetic aspects of human affectional development. In R. Gemme & C. C. Wheeler (Eds), *Progress in Sexology* (pp. 431–457). New York: Plenum Press.

Price, J. S. (2002). The triune brain, escalation de-escalation strategies, and mood disorders. In G. A. Cory & R. Gardner (Eds), *The Evolutionary Neuroethology of Paul MacLean* (pp. 107–117). Westport: Praeger.

Pron, N. (1995). *Lethal Marriage*. New York: Ballantine Books.

Pruitt, M. V., & Krull, A. C. (2011). Escort advertisements and male patronage of prostitutes. *Deviant Behavior, 32*(1), 38–63. doi: 10.1080/01639620903416123

Quinsey, V. L., & Marshall, W. L. (1983). Procedures for reducing inappropriate sexual arousal: an evaluation review. In J. G. Greer & I. R. Stuart (Eds), *The Sexual Aggressor: Current Perspectives on Treatment* (pp. 267–289). New York: Van Nostrand Reinhold.

Raine, A. (2013). *The Anatomy of Violence: The Biological Roots of Crime*. London: Alan Lane.

Rainwater, L. (1971). Marital sexuality in four 'cultures of poverty'. In D. S. Marshall & R. C. Suggs (Eds), *Human Sexual Behavior: Variations in the Ethnographic Spectrum* (pp. 187–205). New York: Basic Books.

Ramachandran, V. S., & Blakeslee, S. (1999). *Phantoms in the Brain*. London: Fourth Estate.

Ramsey, G. V. (1943). The sexual development of boys. *American Journal of Psychology, 56*(2), 217–233.

Ramsland, K., & McGrain, P. N. (2010). *Inside the Minds of Sexual Predators*. Santa Barbara: ABCCLIO.

Rauch, S. L., Shin, L. M., Dougherty, D. D., et al. (1999). Neural activation during sexual and competitive arousal in healthy men. *Psychiatry Research: Neuroimaging, 91*(1), 1–10.

Rawson, R. A., Washton, A., Domier, C. P., & Reiber, C. (2002). Drugs and sexual effects: role of drug type and gender. *Journal of Substance Abuse Treatment, 22*(2), 103–108.

Redouté, J. R. M., Stoléru, S., Pugeat, M., et al. (2005). Brain processing of visual sexual stimuli in treated and untreated hypogonadal patients. *Psychoneuroendocrinology*, 30(5), 461–482. doi: http://dx.doi.org/10.1016/j.psyneuen.2004.12.003

Regan, P. C. (1999). Hormonal correlates and causes of sexual desire: a review. *The Canadian Journal of Human Sexuality*, 8, 1–16.

Regan, P. C. (2000). Love relationships. In L. T. Szuchman & F. Muscarella (Eds), *Psychological Perspectives on Human Sexuality* (pp. 232–282). New York: John Wiley.

Regan, P. C., & Berscheid, E. (1999). *Lust: What we know about Human Sexual Desire*. Thousand Oaks: Sage Publications.

Reid, R. C., & Carpenter, B. N. (2009). Exploring relationships of psychopathology in hypersexual patients using the MMPI-2. *Journal of Sex & Marital Therapy*, 35(4), 294–310. doi: 10.1080/00926230902851298

Reifler, C. B., Howard, J., Lipton, M. A., Liptzin, M. B., & Widmann, D. E. (1971). Pornography: an experimental study of effects. *American Journal of Psychiatry*, 128(5), 575–582.

Ressler, R. K., Burgess, A. W., & Douglas, J. E. (1992). *Sexual Homicide: Patterns and Motives*. New York: The Free Press.

Reynaud, M., Karila, L., Blecha, L., & Benyamina, A. (2010). Is love passion an addictive disorder? *American Journal of Drug and Alcohol Abuse*, 36(5), 261–267. doi: 10.3109/00952990.2010.495183

Rich, P. (2006). *Attachment and Sexual Offending*. New York: Wiley.

Richard, R., van der Pligt, J., & de Vries, N. (1996). Anticipated regret and time perspective: changing sexual risk-taking behavior. *Journal of Behavioral Decision Making*, 9(3), 185–199. doi: 10.1002/(sici)1099-0771(199609)9:3<185::aid-bdm228>3.0.co;2-5

Robbins, R. N., & Bryan, A. (2004). Relationships between future orientation, impulsive sensation seeking, and risk behavior among adjudicated adolescents. *Journal of Adolescent Research*, 19(4), 428–445. doi: 10.1177/0743558403258860

Robbins, T. W., & Everitt, B. J. (1996). Neurobehavioural mechanisms of reward and motivation. *Current Opinion in Neurobiology*, 6(2), 228–236. doi: 10.1016/s0959-4388(96)80077-8

Robinson, T. E., & Berridge, K. C. (1993). The neural basis of drug craving: an incentive-sensitization theory of addiction. *Brain Research Reviews*, 18(3), 247–291. doi: 10.1016/0165-0173(93)90013-p

Rolls, E. T. (2012). *Neuroculture: On the Implications of Brain Science*. Oxford: Oxford University Press.

Rook, D. W. (1987). The buying impulse. *Journal of Consumer Research*, 14, 189–199.

Rosen, R. C., & Beck, J. G. (1986). Models and measures of sexual response: psychophysiological assessment of male and female arousal. In D. Byrne & K. Kelley (Eds), *Alternative Approaches to the Study of Sexual Behavior* (pp. 43–86). Hillsdale: Lawrence Erlbaum.

Rosen, R. C., & Fracher, J. C. (1983). Tension-reduction training in the treatment of compulsive sex offenders. In J. G. Greer & I. R. Stuart (Eds), *The Sexual Aggressor: Current Perspectives on Treatment* (pp. 144–159). New York: Van Nostrand Reinhold.

Rousseau, J.-J. (1781/1953). *The Confessions*. London: Penguin Books.

Roy, C. (2005). *Traditional Festivals: A Multicultural Encyclopedia*. Santa Barbara: ABC-CLIO.

Royzman, E., Leeman, R., & Sabini, J. (2008). 'You make me sick': moral dyspepsia as a reaction to third-party sibling incest. *Motivation and Emotion*, 32(2), 100–108. doi: 10.1007/s11031-008-9089-x

Rozin, P., Haidt, J., & McCauley, C. R. (2000). Disgust. In M. Lewis & J. M. Haviland-Jones (Eds), *Handbook of Emotions* (pp. 637–653). New York: Guilford Press.

Rule, A. (1983). *Lust Killer*. New York: Signet Books.

Rule, A. (2004). *Green River, Running Red*. New York: Pocket Star Books.

Rule, A. (2006). *The Stranger Beside Me*. London: Sphere Books.

Rush, F. (1980). Child pornography. In L. Lederer (Ed.), *Take Back the Night: Women on Pornography* (pp. 71–81). New York: William Morrow and Company.

Russell, D. E. H. (1980). Pornography and violence: what does the new research say? In L. Lederer (Ed.), *Take Back the Night: Women on Pornography* (pp. 218–238). New York: William Morrow and Company.

Ryan, M. (1996). *Secret Life: An Autobiography*. London: Bloomsbury Publishing.

Sachs, B. J. (2000). Contextual approaches to the physiology and classification of erectile function, erectile dysfunction, and sexual arousal. *Neuroscience and Biobehavioral Reviews, 24*, 541–560.

Sacks, O. (1976). *Awakenings*. New York: Vintage Books.

Salamone, J. D., Correa, M., Farrar, A., & Mingote, S. M. (2007). Effort-related functions of nucleus accumbens dopamine and associated forebrain circuits. *Psychopharmacology, 191*(3), 461–482. doi: 10.1007/s00213–006–0668–9

Salter, A. C. (1988). *Treating Child Sex Offenders and Victims*. Newbury Park: Sage Publications.

Samson, L., & Grabe, M. E. (2012). Media use and the sexual propensities of emerging adults. *Journal of Broadcasting & Electronic Media, 56*, 280–298.

Sand, M., & Fisher, W. A. (2007). Women's endorsement of models of female sexual response: the nurses' sexuality study. *Journal of Sexual Medicine, 4*, 708–719.

Savic, I., Berglund, H., Gulyas, B., & Roland, P. (2001). Smelling of odorous sex hormone-like compounds causes sex-differentiated hypothalamic activations in humans. *Neuron, 31*(4), 661–668. doi: 10.1016/s0896–6273(01)00390–7

Savic, I., Berglund, H., & Lindstrom, P. (2005). Brain response to putative pheromones in homosexual men. *Proceedings of the National Academy of Sciences of the United States of America, 102*(20), 7356–7361. doi: 10.1073/pnas.0407998102

Savic, I., & Lindström, P. (2008). PET and MRI show differences in cerebral asymmetry and functional connectivity between homo- and heterosexual subjects. *Proceedings of the National Academy of Sciences of the United States of America, 105*(27), 9403–9408. doi: 10.1073/pnas.0801566105

Schachner, D. A., & Shaver, P. R. (2004). Attachment dimensions and sexual motives. *Personal Relationships, 11*(2), 179–195. doi: 10.1111/j.1475–6811.2004.00077.x

Schein, M. W., & Hale, E. B. (1965). Stimuli eliciting sexual behavior. In F. A. Beach (Ed.), *Sex and Behavior* (pp. 416–440). New York: John Wiley.

Schilder, A. J., Lampinen, T. M., Miller, M. L., & Hogg, R. S. (2005). Crystal methamphetamine and ecstasy differ in relation to unsafe sex among young gay men. *Canadian Journal of Public Health/Revue Canadienne De Sante Publique, 96*(5), 340–343.

Schlesinger, L. B. (2001). The potential sex murderer: ominous signs, risk assessment. *Journal of Threat Assessment, 1*, 47–72.

Schlesinger, L. B. (2007). Sexual homicide: differentiating catathymic and compulsive murders. *Aggression and Violent Behavior, 12*(2), 242–256. doi: http://dx.doi.org/10.1016/j.avb.2006.09.007

Schmitt, D. P., & Shackelford, T. K. (2008). Big five traits related to short-term mating: from personality to promiscuity across 46 nations. *Evolutionary Psychology, 6*(2), 246–282.

Schneider, J. P. (2000). A qualitative study of cybersex participants: gender differences, recovery issues, and implications for therapists. *Sexual Addiction & Compulsivity, 7*, 249–278.

Schneider, J. P. and Weiss, R. (2001). *Cybersex Exposed: Recognizing the Obsession*. Hazeldon: Hazelden Information and Educational Services.

Schore, A. N. (2003). *Affect Dysregulation and Disorders of the Self*. New York: W. W. Norton.

Schroeder, T. (2004). *Three Faces of Desire*. New York: Oxford University Press

Schwartz, M. F., & Masters, W. H. (1983). Conceptual factors in the treatment of paraphilias: a preliminary report. *Journal of Sex & Marital Therapy, 9*, 3–18.

Schwartz, M. F., Money, J., & Robinson, K. (1981). Biosocial perspectives on the development of the proceptive, acceptive and conceptive phases of eroticism. *Journal of Sex & Marital Therapy, 7*(4), 243–255. doi: 10.1080/00926238108405426

Schwartz, M. F., & Southern, S. (2000). Compulsive cybersex: the new tea room. *Sexual Addiction & Compulsivity, 7*, 127–144.

Scorolli, C., Ghirlanda, S., Enquist, M., Zattoni, S., & Jannini, E. A. (2007). Relative prevalence of different fetishes. *International Journal of Impotence Research, 19*, 432–437.

Scully, D., & Marolla, J. (1984). Convicted rapists' vocabulary of motive: excuses and justifications. *Social Problems, 31*(5), 530–544.

Segal, Z. V., & Stermac, L. E. (1990). The role of cognitions in sexual assault. In W. L. Marshall, D. R. Laws, & H. E. Barbaree (Eds), *Handbook of Sexual Assault: Issues, Theories and Treatment of the Offender* (pp. 161–174). New York: Plenum Press.

Sewell, B. (2011). *Outsider*. London: Quartet.

Sewell, J. D. (1985). An application of Magargee's algebra of aggression to the case of Theodore Bundy. *The Journal of Police and Criminal Psychology, 1*, 14–24.

Shaffer, A. (2011). *Great Philosophers who Failed at Love*. New York: HarperPerennial.

Sharot, T., Shiner, T., Brown, A. C., Fan, J., & Dolan, R. J. (2009). Dopamine enhances expectation of pleasure in humans. *Current Biology, 19*(24), 2077–2080. doi: http://dx.doi.org/10.1016/j.cub.2009.10.025

Shaver, P. R. (2006). Dynamics of romantic love: comments, questions, and future directions. In M. Mikulincer & G. S. Goodman (Eds), *Dynamics of Romantic Love: Attachment, Caregiving and Sex* (pp. 423–456). New York: The Guilford Press.

Sherdell, L., Waugh, C. E., & Gotlib, I. H. (2012). Anticipatory pleasure predicts motivation for reward in major depression. *Journal of Abnormal Psychology, 121*(1), 51–60. doi: 10.1037/a0024945

Sherfey, M. J. (1973). *The Nature and Evolution of Female Sexuality*. New York: Vintage Books.

Sherwin, B. B., & Gelfand, M. M. (1987). The role of androgen in the maintenance of sexual functioning in oophorectomized women. *Psychosomatic Medicine, 49*(4), 397–409.

Shope, D. F. (1971). The sociological point of view. In J. M. Henslin (Ed.), *Studies in the Sociology of Sex* (pp. 29–51). New York: Appleton-Century-Crofts.

Shor, E., & Simchai, D. (2009). Incest avoidance, the incest taboo, and social cohesion: revisiting Westermarck and the case of the Israeli kibbutzim. *American Journal of Sociology, 114*(6), 1803–1842.

Shrier, L. A., Koren, S., Aneja, P., & de Moor, C. (2010). Affect regulation, social context, and sexual intercourse in adolescents. *Archives of Sexual Behavior, 39*(3), 695–705. doi: 10.1007/s10508-008-9394-1

Silvio, H., McCloskey, K., & Ramos-Grenier, J. (2006). Theoretical consideration of female sexual predator serial killers in the United States. *Journal of Criminal Justice, 34*(3), 251–259. doi: http://dx.doi.org/10.1016/j.jcrimjus.2006.03.006

Simon, W., & Gagnon, J. H. (1987). A sexual scripts approach. In J. H. Geer & W. T. O'Donohue (Eds), *Theories of Human Sexuality* (pp. 363–383). New York: Plenum Press.

Simpson, J. A., & Oriña, M. (2003). Strategic pluralism and context-specific mate preferences in humans. In K. Sterelny & J. Fitness (Eds), *From Mating to Mentality: Evaluating Evolutionary Psychology* (pp. 39–70). New York: Psychology Press.

Sims, K. E., & Meana, M. (2010). Why did passion wane? A qualitative study of married women's attributions for declines in sexual desire. *Journal of Sex & Marital Therapy, 36*, 360–380.

Singer, B., & Toates, F. M. (1987). Sexual motivation. *The Journal of Sex Research, 23*(4), 481–501. doi: 10.2307/3812226

Skinner, B. F. (1976). *Particulars of My Life*. London: Jonathan Cape.

Smallbone, S. W., & Dadds, M. R. (1998). Childhood attachment and adult attachment in incarcerated adult male sex offenders. *Journal of Interpersonal Violence*, 13(5), 555–573. doi: 10.1177/088626098013005001

Smith, J., R., & Smith, L. G. (1970). Co-marital sex and the sexual freedom movement. *The Journal of Sex Research*, 6(2), 131–142. doi: 10.2307/3811587

Smith, K., Mahler, S., Peciña, S., & Berridge, K. (2010). Hedonic hotspots: generating sensory pleasure in the brain. In M. L. Kringelbach & K. C. Berridge (Eds), *Pleasures of the Brain* (pp. 27–49). Oxford: Oxford University Press.

Smuts, B. (1992). Male aggression against women: an evolutionary perspective. *Human Nature*, 3(1), 1–44.

Smuts, B. (1996). Male aggression against women: an evolutionary perspective. In D. M. Buss & N. M. Malamuth (Eds), *Sex, Power, Conflict: Evolutionary and Feminist Perspectives* (pp. 231–268). New York: Oxford University Press.

Snow, C. P. (1965). *The Two Cultures: and a Second Look*. Cambridge: Cambridge University Press.

Sounes, H. (1995). *Fred and Rose*. London: Sphere.

Southern, S. (2002). The tie that binds: sadomasochism in female addicted trauma survivors. *Sexual Addiction & Compulsivity*, 9(4), 209–229. doi: 10.1080/10720160216050

Spencer, N. A., McClintock, M. K., Sellergren, S. A., et al. (2004). Social chemosignals from breastfeeding women increase sexual motivation. *Hormones and Behavior*, 46(3), 362–370. doi: 10.1016/j.yhbeh.2004.06.002

Spiering, M., & Everaerd, W. (2006). The sexual unconscious. In E. Janssen (Ed.), *The Psychophysiology of Sex* (pp. 166–184). Bloomington: Indiana University Press.

Sripada, C. S., & Stich, S. (2007). A framework for the psychology of norms. In P. Carruthers, S. Lawrence, & S. Stich (Eds), *The Innate Mind: Culture and Cognition* (pp. 280–301). Oxford: Oxford University Press.

Stanislaw, H., & Rice, F. J. (1988). Correlation between sexual desire and menstrual-cycle characteristics. *Archives of Sexual Behavior*, 17(6), 499–508. doi: 10.1007/bf01542338

Stanovich, K. E. (2004). *The Robot's Rebellion*. Chicago: The University of Chicago Press.

Stark, R., Schienle, A., Girod, C., et al. (2005). Erotic and disgust-inducing pictures: differences in the hemodynamic responses of the brain. *Biological Psychology*, 70(1), 19–29. doi: http://dx.doi.org/10.1016/j.biopsycho.2004.11.014

Steele, C. M., & Josephs, R. A. (1990). Alcohol myopia: its prized and dangerous effects. *American Psychologist*, 45(8), 921–933. doi: 10.1037/0003–066x.45.8.921

Steinberg, L. (2007). Risk taking in adolescence: new perspectives from brain and behavioral science. *Current Directions in Psychological Science*, 16(2), 55–59. doi: 10.1111/j.1467-8721.2007.00475.x

Steinberg, L. (2008). A social neuroscience perspective on adolescent risk-taking. *Developmental Review*, 28(1), 78–106. doi: 10.1016/j.dr.2007.08.002

Steinem, G. (1980). Erotica and pornography: a clear and present difference. In L. Lederer (Ed.), *Take Back the Night: Women on Pornography* (pp. 35–39). New York: William Morrow and Company.

Stephenson, K., Ahrold, T., & Meston, C. (2011). The association between sexual motives and sexual satisfaction: gender differences and categorical comparisons. *Archives of Sexual Behavior*, 40(3), 607–618. doi: 10.1007/s10508-010-9674-4

Stephenson, R. M. (1973). Involvement in deviance: an example and some theoretical implications. *Social Problems*, 21(2), 173–190.

Stern, D. N. (1990). Joy and satisfaction in infancy. In R. A. Glick & S. Bone (Eds), *Pleasure Beyond the Pleasure Principle* (pp. 13–25). New Haven: Yale University Press.

Stevenson, R. J., Case, T. I., & Oaten, M. J. (2011). Effect of self-reported sexual arousal on responses to sex-related and non-sex-related disgust cues. *Archives of Sexual Behavior*, 40(1), 79–85. doi: 10.1007/s10508–009–9529-z

Stoléru, S. (2006). Discussion. In E. Janssen (Ed.), *The Psychophysiology of Sex* (p. 376). Bloomington: Indiana University Press.

Stoléru, S., & Mouras, H. (2006). Brain functional imaging studies of sexual desire and arousal in human males. In E. Janssen (Ed.), *The Psychophysiology of Sex* (pp. 3–34). Bloomington: Indiana University Press.

Stoller, R. J. (1971). The term 'transvestism'. *Archives of General Psychiatry*, 24, 230–237.

Storms, M. D. (1981). A theory of erotic orientation development. *Psychological Review*, 88(4), 340–353.

Struckman-Johnson, C., & Struckman-Johnson, D. (1994). Men pressured and forced into sexual experience. *Archives of Sexual Behavior*, 23, 93–114.

Suggs, R. C., & Marshall, D. S. (1971). Anthropological perspectives on human sexual behavior. In D. S. Marshall & R. C. Suggs (Eds), *Human Sexual Behavior: Variations in the Ethnographic Spectrum* (pp. 218–243). New York: Basic Books.

Sullivan, T., & Maiken, P. T. (1983). *Killer Clown: The John Wayne Gacy Murders*. New York: Pinnacle Books.

Sutton, S. K., & Davidson, R. J. (2000). Prefrontal brain electrical asymmetry predicts the evaluation of affective stimuli. *Neuropsychologia*, 38, 1723–1733.

Symonds, C. (1971). Sexual mate-swapping: violation of norms and reconciliation of guilt. In J. M. Henslin (Ed.), *Studies in the Sociology of Sex* (pp. 81–109). New York: Appleton-Century-Crofts.

Symons, D. (1995). Beauty is in the adaptations of the beholder: the evolutionary psychology of human female attractiveness. In P. R. Abramson & S. D. Pinkerton (Eds), *Sexual Nature – Sexual Culture* (pp. 80–118). Chicago: The University of Chicago Press.

Tallis, F. (2005). *Love Sick*. London: Arrow Books.

Thornhill, R., & Palmer, C. T. (2000). *A Natural History of Rape: Biological Bases of Sexual Coercion*. Cambridge, MA: The MIT Press.

Tiffany, S.T. (1990). A cognitive model of drug urges and drug-use behavior: role of automatic and nonautomatic processes. *Psychological Review*, 97, 147–168.

Tillich, H. (1973). *From Time to Time*. New York: Stein and Day

Toates, F. (1986). *Motivational Systems*. Cambridge: Cambridge University Press.

Toates, F. (1998). The interaction of cognitive and stimulus-response processes in the control of behaviour. *Neuroscience & Biobehavioral Reviews*, 22(1), 59–83. doi: http://dx.doi.org/10.1016/S0149-7634(97)00022–5

Toates, F. (2005). Evolutionary psychology: towards a more integrative model. *Biology and Philosophy*, 20(2), 305–328. doi: 10.1007/s10539–004–0756-3

Toates, F. (2006). A model of the hierarchy of behaviour, cognition, and consciousness. *Consciousness and Cognition*, 15(1), 75–118.

Toates, F. (2009). An integrative theoretical framework for understanding sexual motivation, arousal, and behavior. *Journal of Sex Research*, 46(2–3), 168–193. doi: 10.1080/00224490902747768

Toates, F., & Coschug-Toates, O. (2002). *Obsessive Compulsive Disorder*. London: Class Publishing.

Tolman, D. L., & Diamond, L. M. (2001). Desegregating sexuality research: cultural and biological perspectives on gender and desire. *Annual Review of Sex Research*, 12, 33.

Tolstoy, L. (1889/2007). *The Kreutzer Sonata, trans D. McDuff*. London: Penguin.

Tolstoy, L. (1877/1977). Anna Karenina. London: Pan Books.

Tolstoy, L. (2012). *Great Short Works of Leo Tolstoy*, trans. N. K. Dole, L. Maude and A. Maude. Digireads.com Publishing.

Tooby, J., & Cosmides, L. (1990). The past explains the present: emotional adaptations and the structure of ancestral environments. *Ethology and Sociobiology*, 11(4–5), 375–424. doi: http://dx.doi.org/10.1016/0162-3095(90)90017-Z

Torrey, E. F. (1992). *Freudian Fraud*. New York: Harper Perennial.

Trachtenberg, P. (1989). *The Casanova Complex: Compulsive Lovers and their Women*. London: Eden Paperbacks.

Tracy, J. I., deLeon, J., Qureshi, G., et al. (1996). Repetitive behaviors in schizophrenia: a single disturbance or discrete symptoms? *Schizophrenia Research*, 20(1–2), 221–229. doi: 10.1016/0920-9964(95)00104-2

Treadway, M. T., Buckholtz, J. W., Cowan, R. L., et al. (2012). Dopaminergic mechanisms of individual differences in human effort-based decision-making. *The Journal of Neuroscience*, 32(18), 6170–6176. doi: 10.1523/jneurosci.6459-11.2012

Trivers, R. (1972). Parental investment and sexual selection. In B. Campbell (Ed.), *Sexual Selection and the Descent of Man* (pp. 136–179). Chicago: Aldine.

Tsuang, M. T. (1975). Hypersexuality in manic patients. *Medical Aspects of Human Sexuality*, 9, 83–89.

Turner, M. (2008). Female sexual compulsivity: a new syndrome. *Psychiatric Clinics of North America*, 31(4), 713–727. doi: http://dx.doi.org/10.1016/j.psc.2008.06.004

Tuzin, D. (1995). Discourse, intercourse, and the excluded middle: anthropology and the problem of sexual experience. In P. R. Abramson & S. D. Pinkerton (Eds), *Sexual Nature – Sexual Culture* (pp. 257–275). Chicago: The University of Chicago Press.

Tybur, J. M., Lieberman, D., & Griskevicius, V. (2009). Microbes, mating, and morality: individual differences in three functional domains of disgust. *Journal of Personality and Social Psychology*, 97(1), 103–122. doi: 10.1037/a0015474

Udry, J. R. (1990). Hormonal and social determinants of adolescent sexual initiation. In J. Bancroft & J. M. Reinisch (Eds), *Adolescence and Puberty* (pp. 70–87). New York: Oxford University Press.

Udry, J. R. (1995). Sociology and biology: what biology do sociologists need to know? *Social Forces*, 73, 1257–1278.

Valins, S. (1970). The perception and labelling of bodily changes as determinants of emotional behavior. In P. Black (Ed.), *Physiological Correlates of Emotion* (pp. 229–243). New York: Academic Press.

Van den Bergh, B., Dewitte, S., & Warlop, L. (2008). Bikinis instigate generalized impatience in intertemporal choice. *Journal of Consumer Research*, 35(1), 85–97. doi: 10.1086/525505

van der Kolk, B. A. M. (1989). The compulsion to repeat the trauma: re-enactment, revictimization, and masochism. *Psychiatric Clinics of North America*, 12(2), 389–411.

Van Wyk, P. H., & Geist, C. S. (1984). Psychosocial development of heterosexual, biosexual, and homosexual behavior. *Archives of Sexual Behavior*, 13(6), 505–544.

Wagstaff, D. A., Abramson, P. R., & Pinkerton, S. D. (2000). Research in human sexuality. In L. T. Szuchman & F. Muscarella (Eds), *Psychological Perspectives on Human Sexuality* (pp. 3–59). New York: John Wiley.

Wahlstrom, D., Collins, P., White, T., & Luciana, M. (2010). Developmental changes in dopamine neurotransmission in adolescence: behavioral implications and issues in assessment. *Brain and Cognition*, 72(1), 146–159. doi: 10.1016/j.bandc.2009.10.013

Wallace, J. F., & Newman, J. P. (2008). RST and psychopathy: associations between psychopathy and the behavioral activation and inhibition systems. In P. J. Corr (Ed.), *The Reinforcement Sensitivity Theory of Personality* (pp. 398–414). Cambridge: Cambridge University Press.

Wallen, K. (1995). The evolution of female sexual desire. In P. R. Abramson & S. D. Pinkerton (Eds), *Sexual Nature – Sexual Culture* (pp. 57–79). Chicago: The University of Chicago Press.

Wallen, K. (2001). Risky business: social context and hormonal modulation of primate sexual desire. In W. Everaerd, E. Laan & S. Both (Eds), *Sexual Appetite, Desire and Motivation: Energetics of the Sexual System* (pp. 33–62). Amsterdam: Royal Netherlands Academy of Arts and Sciences.

Wallen, K., & Lovejoy, J. (1993). Sexual behaviour: endocrine function and therapy. In J. Schulkin (Ed.), *Hormonally Induced Changes in Mind and Brain* (pp. 71–97). San Diego: Academic Press.

Walter (1995). *My Secret Life*. Ware: Wordsworth Classics.

Wansink, B. (2006). *Why We Eat More than We Think*. New York: Bantam Books.

Ward, T., & Beech, A. (2006). An integrated theory of sexual offending. *Aggression and Violent Behavior, 11*(1), 44–63.

Washton, A. M. (1989). Cocaine may trigger sexual compulsivity. *US Journal of Drug and Alcohol Dependence, 13*, 8.

Washton, A. M., & Zweben, J. E. (2009). *Cocaine and Methamphetamine Addiction: Treatment, Recovery, and Relapse Prevention*. New York: W. W. Norton & Company.

Wassersug, R. J., Zelenietz, S. A., & Squire, G. F. (2004). New age eunuchs: motivation and rationale for voluntary castration. *Archives of Sexual Behavior, 33*(5), 433–442. doi: 10.1023/B:ASEB.0000037424.94190.df

Watson, J. (1930). *Behaviorism*. New York: Appleton-Century-Crofts.

Webster, R. (1995). *Why Freud was Wrong: Sin, Science and Psychoanalysis*. London: Harper-Collins.

Wedekind, C., & Penn, D. (2000). MHC genes, body odours, and odour preferences. *Nephrology Dialysis Transplantation, 15*(9), 1269–1271. doi: 10.1093/ndt/15.9.1269

Wegner, D. M. (1994). *White Bears and Other Unwanted Thoughts: Suppression, Obsession, and the Psychology of Mental Control*. New York: Guilford Press.

Wegner, D. M., Shortt, J. W., Blake, A. W., & Page, M. S. (1990). The suppression of exciting thoughts. *Journal of Personality and Social Psychology, 58*(3), 409–418. doi: 10.1037//0022-3514.58.3.409

Weinberg, M. S., Williams, C. J., & Pryor, D. W. (1994). *Dual Attraction: Understanding Bisexuality*. New York: Oxford University Press.

Wenzl, R., Potter, T., Kelly, L., & Laviana, H. (2008). *Bind, Torture, Kill: The Inside Story of BTK, the Serial Killer Next Door*. New York: Harper.

Westen, D., Blagov, P. S., Harenski, K., Kilts, C. & Hamann, S. (2006). Neural bases of motivated reasoning: an fMRI study of emotional constraints on partisan political judgment in the 2004 U.S. Presidential election. *Journal of Cognitive Neuroscience, 18*, 1947–1958.

Whipple, B., Ogden, G., & Komisaruk, B. R. (1992). Physiological correlates of imagery-induced orgasm in women. *Archives of Sexual Behavior, 21*, 121–133.

White, G. L., Fishbein, S., & Rutstein, J. (1981). Passionate love and the misattribution of arousal. *Journal of Personality and Social Psychology, 41*(1), 56–62. doi: 10.1037/0022-3514.41.1.56

Whittle, B., & Ritchie, J. (2004). *Harold Shipman: Prescription for Murder*. London: Sphere.

Wiegel, M., Scepkowski, L. A., & Barlow, D. H. (2006). Cognitive-affective processes in sexual arousal and sexual dysfunction. In E. Janssen (Ed.), *The Psychophysiology of Sex* (pp. 143–165). Bloomington: Indiana University Press.

Williams, L. M., & Finkelhor, D. (1990). The characteristics of incestuous fathers: a review of recent studies. In W. L. Marshall, D. R. Laws, & H. E. Barbaree (Eds), *Handbook of Sexual Assault: Issues, Theories, and Treatment of the Offender* (pp. 231–255). New York: Plenum Press.

Wilson, A. N. (1988). *Tolstoy*. London: Hamish Hamilton.

Wilson, C. (1988). *The Misfits: A Study of Sexual Outsiders*. London: Grafton Books.

Wilson, D. S. (1999). Tasty slice – but where is the rest of the pie? *Evolution and Human Behavior*, 20, 279–287.

Wilson, E. O. (1998). *Consilience: The Unity of Knowledge.* New York: Vintage.

Wilson, M., & Daly, M. (2004). Do pretty women inspire men to discount the future? *Proceedings of the Royal Society B-Biological Sciences*, 271, S177-S179. doi: 10.1098/rsbl.2003.0134

Wolf, A. P. (1995). *Sexual Attraction and Childhood Association: A Chinese Brief for Edward Westermarck.* Stanford: Stanford University Press.

Wolf, S. C. (1988). A model of sexual aggression/ addiction. *Journal of Social Work and Human Sexuality*, 7, 131–148.

Woo, J., Brotto, L., & Gorzalka, B. (2011). The role of sex guilt in the relationship between culture and women's sexual desire. *Archives of Sexual Behavior*, 40(2), 385–394. doi: 10.1007/s10508-010-9609-0

Wood, J. M., Koch, P. B., & Mansfield, P. K. (2006). Women's sexual desire: a feminist critique. *Journal of Sex Research*, 43, 236–244.

Woodson, J. C. (2002). Including 'learned sexuality' in the organization of sexual behavior. *Neuroscience & Biobehavioral Reviews*, 26(1), 69–80. doi: http://dx.doi.org/10.1016/S0149-7634(01)00039-2

Workman, L., & Reader, W. (2014). *Evolutionary Psychology* (3rd edn). Cambridge: Cambridge University Press.

Yang, Y. L., Glenn, A. L., & Raine, A. (2008). Brain abnormalities in antisocial individuals: implications for the law. *Behavioral Sciences & the Law*, 26(1), 65–83. doi: 10.1002/bsl.788

Yeomans, M. R., Chambers, L., Blumenthal, H., & Blake, A. (2008). The role of expectancy in sensory and hedonic evaluation: the case of smoked salmon ice-cream. *Food Quality and Preference*, 19(6), 565–573. doi: 10.1016/j.foodqual.2008.02.009

Young, A. M. J., Ahier, R. G., Upton, R. L., Joseph, M. H., & Gray, J. A. (1998). Increased extracellular dopamine in the nucleus accumbens of the rat during associative learning of neutral stimuli. *Neuroscience*, 83(4), 1175–1183. doi: http://dx.doi.org/10.1016/S0306-4522(97)00483-1

Zhong, C-B. & Liljenquist, K. (2006). Washing away your sins: threatened morality and physical cleansing. *Science*, 313, 1451–1452.

Zillmann, D. (1984). *Connections between Sex and Aggression.* Hillsdale: Lawrence Erlbaum.

Zillmann, D. (1986). Coition as emotion. In D. Byrne and K. Kelley (Ed.), *Alternative Approaches to the Study of Sexual Behavior* (pp. 173–199). Hillsdale: Lawrence Erlbaum.

Zola, E. (1887/1975). *Earth.* London: New English Library.

Zuckerman, M. (1990). The psychophysiology of sensation seeking. *Journal of Personality*, 58(1), 313–345. doi: 10.1111/j.1467-6494.1990.tb00918.x

INDEX

494 • Index